ONLY GOD

ONLY GOD

A Biography of Yogi Ramsuratkumar

Regina Sara Ryan

Foreword by Jay Martin

Hohm Press
Prescott, Arizona

Cover design: Kim Johansen
Layout and design: Tori Bushert

Library of Congress Cataloging in Publication Data:
Ryan, Regina Sara
  Only god : a biography of Yogi Ramsuratkumar / Regina Sara Ryan ; foreword by Jay Martin.--1st ed.
    p.cm.
  ISBN 1-890772-35-6 (hardbound : alk. paper)
  1. Ramsuratkumar, Yogi 1918-2001 2. Yogis--India--Biography. 3. Spiritual life--Hinduism. 4. Philosophy, Indic. I. Martin, Jay, 1944- II. Title.
  BL1175.R348R93 2004
    181'.45--dc22

                                    2004014422

HOHM PRESS
P.O. Box 2501
Prescott, AZ 86302
800-381-2700
http://www.hohmpress.com

08 07 06 05 04   5 4 3 2 1

To the One who leads us all from darkness to the light,
Jai Guru!

All is the one, beyond name and form, and only God.
– Yogi Ramsuratkumar

ACKNOWLEDGEMENTS

The assignment of this book project was the profound gift of my spiritual master, Lee Lozowick, the spiritual son of Yogi Ramsuratkumar. It is first and foremost through Lee that this writer has learned the nature of devotion, by observing his single-minded focus on and obedience to the Divine beggar of Tiruvannamalai, whom he served for almost thirty years, and whom he continues to serve with every breath. From beginning to end, Lee's encouragement of this writer's work was tangible, both in the benediction that I felt from him as well as in his provision of research materials. Writing the book has been its own reward, and this writer is forever grateful to the one who first offered the invitation.

Next, I wish to thank Devaki Ma, the Eternal Slave of Yogi Ramsuratkumar, and Vijayalakshmi Ma, Yogiji's constant servant and the companion to Devaki, for their inspiration and guidance, before, during, and after this project. The living witness of their faith and surrender to the master will ever remain an incomparable teaching.

Others served this project extensively, providing physical, emotional and spiritual resources. Special thanks to Ute Augustiniak who accompanied me in my travels in 2002 and whose good humor and sisterly friendship made the trip so enjoyable; and to Volker Augustiniak, who with his wife, Ute, has courageously assumed responsibility for Triveni II, the ashram of Lee Lozowick in Tiruvannamalai, India. These friends and sangha mates cared for me and assisted in my research from first to last.

ONLY GOD

I am deeply grateful to Sadhu V. Rangarajan who, together with his gracious wife Bharati, hosted me at the Bharatamata Gurukula Ashram and Yogi Ramsuratkumar Indological Research Centre in Bangalore in October 2002. Sadhuji generously gave of his time and attention in answering my questions about Indian history, language, and culture throughout this project, and provided countless stories from his years of experience in the service of his master, Yogi Ramsuratkumar. The *Tattva Darsana*, a periodical that he began in 1983, and which became the first official periodical for the dissemination of the life and teaching of Yogi Ramsuratkumar, was an invaluable resource in this investigation.

Thanks to the remarkable memory and journal records of Truman Caylor Wadlington, the author of the first English language book about Yogi Ramsuratkumar, so much of the early material about the Godchild of Tiruvannamalai was carefully preserved. Caylor's faith and generosity in sharing this material has been a great service in forwarding the blessed beggar's work in the world.

Thanks to all who allowed interviews about their time with Yogi Ramsuratkumar, especially to Will Zulkowski, Parathasarathy, J. Mukilan and his father S. Jairaj, Kirsti (Sivapriya), Mani and Raji, Ramamurthi, Mr. Dwaraknath Reddy and daughter Sandhya, Jai Ram, Ravi, Saravanan, Selveraj, Chandra, Ashish Bagrodia, and Makarand Paranjape. And to numerous others, whose stories are contained in this book.

I offer my pranams to Swami Satchidananda of Anandashram, Kanhangad, India, and to Swami Nityananda Giri of Tapovanam Ashram whose respect for Yogi Ramsuratkumar was obvious in the words they shared about their association with the beggar saint.

The devotees and students of the Hohm Community of Prescott, Arizona, consistently shared their adventures and insights in traveling with Lee Lozowick to visit Yogi Ramsuratkumar from 1977 onward. Their lilas were given in extensive interviews and in their writings, published in volumes of the *Divine Slave Gita* and the *Tawagoto*, as well as in the *Hohm Sahaj Mandir Study Manual*. Dearest brothers and sisters in the sangha, I honor your contributions one and all.

Acknowledgements

Special commendation to the staff at Hohm Press (Bala, Dasya, Nancy, Erica, Thom, Rabia, Kim, and Becky) who each did their part to move the project forward, and to Tori Bushert for her excellent typesetting work as well as her zeal in meeting our deadlines.

For my husband, Jere Pramuk, whose love and devotion to "this beggar" has grown along with my own, and whose support was constant in the long months during which this book was being compiled, I will ever be grateful.

Finally, there are no words that could adequately acknowledge the beggar king, Yogi Ramsuratkumar, who has blessed this writer so abundantly and guided the work so clearly. The only way to thank him is to follow his directive to chant his name always. May all who read of him be inspired to do so, and thus to remember God with every thought, every word, and every action.

Jaya Yogi Ramsuratkumar, Ki Jai.

NOTES TO THE READER

(1) Most foreign terms are italicized only the first time they appear in the text, and are defined in the Glossary at the end of the book.

(2) The reader will observe an inconsistency in the capitalization of many nouns and pronouns (such as "beggar," "master," "he" or "his" when referring to Yogi Ramsuratkumar). I attempted to limit the use of excessive capitalization by reserving it for proper names, and was easily able to do this with transcribed interview material. However, in drawing from a wide variety of published sources, I maintained the capitalization used in the original source. For unpublished letters or personal correspondence I applied my prerogative of limiting capitalization.

(3) The spelling of certain titles and names (such as Bhagwan versus Bhagavan, and Paramacharya versus Paramacharyal) varies in the text. Here again, I kept the original spelling when quoting from published works.

Some differences in the spelling of names, whether proper or common, is due to a characteristic of the Indians, especially of the northern states, who add "ji" at the end of a name as a mark of respect to elderly persons and persons in high esteem. The reader will therefore encounter such references as "Gandhiji," "Yogiji," "Mataji" (mother), and "Guruji" (teacher). Most often, the South Indian names end with "-an" like Rangarajan, Murugeshan, but those from North India drop the "-an" and pronounce the names as Rangaraj or Rangaraja or Murugesh, sometimes adding "ji" as a mark of respect. The name Vivekanand or Vivekananda becomes Vivekanandan in the south and vice versa. When "ji" is added respectfully, the name becomes Vivekanandji, or Vivekanandaji or Vivekanandanji.

In any case where it is unclear as to whom the name or reference applies, I have attempted to clarify this by a direct insertion in the text.

CONTENTS

FOREWORD

During the time that I was writing my biography of Henry Miller he would occasionally be moved to speak about the great Indian sages who had meant so much to him for so many years. By chance, a mention might have been made of Rabindranath Tagore or Gandhi, and Henry would take wing, speaking rapturously of Aurobindo, Ramdas, Vivekananda, Krishnamurti, and others. He knew their writings, of course, but more important, in his rhapsodies he showed that he had also absorbed their spiritual strivings. Yogi Ramsuratkumar was younger than these others, and not known until much later than they were. Unlike them, Ramsuratkumar did not inscribe his words on paper, so Miller never spoke of him. But had Henry been gifted with the chance to read Regina Sara Ryan's new biography of Ramsuratkumar, "this beggar," as he called himself, would assuredly have been added to Henry's litany, perhaps taking his place at its top. *Only God* shows how Ramsuratkumar emerged from the soil made spiritually fertile by these earlier sages and exhibits in a masterful way how he made his own unique spiritual thrust forward.

Precisely because the teachings of Yogi Ramsuratkumar were delivered in person rather then inscribed in books, Ryan's work has a preeminent importance. Without such written works, his life and words would have no echo in today's world. Those who were fortunate enough to have listened to him teach, either directly or through his disciples, could never forget his voice and message as these passed unto their souls. They lived his teachings. Regina Sara Ryan is one of those who was nourished by his wisdom, both in her own personal contacts with him, and also earlier and more steadily through the teaching of Ramsuratkumar's spiritual "son," Lee Lozowick. The special and arduous mission that she accepted for herself has been to write this biography and thus to give wider dispersal to this beggar's rich wisdom, reaching those who can no longer hear his now-stilled voice or gain access to one who did. She has done this in three remarkable ways.

First, since Ramsuratkumar wrote no autobiography, Ryan has composed a moving narrative of his life – that is, both his "life" in the world, and also of the "liveliness" of his life. She conveys how truly alive his life was. She reminds us that there is as much holiness circulating through life as there is in meditation, sage sayings, chantings, and sacred prayers. From the time of his birth in 1918 in northern India, through the various uncoverings of his enlightenments during his being-in-the-world, Ryan relives his sacred life, bringing him, for us, back to the world from which he has physically departed.

He was, after all, quintessentially, a "hidden saint," unlike many of the other much more publicized modern gurus whose writings called attention to their existence and brought to them many seekers and followers from all over the world. Yogi Ramsuratkumar was nearly sixty years old before this "mad beggar of Tiruvannamalai" began to be known by word of mouth to holy questers outside of India. In the mid nineteen-seventies, Westerners returning from long stays in India began to speak of a person whose existence was "changing the universe" – a strangely compelling and fierce person who had somehow penetrated their hearts. He did not administrate one of those vast "Yogivilles" to which many Western pilgrims flocked. He simply sat in rags, leaning on a pile of old newspapers, and spoke. Hilda Charlton called him a "hidden angel," or a hidden brother of light. He lived his sacredness. Regina Sara Ryan shows this, and more, in her book: he acted his life; she reinacts it in her narrative, which brings his life out of hiding and makes its glory permanently and fully available to those who can be reached by this book.

Further, *Only God*, despite its modest subtitle, is more than a biography. It is itself a book of wisdom, a repository not only of this beggar's life, but also an account of the alteration that he did indeed make in the spiritual universe through his teachings. Ramsuratkumar's life and his wisdom are, of course, ultimately one. By preserving and restoring both for generations that will come, Ryan challenges time and the silence that might otherwise have overtaken Ramsuratkumar after his physical death in 2001.

Finally, Regina Sara Ryan is keenly aware that the life and life-guidance of Ramsuratkumar were not a singular idiosyncratic event, but that in his own individual way he was a profound part of the expansion of spirituality in the universe during the last century and into the present. Thereby she reminds us that countless sages existed before and during Ramsuratkumar's time and, more important, they continue to flourish everywhere in the world today and will in their turn make their own unique contributions to changing the world. By casting her net widely, both forward and backward, Ryan exhibits to us a rhythm in the pulse of the universe that continues to beat despite the deaths of any individual. New gurus are being born every day and emerging from their chrysalises every moment.

Ramsuratkumar is gone, but through this book he remains powerfully at our side – not just on our bookshelf, but *with* us and *in* us. His grace and wisdom dwells in this biographer and continues through her as she recounts his life. It is the transmigration of spirit that we find in this book.

Ryan's account, then, is no dryasdust narrative of the mundane "facts" of Ramsuratkumar's life, but a remarkable tale of the realm of holy "fact" in which he lived and in which he radiated ferocious grace. *Only God: A Biography of Ramsuratkumar* is therefore not merely a book. One of our American sages, Walt Whitman, said of his own *Leaves of Grass*, "This is no book. Who touches this touches a man." The same is true of *Only God*. Who reads this experiences Yogi Ramsuratkumar. "This beggar is everywhere," he once said. To grasp the history and fresh life of Indian spirituality and to catch a glimpse of where it is leading us, the venturesome reader will find in Ryan's portrait of Ramsuratkumar a guide and map of the spiritual world that is even now and always unfolding.

After these reflections I now ask myself: were Ramsuratkumar himself able to pick up this big book with my small Foreword in it, what would he say? I think he would chuckle with delight at my words; and then, as he proceeded on to Ryan's book, I believe I hear him beginning to laugh uproariously. I see his eyes twinkle, kindly but fiercely too, like a holy warrior-saint, and I seem to hear him say: "This beggar knows nothing of such things…All is Father!"…or, "All is the one, beyond name and form, and only God!" What an oddly ripened and rich beggar, this hidden saint and angel of light was. And what a book Regina Sara Ryan has presented to him as a happy and blessed gift to us!

> – Jay Martin, Ph.D.
> Author of *Always Merry and Bright: The Life of Henry Miller,* and *The Education of John Dewey: A Biography.*
> Claremont, California, May 2004

INTRODUCTION

Generally there is some doubt in the beginnings of things – a doubt that lingers in the background of the mind about one's motives, one's intelligence, one's capacity to accomplish the task at hand.

In 1995, in India, sitting on a cold, black marble floor, gazing at a bearded old man wrapped in a blanket, turbaned, and smoking a cigarette with elegant and precise movements, there *was* no doubt. Whatever questions had accompanied me on that trip were burned away, rising in the smoke that gently wafted around his head.

No doubt whatsoever, because love was so tangible in the air that one could eat it. With the body thus satisfied, the mind rested and followed the lead of something else. The heart was in charge here in this cavernous temple in Tiruvannamalai, South India. The old man, a beggar recognized as a saint, was Yogi Ramsuratkumar, and the chamber in which I sat echoed with enthusiastic chants of his melodious name.

No one from the West is ever prepared for India, which is partly what makes it such a compelling destination. The West is the kingdom of doubts, and the kingdom of logic, of critical analysis, of cynicism, of progress at the expense of human values, of the need to prove and be proven. In India, if the pilgrim is the least bit vulnerable, she is disarmed of her logic. One loves and hates India, in part for this exact reason – that the usual rules not only don't apply, but actually seem ludicrous and simply unfounded.

In 1995, at the end of my second trip to this amazing land, *Bharata Mata* (Mother India – its traditional name derived from

"*Bha*" in Sanskrit, meaning "light," and "*rata,*" to revel. Thus India is "the land that revels in the light of Eternal Wisdom"), I described my experience to friends and family. This beggar's benediction, I told them, was as strong as any verdict rendered by some Supreme Court. He had heard the case I had been pleading for the past fifty years (my age at the time) and had unanimously found me "Innocent," with no further appeal. In October 2002, I returned, not for an attempt at a re-trial, but for a recapitulation of the truth that I knew then beyond the shadow of any doubt. I returned to find, once again, the humble beggar who had given me back my life, redeemed me, and forgiven me of my illusory sin.

I came to thank him in the best way I knew how and to live near his ashram for a few months so that I might discover his story for myself. I came for a blessing – praying that this story, as I would track it, would be an act of praise to God, and possibly helpful to someone else. I came to write of Yogi Ramsuratkumar as I had seen and known him myself, and to hear this same story spoken by dozens of others from different cultures, from different times.

In October 2002, a year after the shock of September 11th, as war threatened to engulf the world and as threats of the use of nuclear weapons were being swapped between Pakistan and its neighbors, I was, in fact, making my own pilgrimage of peace. My destination was the foot of the holy mountain, Arunachala, in whose shadow this gentle, peace-loving, and child-like beggar had lived since 1959, and in whose shadow he died in February 2001. The trip to this blessed sanctuary seemed a necessary, and ultimately sane, choice in the midst of a world gone mad. The "Godchild of Tiruvannamalai," as he was affectionately called, offered a different brand of madness. This humble man, who referred to himself only as "this beggar," was the contradiction to ego's reign. Much to the disdain of the sanctimonious, he dressed in rags bearing the dust of the streets, worn day in and day out. He rarely bathed. He was always barefoot. He smoked cigarettes and carried a fan and a coconut bowl, wielding these symbols of his poverty and surrender with regal bearing. He *was* mad, truly – but in the ways that saints are mad when they are lost, completely, to only God.

Introduction

In his madness, Yogi Ramsuratkumar received into his court the Arab, the Jew, and the American; the Brahmin and the outcaste; the destitute and the wealthy. He treated them not equally but uniquely, giving to each one in the capacity to which he or she could receive. To some, who were in fear, he spoke with the tenderness of a benevolent grandfather, assuring them that he was with them, within them, "one hundred percent," and that there was no need to be anxious, ever. Occasionally, his words were delivered on a sharp-edged sword, especially to one who tried to deceive or manipulate him, or brutalize another. As the cacophony of human arrogance reached deafening proportions in the world around him, he sang the praise of the Lord – *Om Sri Ram Jai Ram, Jai Jai Ram* – with greater enthusiasm, and with every breath. He turned hundreds of thousands of visitors to remembrance of the ultimate weapon – the name of God – which alone could penetrate the frozen heart, or disintegrate the wall of insanity that blockaded a suffering world.

Indeed, he was mad. When he was beaten, he did not accuse his tormentors. When he was reviled, he bowed at the feet of his detractors. He brought warring factions together and begged them, with a sweet and lilting voice, to speak together, to heal their differences, to remember God, and to turn everything to him.

Those who found their way to his feet did not always abide by his guidance, but few remained untouched, even forty years after meeting him. Without a doubt, they knew they had encountered a peacemaker of the highest caliber; a light-bearer in a world in darkness; a fool in the face of the technological sophistication that strangles the spirit. Yogi Ramsuratkumar lent his faith to those in doubt, his hope to the despairing, and his love to everyone. This beggar, who never wrote a book, touched a computer, or left India, stood as witness to a universal potential. He forever pointed to the "kingdom within" promised by all the prophets, masters, and saints who preceded him.

But, Yogi Ramsuratkumar did more than indicate a direction. His was an alchemy wherein the individual seated in his presence was rendered new and defenseless. He pronounced us all "Innocent," with no appeal. He showed us who and what we truly were. Nothing but pure magic and benediction could explain how he got in…or how he embodied the truth of "only God" in a way that we could see, and feel, and sometimes even touch. He infected us with a strain of his own madness as he fed us from his own bowl. He blessed us constantly, sanctified us, and sent us on our way to serve as leaven in a bread for the world.

Certainly I didn't need to travel halfway around the world to find him and join in his prayers for peace, since he is as close as the breath, and as constant. But I needed to come to India again to write the story – a story whose time had come; a story that all who would "become as little children" once again would want to hear.

Throughout this trip and for the remainder of this writing project, Yogi Ramsuratkumar's blessing was tangible, and his voice, spoken in the heart, somehow guided me to go more deeply inside the events of his life to ask "why" and "how" and "what does this mean to the men and women of a faith-starved, war-ravaged world?"

Always there was an answer. Not generally a response in words, but always unmistakable, nonetheless – a mood, a sense of benediction, sometimes even the momentary dissolution of the illusory walls of separation that kept me shielded and safe from both the pain of the world and my consequent longing for God.

Insofar as this book sheds one more ray of light on the life and teaching of the Godchild of Tiruvannamalai, Yogi Ramsurat-kumar, for whom there was "only God" in everything, everywhere...all praise and thanks to him. Doubts or no doubts, insofar as this book may inspire and effect something valuable in its reader – something useful to practice, to faith, to surrender, to obedience to the will of God, and to the ongoing progress of the Work – let all praise and thanks resound to the merciful Divine Beggar, Yogi Ramsuratkumar.

ONLY GOD

The Ganges River at Kashi (Benaras)

1

AT THE RIVER'S EDGE, 1918-1947

 December 1, 1918. The First World War has been over for less than a month, the Armistice signed in the early weeks of November. An epidemic of Spanish influenza is ravaging the globe, within one year leaving more than fifty million dead, at least six million of these in India alone. On this day, Mahatma Gandhi, at age forty-nine, is recuperating from a major illness at his Satyagraha Ashram, across the river from the crowded city of Ahmedabad, in northern India. Gandhi is enraged to learn that the wartime restrictions imposed by the British will be continued indefinitely. Within a few weeks he will once again be crisscrossing his beloved Mother India with white-hot fervor, speaking to Muslim and Hindu alike, tirelessly making efforts for peace and unification while repeating the name of God – *Ram, Ram, Ram* – with every breath.

The great nationalist, revolutionary, and spiritual luminary, Sri Aurobindo Ghose, is forty-six and living in Pondicherry. Aurobindo has retired to this quiet French colony to escape British domination and possible imprisonment. He writes feverishly, treatises on spirituality and politics, as a few disciples gather around him.

Bhagavan Sri Ramana Maharshi, at thirty-nine, is already attracting attention from Western visitors, as well as spiritual seekers from all over India. He lives on the slopes of Mount Arunachala in Tiruvannamalai, Tamil Nadu, in a converted cave known as Skanadashram, writing and receiving guests, attended by his ailing mother and a few devotees.

ONLY GOD

On India's west coast, in Mangalore, Vittal Rao, who would later be known as Swami Papa Ramdas, is twenty-four, married, and the father of a child. His life is quickly disintegrating around him as work ventures continue to fail and both his wife and daughter have fallen seriously ill.

In the sleepy village of Shirdi, in the district of Maharashtra, about 285 kilometers from Bombay (now Mumbai), the locals are still grieving the recent passing of their resident sage and prophet. The man they called Sai Baba, held today as one of the greatest saints of India's contemporary history, left his physical body – attained *mahasamadhi* – on October 15, 1918, just forty-seven days ago. Interestingly, in many Buddhist traditions it is asserted that the soul will take rebirth within forty-nine days after the body's physical death.

And, in a small village of North India, along the Ganges River, near the City of Light – the metropolis of Benaras, as it was called in December 1918 under British rule; Kashi as it is traditionally called; or Varanasi as it is known today – Ramsurat Kunwar, later known as Sri Yogi Ramsuratkumar, is born.[1]

The reports vary as to exactly which village in this area held the privilege of being his birthplace. Some say the village was in the state of Bihar; others claim it was in Uttar Pradesh. Since Varanasi lies on the river Ganges near the borders of both states, either one is a good guess. His first biographer, Truman Caylor Wadlington, who received the information directly from Yogi Ramsuratkumar in 1970, gives the location as merely "along the banks of river Ganges in a village near Kashi."[2]

We do know that in later years, when visiting the ashram of Swami Papa Ramdas in Kanhangad, South India, Yogi Ramsurat-kumar was referred to as "the odd Bihari."[3] This descriptor may have been a generic reference to the fact that he was a northerner, rather than a precise historical reference to his birthplace.

Yogi Ramsuratkumar never revealed his native place, except with vague allusions, and in fact made it quite clear that he didn't wish it known. "This beggar has no family," he once said to Lee Lozowick, his American devotee; "Don't go after those people."[4] His reasons for keeping his past shielded in mystery are cause for speculation, and followers are always ready to create elegant metaphysical explanations for the master's ways. In summarizing the life of Sai Baba of Shirdi, a devotee explained: "Like most of the perfect saints he left no authentic record of his birth and early life before arriving at Shirdi. In fact, in the face of his spiritual brilliance such queries do not have much relevance."[5]

Perhaps the reason for Ramsuratkumar's secrecy was even simpler, more human, than one would suspect. Professor Sadhu Rangarajan, an ardent devotee of Yogi Ramsuratkumar's, remembered his master's great reluctance to speak about his past.

"Please tell me the exact village in which you were born." I asked Yogi Ramsuratkumar one day.

Bhagwan took my hand and was petting my palm, saying, "Rangaraja, the people in my village, they are all very poor. If you go there, they will not be able to give you even a cup of coffee."

I said, "Bhagwan, I am not going there for coffee. I just want to go touch the soil and come back. Please tell me what is your village."

"No Rangaraja, my people are very poor, and if you go there and they don't entertain you properly, this beggar will feel very poorly."[6]

We know that Ramsuratkumar was born into a Brahmin family, and that his parents were devout people, although we have no record, to date, of their names. He was the second of three children – all male.[7] His full name means, "the Divine child who always revels in the supreme Consciousness" (literally, *Ram*, the name of God; *Surata*, reveling intensely; *Kumara*, the Divine child).[8] As a young Brahmin he would have been well versed in his heritage, and several stories allude to the early instruction he received from his father in the great legends of Hinduism, the *Ramayana* and the *Mahabharata*. His love of these great works is known through numerous references to them in his conversations throughout his life. As a child, and certainly as a child of his culture, the stories of Ram and Sita, of Hanuman the monkey who flew across the sea to save Sita from the clutches of the evil Ravana as recounted in the *Ramayana*, and the tales of Krishna and Arjuna and the great wars of the *Mahabharata* were not heard as being only about ancient times, and certainly not about strictly mythical beings. These stories and the characters who filled them were rather a living legacy that he himself embodied. "For Yogi Ramsuratkumar this story [referring to a contemporary poetical account written of the love of Sita and Rama] was real! Not only historically, but it was going on now. Yogi Ramsuratkumar was living the *Ramayana* now, in his life. The *Ramayana* was real, and Yogi Ramsuratkumar's *bhava* in response to this work was real. He was living the heartbreak of Sita!…He *was* Sita longing for her lover."[9]

राम

As Ramsuratkumar was born near the Ganges (Ganga), this sacred river exerted a strong influence on his young life. His first glimpse of "her," in conscious memory, occurred at the age of three or four when his father took him to the banks, pointed to the river and asked him, "Do you know what this is?" To which the child answered, "river."

"Do you think this is a mere river?" his father began again, this time with tears in his eyes, as Ramsuratkumar related to devotees many years later. His father continued: "Know that this is a goddess, the mother. Ganga is the mother, the Punya Tirtha [the sacred water of highest virtue or merit]."[10]

This Ganga is no meandering stream, but a massive life-supporting torrent that flows some 1,550 miles from Devprayag at the foot of the Himalayas to the Bay of Bengal. Sometime during the Brahmanical Age (2,500 – 1,500 B.C.E.), the center of civilization in India shifted from the western sectors along the Yamuna and Saraswati Rivers, moving eastward to the fertile area of the Ganges. Much like the Nile, which provided sustenance to the cultures of Egypt, the role that the Ganges played in India is integral to the history of her people. The fact that the Ganges is commonly referred to as "Mother Ganga" and is represented in form as a female goddess says it all. She *is* the creative principle: the birther, supporter, and death-receiving mother. In fact, to die in Kashi, so close to the sacred river, and to have one's remains cast into the Mother's waters, is considered by devout Hindus to be the greatest privilege and the assurance of liberation.

Thought to be the very expression of India itself, the Ganga is tied to the development of yogic discipline from ancient times. Iconography of the great god Siva (or Shiva) – the model of asceticism – shows the Mother river flowing through his hair.

A typical example of the ascetic is the royal sage Bhagiratha, whose exploits are told in the *Mahabharata*. In ancient times, during a long spell of drought, he took it upon himself to stand on one foot for a thousand years and, for another thousand, hold his arms up high. In this manner he compelled the Gods to grant his request that the heavenly river Ganges (Ganga) release its waters to flood and regenerate the parched earth. The downpour from the celestial river was so great that God Shiva needed to slow its speed by catching the water on his head. The water ran through his tangled hair, forming the riverine basin of the Ganges (Ganga) River of Northern India.[11]

As a child, Ramsuratkumar loved the river. He wandered along her shores and surely bathed in her swift-flowing or gentle waters. Being at the river kept him close to nature, which he always loved. Rural Indian village life today is still grounded in nature; it would have been more so in the 1920s. Even those who made their living from merchandising would spend much of their time outdoors – sleeping in open-sided huts, bathing and washing at the river's edge, sitting outside under the stars around a fire, or gathered on the ground or under a tree beside a local tea stall. For the vast majority of his life, until illness made this restrictive, and even though he lived in a burgeoning city, Yogi Ramsuratkumar would spend much of the day, and most of his nights, outdoors. In Tiruvannamalai, Yogiji spent his time under the *ashwathra* tree at the bus station and the *punnai* tree at the town's railway station, and many stories told by devotees include references to these beloved spots.[12]

ONLY GOD

Even in the last year of his earthly life, Ramsuratkumar would occasionally stay in a small screened-in hut located behind the great temple that had become his shrine and is his samadhi site today. Nature was the guise of "His Father," his affectionate words for the All-Pervasive One to whom his life was surrendered.

Young Ramsuratkumar wanted to be under the stars; to hear birds, and the ever-present river; to feel breezes; to be in the communion of trees. He spent numerous childhood nights sleeping on the banks of the Ganges, much to the consternation of his parents, who at first scolded this behavior. When he explained to them that "the river understood and cared for him,"[13] they conceded, allowing him his way even if they did not approve.

Along the banks of the Ganges, young Ramsuratkumar would have seen hundreds or even thousands of ascetics, mostly men, in the course of his childhood. The ascetics who lived along the riverbanks in the 1920s, when he was exploring these territories, were little different from those who live there today. Although some of their twenty-first century descendents may wear watches and carry discarded plastic water bottles, the true sadhu's (wandering sage or ascetic) accoutrements are far secondary to his or her intention – complete and radical reliance upon the Divine, total absorption in the Self.

Some, perhaps, as Bhagiratha described above, would have been posed in extreme yogic *asanas* (postures). Others, perhaps with matted hair, would be sitting silently in deep contemplation, cross-legged, unmoving for hours or days at a time. One would be chanting, repeating the name of God for long periods, or singing *slokas* (verses) of a scripture. Occasionally, small groups would be gathered together speaking with animation. Some would be discoursing on the *Vedas* or *Upanishads* with their visitors or disciples. Others might be sharing the local gossip – about the political climate of the nearby city, or the place where alms were to be had. Ramsuratkumar would have noted the distinguished ochre clothing that many wore, whether they merely wrapped a length of orange cloth around their waists, covered their nakedness with a long orange shirt, or wore only rags, stained or dust-covered. Others, with less than nothing, would have ashes alone smeared over their fully naked bodies. He would have made offerings into their begging bowls, a practice known as *bhiksha*, as it was their code to never ask for anything, but only to await upon God to feed, clothe, or protect them.

These impressions are powerful, even terrifying, for adults to witness. Such radical surrender and trust are both compelling and incomprehensible. Yet, for children, such appearances would be fascinating, frightening, but ultimately magical.

In the 1970s, and later, over half a century after his initial contact with the Ganges sages, Ramsuratkumar still remembered specific occasions when he was invited by some saint to sit by his *dhuni* fire (the ritual fire). He recalled long nights of storytelling in which the myths and legends of his religious heritage were told to him by these wanderers. And he candidly spoke of sharing his own food with them, or even bringing them for a meal to his parents' home or to a neighbor's house.

The feeding of sadhus, as it has been practiced for centuries in India, is more than an act of charity; more than the Christian notion of "giving food to the hungry." Certainly in both traditions there is merit attached to sharing one's goods with those in need, but to give food to a sadhu goes beyond this one-sided service. Such a practice is, in fact, a reciprocal feeding process, something that Ramsuratkumar would have well understood from his earliest days. And something that he advocated with vigor in his later life. The idea of feeding a sadhu was to invite a messenger of the Divine.

In a letter to devotees, Pagal Haranath, a Bengali householder saint (1865 – 1927) expressed an attitude toward sadhus that Yogi Ramsuratkumar would have shared with enthusiasm.

> Sadhus are real magnets, quite powerful to purify everything impure and to turn it all to good. So, with heart and soul, wish [for] the company of these favourites who alone will show you the easiest and proper path to eternal bliss and will lead you to Krishna where...happiness never ceases.
>
> ...Just try once to meet and talk to Sadhus, men at whom you look askance; converse with them about the doings of Krishna, and sing the praise of the Lord with them. You will find that there is no more potent remedy than this on earth to bring peace to the mind.

7

…Hold conversation with these poor wandering mendicants, learn to love them…It is Sri Krishna who has bestowed this honour upon them. The Sadhus have resigned everything to the feet of Krishna, hence it is that Krishna also has enchanced [sic] their honour…[14]

Yogi Ramsuratkumar greatly admired Haranath. "This beggar was once fed by a devotee of Pagal Haranath," he told Haragopal Sepuri, who visited Tiruvannamalai regularly starting in the 1970s. "Pagal Haranath was a Mahatma. His wife Kusuma Kumari was also a Mahatma…" he said.[15] And in fact, with the blessing of hindsight, one can easily say that Haranath's words might have been written about the beggar himself.

राम

Although literacy was far from the privilege of every Indian child, Ramsuratkumar was enrolled in school and pursued his education for many years. We can guess that his studies came easily for him, as higher education followed, and then a teaching career in which Ramsuratkumar rose to the rank of headmaster. But school education seems to have been a secondary influence. Primarily, as the aging saint himself recalled about his early life, it was an event that occurred at the age of twelve, in 1930, that marked the shattering of the protective shell of childhood, introducing him to the great noble truth of human suffering and the nature of impermanence. In much the way that Siddhartha the Buddha was wrenched from innocence by looking upon a poor man, a sick man, and a corpse, Ramsuratkumar was indelibly impressed by an action that resulted in the death of a bird.

On a lovely moonlit evening, at his mother's request, he went to the village well to draw water for the household – a practice that was common for him, and one that has forever occupied the energy and attention of women and children throughout India. As he lowered the bucket via its rope, his attention was captured by a chirping bird perched on the wall of the well not far from his hand. Playfully, without forethought, in the manner of children, Ramsuratkumar snapped the bucket's rope in the bird's direction. The effect was immediate. The tiny creature was dead on the spot, and the boy, shocked with disbelief, slowly moved toward the animal's lifeless body. Taking the bird into his hands, the child tried to pour some water into its beak in an attempt to revive it – an attempt to undo the action that would forever impress upon him the nature of cause and effect, of life and death, and the fragility of the veil between them. When it was obvious that the bird was dead, Ramsuratkumar solemnly walked to the river, waded out a short distance, and entrusted the animal's body to the Mother's waters. Only then did his tears release. Climbing back up the riverbank, he lay for a long time, weeping, tortured in the knowledge of what he had done.

The event heralded an immersion into his own depths, urging a greater introversion, as he reported in later years. It seems that he made no attempt to alleviate his own pain at the time, no attempt to make light of the fact that it was merely a bird. Instead, "he looked for the truth of what had happened, and with such intensity one might think he had committed every act that had ever brought misery into the world. His heart began to feel for all of life, and the suffering he endured sowed the seeds of spiritual growth."[16]

राम

Four years later, in 1934, Ramsuratkumar experienced the second great event of his youth, and the second great event in his spiritual formation. He went to Kashi – Benaras – alone. He was sixteen.

Undoubtedly, since his childhood the young man would have learned by heart and sung the ever-popular songs in praise of Kashi, the Kashi *mahatmyas,* contained in the *Puranas* – the collected ancient stories of Hinduism. Young Ramsuratkumar would certainly have visited this sacred city previously in the company of his devout parents – as pilgrimage is one of India's national pastimes. Whole families flock to the temples or other sacred sites, sometimes hundreds of kilometers distant, for the festivities of a holy day. They come "not sight-seeing but 'sacred sight-seeing.' They want to have the *darshana* of the place itself as well as that of its presiding deity, who in Kashi is Shiva Vishvanatha, the 'Lord of All.'"[17] Benaras is considered to be the permanent home of the Supreme Lord, a place so sacred that it is thought to be both the center of the world and not attached to the rest of the world. A heavenly realm of light, Kashi is also the city within whose walls death equals liberation.

Ramsuratkumar and his family would likely have participated in one or more great celebrations there, as one can hardly visit Kashi without being swept into one. The liturgical year in this city begins in the first nine days of the first month, Chaitra (March/April), with the festival of Navaratra, the "Nine Nights of the Goddess." Greater or lesser celebrations continue on through to Phalguna (February/March), the final month, in which the preeminent holy day – Mahashivaratri, the "Great Night of Siva" – takes place, along with the greatest Hindu carnival, Holi.

One day in his sixteenth year, the teenage Ramsuratkumar was drawn to the railway station near his village, determined to travel to Benaras one way or another. His ardor for the holy city's benediction must have been obvious, as a friendly stranger paid for his ticket and offered him a meal. The stranger's act was probably a small generosity by a fellow pilgrim or a caring elder, as the distance to Kashi was a minor one. But, in any case, it reflected the protective benevolence that the Divine is constantly showing to those who seek for its Heart.

The spiritual heart of Varanasi is the Vishvanatha Temple, also commonly called the Golden Temple because of the 800 kilograms of gold plating on its towers. Dating from ancient times, but destroyed on numerous occasions by Muslim armies, this temple, as Ramsuratkumar would have found it in 1934, had been rebuilt several times, the last in 1776. It was always dedicated to Lord Vishvanatha, who is Siva in his manifestation as Lord of the Universe.

Entering the sanctum sanctorum of this temple, Ramsuratkumar would have found the polished black stone shaft, the *linga* that is the symbol of Siva. From his own accounts in later years, we know that the young man was overcome with the spiritual power emanating from and captured in this place. Here he stood, unmoving, for many hours, held in bliss.

For an ecstatic week Ramsuratkumar wandered the streets of the city, drunk with the Divine Presence he had so unmistakably encountered. Undoubtedly he visited other sacred shrines throughout, and bathed daily in the Mother Ganga, where every morning thousands of other pilgrims would perform their ablutions. Here too he would have met again, in greater numbers, the sadhus and sages who had fascinated him from his youth. He, like all visitors, would have been absorbed in the activities of the burning *ghats*, where day in and day out scores of dead bodies were entrusted to the flames, their ashes strewn upon the Mother's waters.

Whether as a part of this first solitary trip or on another journey soon after, we know that Ramsuratkumar traveled, by foot perhaps, the short ten kilometers northeast of Kashi to Sarnath. This hamlet, formerly known simply as "The Deer Park," was the place where Lord Buddha was drawn following his enlightenment. The taste of freedom that permeates the city's shrines once again intoxicated the adolescent Ramsuratkumar. Perhaps he stood in the shadow of the thirty-four meter high Dhamekh Stupa, the site where Buddha first preached his message of the Middle Path. Perhaps he meditated in the main shrine, in which the Buddhist convert King Ashoka, the preeminent model of compassionate leadership, had sat. In any case, the impressions left upon Ramsuratkumar were strong, and certainly intensified his longing for truth and for a similar freedom and liberation.

राम

The years that followed his illumination in Kashi are hidden years – the first of three such periods in his life. From Yogi Ramsuratkumar himself we know little or nothing about this time until he set off on his spiritual quest, in 1947, thirteen years later. Such disappearances have their historical precedents in the lives of great men and women throughout time. And mythical speculation is generally rife about the goings-on during such years. Jesus, many say, journeyed to India, where he was educated in esoteric yogas after he faded, temporarily, from public view at the age of twelve. The last recorded event of Jesus's childhood also concerned a pilgrimage; also to a sacred site – the Holy of Holies, the great temple of Jerusalem. He too had spent days in this place, during which he discoursed with rabbis and other learned men in much the way that Ramsuratkumar had always found himself drawn to the sadhus at the rivers. When

Jesus failed to meet up with his parents at the appointed time and place, they were distraught. Returning to the city, his mother found him still in the temple among the elders. He seemed surprised at her concern. "Why is it that you searched for me?" he said, his words sounding almost harsh. "Did you not know that I must be about my Father's business?" (Luke 2:49)

Ramsuratkumar would forever speak of *his* "Father" and his Father's work in exactly the same way that Jesus did. Yet, by his own admission, these hidden years were not exalted ones. Studies, an interest in football (soccer), marriage, children, householder *sadhana* (spiritual practice) – the simplicity and predictability of an ordinary man's life – these were his steps and stages.

While Yogi Ramsuratkumar has not confirmed speculation or investigation into his educational past, some evidence points toward an education at Allahabad University, located only 135 kilometers west of Varanasi. A dialogue between the master and Sadhu Rangarajan in the 1990s revealed once again the beggar's reticence, bordering on embarrassment, to admit anything about his past.

"Yes, see, I've got some material about you," said Rangarajan one day, as he sat with Yogi Ramsuratkumar and Devaki Ma.

"What do you know about this beggar?" the older man asked.

"Amitabh Bachchan's father was your teacher."

Amitabh Bachchan, a current megastar of Hindi film, is the son of Harivansh Rai Bachchan, a world-renowned poet and translator of literature and a scholar in both Hindi and Urdu languages. Bachchan's poetic career skyrocketed to fame when his deeply devotional piece, "The Tavern," was first published. He is honored as one of India's greatest writers and a figure of international importance. When he died at age ninety-six in January 2003, the BBC covered his funeral service. Among Harivansh Bachchan's lifelong accomplishments was the translation of Shakespeare's tragedies into Hindi. Bachchan was a professor at Allahabad University from 1941 through 1952 – precisely the time in which Ramsuratkumar would have been attending college, as we know that he finished his secondary education in 1937.[18] It is entirely conceivable that he could have been a student of the great poet's. In Allahabad, Bachchan taught English literature – a subject that Ramsuratkumar always cherished.

"Yogi Ramsuratkumar got a little red" on hearing this news of Bachchan, Rangarajan reported.

"Oh, Rangarajan has done some security work and found out something about this beggar," the saintly man said gently. "How did you get this information?"

"I've got my own source of information, Bhagwan," the professor replied.

"Oh, Rangarajan, you are doing security work, you are probing about this beggar's past," Yogi Ramsuratkumar said, neither affirming nor denying the connection.

All who have spent any time in the beggar's presence have referenced his vast and erudite knowledge of many subjects. That he was thoroughly fluent in English, even in the subtleties of the language, is undeniable. That he possessed a scholar's knowledge of English literature was revealed on numerous occasions. When his American devotee Lee Lozowick and friends visited him in the late 1980s and early 1990s, Yogi Ramsuratkumar occasionally asked for quotes or remembered lines of poetry, like those of Milton or Blake.

Some connection to Bachchan is likely, as we know from other sources that Yogi Ramsuratkumar "had great respect for...Bachchan" and other contemporary Indian poets, and that "he had met them, although details of the talks are not available."[19] We know beyond doubt that Yogi Ramsuratkumar loved poetry, and in fact attracted many superb contemporary poets and writers to his side, as both devotees and friends, during his lifetime.

On another occasion, a location for the place of the beggar's higher education was given as Lucknow, another North Indian city in Uttar Pradesh. Swami Vimalananda, head of the Sivananda Tapovanam, Madurai, apparently met Yogi Ramsuratkumar during the beggar's early years in Tiruvannamalai. They met at the railway station, one of the Godchild's favorite haunts, and spent some time in conversation. As the two men sat together in a railway compartment, the master spoke of his university training at Lucknow.[20]

As to other details of his educational life, we read in *The Gospel of Swami Ramdas* that the "odd Bihari," referring to Ramsuratkumar, "is a B.A., B.T. [a teaching degree], and was a teacher in some High School" currently on a long leave.[21] And this is confirmed in the work of Ma Vijayalakshmi, in an unpublished manuscript about the beggar's life entitled *Waves of Love.*

> He completed his university education, trained to become a teacher, taught in a school for a few years and became the Headmaster...he became proficient in several languages: besides Hindi, English and Bengali, he studied Urdu and others.[22]

With such a brilliant foundation Ramsuratkumar himself might have become a writer, a poet, perhaps even a politician (as he had a great passion for India's welfare), or a distinguished university professor. He was well read, well spoken and full of deep dedication. And yet he left behind all such possibilities for touching the world in these ways. Instead, he would become a beggar, a wanderer, a man living on the streets dressed in rags.

Years later, as he sat with circles of admirers and devotees in places in South India, Yogi Ramsuratkumar would reveal himself as a man of universal education and universal values – a man who could "speak" everyman's language; a man who had seen and known the depths of the human condition, and from many perspectives. He would talk with the uneducated and the most learned in the language of the heart. Simply, practically, he might instruct a struggling food merchant in the making of *puris* (a South Indian food), or direct a woman to the most expedient way of healing her ailing cow. Unmasking pretense and delighting in innocence, he would play with children for long periods of time, yet quickly dismiss or conveniently ignore those who came expecting special treatment for their accomplishments. While there is no doubt that he was well educated in the worldly sense of things, the abilities that Yogi Ramsuratkumar would manifest in his interactions with people over the years would never be ascribed to book learning. Rather, it was his passion for the work of his Father – only God – that allowed him access to such universal knowledge.

In his twenty-ninth year, in 1947, Yogi Ramsuratkumar turned his back on education, scholarship, security and family. Hunger for truth, a fierce dedication to Mother India, and a longing for God –

these were the courses in which his soul was simultaneously enrolled. These were the forces that had weighed upon him during his formative years, and the passions that would eventually triumph.

THE SEARCH OF
THE SPIRITUAL PATRIOT, 1947

The decade of the 1940s was one of most turbulent and exultant times in India's modern history. These were the years during which Ramsuratkumar completed his university education, took a teaching job, married and raised a family in North India.

As a college student in these days, he would certainly have kept current with world events. The superpowers – the U.S., Great Britain, Germany and Japan – were at war, and the effects were felt everywhere. In India, Britain's two-hundred-year reign was coming to an end, encouraged by the relentless and growing internal strife between Hindus and Muslims and by resistance efforts of India's citizenry, inspired by her spiritual patriots.

During the period from 1920 to 1945, Uttar Pradesh was the hotbed of the Indian revolutionary movement. Allahabad University, in Uttar Pradesh, where Ramsuratkumar may have studied, was the womb of patriots and revolutionaries of that period. There is little possibility that the young man could have escaped the waves of political upheaval that were crashing everywhere. The revolutionary activities and the writings of Swami Vivekananda, Sister Nivedita, and Sri Aurobindo were well known – guidebooks of both dharma and dissent. Popular songs, on the lips of schoolchildren across the nation, further impressed the need to honor India's heritage in the struggle against foreign rule.

As a northerner, Ramsuratkumar would have followed closely the progress of India's most publicized patriot – Mahatma Gandhi – who was simultaneously regarded as a living saint. Even forty years later,

Rasmuratkumar's enormous admiration for Gandhi was expressed with unqualified enthusiasm. As the beggar walked the streets of Tiruvannamalai, South India, in the 1980s, he would still spontaneously break into rousing shouts of "Mahatma Gandhi, Ki Jai!"– "Victory to Mahatma Gandhi." He would speak of Gandhi in the same breath with the "many Great Masters" of India, including Swami Ramdas, Sri Aurobindo and Swami Rama Tirtha, all of whom had a profound influence on his life.

In 1942, Gandhi's proposal of a "Quit India" resolution aimed at the British was passed by the All-India Congress. Even as an old man – Gandhi was seventy-three at the time – he was indefatigable. In this year he began yet another campaign of passive resistance. Again he was arrested, together with other prominent Indian leaders, and the demonstrations they had spearheaded were forcibly suppressed by the British administration.

In 1943, imprisoned with his wife and other family friends at the Aga Khan Palace near Poona, Gandhi began a fast, another attempt at drawing attention to the life or death struggle in which his beloved Mother India was engaged. As every action of the much-loved (or much-hated) Mahatma's life was broadcast throughout India twice a day, millions knew immediately where he stood on any issue. The British Viceroy and Indian leaders were deadlocked in their negotiations for a British withdrawal from India. Gandhi's fast was a plea for moving forward.

When Gandhi's wife, Kasturba, died during this detention at the Aga Khan Palace on February 22, 1944, at the age of seventy-four, his own health took a rapid decline. On May 6 of this year, Gandhi was finally released from prison – granted unconditional amnesty for the remainder of his life. This marked the last of the 2,338 days he had spent in jail over his lifetime.

In November 1946, Gandhi initiated a four-month tour in which he visited forty-nine villages in East Bengal. Violence was spreading in this area, as the issue of Moslem representation in provisional government was being challenged. And in 1947, in March, his travels took him through Bihar, where Hindu-Moslem tensions had long been the order of the day. It is conceivable that Ramsuratkumar, as an educated and passionate twenty-nine-year-old living either in the regions of Bihar or close by, was present at some gathering in which Gandhiji spoke.

As the political climate reached blazing intensity on many fronts throughout the country, the ultimate questions of purpose and meaning were certainly stirred in the lives of millions of individuals as well. While Ramsuratkumar never referred to any active engagement in India's political struggle on his own part, he did tell his early biographer that the year 1947 was marked for him by enormous inner turmoil. Undoubtedly, his destiny was calling. But the form that destiny would take was yet entirely unknown.

राम

Swami Rama Tirtha (1873-1906)

Numerous devotees of Yogi Ramsuratkumar's have observed that "he was very fond of Swami Rama Tirtha's teachings."[1] Indeed, Ramsuratkumar's life was a sterling example of these teachings at every turn. As Rama Tirtha lived and died before Ramsuratkumar was born, knowledge of his life and words was probably a part of the younger man's spiritual education. Throughout his life, Ramsuratkumar regularly referred to Rama Tirtha with profound respect and gratitude and often had his guests read from the book *In the Woods of God-Realization*, a compilation of many volumes of Rama Tirtha's lectures.

"Swami Rama Tirtha has said that he will be always in some human form and see that our goal is achieved," Yogi Ramsuratkumar said in later years, speaking of India's role as a spiritual force in the world.

Rama Tirtha began his spiritual life as a *bhakti*, steeped in devotion to Lord Krishna. He was also a single-minded advocate of the *Sanatana Dharma* – or "everlasting dharma," evolved from the Hindu Vedic cosmology. According to this understanding, all things were the expression of one principle of unity, and for Rama Tirtha, God was seen and felt in all names and forms. For Yogi Ramsuratkumar, this truth would forever be summed up in the words that have come to characterize his own teaching, "Father alone exists."

The Search of the Spiritual Patriot, 1947

By the 1940s, Rama Tirtha's teachings were widely known and deeply cherished (although not so consistently practiced), particularly in northern India, as he was born and educated in Lahore, Punjab region (currently Pakistan). In a lecture given in 1896, he maintained that as

> Nature has no prejudice against anyone…a true Sanatana Dharmite must not observe any discrimination against anybody. For him there is no differentiation between the rich and the poor, high and the low, and a Brahmin and a Shudra. They are all equal in his eyes, because the same God is present in all of them. If anybody discriminates between man and man, he, in fact, insults the Omnipresence of God.[2]

Rama Tirtha lived his entire life – of only thirty-three years – in British-dominated India. His enormous passion for his homeland was never diminished, as it was integral to his spiritual dharma. Based in the Vedic understanding, the country of one's birth was no different from the Divine Mother who birthed creation. India itself was the Mother Goddess. Rama Tirtha understood that when his country was in chains, so was his Mother disrespected. His identification of spirituality and patriotism was absolute, as when he announced that "a Hindu is the person who is ever prepared to sacrifice his all at the altar of India, to safeguard her honour, prestige and dignity."[3] Rama Tirtha, like Gandhi, advocated a return to homespun cloth, and called upon his countrymen and women to preserve their cultural heritage by speaking their native language in preference to English. He even likened the freedom struggle to that of the lover longing for the Beloved, and needing to sacrifice everything, no matter what the cost, to achieve unity at last.

> By merely repeating the name of Laila, like a parrot, you cannot become a Majnu [referring to the archetypal Muslim tale of longing between two young lovers]. If you want to be a real Majnu, you have to prove that you can also suffer the same kind of troubles, pain and ordeals to meet your Beloved. So, too, for the good of your country, you will have

to suffer the greatest ordeals, like imprisonment, flogging or even the gallows. If you are thus willing to sacrifice your all, then and then alone, you can hope to free your country from the bondage of slavery.[4]

Despite Rama Tirtha's clarion call to resistance of British rule, he did not see the domineering presence of foreigners as the cause of India's disease, but rather as only one symptom. Rama Tirtha's injunctions were primarily directed at the heart of the matter, the inability of India's people to embrace the truth of their dharma. If they had been strongly based in these principles, he proclaimed, they could not have been subjugated. "Please study your own history with care and attention," he urged, and "you will please mark that, so long as we were strictly following the basic tenets of our Sanatana Dharma which is based on mutual love, unity and selfless discharge of our moral duty, with faith in God, no outside power could dare look at us with evil designs."[5]

One of the most profound influences in Rama Tirtha's young life was Swami Vivekananda, another great patriot-saint revered by Yogi Ramsuratkumar. Rama Tirtha saw Vivekananda, the preeminent spiritual son of Swami Ramakrishna, for the first time at Lahore. The mere sight of the much-revered swami clothed in ochre robes, the mark of his dedication as a *sannyasin*, kindled in Rama Tirtha the desire to commit his own life in a similar way.

Swami Vivekananda (1863-1902)

"Swami Vivekananda's message is the root of India's freedom struggle," Yogi Ramsuratkumar said with enthusiasm in July 1991. "He was responsible for our freedom movement." And on the same day, Ramsuratkumar declared, "What a love Swami Vivekananda had for India and our Sanatan Dharma!"[6]

One of India's greatest poets and mystics, Rabindrinath Tagore, captured the importance of Swami Vivekananda's role in India's history in the advice he gave to Romain Rolland, a Nobel Prize-winning French author, who later wrote biographies of Gandhi and Swami Vivekananda. "If you want to know India," Tagore instructed Rolland, "study Vivekananda."

Swami Vivekananda took to the road shortly after the death of Sri Ramakrishna, his master, traveling far and wide throughout India. As a passionate, highly educated, and articulate spokesman for the dharma, Vivekananda left his mark everywhere. But it was from among the poorest of peasants that the Swami himself realized his greatest inspiration. Even though he had been born and raised in Calcutta, it was on this pilgrimage that the physical poverty of India's masses, combined with its superstitious beliefs and dearth of education, overwhelmingly impressed Vivekananda. It was clear to him that the spiritual, cultural, or political renaissance that he dreamed of for India would never ultimately succeed unless the basic needs of her people were addressed. The poor needed food and some way to affect their future; and their children needed education. Vivekananda's tireless efforts to rouse the "sleeping Lion of India" took him to the palaces of the rich, where he attempted to gain support for a means to renew the hearts, souls, and bodies of his countrymen and women. In a rare few instances he secured the help he needed. His words were inflammatory. "Bread! Bread!" he cried. "I do not believe in a God which cannot give me bread here, giving me eternal bliss in heaven! Pooh! India is to be raised, the poor are to be fed, education is to be spread, and the evil of priestcraft is to be removed. No priestcraft, no social tyranny! More bread, more opportunity for everybody."[7]

It 1893, urged by his supporters, Vivekananda traveled to the U.S., and there delivered a brilliant overview of India's spiritual mission at the First Parliament of World Religions, held in Chicago. This appearance so captured the imaginations of the Americans and the British that Vivekananda's name was soon recognizable throughout the Western world. In his own country, Swami Vivekananda's success abroad immediately earned him the status of a national hero. The message he had delivered to the world reminded his own people of their remarkable heritage. A wave of national pride swept the subcontinent in its wake. From that point on, doors that had been previously closed were opened to him everywhere.

Swami Vivekananda knew that India's youth was India's hope in the freedom struggle. From the end of the nineteenth century and long into the twentieth, his wakeup call was still resounding, particularly throughout Bengal, the region of his greatest influence.

"Liberty is the possession of the brave," he proclaimed, calling upon India's youth to put "first things first." He knew that children needed physical strength and stamina if they were to take their rightful place as future leaders of India. "This urgency of physical fitness must take the topmost priority even to reading the *Bhagavad Gita* itself," he once announced with revolutionary fervor.[8]

It is likely that the youthful Ramsuratkumar was affected in some way by the educational policies that followed upon Vivekananda's efforts. At the very least, Ramsuratkumar would have been exposed in his early years to the Swamiji's life, his words, and his mission, as the patriot-saint's influence was extensive and long-enduring, especially throughout northern India. Furthermore, Vivekananda's central place in India's push for freedom from foreign rule was undisputed. Anyone who participated in that freedom struggle, or studied Indian history, or simply read the newspapers, had no doubt that Swami Vivekananda was India's foremost social revolutionary of modern times.

> [F]reedom is the first condition of growth. What you do not make free will never grow. The idea that you can make others grow and help their growth, that you can direct and guide them, always retaining for yourself the freedom of the teacher, is nonsense, a dangerous lie, which has retarded the growth of millions and millions of human beings in this world. Let men have the light of liberty. That is the only condition of growth.[9]

Vivekananda's mission not only inspired and influenced Mahatma Gandhi but it seeded the work of Sri Aurobindo, the spiritual patriot turned mystic-saint, and the man to whom Ramsuratkumar would first turn in his own spiritual search.

राम

After years of protest and negotiation, on August 15, 1947, India was at last granted independence from British rule. While this was a major victory, it was also a major tragedy. Gandhi and many other freedom fighters and patriots vehemently opposed the Indian Congress's decision to divide the country along religious lines – creating a Hindu India and a Moslem Pakistan. The Mahatma's lifelong struggle to end religious separatism had ultimately failed.

August 15ᵗʰ was, coincidentally, the birthday of Sri Aurobindo, who lived in Pondicherry, South India. Aurobindo, long acknowledged as a great Indian nationalist, was now a spiritual recluse and mystic. In 1947, he was seventy-five years old.

What drove the young Ramsuratkumar to the feet of the great sage Aurobindo rather than to another master is an interesting question. Certainly there would have been many gurus and teachers to be found along the banks of the Ganges in his native place in the north, and Ramsuratkumar had mingled with such men since his childhood.

For many years Ramsuratkumar had kept company in this vicinity with an aged sadhu named Ram Ashram. The elder was a man of profound wisdom and easily commanded immediate respect from his youthful admirer. To him, Ramsuratkumar was willing to pour out the longings of his heart. A few vignettes of their interactions told by Yogi Ramsuratkumar to his early biographer and closest disciples allow us to reconstruct a probable scene of one of the meetings between the old *sadhak* and the young seeker.

As the two friends sat together one night before the fire of the old man's hut, Ramsuratkumar admitted that he had reached a point of near despair. Torn with questions about his life's mission and hungering for some reassurance that he was aiming in the right direction, Ramsuratkumar was desperate. Words alone were unable to soothe his heart.

Recognizing this opportune moment in the younger man's unfolding spiritual process, his caring mentor sent him off to spend some time alone, urging him to contemplate the longing that threatened to overtake him.

Finding a secluded place nearby, Ramsuratkumar raised his eyes and his hands to the night sky and issued a cry to the universe. His lament, coming as it did from the depth of his anguished soul, was an invocation to the Divine, a seed syllable of a prayer of ultimate surrender:

Years of this short life have passed and still I do not stand at your side. Is all that I have learned of religion but a fantasy? Why can't I see you? I am your child, I belong to you. Please, Father, take me away. I will serve you well.[10]

The interior questing obvious in these brief words was not resolved immediately, however. No voices of direction were heard. Rather, after days of wrestling with the options of the next step, and with his guide's blessing, Ramsuratkumar determined to head south, to Pondicherry. The ashram of the great revolutionary, the mystic, the author, the visionary, Sri Aurobindo Ghose, would be his goal.

At the time of announcing this plan to his elder friend, Ramsuratkumar remembered that his mentor had made another suggestion to him. Since he would be so far south, the older man casually told of another saint who lived not far from Pondicherry. Interestingly, however, the elder never used the name of Bhagavan Sri Ramana Maharshi, although it was undoubtedly known to him. Apparently, in the ways of the men and women of wisdom, his mentor deliberately refrained from any additional hints, lest they be forms of interference. In evidence of his own alignment to a surrendered existence, the sage simply relied upon the Divine within the heart of Ramsuratkumar to lead the young man home.

Thus it was that in November 1947, at the age of twenty-nine, Ramsuratkumar began the momentous pilgrimage that would take him eventually to the seat of his heart's desire – absorption in and service to God. He traveled from Bihar or Uttar Pradesh in the north to a small city located on the Bay of Bengal, far in the south. An exotic city, long governed by the French, beautiful Pondicherry had a European ambiance, and horse-drawn carriages with Indian drivers greeted clients with "Bonjour Madam," "Bonjour Monsieur."

His journey was undoubtedly made by train and, based on the distances covered (over 1,500 kilometers), would have taken him at least two to three full days, and probably longer depending upon train schedules or connections. The trip would also have cost him a hearty sum, even in those days; an amount that he probably had to save for, even if he still had an income from his work as a teacher.

A source close to Yogi Ramsuratkumar tells us that someone picked his pocket on this trip and that he lost both his money and his ticket at one point. Nonetheless, he continued on his way, penniless now, relying as he would for the rest of his life on the beneficence of the Divine to show him mercy.[11]

राम

In 1947, Sri Aurobindo's ashram was located in the same place that it stands today – on a quiet street a few short blocks from the ocean. The ashram consisted of a graciously appointed building that housed offices and meeting rooms and served as the residence for Aurobindo and his collaborator in the great work, Mirra. It is she whom Aurobindo had identified as "the Mother," the embodiment of the universal *Shakti*, and the guru to whom all his devotees and followers would surrender. Aurobindo had entrusted to her the complete spiritual and material charge of the ashram. Under her remarkable direction and through the power of her presence, a tiny seedling planted in November 1926 had already, in 1947, grown to a solid oak.

Surrounding the master's headquarters, where the work of administration was managed, in the side streets of the same neighborhood, groups of homes were being purchased, converted into residences, and filled with the many new ventures that the Mother was constantly initiating. A bakery, flower gardens, a weaving department. In 1943, a school for the children of the ashram families was opened. A publishing house was started in 1945. Numerous artistic studios and cottage industries were also founded, an outgrowth of basic self-sufficiency. For fifty years, until her death in 1973 at the age of ninety-five, Mirra was the preeminent presence on the ashram, as Sri Aurobindo was almost always in semi-seclusion.

Since arriving there in 1910, and for the next forty years until his own death in 1950, Aurobindo spent the large part of his days in writing and contemplation. It was Mirra's all-pervading energy and her embodiment of the vision and passion of Aurobindo that Ramsuratkumar would have encountered first. The great man himself was almost entirely inaccessible in these years.

ONLY GOD

Sri Aurobindo, circa 1947

Did Ramsuratkumar actually ever lay eyes on the man whom he later named as his first spiritual Father? The one whom he says "began" the work in his soul? From all reports it seems unlikely. Aurobindo was seen only four times a year, and by invitation: on his own birthday, August 15, as well as on February 21, April 24 and November 24. For a newly arrived and wandering seeker like Ramsuratkumar to have gained entrance to the November 24 darshan would have required some special work on his part.

Such special sightings were reserved to those who had applied via formal letter and been approved for visitation, by name, by Aurobindo himself. "Aurobindo would be handed the list of applicants and would simply look it over, checking with a tick mark who could enter and who not," Mr. Gajaraj S. Dev, an ashram resident since 1947, reported. Since Yogi Ramsuratkumar himself has never mentioned a definite physical meeting, we assume that his visit did not include one.

Another longtime disciple described the elaborate procedures of this darshan process.

[T]o meet in some measure the understandable desire of the sadhaks to see Sri Aurobindo and offer *pranam* to him, the three annual darshan days – of 21 February, 15 August and 24 November – were set apart, and this was to continue till 1938. On these three days the sadhaks and a select number of visitors were permitted to have darshan of the two together (the Mother seated to the right of Sri Aurobindo on a sofa) – and offer pranam to them. The number had grown year by year...The sadhaks and the rest first assembled in the Meditation Hall, and went up in file in an orderly manner carrying the garlands to be offered. The list of the sadhaks and the visitors, and the order in which they were to come, was with Sri Aurobindo and he could take note of the newcomers. Everyone was given a minute or two for making his offering, obeisance and pranam, first to one then to the other. Thus each was in the Darshan Room all alone with the visible divine pair for a blissful interim, and then he (or she) moved off, giving place to the next.[12]

However, from 1939 (whence 24 April became the fourth Darshan day) several changes in this procedure were unavoidable. "Putting up the list of names and indicating the time was stopped for good...as a check on unauthorised intrusion, cards were issued over the signature of the Secretary." Later still, the work of issuing passes was transferred to a Bureau Central. The Darshan time was fixed "almost at 2 p.m. To get an opportunity to touch the feet of the Master became a thing of the past...we had to form a queue and have Darshan while filing past."[13]

Encountering the Mother, however, would have been a different story. Around the block from the main entrance, at the back of the main ashram building, a second floor balcony overlooks the street. "That is where she would give darshan to anyone who happened to be here," Mr. Krishnamurthy, an elderly ashram resident, told me.

"Every day, and twice a day," the Mother would appear on "Second Balcony" to silently bless the gathering of devotees, visitors, or locals. No one was exempt from this siting.

Here, we guess, Ramsuratkumar would have stood, along this clean street with its well-kept sidewalks. He would have looked up to see a slight figure standing at the rail. Her eyes would have met his, and she would have sensed the longing of his heart. After all, she was the Mother. She would know the needs of her children, and her attention would always have been drawn to those most in need of her assistance.

"Finally, the Mother took a personal interest and asked who Yogiji was," Makarand Paranjape, a writer and admirer of both Sri Aurobindo and the Mother as well as of Yogi Ramsuratkumar, reported in a brief interview. "Then she blessed him very amply from her balcony. I think Yogiji said that he had a powerful spiritual experience in her presence, and he also felt that she was blessing his decision to go on to Tiruvannamalai."

Courtesy of Sri Aurobindo Ashram Trust

The Mother, circa 1950

In the late 1970s, Yogi Ramsuratkumar told a close devotee that the Mother, Mirra, had given him a flower and that he got the "madness" on receiving it, but that this Divine madness did not last. "Mother had told him that his foundations needed to be strengthened or meeting with Sri Aurobindo would be too powerful."[14]

"She was everywhere, and could show up anywhere," a worker in the ashram shared with me, as I was shown a photo of what Mirra looked like in 1947 at the time of Ramsuratkumar's arrival. The Mother was already sixty-nine years old when he came there. Still a vibrantly active woman, although extremely thin, she looked almost transparent. Her deep-set eyes were piercing; her otherworldly connection more apparent than ever. Her characteristic smile was ever radiant. Even as a woman approaching seventy, Mirra's ability to keep all things in motion around her was fairly predictable. Echoing the direction of her master, Aurobindo, Mirra believed that work was the necessary bridge over which Divine life would be carried to the earth. Their's was no reclusive dharma. Instead, brief meditations were interspersed throughout a long day of hands-on labor.

For the growing numbers of ashramites who gathered here, the sadhana was threefold – aspiration, or the movement of attention and intention; rejection, of all that is hostile to Truth; and surrender, "of oneself and all one is and has and every plane of the consciousness and every movement to the Divine and the Shakti."[15] One's entire life, therefore, was to be dynamic prayer.

> [A]n outward asceticism is not essential, but the conquest of desire and attachment and a control over the body and its needs, greeds, instincts are indispensable.

> [T]he inspiration of the Master and, in the difficult stages, his control and his presence are indispensable.

> [I]t was not his object to develop any one religion or to amalgamate the older religions or to found any new religion…

The one aim of his Yoga is an inner self-development by which each one who follows it can in time discover the One Self in all and evolve a higher consciousness than the mental; a spiritual and supra-mental consciousness which will transform and divinize human nature.[16]

Ramsuratkumar would have experienced this living dharma during his brief stay near or in the ashram. These teachings undoubtedly impressed him, and fanned a spiritual fire that had long been smoldering. They would influence his own practice; infiltrate his words; and even characterize the approach that he would institute on his own ashram when it was founded almost fifty years later.

In this first visit to Pondicherry, Ramsuratkumar would also have learned more about the man, Aurobindo. Late in his life Yogiji declared: "When this beggar first came to Sri Aurobindo, he didn't know him and didn't know what he was about. This beggar couldn't see him; but when he came to Sri Aurobindo's ashram this beggar felt so much peace, then this beggar knew that Sri Aurobindo was this peace!"[17] And in that understanding he would have recognized his Father.

राम

Born in Calcutta on August 15, 1872, Aurobindo Ghose barely had time to imbibe Indian culture when he and his brothers were taken to England for their education in 1879. Here he lived the formative years of his youth and adolescence from ages seven to twenty-one. And here he received his education.

Aurobindo was a brilliant and passionate student. At King's College, Oxford, he studied Latin and Greek, learned French from his first foster guardians in Manchester, and later taught himself German and Italian with enough proficiency that he was able to read both Goethe and Dante in their original versions. He also studied the great literature and scriptures of his Indian heritage, and in 1892 had a glimpse of spiritual awakening as he read the *Upanishads*. When he returned to his native land in 1893, he reported a "vast calm" that descended upon him the moment he set foot on India's soil – a calm that lasted for several months.

These foreshadowings of his mystical orientation were unknown to those around him as Aurobindo threw himself into his newly acquired employment. His first appointment was a government job in the revenue department in Baroda, the garden city of Gujarat state. From there he proceeded to a secretarial position for the Maharaja of Gujarat, then on to a professorship in English at Baroda College, and finally to an appointment as the college's Vice-Principal.

A man of Aurobindo's intelligence and skill could obviously rise quickly in the ranks and surely was set for great things within the academic world. An illustrious career as an educator was fully assured, and for a lesser man would have promised an easy and lifelong security. But, beginning in 1902, nine years after settling back into Indian society, Aurobindo began to lead a double life, which for many years was unknown to those who shared his career ranks. When he wasn't fulfilling his secretarial duties, advancing his own studies (he learned Sanskrit and several modern Indian languages during this period), or undertaking his class preparations or college administrative duties, Aurobindo was working feverishly, and often subversively, for independence. The cause of ultimate freedom from British domination obsessed him. He knew that such a victory would only be won with long-term preparation of the minds and hearts of his countrymen and women.

Aurobindo's active political life covered a period of eight years, from 1902 to 1910. Even a brief overview of these political years, one of which was spent entirely in prison (mid-1908 through May 1909), reveal the extraordinary character of the man. Like his predecessor Swami Vivekananda, Aurobindo directed his efforts to the youth of Bengal, knowing that this was the way to build a movement that would last. His goal – which he wisely placed some thirty years in the future – was to support a strong foundation upon which a liberated India could proudly and intelligently stand.

Not only was Aurobindo a brilliant visionary, he was also utterly courageous. He withstood indictments for sedition and urged compatriots to refuse to defend themselves in British courts, as this would simply lend credence to the legitimacy of these institutions.

He established his own newspapers and wrote for those of others. He composed essays and articles covering subjects from guerilla warfare to passive resistance – never holding to one extreme or the other and never idealizing either. His path was to use whatever means would be effective, rather than to follow one inspired by some moral, but totally idealistic and hence impractical, stance.

> Sri Aurobindo's first preoccupation was to declare openly for complete and absolute independence as the aim of political action in India and to insist on this persistently in the pages of the journal [*Bande Mataram*, which he founded]; he was the first politician in India who had the courage to do this publicly and he was immediately successful.[18]

What gave Aurobindo courage, at bottom line, was his trust in the unfoldment of God's will. He loved his country passionately. As it was for Rama Tirtha and Swami Vivekananda, Aurobindo's country was more than a political entity. India, "the land of Bharatavarsha, is not a piece of earth or a geographical territory with hills and dales; it is the manifestation of the Mahashakti, the Divine Mother who manifests as Saraswati, Lakshmi and Kali. Hence the Motherland is always identified with Bharati, the name of the Divine Mother who always revels in the Eternal Light."[19]

Who would be foolish enough to try to keep the Mother of the Universe in submission? Who would be stupid enough to stand around idly when she roused herself from her afternoon nap of a mere two hundred years to see the plight of her children?

As revolutionaries before and since, he was absolutely convinced of the moral imperative of his cause. Truth and right would eventually prevail, no matter how long it took, no matter what the cost to his own personal security. In a letter to his wife Mrinalini Devi in August 1905, Aurobindo wrote of his love for India:

> I look upon my country as the Mother. I adore Her, worship Her as the Mother. What would a son do if a demon sat on his mother's breast and started sucking her blood? Would he quietly sit down to his dinner, amuse himself with his wife

and children, or would he rush out to deliver his mother? I know I have the strength to deliver this fallen race. It is not physical strength – I am not going to fight with sword or gun, – but the strength of knowledge…The feeling is not new in me, I was born with it, it is in my very marrow. God sent me to earth to accomplish this great mission.[20]

And then, something changed…and radically. Aurobindo's involvement in political life came to a near-screeching halt in a moment that in retrospect can only be seen as the hand of the Divine. One night in 1908, as he slept in his quarters in the newspaper office of the new Bengali daily, *Nava Shakti,* of which he had recently taken charge, he was arrested. Police, armed with revolvers, charged up the stairs to his room, hauled him off to the nearby police station and then to the Alipur jail, where he remained for one year.

Like so many who experience conversions or transformations under conditions of extreme stress or deprivation, Aurobindo's tenure in prison served as a turning point in his life's story. Aurobindo Ghose was making a rotation – within. The man who entered Alipur jail would be a different man upon his release.

For the first period of his confinement, Aurobindo was placed in a solitary cell. Inspired by his early studies and by the ongoing connection to his nation's spiritual inheritance, he used this valuable time to read the *Bhagavad Gita* and the *Upanishads*, and to practice yoga. His purpose, he openly admitted, was simply to acquire interior strength and guidance to forward the cause of his revolutionary aim. Even when he was removed for an extended period to a large open room in which many other prisoners were also housed, he maintained his rigorous practice amidst noise and near constant disturbance. In one respect it was all the same to him – just another more challenging opportunity in which to practice. After one of the jailers was assassinated, the prisoners in the open room were confined to separate cells, and again Aurobindo resumed his meditation and yoga with even greater vigor. In his notes and letters he wrote:

I looked at the jail that secluded me from men and it was no longer by its high walls that I was imprisoned; no, it was

Vasudeva [a form of Krishna] who surrounded me...Or I lay on the coarse blankets that were given me for a couch and felt the arms of Sri Krishna around me, the arms of my friend and Lover...I looked at the prisoners in the jail, the thieves, the murderers, the swindlers, and as I looked at them I saw Vasudeva, it was Narayana whom I found in these darkened souls and misused bodies.[21]

A fascinating scene occurred during his trial. Confined to a cage within the courtroom, Aurobindo paid little attention to the arguments being raised for or against him. Instead, he remained in nearly constant meditation. At this point, the proceedings were immaterial to him, as "he had been assured from within and knew that he would be acquitted." He wrote these words about himself years later in an essay summing up his political life.[22]

By the time of the trial, moreover, another radical shift had occurred within his soul. His period of intensive practice had changed him. No longer was Aurobindo merely preoccupied with the fate of India and with gathering strength for his role in furthering her independence. His aim now had both deepened and broadened. It was "world-wide in its bearing and concerned with the whole future of humanity."[23]

Leaving prison and returning to the scenes of his life, Aurobindo found that most of his own previous efforts had fallen to ruin without his intensive leadership. The mood in the country as a whole was depressed. Although he was determined to bring new resolve into action, his audiences had dwindled. The old fire was merely smoldering; waiting for something...but for what?

Aurobindo did not stop. But something new was added to his approach. In a public speech at Uttapara shortly after his release, he spoke for the first time of his spiritual experiences, his yoga. In all his endeavors, Aurobindo maintained the fearlessness that had always characterized his political life. "No compromise" was his stand with regard to the conciliatory gestures of supposed reform offered by the British government at the time. "No co-operation without control," he wrote in a letter in the *Karmayogin*, one of the new newspapers that he had inaugurated.[24]

Sri Aurobindo, circa 1915

With this as his central axis, however, he looked in all directions for an expedient solution to India's dilemma. He considered the policies of Home Rule, fearing however that they would ultimately delay independence. He also looked closely, seriously, at the entire movement of passive resistance – an approach that Gandhi would take up in the years ahead. Aurobindo found great merit in this policy but wisely recognized that such a movement was not one that he could lead. Someone else would have to take up this cause, when the time was right.

As his outspoken essays in the *Karmayogin* and his other activities attracted more and more attention, the British Government grew resolute that his voice must be silenced. He would be deported, their first plan, or prosecuted for sedition and jailed. "Leave British India and work from the outside," came the warnings of Sister Nivedita, the valiant British devotee of Vivekananda and a primary force of both advancement and reconciliation in India's struggle for independence from foreign control.

Despite Nivedita's appeal, Aurobindo stayed in place, awaiting his own interior guidance, which he had learned to trust absolutely. The call from within came at last, on the night when he learned that his newspaper office was to be searched and he arrested. Within ten minutes of this revelation, he was at the ghat of the river Ganges, where he secured passage on a boat to Chandernagore in French-ruled India. A few hours later, he debarked in this new city, where he established a secret residence and took up the lifestyle he had established in Alipur prison. Dropping all his political involvement, he "plunged entirely into solitary meditation," until the next inner "call" was heard: "Proceed to Pondicherry."[25] Returning to Calcutta with the help of young revolutionaries, he found passage aboard the *Dupleix*, a ship bound for Pondicherry, the heart of French India, where he arrived on April 4, 1910.

राम

Aurobindo was only thirty-eight years old, but his "life" as others had known it was over. As he had done several times before, in Pondicherry he withdrew into solitude and focused all his efforts on his spiritual work. Friends and enemies alike imagined that his withdrawal was for the purposes of plotting a new strategy, and in a sense they were right. But it was not a strategy that any of his former associates could have imagined. "His retirement from political activity was complete," he wrote of himself. He did not abandon interest in the world or in the fate of India, but rather up-leveled this to an entirely new dimension. His desire to attain "complete spiritual consciousness" was always to include "all life and all world activity." It was simply a shift of context – but one that made all the difference.

As early as 1905 he had begun to speak of the three "madnesses" that had seized him. It is interesting that Yogi Ramsuratkumar would adopt this same phrase – "the madness" – in referring to his own condition of God-realization. Aurobindo's first madness had to do with the recognition that *everything* belonged to God. The third, with his love for India as the Mother. But, "[t]he second madness [which] has recently seized me," he wrote to his wife, "is this: by whatever means I must have direct vision of God…If God exists there must be some way to experience His existence, to meet Him face to face. However arduous this path is, I have made up my mind to follow it."[26]

By 1912, Aurobindo's spiritual life was crowned with "an abiding realization and dwelling in Parabrahman" (the supreme Reality). And that was the beginning of everything. In 1914, the Divine arranged for his meeting with a remarkable European woman, named Mirra. In her, Aurobindo recognized the collaborator – the Shakti – who would bring to manifestation all that he had envisioned, and with whom he would work for the rest of his life.

Their lives together were spent in interior communion, as well as in writing volumes of spiritual teachings about all aspects of life. Ever the journalist, Aurobindo, now assisted by the Mother, announced their "divine Agenda" in a monthly publication known as the "Arya." For six and a half years it ran, 720 issues, accumulating nearly five thousand pages of dharma and practical concerns. In a nutshell, their teaching asserted that the human instrument could be refined, disciplined, prepared and ultimately transformed such that "the greater Light and Force" could be drawn down to work in nature.

His books included *The Life Divine* and the *Synthesis of Yoga*; his essays made commentary on the *Bhagavad Gita*, Vedic and

Upanishadic revelations, the nature of future poetry, and on numerous social, political and national themes. All pointed to a view of evolution of consciousness founded in the great teachings of Hindu culture. All heralded a possibility for liberation from mind to the development of Supermind, or Spirit. Aurobindo and the Mother taught that only when the Spirit is fully released into matter is it possible "for life to manifest perfection."

राम

Aurobindo was a giant within India's political and spiritual history. His accomplishments have ever loomed larger than life. The fact that so few in the West are familiar with his story and his prodigious work – literary, political, and spiritual – is a reflection of the provincialism that has cut us off from some of the greatest influences in world culture and history.

When Ramsuratkumar arrived in Pondicherry in 1947, Aurobindo was already an old man. At seventy-five, he was only three years from his death. A few months earlier, on his birthday, August 15, 1947 – India's day of independence – Aurobindo had announced "the birthday of free India." His message was broadcast on All-India radio throughout that historic day. It is entirely possible that Ramsuratkumar heard this message, or read the text of it in a newspaper in the days that followed. The message that Aurobindo sent across the air to the citizens of his beloved homeland characterized his life's mission.

> I have always held and said that India was arising, not to
> serve her own material interests only…and certainly not like
> others to acquire domination of other peoples, but to live
> also for God and the world as a helper and leader of the
> whole human race.

Yet Aurobindo's warnings were also clear. "India is free but she has not achieved unity, only a fissured and broken freedom…" He was deeply grieved by what he saw as a most serious fracture – "the old communal division into Hindu and Muslim" which has "hardened into the figure of a permanent political division of the country...For if it lasts, India may be seriously weakened, even crippled...The partition of the country must go." In this prediction, which has sadly proven true, he echoed the sentiments of his contemporary, Gandhi, who had always maintained his ideal for a unified India.

Still, in the end, Aurobindo's optimism and sense of complete reliance on the Divine won out over his cautions. Unity should prevail! "Only human imbecility and stupid selfishness could prevent it. Against that...even the gods strive in vain; but it cannot stand forever against the necessity of Nature and the Divine Will. Nationalism will then have fulfilled itself...A new spirit of oneness will take hold of the human race."

That Ramsuratkumar would have turned in the direction of Aurobindo's voice in the second half of 1947 seems more than coincidental. The younger man undoubtedly recognized some affinity of spirit with the great sage – the passionate revolutionary turned mystic; the man of letters speaking for a new world culture; the representative of a spirituality that demanded an embrace of the lowliest and most earthbound elements of creation.

Mr. N.K. Krishnamurthy, an elderly resident of Sri Aurobindo Ashram, Pondicherry, and a great respecter of Yogi Ramsuratkumar, offered his opinion about the reason for the beggar's initial attraction. Ramsuratkumar was an educated man, certainly, and "at the time, Aurobindo was the only one [guru, teacher, master] with intelligence and education for pointing India in a wise and realistic direction for the future."

Certainly Ramsuratkumar would have found in Aurobindo a resonance with the type of universality and open-eyed understanding of the modern world that would come to characterize his own work. When we examine the rare words of the living oral teaching that Yogi Ramsuratkumar left behind, we find again and again his reference to the cause of Indian unity; the struggle for a true and lasting freedom; the role that India as a genuine spiritual culture must play in the world at large. We also find that he stood exactly in many of the footprints that Aurobindo had first impressed upon the earth.

Yogi Ramsuratkumar: "This beggar believes in the vision of his spiritual teacher, Sri Aurobindo, who had a dream and vision of a universal unity and peace on Earth and, furthermore, of a race of spiritual supermen."

"Sri Aurobindo told at the time of Indian Independence that the partition of India itself was wholly wrong. But our leaders at that time did not listen to it. Sri Aurobindo has even predicted that India will be united again. The integration of India is unavoidable. That will happen soon. Then India will lead the entire world. The spirituality of the Hindus will be spread throughout the world. The prediction will come true very soon."

"India has now to play its part in the World. Europe played its part – material part. Now India has to play its part, by taking mankind in the spiritual path, to God."

"In the 21st century, Indians will learn languages of many other nations, go there with the philosophy of Vivekananda, Aurobindo, Mahatma Gandhi and shape the people of the world. We do not want to rob, we want to raise them [these other nations] along a spiritual line."[27]

राम

In 1991, an American visitor recalled that Yogi Ramsuratkumar spoke with awe of the developments at Sri Aurobindo Ashram, where two thousand people currently lived. With the childlike innocence and amazement that characterized his appreciation of the world, Yogiji marveled at the news that their bakery used thirteen *tons* of wheat a month.

"How do they manage such an ashram?" the beggar asked, incredulously. Then he spoke about how Aurobindo wasn't interested in poverty, but wealth, noting that Aurobindo believed that we should "use all wealth for Divine purposes." When this discussion was concluded, Yogi Ramsuratkumar called for the singing of a short Sri Aurobindo chant.[28]

राम

Aurobindo was a radical nationalist, not for the sake of power or special interests but because he held fast to the potential of India as a spiritual force. India's spiritual principles were seeds sorely needed in a world slowly rebuilding itself from the horrors of the Second World War and its entry into the atomic age. Inspired by Aurobindo's vision, Ramsuratkumar, in his own way, would become a sower of these seeds.

THE MOUNTAIN OF FIRE, 1947

 "Ramana Maharshi," the sage of Mount Arunachala, was a familiar name among the pilgrims who passed through Pondicherry in the late 1940s. The city of Tiruvannamalai, in which the holy mountain was located, was only 150 kilometers away – a morning's sojourn by train, or a long bumpy bus ride, or a few days of vigorous walking.

When Ramsuratkumar heard the name of this famous sage from a *bramacharin* (a celibate renunciate) during his visit to the Aurobindo ashram, he recalled the advice of his elder mentor at the Ganges…something about seeing "another great saint who lived not far from Pondicherry." He took the bramacharin's cue as his directive, and continued on to Tiruvannamalai.

The legend of the holy mountain, Arunachala, and its identification with the Lord of the Universe, the great god Siva, is a story that dates back several thousand years. It is told in the *Puranas*, the original folk histories of the *Vedas*, probably written in the early centuries of the first millenium C.E., although originated by storytellers generations before. The marvelous tale involved a long and bitter argument between the Lords Brahma and Vishnu. Whose power was greater? They wanted to know. Creation itself trembled at the force of their rancor, and soon the repercussions were felt in the abode of the destroyer, Lord Siva.

Wishing to awaken both gods from their delusions and so to end this dispute once and for all, Siva took the form of a massive column of light and fire reaching infinitely into the heavens and infinitely into the earth. Shocked by the sight of this sudden intervention, and not knowing what to make of it, Vishnu came up with an idea, which he proposed to his adversary, Brahma. Whoever could first find the origin of this column, either its top or its base, would be declared the victor in their dispute. The other would submit to him.

Brahma, full of pride, did not hesitate to accept the challenge, knowing that in his form as a swan (*hamsa*) he could easily ascend to the loftiest heights with lightning-fast speed. Vishnu, knowing that his manifestation as a boar could dig into the earth with untold swiftness and focus, was likewise pleased with the deal. And so the race was on.

The legend says that their explorations went on for ages, literally *yugas*. Yet, no matter how high Brahma flew, or how deep Vishnu dug, there was the column as strong and radiant as ever, and always with no end in sight.

Vishnu was the first to come to his senses. Recognizing his folly, he climbed back out of the earth, awaiting his opportunity to bow to the Lord Siva, whom he acknowledged as the originator of the column. But Brahma's pride was not so easily tamed. Exhausted and confused at his seemingly impossible task, he refused to be bettered. Instead, he sought some means of deception rather than admit failure to his foe.

As Brahma contemplated his fate, he noticed a small flower, the *kartigai*, floating down from above him.[1] Catching this blossom, Brahma questioned it about where it had come from. "I have been descending for millennia from the head of Lord Siva," the flower replied, and immediately Brahma recognized his advantage. He persuaded the humble flower to attest to his lie that he had found it at the top of the column and, grasping it, he flew to earth, the foretaste of victory already sweet in his mouth.

Standing now before Siva, who had emerged from the blazing column to judge the dispute, Vishnu joined his hands and reverently offered his worship and praise to the awesome power of the Almighty One. But Brahma, holding firm to his delusion, sang no praise, but only lies: "In my flight upwards," the Scripture recounts him to say, "I found the top of the glorious Lingam flame and I have

43

the Karthigai flower as a witness of this event." (*Sivapuranam-Vidyes-varasamhita*, Chap. 7, v. 27-28.)[2]

As great as Siva's blessing was for Vishnu – whom he declared thereafter as his preeminent disciple, and to whom he promised unending love – such was his wrath toward the duplicity of Brahma. Calling upon Bhairava (Siva's own "terrifying" form) to pluck off the fifth head of Brahma, Siva was ready to be avenged. However, he was assuaged by the pleas for mercy offered by the other assembled gods, and thus spared Brahma's life. Nonetheless, Siva did rebuke him with a just punishment for his deeds. Henceforth, declared the Great Lord, there would be no temples erected in Brahma's name, a "curse" that remains even to this day, with the rare exception of the Brahma temples in the city of Pushkar in Rajasthan, North India. In addition, in his extraordinary compassion for the needs of creation, Siva grant-ed another boon. For all time, he conceded, "Even though a sacrifice is complete with all the ancillary rites and offerings of gifts, it will be fruitless without you (Brahma)." (*Vidyesvarasamhita*, Chapter 8, v. 13-14)[3]

And what of the fate of the Endless Flame? This is where the story of Arunachala reaches its climax. The scripture puts words into the mouth of Lord Siva:

This column without root or top will henceforth be diminu-tive in size for the sake of the vision and the worship of the world…

Since the Flaming Lingam rises high, resembling a Mountain of Fire, this shall be the famous reddish Aruna Mountain.

Many holy centers will spring up here. A residence or death in this holy place assures salvation.

The celebration of festivals, the congregation of devotees as well as sacrifices, gifts and offering of flowers in this place shall be million-fold efficacious.

Of all my sectors, this sector shall be the greatest. A mere remembrance of Me at this place shall accord salvation…
(*Siva Puranam Vidyesvarasamhita*)[4]

Courtesy of Ramanashram

Mount Arunachala

It is no wonder that countless thousands of yogis and sages throughout hundreds of years have sought shelter in the numerous caves on the slopes of this holy hill – the reddish Aruna Mountain. "Unlike other mountains, which have become holy because the Lord dwells in them, Arunachala is said to be Lord Siva Himself…[He] identifies Himself with this Hill where the reddish color of the rocks suggests the primeval fire."[5]

The famous sage Adi Shankara (seventh and eighth centuries) recognized Arunachala as being the center of the universe, the mythical Mount Meru. And many legends recount that Siva's consort, Parvati, received her ultimate union with her Lord only after doing numerous *pradakshinas* (circumambulations) of this splendorous hill – a trip of nearly four miles. In the modern era, Ramana Maharshi lived on Mount Arunachala, built his ashram in its shadow, wandered along its endless network of paths, and was known to make frequent pradakshinas.

राम

In 1947, when Yogi Ramsuratkumar first laid eyes on Sri Ramana Maharshi, the elder was already nearing the end of his illustrious life. He was only three years from his death. His physical condition, witnessed in the films made of him in those years, reveals the ravages of time. He is sixty-eight, and his movements are painful to observe. His body is always twisted slightly to the left, and his large rheumatic knees appear to get in the way of one another as he walks, stiff-legged.

Ramana, clothed only in a white *kaupina* (loin cloth), leans heavily on a walking stick, never upon the arm of one of the many devotees who usually accompany him on his walks around the grounds of the ashram, located on the outskirts of the city of Tiruvannamalai. Yet, whether physical discomfort hampered him or not, he is evidently not concerned with the condition of his body. His face is always completely serene, revealing no hint of pain; his gentle eyes and sweet smile, which occasionally can be glimpsed on the film, are completely inviting.

The Mountain of Fire, 1947

At this point in his life Ramana Maharshi is well known, even world renowned. A British news clip filmed in 1937 speaks of him as a man of peace and as one who inspires all who come into his presence. Not only is he surrounded by masses of Indian devotees, but there seemed always to be Westerners, Britishers primarily, crowding him. Some are people with recognizable names and some with reputations, like mystic and philosopher Paul Brunton, the author of *A Search of Sacred India*; Somerset Maugham, who visited Tiruvannamalai in 1938 and used Ramana Maharshi as the prototype for the character of the guru Shri Ganesha in his famous novel, *The Razor's Edge*; and Melissa Marston (Macleod), a British woman who had lived at the Prieure estate with the famous Russian teacher George Gurdjieff in the early years.

Ramana was an extraordinary being, and a magnet for seekers. The beauty and elegance of the Matrabhuteswara Temple, the shrine of his mother's *samadhi* (burial place) that graces the grounds of his ashram, stands in start contrast to the absolute simplicity and

Courtesy of Ramanashram

Sri Bhagavan Ramana Maharshi, circa 1947

47

complete nonattachment of his own presence. He possessed nothing. He asked for nothing. His only apparent interest in life was that of remaining present as a source of help to devotees.

Following his walks, the Maharshi ("greatest sage") would sit upon a divan in the courtyard of the ashram close to the huge well, or in the small house, now used only for silent meditation, that looks out on the yard. Here he would occasionally answer the questions of seekers, read his mail or the newspaper, or, more commonly, do nothing at all that the eye could experience. It was in the silent darshan, those times of wordless communion, that his devotees report he was working in their hearts – turning them from worldly preoccupations; enflaming their desire to be lost in the One; allowing them to recognize, by experience, the answer to the great *koan* of inquiry, the primary practice he had given them, "Who am I?"

राम

Ramana Maharshi's own life story is a relatively simple one. He was born December 30, 1879, in Tiruchuzhi, an ancient pilgrimage center not far from Madurai in the state of Tamil Nadu, South India. Named Venkataraman, he was the second child in a poor Brahmin family that would eventually consist of four children – one older brother and a younger brother and sister. As a child, Venkataraman was given to easily falling into deep states of sleep such that he could not be awakened, even with beatings. His schoolmates enjoyed playing upon this fact, carrying him around and thumping on him amidst their laughter while Venkataraman slept on.

His father died when the boy was twelve, and this event understandably had a profound effect upon Venkataraman. He and his younger brother were sent to his paternal uncle's home in Madurai, where the two boys continued their schooling. Reports from his contemporaries affirm that Venkataraman was a brilliant student, despite his lapses into sleep and otherworldly fascination.

One day, in the midst of his sixteenth year, in the upstairs room of his uncle's house, Venkataraman experienced a profoundly terrifying moment in which he was convinced that he was about to die. What he did, however, was so uncharacteristic as to indicate a type of inner guidance, expressed as intuitive wisdom, that is rare beyond words. Instead of running from the fear, he turned and faced it directly. In fact, he fully invited the experience of death, ready to observe it, to use it as a means to discover the truth.

Venkataraman lay down on the floor, stiffened his body as if rigor mortis had already set in, and began a process of self-inquiry that would culminate in an earth-shattering breakthrough – a spiritual death and ultimate rebirth. His own words, which describe the experience in clear detail, are famous now, as they are so often quoted in stories of his life. They are also emblazoned on the wall of the main temple-shrine within his ashram and within a chamber of the great Siva Temple – Arunachaleswarar – in Tiruvannamalai, where they instruct curious visitors and seekers alike:

> "Well then," I said to myself, "this body is dead. It will be carried stiff to the burning ground and there burnt and reduced to ashes. But, with the death of this body am 'I' dead? Is the body 'I'? This body is silent and inert. But I feel the full force of my personality and even the sound 'I' within myself apart from the body. I am therefore the deathless spirit, untouched by death."

This rare moment in which liberation arose was not fleeting. Venkataraman was maintained in this condition of clear sight, residing in the Self, and occasionally being consumed by the state of complete absorption known as *samadhi*, which exteriorly looked little different from his previous sleep states.

He told no one about this irrevocable change at the time, and for two full months Venkataraman attempted to carry on his normal life of schooling and family responsibilities. However, his taste for studies was completely dry now. As he attempted to work on an exercise in English grammar one day, his observant brother remarked, somewhat sarcastically, "What is the use of study for such a one?" The intimation being that the young man's path was already obvious – he would be a yogi. Venkataraman was struck with the truth of his brother's remark, and actually took it as a direct call from the Divine. It was time to pursue his destiny.

ONLY GOD

The young man left his uncle's house, leaving behind him a simple message. Strangely, the precise words of this message were nearly identical to words used by Yogi Ramsuratkumar more than forty years later and throughout his entire life to express his own departure from the norm, his own absolute reliance upon God. In 1896, the teenaged Venkataraman wrote: "I have, in search of my Father, and in obedience to His command, started from here. This is only embarking on a virtuous enterprise. Therefore, none need grieve over this affair."

Like his spiritual son Ramsuratkumar more than half a century later, Venkataraman was drawn to the city of Tiruvannamalai. A relative had recently returned from pilgrimage to this place and related stories of its power – telling of the great temple at the foot of the red mountain, Arunachala, that is worshipped as Siva, the Lord of the Universe.

Hearing all this, the boy knew his destination. After a difficult journey of three days, traveling mostly by train, Venkataraman arrived at the sacred site, immediately went to the sanctum sanctorum of the temple and, in his own words, "reported his arrival by saying 'Father, I have come.'" It was the first of September 1896.

Sitting within the temple precincts, lost in deep states of bliss, the youth became something of a local curiosity. When the taunting of street urchins posed difficulties, he looked around for a more secluded spot in which to contemplate, and finally retired to a tiny cellar chamber in the temple – preserved to this day as a shrine in his honor. Here he remained, centered in the heart, for a few months, until a caring person removed him from the place and administered to his insect-ravaged body. Whether he had deliberately used the opportunity to practice such severe austerities or was simply oblivious to his physical condition we do not know, although most accounts indicate the latter.

For years thereafter Venkataraman lived in various caves and shrines on and around Arunachala. Unkempt, silent, the boy's radiant features attracted growing numbers of interested and devoted followers. Soon, word spread beyond the city of a previously unknown boy-sage, now referred to only as "Brahmana Swami." In December 1898, his own mother, Azhagammal, and his older brother,

Nagaswami, came, discovered him, and typically urged him to return home. When it was obvious that their "Venkataraman" was dead, resurrected as a God-realized being, mother and brother left. His mother did not return for fourteen years.

In 1900, at the age of twenty, four years after his arrival in Tiruvannamalai, he moved further up the slopes of Arunachala to Virupaksha cave, named for the thirteenth-century saint who had lived and died there. Around this time, one of his most illustrious followers, Narayana Muni, named him Bhagavan Sri Ramana Maharshi. *Bhagavan* (or *Bhagwan*) meaning "Lord" or "God"; *Ramana*, "one who revels in the Self."

Ramana lived for the next sixteen years in the womb-like enclosure of Virupaksha, which he called the "Mother" or the "Heart-cave" of Siva. In 1916, he was joined by his mother, who had moved from Tiruchuzhi to live out the remainder of her life with him, and another spot further up the hill was established for their residence. Here, his mother cooked for her son and his few disciples. Together they sang hymns and worshipped God, establishing a prototype for the ashram life that eventually grew up around them. We know this place today as Skandashram. In 1918, Ramana's younger brother, Nagasundaram, took *sannyas* (vows of renunciation) and moved in as well. It was the start of the Ramana family.

The years at Skanda were full of intense work for Ramana, who wrote treatises, hymns, and poems expressing not only the essential teachings as revealed to him but his blinding love for his Father, Siva Arunachala. In one ecstatic expression we find words that are echoed again and again by Yogi Ramsuratkumar, and interestingly in the poetry of Ramsuratkumar's devotee Lee Lozowick: *Appalvukku Pillai Adakkam*, "The son is absorbed in the father."[6]

In 1922, following the death of Amma, as his mother was called, Ramana moved down to the vicinity of her samadhi site at the foot of the hill and began to supervise construction of a magnificent temple, Matrabhuteswara, erected over her grave. Around this shrine, Ramana Ashram (Ramanashram) was established.

राम

ONLY GOD

Ramana Maharshi never left Tiruvannamalai – even when his physical body passed into death. His own words, spoken throughout his life, pointed to his full immersion in the universal consciousness. He would explain that as the One Transcendent Self is without beginning, so it is without end. In the last months of his life, as sorrowing devotees approached him, Ramana consoled one by saying, "They take this body for Bhagavan and attribute suffering to him. What a pity! They are despondent that Bhagavan is going to leave them and go away; where can he go, and how?"[7] Yogi Ramsuratkumar, also, would say exactly the same thing: "Where can this beggar go? This beggar is always with you."

For thirty-eight years, until his death (mahasamadhi) in 1950, Ramana Maharshi lived a simple, ordered existence. He expected no privilege from the thousands of devotees who were attracted to him from all over the world, and several classic stories tell of his unwavering stand for equality – his recognition that he was not separate from all others.

In one story, witnessed by a young Ramsuratkumar in 1947 or '48, the aging Maharshi refused to receive a specially prepared portion of fruit. Instead, he insisted on taking a piece from the general supply of fruit that was being distributed to all the devotees present.

Another time, sitting as he usually did with his legs stretched before him, he moved into a crossed-legged posture, despite the pain it must have engendered due to the rheumatism that plagued his knees. His position shift happened precisely at the moment when one of the ashram administrators reprimanded a woman visitor for sitting improperly – with her legs outstretched.

As he expected others to submit to ashram regulations, so Ramana himself surrendered to those he himself had placed in authority. Throughout the long and painful illness that preceded his death, "he submitted loyally, one after another, to the doctors who were put in charge, never complaining, never asking for a change of treatment. If ever there was any inclination to try a different treatment it was only so that those who recommended it should not be disappointed, and even then it was dependent on the consent of the Ashram authorities."[8] The parallels in the last years of Yogi Ramsuratkumar's life are eerily astonishing.

Ramana's days were spent primarily at the service of those who came to him. He directed a vast correspondence, wrote more treatises, and walked on the sacred mountain and throughout the ashram grounds daily. His benign and smiling presence was his offering to those who accompanied him or waited for him to pass by. For many hours each day he sat, either on a chair, in the earlier days, or on a divan later, reading the newspaper, answering the questions of seekers, and simply beaming the blessing force of his silence.

Once, when a visitor questioned why he did not preach or teach in a more formal manner, the Maharshi revealed the essence of his "method" of effecting transformation in others:

> How do you know that I am not doing it? Does preaching consist in mounting a platform and haranguing the people around? Preaching is simple communication of Knowledge, and it can really be done in silence only.
>
> What do you think of a man who listens to a sermon for an hour and goes away without having been impressed by it so as to change his life? Compare him with another who sits in a holy Presence and goes away after some time with his outlook on life totally changed. Which is better; to preach loudly without effect or to sit silently sending out inner Force?[9]

Similar questioning of the incongruous methodologies of Yogi Ramsuratkumar would be voiced by many during the years of his ministry as well. He too appeared to give no formal teaching. Instead, the beggar of Tiruvannamalai would invite his visitors to walk with him on the mountain; to sit with him as he read the newspaper; to share equally in the food-alms he had been provided; to chant and sing; and most endearingly, to engage with him in pleasant conversation about seemingly inconsequential affairs, like sports. Yet, the reports of those privileged to speak with Yogi Ramsuratkumar, or simply to sit in his presence, describe an inner-being experience that was going on throughout the interaction. The saint's activities were seen as covers for a much deeper communication – a communion of hearts.

ONLY GOD

राम

In the person of Bhagavan Ramana Maharshi, a complete renunciate, Ramsuratkumar would have found a spiritual force to match the passion of his search. He would have witnessed the result of a life of sadhana that was quietly heroic. Having left the opulent surroundings of the Aurobindo ashram, he would have been struck by the simplicity of the Maharshi's, and undoubtedly moved by the all-pervasive presence of the mountain that hovered above it all.

Yet, in this first encounter, Ramsuratkumar spent less than three days. The Divine, it seems, had other plans for him. This initial visit to the city that would become his home for over forty years served another function. Here, on the grounds of Ramanashram, Ramsuratkumar engaged a conversation with a stranger. This unknown person, learning of the young man's desire to meet with saints, handed Ramsuratkumar a newspaper clipping. It told of another eminent sage of South India, Swami Papa Ramdas, who lived in Kanhangad, a remote village on the western coast of India in the state of Kerala, some 500 kilometers from Tiruvannamalai.

And so it was determined. Taking his lead from the intervention of fate once again, Ramsuratkumar left.

We do not know the details of his traveling, but we do know that in those years there was no other access to Kanhangad except by train. Roads and necessary bridges to this small town had not yet been built. So we can imagine that our pilgrim would have departed from the small train station in Tiruvannamalai, or another nearby city, perhaps boarding the nightly Madras Mail that crossed southern India coast-to-coast, from the Bay of Bengal to the Lakshadweep Sea – a train ride that today takes fourteen hours or more.

He would have spent his few rupees to sit up all night in an overcrowded train compartment on a hard wooden bench. He would have arrived the next day, road weary, at a small junction in the tropical jungle. Alighting from the train at Kanhangad in 1947, he would never have suspected that this place at the end of the line would eventually be the very spot in which he would meet the God he had sought for so long. Here, at the ashram of Swami Ramdas, he would meet destruction.

4

THE PILGRIM'S PROGRESS, 1947

 The year 1947 was the twenty-fifth anniversary of Swami Papa Ramdas's acceptance of sannyas – an event that was celebrated at Anandashram in Kanhangad with great ceremony. By this time, Ramdas's name and reputation were widespread. Men and women from many parts of India, and even from distant lands, were coming to see him, drinking the nectar of love, devotion, and celebration of the Divine name that characterized this little bit of heaven on the west coast of India.

Arriving in Kanhangad, Ramsuratkumar would probably have walked from the railway station to the ashram, a distance of two and one half miles. A devotee who arrived at that same station in April 1948 described her own trip to the property by bullock cart, giving us a glimpse of the roads over which the young seeker would have traveled. Krishna R. Haldipur wrote: "From there [the station] we got into a *jutka* which mercilessly jolted us as it moved along shady cobbled lanes, below the canopy of coconut and arecanut palms…It was dusk when we reached the Panchavatil [also call the Panchavati, the lovely main courtyard of five trees, the place where Papa would meet with devotees]. Papa, who had been waiting for us there, greeted us with great joy…"[1]

This Panchavati was probably the location of Ramsuratkumar's first sighting of the smiling sage, Ramdas. As a first-time visitor and a wandering seeker, he may have joined the residents and guests surrounding "Papa" (as the aged Godman was affectionately called), seated in the shade of these five lush trees. Ramsuratkumar would

Swami Papa Ramdas, around 1947

have observed an entourage of adoring devotees and children attending to the master, and noted the meticulous cleanliness of the Swami's robes.

As generally happened around Papa, laughter may have been rippling through the crowds. Ramdas might be conducting some humorous repartee with a resident or guest. Or he might simply be reading the newspaper while some devotee or child stood by, fanning the master against the extreme heat or the flies that abound in these tropics. Perhaps another disciple was attentively massaging Papa's legs as he sat there. Ramdas suffered greatly from rheumatic conditions and from swelling of his feet and legs brought on by diabetes, and his devotees throughout the years considered it a great blessing to be able to touch him and minister to him in this way. Maybe he was being served tea…maybe he was discoursing on some aspect of the path…we do not know. Yet, for one or more reasons, Ramsuratkumar's first impression was not a positive one. Speaking to Caylor Wadlington in the early 1970s, Ramsuratkumar candidly admitted: "This beggar was not impressed with Swami Ramdas as he had been with Ramana Maharishi and Aurobindo. This beggar was not able to understand Ramdas at that time. He understood immediately that the other two masters were spiritual giants. With Ramdas, however, it was different. It was a kind of reaction…He was living luxuriously and people were serving him like a King."[2]

Admittedly, Pondicherry, where Aurobindo and the Mother lived, offered many more splendors than Kanhangad, but Ramsuratkumar had never actually seen other devotees interacting with the great visionary, Aurobindo. Moreover, the patriot-sage was already a legend in 1947, the year of India's liberation, so Ramsuratkumar had gone to Pondicherry already knowing a vast amount about who Aurobindo was. Papa Ramdas, on the other hand, was an unknown as far as Ramsuratkumar was concerned.

Add to this that when he arrived in Kanhangad, Ramsuratkumar had just come from the foot of Mount Arunachala, from the darshan of a near-naked ascetic, Ramana Maharshi. We know that Ramana rarely spoke, although the emanations of his aura of sanctity were reported to be extremely strong. (Ramsuratkumar himself would note this in his next visit there.) For Ramana, there was no separate self, hence no "one" to suffer. His answers to one and all reflected this perfect *dharma* (teaching) of *advaita* awareness. Papa, in striking contrast, was known to be constantly laughing and joking, even speaking in mocking terms of his own failings, as he played with devotees. He was much concerned with the everyday details of his devotees' daily lives, as well as with the running of an ever-growing ashram, and was avidly involved in setting up a school, medical facilities, programs for the poor.

Papa's companion and first devotee, Mataji Krishnabai, for all her enormous compassion, was a relentless taskmaster – urging Papa himself to constantly give his attention to the needs of his "children" and passionately imploring everyone else to turn to Ramdas in every need. Her single-minded dedication and love served to make Anandashram the abode of bliss that its name signifies, as well as a place where genuine care existed in all domains, even on the physical level.

Besides the usual quota of sadhus and sannyasins, there were always families gathered, and that meant lots of children around Papa. Any one of these factors, if unexpectedly met, might have been enough to put off a serious seeker, and devotees of many masters over the years have reported similar responses in their first encounters. When this writer met her own teacher, Lee Lozowick, in 1984, she was immediately averse to him. Arriving at a public darshan and expecting an atmosphere of sacred worship as she was used to it from her years in another religious community, she judged his antics harshly as he put a pickle jar on his chair and bowed down before it in a mockery of false devotion. It was six months before she was again ready to open herself slightly to even hear about him and his work.

If we are to accept Ramsuratkumar's own words about this period of his life, he was in a very desperate stage of the search. Perhaps his seriousness was such that he too had a very limited view of what to look for, and certainly what to expect around a realized soul such as Papa.

The rational mind of course wants explanations: Why was he "deceived" by the show around Ramdas (as Ramsuratkumar told Makarand Paranjape, the writer, many years later); and why couldn't he immediately understand the greatness of Krishnabai? From innumerable annals of the spiritual path we know that the timing for everything is not in the hands of the seeker, however. Rather, it is the master, ultimately surrendered into the hands of God, who determines the where and the when of such a transformational moment – the moment of recognition. For Ramsuratkumar, there was more to be completed, or more to be started, or more to be learned.

After this first trip south, and after spending only a few days in Kanhangad, Ramsuratkumar returned to his native place in the north. As he told Paranjape, "this beggar once again got engrossed in worldly ways." For the man Ramsuratkumar, this probably meant simply that his focused spiritual pilgrimage had been completed for the time being. But not for long.

Perhaps, although we have no records of this period, Ramsuratkumar attempted to pick up again the life he had left behind in late 1947. Or maybe he simply returned to his sadhu friends at the ashram along the Ganges for additional instruction and support. One way or another, however, we know that what he had received on that first pilgrimage was so strong and so unsettling that it drove him to retrace his steps within less than a year's time. Like a deaf man who can feel the music's vibrations, yet cannot recognize its source, Ramsuratkumar again circled through the south, undoubtedly more distraught, and certainly more impassioned than ever to identify the One who was playing Krishna's flute, which he could hear at a distance – that flute which was calling him home.

राम

In his next trip south, late in 1948, we learn from Ramsuratkumar's own reports that he "went first to the Aurobindo Ashram but could not stay there."[3] It is entirely possible, as some have indicated, that a characteristically beggarly appearance as well as a highly feverish attitude may have begun to distinguish him as an undesirable element in the cultured atmosphere of the Mother's abode in Pondicherry. For whatever reason, Ramsuratkumar moved on, again to Tiruvannamalai, "and stayed for about two months with the Maharshi."[4] This sojourn proved to be highly significant.

राम

ONLY GOD

In India, as in other spiritual cultures in various parts of the world, it is commonly appreciated that a man or woman of grace and/or power (the shaman, a saint, a guru, a priest, a true teacher) can initiate or further the process of internal transformation that the genuine seeker longs for. The master or teacher will typically create this "spark" in one of several ways. According to the *Kula-Arnava-Tantra*, an Indian scripture, there are seven such methods: by mental projection, by energetic transmission, by performing some ritual, by glance, by touch, by word (mantra), and by a process of visualization of sacred letters of the alphabet.[5] These initiations are at times so simple, so subtle, that the casual bystander may not know that such a life-changing event is occurring in the soul of the person next to him. Ramana's form of initiation, according to all reports, was done through his eyes, in a look that could pierce the seeker to the core.

As a spark thrown on damp wood will soon die out, while one applied to desiccated grass will cause an immediate blaze, so too the effectiveness of initiation, or *abhisheka* as it is called in the East, will depend upon the readiness of the seeker. One who is primed, that is, dried out, is one who has seen the uselessness of following his or her own will. Such a one is willing to surrender his attachments in order to move more freely along the path that leads to the ultimate.

By Yogi Ramsuratkumar's own admission to his first biographer, we know that Ramana effected such an initiation for him. Throughout the two months of his second visit to Tiruvannamalai, Ramsuratkumar would spend his days in meditation, or attending to the conversations that the Maharshi had with his disciples and visitors. Whenever Ramana was in the meditation hall, Ramsuratkumar made it his practice to be there too. "Once it happened that while he was sitting on the floor near the Maharshi, he suddenly felt that someone's attention was powerfully fixed upon him. He glanced up from his meditation and beheld the loving and dynamic gaze of the master. Ramsuratkumar looked down timidly, but only a moment lapsed before he raised his eyes once again. Meeting the Maharshi's gaze he went into a visual rapport with him and completely lost himself in the timeless wonder of that godly soul. He felt as though he existed during that short while not as his solitary physical body but something far greater, far more glorious and vast. He sensed that he had lived before…and that the great seer peering into his eyes knew the wonders of the many lives past and those to come. The experience had tremendous impact on him."[6]

And from an article in *Mountain Path Magazine*, the official Ramanashram journal, we read of another powerful incident occasioned by the Maharshi. This one is credited as being in Ramsuratkumar's own words:

> As was the custom in Sri Ramanashramam [also called Ramanashram] after puja was performed at the Mother's shrine, the arati plate was placed before Bhagavan Ramana. One day He took kumkum [sacred red powder, ceremonially applied between the eyebrows] as usual. I happened to be the first to take kumkum from the small pile which Sri Bhagavan had touched. The mere touch of that same plate put me into an ecstatic state.[7]

There is no doubt that Ramsuratkumar was a ripe candidate for the transformation that life in Ramana Maharshi's presence could offer. During the two months of this visit, we can imagine that he absorbed the master's grace and the master's teachings deeply. So deeply, in fact, that Ramsuratkumar would later call Ramana Maharshi one of his "three Fathers," noting, "Most men wouldn't like to say they had three fathers, but this beggar had three Fathers. There was much work done on this beggar. Aurobindo started, Ramana Maharshi did a little, and Ramdas finished."[8]

In a striking parallel to the three primary Lords within the Hindu pantheon – Brahma, the Creator; Vishnu, the sustainer; and Siva, the destroyer – Aurobindo, like Brahma, had initiated the unfoldment for Ramsuratkumar, and Ramana Maharshi, like the sustainer, Lord Vishnu, had nurtured its precious seed. It would ultimately be Swami Ramdas, like Siva, who would effect Ramsuratkumar's annihilation and rebirth.

"Like father like son" is easily applied in the case of Ramana and Ramsuratkumar. With the advantage of hindsight, so many similarities can be observed between the two men as to indicate that Ramsuratkumar had indeed found his ancestry. At the most obvious level of outward signs, interestingly, each man bore the primary name of "Ram." Each had a powerful early association with the great Siva temple in Tiruvannamalai – Ramana had lived in it as a teenager, and Ramsuratkumar, who would later be found within its precincts at any hour of the day or night, had called it "the house of this beggar from ages to ages."

Each possessed enormous love for the sacred mountain, Arunachala Siva. "I came to devour Thee, but Thou hast devoured me; now there is peace, Arunachala" extolled Ramana;[9] while Ramsuratkumar once wrote, "Arunachala is stone mountain to many but to this beggar Arunachala is a great friend who gave help, refuge to this dirty sinner when everyone else denied."[10] Each man chose to live on or at the foot of the mountain for the vast portion of his life, and each eventually built his ashram there.

Both were renunciates – Ramsuratkumar, later a beggar in rags, would carry a coconut bowl, the traditional symbol of the sadhu's dependence upon the Divine for his sustenance; Ramana, dressed

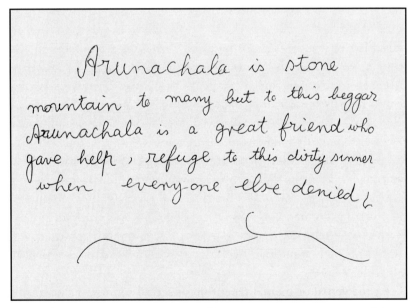

Handwritten by Yogi Ramsuratkumar in the early 1970s

only in a loincloth, carried a water pot and a walking stick, his sole possessions. Despite their own choice of poverty, neither of these "Bhagavans" would encourage sannyas as a necessity for devotees. In fact, both Ramana and Ramsuratkumar were advocates of finding liberation through ordinary life, never through the adoption of some extraordinary station, unless this were obviously one's calling. Furthermore, the fact that each master was fully absorbed in the Ultimate Reality was never a deterrent to his being totally present to the needs of disciples, friends, visitors, children, and even animals. Ramana particularly loved one ashram cow, Lakshmi, and could be seen to stroke her tenderly on his daily walks. Ramsuratkumar had three favorite dogs in succession, each named Sai Baba.

Perhaps what we observe are merely the similarities that all awakened souls possess – elegant kindness, clarity, tenderness, humor, and compassion. Perhaps these similarities indicate much more. Among the strong resonances in their dharmas, each saint was singularly devoted to the Divine and expressed his relationship to God in exactly the same words – "my Father."

Neither attempted to found a new religion, or to align fully within any existing one. They were not looking for disciples to build an organization. Both men sent their visitors away to pursue whatever religion or philosophy was most in keeping with the individual soul's orientation. Recognizing the urgency of giving men and women a more accessible means of Divine communion in an age of darkness (the *Kali Yuga*), they both embraced all paths to truth, merely opening the path wider and providing simple tools that could be incorporated into any existing way. For Ramana, the primary method was to reside fully in the Self, in the Heart, beyond thought and beyond ego. If that were not immediately possible, self-inquiry ("Who am I?") was the recommended practice for orienting a continual movement from the identification with a state of separation toward one of nonduality – recognition of complete unity.

Bhagavan Ramana, moreover, urged devotees to practice *mantra japa*, the verbal or mental repetition of sacred sounds, including the name of God, as a means of constant remembrance. And for those who wanted the most direct path, although for some perhaps much

harder, Ramana Maharshi urged full surrender to the guru as the ultimate way:

"Submit. Submit to me and I will strike down the mind."

"Only keep quiet and Bhagavan will do the rest."

"If one has surrendered himself to God or Guru, the power
to which he has surrendered will take him on the right
course. One need no longer concern himself about the
course. The doubt will arise only if he fails to obey the
Master in all details."[11]

For Yogi Ramsuratkumar, the declaration "Father alone exists; no
one else, nothing else" would constantly reflect his abidance in the
Self. These words would also remind all who came to him that "Only
God" was the Ultimate Reality. The means that Ramsuratkumar
would forever encourage for remembering and praising that Ultimate
Reality was the recitation, quietly or in song, of *nama japa*, the holy
name of God.

Neither Ramana nor Ramsuratkumar are remembered as miracle
workers. Although many disciples can retell stories of unexplainable
events – healings, blessings, even witness to the apparent bilocation
of the master – both men made light of such phenomena, claiming
ignorance of the events or crediting such things to a power that transcended all...themselves included. Ramana would say merely: "As
soon as the devotee turns in prayer to the Jnani [the man of knowl-
edge], the automatic divine activity begins to work."[12] Ramsuratkumar would say: "Oh, this beggar knows nothing of such things...
Father alone exists...Oh, look at the wonder of my Father."[13] The
greatest miracles, however, were being effected in the hearts and
minds of those who came burdened, dark, and suffering to the feet
of either great master and left lightened, "enlightened," and at peace.
These miracles were the norm.

Finally, while Ramana and Ramsuratkumar clearly "ran the
show," in the largest sense of the term, each was a model of surrender to the will, and even the whim, of his devotees. Like Jesus, other

great innocents throughout the ages have served as sacrificial lambs for humanity's transformation. Ramana Maharshi allowed his own crucifixion by submitting to the demands of devotees. Against his own preference, he endured three painful surgeries during the last year of his life – surgeries that only drove the cancer in his arm deeper into other bones of his body. With Ramsuratkumar, the situation was almost identical. He too protested, begged, for nothing but reliance upon "my Father's will" in the handling of his body. Yet, in the end, the pleas of devotees caused him to submit to similar invasions. Both men had come as messengers of the Divine, had offered themselves as our servants, and ultimately took on our sufferings in a way that only a mystical vision can fully comprehend.

राम

Despite the profound experiences that Ramsuratkumar had around Ramana in 1948, the young seeker was still restless – still needing to complete a journey. Repeating the steps of his last round of pilgrimage, and despite the fact that he had been unimpressed with Ramdas at the first meeting, something drew him back to Kanhangad, against all odds. And so he again made the trip west.

5

IN QUEST OF GOD

After leaving Tiruvannamalai and the ashram of Ramana Maharshi, Ramsuratkumar made his second visit to Anandashram in 1948, spent only a few days, and again left disappointed. "Swami Ramdas produced the same kind of feeling in this beggar," Ramsuratkumar related many years later, referring to his initial impression that he did not understand Ramdas and was put off by what he judged as the saint's "living luxuriously."[1]

Ramdas himself would have been the first to admit that his ashram life in 1948 was far different from the life he had lived as a wandering sadhu in the early 1920s. Those years on the road and early days "in quest of God" were marked by austerity and an extremely passionate demeanor – characteristics that would certainly have captured Ramsuratkumar's attention, as he himself had already shown similar tendencies. Commenting on the more sedate style of his years of work at Anandashram, Ramdas once joked:

> You fellows are lucky Ramdas has become a quieter soul, under Mataji's influence. In those days [referring to early sadhana days] he was so nimble-footed that you would have found it difficult to keep pace with him. He would never tolerate any hypocrisy – now he speaks more carefully lest he hurt anyone's feelings. He was like a ball of fire then. He would run up to the hills or take himself to remote places like jungles and graveyards, far from the haunts of men, to spend all night rapt in Ram Nam. He would fast for days together,

unswayed by anyone's pleas to break his fast. He would never engage himself in any talk but that of Ram. Seeing this jovial person cracking jokes, can anyone recognize Ramdas of old? Then, he was like the meandering stream flowing towards the ocean, now, the stream and ocean have become one but the stream continues to flow on, inseparable from the ocean and at the same time enjoying its union with the ocean.[2]

Ramsuratkumar's appearance in 1948 was probably already a source of irritation to those who expected a different protocol. We know that the intensity of his quest led many to dismiss him as a "madman," and Papa's devotee, Mother Krishnabai, would later describe him as "a fire," and therefore a dangerous person.[3] Hence, Ramsuratkumar was denied entrance to many places. It seems that ultimately, according to the will of Ram, Papa was not ready for Ramsuratkumar in 1948, and the younger seeker was not yet ready for Papa.

One thing is certain, however. In two visits to Anandashram, Ramsuratkumar would have heard many marvels of Swami Ramdas's life. The elder saint's amazing transition from family man to wandering mendicant to spiritual master and his complete reliance upon the will of God – whom he called his "Ram" – would have been remembered by the young northerner, at least in context if not in detail. Even in 1948, the parallels between Ramdas's path and Ramsuratkumar's progress in the way were already undeniable.

राम

Biographers are indeed fortunate when their subjects are prolific writers who record their own life accounts. Swami Papa Ramdas wrote his own story in segments, at several different times. At the conclusion of his first pilgrimage of sadhana, when he had turned his back on all the attractions of the world in order to surrender himself completely to God, he spent many months in solitude in a cave, praying and writing. *In Quest of God* details the hardships and triumphs of this first wondrous journey – from 1920 to 1923. Other books followed, written in his own hand, including *In the Vision of*

ONLY GOD

God, At the Feet of God and *The Divine Life*, and devotees over the
years have compiled many more books based on the stories that Papa
told or *lilas* (acts of the Divine play) they experienced in his presence.

What characterizes Ramdas's own biographical narration is a
great teaching in itself: namely, that every detail recorded is set in a
transcendent context. The ordinary man or woman writing an autobiography will most likely relate his or her story from within the context of the dream world in which he or she is separate from God.
Consequently, their stories will be full of the judgements of things as
"sufferings" vs. "successes," casting its characters as "bad guys" and
"good guys." For Ramdas, there were no good guys or bad guys, only
Ram in a myriad of forms. All circumstances were only the hand of
the Divine moving the pieces of creation, and with one purpose
alone, that of expressing Itself. All events were designed to draw the
heart of the devotee into immersion in the heart of Love. Whatever
hardships he, Ramdas, had to undergo were described as gifts of
purification, instruction, and inspiration.

Unlike Ramdas, Yogi Ramsuratkumar left no writing about his
own life. But clearly this same transcendent context – that there is
"only God" – applied whenever he spoke of his journey, and in everything else that he did. Furthermore, Yogi Ramsuratkumar urged
biographers of any saint to avoid negative details in the telling –
details that would distract from the glorious central focus of the
saint's life and mission. He also instructed people to avoid investigations of his own early life. The reasons for this were never fully
explained. However, it is clear that unless one is able to maturely hold
all events as being the Father's Will, one can easily become swept up
in the appearances of things, and try to "fit" the details of the saint's
life into one's own ideas of what is "holy" or "blessed" and what is
not. What Ramdas and Ramsuratkumar have told us in the witness
of their lives, however, is that *all is holy*. Rare indeed is the writer who
can do that genuinely.

As he began his own story, Ramdas, like Ramsuratkumar, wanted one thing made perfectly clear. In all the writing that would follow, he would be concerned only with:

...events, circumstances, influences and environments that awakened, nourished and accelerated the spiritual light and aspiration and, later, the progress towards, and the attainment of, the supreme goal of Self-realization. When he looks back from his present spiritual state, he can clearly see how God's unbounded grace led and guided him through quite a labyrinth of conflicting and puzzling experiences with glimpses of the divine light flashing out now and again all through his career.[4]

राम

Born on April 10, 1884, Vittal Rao was the sixth of thirteen children of Lalita Bai and Sri Balakrishna Rao, devout Hindus of the Brahmin caste and members of the Saraswat community. His birth took place in the family home in the little town of Hosdrug, which faces the Arabian Sea on the west coast of southern India, a short forty-five miles south of the city of Mangalore. The day of his birth was auspicious, as it was also celebrated throughout India as the birth of Hanuman – the monkey-god, the ever-devoted servant of Ram. "Servant of Ram" was the literal meaning of the name "Ramdas" that Vittal would eventually assume when he surrendered himself to God.

This community of Saraswats into which he was born was one that prized education, scholarship, and successful business venturing. Yet, despite the prompting of family and culture, young Vittal from his earliest years was a disinterested student. He tells us quite unapologetically that his teachers were often quite cruel, and that his parents too failed to offer solace during these difficult times. Their responsibilities in raising such a huge family, coupled with the community pressure for distinguished education, were undoubtedly factors in this equation.

Struggling with the systems that attempted to control him, stories abound of how young Vittal hid from teachers, running away to favorite natural haunts instead. Nature, beauty, joy, great good humor, these were his subjects of interest. Art and drama were his favorite pastimes rather than scholarship or business. As a boy he loved nothing better than to spend hours sketching all that he saw, or modeling with clay. As a teenager, he was an avid actor, set designer and costume maker for a local drama group.

Ramdas tells us that his early life was a veritable "tug of war between two forces…one tending to fetter his life and force it into a system which aimed at stamping out initiative and freedom, and the other attempting to release him from the earth-born tangle of a mundane life and raise him up to a purer, greater and illumined spiritual region."[5] How many other young men and women throughout the ages have suffered this same interior tug of war?

Besides the solitude and beauty of nature, young Vittal was inspired by the great songs and stories of his cultural heritage – the *Ramayana*, the *Upanishads*, the tales of the kings, sages, and warriors. He also found inspiration in a few individuals, people whose lives served to nurture that seed of freedom planted in his heart. One was an uncle, a man whom the family regarded as being "lost in God"; outside this family circle, however, this same person might be considered retarded or autistic. Young Vittal would watch this man (who had no functional relationship to the world at large) become ecstatic during the evening *bhajan* (chants and songs) sessions when the families would gather for worship. Something about his uncle's disregard for all things temporal, coupled with his delight for all things divine, made a strong impression on Vittal.

Similarly, Vittal was moved by the example of two sannyasins from the Punjab who visited his family's home when he was about eight years old. Years later, Ramdas recounted that their profound kindness to him left him with a memory that again energized his hunger for truth and contemplation.

A third influence was made by a particular swami, the spiritual head of the Saraswat community at the time. This swami led an extremely austere life, fully dedicated to his spiritual practice. The witness of such a life touched Vittal, who later wrote: "Ramdas used to go for the Darshan of this Swami two or three times everyday [when the man was visiting their town] and he felt that the Swami was exerting on him a strange but powerful fascination."[6] Lastly, Ramdas tells us that he was strongly affected by the devout life of his elderly widowed aunt. This woman was absorbed day and night in the celebration of the Divine name, and from her Vittal received a taste of that special nectar.

On the material plane, Vittal failed to complete his high school studies, preferring instead the "blessed idleness" that allowed him to read at his own leisure, which he did voraciously, to enjoy art, and to contemplate nature. "His was a free spirit and found his joy more in the masterpieces of great English authors than in going through the dull routine of a schoolboy to his textbooks," wrote his younger brother, Sanjivrao.[7]

There was little future in reading English literature or in art, however. Even though Vittal's parents supported him in moving to Madras, where he started art school, within six months his older brother had convinced him to drop that path in favor of one that would provide for the years ahead and for the wife and children who would inevitably follow. When a wealthy member of the Saraswat community offered two scholarships for the Victoria Jubilee Technical Institute of Bombay, Vittal applied and was immediately accepted. The course of study was textile engineering – one that he would never have chosen but one that was available by default.

Once again we find our young subject trapped in a situation that is alien to his inclinations. In order to preserve his inner life, Vittal took to reading philosophy, fiction, poetry, and the great works of Shakespeare (over and over) like a thirsty man seeking for water in a desert. He went through a period of fascination with the philosophy of rationalism, which led him to temporarily put aside the spiritual yearnings of his early days. It was a crisis of faith, we might say, looking at the situation today; and was undoubtedly the gift of God bringing his young devotee to a low point from which he could only go up.

During this period, he read the writings of the great patriot-saint Swami Vivekananda, whose passion for the Divine, knitted with his love for the Motherland, India, reawakened something within Vittal. He also read the works of Swami Rama Tirtha, another of the patriot-sages who would similarly inspire Yogi Ramsuratkumar. The words of these visionaries dragged Vittal back from the edge of an abyss of meaningless where he had precariously teetered. In the years ahead, when Ramdas would confront the human dilemma head-on in the lives of hundreds and thousands of similarly "trapped" and discouraged individuals who would come to him for help, he would be able to speak to them from the intimate knowledge of these painful and unfulfilling states.

Two months before his three-year textile-engineering study was completed, a significant event occurred for young Vittal – an event that would orient his life even more in the direction of his ultimate calling. His best friend, Vadiraj, became deathly ill. Vittal was at the young man's side throughout his final days, as well as at the moment of death as Vadiraj breathed his last. The incident shocked him and marked another degree of loss of innocence in much the same way that Yogi Ramsuratkumar was marked by the death of the bird that he had accidentally killed.

Ramdas later described his condition at the time: "He started crying like a child which had lost its mother…For two days, whenever Ramdas remembered him, he was off and on crying from the sudden separation of this friend. The impression which this sad event left on him deepened his indifferent attitude towards the high aims and ambitions of this transitory earthly life."[8]

With this heartbreak as his graduation present, Vittal finished his studies in Bombay and returned to Madras to embark upon his career of employment, beginning with work in a hand-loom cloth factory under the tutelage of his beloved brother, Sitaram Rao. It was at this time that, after resisting his parents' several requests, Vittal finally consented to take a wife. In 1908, he obligingly married a woman of the Saraswat community, Rukmabai, and in 1913 a daughter, Ramabai (known as Ranne), was born to the couple. In this union, as in so many of the circumstances that the Divine would engineer in Ramdas's life, Vittal found himself again in a situation that was not his preference. He was obviously deeply torn in many directions – unhappy in having to succumb to cultural norms, yet attempting to be kind and responsible to his wife and family. Ultimately, as he reported in his own words, "the marriage was not a success as he fully expected it…Just as the harmonious mingling of two souls provides us with opportunities to realise the beauty of life, so also the constant friction between two souls removes all the dross that covers the soul so that it may appear in all its nakedness before the Great Being from whom it has manifested."[9]

His failures in the daily domestic scene were compounded by his failures in establishing a livelihood. If one were to cast a parable about a God-conscious being who took on the failure of humankind as a way to demonstrate liberation from it, they would find no better example than that of Vittal Rao. Today we might call such well-meaning failures by names that reveal our disapproval. Surely we might assume, in all our psychological sophistication, that he failed because of a bad attitude, laziness, unwillingness to play by the "rules." If we weren't looking with the eyes of faith as we approached the lives of both Ramdas and his future spiritual son, Ramsuratkumar, we could easily assign them the status of irrelevant individuals. *What contribution were they making? Even wife and child could be barely supported!* Yet such judgements would be unfortunate ones, superficial ones. With the gift of hindsight we can see that, in the case of Vittal Rao, and paralleled in similar ways in the case of Ramsuratkumar, "failure" was the Divine's means of purifying and readying the soul for its ultimate great work.

For nearly ten years Vittal struggled to maintain a job or to start up a new business, but he constantly found doors closing all around him. Some businesses simply lost money and he had to be let go. In other circumstances, he took a stand on behalf of underpaid or underprivileged workers and found himself quickly on the outs with his employers, while being loved and respected by the laborers he had defended. Writing of his experiences during these times, Vittal reported that, "Whenever an accident took place as a consequence of which a mill worker had to suffer, Ramdas used to take him immediately on a stretcher to the nearest hospital and wait on the doctor until he had him treated in the proper manner. On these occasions he used to leave the mills without any permission from anybody.[10]

Needless to say, such activities did not endear him to management. He simply refused to compromise his inner principles. From his earliest years, Vittal could not tolerate rigidity in its many forms, nor separation of castes and classes. His efforts were always aimed at attempting to honor all people as equals, even at the risk of his own life, which was not an uncommon occurrence.

As his young friend's death had catapulted him into a new level of spiritual awareness, an event in 1918 served to set his feet firmly on the path of spiritual practice. In this year both his wife and his child became seriously ill. While his daughter recovered quickly, Rukmabai hovered on the brink of life and death, and her husband became desperate. Uncharacteristically, Vittal was swept up into passionate prayer for his wife's recovery. A picture of an eminent swami, Sri Pandurangashram, hung in Vittal's room, and it was to this saint that he directed his intense prayers. He became so deeply immersed in his petitioning of the Divine that hot tears rose to his eyes. The prayer, however, succeeded in calming his heart and his agonized mind, and, synchronistically, from that moment his wife's condition began to improve.

The incident changed him. One might say in looking at the whole panorama of Ramdas's life that his "madness in God" started from this point. This clear Divine intervention, this healing, was a nearly final straw in convincing Vittal that true power abided only in God. With his wife's recovery he began to talk about God, and about the teachings of saints, to everybody who would listen. On almost every evening thereafter, he enthusiastically joined his other family members in their program of bhajan singing. His love for Krishna, the godman and lover of humanity, was obvious in these times as never before. Vittal would often be found ecstatically gazing upon the statue of this beloved flute-playing deity, lost in bliss. It was truly "the beginning of the end" for him.

A few final years of business involvement followed this turning point, and at certain moments it looked as if Vittal, now a middle-aged man approaching forty, would at last find his security. But Sri Sitaram Vittal Company, his last venture in the work of printing fabrics and dyeing saris, would suffer the fate of all his previous efforts. "The scales started tilting dangerously toward the debit side. The expenses became heavy and whatever profits were made they were swallowed up by the day to day overhead expenses," he wrote.[11] A favorite nephew who was close to Vittal at the time noted that, despite the many setbacks, Vittal seemed to him "as irrepressible as ever."

74

While his irrepressibility was undoubtedly true at one level, on another, deeper, level he was suffering greatly. In his own words he reported that:

> It was a period of terrible stress and restlessness, all of his own making. In this utterly helpless condition, full of misery, where was relief? Where was rest. This was the heart's cry of Ramdas. The cry was heard, and from the Great Void came the voice, "Despair not! Trust Me and thou shalt be free!" That was the voice of Ram. These encouraging words of Ram proved like a plank thrown towards a man struggling for very life in the stormy waves of a raging sea. The great assurance soothed the aching heart of helpless Ramdas like gentle rain on thirsting earth.[12]

The power of the name of God began to take over more and more of Vittal's conscious attention. He could be observed walking the streets with one-pointed inner focus, while his lips formed the sacred mantra constantly. If his business associates were nonplussed by his strange behaviors, his wife and family members were often distraught and highly critical of the ways in which his practice affected his abilities to function "normally." In a short time, Vittal began to renounce various bodily comforts, reducing his food intake first to two meals, and then to only one, consisting of plantain and boiled potatoes. He dressed in coarse *khaddar* (the homespun cotton of the poor) and slept on a bare mat. He started staying up long into the night repeating God's name. "I plunged into the depthless sea of life, and came by the rarest gem – Thy Name," he would write years later.[13]

Seeing the condition in which his son was being consumed, Vittal's father was divinely inspired to assist him in the final throes of transformation. Balakrishna Rao, acting in the role of a traditional guru, initiated his son in the *taraka mantra*. Into Vittal's ear he whispered the sacred words, *Sri Ram Jai Ram, Jai Jai Ram*, and instructed his son to repeat this mantra "at all times." The result, he assured Vittal, would be that Ram would "give him eternal happiness." Because of his father's initiation, for the rest of his life Ramdas referred to Balakrishna as "Gurudev" and honored him as others have honored their gurus throughout the centuries.

Later, Papa would add the word/sound *Om* to the beginning of this mantra, making it *Om Sri Ram Jai Ram, Jai Jai Ram.* The addition was not actually an innovation, as some have mistakenly assumed. Rather, it was a return to an original form in which the mantra had been granted.[14]

As his activities became more and more obsessive, the gossip among relatives circulated that Vittal had "really lost his wits." In one revealing story, an older delegate from among his family members came to Vittal's house to talk some sense into him. He found Vittal walking, pacing, back and forth in one particular room, repeating the mantra continuously – a behavior that was becoming more and more consistent. As soon as the older man entered the room, Vittal knew why he was there.

"Look here," Vittal remonstrated, stopping the man in his tracks, "[I am] determined to sing Ram Nam and go on singing it until these four walls resound to the sound of Ram Nam. So please do not waste any breath by telling [me] to stop singing Ram Nam."[15]

The passion evident in this response was not uncommon throughout this transitional period when Vittal was being weaned from normal life and taken to the breast of Ram alone. Ramdas reported that there was some inkling that an ultimate break would transpire, but exactly the form of it was as yet unknown to him. On a night in late December 1922, however, the faraway call was heard at last and answered. As usual, Vittal was deep in his contemplation of Ram when a radical line of thinking unfolded in his mind. In the last few years he had come to trust the Divine in all its dealings with him. He had, in fact, adopted the role of slave, making Ram his "all in all." It now occurred to him to formalize this slavery and complete dependence, and to beg of his Lord to take him completely, removing "the I-ness in him." With that utterance, the desire to renounce all and to take up the role of the mendicant in order to serve nothing but Ram began to crystallize in his awareness. As this thought sunk deeper into this heart, Vittal was prompted to open a book that lay near at hand. It was called *Light of Asia,* and among other things recounted the story of the Lord Buddha's renunciation. Opening the book, his eyes fell upon this passage:

> For now the hour is come when I should quit
> This golden prison where my heart lives caged
> To find the truth which henceforth I will seek
> For all men's sake until the truth be found.

No further confirmation of this radical invitation was needed, yet Vittal was again inspired to turn to his much-used copy of the New Testament, which he opened to the following passage: "And everyone that hath forsaken houses or brethren or sister or father or mother or wife or children or lands for My name's sake, shall receive a hundredfold and shall inherit everlasting life." (Matthew 19:29.)

Finally, opening the *Bhagavad Gita*, he read these words: "Abandoning all duties come to Me alone for shelter; sorrow not, I will liberate thee from all sins."

Nothing more was needed. Through the words of Buddha, Christ, and Krishna, Vittal had been pointed in the same direction. As Ramdas later wrote of this terrible, wonderful moment: "At once Ramdas made up his mind to give up for the sake of Ram, all that he till then hugged to his bosom as his own, and leave the samsaric world."[16]

As his wife and child were away at the time, Vittal Rao used the opportunity to make his preparations for immediate departure. Like a man with only a few hours left to live, he wrote two final letters, one to his wife and one to his business partner. With a small quantity of red ochre powder, he spent his last night dying two pieces of cloth to the traditional shade worn by sannyasins. These would soon become the uniform of his renunciation. Shortly before five the next morning, carrying only a few rupees, his orange "robes," and a handful of favored books, Vittal made his way to the railway station at Mangalore, where he boarded the train, the daily Madras Mail, and headed southeast. It was December 28, 1922.

The letter he left behind to Rukmabai was, in effect, his last will and testament. It is a letter that marks a liberating moment in the life of a great saint, testifying to his absolute love for and trust of the

Divine. But it is also a letter that troubles conventional standards, particularly for those outside the culture of India who have scant appreciation for the stage of sannyas, or renunciation, that has typically characterized the lives of great spiritual masters, sages and teachers throughout the ages. Sri Aurobindo left wife and family for the fulfillment of his mission. Ramdas had now done the same; and later, his devotee Mataji Krishnabai would leave her two children in the care of relatives to serve Papa completely. Anandamayi Ma (1896-1981), hailed throughout the world as an incarnation of the Divine Mother, was married by her family to a pure-hearted man, but never consummated the union. Her husband, Ramani Mohan Chakravarty (typically known as Bholanath), would become her ardent devotee. And, slightly more than twenty-five years after Ramdas's departure, Yogi Ramsuratkumar too would leave a wife and children in northern India and proceed to Pondicherry in quest of God.

It takes a broad vision and a great faith to trust such radical departures and, in this day and age, to avoid diminishing them as acts of irresponsibility. Such simplistic labeling belies the astounding sacrifice that such decisions more likely engendered. To leave behind a predictable, even if uncomfortable, life for a life of complete poverty, radical witness to God, and utter insecurity is not something that an ordinary man or woman can do well. Those who leave for reasons of avoidance and denial of responsibility don't usually end up numbered among the saints.

Dec. 28, 1922
Dear Sister,

You are to me only a sister in future. Sriram, at whose feet I surrendered myself entirely has called me away from the past sphere of my life. I go forth a beggar in the wide world chanting the sweet name of Sriram. You know I have no ambition in life except to struggle for the attainment of Sriram's Grace and Love. To that aim alone I dedicate the rest of my life and suffer for it – suffer to any extent. We may not meet again – at least as husband and wife. Walk always in the path of God and Truth and make Ranne do the same.

Don't give up the spinning wheel. It will give you peace and happiness. Let Ranne also work it.

Sriram's blessings on you and Ranne. He protects you both.

Yours affectionately,
P. Vittal Rao[17]

राम

Two days after leaving his home in Mangalore, having crossed the southern tip of India by train, Ramdas alighted in Trichinopoly and, walking the distance of seven miles, waylaid for a brief time in the pilgrimage town of Srirangam. Here, on the banks of the Kaveri River, he took one step closer to his final aim. Bathing in the river, he removed the white clothes that he had still worn since his departure and laid them upon the swirling waters. As he watched, they were carried away in the strong current, and with them his previous attachments and associations. He then dressed himself in the simple orange cloth that he had dyed, and with a fervent prayer vowed his life to meditation and service of Sri Ram, his Lord; to strict celibacy; and to total reliance upon bhiksha (the receiving of alms) for the maintenance of his bodily needs.

And, in response, he tells us that all the turmoil of his previous years ceased. He wept tears of joy, tears of relief. "Sorrow, pain, anxiety and care – all vanished, never to return. All glory to Thee, Ram."[18] And then from within his soul there arose a blessing which he knew came from Ram alone: "I take thee under my guidance and protection – remain ever my devotee – thy name shall be Ramdas."

राम

For the next six years, Ramdas's life was that of an itinerant sannyasin. From the end of 1922 until sometime in 1928, with short periods of solitary retreat, Ramdas traveled the length and breadth of India – by train, by foot, and always by the grace of Ram. Ramdas tells us that in the first few days of his wanderings the purpose of his journey was given to him. Quite simply, his travels were to draw him away from his previous life and surroundings – to make a clean and absolute break! And, secondly, to take him to sacred shrines and rivers throughout his beloved country. Even though he knew himself to be held in the palm of God's hand from the moment of his dedication, there was evidently an urgent need to practice his faith, his trust, his love, and the celebration of the Divine name in a wide variety of circumstances. Certainly he needed to know if he could be discouraged in his aim by the hardships of the road – in the midst of cold, hunger, ill-treatment – or if he could use all to the glory of God. Certainly, he knew that he had a lot to learn – that he was a mere child attempting to walk and talk, all with the help of his Ram. And from his stories and poems of these early journeys, we know that, paradoxically, despite his full absorption in the Divine, a yearning still existed for something more…something that he would name in his writings at the end of his first year on the road…something that is rarely associated as a distinguishing characteristic of Ramdas but which is seen emblazoned in the life of another itinerant beggar of God, Ramsuratkumar, more than twenty-five years later. What Ramdas longed for and begged for was madness!

A few highlights of these years of sadhana are enough to reveal the courage, the passion, and the complete joy in which Ramdas lived. While we do not have records of Ramsuratkumar's sadhana years before he finally settled in Tiruvannamalai, an astute reader can learn a lot about the details of such a wandering life from what Papa has left us. His experiences of sadhana led Ramdas to the lowliest places and demanded the most severe tests of endurance. Yet, no matter what was offered to him, he turned absolutely everything into praise of God. As far as he was concerned, sleeping on the bare urine-soaked ground under a tree near a train station (as he did in Ajmere) was as much Ram's unique and personal expression of love and protection for his "Das" as was a clean room in a palace (as he was given in Limbdi). Whatever the circumstances, Ramdas took what was given as a means of advancing his detachment from the body and his realization of impermanence. In all that transpired, "Ramdas, the child of Ram slept soundly till morning in the loving embrace of that all-powerful Being – Ram."[19]

Swami Ramdas as a sannyasin

ONLY GOD

It seems more than coincidental that Ramdas, like Ramsurat-kumar, was drawn to Pondicherry in the initial stages of his first journey through India. Ramdas sorely wanted the darshan of the great Bengali patriot and mystic, Sri Aurobindo, who even in 1923 was renowned throughout India. Together with a fellow sadhu (a *sadhuram*, as Ramdas called his sannyasin companions), he walked the twenty miles from the town of Tirupapuliyur to the outskirts of the lovely French colony. Inquiring about the location of the Aurobindo ashram, they were finally directed to the gate of the palatial building where, they were told, the saint was living. When he entered the grounds, however, Ramdas learned from two young Bengalis that "Sri Aurobindo is in retirement, he will not give audience to anybody for a year to come." This was 1923. Aurobindo had been in Pondicherry since 1914, and accompanied by the Mother since 1920. Nonetheless, he was as physically inaccessible to Ramdas as he would be to Ramsuratkumar in 1947 and '48.

Ramdas was not immediately discouraged, however. Nor was he afraid to beg...which he did, imploring a mere glimpse of the great man – the briefest darshan. But there was no granting of such spontaneous favors in those days, or ever, perhaps.

Ramdas was thwarted, according to Ram's will, in his desire to meet the saint. He was also severely tested in the hours that followed. Outside the gate of Aurobindo's ashram, as he reported to his companion-sadhu the news of what had transpired inside, the two were approached by a policeman and told that they were wanted immediately at the police station. There they were sternly rebuked (in French) by a fierce-looking police inspector and informed that they had only two hours in which to leave the city or suffer more serious consequences. When the sadhuram heard this, he proceeded to argue their case, trying to explain the great fatigue that the two wanderers were suffering. They had, after all, walked twenty miles that morning already!

Arguments were not expected, however, and the inspector became more stern than ever. Spicing his commands with "some finely selected epithets of abuse," he changed his ultimatum for getting out of town from two hours to one! Needless to say, the two sadhus complied. While Ramdas took all as Ram's directions to them, his

companion did not. As they walked away from the city, heading back
to Tirupapuliyer, the other sadhu complained hotly, with his own
choice words of abuse for the inspector, before falling silent at last.

Their next destination? Mount Arunachala!

By train from Tirupapuliyur, Ramdas and the sadhuram arrived
in Tiruvannamalai, where his companion secured lodging for both of
them with a local goldsmith. For a few days in this quiet city Ramdas
had the use of an enclosed verandah, where he would meditate and
rest. At night, with his friend he would visit the great temple,
Arunachaleswarar, "the huge temple of Mahadev [Lord Siva]," as
Ramdas referred to it in *In Quest of God.* [20] On one day, his companion sadhu was only too happy to take Ramdas to a thatched shed at
the foot of the mountain, about a mile or so from the great temple.
This simple dwelling was the heart of the ashram of Sri Ramana
Maharshi, who was now, in 1923, in his forty-third year of life.
Entering the presence of the holy man, both Ramdas and his friend
prostrated themselves. In his own words, Ramdas described the incident, speaking of Ramana:

> There was on his face a calmness, and in his large eyes a pas-
> sionless look of tenderness, which cast a spell of peace and
> joy on all those who came to him. Ramdas was informed that
> the Saint knew English. So he addressed him thus: "Maharaj,
> here stands before thee a humble slave. Have pity on him.
> His only prayer to thee is to give him thy blessing."
>
> The Maharshi, turning his beautiful eyes towards
> Ramdas, and looking intently for a few minutes into his eyes
> as though he was pouring into Ramdas his blessing through
> those orbs, shook his head to say that he had blessed. A thrill
> of inexpressible joy coursed through the frame of Ramdas,
> his whole body quivering like a leaf in the breeze. O Ram,
> What a love is Thine![21]

Shortly thereafter, Ramdas felt prompted by Ram to enter into
solitude for a longer period. Discussing his desire with his friend, the
sadhuram immediately took him on a little pilgrimage to several different caves all located on Mount Arunachala. One small place, not

far up the mountain and a ten-minute walk from the entrance to the Arunachaleswarar Temple, was chosen for Ramdas's retreat. Here he spent one month, dedicating his time to meditation upon Ram. It was the first period of solitude in his journey of sadhana, and it proved to be a time of profound joy and ecstasy for him. He described it as "rolling in a sea of indescribable happiness."[22]

The interior of the Banyan Tree Cave as it looked in 2002

In this auspicious spot, Ramdas was gifted with a great revelation – a universal vision in which he experienced that Ram was in all, in everything. If indeed his madness for God had been growing prior to this event, now it was filling up and spilling over. One day, for instance, "lost in the madness of Ram's meditation," Ramdas rushed from the cave into the outdoors where he embraced rocks, trees, and even an unsuspecting man who happened to be walking on the hill. The poor man ran away in fright, thinking that Ramdas was "a mad man who was behaving in this manner and so was afraid of harm from him." Years later, in telling of this wondrous moment, Papa would laugh, remembering the sight of this man whom he had embraced in his God-intoxicated state. In his writing at the time he reported, "It was true, he [Ramdas] was mad – yes, he was mad of Ram." [23]

राम

As the months rolled by, this journey was marked with so many wondrous incidents. On several occasions Ramdas was literally saved from near-imminent death by the intervention of his Lord Ram's grace. There were other times in which he was met and led by wise and caring sages, or served by fellow sadhus who easily recognized the extraordinary nature of this humble, ever-smiling brother. Each incident relates a story and a teaching lesson. In Raipur, for instance, we learn something more of Ramdas's universality when he was approached by a young Muslim who politely inquired if he had faith in Muhammad.

"Why not?" Ramdas replied. "He is one of the greatest prophets of God."

His youthful inquisitor was put off by the response, wondering why Ramdas had used the phrase "one of the" rather than the "only one." To which Ramdas answered: "Young brother, although Muhammad is a world Teacher, there are others also who are as great Teachers, for instance – Buddha, Jesus Christ and Krishna – and in our days – Mahatma Gandhi. If you would try to understand the message they deliver to the world, you will find that in the essentials they all agree and hold out the same goal to mankind." [24]

Such stories round out for the reader the full scope of this remarkable and amazingly wild personality whom we know today as benevolent "Papa," the Father of Yogi Ramsuratkumar and the guru and beloved of thousands of devotees throughout the world. A few more tales, however, bear special recounting here, in an attempt to capture an essential parallel to the life of another mad and wild lover of God, the "odd Bihari" – Ramsuratkumar – who would visit Papa in the late 1940s and early 1950s.

ONLY GOD

In Ramdas's first trip to the city of Calcutta, he visited the ashram of Sri Ramakrishna in Dakshineswar. Guided by the hand of Ram in the person of an ashram attendant, he and another sadhu were taken to the small room that had been occupied by the great saint. It contained a bed and two cushions used by Ramakrishna. Approaching these sacred artifacts, Ramdas placed his forehead upon them in the traditional act of imbibing the *shakti* (energy) contained in such objects. The impact was electrifying and immediate. As he described in *In Quest of God*:

> By this time he [Ramdas himself] was beginning to feel the electric influence of the very air inside that room. Thrill after thrill of joy passed through him. He then laid himself flat on the floor of the room and began to roll all over the place, feeling all the while, an inexpressible ecstasy of bliss. O Ram, the floor was blessed by the tread of the sacred feet of that holy man. About half an hour passed thus and he was still rolling on the floor, his face beaming with a strange light of infinite joy.[25]

The image of Ramdas the sadhu literally rolling on the floor in ecstasy in order to absorb the energy of a saint's footsteps is a powerful picture. It points to a sense of complete freedom and a degree of divine madness that frequently possessed Ramdas in those early days, and he wanted more! There were obviously no rules for him, except his passion for Ram. No false appropriateness was to prevent his "getting the goods" – in this case, the blessings of a saint, Ramakrishna, who was also completely mad in the Divine.

Following this thread of madness a little further, we find Ramdas at the conclusion of his first pilgrimage of sadhana ensconced in another cave, called "Panch Pandav," on the Kadri hill, not far from his family home. Here he had entered into solitude and lived for many months as he wrote the narrative of that initial trip, which we know today as *In Quest of God*. Here Ramdas also wrote poetry – line after line, verse after verse of God-intoxicated expressions. It is from these marvelous lyrics that we learn so much of the state of longing and heartbreak that he still endured, despite his ecstatic immersion in the One. We learn of his impatience with his own weaknesses, his remorse for his imperfections, and at the same time his glorying in Ram, who had made him strong, courageous, and still. For those who have read the diaries of other mystics and saints, however, such seeming contradictions come as no surprise.

O Ram, Thy slave cries to Thee repeatedly to make him mad of Thee, but Thou dost not listen to his heart-felt prayers. Thou bringest on the madness only for a short time. Why not always? Let his mind think on nothing else but Thee, Thee and Thee alone – that is the madness he craves for. Have pity on him![26]

Madness of Ram, Madness of Ram's love. Come on, take possession of Ramdas and make him swim for ever and ever in the ocean of Thy unfathomable love.[27]

O Ram, save, save Thy child, Thy slave. Let every fibre of his being thrill to the music of Thy madness; the very blood of his veins rush impelled by the fury of Thy madness; his very bones tatter and shatter in their seats by the repeated blows inflicted by Thy madness; his whole frame quiver, tremble and shake by letting fall on him an avalanche of Thy madness. Om Sriram![28]

Ramdas, you are now mad, completely mad, O sweet madness, madness, madness! O Love, O Love! Ramdas, you are really mad. Now, Ram is the theme of your madness. You are stark mad, Ramdas. Drink, drink Ram's love, Ram's nectar. Ram's light dazzles everywhere.[29]

राम

As he traversed Bharata Mata's sacred pathways, Ramdas attracted the attention of many, some of whom followed him for significant periods, others who waited for his return as an occasion for great celebration and the receiving of his transmission of truth. His earliest devotees included many members of his own huge family – brothers and sisters, nieces and nephews, and perhaps most poignantly, his own daughter. Ramabai was, in 1926, married to Chandrashkar Trikannad, a nephew who had treasured the presence and great good humor of his Uncle Vittal before the latter's sannyasin days. Ramdas attended the wedding of the young couple and declared with a hearty laugh of profound sincerity, "Ramdas saw Ram and Sita in the pair!"

In Chandrashkar's book, *Passage to Divinity*, besides his own testimony about his uncle, we also read another tender and revealing first-hand account by another nephew, P. Ramanand. The story bears repeating because of what it tells us about the irrevocable change that took place in Vittal Rao, and about the transformed relationship that Papa now witnessed to one and all – blood family or not.

Ramanand as a boy had always appreciated the visits of Uncle Vittal to his family's home. But when Ramanand was a high school student their relationship hit a high point. For literally days on end, Vittubappa (as he affectionately called his uncle) would regale his young listener with story after story based in Vittal's deep knowledge of English literature. This was not formally a teaching, but rather an outpouring of one who simply loved Shakespeare, Ben Jonson, Addison and Steele; from the sublime classicists to the contemporary humorists, Vittal knew it all, and savored it all.

Ramanand was equally impressed with the tremendous good humor of his Vittubappa. His jokes, his repartee, his artistic and dramatic skills, all these attributes served to make him the kind of uncle that a creative and intelligent nephew could look upon with overwhelming admiration.

The uncle and nephew actually shared a voluminous correspondence for a significant period. Twenty- or thirty-page letters between them were not uncommon. Herein they each expressed unrestrained writing: poetry, satires, and commentaries on this and that.

It came as a complete shock to young Ramanand to learn that his uncle Vittal had renounced the world. He wasn't concerned for what other family members expressed about the departure – which was all generally gossip and criticism. But, personally, his young heart felt fear and sadness for his own loss of a special place in his uncle's world, as well as for Rukmabai and Ramabai, the wife and child left behind. He grieved to think of Gurudev Balakrishna, the father who had "lost" a son. He also feared for the hardships that his much loved uncle would be called to undergo.

When Ramanand saw his uncle at last, upon Ramdas's return from his one-year journey, and during the time that Ramdas was living in the Kadri cave, he felt the greatest pain of all – a unique type of abandonment. His own words express the depth of his bittersweet dilemma:

> I saw before me a picture that was all holy and sublime, the very picture, in fact, of the Emaciated Buddha, the Enlightened One, in meditation…When he saw me near him, a smile immediately flashed across his emaciated face – but was it a smile of recognition? I did not know. There was some all-embracing universality about that smile that I could not understand. For all my former intimacy with him, I had become just another "Ram" to him. Tears welled into my eyes.
>
> And when I walked back home, I was proudly conscious of the fact that my uncle did return to us and to the world as Swami Ramdas – as an Enlightened Soul.[30]

By early 1928, his travels as a sadhu were coming to an end, and Ramdas planned a return to his native region on the west coast of southern India. He informed his uncle Ananda Rao by letter that he was ready at last to settle, and in an isolated place. Arriving there in April, a plot of land was leased on nearby Pillikunje Hill, in the township of Kasaragod, and plans were drawn up for the construction of a simple one-room monastic dwelling with a verandah. By the end of May, in record time, as the monsoons threatened, Ramdas's newly named "Anandashram" was ready to be dedicated and inhabited.

Ramdas lived at Anandashram, Kasaragod, from 1928 to 1931, visited daily by family members and a growing body of devotees. It was in these early ashram days that a remarkable young woman, deeply pained by the death of her husband, and near suicide with

Mataji Krishnabai

grief, was drawn irresistibly to the bliss and peace that she found at Ramdas's feet. Her only wish was for his service. This woman, Krishnabai, above all others, had recognized in Ramdas the fullness of the Divine, and would very quickly surrender herself without reserve. Years later, Papa would say of her readiness for absorption into Ram: "All others were like green wood. Mataji was dry tinder."

In January 1931, an event occurred that indicated a new direction for Ramdas. Since 1930, a campaign of vilification had been waged against the saint and his ashram. It also affected his blessed disciple, Mataji, who was now spending more and more of her time in complete service to him. This campaign culminated in a physical attack on both Papa and Mataji by two hired thugs, and left Mataji with back and neck injuries that would be a source of pain to her for the rest of her life. Yet, like her beloved Papa, who took everything as Ram's will, Mataji too refused to retaliate in the situation, even with harsh words for their attackers.

The assault was a sign, however. Within the hour, both Ramdas and Mataji had vacated the Kasaragod ashram, never to return. Awaiting Ram's will, they took up asylum for the night in the nearby home of Chandrashekar and Ramabai. The next morning they left by train, traveling a short distance to the town of Kanhangad, at the invitation of Chandreshekar's parents. Within a few days, Papa was scouting the environs to locate what was to be his second and final ashram – the place where he would live out his remaining thirty-plus years.

राम

Located on a lonely stretch of bare land, slightly inland from the Malabar coast, near the city of Kanhangad, Papa found his favored spot. In ancient times, it seems, this area had been made sacred by the presence of many sages and rishis who lived in a small range of hills that now comprises Anandashram. There is also a legend that it was here that Hanuman stopped on his journey to Sri Lanka when he was carrying the Dronachal Mountain, and that a small piece of that mountain broke off and remained here. In fact, devotees in Anandashram have claimed for many years that they have seen the great warrior, Hanuman, the monkey-god, walking along the ashram paths and standing in the bhajan hall late at night.

With Papa's own hands, the ashram was transformed from a barren hill to a garden; the place of refreshment for body and soul, which it is today. "Rain or shine, Papa would work on mornings and evenings with a small shovel. Papa loved flowers and he planted many flower plants in rows around the Ashram."[31] A story of one particular mango tree characterizes Papa's relationship to these gardens. This tree, which grew outside his window, had been attacked by weevils and was nearly dead. When others in the ashram had given up hope for it, Papa did not. He asked for the tree to be cleaned and fertilized heavily with manure, and then he spent days and weeks giving it his attention. Despite all odds the tree survived, and still bears fruit to this day.

This care for trees and plants was typical of the care for everything that Papa and Mataji demonstrated in their isolated ashram. Slowly and steadily, from a following of family and friends, the number of visitors and guests grew. Papa hosted his devotees and their families, and "instituted a programme of one hour of Bhajan in the morning and one hour in the evening…reading of scriptures of one hour during the day and one at night…and…At other times…discours[ed] on what Sadhanas one should do to attain Self-realization and how one should face obstacles on the path."[32]

These early years were marked by intense physical labors by both Papa and Mataji. And as Papa himself notes, "the brunt of the work was borne by Krishnabai."[33] Day in and day out, month by month, year by year, the master and his disciple labored ceaselessly to maintain the grounds, cook the food, care for the animals, answer a wave of correspondence, and supervise building projects that were necessitated as their visitors increased in numbers. A school was founded, to which Papa and Mataji gave their lavish attention. The ashram also became a stop on the route of wandering sadhus, and a special building was constructed which allowed these renunciates to live in private quarters where they could practice, undisturbed by the active lives of other residents and guests. A few wonderful stories of Krishnabai in those years, as related by Papa himself, tell of her constant generosity, her exorbitant kindness, and her management of everything from the grandest plan to the smallest detail.

A poor man once approached Mataji in great desperation, as he had not enough money to feed and support his wife and children. The ever-gracious Mother gifted this poor man with one of the milk-bearing cows from the ashram cowshed. In fact, because Mataji was a genuine mother, she gave her son the best cow – the one that produced the highest quantity of milk.

Overjoyed at first, the man soon became dismayed. Approaching Mataji again, he declared: "But where shall I keep this cow, as I have no shed?" Whereupon Krishnabai immediately agreed to have a shed built for the cow, adjoining the man's hut.

As the man considered further, however, he wondered how he would ever feed such a cow, knowing that his own meager resources were inadequate to cover the needs of his family, let alone the insatiable appetite of a four-stomached animal. But Mataji was again unperturbed. "I will send you hay," she said.

"What about oil cakes?" the man asked, to which Krishnabai replied that she would send him whatever he needed, and daily.

The man went home singing her praises, only to return grumbling, a few days later, saying that he was unable to get a fair price for his milk at the market.

Krishnabai had no word of recrimination whatsoever. Instead, she proposed a plan of tremendous ingenuity. "Why are you afraid?" Mataji first asked, wisely reminding this man that the benediction of God is unlimited, and urging him to trust in the face of such tiny wrinkles in the plan. Then, she suggested that the ashram itself would buy the milk, since they always had a great need. The man received the benediction, and did exactly as the Mother had recommended. He and his family were now satisfied and "lived happily ever after." While Mataji was supremely overjoyed that one of her children could be so completely served.[34]

राम

From 1931 until 1947, when Ramsuratkumar caught his first glimpse of Papa and Mataji, their lives were solely dedicated to creating of this earthly home a haven for prayer and practice, which it remains to this day. With occasional trips to other parts of India, necessitated by the longing of his devotees, Papa remained in Kanhangad, living for one reason only. Although Papa had a continual stream of personal health problems, including diabetes, "yet when someone fell ill in the Ashram, despite his own physical ailments, Papa would unfailingly visit the devotee and spend time with him."[35]

Once a disciple spoke to Papa, concerned about the strain he was putting himself under in making such visits, but Papa would not hear of such a thing. He immediately contradicted the interrogator by saying that such activities were not strain for him:

> Let Ramdas make one thing clear. God has kept this body alive so long only to serve His devotees. There is nothing more for Ramdas to achieve in life. By God's Grace Ramdas has attained That for which he had taken this birth. He now lives only to serve the devotees of God. But for this supreme justification for its existence, Ramdas' body would have dropped off long back, in fact as soon as he had attained what he had come into this world to attain. As long as this body lives, it shall be spent in the service of Ram's devotees.[36]

Papa's ultimate act of service to Ramsuratkumar would begin in 1952.

6

THE MADNESS OF THE SAINTS

 It was already late in the year 1948 when Ramsuratkumar left Anandashram and began his journey north again. Maybe, in fact, he celebrated his birthday on the road. On December 1, 1948, he turned thirty – still a young man by today's standards. Yet, for one who had so passionately determined to find his life's purpose, and who had twice been frustrated, this thirty-year milestone must have seemed like a signpost to the grave. *Already thirty, and still no master! Still no "home"!*

Like Ramdas before him, it seems that Ramsuratkumar was living out his own grand series of failures and disappointments. With the knowledge of hindsight, we can clearly see how his growing desperation was increasing his desire for liberation, and pointing the way. Yet, at the time, such periods of confusion, darkness, searching and evaluating may have been excruciating, as the very Divine who is sought seems to be playing hide-and-seek with a vengeance. The seeker may easily begin to doubt – his own intentions, his own experiences, and even his Lord. Left alone, seemingly to his own devices, sometimes with only the thinnest thread of a lifeline floating upon a raging sea, the seeker can pitch and thrash around for a long time. Such times are purifications in the truest sense of the term. These are the times in which one's ideas of God are seriously brought into question. Times in which all one's expectations are crushed. The once-blissful spiritual path may now seem to be leading one to the depths of hell.

Among the Christian mystics, St. John of the Cross has brilliantly annotated the characteristics of this period, which he called the
"Dark Night of the Soul." The Sufis have described *fana*, in which
the soul is literally stripped, leaving it ready for annihilation in the
Beloved's heart. Yet, such poetic renditions belie the fact that when
one is in the midst of such a "dark night" one sees *no* light. If there
were a light – some hope, some promise – it would be no "dark
night." From 1948 until 1952, when he finally recognized Papa as his
spiritual Father, Ramsuratkumar probably suffered this same fate of
purification and longing that all genuine lovers of God suffer.

We know from Ramsuratkumar's own narration that for some of
this period he was in the far north, in the Himalayas, searching for
masters and saints. A swami named Vimalananda reported that, in
Rishikesh, Ramsuratkumar visited the famous Swami Sivananda during this period.[1] Shortly after April 15, 1950, wherever he was,
Ramsuratkumar read in the newspaper of the death of Ramana
Maharshi and was struck with a powerful sense of loss. Seven months
later, on Dec. 5, 1950, he read of the mahasamadhi of Sri Aurobindo.
We know that these two pieces of news together were received like a
heavy blow, as Ramsuratkumar noted: "This beggar felt a type of
restlessness that he had lost the golden opportunity of keeping company with those two great Masters."[2] He reported to his biographer,
Caylor Wadlington, in the 1970s, that since 1947 he had felt guided
by both Aurobindo and Ramana Maharshi.

From the time in which he learned of the death of Aurobindo, in
late 1950, it was slightly more than a year before Ramsuratkumar
began the final "searching mission" that would take him, for the third
time, to Ramdas's ashram in Kanhangad. Perhaps Ramsuratkumar
intuited that this trip would be his walk to the guillotine, and perhaps this pre-conscious knowledge stalled him for some part of that
final year; or maybe there was simply unfinished business to complete; or possibly the journey was undertaken by foot and required a
long time in the making. Regardless, Ramsuratkumar's intention was
formed and remained firm: "One thing [was] very important; it was
the third chance to visit Ramdas…This beggar thought to himself,
'Let me try again to visit Ramdas, for he is recognized as a great Sage.'
So in 1952 this beggar did not go to Tiruvannamalai, nor did he go

to Pondicherry, for the Masters were not there."[3] And so he left for the south, to that tiny ashram on the west coast, to once more take the darshan of "Papa."

राम

Four years (1948-1952) had transpired since Ramsuratkumar had laid eyes upon Ramdas. The young northerner was different, undoubtedly closer to the bottom of the pit through which the soul must traverse on its way to heaven. Tempered, in some respects, by the benefit of years, with a more refined vision, but also more fired-up than ever in his desire for truth, Ramsuratkumar again set out to meet his Ram.

Because Ramsuratkumar was different, Ramdas seemed different too – as a master often reflects the devotee's state of being. Yogi Ramsuratkumar described this third meeting:

> Swami Ramdas turned out to be an entirely different person. At the very first sight, Ramdas could tell a number of intimate things about the life and mission of this beggar which nobody but this beggar knew.
>
> Not only that, but the Master started to take a special care of this beggar. This beggar felt that he had come to a place where he had a number of well-known intimate friends. This beggar began to feel from the environment of the ashram that Ramdas was a great Sage, a truly great Sage. It was then that this beggar first understood the great Master. Ramdas is this beggar's Father.[4]

When Yogi Ramsuratkumar spoke these words, in the early 1970s, describing this 1952 meeting with Ramdas, he included only the essentials. So many smaller and curiously interesting details were left out. As far as Ramsuratkumar was concerned, the only thing that mattered was that he was blessed by Papa to see and understand him. He was given the mantra, *Om Sri Ram Jai Ram Jai Jai Ram*, with which hundreds and perhaps thousands of other devotees had been initiated before him. He was similarly instructed to "chant the mantra all the 24 hours." Ramsuratkumar did as he was instructed, and after seven days he found himself in a state of complete and utter union with his master, and his master's Lord, the Eternal God, the Father of all.

> This Beggar tried [repeating the mantra] for one week and then Papa was with Him all the time, everywhere and everything, nothing else, nobody else but my Father.[5]

How "it" was accomplished – this irrevocable transformation and this immersion in madness – Ramsuratkumar summed up in one all-revealing sentence, "Ramdas killed this beggar in 1952"; a sentence that he repeated over and over, with only the slightest variation and elaboration, over the forty-plus years of his life following the event.

> This beggar ceased to exist in 1952. After that, a power has pulled him here and there. Even now, this beggar is controlled by the same power, the power that controls the whole universe! This beggar has no consciousness! No mind! All has been washed away! No thought, no planning, no mind to plan. No sense of good and evil. Swami has killed this beggar, but life has come. Millions and millions of salutations at the lotus feet of my Master, Swami Ramdas! The same madness still continues. He has initiated this beggar in Ramnam and has asked to chant it all the twenty-four hours. This beggar began to do it and in the space of a week, this beggar has got this madness.[6]

Years later, in the 1970s, Yogiji discussed with a Western friend that "kundalini shakti was the key to wholeness and unity with the universe, since the same serpentine fire was pervading the universe that was alive and active within man. He said that it was this force which his master Swami Ramdas awakened in him."[7]

The beggar's own words make "the killing" sound fast, clean, and complete, which it certainly may have been when viewed from the perspective of eternity. Yet, in the dimension of time and space, and from the testimonies and clues left behind, we know there was a dying *process*, and that Ramsuratkumar, like any man or woman who approaches the dissolution of ego, he did not fancy that process! In 1991, in the presence of Lee Lozowick and several American devotees, Yogi Ramsuratkumar again spoke of his dying "at the lotus feet of my Master Swami Ramdas." But this time he added some startling words: "It was not This Beggar's wish," Ramsuratkumar admitted. "Ramdas did it by force."[8]

The small twist created by these two short sentences invites a different view on the matter of the beggar's subsequent madness and surrender. What were the actualities of such a "murdering" process, the type that creates an irrevocable change in the victim? What kind of force *did* Ramdas use?

After Ramsuratkumar had received the mantra and had apparently fused with Papa's essential nature, Ramdas refused to allow the young devotee to remain in close physical proximity, or even to stay on at the ashram, even though Ramsuratkumar passionately desired this closeness, and asked for it several times. Three weeks after his arrival, Papa sent him away. In *The Gospel of Swami Ramdas*, which describes Ramsuratkumar's visit, and first refers to him as the "odd Bihari," we read that "his behaviour was not satisfactory. He was highly emotional," and hence, was asked to leave.[9] In fact, Ramsuratkumar was Divinely *mad*, and so obsessed with his love for both Papa and Mataji, whose sanctuary and benediction had provided the context for his absorption into God, that his activities took on the vestiges of insanity.

Ramsuratkumar couldn't stay, and yet he found it nearly impossible to go. For a while, perhaps for the first time in his life, he became like a beggar at the city gates, living outside the ashram boundary, standing and waiting at the entrance in the hopes that he might catch a glimpse of his Father, Ramdas. "It was monsoon time, and he got thoroughly wet standing there," reported one close devotee who had heard this story from Yogi Ramsuratkumar in the 1970s.[10]

राम

Today, the thousands of visitors to Anandashram in Kanhangad cannot help but notice a larger-than-life-sized photograph of a bearded, green-turbaned saint above the front door inside the massive dining hall. Yogi Ramsuratkumar's sparkling eyes join in blessing with the other four photographs that grace this passageway: Ramdas, Krishnabai, Swami Satchidananda (the current head of Anandashram), and Swami Shuddhananda (formerly Sriram Trikannad, a renowned devotee of Papa and Mataji).

Had these same visitors or guests witnessed some of the interactions of Ramdas and Ramsuratkumar in 1952 or 1953, or if they have read the passages referring to the "odd Bihari" in *The Gospel of Swami Ramdas*, they may indeed have cause to wonder why he holds such a place of honor here, now. Is this not the one who was sent out from Papa's ashram because his behavior was so highly emotional that it was disruptive to the other ashram programs? Is this not the same man whom Papa and Mataji rebuked strongly on several occasions? Is this not the man to whom Mataji asked, "Why do you talk like one gone off one's head?"[11]

Records of the time (1952-1953) tell us in no uncertain terms that, despite whatever "special care" was transpiring in the heart and soul between master and disciple, on another level Papa was hard and uncompromising in his dealings with Ramsuratkumar. Actually, even "hard" is too soft a word to describe some of the tests and trials of sadhana – the strong words, and the sending him away – to which Ramdas subjected his wildly ecstatic devotee.

Such tests are not at all uncommon in the annals of spiritual history. The great Tibetan guru Marpa demanded ceaseless and seemingly pointless work from his aspiring student, Milarepa. Marpa enlisted Milarepa's energies to build a house, but each time the structure was nearing completion, the master changed his plans for its location. Nine times Milarepa built it, and eight times he had to tear it down and start over from scratch. This testing went on for several years to the point where Milarepa was exhausted, emaciated, malnourished, bruised and battered, and, most of all, completely disheartened. All was done, however, in the master's compassionate wisdom; his way of tearing down the facades of his devotee's resistance.

Ramsuratkumar was thirty-four in 1952; Ramdas was exactly twice his age. Papa had "seen it all," in terms of the behaviors and habits of sadhus and seekers, and was strongly critical of those who wore the garb but lacked the spirit of absolute madness that must accompany such a divinely foolhardy act as radical reliance upon God. "Complete renunciation is not a joke," Papa had lamented in 1951. "It is like climbing up a coconut tree and letting off your hands."

> You have to give up everything – money, position, name, relations, friends, etc., and rely on God entirely. There are people who take sannyas, keeping a decent bank balance, or having a good pension. What kind of renunciation is it? They simply say they do not depend upon anybody, while in truth they depend upon their assets and not on God. If they happened to hear about the crash of any bank, their mind at once turns to anxiety to their deposit. How can they progress? Spiritual sadhana is not easy. It is as hard and perilous as walking on a razor's edge.[12]

राम

This "razor's edge" was well known to the renunciate Swami Satchidananda, who was Papa's secretary and the author of *The Gospel of Swami Ramdas,* and therefore a first-hand witness to Ramsuratkumar's encounters with his master, Ramdas. In fact, in 1952, Ramsuratkumar had approached Satchidananda and spoken of his urgent desires for a life in God. It was the Swami who had encouraged Ramsuratkumar to approach Papa and to ask for initiation in the mantra.

Clothed in the traditional ochre robes of the sannyasin, Swami Satchidananda today walks the paths of Anandashram quite slowly, in the actual footsteps of his beloved Swami Papa Ramdas and Ramdas's saintly collaborator, Mataji Krishnabai.

Satchidananda first came to Anandashram in January 1949, at the age of thirty, and was initiated into sannyas in 1950. He stayed on to serve both Swami Papa Ramdas and Mataji Krishnabai in the ashram for over fifty years. Writing of his own sadhana, in words not unlike those that Ramsuratkumar used about his experience with the paradoxically "all-compassionate" Papa, Satchidananda explained: "I came to them [Papa and Mataji] absolutely raw and shapeless like a lump of clay and surrendered to them. They graciously took me in hand, pressed, crushed and moulded me to give shape to make me their instrument to serve all."[13]

During a period from 1951 through 1959, Swami Satchidananda kept a daily journal in which he recorded all that both Papa and Mataji publicly said and did. This journal, first published in 1979, is now known as *The Gospel of Swami Ramdas*. The book is not only a testimony to the extraordinary life and teaching of Ramdas and his selfless servant Mataji, but a reflection of Swami Satchidananda's profound devotion and discipline that allowed him to undertake such a demanding project.

The entire play of the devotee Ramsuratkumar with the master Ramdas is perhaps one of the most enigmatic lilas in the beggar's life. Yet, the pieces fell into place more clearly as Swami Satchidananda narrated the story once again during an interview with this biographer in 2002. With the wisdom of his years made obvious in his careful choice of words, Swamiji let me know without having to say so that despite the most outrageous aspects of the stories reported about the "odd Bihari" in *The Gospel*, he (Satchidananda) clearly held a context of love and deep respect for Yogi Ramsuratkumar. He, more than many others, would have known that the master's ways are indeed enigmatic, difficult, at times excruciating to bear as the disciple is "moulded into an instrument."

Swami Satchidananda:

"In 1951-52, bhajans were taking place in the Hall [at Anandashram, Kanhangad]. He, Ramsuratkumar, would have come as a casual visitor, staying two or three days [actually the *Gospel* narrative says that Ramsuratkumar stayed three weeks]. When he was here in the beginning, in the few days' visit, he took the mantra from Papa, and, wherever he was, even though he was sent away from the ashram, his devotion to Papa and Mataji endured as intensely as before.

"When he was here he was so devoted to Papa and Mataji that he almost wanted to possess them. That possessive devotion was not liked by Papa and Mataji. One day, after bhajans were over, he started shouting, 'Mataji, Mataji, Mataji,' and fell down as if in a swoon. When she came to know about it (Mataji was not there at the time) she did not like it at all, because her tendency was that all should be more devoted to Papa than to her.

"After this incident, perhaps discouraging him to be more devotional to her, Mataji started avoiding him. Later, his possessiveness was not appreciated by both of them, and they asked him not to stay in the ashram but to go home and practice his sadhana there. This upset him completely and he started behaving in an unseemly way, with the result that Papa had to strongly tell him to leave the ashram.

"We don't know what happened immediately after that. He was wandering as a demented person due to his love of Mataji and Papa, and he had a minor accident at a railroad station."[14]

The Gospel narrative is stronger, noting at the time that Papa "gave him sound advice," and after this, Ramsuratkumar "was so much ashamed that he could not raise his head." The pain and the dilemma implied in these brief words was enormous. The devotee, Ramsuratkumar, fully desiring for nothing but to worship his Beloved, is given to understand that his demonstrations of devotion are neither approved nor appreciated. He is deeply ashamed. And yet, he is helpless. Madness has overtaken him, and his actions are not in his own control.

And so it was that after repeated visits, long and often grueling travels, pilgrimages back and forth between Kashi and Kanhangad, Ramsuratkumar has found his home, his Ram, and almost immediately is thrown from the nest. From numerous sources we learn that the final interchange of this visit in 1952 with Ramdas came in the form of a brief question and a spontaneous, unpremeditated answer. Ramdas asked him, "Where will you go?"

Ramsuratkumar replied: "Arunachala."

103

Although this destination was his intention, an incident along the way would turn Ramsuratkumar around, sending him back in Papa's direction, again driven by the madness.

राम

In the railway yard of a small station on the line between Kanhangad and Tiruvannamalai, a young man stood transfixed with his left foot on the train tracks. Windblown, unkempt, his head thrown back slightly, he appeared to be gazing into the face of some unseen entity.

As fellow travelers observed this strange sight from the platform of the Erode station, they were suddenly thrown into panic. A train was approaching fast, bearing down on the same track where the man was standing. They shouted to him; they waved, but he was seemingly oblivious. Unable to move his body, Ramsuratkumar, having left Papa in a state of Divine intoxication, had suddenly been consumed by his attention to God. In an instant, the train was upon him. Its steel wheels grazed his left foot, severing the tips of his big toe and his second toe, and he was thrown back from the tracks as the train passed through.

Immediately, he was surrounded by curiosity seekers and railway personnel and rushed to the railway hospital. Here, in response to inquiries, he did not give his own name. All he could say was his master's name, "Ramdas."

Years later, in the 1970s, in reporting this story to a devotee from Finland, Ramsuratkumar said that he heard a voice speaking to him at this critical moment. As the train approached, and as his own paralysis deepened, the words that came through were radical and revealing. "This is what happens when you work with Ramnam," the voice cautioned.[15]

The incident at Erode obviously delayed his intended journey to Tiruvannamalai. Some time was spent in recovery, but the details of the next few months are not completely clear. From *The Gospel of Swami Ramdas* we learn that he was cared for by a devotee of Ramdas, a Gujarati man, but his ongoing state of madness soon moved him away.[16] When he left, it was not to continue on to Mount

Arunachala, as he had originally intended. Instead, this shock to his God-mad condition drove the young seeker "back to his house," apparently back to the north, where he stayed for several months. But life here was undoubtedly more unbearable, as his madness was probably taken to be insanity. *The Gospel* recounts that people there "found him to be out of his senses."[17] Without warning, he left the environs of Kashi and wandered, lost in God.

Above all else, Ramsuratkumar longed for the sight of Papa. But as he could not return to Anandashram, since he was clearly not welcome there at this time, Ramsuratkumar was led elsewhere, across the northern states, toward Ramdas's other ashram, located in Bhavnagar, a small seaport city in Gujarat province. From this center, Swami Ramdas and Mataji Krishnabai made frequent short trips to neighboring towns and cities, at the requests of their devotees. These visits provided more available access to the master. Evidently, Ramsuratkumar knew of Papa's schedule at this time, as we hear that he was seen at the airport "as soon as Papa alighted from the plane at Bhavnagar on the 3rd [December 1953],"[18] and in other places where Ramdas was present. According to Swami Satchidananda, Ramsuratkumar "was following Mataji and Papa wherever they went in Gujarat, Porbandar, Nagpur…so many other places, waiting to see Papa. How he knew where Papa and Mataji would be, and how he made his way there is a mystery. Wherever Papa went, he was there."[19] It was in Bhavnagar that the "odd Bihari" would enhance his reputation for being a disruptive force, and here once again be singled out as a madman, lost in God.

Swami Satchidananda:

"After two or three years [in December 1953] we saw him as a sadhu with not clean clothes. In Bhavnagar, Gujarat, there is an ashram started in Papa's name, where Papa used to spend two months in winters. Yogiji would attend bhajan programs there in that ashram. His love and devotion to Papa was so great that he didn't want to go to any other saints. He strongly objected to other devotees singing songs about Sai Baba and other saints. He wanted them only to sing about Papa and Mataji. He had mentioned to others with whom we were staying that he was asked by Mataji to wander about.

"When this was going on, Papa told him to go to a quiet place, Girnar, where footprints of the Lord Dattatreya are worshiped. He did not like to go. He started saying, 'Why should I go to Girnar. Papa is my Krishna, Rama and Shiva. Mataji is my Radha, Sita and Parvati. I am a worshipper of images and personalities, I don't worship the impersonal – so why should I go to Girnar.' So he almost refused to go."[20]

In *The Gospel*, the words of this encounter are more precise, as Ramsuratkumar proclaimed, "Why should I go to Girnar leaving my *ishta devata* here? I am not a *nirguna upasaka* and have nothing to do with Dattatreya."[21] The *ishta devata* refers to the chosen form of the Ultimate God that the devotee will use as his object of worship. For some it is a particular manifestation of the One – like Krishna, or Kali, or Dattatreya – while for others, the human guru is the ishta devata, and is fully adored as inseparable from God. In saying that he was not a "nirguna upasaka" – a devotee of the timeless eternal essence, who sees all as One, all as the same – Ramsuratkumar was saying that, for him, the relationship to God was an embodied one. God was found through his guru, Swami Papa Ramdas.

Swami Satchidananda continued his narration saying: "But when asked not to enter the gate, he finally agreed to go [to Girnar] and was provided with a woolen blanket, a bed sheet, etc., and he went for a few days."

Papa left Bhavnagar shortly thereafter, and journeyed to Rajkot to visit other disciples. Ramsuratkumar, meanwhile, "threw away the blanket and money and had a few hot words" with the man who had given them. Then, following Papa's suggestion, he left for Girnar, but after two days he was back. When he entered the ashram compound, he was stopped by the gatekeeper and was not allowed to enter the darshan hall. "I had been to Girnar. There is nothing there. I want only Papa and Mataji. I cannot live away from them," Ramsuratkumar pleaded.[22]

Papa arrived back on the morning of December 12, and that afternoon, as he sat in the hall, suddenly the Bihari "dashed in and fell at Papa's feet."[23] When Ramsuratkumar stood up at last, he gazed intensely into Ramdas's face.

"Why did you come back from Girnar?" the guru asked the wild-eyed devotee.

"I did not find anything there. I wanted to obey you and went with the idea of staying there, but something pulls me back to you. How can I live away from you and Mataji? I have no control of myself. Some strange power has taken possession of me. I will stay on here with you and follow you wherever you go," Ramsuratkumar declared with conviction.

"Nothing doing," said Papa with fierce compassion. "We cannot permit one like you to stay with us. You may have love for us, but you abuse and insult those who love Ramdas. Is this the way you love Ramdas? You had angry words with Sumatilal. The other day you spoke in insulting terms about Sai Sattar Shah and Bindu Maharaj. How can you spiritually progress if you go on insulting saints? Ramdas cannot permit you to stay here."

"Where can I go?" the Bihari asked, heartbroken.

"How and where did you live all these days? Carry on like that," Ramdas instructed.[24]

And so, once again, Ramsuratkumar was driven from his master's sight, and forbidden to enter the ashram compound. But, despite the harshness of his guru's words, Ramsuratkumar remained, much like a faithful dog, waiting outside the gates, hoping for another opportunity to make his way in.

Three days later, the Bihari was back in the bhajan-hall. When Papa heard of this, he decided to take a new approach with his persistent devotee.

"Ramdas has to tell you something," Papa began. "You must have your hair cut, have a clean shave, put on clean clothes and then come here."

"May I do that after bhajans?" Ramsuratkumar asked, overjoyed at being allowed to remain for even a moment in the master's presence.

This time, Papa was demonstrably affectionate. He patted the younger man on the back as he said, "Yes, you do that after bhajans."

Ramsuratkumar was now beaming with happiness, completely ecstatic at receiving his master's touch. After the bhajan singing concluded, he was taken to the barber, and soon after returned looking like a new man, "with close cropped hair, shaven face, white dhoti and chaddaer."

"Ah, that is good, it looks as if you have taken rebirth. It is clean outside. Do not create any more trouble here. Be quiet. Do not snatch away the Ramnam books from people who are writing Ramnam," Papa instructed kindly, and with a twinkle in his eye.[25]

An interim of quiet and acceptable behavior followed. But on December 18, as Papa was at work dictating a letter, Ramsuratkumar entered "in his usual unkempt way" and threw himself at the guru's feet. The madness was consuming him; he begged for help.

"Papa, what shall I do? Tell me," the young man begged.

"Ramdas has told you what you are to do. You do not listen to what he says but go on asking what you should do."

But Ramsuratkumar, distraught, protested: "I try to obey you. I went to Junagad, but some other power forced me back to you. I cannot stay away from you. I do not know what is pulling me back to you. I have no control over myself."

Papa was ruthless. Despite his young devotee's God-intoxicated condition, some remnants of ego might still have remained, and the master knew that these needed to be burned away, and quickly. His words cut like a sword: "It is only the ego residing within you that makes you dance like this. You want everything done your own way. You have to get away from Ramdas. There is no place for you near him. You will not gain anything thereby. It is found by experience that those who associate always with us do not improve. They start finding fault with us and that becomes the cause of their regression. Even before starting to stay with Ramdas, you have begun to find faults. You asked the other day why Ramdas went to Rajkor and Bombay for attending marriage functions. You considered it a folly on the part of Ramdas and remarked he should not have done so. Is it with this attitude that you are going to stay with Ramdas? Give up that idea and go to Girnar. If you do not go to Girnar now, it is not going to leave you. Girnar will pull you. Believe it; this is true. If you lead an ill-regulated life like this, Ramdas can tell you, you will go off your head."

Ramsuratkumar was devastated, speechless. He wept openly, in desperation. The thought of having to leave his Beloved was more than he could bear. "No, Papa, I cannot leave you and go away," he cried, speaking slowly and deliberately, with the pain of a disconsolate lover. After that, he prostrated and left the room, his tears still flowing. It was shortly after 2 PM.[26]

For the rest of the day, Ramsuratkumar was inconsolable. He restlessly ran about "in the hot sun...like a mad man," outside the ashram boundaries, as he was again forbidden to come in. At about 8 PM, when Papa heard of the goings-on, he and Mataji exchanged words in the presence of a few other devotees.

Mother Krishnabai began explaining gently, "Looking at his condition, Papa feels sorry for him. He has great love for Papa. If he obeys Papa's instructions, he will soon come up."

Ramdas, for his part, was still in the mode of cutting away whatever was not needed. His words were uncompromising: "Really, Ramdas feels sorry for him. True, he has great love for Ramdas and Mataji. But all others are less than straw to him. He does not care for them and falls out with them when they do anything that he does not like. He is not mad. He understands everything. The only thing is that he is bent upon his own way, which is harmful both to himself and others."[27]

Later, at about 9:30 or 10 PM, one last report of the Bihari reached Papa's attention. Mrs. Kamdar, one of Ramdas's hosts in Bhavnagar, informed him that the "Bihari sadhu beat our gateman. He wanted to force himself in and, when prevented by the gateman, gave him some blows and ran away."[28]

Swami Satchidananda, in 1953, described Ramdas's reaction. "Interestingly, Papa laughed awhile on hearing the new development, but made no comment." And the Bihari disappears from the pages of The Gospel at this point.

It was late January or February, 1954, when Papa finally turned south, to Anandashram. Swami Satchidananda remembers that Ramsuratkumar "also came here, but not coming inside. After waiting for a few days, he disappeared."

ONLY GOD

राम

Throughout the years, Yogi Ramsuratkumar revealed little about the pain of his interactions with Ramdas. Quite the opposite, he consistently expressed nothing but gratitude for the ultimate gift, the "killing," and the merger with the One. In the 1970s, Ramsuratkumar simply explained that, "Thrice this beggar approached Swami Ramdas [asking to stay]; every time he was refused."

Ramsuratkumar never forgot a teaching that Ramdas gave him at the time of these refusals. It was a story about trees – a subject with which both saints were familiar, as both loved trees, and had sheltered themselves among them on numerous occasions. Ramdas told his young devotee, Ramsuratkumar, that wild trees – trees that must battle the elements in order to survive – are much taller, stronger, and more vital than domestic trees that are constantly watched over, even pampered, and fed. The trees that grow on their own, furthermore, "gradually become a haven for numberless forms of life seeking refuge from predators."[29]

In this references to the free trees, Ramdas was speaking about the destiny of certain souls. He was certainly speaking prophetically of Ramsuratkumar. Some are *meant* to stay close by the master and the ashram, obviously. Perhaps it is the only way they learn what must be learned in this lifetime. Perhaps they are indispensable to the master's current work. But for others, the situation is exactly the opposite. Were they to stay close in, they would never fulfill their mission. As Caylor Wadlington understood from his conversations with Yogi Ramsuratkumar, "Swami Ramdas brought him [Ramsuratkumar] to understand that his own nature and that of his spiritual mission required him to enter into the tumult of the world."[30] And this understanding was reinforced by Vijayalakshmi, writing in 2002: "Swami Ramdas was aware of the Yogi's great mission in life and knew that he had to be sent away in pursuance of that mission."[31]

Papa's instruction about the trees reflected a theme that he reiterated often. Early in 1954, when another devotee asked him if it was more beneficial for one to stay in the guru's shadow or to stay away and work, Ramdas responded that the people who stay in the shadow can actually be more trouble. If such people are merely hanging around to be cared for, they are not benefited ultimately. Mere proximity is never the answer. Despite Papa's usual recommendation that devotees keep the company of saints, in this instance, within a different context, Papa said: "Nobody has benefited by the constant company of a saint. No plant grows well under the shade of a big tree. People think that by living with a saint in an ashram, they will realise God. That is not correct. Ashrams have not produced mahatmas."[32]

Clearly, Papa's directives to the Bihari served to launch the God-mad Ramsuratkumar into the ocean in which he would have to sink or swim.

राम

Many years later, when Yogi Ramsuratkumar was fully recognized as a saint, a mahatma in his own right, a man in the crowd around him became highly emotional, crying out: "Krishna, Krishna," and swooning uncontrollably.

Seeing this, Yogiji's response was identical to Papa's. Turning to Sadhu Rangarajan, who was seated nearby, Ramsuratkumar directed, "Go lift that man and throw him out. He is disturbing things."

During his early interactions at Anandashram, following his "death" at Papa's hand, Yogi Ramsuratkumar was in the initial stages of his God-given madness – a stage typically characterized by emotional behavior. "The apparently eccentric and odd behavior of the Yogi, the sign of the spirit's fusion with the infinite, caused problems on the material plane. Nobody understood the terrible internal suffering that the Yogi was undergoing in the process of the merger with the infinite," explained his close devotee Vijayalakshmi.[33]

"But gradually the emotional stage fades and silence enters," Sadhu Rangarajan elaborated. "Even Ramakrishna, in the early stages, was crying 'Ma, Ma,' and taking the food left for the goddess. But, as time went on, reaching the higher levels of manifestation, such souls become deeply silent." And further, "In the early stages, Yogiji was walking through the town shouting, 'Mahatma Gandhi, Ki Jai.' But as he came to later stages he simply sat, giving darshan."[34]

राम

As Swami Ramdas had wandered throughout India for many years, he had witnessed "spiritual" manifestations that ranged from the sublime to the ridiculous. He had sampled his own wine of madness and exhibited his own odd behaviors, as he rolled on the floor in the room of Sri Ramakrishna to absorb the saint's vibrations. Papa had, in fact, *prayed* for madness unceasingly, until there was no "one" left to pray. Ramdas too had been an educated man who had "failed" in terms of the world. He too had been a desperate man.

Papa knew that one could not judge a book by its cover. He and Mataji in their travels over the years visited the ashram of Upasani Maharaj in Sekuri. Both had the highest regard for Upasani Baba, a guru of eminent renown who was wild with everyone. This saint was known to beat, kick, and shout at his devotees; even those who most adored him. When Ramdas's devotees questioned him about the stories of Upasani Baba's behavior, Papa said that there are three types of saints: *bala avashta*, who always remain like children – playful, gentle and cheerful; *unmatta*, who avoid contact with the world; and *pishacha*, who beat, abuse and curse others.[35]

Ramdas himself had, at many other times, been strict to the point of demand with those who loved him so much that they tried to attach themselves to him forever. During his days of sadhana, Papa had a faithful companion for a long period of time named Ramcharandas – a man of enormous devotion and unceasing sacrifice. Ramdas loved Ramcharandas greatly, as he always spoke of him with deep tenderness throughout the years that followed. Yet, in their journeys together, repeatedly "Ramdas had sent him away with the same firm advice…'When Ramdas sees you next you must be shining with God-realization'…because Ramdas wanted Ramcharandas to get over his attachment to Ramdas' body and to transmute it into universal vision…"[36]

Papa enjoyed telling a story of a devotee who had pursued a silent saint for years, without hearing a word of advice or direction from him. "Then, one day, the saint opened his lips to tell him *Ja Marja* (go and die). Those seemingly rude words were joyfully welcomed by the devotee who took them as a blessing addressed to his ego."[37]

Having lived as the guru of an ashram for twenty years, Ramdas had seen scores of phenomena, including many varieties of ecstatic states of "divine madness." He had also heard countless protests of never-failing love, which, as the years went by, either faded into background noise, or continued as rote prayers or requests for favors. These lovers of Ram, for all their good intentions, wanted more to stay as Papa's irresponsible children than to practice the sadhana to which he directed them with every breath of his life.

One day in the late 1950s, for example, a few years before his death, Papa overheard Mataji speaking to a woman visitor to the ashram, and he later asked what she had been lecturing the woman about. "'My usual refrain,' replied Mataji with a short laugh, 'I was telling her, what was the use of coming to this place, prostrating before you and saying you were theirs and so on, if nobody cared in the least to follow your teachings?'"[38]

"Who wants God-realization these days?" Papa continued where Mataji broke off. "They talk about it, they like to hear Ramdas talk about it, but who will put in the least effort for it?"

For Ramdas, the situation often brought him to a point that sounded like heartbreak. He looked around at devotees who were willing to "go to any pains for a worldly object like a desirable son-in-law, a new business contract, a new job and things like that, but when it comes to giving a little time to remember Him and meditate on Him, they are too busy."[39]

Using the dharma to justify their lack of practice, these would-be devotees waited and hoped and expected that Papa would show God to them. They demanded it, in fact, but did nothing to prepare their own hearts for such a transformational vision. They still kept their eyes focused in the direction of money, power, and security, and Papa knew it:

> They must show some inclination at least to want God. That is all Ramdas asks of them. "Show some desire to seek God and Ramdas will do the rest," he tells them. But, even this desire is absent. When there is so much wealth to be garnered, such fineries to be worn, so many cinemas to be seen, who has time for God?[40]

It was a paradoxical lament, because at the same time Ramdas knew that everything, timing included, was in the hands of Ram, and was to unfold according to Ram's will. He expressed that so beautifully, saying, "Sooner or later the seed of God realization will take root in their lives and blossom forth to fruition."[41] Still, knowing that the timing is God's seems not to make the master's heartbreak any less. He sees the enormous suffering of his devotees, whom he has adopted as his children, in fact, and he wants to bring them to the place where they can live their birthright. And so, he never gives up.

Would this "odd Bihari," Ramsuratkumar, who, in 1952 and '53, repeatedly threw himself into ecstatic states in his declarations of love for Papa and Mataji, and who shouted at those who sang songs in honor of any other saints, turn out to be one of those rare souls who would endure, and thus realize Oneness with Ram? Or was he just another wild man who would prove to be a backslider?

Probably, Papa did not know at the time. It was not his business to know, only to act as Ram directed him in the moment. The process for Ramsuratkumar, as for every other disciple, from beginning to end, was in the hands of Ram.

7

"THIS BEGGAR BEGS OF YOU"

 Severed completely from the physical presence of his Lord, it was now Ramsuratkumar's task to integrate fully what this "union in separation" would mean to his life and work. Immediately, he was faced with a new dilemma. Mad in God, obsessed with his master, infused with the mantra that kills ego, Ramsurat-kumar was, in 1954, at the same crossroads that Ramdas was when *he* started his journey of sadhana back in 1921 – where to go, and what to do?

Leaving the environs of Anandashram, Ramsuratkumar undoubt-edly boarded a train…for anywhere! Like Swami Papa Ramdas, he would live solely without purpose except as directed by the Divine; relying completely upon the guru within his own heart, the One whom he called his "Father." In *In Quest of God*, Ramdas explained that, in the first few days of his initial pilgrimage, he came upon his purpose – which was to visit various shrines and holy places through-out India. He would carry the name of the Divine with him, con-stantly singing the praises of his Ram. Ramsuratkumar, however, had little interest in shrines and holy places at the time. He had been to Girnar briefly, at Papa's request, and he knew that nothing there could compare with the light that shone from his living master. He was not interested, he told Papa, in worshiping the impersonal. His was the path of the immanent Divine – *Papa* was his Rama; *Mataji* was his Sita. Without them close at hand, where would he go; how would he occupy his life, his time?

From early in 1954, the date that marks the last recorded trip to Anandashram, until the summer of 1959, when Ramsuratkumar arrived in Tiruvannamalai, he was a wanderer and mendicant. From his own narration we learn that he traveled often by train, and from other anecdotal evidence we hear that he wandered throughout India. Speaking one day in 1988 of the fact that the great patriot Swami Vivekananda had spent years traversing the length and breadth of India, and that he had begged for his food along the way, Yogi Ramsuratkumar commented:

> I was also wandering like a beggar from 1947 to '59. Once I had to leave a town since I was told that beggars were arrested there. In Gujarat it was different. Once this beggar was caught along with a few beggars. But the "beggars" escaped by "paying" something. Only this beggar and some sadhus were detained for 5 to 6 hours. And at that time a police officer came in and asked, "Oh! How were you caught?" and [then they] released me. Once I was travelling in a train, in Gujarat, of course ticketless, and was sitting in the seat of the TTE [Traveling Ticket Examiner]. When the TTE came in, this beggar left the seat for him. But the TTE said, "No, Swamiji. You can sit." These happened in the land of Mahatma Gandhi.[1]

As we piece together the puzzle of his sacred life, this story indicates that Ramsuratkumar was distinguished, early on, from the ordinary beggars, and even from the other sadhus. The police officer's remark, "How were *you* caught?" indicates that the man saw, or felt, or knew, that something was different about this fellow, Ramsuratkumar. When the TTE gave up his own seat and referred to the beggar as "Swamiji," he was acknowledging a similar recognition. As with his Father, Ramdas, who was often singled out of a group of sadhus by the radiance of his smile, his laughter, and the light from his eyes, one can guess that such was also the case with Ramsuratkumar. An astute observer would have noted an air of elegance that surrounded this beggar in rags. Obviously, here was no pauper; nor even an everyday seeker after wisdom. This one had already *found* or *been found by* something, and showed it. While he might appear mad or obsessed, it is likely that he also sang the name of God, or danced along with a chant or mantra, thus infecting all around him with some remembrance of the Divine. Like Ramdas, he was probably laughing his way through difficulties, cracking jokes, chuckling with the innocence of a child of God, as future visitors and devotees would consistently mention these qualities about him.

The wanderer Ramsuratkumar spent some time in Eastern Gujarat, near the city of Ahmedabad, sitting on the banks of the River Sabarmati, in the midst of the other beggars and sadhus who had gathered there. One can imagine that this sacred site held a special attraction for him because of its proximity to Satyagraha Ashram, Gandhi's headquarters during the long struggle for India's independence. From this ashram, located on the banks of the Sabarmati, Gandhi had set out in March 1930 on his famous Salt March to the sea. Reflecting that Gandhi was assassinated in 1949, and that Ramsuratkumar's wanderings in this area probably took place in the mid-to-late 1950s, one can hypothesize that the location was still highly charged with the energy of Gandhiji's life and work.

In speaking of his time along this river, Ramsuratkumar explained that ladies from the area who came here for their daily bath would make regular offerings, throwing coins to himself and other beggars:

> The offerings this beggar would get from one day would be sufficient for him for two days. So, if one day he would beg, he would not have to go there to beg for two days, because that money would be sufficient to maintain him for that period. Therefore, this beggar was able to sit in some corner and do meditation and sadhana without the need to beg every day.[2]

As he sat in meditation, or walked the lonely highways, wherever he was led by the direction of his Father, Ramsuratkumar had the opportunity to absorb "the Divine into every pore of the being."[3] That is, he moved from the initial realization of God-unity into the firmly established state of *sahajiya*, or natural manifestation, a transition that would ordinarily take a number of years. The lives of many other great saints, including Ramdas, Ramana Maharshi, and Sri Ramakrishna, have witnessed to the time necessary to accomplish this same process.

Of this transitional period, as we learn from Ma Vijalakshmi:

> There was neither the means to buy food nor the thinking to plan a meal…Clothing, bathing, cleaning, eating, etc., became of no importance to him. The inner call urged him on to places where there was divine work. His inner consciousness now merged with the infinite that operated at various levels to alleviate suffering, to understand and help in solving the problems faced by the vast multitudes inhabiting the country. His innate patriotism and love for people strengthened. His faith in the Vedas and the Sanatana Dharma was reinforced during this period.[4]

For the uninformed observer, the activities of this strange and unkempt Hindu must have been cause for curiosity, if not outrage. Ramsuratkumar might be instructed (from within his heart) to visit a particular temple, but once he arrived there, he might refuse to enter. Here he would remain outside the gates unless it was clear that the internal instructions from his Father had changed. At another time, he might be directed to talk to a certain person or even to bow before someone, and in his submission to the will of God, which he came to trust beyond all else, he obeyed without question. He was an instrument, used by the Divine hand; there was no longer any independent will.

One day in these early years, on a road near Tivandrum in Tamil Nadu, after visiting the great monument to Swami Vivekananda on Cape Comorin, at the southernmost tip of India, he observed a stalled truck far in the distance. The driver of the vehicle had been working for a long time in a vain attempt to start the engine, when Ramsuratkumar "drew near to the truck, stopped, and observed the work."

"You are having trouble starting your car?" Ramsuratkumar asked, and then added, "Please start it now." He touched the engine and said aloud, "By the Grace of Ram your car will start."

"The words of this 'lunatic' [Ramsuratkumar] were an outrage and because their tempers had grown short with their failing efforts they weren't about to spare him their wrath," wrote biographer Caylor Wadlington, who heard this story directly from Yogi Ramsuratkumar in the 1970s. "Then, to everyone's astonishment, the man in the cab was able to start the engine with ease. They were so surprised and delighted that they extended their heart-felt thanks to this mysterious mendicant and saluted him as they drove away."[5]

Makarand Paranjape, a writer, poet, and university professor, was gifted by Yogi Ramsuratkumar with a few other intriguing stories of this "lost" period. Paranjape reports that Ramsuratkumar "was interested in meeting some of the great people of India; those whom he felt had something to offer or do for the future of the country."[6] It is fascinating to note, in this regard, that Ramsuratkumar's interest was exceptionally universal, even in these early years of his developing work. His visits to and attempted meetings with distinguished people at this time, and in the coming decades of the sixties and seventies, were not limited to great philosophers (like Krishnamurti, whom he saw on a few occasions in the 1960s) or saints (like Swami Muktananda of Ganeshpuri, whom he encountered in Tiruvannamalai), as one might expect. His madness, and his Father's direction, took Ramsuratkumar to the door of a Nobel Prize-winning physicist, Sir C.V. Raman, at his institute in Bangalore. ("Great advances in knowledge came through questioning the orthodox view," wrote Raman; a statement which Ramsuratkumar would have supported heartily.) He also traveled to meet a renowned politician, governor, and minister of culture in Bombay, "K.M. Munshi, the founder of the Bharatiya Vidya Bhavan [a prestigious institute for Indian art and culture] and the governor of Hyderabad at the time of the independence. K.M. Munshi, who was a barrister and a follower of Mahatma Gandhi, however, proved hard to meet. Munshi was also a well-known writer and scholar. He lived in a huge house and in great luxury. I think Yogiji said that Munshi drove away without seeing him, even after he kept Yogiji waiting for several hours."[7]

Why Ramsuratkumar went to one person and not another is purely conjecture. He was simply driven by God, often unaware of why he was doing what he did. In later years, the God-mad beggar would deny any knowledge of having a hand in the numerous miracles that appeared in the lives of his devotees when they called upon him in their need. "This beggar knows nothing," he would say with laughter, as his eyes grew wide with wonder at the story being told to him. Those who asked him to explain his actions would forever set themselves up for frustration – there simply was no answer, in many cases. Moreover, he cautioned that attempts to explain things would actually undermine the work that was being done or given. "Why, Bhagwan?" was simply not a question to be entertained. Undoubtedly, in these early years of integrating his Divine absorption, Ramsuratkumar himself had learned that it was a question not to be asked of his Father. Rather, all that was necessary was to listen and to obey.

राम

The *Matsya Puraana* relates that Lord Siva, in the form of a naked mendicant, and accompanied by a dwarf who carried a *paatra* (alms-bowl), left his abode of bliss on the summit of Mount Kailash and wandered about the country until he reached Benaras, where he settled down.

In ancient times, the great *rishis*, from whom all Indian culture and spirituality was learned and evolved, wandered "with no stone to lay their head upon and did not know where their next meal would come from."[8] Their quest was singular, however: to move beyond the unreal in order to rest completely in the Real.

This tradition of having nothing, while relying solely upon the benevolence of God as mediated through nature, circumstance, and the hands of other humans, is one of the great treasures of the Hindu/Buddhist cosmology. Countless men and women throughout the ages have cast aside their "self-dignity and ego" as they abandoned themselves to the love and generosity of others. "To them, food is [merely] fuel for the body, and the place to rest or a rag to wear a sheer necessity to preserve the tabernacle of the Spirit."[9]

Not only in India was beggary of this type recognized as a form of asceticism, a witness of humanity's poverty of spirit, and a profound declaration of faith. Many Sufi groups of the Middle East have a long history as mendicants. In Italy, St. Francis of Assisi built his order of friars upon this noble foundation, which he learned from the example of his master, Jesus. When an educated man approached Jesus saying that he would follow wherever the master led, Jesus proclaimed a deep metaphysical truth when he uttered: "The foxes have their holes and the birds have their nests, but the Son of Man has nowhere to lay his head." (Matthew 8:18-20) Regarding such exalted beggars of God, scholar and devotee Dr. Sujatha Vijayaraghavan writes:

> Such beggary was the right and privilege of only those who had the courage to bid the world to get behind them...[they are] appropriate illustrations of those yearning for the vision of the truth and begging for it with their dare-devil *askesis* [Greek, meaning "disciplined training"]. These men sanctify the face of earth wandering among men whose fold they return to, to bless and guide. In their piteous pleas, they win the eternal treasures and teach us that begging for Truth is the only way to join the ranks of the gods."[10]

राम

"Don't be deceived by His beggarly appearance. He is Lord Rama Himself in the guise of a human being."
– Ma Devaki, words to a fellow university professor, describing Yogi Ramsuratkumar[11]

As he traveled the country during these "lost years" – 1954 until 1959, and even prior to that, when setting out from Varanasi in 1947 – Ramsuratkumar differed from his Father, Ramdas, in one noteworthy external aspect. From the beginnings of his life on the road, Ramdas had wrapped himself in a single piece of orange cloth, a mode and color of dress that was recognized and honored by devout people throughout India. To wear the "ochre robe" was to be marked as a sadhu or sannyasin, one who had formally given up everything to pursue realization of the Divine. In some cases, it also meant a type of affiliation, such as becoming a monk under a teacher, or within a particular lineage or organization. Ramsuratkumar, by the will of his Father, never engaged this external formality of dressing in ochre. From first to last, despite some of the most exalted names that others called him – including, "Maharaja" (great king), "Swamiji" (wise man), and even "Bhagwan" (God) – or regardless of the privileges and acts of obeisance afforded him by those who apprehended who he was, Ramsuratkumar always remained only "this beggar" by his own description. "This beggar himself wandered all over the country begging for food, for twelve years. He never used to wear *rudraksha* [a necklace of sacred prayer-beads] or put *bhasma* [holy ash] on his forehead. He wandered in rags like any other beggar."[12]

His clothing might consist of a single piece of cloth, or a collection of this and that: a shirt, a dhoti, a shawl, another shawl, a turban casually wrapped. Often brilliant in color – bright pink, orange, emerald green, yellow – his "robes" were worn until changed by the whim of God; old scraps, worn layer upon layer, and never washed.

To have taken up the sannyasin's robes, although Ramsuratkumar was offered them on several occasions, would have identified the beggar in a way that was either not useful or not necessary. His was the truest state of sannyas, the truest renunciation and dependence, but without the badge of its dress. One day in 1988, when Yogi Ramsuratkumar was presented with a copy of the *Chidakasha Geeta*, the spiritual testament of Swami Nityananda, he asked a young devotee to open the book at random. When a page had been determined, Ramsuratkumar asked Rangarajan, an orange-clad sadhu, to take the book.

"Read any paragraph," Yogi Ramsuratkumar directed. Interestingly, the lines on which Rangarajan's eyes turned were about the essence of sannyas. He then read aloud, to the delight of Yogi Ramsuratkumar, these words of Nityananda:

> He who deliberates upon the Truth is Sannyasi, Yogi. Even if he be a cobbler, pariah, he is so only in outer action. [Cobblers, or shoe-repair persons, even today are considered among the lowest class of Indian society because they must touch the foot and its coverings, thought to be unclean.] Pariahhood [does not endure] after death. He who has pride

and jealously, who debates and argues, who criticizes others, *he* is the pariah. To cobble does not mean to stitch cloth. It really means to stitch by placing the *chitta* [basic consciousness] in the *buddhi* [intellect, mind].[13]

Yogi Ramsuratkumar then asked that this passage be read aloud three more times.

To call himself a beggar, as Ramsuratkumar did, was one of the great mysteries surrounding this Godman. But this quote of Nityananda's sheds one interesting beam of light on this multifaceted enigma. No matter what he or his work looked like on the surface, this cobbler (this beggar) was in fact forever stitching "the chitta in the buddhi." To place the essence of consciousness within the minds of men and women, to allow them to remember the essence of who they were, this was the job that Yogi Ramsuratkumar would continue to do for the rest of his life. His visitors would constantly report that he had touched this essence in them; that all their worries would disappear upon simply having sight of him; or that their longing for God would be unbearably intensified. Merely by sitting with him, or gazing upon him, with nothing else necessary, they were transported to the plane of clarity, sometimes filled with inner peace and joy.

Dev Gogoi, a young resident of Tiruvannamalai who met Yogiji in the 1980s, affirmed that his communion with Ramsuratkumar often took place at this level beyond words. One night, as Dev sat with the beggar, he felt his heart being broken open. Intense longing arose in him – this unquenchable thirst for the truth, for liberation, for a deep draught of the water of eternity. As night descended, and Yogi Ramsuratkumar made no request for light, the room grew very dark, and the urgency of Dev's longing only increased. When the pain in his heart became terrible, his tears began to flow silently. Just then, Yogi Ramsuratkumar stood up, walked over to where the young man sat, and handed Dev a single rose. No explanation was necessary. Dev was absolutely clear that this rose was the saint's tangible response to his deepest and most urgent prayers.

राम

Referring to himself as "this beggar," Ramsuratkumar fully identified with those who had no property, no source of regular income, and certainly no status in the culture. Throughout his life, Yogi Ramsuratkumar would remain as one with no affiliations other than his complete surrender to his Father, and with no possessions other than the clothes on his back, and the fan and coconut bowl in his hand.

"I don't understand how you are a beggar," questioned young Nivedita, a high-school-aged devotee of the master Ramsuratkumar, in 1988.

"I don't do any work and I live by begging," Yogi Ramsuratkumar explained with his characteristic chuckling laughter. "I live on the earnings of others who work hard. Do you understand now?"

"But the Brahmins are *supposed* to live on alms," Nivedita retorted, with her usual quick wit. "They *have to* depend on the society for their food. You are a Brahmin. How can you say that you are a beggar?"

"No, I am not a Brahmin," Yogi Ramsuratkumar corrected, "I am a Chandala." When she appeared to question the meaning of this word, he merely recommended that she ask her father to explain it when she returned home.[14]

To have called himself a "Chandala" was tantamount to placing himself among the most downtrodden people of India, the untouchables. The Chandala were without caste, the "outcastes" within the original Aryan system of separating people according to color. Any contact with a Chandala was considered a form of pollution, so that even if a Chandala's gaze happened to land upon foods or drinks, such foods would be considered worse than rotten. The mere shadow of an outcaste was polluting, therefore the outcaste or Chandala could not set foot in a town in the daytime. The Chandala must keep his head lowered at all times, lest his eyes meet those of an Aryan master. In such a case, the Chandala's eyes might be cut out. This one had less than no identity. He could only wear clothes taken from corpses of dead people and was required to tie a broom to his back to cover his footprints, or any other evidence that he or she had been around. A Chandala could only eat a meal from a broken plate, and his sole possessions could be a donkey and a dog – two equally despised animals. If a Chandala were to hear Brahmin teachings, moreover, molten iron was to be poured into his ears.[15] Such was the realm of society with which Ramsuratkumar affiliated himself.

Identification with the pariahs among the culture was the lila of the Godman Jesus too, who ate with tax collectors and allowed prostitutes to touch his feet. Other great saints and spiritual masters, both in India and in the West, have lived their own variations of this theme.

राम

In Tiruvannamalai, India there is a little beggar
who lived on a garbage heap for 25 years
before He was found out
and they started coming by the thousands
to worship Him. The King of the World
is always a Master of disguise…[16]

These words were written by a prize-winning American poet late in the 1990s. While this poet, Red Hawk, had never met Yogi Ramsuratkumar in the physical body, still he had been deeply touched by the beggar's spirit and his poem captured the essence of the beggar's profound mission interwoven with his hidden nature.

Ramsuratkumar looked for no kingdom other than the kingdom of hearts in which his Father lived. "This beggar is a *disciple*," and "everything is my Father," he would say to a group of American visitors in the 1980s.[17] All praise belonged to God alone. It made no difference to him whether he was acknowledged or not. In fact, at times, he even went to humorous lengths in obscuring his "status." One day, when Sadhu Rangarajan was sitting with Yogi Ramsuratkumar, a large crowd of "rustics," country people, entered the master's residence to receive his darshan. Because Rangarajan was dressed in the ochre robe, one man in the visiting group assumed that the sadhu was the one whom they had come to see. He prostrated to Rangarajan, and the others in his party soon followed suit. The sadhu was aghast, immediately objected, and tried to point them to the elder, his master, Ramsuratkumar, who sat off to one side of the room, smoking. But, before he could say anything, the beggar had gotten hold of the sadhu's hand.

"Rangarajan, would you keep quiet!" Yogi Ramsuratkumar said in English, so that his country guests wouldn't understand. Sitting silently, he merely watched as one after another prostrated to the sadhu and then went out.

"Bhagwan, what is this *tamasa* [a tendency not to move or change, even when change may be appropriate]?" Rangarajan asked with embarrassment when the guests had left. "They came here to have *your* darshan."

"What is wrong!" replied Yogi Ramsuratkumar. "They have had my darshan in your form. What is wrong in it?"

Still the sadhu objected, trying to argue that these people had come such a long way…and so on.

"No, Rangarajan, this beggar is not different from you." Yogi Ramsuratkumar was instructing all of his hearers in this profound teaching. "All praise goes to my Father!"

Then he went on, "Second thing, you know their respect and regard for that dress. This beggar is in this beggar's garb, but you are in this ochre robe, and this is our country's tradition. You must appreciate those values. You must not complain. It makes no difference whether they prostrate to you or to me."[18]

Ramsuratkumar's interactions with humanity had no caste or religious limitations. In later years, he would be available to a high-ranking statesman who was driven to his door in a Mercedes Benz, and even more available to the man's hired driver. His heart was open to the suffering Muslim as much as to the suffering Hindu, and these early years on the road would have exposed him to all of it. He himself would be despised, or he would be honored, as his Father Ramdas was, and he would take it all the same.

Ramsuratkumar's approach as a beggar on his own behalf was never insistent or demanding. "He would never *really* beg. If he were feeling hungry, he would just stand silently before a house, before a hotel, before anywhere. And if they came with something he would accept it, eat it, and go away. He would put all the eatables into his coconut shell and eat from that," explained a close devotee.[19] This was the way in which surrendered sadhus conducted themselves.

That his begging was part of his broader mission is demonstrated in a small incident that took place in 1990. Surrounded by a large crowd of followers as he walked through the temple, Yogi Ramsuratkumar was offered some biscuits, which he received in his bowl. Turning to a woman devotee who stood nearby, he looked at the many people surrounding him and said, "I am in all these," as he pointed at the gathering. "Distribute to them also. I eat not only through this mouth [pointing to his own] but through all these mouths." The woman obeyed and gave the biscuits to the crowd.[20]

At another time, when some visitors from South Africa brought a large offering of fruits and other specialties to Yogi Ramsuratkumar, the beggar asked: "Why all these? This beggar doesn't need all this."

At that same moment, a voice was heard nearby, crying out, "Yogi Ramsuratkumar Maharaj Ki Jai!" It was a destitute beggar, standing at Yogiji's door.

Summoning his devotee Swaminatha, Yogi Ramsuratkumar instructed him to "take all these and give it to him [the beggar]." When all the fruits were placed into the outstretched hands of the beggar, Ramsuratkumar called after the man: "Go and share it with all others sitting there (around the temple)."[21]

Driving out beggars "is not proper; they have a right to beg," Yogiji spoke imploringly one day to Sadhu Rangarajan in 1988, urging him to write an editorial for his journal, *Tattva Darsana*, about the rights of beggars in India. At the time, the government was systematically rounding up beggars and prosecuting them. Ramsuratkumar, who was passionately opposed to this harassment, explained:

In this land begging has never been a crime. Sudhama was a beggar and he went to Krishna begging for alms. Krishna received him with all honours. All great saints have been beggars. My Master, Swami Ramdas, explains in his *In Quest of God* how he went around as a beggar…I am not speaking only of Sadhus, Brahmacharis and Brahmans who are enjoined to beg in this country. I am speaking for ordinary people who go out begging for alms when they find it difficult to make both ends meet. They are not criminals. They beg as there is no other [way to] go.[22]

Yogi Ramsuratkumar's request for an editorial followed upon one incident that was both humorous and significant. Sometime in early 1988, Justice Venkatriamiah, a judge of the Supreme Court, came to Tiruvannamalai to see Yogi Ramsuratkumar, who on this day was sitting somewhere in the midst of the beggars within the Arunachaleswarar Temple. Suddenly, the police started driving out all the beggars from the temple, and when Yogi Ramsuratkumar asked a police officer, "What are you doing?" the man explained that a special person (meaning Justice Venkatriamiah) was coming around, and that security had to be maintained.

Without resistance, Yogi Ramsuratkumar joined the other beggars in leaving the temple complex. He retired to one of his other usual haunts, nearby the temple walls.

When the Justice arrived in the area, he asked directions from someone, and finally located the spot where Yogiji was sitting, made his obeisance, and sat before him.

"You are the judge of the Supreme Court," the beggar declared. "I want justice from you."

Venkatriamiah, surprised, said, "Bhagwan, what can I do for you?"

"How much monthly salary do you receive?" Yogiji asked.

The judge answered, quoting a large amount.

Ramsuratkumar's eyes must have twinkled with his characteristic playfulness as he said, "You are getting *so much* salary, why should you drag us all out from sitting before the temple?"

Venkatriamiah was confused. "Bhagwan, I am not understanding what you are saying," he admitted, somewhat ruffled.

"These police officers were telling us that because you were coming we must all get out, and I was wondering why *you* should have to come and sit there for begging? We are beggars. Why should *you* come to this small place and drive us all out?"

Then the judge burst into laughter, as Yogiji laughed, knowingly, along with him.

When the editorial, "The Right to Beg," was published in 1988, the beggar, Ramsuratkumar, was very happy with it.[23]

Yogi Ramsuratkumar also begged on behalf of the work he was given to do by his Father. In later years, when something was needed for the ashram temple construction, for instance, he had no hesitation in "begging" it, by simply assuming that his requests would be honored and immediately fulfilled – which miraculously in most cases they were. "This beggar never orders, he only begs," he said.[24] Even a simple demand to a devotee might be prefaced with the devastating words, "This beggar is begging you" – Yogi Ramsuratkumar's way of indicating, often enigmatically, an issue of utmost importance to Father's work, as he burst into laughter.

But the most radical expression of his begging, which would come to characterize his entire life, was in the constancy of his prayers to his Father. It is this type of beggary that is explained in the tender poetry of his devoted American son, Lee Lozowick, who wrote in December 1988:

> Oh! Do you know the root of the word beggar?
> The Latin word "precare," which has come
>   to us in English as prayer:
> "Precare" means "to beg."
> Yogi Ramsuratkumar:
> Begging, Begging, Begging,
> Praying, Praying, Praying.[25]

Yogi Ramsuratkumar would beg the rain of his Father's blessings on all who approached him with their requests for help. "That's the beauty of the beggar – he's not an Avatar, he's not a Godman – he's just a beggar. Whatever is brought to him he turns over to his Father in Heaven, over to God," Lee Lozowick affirmed.[26]

Not only did he intercede with God on humanity's behalf, he went further. He bequeathed, as his only legacy, the name of God – first, in the form of the Ramnam mantra, *Om Sri Ram Jai Ram Jai Jai Ram,* as his Father Ramdas had given it to him, and later in the invocation of his own name, *Yogi Ramsuratkumar, Yogi Ramsuratkumar, Yogi Ramsuratkumar, Jaya Guru Raya* – so that men and women of all the ages to come might also become beggars, "prayers," going directly to the heart of God, the source of all benediction.

E.R. Narayan, calling Yogi Ramsuratkumar the "King of Beggars," summed up his mission perfectly when he wrote:

But here we see a beggar who had a very good life in early years and turned into a beggar by virtue of his own will. He is now a king of all beggars. He reigns in his kingdom in the hearts of people throughout the world who come to know him, even by accident. There are no boundaries to his influence. Unlike the common beggar who begs for food, clothes, and materialistic comforts, here is a beggar who yearns and begs for the well-being of all the creatures in the world, praying to his Father to relieve their sufferings…He does not beg anything from you, He begs to God for you.[27]

8

CHANTING THE NAME OF GOD

 All [this beggar] knows is Ramnam. For him there is no need for realization, visions, experiences or anything else. Ramnam is everything. Chant the name all twenty-four hours! I do as ordained by my Master. That's enough for this beggar.

— Yogi Ramsuratkumar

Two things are certain about Ramsuratkumar's sojourns throughout these hidden years, 1954-1959. First, we know that he lived and traveled as a beggar, and secondly we know that he praised the name of God, as his father Ramdas had instructed him.

In assuming this practice, known colloquially as "Ramnam," or more formally as the taraka mantra, Ramsuratkumar joined with millions of others throughout the ages in India for whom this sacred name was a bridge across the ocean of unreality.

Mahatma Gandhi, a great hero of Ramsuratkumar's, had died in 1949 with the name "Ram" on his lips. Since Gandhi's youth, this revered mantra was his constant companion. In 1924, writing about how to overcome the plague of desires, Gandhiji recommended the invocation of this name. "I have suggested the word Rama because I was brought up to repeat it in my childhood and I have ever got strength and sustenance out of it."[1]

In later writings, Gandhi affirmed what ancient teachers had always taught about the use of mantra: that it may begin as a physical activity, a mere repetition, but eventually sinks into the core of the heart. "Psychologists also believe that man becomes what he thinks.

Râma-nâma follows this law."[2] In 1935, as Gandhi carried on a dialogue with a visiting mathematician, the subject turned once again to nama japa. The man expressed to Babuji (an affectionate yet respectful name for Gandhi) that he was annoyed by repetition in any form, even in the most sublime music of Bach. When Gandhiji pointed out that recurring decimals were a fact of life in the field of mathematics, the man countered that each "recurrence" marked a "new fact." Hearing this, Gandhi, ever the brilliant advocate, drove home his point about using the name of God:

> Each repetition or japa, as it is called, has a new meaning; each repetition carries you nearer and nearer to "God." This is a concrete fact and I may tell you that you are here talking to no theorist, but to one who has experienced what he says every minute of his life, so much so that it is easier for the life to stop than for this incessant process to stop. It is a definite need of the soul.[3]

All theistic spiritual traditions offer a variety of practices to those who wish to progress in their knowledge and love of God. Yet, despite their variety, all have essentially the same aim – to keep the remembrance of God ever present. With such remembrance, everything changes; particularly the limited, time-centered view of things that keeps the human mind in bondage. With remembrance, on the other hand, anything is possible. Remembrance of the One, the All-Pervading Reality, is the means whereby ordinary men and women enter into the broad, unlimited stream of eternity.

One of the easiest ways to keep remembrance is by reverent repetition of the name of God, since "the name" and "what is named" are not considered separate within many spiritual traditions. In the Psalms, King David sings: "I will tell of Thy Name to my brethren." – Psalm 22; and, "Our help is in the Name of the Lord." – Psalm 124. In Christianity, in the Gospel of John, we read, "In the beginning was the Word, and the Word with God, and the Word *was* God."

To speak or sing God's name has long been a means of worship, since God's name invokes the Divine Presence. Swami Papa Ramdas indicated that such invocation was not about crying out to the heavens in search of a God who will lend an ear to our petitions. Rather, "when you take the Name, you are taking the Name of the Lord who dwells in your own heart."[4] The repetition of God's name is all about awakening and keeping alert the already inherent Divinity that resides within each human being. And again, Ramdas has informed us, "Contact with the Name is contact with God, because Name and God are not different. Name is God and God is Name."[5]

Many other contemporary spiritual teachers have reinforced the age-old practice of nama japa (repeating God's name) or *nama kirtana* (singing God's name). They have cited it as an ideal activity for the times in which we live – the Kali Yuga, the age in which breakdown and dissolution naturally take place. We see the results of such breakdown around us in every domain of culture. For those who are over-busy all the time, "it is too much to expect the human mind to be able to directly absorb itself in meditation on the Universal Almighty…In this age of modernity in everything and weakness of will, generally speaking, japa or the constant taking of the Divine Name may be regarded as the best and perhaps the only means of maintaining a spiritual awareness in one's daily life."[6] Ramsuratkumar affirmed this himself. In later years, he would readily quote, and often sing, from memory these lines from the great poet Tulsidas (1543-1623), saying: "The name of Rama is a wish-yielding tree, the very home of beatitude in the age of Kali."[7]

राम

From the earliest written accounts (mid-1960s) of his life in Tiruvannamalai, we know that Yogi Ramsuratkumar chanted the name of Ram, sang the Taraka mantra, and engaged others in this heart-opening practice. In many remembrances by devotees throughout the years, we hear such reflections as "and after we had finished food we spent some more time chanting Ramnam."

In the 1970s, one of his Western visitors noted, "Swami was telling us how powerful is the repetition of the name of God and praising this as the most wonderful and direct of all paths to God realization. 'If in a time of need or sorrow you repeat the name of God, then God will be with you,' he said."[8]

Yogi Ramsuratkumar loved to sing, and would spontaneously break into song to the delight of his companions. "Sometimes he would sing Bengali devotional folk songs," wrote an early disciple. "He said he learnt these devotional melodies traveling with the nomadic (East) Bengali minstrels in His younger days."[9] (This information readily leads to speculation that perhaps Yogiji actually had some affiliation with the legendary Bauls of Bengal.)

One day in 1988, when asked to sing one of his favorite songs, the beggar intoned: "*Yug Yug se aarji raahtra shan hai Ram naam, Ram naam*," meaning, "The national wealth acquired in ages is Ramnam; the country's wealth worshipped through ages is Krishna-nam; the wealth adored by the community through ages is Shiva-nam; the wealth worshipped by the nation through ages is Rama-Krishna-Shiva-nam."[10] Not only was such chanting an activity of Divine worship, it was for him literally the heartbeat of his beloved nation.

Also in 1988, Yogi Ramsuratkumar issued a rare public statement, the entire content of which was a plea for the invocation of the name of God. His statement came in the form of a letter addressed to "My Friends!" to be read on the occasion of a conference held in Pondicherry, India, on May 7-8 of that year.

This beggar learnt at the feet of Swami Ramdas the Divine name of Rama, and beg[s], beg[s] all of you not to forget the Divine name Rama. Whatever you do, wherever you are, be like Anjaneya-Maruthi thinking of Rama and doing your actions in this world…There are people who like to remember the name of Siva. It is equally good – there are people who like to remember the name of Ganapathi – equally good. Whatever name you choose, whatever form you choose, but give to this beggar what he wants…This Divine name has been always of great help to all in the world. So I think none of you will shirk away when this beggar begs of you, "Don't forget the Divine name." This beggar prays to his Father to bless you all who have come here. My Lord

Rama blesses you – My Father blesses you. Arunachaleswara blesses you.[11]

राम

Lord Krishna's words, recorded in the *Bhagavad Gita*, describe his all-pervading, transcendental nature and proclaim that he is the greatest of everything – the greatest animal, the greatest mountain, the greatest river. He says that *japa yoga* is the greatest form of worship and the greatest form of sacrifice, and, therefore, that he, Krishna, *is* that.

The use of the name "Ram" or "Rama" as a mantra was first written about in the *Ram Tapani Upanishad.* Yogic scholar Georg Feuerstein quotes a source as dating this writing from about 300 BCE, although others have claimed it to be much older. For how many centuries it was used before the writing about it, however, none can say.

A Sanskrit lexicon defines "Rama" as "that which revels in the bosom of every being." Swami Papa Ramdas echoes this meaning in saying: "Ramdas's Ram is the all-pervading, Omniscient, Omnipotent Supreme Being who is seated in all hearts, who has donned all forms and Who alone Is."[12]

As its expression expanded over the ages from the singular *Ram* to the familiar *Om Sri Ram Jai Ram Jai Jai Ram,* the Ram mantra came to be called a taraka mantra (*taraka* means "superior") because of its "infinite potency." It is one of the *mahamantras* (great mantras), ranking alongside the *Om Nama Shivaya* mantra, the Gayatri mantra, and a few others.[13]

About four hundred years ago, there lived a great lover of Rama, Sri Samarth Ramdas of Maharastra (1608-1681). During his own years of wandering through India and performing of sadhana, he had chanted thirteen *crores* (130 million repetitions) of this taraka mantra sitting on the banks of the Godavari River near Nasik. As followers were attracted, he initiated serious disciples in this mantric practice and then sent many of them throughout India to teach the religion of Hinduism. Aware that this initial sound, "*Om,*" had such profound potency, he removed it, leaving the mantra in the form of thirteen Sanskrit sounds, *Sri Ram Jaya Ram Jaya Jaya Ram.*

When, in the twentieth century, Vittal Rao (Papa Ramdas) received the mantra from his own father, whom he thereafter referred to as Gurudev because of this initiation, it was in this abbreviated form that he was given it. Later, Papa Ramdas added back the *Om*.

ॐ श्री राम जय राम जय जय राम

Om Sri Ram Jai Ram Jai Jai Ram

Ramdas tells us:

Sri Samarth Ramdas assured the aspirant that if he takes "Sri Ram Jai Ram Jai Jai Ram" 13 crores [130 million] of times, he will have the vision of Sri Rama. The Mantra mentioned by Samarth Ramdas was without "OM." The Mantra Ramdas gives you is "Om Sri Ram Jai Ram Jai Jai Ram." "OM" has untold spiritual power. Hence Ramdas from his own experience, tells you that by repeating this Mantra with "Om" six crores [60 million] of times, you will attain salvation. Repeat the Mantra at all times until the target is reached. You need not keep count of the Mantra. When it reaches six crores you will automatically realize Ram – the Supreme Self. Chanting His name is the way to make Him manifest Himself in you.[14]

Understandably, when one knows the potency and significance of a chant, it is likely more powerful. Papa Ramdas spelled out the meaning of the mantra in simple terms: "Om = Impersonal Truth; Sri = Divine Power; Ram = God who is both Truth and Power, both personal and impersonal. Ram represents the Purushottama [ultimate Lord] of the Gita who is at once Purusha and Prakriti and also the supreme, transcendent One beyond both. Jai Ram = Victory to God; Jai Jai Ram = Victory, victory to God." Thus, the whole invocation means: God who is at once Truth and Power, Impersonal and Personal! Victory to Thee; victory, victory to Thee![15]

राम

Nama Japa can be expressed in a variety of ways. These prayers can be said as one fingers a *mala* (set of beads, a rosary), or not. The sacred words/sounds can be repeated mentally (*manasika japa)*; whispered or hummed under the breath (*upamshu japa)*; said aloud (*vaikhari japa)* in such a way that other sounds are obliterated, and sung to a repetitive chant. *Likhita japa* is a form in which one writes the mantra for an established period of time, daily or regularly. Then there is *pashanti*, wherein the chant runs fast before the mind, without verbalization. In the most advanced stage the mantra has taken hold of the being, beats with the heart, and even in sleep the chant is still going on. As Ramdas writes: "It is not enough to sing the praise of the Name. You must keep it constantly on your lips. Gradually, you will find the Name taking hold of you. Now it is not you who possess the Name, but the Name takes possession of you. Then the mind will refuse to wander here and there. It gets absorbed in the Name and derives great peace and joy."[16]

The state that Ramdas describes sounds very much like a state of liberation. It was obviously that for Ramsuratkumar, as one of his devotees described:

> Shastras say that one becomes what one thinks intensely and constantly. Immersed in the japa sadhana from the moment of his initiation, my Master [Yogi Ramsuratkumar] has become "That." The death he speaks of [when he says "Ramdas killed this beggar in 1952"] is the cessation of the subject or individuality in Him and its merger into the object of His meditation. The salt doll merged into the ocean. Yogi Ramsuratkumar became Rama.[17]

Esoterically, the word "mantra" is derived from *manana* – thinking – and *trana* – liberation. Therefore, it is a potent form of thought that becomes an instrument of conscious intention.[18] When a mantra is chanted, there is a vibration created within the body, because each sound has a particular vibration and hence a particular potency.

Various combinations of sounds are known to intensify the vibration, creating effects on many levels – body, emotions, and spirit. These combinations that we know today as mantras have a strong spiritual vibration. They were initially received as revelations to advanced yogis or masters in heightened states of awareness.[19] "Om," for instance, is known to have a potency that can literally transform the physical body. Anyone who has ever intoned this sound for a period of time will generally testify to feeling "something," if only the "buzz" that accompanies an increase of oxygen to the brain.

When a master or qualified teacher speaks a mantra to his or her devotee, or whispers it into the ear, it carries substantially more potency than if it is simply found in a book about mantras or heard on an audiotape or CD and then repeated. The mantra that springs from the bottom of the heart of the master carries with it the power of all the *tapas* (spiritual practice and austerities) that he or she has done, as well as a potency passed along through a lineage. If one is associated with that lineage, one enjoys the benefits of significant empowerment in its use. *Vag-diksha*, one of the traditional forms of initiation, or transference of the potency from the master to the disciple, is done through such mantric utterance.

While Yogi Ramsuratkumar rarely conducted any formalities of initiation, he constantly offered these empowered mantras to those who came into his presence. Yet, understandably, only those with the prerequisite hunger could receive them. Once received, it remained the devotee's task to cultivate the precious seeds that the master had planted by continuing the practice. As Lee Lozowick wrote in one of his many poems of praise to and longing for his master: "Let me be strong enough to be surrendered to You – whisper Ram in Your son's ear / oh Favorite of Your Father in Heaven./ Om Sri Ram Jai Ram Jai Jai Ram."[20]

राम

All who set eyes on Yogi Ramsuratkumar noted several distinguishing characteristics of his activity that might be ascribed to his continual remembrance and use of the Divine name. When his hands weren't occupied otherwise, Yogi Ramsuratkumar's fingers on his right hand moved as if he were plying invisible mala beads. Others have noted that he often used the index finger of his right hand to trace a pattern of symbols into his own left palm, on the hand or arm of a devotee whom he drew close to him, or on the floor or carpet in front of him. Some have said that the "patterns" seemed to be identical to those used in writing "Ram."

Ramsuratkumar, as we noted earlier, was always asking the Divine names to be sung by those in his presence, and often singing them himself. He recommended to devotees to chant constantly, "like the pouring of oil from one pot to another, without break. Namajapa should be sustained, just as pouring of oil is not broken."[21]

Some of his closest devotees in the later years of his life, Devaki Ma and Vijayalakshmi Ma, who attended him in public darshans from the early 1990s, would sit on the far corner of the dais, at a right angle to him, carefully fingering their malas for hours at a time. To others he gave encouragement in the writing of the mantra – Ramnam; or his own name, Yogi Ramsuratkumar. Visitors and guests to his ashram might observe one or more of his male attendants sitting against a side wall, eyes either riveted on the master, awaiting his call, or focused in a notebook, as line after line of a mantra was carefully transcribed.

Using the name of God was Yogi Ramsuratkumar's remedy for all ills, as it had been for his Father, Ramdas. "We have got so many problems all around, This Divine name is just like an umbrella in the heavy rainfall. Catch hold of the Divine name and go on doing your work in the world," he advised.[22] In the 1970s, when one of his Western visitors asked him about the repetition of *his* name, which they regularly chanted together, the beggar said: "If someone repeats this beggar's name he will be helping the work of this beggar, he will be helping the world, and he will be helping himself. You repeat the name of this mad fellow then I will be with you."[23]

Occasionally, detractors questioned this recommendation to say the name, Yogi Ramsuratkumar, thinking it was some means of self-aggrandizement. But the Godchild's explanation was simple. "'Yogi Ramsuratkumar' is not the name of this beggar. This beggar died at the feet of Papa Ramdas in 1952. 'Yogi Ramsuratkumar' is the name of my Father."[24]

Furthermore, according to him, there was no activity or place wherein it was not appropriate to be absorbed in Divine Remembrance, or chanting the name of God. One evening in the late 1980s, when Devaki Ma and several other devotees gathered at the master's residence, she questioned him about proper times for the chanting of Ramnam. Yogi Ramsuratkumar replied that he would talk more about it in the morning, and then left his visitors for the night. Early the next day these same devotees all heard the joyous voice of Yogi Ramsuratkumar coming from the toilet building. He was singing, *Sri Rama Jaya Rama, Jaya Jaya Rama*. And with this demonstration, Devaki Ma had received the answer to her question.[25]

राम

Reflecting back to his sojourns of the late 1950s, we can imagine Ramsuratkumar with quick and lilting steps, and chanting the name of God, now moving closer and closer to Tiruvannamalai, his ultimate home. With the days of his wandering sadhana drawing to a close, was it *Om Sri Ram* that he sang? Or was it *Arunachula Siva* that he intoned in praise of the inexorable power of the Lord embodied in the holy mountain to which he was headed? For him, all names were one, all were variations on the same theme – only God.

THE MOTH TO THE FLAME, 1959

 From whichever direction he approached the small city of Tiruvannamalai in the summer of 1959, whether by train or on foot, Ramsuratkumar would have seen the sacred red mountain, Arunachala, towering majestically in the distance long before he viewed the massive *gopurams* (entryway towers) of the great temple that stood at its base. Arunachala, reaching to a height of 780 meters (2,259 feet), rises like an imposing monument on a relatively barren plain.

Ramsuratkumar had journeyed far, and at last the weary traveler had reached the place that would soon become synonymous with his name. Tiruvannamalai and its environs would ever after be his home, and the final resting place of his physical form.

But let us not be deceived for a moment in imagining that "coming home" meant any security, any comfort, or any respite from the all-consuming work that his Father had given Ramsuratkumar to do. He was a beggar, a *sadhika*, a man without home except in the heart of God. This rugged mountain, Arunachala, was for Ramsuratkumar no mere friendly landmark or natural wonder. Rather, it was the embodiment of God Himself, Lord Siva dwelling on the earth. In this capacity alone could he call Arunachala home.

From one source we learn that Yogi Ramsuratkumar apparently spent about six months in one cave, Guhai Namashivayar, on the Arunachala hill in 1963-64. And speculation is that he probably spent much more time in other caves. He certainly would have visited the famous Skandashram, a cave in which Ramana Maharshi lived; and the cave where Swami Ramdas made his retreat would have been easily accessible, as close as it was to the temple entrance. In the 1980s, several devotees tell of meeting Ramsuratkumar at "Papa's" cave on at least one occasion.

His love for Arunachala was obvious too in the chants he invoked to honor this One. "*Arunachala Siva, Arunachala Siva, Arunachala Siva Aruna Jathaa*" he would sing as he walked along the streets and back roads of the city, or as he sat with his many visitors under the punnai tree near the train station in Tiruvannamalai, a prime spot from which to gaze upon the mountain's verdant and rocky slopes.

Many stories told by Ramsuratkumar's visitors and devotees throughout the years concerned their climbing to the top or circumambulation of the mountain. When a devotee of Ramdas's visited Yogi Ramsuratkumar in the mid-1980s, the beggar told the woman to go to do pradakshina of the mountain, saying "Everybody is always asking for something else, money, wealth, something, but no one is asking for blessings from Papa." Apparently, as far as Ramsuratkumar was concerned, to walk the sacred road around the mountain was the same as invoking the blessing of his master, Swami Ramdas.

Some of these stories mention the beggar's injunction to his guests that they come to visit him only *after* doing pradakshina, while others link Ramsuratkumar with mysterious, even miraculous, happenings on this mountain.

The writer and professor of literature Makarand Paranjape, who first met Yogi Ramsuratkumar in 1992, recalled a delightful incident that occurred during his second visit. Having taken the bus from Bangalore, he arrived in Tiruvannamalai at precisely 4:30 in the morning. Deeming it much too early to visit the master, Paranjape waited at Ramana Ashram, attended early ceremonies there, had breakfast, and decided to take a brief walk on the mountain, to the Virupaksha cave, before moving on to the Yogi's residence. His intention in the walk was to be gone for little more than an hour, but when he reached his destination, a Tamil man, who spoke neither English nor Hindi, through signs and gestures indicated that he would show Paranjape around to various sites on the hill. Forgetting his original plan, or thinking he could do it all, Paranjape agreed.

As they climbed on Mount Arunachala, Makarand was taken by the beautiful and mesmerizing view of the town below. But then, as the morning progressed, and the trail wore on and on, the trip became more difficult. Paranjape had made the journey without shoes out of respect for the holy ground upon which he walked, and when they finally reached the summit, his feet were in great pain.

"It is said that whenever you are at the mountain, whatever you wish for comes true," Makarand remarked in an interview in 2002. "When we were coming down, the only thing I felt was, 'Oh God, I wish I had a pair of *chappells* [sandals].' Any old chappells would do, because my feet were really killing me, I was just not used to it, and this was almost a three-and-a-half-hour climb, or maybe only two-and-a-half, I can't remember now."

Immediately upon the invocation of this wish, his climbing companion stopped them. "'Wait a minute,' he says to me," Makarand reported. "And behind a rock he puts his hand inside and fishes out a pair of chappells. And I said, 'What an idiot, that the only thing I asked for was a pair of chappells!' "

By the time Paranjape returned from his grueling sojourn it was already 2:30 in the afternoon. He had missed lunch, and was thoroughly spent from this exhaustive climb.

"I trudged my way to Sudama [Yogi Ramsuratkumar's residence] and reached there for four o'clock darshan, around 3:30. As I'm standing in queue, a person comes up to me and says, 'Are you Makarand Paranjape?' and I say 'yes'."

"Bhagwan has been waiting for you from 4:30 A.M.," the questioner informed him.

Ushered into Yogi Ramsuratkumar's presence, Makarand at last received the master's smile. "So," he remarked, his eyes twinkling, "Arunachala has played a trick on this beggar."

To this day, early in the twenty-first century, Arunachala remains one of the great centers of pilgrimage in south India. On the full moon of every month, the population of the city of Tiruvannamalai swells from 200,000 to as much as two million. From all over the southern regions and beyond, buses and hired vans aim for the mountain, some of them traveling for thousands of kilometers, and over several days, to reach their destination.

Pilgrims typically dress in their finest clothing, remove their shoes, and begin to chant "*Arunachala Siva*" in one of its many variations, as they commence the clockwise journey that typically lasts from three to four hours, and often much longer.

Beggars and sadhus line the pradakshina route, awaiting the generosity of the pilgrims who know that money offered during this particular season will earn the giver greater merit. Well-off merchants, now selling everything from stainless steel pots to pirated CDs, set up elaborate stalls to display their wares, while their poorer competitors may simply throw a burlap sack upon the ground on which they have carefully arranged a meagre assortment of plastic combs. A festival atmosphere predominates, as the rest of the city grinds to a near standstill. Residents and visitors alike have all turned their attention to the mountain, the body of the Holy Lord.

Because the mountain *is* Siva himself, pilgrims come for a purpose. They do their pradakshina to earn his favors, and to thank him for his boons. They further know that Siva Arunachala, also known as the "Arunagiri Yogi," throughout the ages has attracted rishis, sages, sadhus and thousands of other entities – embodied or not – who still dwell here; and stories abound of visions, meetings, and special aromas that indicate the presence of both celestial and underworld beings.

Into this circus at the center of the world – this meeting place to which both rich and poor have been called for thousands of years, from north and south in India, and more recently from Europe and the United States; this marketplace of the sacred and the profane – Ramsuratkumar entered fully, at last.

राम

From 1959 until 1964, when he met a shopkeeper named Perumal who would later write of their early adventures, we have little to go on in reconstructing Ramsuratkumar's life.

It stands to reason that he began his tenure in Tiruvannamalai with a short stay at Ramanashram, as every pilgrim knows of its longstanding hospitality. This place, moreover, held vivid memories for him. Here he had met the eyes of the beloved Maharshi in 1948, and been deeply affected by this transformative glance. Having been absent from this ashram for ten years now, the site of Ramana's samadhi (place of entombment) undoubtedly stirred him; not in the way of sentimental attachment, certainly, but in the way in which Ramsuratkumar was forever grateful to those who had served and guided him in his spiritual quest.

The man, Ramsuratkumar, who now stood before his mentor's grave imbibing the vibrations of Bhagawan Ramana Maharshi's eternal spirit, was no longer on a search. He had been driven to divine madness by Ramdas's hand, and now was "found." Merged with his own master, identified eternally with the One, he had been sorely tested, plunged into the fires of deprivation and abuse, and had emerged with the cry of victory – "Jai Jai Ram!" – on his lips. His own descriptions of his condition then, and forever after, are incomprehensible to the logical mind; only by feeling with the heart into the mood of emptiness and absolute surrender they convey can we glimpse the radical transformation that occurred for him.

> This beggar doesn't know what is right and what is wrong. He has no mind. No reasoning. No individual here! So don't expect this beggar to do only what you thing is right…This beggar does not live for happiness. This beggar lives only for Father's work. Every minute, every thought, word and every movement…every gesture of this beggar is controlled by Father – Father who runs the whole Cosmos. Father governs us all. He governs this beggar, you and everyone. This beggar is nothing. Do you hear? There is no existence. Only Father here! No conscience, no will of his own, no decision of right and wrong. All washed away!…Gone…Totally gone, nothing remains…[T]his beggar cannot be in one state all the time. Whatever state Father keeps this beggar in is perfect. No questioning. For him everything is Father's will. This beggar ceased to exist in 1952. Only Father is everywhere…limitless…only Father is…Father alone is.[1]

Yet, the unfolding details of his profound service to humankind and to God, the recognition of *who* he actually "was," were revealed to others only slowly, in tiny incidents, in chance meetings, in the moods of ecstatic song and dance that emerged from him to captivate and infect his observers, many of whom delighted in coming back for more.

Neither at this time, nor later, was Ramsuratkumar's lila ever characterized by grand gestures, by brilliant discoursing on religion or philosophy, by the teaching of various yogas, or by initiation of social-action programs. Simplicity, pure joy, ecstasy, child-like wonder, celebration, gratitude, humility, patience, silent bearing with his own suffering, and the relief of the sufferings of others...these were the "programs" he followed and the yogas he taught by example.

> Father gave the work of preaching and teaching to Sri Aurobindo, Bhagavan Sri Ramana Maharshi and Swami Ramdas. But, for this beggar, Father has given the work of alleviating the suffering of others alone.[2]

Entering Tiruvannamalai in 1959, Ramsuratkumar probably knew no one. There is the chance that some person from Ramanashram remembered him from his two-month stay in 1948, but unlikely. There is the chance that he might have recalled a name or two of Ramdas's disciples who lived in the area, since he had spent so much time around devotees of Ramdas in the late 1940s and early '50s. Yet, for all intents and purposes he was unknown and unaffiliated. But not for long.

The Tiruvannamalai of the early 1960s was a vastly different place from the city of today. Even in the 1970s, Western visitors from the U.S. described it colloquially as "a one-horse town." All told, it consisted of a massive temple, dating from the thirteenth or fifteenth century, depending upon whom one consults; an assortment of smaller temples lining the route around the mountain which dominated everything; the ashram of Ramana Maharshi, attracting ever larger numbers of dropouts from the technologized, depersonalized and despirited West; the ashram of Sri Seshadri Swamigal, a saint who lived here for over forty years and attained mahasamadhi in 1929; a humble assortment of shops; a vegetable market.

To the north, in those days, large open fields and a single dirt road lay between the great temple and Ramanashram. To the south, a straight view from the railway station allowed one to see the temple towers. Today, these routes are choked with diesel-fueled buses racing at breakneck speed amidst crowds of residents and pilgrims, animals, private automobiles, bicycles, motorized rickshaws. Shops of all sorts, some two and three stories high, line the streets, with large, brightly painted signs announcing Xerox, or Internet Café, alongside #6 Tailor Shop or Family Fun Food.

Yet, despite the huge increase in population and industry, Tiruvannamalai still retains some of its small-town feel. One still runs into the same people one has met only the day before, and finds certain "characters" showing up on a regular basis – like the "one-armed" beggar who hides his arm under his cloak; or the young French sadhu who stands talking to the mountain. If such a small-town feel is the case today, even amidst growing depersonalization and the speedy adoption of the worst of Western "values," how much more it would have been true of the place in 1959, when the city was actually an oversized village. It would not have taken long for one such as Ramsuratkumar to begin to attract attention, if only for the exuberant joy that he radiated, day or night, whenever one might encounter him.

Sri V. Ganesan, a grandnephew of Ramana Maharshi, raised in the Ramanashram family, was a young man in the early 1960s. He has a vivid memory of seeing Yogi Ramsuratkumar in those days leaping from slab to slab in a local cemetery, ecstatically chanting Ramnam all the while. What impressed Ganesan was the sense of the "enormous energy that poured from him," and the fact that the beggar might do this for hours on end, regardless of what was going on around him.[3]

What Ganesan describes was a type of dance, an activity that became one of the distinguishing characteristics of this ecstatic swami, Ramsuratkumar, in the years to come. Many people, in describing him, have told of his lilting steps, the waving of his arms, his twirling movements, and his song. In the 1970s, Shri V.

Ramanujachari asked the beggar, half in jest, "How come you have this dancing gait?" With "sudden earnestness in crisp but nostalgic tone" the Yogi explained: "This beggar was not like this before. But something happened to him when He met his Master Ramdas. From then on due to My Master's Grace, I have this joyousness reflected in this way of walking."[4]

A woman who met Yogiji in 1975, Smt. Tilakavati, reported a similar type of behavior, calling it the dance of Siva, "leaping, twirling, his limbs moving in graceful arcs as he chanted Ramnam or Om Namashivaya…once he danced to the sound of Damaru, the sound being made not by the instrument but by his own voice." The *damaru* is Siva's drum, and iconography frequently depicts the great Lord waving or playing it as he performs his periodic cosmic dance that destroys creation so that it may be renewed. "The sounds [of Yogiji's voice] were such as no human voice could reproduce; it was most awesome, inspiring and thrilling."[5]

When Hilda Charlton, an American woman who had lived in India for twenty years, and one of the earliest teachers of Indian spirituality in the West, visited Yogi Ramsuratkumar in 1978, she too was overjoyed in witnessing this dance. The very first night that she met him, Ramsuratkumar spontaneously danced, all the while singing "*Sri Ram Jai Ram Jai Jai Ram.*"

In awe and deep respect, Hilda reached down and touched the ground by his foot. "Was that necessary?" Yogi Ramsuratkumar asked her kindly, as he was often shocked by the reverent attention paid to him by others, and was always putting his guests above himself.

"Yes, it was," said Hilda with firm resolve, recognizing the magnitude of the being in whose presence she sat.

Later that night, in conversing with Will Zulkowski, who was among her travel companions, Hilda remarked, still vibrating from her experience with the beggar: "O Will, you wouldn't believe it. Your master is so far out there. When he was singing and dancing he was bringing in light from other universes. You have no idea how great he is. He is just beyond, beyond, beyond."

His singing, too, had similarly profound effects upon those who heard him. Kirsti, also known as Sivapriya, a Finnish sannyasin and long-time devotee of Ramsuratkumar, recalled that:

His tunes for the mantras were joyful, like dancing. I had the
feeling like moving my limbs to all directions – above, below
and all around, in all the directions of His Father's presence
– when hearing them. They touched what Sri Aurobindo
called the "psychic being," the soul consciousness around the
heart area. They awakened intensive vision, not only brought
about mental silence.[6]

With activities such as these it is no wonder that the stranger
from the north was soon being noticed, and then sought after – for
good or for ill – by many people of this day. Some certainly saw only
the vestiges of madness – the ill-assorted dress, the blazing eyes that
looked through and beyond his visitors, the constant singing of
Ramnam, or the seemingly erratic movements. From Ramsuratkumar's account to a close disciple, we learn that an official at Ramanashram had taken him aside and berated him for his appearance, saying, "Whenever you come to this ashram you should take a bath and
you should come neat and clean, and well behaved, and put your
cloth in a proper way. Then only you should enter the ashram."[7]

Nonetheless, for those who had the eyes to see, "there was a
growing awareness among the people that this was a Godman."[8] A
strong and close disciple of Ramana, named Sundaresan, started
speaking of Ramsuratkumar as "a great yogi." And years later, the
beggar told his devotee Parathasarathy that "Sundaresan called this
beggar first 'Yogi.' " Before that he was simply "Ramsuratkumar."

राम

For the first two years of his residence around Tiruvannamalai,
Ramsuratkumar stayed mostly within the environs of a graveyard
located near a small ashram, the Eesanya Mutt, on the western end
of town. Will Zulkowski, who spent many months with Yogi
Ramsuratkumar starting in the mid-1970s, frequently talked with
the master about his early years in this area. "He stayed in the graveyards because nobody bothers you there," Will remarked in a personal interview. "Nobody wants to sell you anything there, nobody
wants to hassle you for any money. People avoid graveyards."

Yogi Ramsuratkumar on Mount Arunachala, 1960s

After this initial phase, we know that Yogi Ramsuratkumar spent time in other favored haunts. He could be found sitting under a peepul tree near the bus station; he took shelter under the punnai tree at the railway station; he slept on the verandahs of shops in the markets near the temple, and in the vicinity of the Ganapathi Temple known as Pillaiyar Koil. This structure was not far from the compound owned by the Theosophical Society of Tiruvannamalai, and here Yogi Ramsuratkumar made use of the library that must have provided great food for the mind and soul of one as well educated as he was. At this place he met Sri Sriram, who was later to become the president of the Theosophical Society, and a friendship was established that lasted throughout their lives.

Until illness curbed his physical energies later in life, Ramsuratkumar did a great deal of walking, wandering around the mountain, and venturing into nearby villages. From a scattering of stories we know that he soon endeared himself to local people throughout the region. Many years later, when residents of these neighborhood towns would come upon him in Tiruvannamalai, there was frequently a note of sadness and even gentle reproach in their voices as they urged him to return to them, and to once again bless them by accepting their simple food.

राम

The fact that Ramsuratkumar also made several more lengthy trips in the 1960s may come as a surprise for some. At Anandashram in Kanhangad in 2002, I met Smt. Lakshmi, daughter of Sri Devasenapathi, a longtime disciple of Papa Ramdas. Although Lakshmi was only fourteen in 1966 when she first met Yogi Ramsuratkumar, she clearly remembered his stay of two months at their family home in Madras (Chennai) during that year (although another biographer reports this as being 1962), just prior to the wedding of her eldest sister. Ramsuratkumar helped her father in these preparations. However, when Mataji Krishnabai learned of this arrangement, she cautioned that Yogiji should not be left alone at their home. "He is a fire, he is a fire," Mataji warned enigmatically.

"Tiruvannamalai itself is the place of fire," explained a wise son-in-law who was present in this 2002 interview. "Ramsuratkumar had joined with that Fire!"

In 1964, the year that marked the death of Jawaharlal Nehru, one of Ramsuratkumar's admired icons, and a short time after the death of Swami Ramdas (1963), Yogi Ramsuratkumar once again visited Madras. Here he encountered J. Krishnamurti, who at that time was back in India after a trip to Europe, where he had stayed in Rome, London, Paris, and Switzerland in the propagation of his mission, or "non-mission" as the case may be.

The story varies somewhat as it has been told by several different devotees, but the essence of the meeting between the two men remains much the same in all accounts. Following Krishnamurti's public lecture, Ramsuratkumar went to the great philosopher's residence at Adyar. Standing in the courtyard, he was informed that Krishnamurti had retired for a rest and would not be seeing visitors. Before Ramsuratkumar could turn to leave, however, he was noticed by the aged Krishnamurti who happened to be looking down from his upstairs window.

Leaving his room and coming to the courtyard, the philosopher approached his young admirer. At seventy-three years of age, Krishnamurti was a model of elegant action and refined spiritual discipline, and Ramsuratkumar, who was only forty-six at the time, afforded his elder the highest regard – he attempted to prostrate to him. However, the gesture was never completed, as "Krishnamurti held him by the shoulder, thereby preventing him from prostrating." Instead, "the two Mahatmas gazed at each other in silent communication."[9] At another time during this period, Ramsuratkumar followed Krishnamurti to Bombay for a continued series of lectures. An even more remarkable tale unfolds of this meeting, as Vijayalaksmi notes in her biographical account:

One day when Yogiji was walking towards the place of lecture, a car stopped by, and Krishnamurti, who was in the car, invited the Yogi to accompany him. Not only that, he had Yogiji seated by his side on the dais of the lecture hall.

Krishnamurti's lecture was listened [to] in rapt silence. Some conservative Brahmins raised the issue whether Krishnamurti's methods would apply to persons who had deep faith in God. Krishnamurti clarified that those with faith would not need his advice. Bhagawan [Yogi Ramsuratkumar], while narrating this event, had mentioned to a devotee (Appan Iyengar) that Krishnamurti insisted on his speaking to the audience and so Yogi Ramsuratkumar also spoke.[10]

Others have reported bits and pieces of conversations that Ramsuratkumar had with the eminent philosopher, whom he often mentioned in later years, ranking him among the great saints of the time. The writer Makarand Paranjape heard Yogi Ramsuratkumar say that Krishnamurti had told him (Yogiji) that there was no need for a guru. In telling of this incident later, Ramsuratkumar had commented, "But when I went to listen to his talk, I saw that everyone was treating him as a guru, so I understood that he was also saying the same thing."

That J. Krishnamurti admired Yogi Ramsuratkumar is also clear from another source. Henry Tabman, an American, had met Krishnamurti in New York City prior to Tabman's embarking on an extended trip to India. When Krishnamurti asked him why he was going to India, Tabman said that he desired to meet Yogi Ramsuratkumar, adding that "people believe he is a great man, a great yogi."

Hearing this, Krishnamurti smiled, and so Tabman asked him, "Do you know him?"

To which Krishnamurti clearly said, "I *know*; I don't believe."

At the time, Henry Tabman was upset, thinking that Krishnamurti had somehow disparaged the beggar. In India, however, when Tabman brought this conversation to his friend Sadhu Rangarajan, the sadhu was able to clear the misunderstanding, explaining to him that Krishnamurti had been making a refined distinction between *belief* and *knowledge*. Belief was unnecessary when the higher knowledge was, in fact, present.

Eventually, Tabman told his story to Yogi Ramsuratkumar, saying, "Krishnamurti made this remark about you."

Hearing this, Yogiji started laughing.

Another series of remarkable trips during the 1960s took Yogi Ramsuratkumar to Ganeshpuri, near Bombay, the site of the ashram of Swami Nityananda, and later to the Nityananda Ashram at Kanhangad in southern India before returning to Tiruvannamalai.[11] No reports verify that Ramsuratkumar ever met with Nityananda prior to the elder saint's mahasamadhi in 1961. But interested devotees may wish to further pursue the life and teachings of this great *mahasiddha*, about whom Yogi Ramsuratkumar once said: "Swami Nityananda has agreed to take care of this beggar's work outside India and this beggar has agreed to do the work of Swami Nityananda in India."[12] Furthermore, Ramsuratkumar impressed upon devotees that anyone who had understood even a small part of Nityananda's life and teaching was certain of some insight into his own (Ramsuratkumar's) life and teaching.[13]

As interesting as these early chronologies may be, a list of Yogi Ramsuratkumar's trips or meetings pales in comparison with absorption in the day-to-day life that the God-intoxicated beggar was living in the 1960s and early 1970s in Tiruvannamalai. To feel inside the life, we must let ourselves be taken in by one story in greater depth. A wondrous story that rounds out the full scope of his grace and majesty in these early years.

Let us stop for a while in the year 1964, then, and hear from one who was to be his companion for nearly forty years. Let us meet Perumal.

10

THE MAN OF LIGHT, 1964

Emancipation was not the end for this beggar, rather it was the beginning for him.

— Yogi Ramsuratkumar[1]

The brass market of Tiruvannamalai is a series of independently owned shops, lined up one beside the other on both sides of a small street in front of the east entrance tower (Ammani Ammal Gopuram) of the Arunachaleswarar Thirukoil (Temple). Today there are perhaps thirty or more such shops, each with a similar variety of offerings — from tiny peacock-shaped ghee lamps, which tourists can purchase for forty rupees (less than one dollar, U.S.), to stainless steel plates, cups and tiffins (handy, two- or three-tiered containers, which can hold the various items of a typical meal), to water pots and vessels too large to lift, to life-size representations of Hindu deities.

The brass market's location has not changed since the 1960s. As one walks the busy thoroughfare of this bazaar today, listening to the shouts of hawkers and feeling the electric hum of the crowds, one senses this as a hub of the city's life; a crossroads of the sacred and the profane; the marketplace at the temple. Down these streets pass well-shod tourists looking for mementos as they wind their way around barefoot locals on bicycles to which enormous loads have been strapped. Families on pilgrimage to Arunachaleswarar wander here, as well as homemakers looking for bargains. Beggars, however, must be wary as they will be accosted by police if shopkeepers complain of their persistence. Nothing must deter the flow of commerce.

ONLY GOD

Early on a Sunday evening, sometime in 1964, a prosperous young brassware merchant sat alone in the growing shadows before one of his two thriving shops, which were closed for the day. Enjoying the mood of an uncharacteristically quiet street, he was "wrapped in a meditative solitude" as he contemplated the east gate of the temple and the majestic mountain that rose above it.[2] It had been a day like any other, except that this evening his meditation held a note of poignancy – a longing – that he had not known to such a degree before. His life, certainly, was good. He was married. He was a father of children. He was a well-respected businessman. But still, he longed for...*something*. What that was, however, he was unable to say.

An instant later, his reverie was interrupted by an extraordinary sight. Little did he suspect in that moment that he was about to encounter a force, a living presence, that would completely transform his life, down to the last detail. He noticed a "streak of something like a beam of light, swift and sudden like a lightning." The strange sight had occurred at the foot of the temple's east tower.

Immediately, the "light" moved toward him, but now it had assumed the shape of a man. Memorably, this man of light was characterized by a remarkable "gait and manner of bearing." Although he could not see the features of the face, the merchant, whose name was Sivananainda Perumal, would describe the experience years later, saying, "I felt that it was the supreme Lord walking in a human form."[3] As the wondrous figure moved closer, Perumal began to take in the details of its appearance. He noted especially the palm-leaf fan and small bundle of four or five newspapers the man held in his hands; the green shawl that regally draped his body; and most significantly, the soft and welcoming eyes and smile.

Unnerved by what he saw and felt, the merchant's gaze flashed away from the approaching form. He looked to the temple tower and the mountain, then back to the oncoming figure. Reading Perumal's feigned indifference, undoubtedly his typical strategy for survival in the face of the unknown, the light-filled "Lord" looked at him all the more intensely. Smiling still, the stranger began to shift his body from side to side. It was a dance of sorts; the beginning of a playful lila. The elegant swami's movements were precisely calculated to block the merchant's clear view of the tower and the mountain. From mild annoyance and insecurity, Perumal's response flared into anger. But, before he could speak or move, the eyes of the kingly stranger had penetrated his, and the rage melted as quickly as it had erupted.

Affection replaced his fear, for the moment, and without saying a word, Perumal gestured to his new companion to sit by his side. The swami did so without hesitation. The two men then sat in silence for twenty minutes – the young Perumal still gazing at the shrines in the distance, while the elder seemed to be studying, staring at, the one who looked away.

At last Perumal spoke, offering hospitality. "Sir, please take some coffee," he addressed the other kindly.

"Yes, alright," the elder replied in a tone of voice that Perumal says woke him from his reveries.

Clapping his hands to call some youngsters who were playing on a nearby terrace, Perumal intended to invest their services in fetching the coffee. To his surprise, however, the swami interrupted the plan.

"Not them," Yogi Ramsuratkumar directed, gently but unquestionably, like a king to a knight who has come asking for a quest. "You go yourself to get it."

In that moment, however, Perumal did not yet know that what his heart had longed for was to *be* this bidden knight. Instead, his ego was stabbed, and he heard these simple words as a threat to his position. Anger again rose up. "Who is this man, anyway, to bid me?…He does not know who I am. I am a merchant of some standing, the owner of a shop. It was I who invited him to coffee."[4] And so thinking, Perumal became confused. Lost in the logic of what to do next, he hesitated. "Now, if I do *not* get him the coffee, I would be guilty of a lapse," his mind argued. "So I must go to fetch it myself."

As he rose to his task, albeit reluctantly, Perumal looked around to see if his activity was being noticed. "Bring two coffees!" the swami called after him, sending another tiny arrow straight to the target of Perumal's pride. Now, anyone watching would have no doubt that a "man" was being sent to do a boy's job.

By the time he reached the nearby hotel, where he ordered two coffees to be freshly prepared, Perumal's heart had softened slightly. When the hotelkeeper offered to send a shop-boy to deliver the refreshments, Perumal refused politely but firmly. He did the same when two or three more people stopped and offered to carry the coffees for him as he returned to his spot in the bazaar. "I am taking this coffee for a venerable person. Therefore I must take it myself," he informed them.[5]

This use of the word "venerable" is an interesting one. It denotes not only a person of advanced age, which Ramsuratkumar may have seemed to the young Perumal (although the beggar was only forty-six) at the time, but refers also to one deserving of respect or reverence based on nobility of character. That Perumal chose this word to describe a guest whom he had only known for twenty minutes is probably indicative of the nearly instantaneous magnetic pull that Ramsuratkumar had begun to exert on him.

Arriving with the coffee, Perumal noted that the swami was "seated majestically, facing west, smoking a cigarette" – the first mention, historically, of the smoking that was to be a life-long trademark of the beggar's.[6] Continuing his playful exchange, Yogi Ramsuratkumar's eyes probably twinkled mischievously as he asked Perumal if anyone along his way had offered to fetch the coffee on his behalf. "I did not give it to them. I brought it myself," Perumal admitted, probably with great seriousness.

As the younger man watched with curiosity, Ramsuratkumar poured the two cups of coffee into four vessels, back and forth, to cool it. Giving half the quantity to Perumal, the elder took his from the coconut shell he had been carrying, and the two men looked at one another closely as they drank.

"You go and return it," Yogi Ramsuratkumar again directed, as he gathered the coffee containers. To test Perumal's pride and obedience may have been the furthermost thing from the beggar's mind. Yet, for one surrendered completely to the will of God, as Ramsuratkumar was, such seemingly inconsequential requests could take on enormous proportions. In the give-and-take of their first meeting, the master had lost no time in laying the groundwork for what was to be a forty-year relationship. Yogi Ramsuratkumar offered Perumal a gift that he would offer to thousands of others in the years ahead – the gift of seeing oneself more clearly. In Perumal's case, as in most others, this revelation was not necessarily a pretty sight!

Despite his instinctive regard for the man who had transformed the drinking of coffee to an act of holy communion, Perumal continued to suffer annoyance, anger, and even outrage. When Ramsuratkumar laughed joyously upon learning Perumal's full name, the young man was affronted, as if he were being mocked. When the beggar, who himself was bearded, quietly asked his new friend why he too wore a beard and matted hair, Perumal "was inflamed with a great anger." With his ego struggling to maintain some guard on its territories, Perumal indignantly exclaimed, "This is one thing you should not ask!"[7]

Yet, despite the fire that blazed from Perumal's eyes, Yogi Ramsuratkumar's gaze offered nothing but tenderness. Slowly, inexorably, that gaze was boring through layers of defense and resistance, working itself to the center of the younger man's heart.

When Perumal needed to transact some business with an associate who had arrived on the scene, he took his leave of Ramsuratkumar, warmly inviting him to come again to the metalware shop on the next day.

The two businessmen left the vicinity and proceeded to walk to the temple, passing in through the east gate. Of this separation Perumal notes: "I turned back often to see Swami and found him watching us from where we had left him."[8] Although their parting was a sweet one, and although Perumal definitely wanted to see this regal swami again, he was not prepared for what was to come next. When he and his business associate engaged the services of a pious temple priest to offer their prayers of adoration to the Lord Siva in the inner sanctum of the temple, Perumal unexpectedly found himself weeping uncontrollably. As he described the moment: "Although I was standing in front of the holy of holies, my mind was still outside the temple, contemplating Swami." When they ventured further, entering into the Divine Mother's shrine, an even stranger experience awaited Perumal.

> I felt the entire sanctum sanctorum was illumed with a green light. I could see that in a corner…a figure was seated. I asked my companion "There is a figure seated there. Are you able to see?" He looked carefully and said, "Only the garlands

offered to the deity are heaped. It is this that looks like a figure to you." I remembered at once the proverbial saying that for the cowherd who has lost his cattle every fence has the likeness of a cow. I felt convinced that my mind had become obsessed with the thought of the person I had met in front of my shop.[9]

The obsession that Perumal experienced on this first auspicious day never left him. Even though his faith and obedience wavered many times in the early years, as his emotions seesawed from wonder to rage, Perumal had unquestionably received the master's initiation and would never be able to undo it. Little did he know, then, that this One who had captured his heart would become his ishta devataa, and that he, Perumal, the prosperous merchant, would soon be as poor (and as rich) and as the kingly beggar, as yet unnamed, who this day had emerged from the light.

राम

Ramsuratkumar and Perumal were soon spending time together regularly, often every day, and sometimes several times a day. The two men ate together, walked through the temple together, and crisscrossed their way from one end of the city to another. In 1998, Perumal wrote a book entitled *Treasures of the Heart, The Unforgettable Yogi Ramsuratkumar*, detailing those first few years following their initial meeting. Not only has this work left us a testimony of love and devotion, but for biographical purposes it is also a treasury of details and clues that help us flesh out this period from 1964 until the early 1970s.

We learn that at the time that he met Perumal, Ramsuratkumar was already using the title "Yogi" before his name. "Do you know the name of this beggar?" the older man had asked a boy who had brought him and Perumal a meal that they shared. "It is Yogi Ramsuratkumar," the beggar announced himself, speaking his own name for the first time in Perumal's presence.[10]

We learn from Perumal's initial description that the beautiful swami was carrying a palm leaf fan. (Ramsuratkumar told another close devotee years later that he had received that fan from a swami, Sri Vasudevananda Saraswati, whom he had accompanied from northern India to Tiruvannamalai. Sri Vasudevananda had a large number of these fans with him, and had given one to his companion.) "Visiri swami," meaning "country hand fan swami" would become one of the affectionate titles bestowed on Yogi Ramsuratkumar by admirers in those early years. The palmyra fan, along with his coconut bowl, would figure prominently in many future lilas, and eventually become the symbols of this beggar's reign – outlined in lights over the main gate of his ashram, as well as inside the massive temple that would eventually be built in his honor.

The beggar also introduced Perumal to a deserted cottage that he had previously occupied for some time during this period. (Coincidentally, the cottage was located in an area not far from his future residence and ashram.) It was a dreadful house, infested with scorpions, snakes, and white ants that ate their way happily through Ramsuratkumar's treasured issues of *The Hindu* and *Indian Express* – newspapers that he read every day.

> The room itself was a strange artifact. It had a roof of coconut palm leaves. But they were so old, the palm fronds has dissolved into dust for [the] most part. Most of the roof was open to the terrible sun as well as rain. This run down, dilapidated and dangerous room frightened me. I held the bars of the window and turned around. Two black scorpions, with their stings upraised, had begun to crawl towards my hand. Seeing this, Yogi Ramsuratkumar, whom I had turned around to watch, urged me to move, saying "Hmm! Hmm!" and I snatched away my hand just in time.[11]

Sharing this bit of his personal history was rare for Ramsuratkumar, and Perumal preserved the story well. What it further points to, without much imagination, is that these and similarly dangerous conditions were not foreign to the Divine beggar's experience. As Perumal reflected, "Yet how patiently he bore with all." Dare we venture a step further in saying that the beggar deliberately chose the most dreadful circumstances in which to practice his sadhana on behalf of suffering humanity? Such a conclusion, it seems, is easily warranted.

Following another series of clues, we learn that in 1964, when he first met Perumal, the beggar was not a regular visitor to the area of the brass market, a place that would become one of his favorite haunts and sleeping places in years to come. Had he been walking that street of shops before then, since 1959, it is likely that Perumal and other local merchants would have remembered such a striking figure. Yet, Perumal speaks of Ramsuratkumar as someone he was laying eyes upon for the first time. Furthermore, in the first few days after their meeting, when the beggar began to spend more time at Perumal's shop, the laughter that poured from that tiny hut was enough to attract the attention of his fellow merchants. They soon approached Perumal, asking with great curiosity, "Who is this man?"

Two days after their first encounter, in fact, Perumal was summoned by the president of the merchant's association, who inquired: "The entire bazaar was amused by a sound of laughter from your shop which was like a roar of a king elephant. Everyone, who heard that laughter, is still laughing. Even those that are standing nearby are laughing. Who is the Swami who laughed such a laughter?"[12]

With simplicity and reverent insight, Perumal replied: "Sir, for the past two days a saint is seen moving around our bazaar. But I have not asked his name or the place he hails from. However I am certain that he is a man of great penance, that he is a good and great man. He is a man advanced in years, seems very learned, wise, a ripe fruit of wisdom."[13]

Before he encountered Perumal, Ramsuratkumar had obviously made numerous acquaintances among sadhus, renunciates, and "madmen" of the locale. "Such renunciates seem to gather in your shop and make merry," Mr. Chettier, the merchant association president, had laughingly remarked. And as Perumal and the ecstatic beggar moved around town, Ramsuratkumar recognized and was recognized by many others.

One semi-mysterious story tells of a Muslim, dressed in a green shawl and white cap, who stepped out of the shadows near an ancient tamarind tree on the western outskirts of the town. The Muslim had rushed forward with arms outstretched and was warmly embraced by

Yogi Ramsuratkumar. Both men laughed joyously, delighted in one another's company, but more delighted in the shared intoxication with the Divine that was generated in their meeting. As Perumal recounts in describing the meeting: "I too laughed. This laughter lasted for several minutes though none of us knew why we were laughing."[14] Interestingly, Perumal also notes that the Muslim addressed a question to the beggar in Urdu, and that Ramsuratkumar's response was more laughter. Urdu – the national language of Pakistan, consisting of many linguistic elements of Arabic, Persian and Sanskrit – was a language with which Ramsuratkumar was familiar. The fact that it was the language in which many great Indian poets and literary geniuses wrote their works may account for this, as Ramsuratkumar was well educated and widely read.

On the other side of town, near the small ashram Eesana Desika Math, an area frequented by Ramsuratkumar before 1964, the beggar would stop to visit the hut of another friend, identified only as a "Kerala Nair." The Nairs were a strong, warrior caste or subculture of Hindus with their own traditions and customs, based in the state of Kerala. In one story, when the Nair saw Ramsuratkumar approaching, he too rushed forward with great affection, offering him water to drink. The Nair acknowledged Perumal's great "good fortune" in being able to offer "fine service" to their mutual friend.

From Perumal too we learn of Yogi Ramsuratkumar's close friendship with a congressman, "a patriot" named Subhan Bhai. These two also carried on their discussions in Urdu, and one day, over a cup of tea, and in the midst of their gentle joking together, the beggar offered both Bhai and Perumal a profound teaching.

"I rest on the *payol* of my house in Moghulpura," the congressman remarked on this day. He was speaking of the widespread custom of sleeping outside on a house's covered verandah or porch in order to capture any breeze in this torrid climate.

Ramsuratkumar himself had, for years, slept out of doors, and the payols of the shops in the brass market itself were soon to become his favored sleeping places after dark.

"Perumal, the payol is the best place for men to rest," Ramsuratkumar indicated matter-of-factly. But then he added something that drove his meaning to a much deeper level. "This fine man, Subhan

Bhai, has built a palatial house. But in the end they will put him on the payol,"[15] the beggar said, with great tenderness in his voice, painting the image of a dead man wrapped in burial clothes, laid out on the verandah of his home, awaiting the pallbearers to his funeral.

Although these details are small ones, they point dynamically and once again to the universality of Ramsuratkumar's associations. Hindus, Muslims, penniless sadhus, wealthy merchants, Brahmins or Chandalas, all were held equally in the Godman's heart. These vignettes also indicate how graciously he was regarded by one who had the eyes to see, or one whose own heart was wounded enough to allow in such tender mercies as Ramsuratkumar offered.

Not everyone could receive him, however. As the unlikely pair were seen together more regularly, and especially as Perumal began to leave his shop unattended at odd hours of the day, the merchant was approached by the naysayers. Besides certain members of Perumal's own family, numerous business associates urged him to steer clear of this strange madman, "this crackly fellow…[who] wanders around Ramanashram."[16] Such warnings are understandable, although regrettable. The unpredictable behavior of the God-intoxicated person is bound to make waves, upsetting the established rules of commerce, as well as the often inflexible order of any longstanding institution.

When dislike and mistrust for the beggar's odd ways resulted in critical gossip, that was one thing. When that dislike erupted into violence and abuse, directly leveled against him, it was quite another matter. Sadly, this period of the mid-to-late 1960s was repeatedly marked by such more serious attacks.

राम

Humanity's ignorance of its true divine condition lies at the root of its self-imposed suffering, just as such ignorance motivates the imposition of pain and suffering upon others. To those who seek power in an attempt to deny their suffering, the innocence and simplicity of those who speak only truth is a terrifying threat. But so is any activity that tends to pry open an old wound. Why else would parents hurt their crying children, if not because of their own pain? Why else would once-amicable neighbors suddenly start killing each other when imaginary political lines are drawn between them? Fear fuels violence and abuse.

While we know that such violence has been done to the prophets and saints of all religious traditions, it is disturbing and surprising nonetheless to learn that Yogi Ramsuratkumar was the victim of numerous harassments, threats, and attacks. Perumal has supplied us with the details of many of these events.

One day, as they walked on the road leading westward outside of town, in a semi-deserted area where cattle fairs were held, Ramsuratkumar told Perumal of the trials he had suffered there. These reports were further confirmed by an observer who reported seeing the beggar at rest under one of the generous trees along this way, when several "miscreants" arrived on the scene. Grabbing the newspapers that Ramsuratkumar always kept on hand, the abusers would scatter them about. They would snatch his fan and throw that to the ground, tear away at his shawl and his blanket, all the while belligerently shouting at him in an attempt to drive him away. "Don't come here again," they would scream. "Get lost!"

When Perumal gallantly tried to assure Yogi Ramsuratkumar that he need not fear, telling him that a local friend would watch out for him in the future, the beggar was apparently neither assuaged nor convinced. While he never lost absolute faith in his Father's benevolence in all things, Ramsuratkumar was unquestionably affected by such attacks. "Only he who has suffered pain can understand fear," the beggar quietly told Perumal, reflecting wisdom honed by the razor of humanity's grief, which he had long observed and felt. "It is not possible to explain pain and fear to anyone [who has not gone through it]," Yogiji said.

Taunts and threats against the beggar escalated to beatings. (And later, incredibly, to stabbings and attempted murder.) As Perumal sat in his shop one day, a friend ran in breathlessly. "Sir! In the northern quarters near the Durgamma temple in the small bazaar two ruffians are beating up your Ram Ram Swami."[17]

Perumal jumped up and ran out without a moment's hesitation. As he neared the main entrance of the temple, he spotted two men, one a friend and the other "a sturdy watchman," who stood there. Perumal informed them of the reason for his haste, and the two fellows joined him in his northward aim. Nearing the small bazaar, they were confronted with a heartbreaking sight. A crowd had gathered to watch the curious drama. In the center of the spectators' circle stood Ramsuratkumar, bent against the furious blows of an attacker. His clothing was torn, and he was bruised and bleeding all over, yet he remained silent. His coconut bowl was still in his hand, but his shawl had been ripped away and his newspapers scattered, while insults and threats were screamed at him. Still, he made no reply.

When Perumal and his two companions pushed their way through the hypnotized crowd, the attacker spotted them, knew they meant business, and immediately fled. Perumal's friend, Guruswami, who had followed him from the temple, shouted passionately, "Don't let him escape. Catch the rogue," and ran after him. Only then did Yogi Ramsuratkumar raise his voice.

"No Sir! Don't catch him," implored the benign beggar. "Let this be for me alone."

Perumal was understandably shocked, and then angered, by what was obviously to him an act of injustice. He tried to explain that letting the man go would only encourage him to try such violence again.

"Let him come," responded the beggar. "We shall bear it. Let us do Father's work."

Only then did Perumal's tears flow.

Seeing his friend's disturbance, it was Ramsuratkumar who then assuaged and encouraged him. "Don't worry, Perumal," he said. "Father will look after everything. Let us do Father's work."[18]

Years later, as he reflected upon his reaction to this incident, Perumal wrote: "My mind had one thought then. *How does he bear all this to serve the world and protect the people?*"

It is the same question that has been asked of other Godmen and women throughout the ages, and Perumal certainly knew this. The chapter of his book in which he reports this particular story is appropriately titled "Crucifixion."

राम

Two days after he met Ramsuratkumar, Perumal heard the death knell to his own life as it was. He and the merchant association president were lightly conversing about the new sadhu and the other mendicants who had suddenly shown up in Perumal's shop. With unconscious precognition, the president good-naturedly remarked: "One day, you will also give up your trade and shop and become a mendicant yourself."

While he dismissed it as casual chatter at the time, Perumal was not able to shake the man's words that night as he lay sleepless. "I feared that the words of a good man would prove true,"[19] he admitted, as he tried to come up with excuses that would drive these renunciates from his shop. But, by the next morning, he found that his mind kept returning to the loving remembrance of "the elder" who had stepped so gracefully into his life. As he ate his breakfast and drank his coffee, his thoughts went out to the welfare of this blessed other. "Ah, did this elder find something to drink this morning?" he wondered.[20] Only when he arrived at his shop and found Yogi Ramsuratkumar pacing back and forth before the entry was he soothed in his concern.

The more time and attention he gave to and received from the gentle beggar, however, the less care Perumal took of his shop and his other worldly responsibilities. Together the two men wandered on the mountain, lingered for hours in the temple, ran here and there across the city, and sat up late in the night chatting, singing songs in praise of God, chanting the name of Ram. Many nights Perumal would not go home at all, choosing instead to sleep in the bazaar, on the front step of the shop, keeping the company of the Godman. The hard-packed soil of Perumal's soul was thus being turned over, oxygenated, exposed to the sun. Previous attachments and interests were quickly losing their lustre as Yogi Ramsuratkumar's smile over-shadowed everything. Perumal admits that the beggar's songs drowned out his memories of anything else.

Was this Ramsuratkumar's intention for his new devotee? The guru, it seems, has one purpose and one purpose only, which is to woo us from our attachment to self and plant us firmly in the soil of his heart. To do that, he, as the agent of the Divine, will enact whatever it takes. As his influence starts to tear away our long-held defenses, we

Yogi Ramsuratkumar (right) and Perumal

may find ourselves drowning in confusion, losing our grip on a once firm reality. When this happens, he may throw us a lifeline, or send in a lifeboat anchored to him. But how and when we finally start to pull ourselves in to his shore – that part is up to us.

Perumal's story is filled with examples that parallel those that most devotees have experienced; examples in which one has disregarded the master's words, choosing instead to follow one's own will, often with nearly disastrous consequences. That the beggar was concerned for all aspects of the young man's well-being is obvious. Besides feeding Perumal, and even reminding him that it was time to return to his shop, Ramsuratkumar by example and joyous invitation tried to steer him in the direction of a deeper trust and surrender. When the young merchant suffered upset from a disturbing dream – a dream that he interpreted as foreshadowing a life of poverty and hardship – the beggar urged him to dismiss it as nothing. "Such a situation will not come to pass. Don't worry," Ramsuratkumar assured. But, despite his master's faith, Perumal was adamant. "No, Swami," he declared, resolutely designing his own future path, "I am sure I am going to suffer a great deal."

To this, Yogi Ramsuratkumar could only laugh, compassionately, patting his friend on the back and consoling him. "Perumal! What you saw was just a dream. Don't worry about it," tenderly adding, "This Beggar is with Perumal."[21]

Besides reminders and assurances, the wise elder also gave more serious warnings and direct advice to his younger protégé. "No, Perumal. Do not go into partnership with that man," Yogi Ramsuratkumar had implored one day, having heard that Perumal intended to join forces with an associate and establish a new business in grain sales. "This business is not good for you."[22] But Perumal had already moved beyond the point of turning back. Without consulting his mentor, he sold most of his worldly goods, including his wife's jewelry, to raise the money for the venture. As Perumal and his new partner left town to enact their first major transaction, Perumal lay down in the cart so as not to be noticed by Yogi Ramsuratkumar as they passed the bus-stand, one of the beggar's familiar haunts. Only when he was convinced that he had not been spotted did Perumal chance to sit up again, climb out of the cart, and proceed to walk beside it.

Not a moment later, as if materialized from the ethers, Yogi Ramsurat-kumar came walking toward him, "glowing brilliantly," as Perumal remembered the event.

Despite the beggar's urgings to stop and turn away from this deal, Perumal argued: "I cannot let go of this." And years later, in detailing the incident, he wrote: "I could not accept what he said. The man who had entered into partnership with me was a man who held me in high regard. He was trustworthy. So I ignored Swami's words and left with him."[23]

The association turned out to be a travesty – a devious scheme on the other man's part, which ultimately left Perumal penniless. Ramsuratkumar, however, never abandoned even the most foolhardy of his devotees. Although his advice had been ignored, like a slap in the face of the Divine, the beggar's concern for Perumal was true. Hearing what had come to pass for his young friend, Yogi Ramsurat-kumar wept.

"Do not worry, Perumal!" the beggar spoke comfortingly as he stroked Perumal's arm with his left hand.

"His soft words and loving touch had the power to revive me," Perumal wrote. "They could give life to a dying man."[24]

राम

Perumal's formal life of service to Yogi Ramsuratkumar began in the humblest manner. With a simple request, the beggar showed up one morning at Perumal's shop. In his hands, and grasped close to his chest, the swami held a small bundle consisting of some newspapers, a book and a new *dhoti* (item of clothing). "Perumal! Hold this. Put them inside the shop," Yogi Ramsuratkumar said as he handed over the bundle.[25] How could Perumal, or anyone, have known the significance of this tiny gesture? And yet, what transpired in that moment was an act that would have profound implications for both men. It was, in fact, another aspect of Perumal's initiation. Herein, although he did not know it, Perumal was being given a sacred trust disguised as a seemingly mundane task. This trust – as guardian of the master's treasury of discarded rags, newspapers, letters, and various things that were later to prove of utmost significance – was to be his lifelong sadhana. He had no idea! (Little do any of us know in what way our lives will ultimately serve something larger than we are, something far beyond anything we may have aimed for.) Yet, around Yogi Ramsuratkumar, every gesture and every word was significant. Nothing was casual. Nothing was wasted.

Before he could be knighted in his role, however, Perumal had to be tried and tested. Unfortunately, yet predictably, he had to learn his most sublime responsibility by first seeing clearly how irresponsible he was. And so, with an air of confidence bordering on arrogance, Perumal took that small bundle from the master's hands and placed it in a corner of his shop, covering it with a piece of gunny sack.

Weeks later, Ramsuratkumar again arrived at the merchant's door with more newspaper. "Let us put these along with the old bundle," he instructed Perumal, who noted that his concern for these items was understated, but obvious. Because his shop was full of many things, of which he took great care, Perumal had assured his older friend that this little pile of newspapers would not be damaged.

At last the day of reckoning arrived when, unexpectedly, the master asked to see the entrusted bundles. Upon lifting the wooden seat under which the beggar's things had been stored, Perumal gasped in horror. The newspapers had been attacked by crazy white ants, and so well eaten that not one sheet could be lifted without crumbling in Perumal's hands.

Full of fear and shame, Perumal looked at his master, who was examining the whole scene with intensity. Before Perumal could say a word of apology, however, Ramsuratkumar immediately directed him to examine the shop's account books, which were stored adjacent to the pile of newspapers that was now "ant food." To his complete amazement, Perumal found that not one page of the account ledgers had been touched by the insects. "Everything happens by Father's will," Ramsuratkumar would conclude that day.[26] All things had worked together unto good. Yet, a sadder but wiser Perumal remained. He had been instructed in a lesson that many would see enacted around Yogi Ramsuratkumar in the years to come. Namely, that the master will constantly sacrifice himself (in the form of anything from his newspapers to his life) to bring about the disciple's awakening from arrogance and self-obsession.

राम

"Swami, I wish to go to Kasi," Perumal moaned, lamenting the unraveling that was occuring in his once-secure life. These words had become a mantra of sorts for Perumal, spoken more and more now as his business interests waned, his finances drained, and his spirits depressed.

Ah, to pilgrimage to "Kasi" – Kashi…Benares…Varanasi, the city of many names! Or, better perhaps, to die in Kashi! – the ultimate fantasy of escape. To die in Kashi was considered the greatest boon for a devout Hindu: *Kashyam marannam muktih* – "Death in Kashi is Liberation." Whereas death anywhere else was to be feared, here it was welcomed. Kashi was forbidden territory to Yama, the terrifying Lord of Death. To have one's remains cast into the Mother of Waters, Ganga, assured salvation.

Ramuratkumar knew all about such dreams of salvation. Having been born near Kashi, he would have known of the endless streams of ardent pilgrims who approached these sacred precincts year after year. In visiting the city as a young man of sixteen, and perhaps many times earlier, he had probably bathed numerous times in the Ganges' waters, and would have known its transcendent powers to heal both body and soul. He would have seen, "leaning against the walls of the shops on Lanka Street, stacks of bamboo litters for carrying the dead."[27] He would have heard the unmistakable "chant of a funeral procession on its way to Manikarnika [the great burning ghat]: *'Rama nama satya hai! Rama nama satya hai!'* 'God's name is Truth! God's name is Truth!'"[28] He would have met the Kashivesa, those who come from all over India to live in Kashi until they die.

Nonetheless, every time Perumal invoked this urgent request, his cry for liberation, Ramsuratkumar gently directed him otherwise. "Not now, Perumal. This beggar is here now."[29]

The Godman Jesus had said a similar thing. When a love-drunk woman devotee used precious oils to bathe her master's feet, some of Jesus's disciples criticized the extravagance. This oil, they argued, could have been sold for a lot, and the money used to feed many poor people. Of course they were right. But the master Jesus pointed to a higher principle in saying: "The poor you will always have with you. Me, you will not always have with you." (John 12:8)

One day, many years later, when Yogi Ramsuratkumar's "eternal slave" Devaki Ma expressed her desire to join the thousands of pilgrims who were making pradakshina of Mount Arunachala, the beggar's response was much the same for her as it had been for Perumal. He told her that she didn't need to do it. He told her that circumambulating the ashram property, a trip that took fifteen minutes at most, was equivalent in the blessings gained by circling the mountain. At another time, he told her to simply walk around his chair, three times. Which she did.

Such guidance about the genuine nature of things is always being given around such exalted ones as Jesus and Ramsuratkumar. Yet, the human tendency still persists to look elsewhere for the "pearl of great price" that glows in our midst, the source of light within our own hearts.

Eventually, Perumal gave up his fantasy of going somewhere else and surrendered to his fate, his place, beside the Lord of Kashi himself. But when he first began voicing this request, such surrender was the last thing in Perumal's mind. Quite the contrary, one day, despite his master's words, he planned to escape from Tiruvannamalai. His "escape" would be to Madras at the invitation of a friend who had urged him to leave his familiar surroundings in order to get his life together again. His relatives, including his wife, were in agreement that the move would be a good one. Also, Madras was one step closer to Kashi.

As he had done before, Perumal tried to hide his actions, knowing predictably that the master's concern would discourage him. So, on this day, as he came closer to the bus-stand, he made his way furtively along the walls of the shops, hiding behind cars and lorries. Little did he know, however, that Ramsuratkumar had witnessed the whole ridiculous act. The beggar had been seated between the huts of two flower sellers in such a position that he could see all the way up the street. Yet, to one approaching, he remained out of sight.

When he was still about 150 yards from the Madras bus, Perumal noticed to his dismay that it was about to pull away. With all the speed he could muster, the young man charged ahead. He was determined to catch that bus, no matter what might get in his way! Or so he thought. Just as he approached the flower stalls, however, Ramsuratkumar leaped forward and lovingly called his name, "Perumal!" and the race was over.

"Where are you going in such speed?" Ramsuratkumar asked innocently, as if he knew nothing.[30] But Perumal was too winded to speak. Looking into the beggar's face, he could no longer contain the tears that had been burning behind his eyes for too many days, too many lifetimes perhaps. Yogi Ramsuratkumar then lovingly took his hands and put his arm around Perumal's shoulder, as the two men stood like star-crossed lovers in the middle of the street. By the time the beggar asked him again about what had happened, Perumal had seen the archetypal humor in the situation – how we try to deceive ourselves, fleeing from the very source of our life! Laughing now, Perumal reported what was already a thing of the past: "Swami, I am leaving for Madras! I planned not to see you or tell you about it. That is why I was running." And, in the midst of his laughter, the tears flowed.

Yogi Ramsuratkumar slapped Perumal's palms and placed his hand upon the young man's head in a gesture of blessing. Again slapping Perumal's left shoulder, the beggar pronounced his sentence: "Perumal! Henceforth we shall stay with this beggar. We shall trust this beggar and believe in him. We need not leave Tiruvannamalai and go anywhere. This beggar and Perumal shall stay here."[31]

"Yes! Swami," said Perumal as he prostrated to the Godman's feet. "I shall do so. Henceforth I shall stay with you."[32]

राम

Perumal did as he promised. For the rest of his life he stayed in the service of Yogi Ramsuratkumar. He carried his bundles, he attended his needs, he spent days and nights guarding the precious One who had taken everything from him, and given everything back. When Yogi Ramsuratkumar moved from the house near the temple in the 1990s to the environment of the ashram on the west end of town, Perumal stayed at his post, guarding the master's gunny bags that were piled up within the *mandapam* (covered area) across the street from the beggar's Sannadhi Street residence.

When Lee Lozowick and his students made their first contact with the beggar, Perumal was there. In 1997, prior to the publication of Perumal's book, Lee composed a tribute to the man who had served their master so well:

> When I first came to Yogi Ramsuratkumar in 1976, I was most deeply touched by the extraordinary service I witnessed on the part of Perumal. I again visited in 1979 and 1986 and each time my faith in the possibility for one as selfish as I to serve [F]ather, Yogi Ramsuratkumar, was graced through a deepening friendship with Perumal.
>
> Yogi Ramsuratkumar's eternal blessings go to Perumal. It is always a thrill to see how Perumal guards Yogi Ramsuratkumar's bags of sacred Treasure and to see the love and surrender in Perumal's eyes.
>
> Happiness, health, and above all, to be the beloved devotee of God in human form, Yogi Ramsuratkumar, are Perumal's. I pranam at his feet. (2-12-97)[33]

THE GODCHILD OF TIRUVANNAMALAI

 The 1960s and 1970s were a time for exploration into the spirituality of the East, and squadrons of Westerners made their way to the subcontinent of India in order to find a teacher, a guru, or some exotic way to "turn on, tune in and drop out." A few seekers had experiences that genuinely changed their lives. Irina Tweddie, a Russian-born British woman, had traveled to India to visit the Theosophical Society in an attempt to heal the grief of her husband's death. Unexpectedly diverted, she met her guru, whom she referred to as Bhai Sahib, in 1961, and after his death, she carried his Sufi teachings back to London and the West. From the U.S., Albert Rudolph, born and raised in Brooklyn, New York, journeyed to the East, where he first met Swami Nityananda in 1958. Rudolph was recognized by Nityananda's successor, Swami Muktananda, and renamed "Swami Rudrananda" (commonly known as Rudi) in 1966. Returning to the U.S., Rudi's antique shop in New York City became a popular meeting place for hundreds of hungry Western souls, and soon kundalini yoga was being taught to thousands. For so many others, traveling through India was an interesting diversion, an alternative lifestyle, a fascinating way to grapple with the growing sense of meaninglessness engendered by the isolated and impersonal cultures in the West.

The Beatles had first met Maharishi Mahesh Yogi in 1967 and then visited him in India in 1968. Their short-lived affiliation helped to make "Transcendental Meditation" a household word and a cultural phenomenon. Richard Alpert, Harvard University professor and friend of drug-guru Timothy Leary, left the States in 1968 and traveled to India to find another type of guru, Neem Karoli Baba. This passage eventually received widespread publicity, as Ram Dass (Alpert's new spiritual name) wrote of his sojourn in his now classic, *Be Here Now*. Thousands of readers found it to be their handbook for the quest, and it encouraged countless Westerners to turn to the East.

राम

It was 1969, and nineteen-year-old Truman Caylor Wadlington had just dropped out of college in his sophomore year at the University of Indiana. The Vietnam War was at its peak, and he was "not doing well." Introduced to psychedelic drugs, like so many of his contemporaries in the 1960s and '70s, Caylor underwent "amazing, truly cosmic inner experiences," which were surprising to him since, as he put it, "I was a very unspiritual person. I didn't know spirituality apart from religion."[1] These openings, however, served to initiate his quest for another level of understanding, leading him first to a Sufi group and then to a yoga class, and within a short time he was "living with a small handful of people who were diving deep in search of God." Among those housemates were Will and Joan Zulkowski, who would play a major role in supporting Caylor's pilgrimage to India and his work with Yogi Ramsuratkumar.

"One person in our house was in his late twenties. He had just come back from India, where he had been in Tiruvannamalai," Caylor explained. The stories that this seeker told awakened a longing in other members of the group to make a similar pilgrimage of self-discovery. One by one, the original circle of friends disbanded, leaving Indiana with the intention to travel through India and rendezvous at the site of the sacred mountain, Arunanchala, in Tiruvannamalai, and the location of the ashram of the widely renowned saint, Ramana Maharshi.

"My friend gave me one contact name, that of Maurice Friedman, an old man in his seventies who had known Ramana Maharshi personally. Friedman had lived in India for most of his adult life. He had been an engineer in the 1930s and '40s, and had

177

retired there and dedicated himself to the spiritual quest." It was Friedman who transcribed the tapes of yet another famous saint, Nisaragadatta Maharaj, and had compiled them into a now classic book, *I Am That*, which was published in the late 1970s. Caylor met Friedman in Madras in the spring (April or May) of 1970, spent a day of orientation under his care, and then, with the older man's assistance, found himself aboard a train bound for Tiruvannamalai. "And I was determined, with all-American zeal," Caylor reported with a laugh, "to meditate my brains out, until I was enlightened." It was this zeal that furthered the course of events and resulted in his desperate need for help – a need that would lead him, fortuitously, to the feet of "this beggar."

"Even before I went to India, I started to have pulsing, throbbing energy moving in my head, right on the front of my head, at the third eye," Wadlington noted. "It became painful, like my head was in a vise; not like a headache, that you could take something for. So, I had decreased my meditation time back at home. But, diving back into meditation in India, within a few days the pressure was returning. Whenever I was relaxed or focused it would also come with a vengeance.

"I started getting desperate, and went to some of the senior disciples of Ramana, who were teachers in their own right at this time. They all said I was meditating wrongly, and should do this or that. But there was one Swedish woman, Gilda, who told me of having been to see a yogi who had answered for her the questions and family problems that she had come to India to try to solve. She said he was exceptionally kind, that he wandered about the town, and often feigned madness. But, in fact, according to her, he was very powerful and certainly aware of the highest truth. This yogi had met Gilda and another woman, Aruna, a long-time resident of the city, as if by chance, outside the Ramana Ashram. On the day prior to her departure from Ramana Ashram, Gilda had been with Aruna, a French woman residing outside the compound, and together they had been walking in the village behind the Temple when suddenly Aruna looked up to see this dirty beggar man with a stack of newspapers balanced on his head, clad with a dirty and torn green blanket wrapped about his shoulders and a peculiar stick and a small black pot as well. She became very excited at having seen him and rushed to greet this beggar without question. Gilda assured me that at the first glance of this man she knew him to be a Holy One.

"Hearing this I remember thinking to myself, *A yogi, wow!* and I was enamored by the general impression I got of him. I met Aruna at Mr. Osbourne's funeral [Arthur Osbourne, who had been an early disciple of Ramana's] and asked her to introduce me to the yogi, but she said no. 'That's not the way it goes,' she instructed. 'If you are meant to meet him, you will.' I urged her that if she ever saw him again to tell him about my problem and that I would really like to meet him.

"Amazingly, Aruna did meet him [the beggar] the very next day, and hearing my story he asked her to send me at sunset of the following day to the [Arunachaleswarar] Temple entrance. I was beside myself. So much distress in my body!" Caylor reported, his voice still relaying the urgency of an event that had occurred over thirty years ago. "For the next day I just paced, since distraction or movement was the only thing that helped the pain.

"I went early to the assigned spot. It was still hot; it must have been half an hour or maybe a full hour before sunset. (It was on June 23, 1970.) I entered the temple and sat off to the side. Within twenty minutes *he* came in through the temple entrance with his staff in his hand – the one with lots of little twigs attached to it – and he was surrounded by bunches of little kids pulling at his clothes and laughing, laughing; himself and the children, all laughing. It was quite a sight. Such a colorful sight, because he used to wear bright colors, and he had a long, white beard, and long black hair, not quite to his shoulder. But his face was young and radiant, with clear and pure eyes. These children were quite a ragtag bunch, with all sorts of little energy sparks about them. He smiled like a child when he saw us. Seeing him in this way I just knew I was going to be okay. From then on he was to me an eternal friend, father, brother."

That first sighting was revelatory for Caylor. He wrote of it: "He gave me a looking through, to the very core of my being. Without question, this new friend must have learned everything of my past, present and future. For perhaps five minutes, without interruption, his gaze opened me in order that he could enter my very being."

Continuing his narration of these initial events, Caylor went on: "We talked for a while, got to know each other, and he asked me about my problem. I told him a little, but he soon said not to talk anymore, and that we would deal with it later. When sunset came we moved to a secluded area, with a few of the children along. It became dark and we still continued to talk, not about spiritual things, mostly about family, politics, general topics. It was not intended to be a probing discussion, but simply an occupying of some time – a time for him to get to know me. The topics themselves really had *nothing* to do with getting to know me, but it was just the chance for him to be sitting there, looking at me. He would ask a question and have me talk, and then he'd be smoking, and like a huge energy furnace he'd just go into some internal space and explore, examine or work, or help, or…something." Caylor was reliving the moments as he spoke to me, and I could feel a resonance with the power of the saint's influence as it had penetrated my own being the first time.

"He asked me if I had been initiated by any masters. He also had me talking about UFOs, because the stars were so bright, and about other things that interested me. Maybe about eleven or twelve o'clock, which is really late in India, he got me up and we walked back out of the temple to a little soapstone-sculpture shop [known as Ramaswami's shop] – it was in the row of shops in front of the temple. It was closed, but there was a friend of his in the back with a candle who let us use his space. Yogi Ramsuratkumar took a folding chair out from the shop and sat me out into the street, about twenty feet from him. He was on the shop floor, on a step about two feet off the ground. He just sat there, smoking, in the pitch dark; hardly a light in the area. He began to focus on me. It is possible that he said, 'Don't think about anything. You don't have to meditate or pray about anything, just sit there for a moment.' Then he would smoke, almost feverishly for a few seconds, and then seemingly go inward, dropping his hand to his lap. Again he would look at me in a focused way, a piercing way, for a few minutes, and then take a couple more drags on his cigarette, and then go inward. Then come back 'out,' and focus on me…It must have been less than ten minutes.

"Suddenly he got up and walked to me, and he put his hand on my head, very casually, not in any determined fashion, and he said:

'This is going to come back in two weeks. At that time, you can come back and see this beggar.'"

राम

Yogi Ramsuratkumar's ability to see beyond appearances and to affect the physical, emotional, and spiritual states of his visitors is unquestioned by those who knew him. Shri V. Ramanujachari, a trusted devotee who spent considerable time with the beggar in these early years, shared his educated insight into the beggar's skill in these domains.

"Swami was very particular that he should be called Yogi," the Indian man explained. "When I once started the conversation by saying 'Swami Ramji,' he immediately corrected me authoritatively – 'Yogi Ramsurat Kumar.' He *is* a yogi. It was not always patent what yogic practices he has practiced earlier, although one was certain that he was an adept at *samyama* in the classic methodology of Patanjali. [*Samyama* is constraint brought about by the combination of concentration, meditation, and ecstasy. It is focused upon one internalized object.] Sometimes he would sit cross-legged, his right arm at his chest level, with fingers giving an impression that he was counting the beads of a japa mala, with his lips silently intoning a mantra. I got the feeling that simultaneously he was drawing the breath, *prana*, from *muladhara* [the root chakra] step by step upwards. There used to be a purposive concentration on the person before him, as if he was working a transformation within the visitor."[2]

राम

"That was it," reported Caylor of his first experience under the beggar's eye. "I was just in seventh heaven. I knew my prayers had been answered, since I'd been praying for that kind of help for such a long time. For a full week or ten days I had no problems, no head pressure. But then it came back, and so intensively that I was again beside myself. And since I had walked away from our first encounter so happily and feeling so safe, I hadn't even thought to ask him *where* I could meet him again.

ONLY GOD

"The day that the pain came back I spent over an hour walking around the samadhi of Ramana Maharshi, praying that he (Ramana) would help me to find Yogi Ramsuratkumar. I knew this had to work. I kept thinking, 'At the main intersection, in front of the temple, at that little shop where we had been a week or so before. I'll meet you there,' and I thought of a particular time that I would meet him.

"But, as the time drew near when I had prayed to meet him, I couldn't relax or focus, so I left early to go to town, and by the time I got there the sky was black. It was going to storm, which it did, quickly thereafter, raining cats and dogs. All the shopkeepers had bundled up their wares and were seeking shelter under the temple mandapam [a covered area with open sides, supported by pillars], which is where this little shop was that I had designated. There were crowds of people, and I had to push my way through the crowd to get to this shop, and then pull back to a place where I could see the whole street, and look for his staff...look for his little entourage of people. Every now and then I would run out into the rain, into the intersection, because I knew that was the only place where someone else could see *me*, because it was so crowded and dense under the mandapam. I would look around and present myself for him to see me, if he was there.

"A long time passed. Maybe I did this for about an hour, and I was getting desperate. I ran out into the street in sort of a frantic fashion. I turned one way and looked; then turned another way and looked. I really was upset. Then I turned around quickly to run out of the rain...and ran right into his chest! He was standing two inches behind me. He bounced off me and I bounced off him. He stood back with his staff raised, and his group of friends behind him, and looking surprised said, 'Mr. Kay, what are you doing here?'

"My heart melted. My whole being relaxed in utter relief, and I said, 'Ohhh, Swami,' and I gave him a big hug. I embraced him. It was like being saved, or something.

"He said, 'Come on, let's go. Let's go have some tea.'

"He took me to a little shop down the road that was owned by a Hindi gentleman. And since Yogi Ramsuratkumar was from North India he had occasionally found some companionship, or some

182

friendship, and shared some common cultural affinities there. That shop was open for a while, so we sat and he again started to talk to me...once it was about cowboys and Indians – anything to keep me talking and to have me engaged with something, and not focused on my problem. It was a chance for him to just see me on another level, while he smoked and focused and looked at me and laughed and talked.

"When the shop was closed and the old man was cleaning up, Yogi Ramsuratkumar again had me sit away from him, five or six feet this time, and he again did this thing where he really focused on this energy problem in my head. This went on for maybe fifteen minutes. Then, he took me by the hand and walked me down the street to a restaurant and fed me, and then sent me back to Ramana Ashram where I was staying.

"That was the last time I ever had that pain." Caylor smiled, thoughtfully, remembering. This healing, he noted later, contained a strong teaching for him: "He recommended that I simply relax and reduce my meditation. To some extent I did loosen myself up; however, the source of the problem lay in my entire approach to spirituality. That is to say, spirituality, to me, had become entirely divorced from living. So long as I was not absorbed in 'meditation,' then so long was I apart from spiritual sadhana. It was a dangerous and fatal misconception.

"We became tight friends after that," Caylor explained. "I used to hunt all over town for him. Every few days, or a week later, I'd go into town and I'd search till I found him. I'd get clues from shopkeepers, and ask for 'Ram Ram Swami,' which is what the children called him. I didn't know at that time that his name was Yogi Ramsuratkumar. Sometimes I'd find him, and sometimes I'd spend a long time and not find him. But, within a month, I knew all of his major haunts, and I had become a little bit a part of his entourage by then. He would have me walk with him out into the country; we'd spend all day together. Or we'd walk up onto the mountain. And at some point he'd send me away. But it wasn't long before I was spending three or four days a week just tagging along.

"We just were pals. I told him that my siblings all called me 'Kay-Kay' and after that he called me 'Mr. Kay,' and later he called me 'Dr.

Kay.' Names were very important to him. He could tune into some-one by the name.

"Actually, Yogi Ramsuratkumar was much more like my mother than he was like a teacher or a guru. He would always just welcome me, hold my hand, have me talk about my family. He'd feed me, or have me run out and get tea or *tiffin* [a plate or container for food] for everybody. So, I was a part of this little group for about six months or so. Then he sent me to Madras to the Theosophical Society.

"Every few months I'd make a trip down to see him. I'd write him letters, to which he'd reply with one or two sentences indicating that he'd received my letter, that he was happy that I was doing well, and that I should continue reading the *Secret Doctrine* of the Theo-sophical Society [the headquarters are located in Madras]. He really wanted me to get some special kind of education. Then he would include that I should come to Tiruvannamalai on such and such date and he would meet me.

"During those days I would spend the whole day with him, out in the countryside, near the railroad tracks; and I'd sleep with him and his group in the bazaar near the temple at night. He didn't want me to meditate. *He wanted me to be around him.* He said that medi-tation was not important, but that finding a great teacher and serv-ing that great teacher had been his way, and it was the best way, *The Way*. How we come to God is a mystery, and the guru can do this.

"I had the opportunity over the years to hear him speak to all people at all levels, and I had the opportunity to sit with him when he was visited by other yogis, priests, mothers and their kids, pil-grims. He never encouraged people to meditate, but if some other teacher had given people a path, he would always boost their opti-mism about *that* way: 'Ohhh, Swami such-and-such, he is so great. He is so inspired by God. You follow every word he says.' Yogi Ramsuratkumar would always try to bind that person to his guru ever more closely.

"But when people came to him for guidance, meditation wasn't something he encouraged. He would often encourage people to do bhajans, to sing. Or to go to the temple every day to do *pujas*, those kinds of things. Most often, the real emphasis would be to serve one's teacher. That was the great path for him!

"So, I always hoped that I could be a true disciple to him, and serve him. But he would never let me stay with him and serve him in that way. He didn't let anyone do that except for Perumal – he was a truly spiritual man. Yogi Ramsuratkumar occupied *all* of his time. Perumal had very little time even for his own children or his family concerns. He was the one person that Yogi Ramsuratkumar allowed to give *everything* to him – every ounce of energy that Perumal had, every ounce of care, Yogi Ramsuratkumar accepted that from him, and set it up for Perumal to be that servant person. Very much the relationship of Hanuman to Rama."

राम

While Caylor could not be Hanuman to Ram in the way that Perumal was, he was given other tasks of importance. From his first meeting in June until he left for his tenure at the Theosophical Society at the end of 1970, Caylor spent most days and many nights with his newly found and much beloved "teacher." They ate many meals together. They wandered the holy hill. They talked for count-less hours. The teachings were given as a part of every day's activities.

In August 1970, as they sat together in Ramaswami's stone-carv-ing shop, Yogi Ramsuratkumar spoke about his love for a particular stone Nandi, the bull of Siva. In simple and nonesoteric terms, the master explained the role of this deity to his young Western disciple. The beggar also revealed an interesting agreement that he had with the shop owner. Basically, at Ramsuratkumar's prompting, Ram-swami had consented to display the object for a period of thirty days, but not to sell it. At some point within this time, the beggar would then bring a sum of not less than twenty-five rupees with which to purchase the piece.

Yogi Ramsuratkumar would visit the shop regularly during this allotted period "to sit and gaze at his lovely little pet. He honestly loved it, in his own way. So for quite some time he would sit at the shop to infuse part of his self within the beloved little friend."

Asking the shop owner to remove the artifact from the shelf, Yogiji placed it lovingly in Caylor's hands, and asked him to hold it for a while. Feeling at first honored, but quickly insecure about how best to treat the object, and completely unaccustomed to how to "love the small thing," Caylor's attention wandered. At this moment, Ramsuratkumar gently took the little bull, and placed it in his own lap. Caylor's journal records what happened next, and lends additional insight into the many ways in which the Godman worked with those close to him.

It was then that the Yogi began to express verbally his love for the Temple image. [There were several large and small Nandis in the great Siva Temple that was Ramsuratkumar's "home."] His emotions were authentic and his movements so childlike that I began to accept the pet as truly something special. I understood further that what he did so often to flowers and other objects had been done in a special manner and in an intensely careful way to this carved image so endeared and loved by its spiritual "father" [meaning Ramsuratkumar].

Yogi Ramsuratkumar asked me if I would like to have it to keep in my room. He explained that he would lose this friend if he did not give it to someone he cared for. He thought I could love the thing as he had loved him.

I was to receive it, look at it often, and love it with all my heart. I did so first because it was advised by my teacher. It was at the same time a treasured opportunity for furthering my inner development and a difficult and not well understood task to fulfill through the determination and awful respect for this beggar man whom I understood well enough was a Kosmic Man [using words applied by Sri Aurobindo].

I parted my company that morning without carrying with me Nandi-Shiva. As I hadn't enough rupees in my purse to pay for the piece, I left him behind and promised to return the next morning to receive the little one at the exchange of 25 Rps.

I always, even from the beginning, considered the figure not as a purchased item but a *gift* in the most true and almost holy sense of the word. Where was there money and riches enough to pay for one's own spiritual development! I was made to understand that Nandi was going to be good for me and was to accompany me as a spiritual companion for a good long time.

I was instructed: Never to disfigure the stone image in anyway. To keep him with me whenever I travel or wherever I lived, and to keep him for however so long a time as is necessary. Yogi Ramsuratkumar added that someday I would be told when Nandi was no longer needed.

Never to expose him to the eyes of anyone but those who are my friends. In any cases other than that, he should be covered with cloth or in some other way shielded well.

I should try to love Nandi, for his true master, Yogi Ramsuratkumar, was unable to watch over him and care for him. I had been entrusted with the image so that it shall be with one who loves the master as well as the art carving.

It has occurred to me on more than a few occasions that this "small one" is my link with my beloved teacher and friend. Often I was told that Nandi was to serve as a meditation for me – all that need be done is look at him and remember too his benefactor.

The next day, Caylor returned to the shop and received the Nandi for twenty-rive rupees.

Months later, in that same year, when the master and the young disciple discussed many topics of interest to both of them, Caylor asked: "Shiva rides on the back of Nandi Shiva. The Buddhists also are pictured riding on the back of a bull, aren't they?"

To this Yogi Ramsuratkumar replied, "I don't know. Do you think I will ever get to ride on the bull? Sometimes I feel like He has been riding on this body."

Then, peeking out of the corner of his eye, he seemed to know that Caylor's thoughts had been instantly stopped by what he had just said. Yogi Ramsuratkumar took the young man's hand and burst out in laughter.

राम

Before moving to Adyar, the headquarters of the Theosophical Society located in Madras, Caylor was present for the beggar's birthday, December 1, 1970, and his journal leaves us a description of the ordinary and the extraordinary aspects of any day in the master's life during this period.

As had happened on so many occasions, on his way to town to purchase roses for "Swami" – as he referred to Yogi Ramsuratkumar – Caylor was surprised and delighted to find that the beggar had anticipated his arrival and was waiting at the side of a tea stall. While Caylor intended to gift his master with roses, Yogi Ramsuratkumar turned the tables. Leaving the young man's side for a few minutes, the beggar returned with a string of fresh marigolds. "He tied the two loose ends together making it into a necklace: he took those flowers and reverently placed them around my neck," Caylor wrote, feeling in this act a type of initiation, in which the master was performing a sort of mystical ritual that he, Caylor, was ignorant of. Such gestures of surprising generosity and tenderness have been reported throughout the years by those who have met Ramsuratkumar and spent time with him. To read of this lovely moment in 1970 indicates that such generosity and caring have always been Yogi Ramsuratkumar's hallmarks. Probably these activities were full of much more significance. But few who received them could say what that meaning was at the time.

When they shared tea, Yogi Ramsuratkumar spoke of many things. What Caylor most strongly remembered came in the form of gentle instruction, and perhaps warning of what the future might hold for one who approached a master closely: "There are saints, Mr. Kay, who will throw stones at those people who come near them. But whoever is hit with those stones is blessed by them."

The birthday "party" had been arranged for three in the afternoon at the deserted temple – Sri Pacchai Amman – at the base of Arunachala on the north slope. With another Westerner, Robert Lee, who had just met Yogi Ramsuratkumar, Caylor walked to town to buy more flowers, cake, and cigarettes for the beggar. When the two men arrived at the temple about three, they met Aruna, and about twenty minutes later were joined by George, a devotee and guardian to Yogi Ramsuratkumar, as Caylor described him. "George was a

Christian convert, very poor, but he was a truly wonderful person and of a fine character. Swami and George help one another as best they can." George had been sent by Yogi Ramsuratkumar to escort the group up to the place that he had chosen as being more secluded, and thus more appropriate for the occasion.

George stepped to attention when a drunken man threatened to disrupt the harmony of the gathering. The fellow was delirious, in fact, and George's service to the master expressed itself in carrying the man down the rocky slope to the roadway – a distance of almost a third of a mile. "When he [George] finally returned," Caylor reported, "everyone was somewhat surprised to see that he had brought with him about eight or nine of his family and relatives." The party had grown to a group of thirteen.

Caylor remarked that Yogi Ramsuratkumar "was not in such a joyous mood. He was obviously absorbed in the 'work' that he was doing on us." It is entirely possible that the beggar's "mood" was brought on by his need to bear the burdens of expectation and nostalgic association that his Western guests had about the "birthday party." Whether he was suffering the effects of such a situation or not, Ramsuratkumar's "childlike manner, innocence, and beautiful smile prevailed over everyone," Caylor wrote.

It is interesting to note that one of the guests invited by Yogi Ramsuratkumar was the head officer of the Tiruvannamalai railway station. This man, Caylor notes, was "a very good friend of his [Yogi Ramsuratkumar's]." How telling, that the beggar who lived in the fields and under the trees and spent much time around the railway station had attracted the devotion and respect of an official.

Tea was made and oranges and other fruits were peeled and passed around, and then it was time to enact the ritual of the birthday cake. When the procedure and the "significance" of the blowing out of the birthday candles had been dutifully explained to the guest of honor, Yogi Ramsuratkumar obliged with the most elegant simplicity. He "made a wish" and blew out the candles! "I love my friend," Caylor wrote, in describing this moment. We can surmise that whatever mood had previously prevailed had been redeemed by the master's willingness to accommodate the wishes of his hosts.

Caylor wrote that throughout this whole rigmarole, for the full three-and-a-half hours of their time together, "Yogi Ramsuratkumar sat in the direct glare of the sun's searing rays. His forehead was perspiring heavily. But even at the repeated suggestion of a number of us he persisted to remain in the sunlight while the others sat in the shade from the giant boulders and overhanging rocks." It was Caylor's view at the time that the spiritual master was directing his transformative energies at those who gathered with him. "Perhaps others as well as myself could feel tangibly within their heads the effects of the spiritual currents he was driving forcefully towards us all. Much of the passing hours were spent observing quietly that great spiritual Master labour selflessly for our benefit."

For an hour or more following the cake ritual, Subramania, another of the men who served as a friend and guardian of the "child-like beggarman," kept up his singing of Tamil spiritual songs. "He is not really such a fine singer, but his devotion and attitude were gracious," Caylor noted. When Subramania was finished, the group lapsed into a sweet silence. With his unfailing sense of cosmic humor, the master, who had long ago realized the death of every desire at the feet of his master, Ramdas, said, "It has always been the desire of this beggar to celebrate his birthday. Today that final desire has been fulfilled. It is written in the Hindu philosophy that when all the desires are washed away – when one has become desireless – that person is freed from the wheel of rebirth. When one is desireless, he will be reborn no more into this world. This beggar's last desire has been fulfilled." Even the rocks must have chuckled at this point.

"Swami," Caylor responded, maintaining the mood of joyful gratitude and playful camaraderie, "this world has suffered a great loss today."

At this Yogi Ramsuratkumar slapped his hands on his knees as he broke into a fit of rollicking laughter. "It was a sight to behold – his laughter is so so beautiful and free," Caylor wrote.

A little later in the afternoon, the beggar quietly asked Caylor if he had any spare money. Three rupees were immediately presented. Seeing this, Robert also gave some money. It was all well and good. But when Yogi Ramsuratkumar made the request a second time, and Caylor produced another five rupees, and when the beggar distributed all the funds to George's family and to Subramania, Robert became exceedingly uncomfortable. "This emphasis on money and its distribution shook Robert's confidence and faith in Yogi Ramsuratkumar. Robert was obviously disturbed about having been asked by a 'so-called saint' for money," Caylor noted. "I wasn't too surprised at this behavior, for Robert had made some fuss earlier about having to give some change to beggars."

Yogi Ramsuratkumar's generosity, involving the equivalent of something less than a dollar, had proven a huge stumbling block to one who had expectations about the saint's behavior. In retrospect, it is hard to imagine this being a problem for anyone. Yet, for this young Westerner, as for all who approach a saint or master, the holy one's Presence is a powerful force. In the saint's aura, areas of unresolved conflict are brought to the fore and exposed to the light. In Robert's case, a few coins and his faith was shaken.

By 5:30 or 6:00 P.M. the festivities of the day were clearly over, and the group prepared to depart. As George's family returned to the village, Yogi Ramsuratkumar requested that the three Westerners – Aruna, Robert, and Caylor – spend some time together, with him. Robert's questions were raised then, and with patience and tenderness, Yogi Ramsuratkumar answered them, one by one.

"What have *your* spiritual experiences been?" Robert boldly inquired of the Godchild, as if assuming that he could evaluate their merits.

Silence. And then Yogi Ramsuratkumar spoke, echoing a consistent theme: "This beggar has had no experiences." He proceeded, however, to tell the group of his past search, of his three masters, and of his dissolution at Ramdas's feet.

राम

In a 2002 interview, Caylor explained something about Yogiji's use of money.

"Besides Perumal and George, there were others too, people who came and went; who had lesser roles, more like lieutenants in the entourage. Most of them were out of work, had no money, couldn't feed their families; had family problems. They knew they would be paid; that if they served Yogi he would give them money, and he did. Every day he would give them a few rupees.

"People would send Yogi Ramsuratkumar money: three rupees here, ten rupees there. He would open little letters of concern from people who had problems and questions. People were always giving him flowers and fruits, but often when they were giving the flowers, from their hand, which they would close into his when they greeted him, they would try to push some money into Yogi Ramsuratkumar's hand. Sometimes he would accept it, and sometimes he wouldn't. It depended on…" Caylor paused, obviously recognizing the foolishness of trying to interpret the actions of a saint.

"Who knows why. But he always had money rolled into the cloth, the dhoti around his waist. He'd have his smoking paraphernalia – his little box of Indian matches and cigarettes – rolled into a corner of the cloth that wrapped up his newspaper bundles. In those days, all his newspaper bundles were carried, so there could be three or four people carrying forty or fifty pounds of newspapers *each*. Certainly not less than twenty pounds each, over their shoulders, a bundle or two. Those papers would be wrapped with common cloth, and in a corner of those he might have some of his smokes, and two or three rupees, or eight or ten rupees. You'd always see a little bit of money stuck away somewhere – these little crumpled up ones or two-rupee notes.

"He would basically feed those people who were looking after him, and often give them money for their health problems, and their children's health problems. He never had much money – but he always had enough to feed the people around him."

From Caylor also we are left a tender report of the odd behaviors of the Godman, Yogi Ramsuratkumar – the enigmatic ways in which he used material things, shamanistically. "I learned how every single thing he touches – even if it's a cigarette butt or the package or a twig he plays with or a string that he's taken off a little wrapper of food – anything he's ever touched you can't just throw away, because there's power in there. There's something; there's an essence, there's a quality. It may be months before he finds time to empty his pockets and place everything where it will do some work. It takes a long time to see him doing these things. He doesn't talk about them. He's a beggar. He calls all these things his 'madness.' He loves to talk about how bizarre he is. It's really remarkable."[3]

राम

The first report by a Westerner of the beggar's ecstatic dance is found in Wadlington's journal for December 3, 1970. As Caylor and Ramsuratkumar sat together late that night inside the temple compound, a small girl, a beggar child, approached them. Keeping her distance at some ten or more feet, she gestured her need – for something...money, perhaps, or something to eat. Usually, Yogi Ramsuratkumar was forthcoming with a handout to such beggars, but this time not. Caylor had the impression that the master had obviously been disturbed by "the vibrations of the innocent little visitor" and was concentrating some of his energy in asking her to leave them, although not verbally. After a short time the child left.

A few minutes later, however, she reappeared, and the beggar's reaction to the situation completely startled Caylor. He wrote: "This time, Yogi Ramsuratkumar got up and did a peculiar dancing or skipping step for the complete length of one side of the tank [a reservoir of water within the temple precincts]. After having returned in the same manner and sitting down, the little girl went away. Swami's childlike dance was a wonder to behold – it was the first time I had seen him do such a thing."

This story is instructive in that it points to multiple purposes of his Divine dance. While it would be easy to interpret Ramsuratkumar's dancing primarily as an expression of bliss or celebration, we see here a case in which it seems to have been directed to accomplishing a tangible end.

राम

On the evening of Caylor's last meeting with Ramsuratkumar in 1970, just before the young man left for Adyar at the master's instruction, a most unusual conversation occurred between them. For two or three nights previously, the beggar had expressed to Caylor the need to talk about the mechanics of computers. "There was some need in his work to understand these 'superminds,'" Caylor noted.

Fortunately, Caylor had made the acquaintance of a German friend, Andy, who had a vast knowledge of the subject, and was able to explain and diagram a simple model that Caylor shared and discussed for hours with his Swami. The conversation focused not only on the mechanics, but upon the "potentialities, the function, and the likenesses to the human mind of the modern day computers."

Although Caylor's own facility with the subject of computers was limited, he had the distinct impression that Yogi Ramsuratkumar was using him to access knowledge he had forgotten or didn't even know he had; information that would be useful, in some way, for the master's work.

This is an interesting and somewhat paradoxical bit of data, considering the fact that Ramsuratkumar had spoken strongly of the interference that modern technology was having upon the environment. On one occasion he mentioned to a Western visitor that radio waves were disturbing the air in such a way that one's ability to work on this earth in this age was being compromised.

The larger context for this incident, however, as Caylor noted, seems to be that Yogi Ramsuratkumar's work on behalf of humanity required this knowledge of computers, in some way. Nothing was outside his field of interest and influence. In later years, when he was visited by Lee Lozowick, one revealing photograph finds the gentle beggar wearing earphones, listening to a CD of the American devotee's rock and roll music.

Whatever significantly altered the mind, and thus affected the heart, of man or woman, Ramsuratkumar knew about it.

राम

In 1970, prior to his receiving his characteristic hand fan, the beggar carried a stick, a coconut bowl, and his newspapers and bundles, except when these latter items were being transported by those around him. One day in December of this year, he added a string of *rudraksha* beads to his variety of implements. These sacred beads, mentioned in the *Siva Purana*, are typically used for the repetition of the mantra "Om Nama Shivaya," or any other mantra, and are often worn as the one item of decoration by a sadhu, a sign of identification with the Lord Rudra, another aspect of Siva. From this point on, photographs of Ramsuratkumar frequently reveal the rudraksha mala around the beggar's neck.

Throughout his life, Yogi Ramsuratkumar made use of many ordinary items in ways that his visitors were aware of, but generally did not fully understand. A stick, a rope, a fan, a coconut bowl. He was extremely careful of the use of these things, as they became for him tools in the same way that the shaman uses tools at one level of reality to affect the energy on other levels. On the day that Caylor noted the addition of the rudraksha mala, he was gifted with additional insight into the beggar's use of the decorated staff, or stick. As often happened, the crowd that surrounded Ramsuratkumar consisted of both friends and detractors, and the latter group was increasingly troublesome and threatening to the Godman. In Caylor's journal he wrote: "Swami handed me his invaluable and treasured tool – this stick. I was instructed to hold it in the air for some time. I did so happily, for it was a rare occasion to get to hold this instrument and to be of some service in his work. Those people who were interfering with his work soon left. I was shown where to place the stick. I did so. It probably remained working for him as a vigilant guard against ill-intentioned intruders."

राम

Caylor Wadlington's purpose in handling that stick as a means to guard "against ill-intentioned intruders" was greatly magnified in another task that Yogi Ramsuratkumar begged of him, on May 17, 1971, during one of Caylor's return visits from Madras. On this auspicious day, as the beggar told his young Western visitor many stories of his early life, Ramsuratkumar entrusted Caylor with the job of writing a book, in English, about him and his activities.

The purpose of this book is not simply to externalize an unknown Adept. Its true motivating impulse is incrusted in matters of far greater import and urgency than the inspiration which this book may create in the minds of a few men. I will convey here something of its secret purpose, for doing so is extremely important to the overall work of accomplishment which it has been designed to fulfill.[4]

These serious words in the introduction to Wadlington's book, *Yogi Ramsuratkumar, Godchild of Tiruvannamalai*, greet the casual reader with a small jolt, and inspire a different level of attention.

> …there is a group of political-minded men who, day and night for the past four years [from around 1966 until 1970 or so] have set themselves to the task of systematically perse-cuting this man [Yogi Ramsuratkumar]. In very subtle but methodical ways he is constantly threatened and mercilessly tormented, while attempts on his life are never infre-quent…Men are consciously and knowingly seeking to extinguish the life of one who, with the light and power of the Divine, slaves to solace this needy world.[5]

The urgency of Caylor's mission was undeniable. When I met him in 2002, over thirty years later, he was still serious about his responsibility, one that had evidently been communicated to him by the beggar. Caylor's love for his exalted subject was obvious, coupled with his inherent appreciation for the work that Yogi Ramsurat-kumar was effecting in the world.

> It is too often true that men worship the dead and not the living, but this must not be allowed to happen to a man such as this…The moment is urgent, for the Adept has great work to do in this world, and it has become difficult to do that work under the conditions which now exist.[6]

For Caylor Wadlington in 1971, although he had only known Yogi Ramsuratkumar for less than a year, there was no question that what was being asked of him was of the highest importance. Whether he knew all the details or not, he knew that the enigmatic presence of this beggar was a gift to the world, a gift beyond accounting, and that this gift needed to be recognized and protected.

"This was a time in South India's political history that was very troubled," Caylor explained, commenting on the incendiary political atmosphere of those years. "There was a secessionist group in South India that ruled the political scene. The Naxolites, I believe they were called. A very right wing, Tamil-speaking, ethnic political movement that resented the federal government of India's prejudice in favor of the northern Indian states. Most of the laws, funding, and language were preferential to the northern Indian states. The national language was Hindi, and the school systems, and government jobs, and civil job opportunities were all affected by that preferential treatment of northern India. So Yogi Ramsuratkumar, being from northern India, and other people from northern India, were often harassed – business people, businesses, spiritual people.

"The Naxolites were an atheistic group who believed that Hinduism and the religious establishment was out-and-out discriminating against low-caste people. For them, the religious establishment didn't work in South India in the social situation, and the federal government, the Brahmins and the Hindis, were their nemesis.

"Yogi Ramsuratkumar was a Brahmin. He had been born a Brahmin, although he didn't wear any Brahmin thread anymore. But he was from North India, and he was obviously a very powerful spiritual person. They knew he was from the north, and he even dressed with his cloths tied in the way of a North Indian. Also, his Tamil wasn't that great, he would say."

It was known that Yogi Ramsuratkumar openly opposed "separations and divisions based upon race, religion, language, and politics," Caylor wrote in his 1970 journal. "That is to say, he professes the innate unity of men, the spiritual power of India, so long as it remains harmonious within and between her peoples." What was probably one of the central factors, as well, was that Ramsuratkumar was "a recognized sympathizer to the political and social order which the beloved Gandhiji expressed." This would definitely have inflamed the hatred of his opponents.

As others have pointed out, Ramsuratkumar was completely open in expressing his sentiments. "Mahatma Gandhi, ki jai!" he would shout as he walked along the roads of this South Indian town.

"He would point all this out to me," Caylor explained. "The situation was getting very heated. Sadhus from the north were being beaten up and killed on the back roads, and were being arrested and thrown in jail and tortured. He would show me these things in the newspaper. He apologized to me, because he didn't really want me to have to get involved, and I really didn't *want* to know anything about it. I didn't want to know about politics, especially not there, not in India. And I didn't *really* believe, for the longest time, that this had anything to do with him. I couldn't figure it out. He had no money. He spent his days under little thorny bushes, and didn't talk to anyone about political stuff. I couldn't get it.

"Wherever we were, people used to come and stand, just staring at him. He used to say that these people were sent, instructed to come and just watch him, and in a way harass him, and come up and ask for favors, like other sincere people. But they came with an air of mocking. Sometimes he would stand up and shout at them, or order them to leave, and sometimes he would just ignore them. Sometimes he would get up and move.

"But I think the real problem was in the predawn or late night hours, when there were no other people around; those were the times that were dangerous for him. Some nights, when he would be 'called' to someone who needed him – an inner calling for him to just get up and go – for him to go in those late hours, without light on the street, this was scary for him. Actually, it scared him. I can say that he used to apologize that these things upset him. Yet, he would always credit his protection to his Father.

"There were occasions when he was assaulted, at least two or three times over a couple of years before I was there. The last time was on an occasion when he had been walking around the temple at night. He told me that, on the road ahead of him, suddenly car-lights blinked on, and he was in the headlights. And this car turned on its engine and came forward, and sped up as it approached him, and then turned in towards him. It was going to try to kill him, or maim him, or smash him. He backed up against the temple wall, and he said that by some mysterious power that he couldn't understand, that car smashed there [against the wall] but never touched him. It was as if it had hit some [invisible] wall in front of him. That's when it got really intense and he asked me to write this book."

Caylor's journals of the time point out numerous events that he himself had witnessed – incidents of cruelty, bordering on malicious threat. "He suffers no end by the ignorance of men about him. Seeing only a madman in him, they stone him, beat him, and persecute him all his waking hours. For three years he has endured torment and torture which no man could endure for more than a few days. The author, this boy [meaning himself, Caylor Wadlington] has witnessed the plots and endless schemes which are forever put to him. By God, I testify that his greatest miracle of all is that still he lives. For no man, lest he be a child of God could survive the treatment that men have made him suffer. Anyone else would be crazed and deranged in only days' or weeks' time."

One night, as they retired to a café for a late meal, Caylor noted that "certain people employed at the restaurant consciously abused and tormented my beggar friend." It was not the first time he had witnessed and been at the effect of such behaviors. On another occasion, in a tea shop, when he and Ramsuratkumar were delighting in an antique wooden book that Caylor had brought with him from the States, some of the patrons in the shop began to cast disparaging remarks, "ugly comments about the worth and age of the art piece," although they knew that the piece held both sentimental value and some significance to both Yogi Ramsuratkumar and his young companion. The beggar, in fact, had been pouring his attention over the pages, as if to imprint his own power upon them.

Initially, Caylor thought these comments to be reflective of "simple ignorance and lack of culture" on the part of the detractors. Soon, however, he realized "that these men were purposely tormenting this beggar with their subtle remarks." Caylor noted that Yogi Ramsuratkumar looked at these men in "a funny way," and they soon left the shop without further disturbance.

While the incident was minor when viewed alone, it was indicative of the constant harassment to which the Godchild was being subjected. As he wrote about the events of this day in the early 1970s in his journal, Caylor's outrage and heartbreak were clear:

> It had become obvious to me – VERY VERY EVIDENT – that a great deal of malice was always being dealt to my friend. More and more, he was purposely putting me in positions where I might see these things with my own eyes. Today, as the town's streets were crowded and it was too dangerous for him to walk unguarded, I offered my assistance by walking him back to the great Ashwathra tree which serves as his shield against evil, and more than that, his home and companion…The Ashwathra tree was an island apart from the world for him. Whenever he would come to one, he would assure me I could put all my things down and rest for a moment. He too seemed to become quickly and thoroughly relieved of his burdens. The great Spirit of the Tree watched over him. When we finally arrived at the Bus Station where Swami's tree is, we sat together for a few moments. He dismissed me and then I went back to the Ashram.

Their work together was intense during this period when Caylor was interviewing or Yogiji was reading. The fact that he had been so threatened on so many occasions caused Yogi Ramsuratkumar to be extremely vigilant. Caylor wrote: "I was sitting with Swami in the country side and we were doing some very concentrated work…in connection with [the] book…Here came two very close friends of mine across the field. And they saw me sitting on the rocks, and although they had not met Yogi Ramsuratkumar they knew who he was. And thinking that for them to meet him, not to intrude or anything, but just to meet him, they came with open hearts. Swami was very [focused, concentrated]. He wasn't paying attention to anything outside of him. They walk towards us and about twenty feet away he [Yogi Ramsuratkumar] jolted himself out of this state, looked over his shoulder to see who it was, and then jumped up and ran away. These presences, the penetration of their auras, interfered with his established field of work. My friends felt horrible. They apologized and left. The master adjusted himself and returned."

In my interview with him in 2002, Caylor summed up the connection between these threats toward Ramsuratkumar and the reason for the book. "Yogi Ramsuratkumar said that for his work in India and India's great place in the world, he had some role in that, and that his life as a little-known beggar was the ideal for his work. But that because of this [the attacks and threats], he needed to change this situation so that more people were around him. He needed some protection. If he could bring himself out a little he would have people around him who would protect him. Even though many other people were drawn to be around him, it wasn't as if he asked them to protect him. But the book served the purpose to protect him."

A published book, in the early 1970s in southern India, *would be* a legitimizing factor, and a means to make the saint's presence known. After all, the book was to be written neither in Tamil nor Hindi, but in English, and by a Westerner (probably an added note of legitimacy). Those who possessed the ability to read English might be people of some education, perhaps people of some influence, who could offer the protection needed. "This book will bring a new chapter to the life of this beggar," Ramsuratkumar had told Caylor.

And as one reads the book today, it is clear that Caylor's simple, yet erudite and even scholarly, approach was exactly what was called for. Within a few pages (the small volume is less than one hundred) he succeeded in placing a relatively unknown beggar, whom some even deemed a madman, within a context that spiritually-minded Indians (from north *or* south) could not deny. The great Realizers – the great Awakened Ones – of India's spiritual history (people like Chaitanya, Rama Tirtha, Ramakrishna, Shirdi Sai Baba) now had a new peer. In Yogi Ramsuratkumar, as Caylor honestly portrayed him, the parallels to the work of these renowned predecessors was obvious. Here, in this beggar, was one who was not separate from the "Father," and one whose dedication to humanity's spiritual evolution was unquestionable. Caylor found in Yogi Ramsuratkumar one whose entire existence was a reflection of the tenderness, the simplicity, the innocence and the power of God. And he wrote about that.

The small book was originally conceived of as a much more extensive work, Wadlington reports in the Author's Note – a work that would be "an attempt at placing Ramsuratkumar in the correct perspective amidst the fraternity of spiritual Adepts," one that covered his life from 1959 until the present, and then addressed itself to the Yogi's vision on the "scheme of humanity's collective evolution."[7] That master plan, however, never materialized. The urgency of the moment inspired Caylor's efforts to complete only the second part for immediate publication – the brief life-sketch, "Born of Three Fathers" – the entirety of what we now know as this first biography. In that one piece he incorporated the essence of all the others.

राम

The title of the finished book became *Yogi Ramsuratkumar, The Godchild, Tiruvannamalai.* "The whole 'Godchild' thing was something that just occurred to me, based in his actual name," Caylor remarked in answer to my question about this affectionate descriptor that he had used in the title of the book. "I knew that 'kumar' meant child, and 'Ram' was God. So, I put them together and he really liked that.

"He had sent me to live at the Theosophical Society to have connection with other Europeans. In these writings that I was studying, they talk about 'the seven kumars' from the Vedic writings, and I happened to come across those terms. They were the seven immortal youths who came from some other solar system. They were a part of this group of '*petris*' or fathers of human evolution. Only one of these kumars was in this planetary system. So, I thought this name was really appropriate. He *was* so childlike.

"When I finally showed him the book he spent quite a lot of time focusing on the cover. He had wanted the word 'Tiruvannamalai' on the cover under his name, and although I never went by the name of Truman he wanted that on the book too.

"I wrote the book while I was living in Madras," Caylor explained in answer to my question. I wanted to know how much of the book was his own extrapolation, since many passages contained theosophical terminology, and how much was given to him directly,

YOGI
RAMSURATKUMAR
THE GODCHILD
TIRUVANNAMALAI

Truman Caylor Wadlington

The cover of the book written and published by Caylor Wadlington

203

verbatim, by the saint. So many interpretative passages analyze Yogi Ramsuratkumar's inner states as he made his various journeys prior to settling in Tiruvannamalai. For instance, in covering the beggar's experience in Pondicherry at Aurobindo's ashram, Wadlington wrote: "Ramsuratkumar made a searching analysis of himself in the light of the Master's writings and mode of life."[8]

"He said that almost word for word, I think," Caylor replied. "Yogi Ramsuratkumar spoke several times about his spiritual dilemma, or spiritual crisis at that time in his life. How he was quite desperate to find some guidance or some opening, and how each of those three teachers guided him as if a next step. I got the impression that he had sought long and hard and was very stuck, or frustrated, or disillusioned. Feeling very unfulfilled up to that point."

Doggedly, I asked Caylor of his descriptions of the Yogiji's experiences during a meeting with Ramana Maharshi, about which he wrote: "He [Yogi Ramsuratkumar] sensed that he had lived before in forgotten times and that the great seer peering into his eyes knew the wonders of the many lives past and those to come."[9] My questions were not directed as challenges, but simply as one writer to another, wanting to know how the process had unfolded. Caylor honestly explained: "Yogi recounted these experiences to me. And how much I put in my own words and how much I took from his words it would be very hard for me to say anymore. But it *is* an experience that he related to me. It would be hard for me to imagine Yogi speaking of past lives, at least his own. So, definitely this incident where their eyes met, where this deep 'soul examination' took place, where this powerful gaze of Ramana, in which Yogi felt himself completely seen, no doubt happened. 'Lives past and those to come'? I could have written that based in my own ideas. But, throughout the whole process, I read this material out loud to him many times. If it were very wrong, he wouldn't have let it stand. Actually there were only two or three things that he stopped to change in that book. Something about the way he related that experience to me must have conveyed to me the impression that Ramana saw *everything*, past and future.

"I would come down to Tiruvannamalai, and Yogi Ramsuratkumar would tell me just two or three little bits of his life and ask me to write something. Like the little story about hitting the bird – that was one of the very first stories. And he also confided to me that he had a family in Benaras, but that for the protection of his family and for other personal reasons, that information couldn't be included in the book."

Both from Caylor's reports and from my own experiences in working with a master, it seems obvious that Yogi Ramsuratkumar's single-minded purpose was all that mattered to him. He was probably not concerned with presenting the world with his memoirs, nor some precise historical narrative. By supplying his young biographer with only the briefest details, the saint probably expected that Caylor would "live" the life within himself, writing it in his own words. Caylor's job was merely to be an instrument in the hands of God.

Admittedly this was a job that required a great deal of trust on the young man's part, and Caylor was clear about the difficulty of the task. Ultimately, however, it would be his degree of alignment with Yogi Ramsuratkumar that would accomplish the work and bring about the master's desired result. In having Caylor read the passages to him over and over, all along the way, Yogi Ramsuratkumar was no doubt testing their effectiveness as much as he was correcting their accuracy. In so doing, he offered an invaluable object lesson to those of us who primarily need legitimacy and reasonableness to affirm our efforts. In the domain in which one such as Yogi Ramsuratkumar was working, reason was always superceded by his own receptivity to Father's will, something that the master knew instinctively, because in reality he was not separate from the Father.

"Every word was to be left to my discretion, and what was eventually written was to be left unchanged, even to the last punctuation mark; for Divine guidance was to be, in truth, the actual author," Caylor wrote. Yogi Ramsuratkumar also stressed the importance of the few photographs (there are four) that the book would contain. "Seeing the photographs, people will come to understand this beggar," the Godman said. And indeed, as one examines these photos today, they contain not only visual representation, but an energetic transmission that is characteristic of all the photos of this remarkable being, Yogi Ramsuratkumar.

*One of the photos of Yogi Ramsuratkumar included
in the book written by Caylor Wadlington.*

राम

On occasion, in these early days, Yogi Ramsuratkumar would speak briefly, revealing something of the nature of his work. Caylor remembered these injunctions very clearly, as they were often repeated several times in one sitting, as if they were seeds being planted and watered in the young biographer's field of awareness.

"This beggar has been assigned a great mission. And this beggar does his work in every step he walks," Yogi Ramsuratkumar explained. "This beggar has been assigned a great mission. His work could not be done by others. Please excuse him for giving some importance to this body." And on another occasion: "The name of this beggar will be left behind. When his mission is completed, this beggar will pass away. But the name, Yogi Ramsuratkumar, will remain in the history of spiritual India. And to a few chosen individuals, his name will be a source of inspiration."

"This beggar is working to uplift this country. He gives advice or help to those few people who come to him. But as a general rule – his real work goes unnoticed." As Caylor attempted to draw the master out on the nature of this "real work," however, Ramsuratkumar stopped him: "Please, Mr, Kay. Do not ask about this work. It could not be understood at this time."

"When a building is built, tools must be brought from far away. Those people who offer food and shelter to this beggar are his tools…A yogi's work is never left unfinished. Though obstacles may come, it is certain they (the obstacles) will never succeed. That job, which he had been sent to do, will be completed. No obstacles can stop it. HE [the Father, God] will see to it." As these last words were spoken, the Godchild pointed his finger skyward. "Whenever he spoke of God," Caylor described in his journal, "he would often tilt his head in a childlike manner and point gently to heaven above. Where are the words to capture such synchronous expressions of body and soul? This particular gesture I had seen a number of times. I never could fail to smile inside or to shrink in awe at the Forces he made such vivid reference to."

राम

207

ONLY GOD

When the Godchild, Ramsuratkumar, referred to the unknown nature of his work, the remark came as no surprise to the young Westerner who, in a few short months, had observed many things about his mentor's paradoxical ways. He knew Ramsuratkumar in a number of guises, from the stern taskmaster, to the most solicitous friend, to the protective mother. "If playing a role were necessary to produce effects desired in his work," Caylor wrote in 1971, "then he would resort to such means. Not at all are such things distasteful in such a man as he. His childlike disposition, his innocence, his humor, his awesome seriousness, even in his feigned enthusiasm or humor bordering lunacy – still it was Yogi Ramsuratkumar." Further, Wadlington claimed that, in his view, the master "was never to be misunderstood; for all of it was his method and way of living the work he did.

"On the other hand," Caylor went on, "it may be truthfully said that the beggar was not to be understood whatsoever. That is to say, one could not detect much coherence or fluidness in his behavior. Balance, in his company, was to be derived by renouncing all hopes of understanding what 'this lunatic' (as he often referred to himself) was doing. 'Why had he behaved so?' Such questions could easily sever any hope of retaining any relationship, particularly a spiritual one, with him, except for the fact that one very quickly begins to observe in him a kindness and a childlike consideration and love towards those who harbor good-will and desire understanding of things not oft considered by men. As I say, it is this attitude pervading his lunacy, his enthusiasm, his reprimands – all of his behavior – which proves the underlying purity and holiness of his work and his very inner nature. He becomes an open book more easily read than a 3rd-grade reader."

A tiny incident indicative of Ramsuratkumar's "madness" occurred one day as Swamiji and Caylor sat together in the temple precincts. When a village woman moved to a position behind Caylor, her presence was felt as an ominous intrusion on their discussion. The master had a small marigold flower in his hand at the time, and had been slowly turning it over and over. Suddenly, Ramsuratkumar erupted in what seemed like rage, throwing the tiny marigold to the ground. Immediately, the woman turned and headed for the exit of the temple.

Caylor was confused at first, thinking that his master's behavior was occasioned by something that he had done. But Ramsuratkumar soon quelled the younger man's fears by explaining that the woman had intended ill will (she was acting in alliance with the DMK movement, part of the political faction that was harassing him), and that his play had been to impress upon her that he would not tolerate her activities.

An instant later, Yogi Ramsuratkumar picked up the flower, focused his attention directly upon Caylor again, and continued to speak as if nothing had happened.

This type of event, repeated hundreds of times in different ways over the years to follow, would have similar results. Devotees would report that what they observed as incomprehensible or mad, at the time, was in fact proven to be prophetic utterance, or protective activity on the part of Yogi Ramsuratkumar, the ever-compassionate saint.

राम

When the book was completed, and distribution had begun, the effects were felt almost immediately. In a precious testimonial to his young disciple's efforts, Yogi Ramsuratkumar explained to Caylor: "Finally it has become apparent as to why this beggar was made to endure the last five years of pain and persecution…If that had never developed, this beggar would never have called upon you to write this life sketch. It was [this beggar's] only recourse; it was no longer possible for [him] to live and work unnoticed, nor could [he] even remain in Tiruvannamalai. Already the book has begun to alleviate this situation … At least to the extent to where it is possible for this beggar to continue with his Master's work. But what the book has done for me is not important compared to what it may do for others. No book may fail to uplift or inspire, Mr. Kay. Every book shall touch the heart of a brother."[10]

12

A FRIEND AND PROTECTOR, 1971

Caylor Wadlington had just returned to Tiruvanna-malai after spending many months at the Theosoph-ical Society headquarters in Adyar. Arriving back to the foot of Mount Arunachala on May 12, 1971, the young disciple went in search of his master, who could not be found anywhere. In vain he visited Ramsurat-kumar's usual haunts. He asked the beggar's friends at the tea stalls, the stonecutter's shop, near the protective trees, in the temple com-pound. Yet, no one had a clue. So, as he typically did, Caylor spent time at Ramanashram, meditating in the Mother's temple, writing in his journal, and wandering the city.

On the very same day, two other Westerners, who would figure prominently in the regard of Yogi Ramsuratkumar in those early years, arrived in Tiruvannamalai. Will and Joan Zulkowski had been housemates of Caylor's in their little "ashram" back in Bloomington, Indiana. Like him, they had been inspired to pilgrimage to India, and like him, they had no previous knowledge of the beggar saint of Tiruvannamalai.

Will had been extremely generous toward Caylor, and had, in fact, given him the money to make his initial trip to India. In addi-tion, when Caylor's biography of Yogi Ramsuratkumar was complet-ed, Will gave him a significant sum of money ($500-$1000, U.S.) to finance its publication. Besides his personal support, Will had con-tacted others from the New York area, where he was living at the time, who might be willing to put up some funds. In one delightful coincidence that could be termed a meeting of saints, Will headed for a particular Oriental art and antique shop in Greenwich Village on 7th Avenue, where he knew he would find Swami Rudrananda, a well-known spiritual teacher of the day. When Will told the robust swami of his friend Caylor's need, Rudi (as he was affectionately called), looked at him intently as he handed over a moderate donation to be used toward the publication of *Yogi Ramsuratkumar, The Godchild, Tiruvannamalai.*

The Zulkowski's first trip to India had begun eleven months ago, and in May of 1971 was fast drawing to a close, as Joan had previously contracted hepatitis and was anxious to leave. The couple had spent most of their year in Puttaparthi, near Bangalore, at the ashram of Satya Sai Baba. They had also visited other saints before finally journeying further south to the city of the sacred red mountain.

Will and Joan actually made two trips to Tiruvannamalai that year. The first time they stayed for six weeks, but Caylor was away in Madras at the time and without guidance they never met up with the "Ram-Ram" swami. On this current visit (approximately May 12-23), they ended up spending only two weeks before heading back to Bangalore in preparation for their departure to the States. Until the very last day of their stay in Tiruvannamalai, Ramsuratkumar was not to be found. He too had been away, as Caylor learned. When Swamiji at last returned to the city, Caylor asked him whether his American friends could meet him on the evening of their last night in town, but the beggar told him that the time was not right. However, when Caylor mentioned their names to Yogi Ramsuratkumar, Swamiji said, "Oh yes, I know those two." To Caylor's amazement, the Godman told him many details that specifically described both Will and Joan.

"Well, we'll meet again. Don't worry," Yogi Ramsuratkumar told Caylor, referring to the couple, calling them "Will-Joan" – their names had immediately become an amalgam in the beggar's mouth.

Will and Joan would not return to India again until 1973, at which time they would finally meet "Caylor's Swami."

राम

On May 16, having been back in Tiruvannamalai since May 12, and not having found his master, Caylor was frankly disturbed. "I will concede that I am disheartened at not seeing the one to whom I owe my very life," the young man wrote in his journal at the time. On that morning, however, a visit from another Western acquaintance would solve the mystery of the master's whereabouts in a most delightful and even magical way.

Mark was a friend whom Caylor had met at the guesthouse where they both resided during this sojourn in Tiruvannamalai in May 1971. Mark's interest was in visiting many different sadhus and saints, and Caylor obliged him in the search. He showed him a photo of Poondi swami, who lived at the base of Mount Arunachala's east side, and suggested that Mark meet the old sage. Interestingly, encased in the same plastic folder that held the Poondi swami photo was a photo of Yogi Ramsuratkumar – one which had been taken by Robert Lee on the occasion of Yogiji's birthday celebration in 1970. When Mark inquired who the man was, Caylor feigned casualness. "He is another yogi I know," he said without emotion, as he surely wanted to keep his master's identity protected from the merely curious.

Later that day, after meeting Poondi Swami, Mark met a man from Calcutta who drove him and a few others to see yet another saint, this one residing in a village not far from Tiruvannamalai. Mark had learned that Swami Gnanananda Giri was reported to be 150 years old; however, when they arrived at the saint's ashram, known as Tapovanam, Mark was disappointed to learn that the swami was not giving darshan to anyone, as he was involved deeply in his own tapas (ascetic practice).

The trip was far from being a complete waste of time, as Mark later told Caylor, because at Tapovanam he had met a great yogi, "a wise old man," who was obviously a person of intense spiritual accomplishment. For three or four hours Mark had experienced the wise man's company, and had asked him numerous questions. The "great yogi," however, would only speak to Mark through a third party, and in response to the young seeker's questions had generally "feigned spiritual ignorance." Furthermore, he demonstrated what Mark later described as "lunacy, laughter, and joking." At some point in their encounter it occurred to Mark that this crazy-wise person was not unfamiliar. In fact, that he had seen the man's picture only a short time before, from Caylor. It was Yogi Ramsuratkumar whom Mark had stumbled upon!

"The beggar man spoke in seemingly nonsensical paradoxes, somewhat as Zen masters are said to do," Mark told Caylor. The young seeker was deeply impressed in this encounter, but also told Caylor that he wasn't sure how to interpret all that he had experienced. "Was he the lunatic he claimed to be? No. That much Mark knew was absolutely false," Caylor reported. "Was he a great sage or wise and gentle sadhik? Mark received him only as a comrade, and recognized the spiritual joy about him."

"Where have you become so well versed in Zen?" Mark asked Yogi Ramsuratkumar directly, relating to the only point of reference he had for such enigmatic behavior.

"This beggar hung about ashrams for some time," Yogi Ramsuratkumar replied, skillfully relating to Mark in a way the man could hear. "Others have acquainted this beggar with the Oriental Path."

To say that Caylor was overjoyed to learn of his master's whereabouts would be an understatement. He was ecstatic! Mark had unknowingly been the means to connect him with the man of his heart. The next morning, May 17, the two Americans left town to find the laughing beggar.

They traveled by bus, to the outskirts of the small but historically significant village of Tirukoilur, a city of three remarkable temples – two dedicated to Siva, and one to Vishnu Perumal. It was in this town in 1896 that Ramana Maharshi had exited the train on his first and final journey from his uncle's home in Madurai enroute to the city of Tiruvannamalai, as he hadn't enough money to make the full trip. Spending the night in one of the Siva shrines in Tirukoilur, he had a vision of light, *jyoti,* emanating from the peak of Arunachala and calling him to "himself."[1]

Tapovanam Ashram, located on the main road about two miles before the city, was the first and only stop for the two Westerners. Arriving at the colorful and ornate gateway to the small ashram at about 9:30 A.M., they immediately set out searching for Yogi Ramsuratkumar. The compound, however, was vacant except for a few workers, who spoke no English. By gesturing and with a few carefully chosen words, the men communicated their aim. *A yogi...a bearded beggar man...a coconut bowl...*and the workers informed them, through similar gestures, that the man they sought had gone to the river early that morning, accompanied by a friend. He would, very likely, return shortly.

The entrance to Tapovanam Ashram

As Caylor and Mark were on a mission, they were not inclined to wait. Walking out onto the road and heading a short distance in the direction of the river, they met Ramsuratkumar, "Our Friend," as Caylor referred to his master in his journal entry on that day. The old beggar was walking toward them in the company of a man named

Ganapati. Caylor wrote: "I honestly gasped as I turned around and by 'chance' saw him approaching us. He too seemed thoroughly astonished to see me. Not only that, but he somehow failed for a moment to recognize Mark."

The foursome retired to a nearby hotel – probably a simple dwelling that allowed for overnight guests, with a few shaded tables in front – and had two cups of coffee each. Ramsuratkumar insisted that his companions take the coffee whether they wanted it or not, and himself paid the bill for all of it, which amounted to two rupees. Their reunion was a joyous one, full of the laughter and tender regard of the Godman for those who turn to him.

It was during this coffee break that Ramsuratkumar related to his guests a most extraordinary event that had taken place early that same morning. Swamiji and a few others had gone to bathe in the river just a mile distant from the ashram. There, while wading in the current, a man had stumbled, wedging his foot in a crevice of the rocky riverbed. For more than three hours people from the village or from the ashram had vainly attempted to release the man's foot from the trap. "Everything anyone could dream of was put to the test, but still his foot was held firm in the rocks," Caylor reported. "The man's leg had been pulled and twisted until the slightest pressure caused an awesome pain to his foot."

The man himself, Sri P. Radhakrishnan, an officer in the Public Works Department of Madras, was in a state of near desperation. His foot had been so bruised and lacerated, and his pain was so great, that the man was rapidly losing bodily strength and mental balance. He could bear no more manipulation. Several of the villagers suggested amputating Radhakrishnan's foot, which seemed the last available resort.

Caylor's written account of the events that followed are full of a mood of magic:

Yogi Ramsuratkumar had returned to the Ashram and there he had fallen into some peculiar state of consciousness. His outward behavior and appearance…had lost most all similitude of that of a normal man. Then, with two friends looking after him, he journeyed down the road till they arrived at the scene of the incident. Villagers were all about, waiting for something or someone to find release for their friend.

Establishing his two cohorts (accompanists) at a carefully chosen point along the riverbank, and making it perfectly clear to them that under no circumstances were they to move from that spot,…Yogi Ramsuratkumar stated emphatically to them that at exactly 8:40 A.M., ten minutes from the present time, Sri Radhakrishan would discover himself free from the trap which mercilessly held him. For anyone to have said such a thing after so many people's tricks and schemes had failed to bring any result other than agonizing pain, could surely have been nothing less than a clear indication of a man's lunacy – or of his divinity – for no less than three and one-half hours he had been trapped.

Yogi Ramsuratkumar at first waded into the river toward Radhakrishnan, but a group of village children, intrigued by the Yogi's appearance, began to splash him. Retracing his steps to the riverbank, the Beggar then moved upstream at a location behind the trapped man, and somewhat distant from the villagers. Caylor went on:

It was then, at that very moment, that the ensnared man turned and glanced, only for an instant, into the fixed gaze of Yogi Ramsuratkumar. The foot lodged in the rocks of the riverbed slid free.

The village people became exultant. And because it had happened precisely as foretold by the Yogi, the two men, instructed to remain stationed along the riverbank, who had been instrumental to him in the event, jumped up and down cheering out, "You have saved him. You have saved him."

Sri P. Radhakrishnan went to the Ashram later that morning. In religious gratitude he prostrated himself at the feet of the Yogi and presented to him an offering of plantains.

Swami accepted his offering graciously and extended further blessings to him, foretelling a revolutionary change that would come to his life from that moment onward. Goodness was to come to his life!

Following the telling of the story, Yogi Ramsuratkumar, Caylor, and Mark (Ganapati had already left) moved from the coffee stall to a spot across the road. Caylor remembered the place well, as it was the foundation of a ruined house and was shaded by towering trees. Sitting amid the ruins, the men remained together for three hours, "absorbed in his [Swami's] spiritual current," as Caylor described it.

Here Yogi Ramsuratkumar did two memorable things. First, he spoke to Caylor of the history of his sadhana – his progression from Aurobindo to Ramana to Ramdas – and expressed his intention for a book project – the work that Caylor would eventually write, entitled *Yogi Ramsuratkumar, The Godchild, Tiruvannamalai*. Secondly, the master did some powerful energetic work with his new disciple. "I don't know *what* he was doing," Caylor reported. "He would have me stand in front of him, a short distance away, and would shout at me. With these shouts each of my chakras would literally explode." After that, as Caylor remarked, he was "so blown open that I could hardly walk." That's when the beggar took his hand and led him, and Mark, back to the Tapovanam Ashram to meet Swami Gnanananda Giri.

"I could never be very surprised by anything Yogi Ramsurat-kumar did," Caylor wrote about that day, "but I will concede that I felt it a bit odd that such a lofty Soul as my Yogi friend should imme-diately prostrate himself to Swami Gnanananda." Little did Caylor know that the one to whom his master prostrated was a spiritual per-son of the highest attainment, a man who not only had a wide-rang-ing influence, with hundreds of disciples, but one who also served as an important source of help and support to the God-intoxicated Ramsuratkumar.

Mark and Caylor then gave their *namastes* to Swami Gnananan-da, although Caylor remembers nothing that the swami talked about that day. Following a long puja ceremony, Yogi Ramsuratkumar pre-sented Caylor with a photo of the saint of Tapovanam, but not before he had touched the photo to Gnanananda's sandals in order to secure additional blessings on the artifact. Ramsuratkumar instructed Caylor to look at this photo at special times, "as it would be of immense help" to him. He furthermore instructed him that "it is not merely a photograph, but something much more."

ONLY GOD

राम

The Tapovanam Ashram of Swami Gnanananda Giri was already a familiar place to Ramsuratkumar when these young Westerners found him there in the spring of 1971. For how long exactly he had been coming to receive its spiritual vibration through the chanting of the Vedas, and to honor the guru who made his residence there, we do not know, although some sources indicate that he was there in the 1960s. We do know that even after Ramsuratkumar's own ashram was thriving in Tiruvannamalai, and long after the passing of Gnanananda Giri, who attained mahasamadhi in 1974, the beggar maintained his contact with the place, and with Gnanananda's successor, Swami Nityananda Giri. He also continued to visit there on occasion, most notably on July 30, 2000, in the midst of his illness, and as he returned from the hospital less than a year before his death, he also visited there, and gave darshan for several hours.

That Ramsuratkumar was a well-known figure at Tapovanam is confirmed by the inclusion of an early photograph of him taken in the ashram and included in a book about the life, personality, and teachings of Sadguru Gnanananda. This same book, first published in 1979, contains the following acknowledgement:

> Encouragement, guidance and transmission of strength and grace to carry out this work has been received in a most liberal but totally unreserved measure from Yogi Ram Surat Kumar of Tiruvannamalai. We bow in prayer to him for his blessings.[2]

When the compiler of this book brought Yogi Ramsuratkumar its "rough draft of about 600 typed pages...for approval, he leafed through every page and said 'let us condense it to about 200 pages.' When the condensed version, titled *Sadguru Gnanananda,* was brought to him for final approval e gently caressed the manuscript and said, 'Father blesses the book. It will be read widely in India and abroad.'"[3]

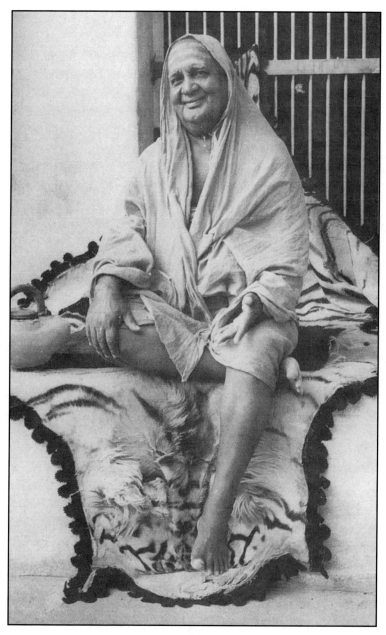

Swami Gnanananda Giri

ONLY GOD

राम

In the person of Gnanananda, Ramsuratkumar found not only a wise elder and friend, but an initiator, of sorts, who served to further empower the Godchild's work, introducing his name to the world beyond Tiruvannamalai.

Gnanananda Giri settled in the area around Tirukoilur about 1950. The city is a pilgrimage site in south India, about forty kilometers from Tiruvannamalai. Here the swami established Tapovanam, a name meaning "forest of penance," in 1954, and from 1966 until his death in 1974 made it his primary home. Visitors to the clean, brightly painted premises might be greeted by an orange-clad, round-faced, laughing fellow who would immediately see to their needs – directing them to a place to wash up, a place to eat, a place to rest. How shocked many of the guests were to learn that the friendly doorkeeper and guide was none other than the most revered saint himself, Gnanananda – the one whom they had come to see.

The early life of this saint is shrouded in mystery, and like many others, including Ramsuratkumar, he was always very reserved in speaking of his former life. Invariably, when the subject was raised, Sri Gnanananda would put off the questioner with "Oh, we can talk about that later," or vaguely reply, "Oh, that happened a long long time ago."

That he was born in Mangalagiri in the state of Andhra Pradesh is somewhat assured. That he ran away from home at an early age; that he selflessly served his one guru, the Sankaracharya Swami Sivaratna Giri, for nearly twenty years, as his primary disciple; and that he surrendered his post as lineage holder to his guru in order to spend as much as forty years in wandering, isolation, and practice in the Himalayas and in travels throughout the length and breadth of India, we are fairly certain.

His age has long been a subject of both curiosity and controversy. Gnanananda probably lived no less than 120 years, as his experiences testify, and some sources list this life span as being 250 or even 300 years. During his blessed life, moreover, he had contact with some of the great saints of contemporary India. He spoke once of having conversed with Sai Baba of Shirdi; having personal knowledge of an initiation given to Sri Ramakrishna Paramahansa, whom he met at Dakshineswar; and of a similar meeting with the latter's disciple, Swami Vivekananda. He had also met Saint Ramalingam of Vadalur, who lived from 1823 to 1874, and he reported discussing spiritual matters with Sri Aurobindo in Pondicherry. Gnanananda had come across the boy Venkataraman (later known as Ramana Maharshi) in the Madurai temple when the youth was just thirteen years old. And later, when young Ramana Maharshi was living in the Virupaksha cave at Tiruvannamalai, Sri Gnanananda Giri used to meet the young ascetic frequently.

The path of bhakti (devotion) coupled with the realization of advaita vedanta (non-dual awareness) had been his own way, and he therefore advocated complete surrender to guru and God as being the best suited and the easiest form of practice in this age. One of his outstanding admirers, a Benedictine monk named Swami Abhishiktananda, wrote of this guru-disciple relationship in a small book that celebrated his time with Gnanananda at the Tapovanam Ashram in 1955-56:

> Guru and disciple form a dyad, a pair, whose two components call for each other and belong together. No more than the two poles (of a magnet) can they exist without being related to each other. On the way towards unity they are a dyad. In the ultimate realization they are a non-dual reciprocity.
>
> The guru is certainly not any kind of teacher; not a professor, nor a preacher, nor an ordinary spiritual guide or director of souls, one who has learnt from books or perhaps from someone else that which he in turn passes on to others. The guru is one who in the first place has himself attained to the Real, and who knows by personal experience the path that leads there; one who is capable of giving the disciple the essential introduction to this path, and causing the immediate and ineffable experience, which he himself has, to spring up directly from and in the disciple's heart – the lucid and transparent awareness that *he is*.[4]

221

Music and singing were also dear to Gnanananda, and he told followers that sincere chanting of the names of the Lord was a means of attaining liberation. For those who had the will, he further exhorted the practice of self-enquiry. It seems no accident, therefore, that Ramsuratkumar would have found sanctuary and encouragement at this place, as his own life witnessed to these same values and practices.

Since the realized being is never separate from the One Reality – "Father is everything," as Yogi Ramsuratkumar would say – still we can guess that companionship with those who have attained a similar degree of surrender or enlightenment would be enormously useful and satisfying. Since his own master, Swami Papa Ramdas, had left the physical body in July of 1963, it is likely that Ramsuratkumar's association with Gnanananda and the mood of the Tapovanam Ashram were additional means of stoking this fire of devotion. The ashram was also a place of safety for him – a place where he could be free from the constant threats to his life that plagued him in Tiruvannamalai.

Swami Gnanananda, besides offering his spiritual joy and sharing in Ramsuratkumar's devotion to God, was instrumental in helping to protect him from the harassment of these threatening elements. In 1971, the Tapovanam saint not only introduced Ramsuratkumar to Pon. Paramaguru, the Director General of Police in Tamil Nadu, but arranged with Paramaguru to provide ongoing protection for Yogiji.

The form of that protection was sometimes grand, bordering on the humorous. In the 1970s, a Tamil Nadu police inspector (perhaps Paramaguru himself) was visiting Tiruvannamalai, when he came upon the beggar swami. Offering obeisance, the man "took his feet," that is, he touched the Godchild's feet in the manner of those who pay deep respect.

The police inspector then invited Yogi Ramsuratkumar and his two companions, Will and Joan Zulkowski, up to his bungalow. He had Yogiji sit with him in the back seat of his car, while Will and Joan took seats up front with the driver. As they proceeded along Chengam Road, en route to the man's residence near Ramanashram, every policeman in town, recognizing the inspector's car, stopped and came to attention along the side of the road. Each one saluted the car as it passed, and, needless to say, noticed who it was that sat in the seat of honor.

The other influential person who Swami Gnanananda Giri introduced to the beggar was Sri A.R.P.N. Rajamanikam Nadar, a wealthy businessman from the industrial city of Tuticorin, on the southeastern coast of India. In the hidden ways in which the Divine stream winds its ways through the desert of human history, this connection was to prove transitional in the life and work of Yogi Ramsuratkumar.

Sri Rajamanikam was a man of expansive means, both in worldly wealth and in the qualities of his heart and soul. An ardent devotee of Gnanananda Giri, he had been asked by the saint to involve himself in the activities of the Tapovanam Ashram. His visits to his master's residence were regular as he, together with his wife and children, traveled the long hours from their home in Tuticorin to Tirukoilur to pay homage to his guru and to provide the support his master had requested. It was largely through the early efforts of Rajamanikam, at the request of Sri Gnanananda, that Yogi Ramsuratkumar's name came to be known throughout South India.

An article in *The Hindu* newspaper, September 7, 1979, written by Justice P. Ramakrishnan, described Rajamanikam as a man who "accomplishes all that he sets his heart on, as he had earned in full measure the grace of the Swami [Gnanananda]." This same article tells of an event that occurred on April 27, 1973 (another report by Rajamanikam himself says April 29), when Yogi Ramsuratkumar was visiting the Tapovanam Ashram. According to Ramakrishnan, "Swami Gnanananda commanded the Yogi [Ramsuratkumar] to reveal himself to the world and gave him a palmyra fan and an incense stick symbolizing that a fragrant spiritual breeze could begin to flow from his presence." (Prior to this date, Ramsuratkumar carried the one fan that he had received many years before. Now, with this symbol of empowerment from an ageless saint, he had two fans, tied together. From this point on, the country hand fan was doubly empowered as the beggar's royal scepter.) "Two days later, in accordance with the plan that Swami Gnanananda and the Yogi had made, the former gave a pair of Padukas [sandals] to Sri Rajamanickam and told him, 'Just as Sri Rama gave his Padukas to Bharata, I am giving this to you.'"[5]

This reference to sandals relates to an important incident from the *Ramayana*. Prince Bharata has journeyed to the forest to find his brother, Lord Rama, who has been in exile there for several years. Bharata has come to tell Rama that their father, Dasaratha, has died, and to encourage Rama to return to Ayodhya and assume his rightful place on the throne. Rama, however, is adamant that he must fulfill the sentence of a fourteen-year exile that his father had rendered upon him, and refuses to return. Prince Bharata is heartbroken. As he does not wish to rule in his brother's place, Bharata asks Rama for his sandals, his wooden padukas. These he takes back to their kingdom. He has the royal throne brought from the palace in Ayodhya to a nearby village, Nandigrama. Here, Bharata places the padukas with great ceremony on the throne. He clothes himself with rough garments and seats himself on the ground before the throne. He swears that he will not take the royal seat, but only govern in his brother Rama's absence. Every day, the ministers and noblemen of the kingdom also put on rough garments and make the short pilgrimage to Nandigrama where they bow to Rama's shoes as to a king. It was said that if justice was being done, the sandals would lay quiet. If someone was wrongly judged, however, the sandals would beat together, creating quite a racket with their loud wooden soles.

Swami Gnanananda's gift of his padukas to Rajamanikam was no casual affair, although it was probably done with laughter and lightness. It linked the three men in one mission – the message of Rama Rajya, i.e., the proclamation of the word of God. Rajamanikam was to take the sandals, representing his master's spiritual power and presence, and carry them throughout Tamil Nadu. He was to witness to the grace that flows from the word of God. Outfitting a small van adorned with the portraits of Swami Gnanananda and other saints, including that of Yogi Ramsuratkumar, the beggar of Tiruvannamalai, Rajamanickam and a band of *bhaktas* undertook several pilgrimages in the 1970s and '80s. The most significant "*padayatra*" – as these journeys were called – was a two-year odyssey beginning in 1977 that took him to towns and villages throughout South India. Despite numerous obstacles, Rajamanickam maintained his enormous zeal and love for his guru, Gnanananda, as well as for the beggar-swami who had similarly captured his heart.

224

A Friend and Protector, 1971

It was through Rajamanickam's efforts that countless villagers and city dwellers throughout Tamil Nadu first heard the name of Yogi Ramsuratkumar. Those who visited Tapovanam in those early years, drawn by the energy of Gnanananda, would soon hear more of the mad beggar saint who had also loved this master. The trail from Tirukoilur to Tiruvannamalai, once walked by Ramana Maharshi, was becoming well worn to another end, as more and more devotees of Gnanananda's began to link the two places in their pilgrimage rounds.

From family and friends of Rajamanickam, and many others related in some way through the Tapovanam ashram, the stories are consistent: "We met Ramji swami at Tapovanam"; or "My parents would take us to Tapovanam and always we would go to Tiruvannamalai to have the darshan of Ramji Swami as well." In December 2002, as I visited with Rajamanikam's daughter, Vasugi, in Sivakashi, her voice was deep and resonant as she shouted out her praise, "Jaya Yogi Ramsuratkumar ki jai!" A woman in her forties, her approach to her faith and her devotion was completely without apology. As she spoke, even a pause of ten seconds was filled with saying the name of the beloved beggar whom she first met as a young girl of thirteen. "And will you have some tea? *Yogi Ramsuratkumar, Yogi Ramsuratkumar, Yogi Ramsuratkumar*. And how about some cookies? *Yogi Ramsuratkumar, Yogi Ramsuratkumar*. How long did your travels take you?" As her guests politely answered her, she continued to softly vocalize the name: *Yogi Ramsuratkumar, Jaya Guru Raya* (Victory to Him).

Vasugi explained that Yogi Ramsuratkumar could and would, in fact, mind the business of his devotees to the degree that they held themselves open to his direction. In her own case, the beggar actually helped in the arrangement of her marriage to her husband, C.A. Jairaj, as both their parents were devotees of Swami Gnanananda, and had therefore known Ramsuratkumar for many years at Tapovanam. Furthermore, after Gnanananda's death, her father and husband both sought the beggar's guidance in both personal and business matters. In fact, before building their home in Sivakashi, the city where Yogiji recommended that they live, the architectural plans were brought to the beggar for his approval and blessing.

ONLY GOD

The relationship between Yogi Ramsuratkumar and Swami Gnanananda is further linked through Rajamanickam in one lovely story. The beggar once gave a statue of Mahatma Gandhi to Rajamanickam and directed him to walk from Tiruvannamalai to Tapovanam to deliver the gift to Swami Gnanananda Giri. The statue of Mahatma Gandhi was "a symbolic gesture of showing to the world what is in store for the future of mankind," wrote A. N. Balasubramanian, a professor of economics, who shared the incident in his recollections of the beggar saint that were compiled in 1988.[6]

राम

Other stories of the interrelatedness of Gnanananda Giri and Ramsuratkumar are conveyed by those who knew both of them in these early years. Swami Nityananda Giri, who is currently the spiritual director of the Tapovanam Ashram, spoke at length about his knowledge of their relationship.

"Ramsuratkumar used to come here quite often; he was one of us," he told this biographer in an interview in November 2002. Apparently it was T.K. Sundaresan, a disciple of Ramana Maharshi's, who brought him first to Gnanananda. While at Tapovanam, Yogiji would often spend much time along the riverbank, or "there is a big hole in the trees and he'd be sitting there, so we have heard," Nityananda reported. To those who know of the beggar's love for trees and his affinity for the embrace of nature, this comes as no surprise.

"Gnanananda would never tell him – 'Come here' or 'do this' or 'do that.' He would allow him to be free," said Nityananda sweetly in recalling the exchanges between the two men. This freedom to come and go as he pleased was undoubtedly a great blessing for Ramsuratkumar, owing not only to his restricted situation in Tiruvannamalai, but to his wanderer's spirit.

While the beggar gave profound regard and homage to the saint of Tapovanam, Swami Nityananda was quick to assure me that there was never any doubt as to who Ramsuratkumar's guru was. Swami Ramdas was his master *first, last, and always*, and all who met the beggar knew this. Mother Krishnabai also was acknowledged. "There is only one mother," Ramji (as they affectionately called Ramsurat-kumar) would say.

On Guru Poornima day, a July holiday celebrated throughout the world to honor the guru, Yogi Ramsuratkumar would often come to Tapovanam. Ochre clothes were typically given to sannyasins on this occasion, and the beggar several times received this gift from the hands of Gnanananda himself.

One of the clearest recollections that Swami Nityananda had of the Godchild of Tiruvannamalai in his visits to their ashram was his wonderful songs. "In the night he would be chanting, *Om Sri Ram*, very often," the Swami related. "He also used to sing Mira bhajans, beautifully…very melodiously." Typically, these chants of the poet-saint Mirabai extolled the beauty of her dark-skinned Lord and Lover, Lord Krishna. For a bhakti such as Ramsuratkumar, these songs would naturally have been favorites. In fact, guru bhakti was so strong for the beggar that he would frequently drop into a type of ecstatic trance at the mere sight of something connected with the guru, Nityananda reported.

Yogi Ramsuratkumar was extremely fond of Vedic chants as well. "Every month we would have a day of remembrance of Gnanananda, a monthly celebration of his *mahanirvana*, and at that time a lot of Vedic pundits would come and chant Vedas. He [Yogi Ramsurat-kumar] would be walking with me around these mango trees, putting his arm around me. At that time I was not yet sannyas – I was not initiated. He would tell me, 'Sundarishi, are you not seeing here the rishis, Vedic rishis? I'm seeing them! I'm seeing them! They are here now!"

One day, returning from a trip to Madras where he had gone to pick up the newly printed copies of a book about the life and teach-ings of Gnanananda Giri, Swami Nityananda Giri found Yogi Ramsuratkumar "sitting in front of the *vigraha* of Gnanananda. He had already started a continuous chant of '*Gnanananda, Gnana-nanda, Satguru Gnanananda.*'" The chant was carried on throughout that auspicious day and on into the night. One could say that it con-tinues to this day, as this same chant, originally invoked by Ramsuratkumar, is still sung at the Tapovanam ashram in the dining hall prior to the serving of meals.

ONLY GOD

The Godchild of Tiruvannamalai seems to have found a worthy helpmate as well as a playmate in the person of Swami Gnanananda. Nityananda told of a morning when his master was sitting on the low wall of the verandah outside the puja hall. When Ramsuratkumar approached, "suddenly Gnanananda jumped up and said, 'Let us run a race, one, two, three, shoot!'" At which point the two saints, like children, immediately took off down the walkway. Laughing, Nityananda reported that his master, Gnanananda, had won the race, despite the fact that "he was fat and all that."

Prior to his death, Swami Gnanananda Giri had a life-size representation made of himself. Known as a *vigraha*, a Sanskrit word meaning "a form," Gnanananda invested the piece with much care and attention. It was to be a living memorial to which his devotees could come; a place from which blessings could be received. "He [Ramsuratkumar] was extremely fond of that vigraha – the black one. He used to give great importance to that. Ramji used to tell devotees: '*He* is *there* [meaning Gnanananda]. You can feel his presence,'" Swami Nityananda recalled with delight. This anecdote is all the more interesting when we know that Ramsuratkumar too left behind a large standing vigraha of himself, which is the central focus of the interior of the temple dedicated to him in Tiruvannamalai. "In fact," Swami Nityananda continued, "when a group of devotees joined together and wrote a book about Gnanananda, Ramsuratkumar wanted to see this chapter about the vigraha."

Ramsuratkumar had very many devotees – those who honored and loved him – at Tapovanam.

After the mahasamadhi of Gnanananda, in January 1974, Yogi Ramsuratkumar stayed at the saint's shrine for nine or ten months. At that time, Nityananda was hard at work compiling the teachings of Gnanananda that would later become a book. "We used to stay in the room upstairs," the Swami recalled. "Yogiji used to sleep there on the terrace, and he was very particular that nobody disturb me. He would not allow anyone to go upstairs. He would say, 'He [meaning Nityananda] is doing master's work. You should not go and disturb him.' He was very serious about it, and I cannot forget that."

"He used to take *bhiksha*, from people here. He gave a lot of importance to sadhus, sannaysins and Vedic chants, which is now

228

exactly what the Ashram [in Tiruvannamalai] is trying to do. In fact, it is a peculiar coincidence. I was also...with his samadhi. When Ramji Swami attained samadhi, they came to me, and I came there, and his mortal remains were laid to rest according to his own instructions and according to standard [Vedic] procedures."

Another devotee, who observed Yogiji in the Tapovanam Ashram at this time, remarked that the Godchild frequently sat quietly in front of a painting of Lord Rama, and in this way encouraged others to practice remembering the presence of the great god. "One day, immediately after the mahasamadhi of Swami Gnanananda, he was very much touched by the intensity of the grief of the lady devotees. He said, 'You are very fortunate people. Your love for Swami is like an *atma nivedana* [surrender]. You are like gopis who could not bear the separation of Sri Krishna. You are engulfed, totally taken over by Him. You are totally merged in Him."[7]

राम

As the years rolled on, and as more people came from Tapovanam to visit Yogi Ramsuratkumar in Tiruvannamalai, he would turn them back to the source of their devotion – back to Gnanananda and the incomparable teaching they had received from his presence and his words. "Everything is for you *there*," the beggar would direct. He never wished to draw anyone to himself but only to point one and all in the same direction, that of surrender to God and the remembrance of the Divine name.

"The main teaching of Gnanananda himself was *guru tat tvat* – the principle of the guru which transcends name and form," Swami Nityananda explained. "The real guru is beyond name and form. Therefore the same guru is in all teachers. There is no question of 'your guru' or 'my guru.' [Such distinctions come about] only because of ignorance. That being the teaching, it was easy for the devotees of Gnanananda to very well recognize a master, another master [such as Ramsuratkumar], too."

The disciples of Swami Gnanananda were not at all left in the dark about the sanctity of Yogi Ramsuratkumar. From Vasugi, one of the daughters of Rajamanickam, we learn that Gnanananda was quite direct in revealing the beggar's true identity to those who were close to him. "Gnanananda Swami showed him [Rajamanickam, her father] that he [Ramji] is a great *mahaan*. 'He is a great mahatma,' my father would tell us, and we blindly followed my father's footsteps in travelling to Tiruvannamalai since 1972 to seek Swamiji's blessings." And from another source we learn that Gnanananda himself told his disciples, speaking of Ramsuratkumar, "He is a great *siddha purusha* [enlightened saint]."

Another Tapovanam resident, Tennangur Sri Namaji Swami, recounts that one day his master, Gnanananda, asked the assembled crowd if they had seen Kabir, the famous poet saint of the fourteenth century. Of course people looked dumbfounded at such an inquiry. No one responded, so Maharaj (Gnanananda) asked again if they would like to see Kabir. This received an enthusiastic and expectant agreement. With everyone's eyes fixed on him, Gnanananda pointed to Yogi Ramsuratkumar, who stood silently among the assembly, and said, "He who was Kabir then is now Yogi Ramsuratkumar."[8]

Yogiji's teaching method, Nityananda pointed out, was essentially *namas* – japa and chanting of the name. "In fact, we used to have very humorous exchanges with him, because we monks here are brought up in traditional advaita vedanta, and the emphasis here is on overcoming name and form." Ultimately, however, there was no contradiction between the teachings of the two saints – between love of God's name and advaitic consciousness. As Swami Nityananda reminded us, "The absorption in the name of God will take you beyond name and form, and even great masters among advaita vedantins have talked about the glory of name." Swami Gnanananda Giri was certainly one of those. Here was no lightweight on the spiritual landscape. While never receiving the notoriety of Ramana Maharshi or Vivekananda, Gnanananda stands shoulder to shoulder with these remarkable figures of our modern times.

> To attain Divine Grace, meditation is more important than prodigious learning. Yearning is more important than skill in discussion; tears flowing from eyes are more important than verses recited by the tongue and worship is more beneficial than research into books.[9] – Swami Gnanananda Giri

13

WIDENING THE DOOR, 1973-1975

 Caylor Wadlington's relationship to the wondrous beggar, the Godchild of Tiruvannamalai, drew other Westerners intent on meeting "Caylor's swami." Some of these visitors left barely a trace of their presence. Others, like Will and Joan Zulkowski, stumbled into the Godman's chamber, where they stayed for several weeks almost every year. In the process, they left behind them a long list of classic teaching lessons, a legacy of interactions that illuminate the wisdom, compassion, and wonderful humor of the beggar-saint.

In 1973, two years after their first trip to India (1970-71), in which they had failed to meet Yogi Ramsuratkumar, Will and Joan wrote to their friend Caylor, "Would you please go to the swami and ask him if it's alright for us to come back?"

The answer arrived promptly. "It was a beautiful letter," Will recalled. Caylor had written: "Swami says yes, you've delayed your trip for a year, come." Yogi Ramsuratkumar had signed the letter, himself: "My Father blesses Will, My Father blesses Joan. Mother India's arms are always open to you." The beggar had also added an "Om sign, and what looked like a little mountain."[1]

Needless to say, the Zulkowskis were both elated by the letter. They flew to Madras in November 1973, where they met Caylor, and soon after had their first memorable darshan of Yogi Ramsuratkumar.

"We came into Tiruvannamalai in the late afternoon on the bus," Will began. "We asked around town if someone knew where Swami was, and on that particular afternoon, we learned, he was staying at some judge's house. Caylor went to see him and once again reported that it wouldn't work out for us to go. Swami had said, 'Oh, come back tomorrow. This beggar has a fever today, so it's not good to talk today.'

"We were staying at Ramanashram, and the next morning we rented bicycles and rode out to the railroad tracks. Caylor knew exactly where the place was, so we parked our bikes near there. And then we saw Swami! He was very friendly, very jovial, and his pockets were bulging. I asked him, 'Swami, what do you have in your pockets?' He just reached in his pants and pulled out *nellikkai* (gooseberries), a little dried herb, the chief ingredient in Tibetan medicine and also Ayurvedic medicine. It's very bitter, but when you chew it, after a while, it does take on a sweetness.

"From the beginning Swami was concerned about our being in the sun. 'Oh, you're not used to this tropical sun,' he said. 'Sit here,'

The railway station platform, Tiruvannamalai

pointing to a tiny palm tree, about four feet high, nearby. The three of us Westerners huddled together under it. Of course, when Swami makes a suggestion, I didn't know it so well at the time, but I came to appreciate that you don't argue, you just do it. Anyway, we sat there, and Swami started talking, and thanking us so sweetly for a favor we had done for him [in supporting Caylor]. 'No, no,' we told him, 'it is our pleasure to serve you.'"

Yogi Ramsuratkumar looked at Will for a while, studying him intently, as he often did to his visitors, and put up his hand in a typical gesture of blessing. Almost immediately, Will lapsed into a deep state of ecstasy.

"I closed my eyes and I was *gone*. I just went into a samadhi-like state, and I stayed that way for at least half an hour. I went so deep in my consciousness that the whole world was gone. I could *hear*, but I was in a pristine blackness. It was not a negative thing, at all. A luminous blackness, rather than a flat blackness, and it was extremely peaceful and extremely quiet there. So I thought to myself, 'I'm never, ever, coming out of this state.'"

Yogi Ramsuratkumar, however, soon interrupted Will's ecstasy, calling him back to reality. "Mr. Will, come this side. No good tea, coffee, and cigarettes on that side," the beggar directed.

But Will was not persuaded. "I still said to myself, '*No, this is so beautiful, I'm never coming out of this state.*'"

Again, Yogi Ramsuratkumar said, "Mr. Will, come this side. No good tea, coffee, and cigarettes on that side."

"*Nope, I'm never, ever coming out of this state. It is too beautiful, I don't ever want to leave it,*" Will still affirmed to himself.

Finally, Yogiji was firmer than before, saying strongly, "Mr. Will, no good to be on that side. No good to be on that side."

When Will failed to respond, Yogi Ramsuratkumar took control. "I felt like someone had drawn a complete circle of light around me," Will explained, "and then Swami did a very strange thing. Slowly he said the words, 'Nine, eight, zero, two,' and the instant he said, 'two,' I was back in my body, with my eyes open. Then he just roared with laughter, for at least a half an hour after that, and was playfully slapping Caylor on the back. 'I think that's Mr. Will's number,' Swami said. And laughed some more. I've never seen him laugh so much.

"For years, whenever I'd see him, I quizzed him about what that experience was, and what that number was. I would joke, 'Swami, is this my room number in heaven?'

"'Oh, it's just this beggar's madness,' he'd say, avoiding the issue. 'This beggar doesn't know what he did.' He'd never give me a straight answer. After I had that experience I figured that Yogi Ramsuratkumar was my guru."

राम

When Yogi Ramsuratkumar sent Caylor to Madras, it was Will-Joan who shared the privilege of spending long hours, both day and night, with the master. As Caylor had done, they stayed with him many nights in a shop in the brass bazaar. They would typically meet him about 8 P.M. and leave at his bidding about 5 A.M.. Although the two Americans often wanted to sleep during these hours, most of the time it was clearly not the beggar's intention that they drift off.

"Sit down, Mr. Will," Yogi Ramsuratkumar would say, meaning "sit up," as Will would start to doze. It was his way of calling his visitors back to attention. The nights were times of instruction and communion, unimpeded by the activities and distractions of the day. Will remembers conversations that occurred at 3 A.M. in which Swamiji spoke of Will's healing abilities and his future work.

"Swami, how can I do this, I'm just an ordinary person?" Will would ask, at which point the beggar would raise his hands and say only: "Father's will, Father's will, Father's will."

"I didn't argue. But I was a little surprised, shocked," Will remembered.

Different people would stop in to pay their respects to the beggar-swami, but most of the time the three would be alone. When they assembled for the night, and if no other attendants were available, Will or Joan might be asked to lay out his bedroll, which had been stored in the shop of some friendly merchants. Actually, "bedroll" is a euphemism for what Will and Joan saw as a terribly ratty mat, full of holes. At one of their early meetings, this bedroll became the subject of a strong teaching lesson that Yogi Ramsuratkumar enacted with Joan.

When the spot for the night had been determined, and the beggar's burlap bags of newspapers and assorted trash and treasures had been arranged, Yogi Ramsuratkumar addressed Joan, saying sweetly, "You can do some work for this beggar?"[2]

Joan, of course, was thrilled at the insinuation that she could be of some service.

"Perumal isn't here," Swamiji said, "you can unroll the bed." And with that, Yogi Ramsuratkumar began to carefully instruct the young woman about exactly how she was to do the job.

"He told me in detail how I was to proceed," Joan reported years later in speaking about Yogi Ramsuratkumar to a gathering in New York. "Don't get up now," the beggar warned her again, as Joan was probably already in motion before her instructions had been fully received. "This beggar will explain how you must do this nicely."

Such a simple task, to roll out a bed! And yet the mind, driven by ego's need to have its own way, would not allow Joan to hear. As the Godchild explained how he wanted it, Joan heard only what she expected to hear, blocking out everything else. As she jumped up to finally "do the work," she moved the bed materials in such a way that left the usually gentle beggar aghast.

"What are you *doing*?" he shouted, astonished at her activity.

"I, uh, well, you know, Swami..." Joan tried to defend her unconsciousness, but could only stumble over her words.

"Sit down," he said firmly, and Joan reported that she felt mortified.

As her mind raced for a justification, wanting to blame the master for his lack of proper communication, Yogi Ramsuratkumar turned to Will. "Mr. Will," he said sweetly once again, "Joan thinks this beggar is very arrogant."

These words shocked Joan. This was precisely the direction that her thoughts *had* been taking. Yogi Ramsuratkumar, meanwhile, grew serious again and, looking at her with firm resolve, said, "After some time, when you've been with this beggar, sometimes he treats you differently."[3]

The lesson for Joan was obvious. If she *was* serious about taking the benediction of a master's teaching, she would have to pay attention in a way that she was currently unaccustomed to doing. She would have to surrender her own expectations in order to hear exactly what was being asked of her. She would have to attend to the smallest details that she might have previously conceived as inconsequential. And, she would have to be ready to bear both the sweet, embracing words of her "Swamiji" as well as the cutting edge of his sword.

That Yogi Ramsuratkumar was only interested in working with those who could "hear" him was made perfectly clear to both Will and Joan on another occasion. As they sat in the beggar's presence, a visitor from Canada talked on and on. Swamiji fell asleep, and after a while the man left. When the master woke up, Will asked him, "Swami, why did you fall asleep when that man was here?"

"Oh," said Yogi Ramsuratkumar quite unapologetically, "that man couldn't hear what this beggar had to say."

राम

Like Joan's experience with the bedroll, Will had a similar story to relate about how small things would take on enormous significance in the work-field of a Godman. One day, as the Zulkowskis sat with Ramsuratkumar and a couple of other Western women, their host sent a little boy to get tea. "Swami would place the teacups very specifically in front of you. That was the protocol. He would serve the tea and then you'd wait for him to take the first sip, and then you could take your tea. In one of these little escapades I wasn't thinking and I just moved my teacup a little closer," Will reported candidly.[4]

Immediately, Yogi Ramsuratkumar stopped what he was doing and looked directly at Will. "Oh, you don't think this beggar knows what he's doing? Do you? But this beggar put that cup there for a purpose."

Yogi Ramsuratkumar was quite upset by Will's tiny gesture. Leaving his guests to wonder about what had just happened, the master left, temporarily. When he returned, he walked around and around the group, holding up his staff. Ten minutes later, his ritual was finished. "Well, this beggar did what he could. Let's do it again," he said, and with that he replaced the teacups and started their meeting all over again.

"After that, I never, ever touched the teacups," Will reported. "He made no gestures that were outside of his work. Everything was a part of what his mission was. There were no wasted movements. Even the slightest move, even the slightest thing, had great meaning to him. We were not aware of it. Swami was always very gracious, very gentle. But after we had been with him for about two weeks he started to get a little peppery. He said, 'When you are with this beggar you must pursue *his* program.'"

"Once, he was reading a newspaper, and it was folded a certain way, and he got up to do something and I started looking at it, and when he came back he was really upset."

Several years later, in hearing these stories, Hilda Charlton, a prominent spiritual teacher in New York City, drew out the principles underlying the mad beggar's behavior, since few in her group had experience in the domain of spiritual work. Because she had lived in India and studied with several remarkable masters, Hilda was able to see what most Westerners would completely overlook. On November 11, 1976, she said:

> Do you comprehend what he was doing, kids, when he put a teacup here and one over here and one over here and one over here and nobody could move them? He was working with the Infinite. So you understand? Do you comprehend at all? He was placing something that had power to change the world. He might have been working with religions. He might have been working with countries. He might have been working with ideas. But he was shaping things.
>
> And he hides behind his craziness; he hides behind his laughter. But he's stern, stern, so stern you have to do it just right. And people don't understand – why can't you just do it sloppy?
>
> Why not? Because he puts a stone there, he's placing it for the universe; he's placing it for the world. He's changing the world with his thoughts, with his power...These hidden angels, these great ones, help hold the world in balance.[5]

राम

Yogi Ramsuratkumar's sternness most often took the form of temporary reprimands, while at other times harsher methods were necessitated, as those around him continued to violate protocol, or refused to listen to his directions. In 1974, shortly after the mahasamadhi of Swami Gnanananda Giri, Will and Joan visited Tapovanam with the beggar. After they had been there for a few days, "we were getting to be a nuisance, so that when he would see us, Swami would just run the other way," Will confessed without trying to defend himself. As the threesome sat in a tea stall one day, Yogi Ramsuratkumar turned to the couple and said without emotion, "Better you clear out of the place."[6]

His directive was unequivocal, and Will said that he and Joan felt "like our universe was dashed." They obeyed, however. They got on the bus headed for Madras and the Theosophical Society, and stayed away for eight months. In Madras, however, they got involved with a powerful tantric teacher. Joan actually ended up going off with this teacher for a period of time, and Will was greatly upset, and depressed to the point that he wanted to kill himself.

Finally, when all hope was exhausted, Will returned to Tiruvannamalai and went back to see Yogi Ramsuratkumar. When Swamiji saw him, he simply took Will's hands and held them, for hours, looking at him and "working" on him, as Will described. Whenever Will felt some urgency to do something or say something, Yogi Ramsuratkumar would just look at him and say, "Will, silence is the greatest power." Will interpreted these words to mean that "the great work is being done at another level. You don't have to try to force anything."

As soon as the beggar did this, Will felt better. In his enormous compassion, Yogi Ramsuratkumar kept Will close to him for ten or twelve hours a day for several days. Eventually, Joan returned, and with the beggar's benediction everything got "patched up," Will said.[7]

राम

"We used to carry his burlap bags, every night, out to the fields, and then back. Joan got to carry the light stuff, and I, or Perumal, or

George, we got the heavy stuff. Swami never threw anything out," Will explained.

One day, as the Americans followed Yogi Ramsuratkumar along a narrow path between the rice paddies that were cultivated near the railway station outside of town, they learned another invaluable lesson about paying attention. It was a gorgeous morning, blessed with fresh air and the sounds of birds, and crowned with the ever-present spirit of Arunachala which loomed above them. As usual, Will and Joan were carrying one or more heavy burlap bundles, the beggar's accoutrements.

Without warning, Yogi Ramsuratkumar stopped in his tracks. Joan, who was next in line, was unprepared for his action. Distracted by her own thoughts, her absorption in the beauty of nature, or whatever, she bumped into him as if walking into a wall. Will, behind Joan, and similarly distracted, bumped into her. Startled and embarrassed, the couple immediately felt the sting of the master's disapproval. His words were clear: "This beggar doesn't want you to think about mantras. Don't think of any gurus. Don't even think of God. Be observant and do what he says to do. We have this work to do nicely and that's all you have to be concerned with."[8]

In related incidents involving his Indian attendants, Yogi Ramsuratkumar made many valuable teachings about intention and attention, as well as how he expected work to be done. When Yogi Ramsuratkumar still lived under the punnai tree, an Indian man named Jagannathan was his primary attendant. At this time, another entourage of men was usually available to carry the large bundles that the beggar wanted near him, leaving Jagannathan free to be fully available to the master's needs. As they walked through fields and along narrow paths, Jagannathan was to be especially attentive. Yogi Ramsuratkumar expected the younger man to hold his hand, either walking before him, or immediately after.

During one celebratory event at the Arunachaleswarar Temple, a Chettiar (one of a sub-caste of Hindus native to Tamil Nadu) paid a visit to Yogi Ramsuratkumar and gave him a gold ring, as a tribute. As in many cases, the beggar submitted to the devotee's wishes and put the gold ring on his little finger, where he wore it for several months.

One evening, a dispute arose among the men who were carrying Yogiji's bundles, and resentment was expressed to Jagannathan. *Why did he not share in the load?* the other men wanted to know. At one point, the attendants actually put down their packs and refused to proceed until Jagannathan picked one up. This pacified the men and so Jagannathan, still carrying the bundle, ran to catch up with Yogi Ramsuratkumar. As soon as the Godchild saw Jagannathan with the sack, he became agitated and told his attendant to put it down immediately, explaining to him very strongly that it was not his work. Jagannathan did as he was instructed and the group proceeded to the protection of a vessel shop where Swamiji and Jagannathan would sleep the night.

The next morning, as they had tea, Yogi Ramsuratkumar noticed that the ring was no longer on his finger. Considering this circumstance for a moment, the beggar turned to Jagannathan and gently but seriously addressed him, saying: "See Jagannatha [as Yogiji referred to him], when you do somebody else's work, Father's work gets upset."

The Godman was not declaring a precise cause-effect relationship between the disputes of the previous day and the disappearance of the ring. Nonetheless, Jagannathan was clear that his own inability to keep his priorities straight, as far as where his attention should have been placed, had direct bearing on the situation. In some way, Yogi Ramsuratkumar's intentions had been frustrated, since his wearing of the ring had some significance for him. People who do not appreciate that such distinctions can make a big difference will easily get lost in trivialities, thus missing the larger picture.[9]

राम

Yogi Ramsuratkumar had worked with enough Westerners to recognize the phenomena of drug-induced states. "It is very hard for this beggar to work with too much drugs," he told Will and Joan, referring to such people. He proceeded to tell them that drugs were a deadend for humanity, a spiritual deadend. "He was very firm about this. Caylor was considering writing a book about the relationship of drugs to spiritual experience, and when Yogiji heard of this he was very upset. He didn't want him to write anything that might encourage somebody to take drugs," Will reported.

राम

The beggar's practice of smoking cigarettes was noted by almost everyone who visited him. For some, it was miraculous – no matter how much he smoked, they claimed to never smell cigarette smoke lingering on or about him. For others, the action was enough to turn them away, as they surmised that no "spiritual" person should engage in such a habit. In 1995, as this biographer left Yogi Ramsuratkumar's darshan one morning, she was approached by a pristinely dressed Western woman, who introduced herself as a journalist from a widely read yoga magazine published in the U.S.

"What's going on here?" the woman asked, initially dumbfounded by the fact that no spoken instruction had been offered by the master during the meeting. "He was smoking!" she added, as if I didn't know. She looked horrified, and was unable to contain her disapproval.

Her response was overt and honest, however. Many others might have said nothing but simply left the scene without bothering to question their assumptions. (This woman, in fact, stayed around long enough to interview Lee Lozowick, who was visiting at the time. She opened herself to a new level of understanding as Yogi Ramsuratkumar's spiritual son held her questions with compassion and answered her candidly. In the end, the journalist wrote a short, positive description of the beggar's ashram in a publication for Western readers.)[10]

From Will Zulkowski's early reflections, and from his conversations with Hilda a short time later, we hear for the first time a new interpretation of the beggar's use of tobacco.

"Swami was always telling us, 'Oh, this beggar is so sick of smoking, it makes him so sick.' But then he told Caylor that the only reason he smoked was because he couldn't stand to be around human beings. He had to smoke because it made him more dense, and then he could stand to be around humans. It seemed that he smoked a lot more when people came around, and Hilda had the impression that he was burning up the karma of the people who would come. When people came he was chain-smoking. When people weren't there, he didn't smoke as much."

These observations were definitely confirmed by others in the years that followed. From Ma Vijayalakshmi's unpublished biography of the beggar, entitled *Waves of Love*, written in 2002, we learn:

> The pulls on his Charminar cigarettes put off some devotees who thought it strange that a "Swami" would smoke. But this was a way of work for the Yogi. He used to say that before the "madness" seized him, he never liked to smoke. In fact the smoke nauseated him – "this beggar used to feel like vomiting." But Father's work introduced new parameters including smoking. Many are the devotees who narrated their tales of woe to Bhagawan, who just sat and smoked and blessed them with "Father's blessings." Within a short while they found their problems solved – be it health, finance or business. Shri T.P. Meenakshisundaram, a great devotee of Bhagawan, who had also been closely observing him over the years, has written many songs in praise of Bhagawan. In one of the songs, he recorded that the smoking of Bhagawan alleviated the sufferings of devotees and elevated them to a higher place. "You continue your endless smoking and your delight in the immediate relief and uplift of the sufferers, be praised," he writes.[11]

Besides his use of smoking to handle the karma and health of those around him, Will also noted Yogi Ramsuratkumar's various gestures that seemed to be addressing unseen forces. "When he would talk," Will said, "he would always be looking above your head, making motions with his fingers." It was Hilda's observation that he was looking into the future and warding off the karma that might be coming one's way.

Whatever the Godchild's smoking meant, however, it was not the devotee's job to analyze it. "Don't try to figure me out, because you can't do it. Just do what I say," Yogi Ramsuratkumar repeatedly told Will and Joan.

राम

Whether it was the need of a mother for her child's welfare, or the need of a nation for a leader with integrity, Yogi Ramsuratkumar's attention was constant and unshakable. As many people before and since have noted, the beggar held the whole world as his field of endeavor.

"In the early years we would talk about world politics," Will said. "And he knew more about world politics than anybody I had ever met. He had the overview on everything. He knew who was specifically responsible in every country if there was anything bad going on. Once he told someone that he was aware when the satellites went overhead. He said they were interfering with his work. He also said that he didn't like the advance of technology, because 'the scriptures are all in the air [referring undoubtedly to the Vedas, which were traditionally believed to have been transmitted to the great rishis through the air], and those radio waves are disturbing the scriptures.'"

Such a refined sense of energy is so far beyond common understanding that it could easily be dismissed as sheer madness. Unless one had some inkling of the yogic traditions, or some appreciation for the energetic matrix that contemporary physicists describe at the subatomic level, such references sound incredible. "He was really 'way out there,'" Will himself exclaimed.

राम

The stories of attack and harassment that Yogi Ramsuratkumar had begun to tell Perumal about in the early 1960s, and Caylor about in 1970, were enhanced with some details as noted by Will and Joan. The DMK party, which sought to drive out all non-Tamil elements, had actually hired "*gundas*" – thugs, terrorists – Will was told. A person who wrote an editorial that criticized DMK tactics might coincidentally meet with a bad accident going home on his bicycle or motor scooter. The accident might happen to another family member – a child coming home from school. The ongoing intimidation was strong.

243

Will was unaware of how this harassment was affecting his much-loved swami until he moved out on the street with Yogi Ramsuratkumar. As they walked along, Will noted that the beggar was constantly on alert, looking all around him. On these excursions the saint made use of his power staff, which Will described as looking like an archer's bow, decorated with peacock feathers and bits of string that had been saved and tied in place. He might suddenly raise the staff, turn to Will, and point in a new direction, saying, "Stop. Go over to the side." With that, Will noticed a previously unobserved car come roaring out of a small street or alleyway, precisely aimed at the spot where the two men would have stood had they not moved unexpectedly.

The Godchild told Will that the people who gave him food at various restaurants around town had also been approached by these gundas. These generous merchants were systematically harangued and threatened with mishaps to their businesses if they continued to serve the Bihari, the beggar.

Ramsuratkumar told Will that, within six months of his arrival in Tiruvannamalai in 1959, he overheard two men within earshot of him speaking. "We think this guy should leave this place," they said. At the time, the beggar simply ignored it. But then things got progressively worse. "A few times they tried to stab him," Will related, with tears in his eyes as he remembered. "Sometimes he would wake up and we would find that his arms had been cut. But he would rub them to heal them, saying *Rama, Rama, Rama.*"[12]

After one particularly grueling day, Will asked Ramsuratkumar directly, "Swami, why do you take this? Why do you do this?"

Gently and sweetly the Godman replied, "This beggar's here not to defend his ego. He's only here to do the Father's work."[13]

For Will, this provided a very strong lesson, as he compared Yogi Ramsuratkumar's response to the typically pushy way in which he, Will, attempted to conduct affairs.

Once, at 4 A.M., some drunken men approached Swamiji, cursing him as evil, and fully intent on beating him up. "Oh, Ram is here," the Yogi shouted with enthusiasm as they lunged at him. "Sita is here, Lakshmana is here!" The two attackers were so stunned by their victim's mood that they quickly backed away and, with quizzical looks, wandered off in another direction.[14]

In a similar act of faith, innocence, and skillful means, Yogi Ramsuratkumar once encountered an arrogant Brahmin man who was associated with the DMK. As the beggar left the premises of a house, following a wedding to which he had been invited, the Brahmin, who was sitting outside the door, remarked with dripping sarcasm: "Oooh, it's the godchild."

Yogi Ramsuratkumar stopped on a dime, turned to the Brahmin and immediately pranamed, reverently touching the man's feet, saying, "Ooooh, it's God Himself!" And with that, the mad beggar rose up and walked off. Needless to say, the Brahmin was left in a state of profound astonishment.[15]

Linking the publication of the biography written by Caylor with a lessening of these threats to his life, Yogi Ramsuratkumar told Will, "You gave the money for this book, thereby this beggar was helped; thereby this universe was helped. This beggar is always in your debt."[16] He further explained to Will that the small book had enabled him to stay in Tiruvannamalai because some of the people who read it were journalists from Madras and Bangalore. These people had influence, which allowed him to remain in relative safety.

राम

"Joan and I came one evening and Swami was eating a big gourmet meal that some devotee had brought. With tears in his eyes, he said: "That lady used to cook for Nityananda." It was moving to him to think that this woman would cook for him, when she had also cooked for this great saint. I asked him about Nityananda, and he said he thought Nityananda was one of the greatest saints that ever walked the earth, although he said he had never met him."

राम

The life of a beggar stood in stark contrast to the "values" and habits of many Westerners, and these differences were strongly highlighted in Will's interactions with Yogi Ramsuratkumar. For one who had lived on the streets, fed from the scraps of others' meals, and slept on the ground, some of his guests' behaviors appeared ridiculous.

"Sometimes, he said he was sick of sweets, and he would have us go to the bazaar and get some really sour purple grapes, real bitter. Joan would be washing the grapes, and he'd say, 'Why are you washing the grapes?' because from a Western standpoint, they were filthy. They had been right on the roadside. He would take one and say, 'Oh, these are so refreshing. So good.'"

"Caylor's friend wanted to open a 'health food' restaurant in Madras. When Swami heard this, he was totally cracking up by the concept, because for him food *was* for health." For one who had known hunger, as Yogi Ramsuratkumar certainly had, and one who had seen the hunger of India's poor, such an idea as special health food was ridiculous. A lot of times the beggar lived on only puffed rice and water, which was very inexpensive. "For ten paise (less than a penny) you used to be able to get a big bag. He lived on a lot of puffed rice."

And likewise, his behavior was a constant source of wonderment to those who observed him carefully. "What he did for a bath every day – his morning bath. He would have Perumal go get him some water in his coconut bowl and he'd sprinkle a few drops of water over his head and he'd rub it over his face a little bit, then he'd say, 'Oh, now this beggar is awake.' Most times he wouldn't get a bath for over a year. I would ask him about this, and he'd say, 'Oh, this beggar didn't have time to have a bath this year.' His idea of a bath would be to walk into the bathing ghat at the temple. He would walk in and walk out, and that was his bath for the year."[17]

In a somewhat related "bath" story, told by a resident swami in Tiruvannamalai, who heard the story from Yogi Ramsuratkumar: one day the beggar received a visit from a highly-renowned and extremely orthodox Vaishnavaite sadhu from North India. This man was well known for his sanctity as well as for his habit of ritualistically bathing up to ten times a day. He was also reputed to be completely lacking in fear for the consequences of any of his actions.

As the two men walked together within the compound of the great temple in Tiruvannamalai, the visitor expressed his wish that they both take the darshan of the temple deity, within the Holy of

Holies. An obvious requirement of such a visit, for the Vaishnavaite, included fresh ablutions just prior to entry.

As the men approached one of the large water ponds within the temple precincts, the Vaishnaivaite turned abruptly, placed his hands on the beggar and pushed Yogi Ramsuratkumar into the water, declaring, "Now, take your bath!"

A day later, when asked about how the visit from the sadhu went, the gentle Godman's only reply was, "It is true what they say about him. He really has no fear."[18]

राम

"Do as you like, but this beggar feels…" was the way in which Yogi Ramsuratkumar indicated his wishes for those who asked his advice. Will would always write and tell Yogiji of his plans to visit India, which he did almost every year for six weeks in January-February. He would spend time at various places, including Tiruvannamalai, and also at Sai Baba's ashram in Puttaparthi. One year, Will had come to India intending to spend his first two weeks in Tiruvannamalai before moving on. When he arrived, Yogi Ramsuratkumar was sitting on the front steps of his residence at Sannadhi Street, and when he saw him he grabbed Will's hands and said, "This beggar wishes you a good trip."

Will was shocked. "But Swami, I just got here, I'm going to spend two weeks with you," Will tried to reason. Yogi Ramsuratkumar looked at the Western man and said, "Do as you like, but this beggar feels…," and then followed these words with specific instructions. Will knew that this type of command was best obeyed. So, he left according to Yogi's "feeling."

"He was very precise in the way he wanted things done." Will was adamant. "There was no 'doing it your way.' Absolutely none. It wasn't even in the equation."

When Hilda heard this story from Will, however, "she interpreted it that Swami was picking up on my capacity to only absorb so much, and that after that it doesn't pay to stay any longer. She said, 'You have to consistently trust Swami. He is knowing what your capacity is, what your limit is.' That's a big one to crack, because the ego wants to be in control. But when you are dealing with those people [the saints], control is not an issue. You have to tell the mind to shut up."[19]

Ramsuratkumar delivered a similar message to Will and Joan one year when they asked to go to the Kumbha Mela, a massive gathering of sadhus and saints from all over India. The beggar looked at them incredulously as he said, "You can't even handle what is *here*. Don't even think about the Kumbha Mela."

Another day, as Will was considering the issue of helping other people, he asked Yogi Ramsuratkumar about this strong desire. Without pausing for breath, the Godman replied, "Will, who can a drowning man help?"

राम

A young man, John Gilbert, used to visit Yogi Ramsuratkumar during the early 1970s when Will and Joan were in Tiruvannamalai. John was diagnosed with cancer. But when he told this to Yogi Ramsuratkumar, the beggar looked at him for a long time, up and down. Finally, Yogiji said: "This beggar doesn't see anything; he sees nothing. And if John Gilbert thinks he *has* anything, John Gilbert should say, 'I am not the body. I am not the body. I am not the body.'"

Within three or four years John had died of cancer, but the instruction he had received from Ramsuratkumar had addressed the issue of his illness at a much deeper level than his physical symptoms.

राम

"He wouldn't begin to talk about who he really is," Joan reflected years later, "until the quiet of the night had settled in and the village had stopped its activity, and people had been sent away. [Then] those who were lucky to stay would hear some fantastic things from that beggar. He would tell us with no uncertainty that he is a master, and that he is doing his Father's work perfectly, and he would also say that the Father is pleased with this beggar's work. He would say that it's not this beggar's lot to live in an ashram and have that kind of sur-

Yogi Ramsuratkumar, circa 1959

Yogi Ramsuratkumar at Tapovanam Ashram, circa 1970

Yogi Ramsuratkumar and Caylor Wadlington at the bus stand, Tiruvannamalai, 1972

Caylor Wadlington, Yogi Ramsuratkumar, and Joan Zulkowski, 1973

Caylor Wadlington, Yogi Ramsuratkumar, and Will Zulkowski, 1973

Yogi Ramsuratkumar, early 1973

Yogi Ramsuratkumar, 1975

The beggar-king, Yogi Ramsuratkumar, and his dog, Sai Baba, circa 1976

The Godchild of Tiruvannamalai and Hilda Charlton, 1978

Yogi Ramsuratkumar on Sannadhi Street, overshadowed by the temple gopuram and Mount Arunachala, late 1980s

Lee Lozowick and Yogi Ramsuratkumar within the Arunachaleswarar Temple, 1988

The Divine beggar, Yogi Ramsuratkumar, circa 1989, at the Krupa estate of Dwarakanath Reddy

Yogi Ramsuratkumar with the Sudama sisters, early 1990s

Tending the flowers in Reddy's garden, early 1990s

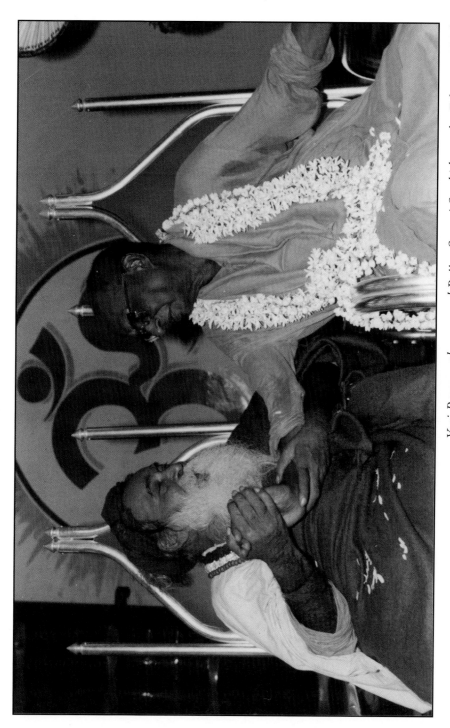

Yogi Ramsuratkumar and Pujya Swami Satchidananda, February 1994

The laughing Godchild garlanded with flowers

rounding. He said it was his lot to live the life of a beggar and he does it very well." Then he would laugh.

"One night I said, 'Swami, it looks as though there are kings sitting before a beggar,' because the Westerners who were visiting him were dressed so nicely, 'but it is really beggars sitting before a king.'"[20] Yogi Ramsuratkumar was delighted by her comment.

राम

In these early years of his ministry to the West, Yogi Ramsuratkumar's dogma was the same as it had always been, and always would be. He told Will that all the practice he ever had to do was "to remember God all the time." Many years later, in a letter to Will, he wrote reminding him of this, urging him above all else to remember God.

राम

Besides the narratives left by Wadlington and the Zulkowskis during the years 1971-1973, another brief but fantastic portrait of the beggar is drawn by a brilliant Canadian writer, Paul William Roberts, who met Yogi Ramsuratkumar in 1975. Robert's book, *Empire of the Soul*, published in 1994, diaries the author's journeys through India in the mid-1970s, and again in the 1990s. In a chapter about his adventures in Tiruvannamalai in 1975, Roberts describes meeting the beggar-yogi sitting at a vacant stall in the brass market.

On a bench in the shadows sat a powerfully built man, perhaps in his late sixties – it was hard to tell – [Yogiji was in fact fifty-eight] with a huge, graying beard. His dirty robes had something of ancient Rome about them. He was flapping a circular fan of some sort of dried leaf attached to a wooden handle, powerfully, urgently, as if the heat really bothered him. His hand moved in a blur below his face. A large, soiled rag worn bandanna-style was drenched in perspiration…His English was excellent, and judging by the pale skin and the accent, he was certainly not from these parts, not a Southerner. His body, too, was different: large-boned, with sizable muscles in the legs, big feet, and large but slender and well-formed hands. A Bengali, I decided, mainly because he resembled the poet Tagore.[21]

Like so many Westerners before and since, Roberts was immediately taken by the oddly dressed beggar with the "bright eyes" and look of "impish amusement" in his face. He was even more surprised when Yogi Ramsuratkumar took his hands and warmly welcomed him – "Oh! You have come!" – as if he were expected.

Roberts also noted that the beggar smoked, and that, "[w]hen his other hand was not fanning...it was performing a rapid motion like counting the beads of an invisible rosary. Indeed he was all motion."[22] This same gesture, of apparently saying the name of God as he moved an invisible mala, was observed throughout the beggar's long life.

Their discussion ranged from the specifics of yogis who smoked to the purpose of life, as the Westerner tried to grasp the essence of a life that was spent in such relaxed disregard and yet kingly bearing as was Ramsuratkumar's. When Roberts observed that many people would judge such a life as being an evasion of responsibility, the beggar calmly responded, "There are many tasks in this world. Many jobs that must be done by those who God wishes to do them..."[23] And with that, Ramsuratkumar briefly explained that such jobs might actually be affecting the outcome of world events in a way that most people could never understand.

"There was a great teacher," the Godchild remarked, without mentioning the name of Swami Ramdas, "who took this beggar and made him function for the will of God. Just as a broken automobile can be repaired so the driver can drive it again..."[24]

When Paul questioned the beggar about how such influencing of world affairs might be accomplished, Yogi Ramsuratkumar's answer was to swat a fly that had landed on the counter in front of them. Then,

[H]e picked the creature up by a wing and gave it to me. I tentatively accepted it, trying to appear grateful, and examined the insect in the palm of my hand to see if there was something I had missed. Mangled, oozing, one wing buckled into a squashed abdomen, it looked like any other dead fly I'd ever encountered.

The yogi watched me intently, puffing and counting those invisible beads, a big, generous smile swelling through his high cheekbones.

"Very dirty," he said, nodding at the fly. "Put it there." He indicated the spot where the fly had just met its abrupt end. A tiny stain was still visible on the wood.

I tipped the speck down near the stain.

"What can death be?" the yogi asked.

I shrugged, not about to offer an answer to that.

"It is a question we are interested in – is it not so?"

I nodded.

"Watch." He pointed to the fly.

I watched the raisinlike blob, hearing the yogi's breathing become faster and faster – until it suddenly stopped. He then held up his right hand a yard or so from the fly, becoming incredibly still. This stillness was all the more dramatic after his perpetual motion – and it really *was* stillness. As I continued to watch, the fly started twitching, shaking its buckled wing out, then getting up, testing its legs with a few unsteady steps. A second later, it flew away.

The yogi remained motionless for another minute, then immediately became his old self again, lighting up and fanning.

My first thought was just how dead the fly had been. Surely I had seen enough dead flies to know the difference. This fly had been crushed, split open.

"How did you do that?" I asked.

He looked over through the gloom, the whites of his eyes sparkling. "Life is a force," he said quietly. "Death is the absence of that force – is it not so?"

"I suppose…"

"Fly needs less force than the human – is this true?"

"Probably…"

"Can this beggar not give the fly enough force to live?"

I asked how he could transfer his life force and how the fly could repair the damage to its body even it received new life force.

"Is it not so that God can do anything he wishes?"[25]

At the end of this first encounter, Yogi Ramsuratkumar suggested that Roberts make a pradakshina of the mountain, Arunachala, rather than climbing it, as the Westerner had originally planned. The trip proved to be well beyond the man's expectations, as it took him much longer and taxed his energy reserves in the intolerable heat. By the time he staggered into town at the end of the circumambulation he was thoroughly dehydrated. So much so that he had to drink nearly a dozen sodas to satisfy his enormous thirst – a story that he tells with great humor.

That evening, when he met Yogi Ramsuratkumar again, Roberts reported on his adventure, emphasizing the fact that he had nearly succumbed to the terrible heat.

Yogiji agreed. "It is far…the heat will make you sick."

"Thanks," Roberts replied, incredulous, as he asked, "So why did you tell me to walk around it instead of up it?"

"Who listens to this beggar?" Yogi Ramsuratkumar said. These same words would be repeated many times in the years ahead, as visitors and even devotees rarely followed his instructions![26]

When Paul Roberts announced that he was leaving Tiruvannamalai on the next day, the beggar inquired if he remembered his (Yogiji's) name, and then asked Roberts to repeat it, *Yogi Ramsuratkumar*…nine times.

"Oh, oh, You are too kind to this old beggar. When you write about him, you must write only the truth…"[27] said Ramsuratkumar.

In 1975, this young seeker had no such plan. But, in the years that followed, Paul Williams Roberts became a highly respected and distinguished writer and journalist.

14

A LIVING FAITH

 At the same time that Westerners were discovering the hidden saint of Tiruvannamalai, more and more Indian people were also attracted to the feet of the beggar. They came from local villages as well as from cities all over South India, and further beyond. Those on pilgrimage to Arunachala began to hear stories of a radiantly joyful swami who frequented the temple compound and was often found among the beggars at the temple entrance. But, rather than taking from you, this beggar was known to grant wishes, even to perform healings and miracles. "If it was a problem to humankind, it was equal to him. He doesn't see any discrimination," remarked Parathasarathy, a passionate Indian devotee who first met the Godchild in 1976.[1] Yogi Ramsuratkumar was willing to spend time with anyone who came to him expressing the smallest grain of faith.

One day, for instance, as Parathasarathy looked on, a village woman lamented a long, sad tale about her sick cow. The beggar listened to her seriously, respectfully, for half an hour. Finally, he spoke carefully and with the force of his full authority: "Ma, you will go to the temple and take the abhisheka water. Force it to that cow. You will *do it*. Go immediately to the temple and force the cow to drink the water. Do it immediately." Such a commanding tone was necessary, Parathasarathy explained, in order to inspire compliance. And, without hesitation, the woman did as she was instructed. "Swami, my cow is all right!" this same woman cried out in praise and gratitude the next day, returning to the one who had granted such a boon. "Thank you, Swami!" she repeated again and again. With such stories circulating through the city it was no wonder that the beggar was becoming an attraction to rich and poor alike.

While some Westerners and more sophisticated Indians were asking for his spiritual direction, Yogi Ramsuratkumar was demonstrating the essence of Godliness by the ways in which he reached out to touch those who, like himself, had long struggled from day to day, some just to survive.

An Indian woman came to him one day in the 1970s asking for his help in achieving a relationship with God. Saying little, he allowed the woman to simply sit in his presence. A short while later, as she waited for her answer, the master called out to a vendor of *pakoras* [deep-fried vegetable fritters] who was passing by with his cart on the street, "How is your business?" The beggar then invited the man to come and sit near him. Taking hold of the man's hands, Yogiji looked at the food vendor with great tenderness.

"Swami, my business is not well," the man recounted regretfully.

"Oohhh," said Yogi Ramsuratkumar with obvious concern in his voice. "And how are you preparing these pakoras?"

"Oh, I would blend with some chilis and other things, and fry it in the pan, and that's it, Swami."

"You fry it thoroughly?" Ramsuratkumar asked for specifics, entering fully into the man's life and work situation.

"No, Swami, sometimes I would fry it thoroughly and sometimes I would half fry it," the pakora-seller explained.

Yogi Ramsuratkumar considered the man's words for a moment. "You do one thing." He spoke like a solicitous father guiding his son. "Don't fry it thoroughly. First fry half, then try to sell it in the market. The next day, if anything remains unsold, you will again fry the same thing a little bit more. And the next day you can sell it."

"In such a way, he gave the man some formulas as to how to produce better pakoras!" Parathasarathy explained. All told, Yogi Ramsuratkumar spent forty-five minutes with this fellow, after which he gave him some rupees for a plate of pakoras. The beggar then passed the food around to those who sat with him, before dismissing the merchant.

Turning at last to the woman who had inquired about the best way to attain Godhood, Ramsuratkumar's "spiritual direction" was evidently complete: "Amma! Now this beggar leaves you. You can have some pakora, and you can go."

राम

Yogi Ramsuratkumar was not looking for disciples, or even for admirers. He had no intention of starting an organization, building an ashram, or acquiring anything. Many people who tried to get closer to him were turned away, and more were turned back to their original path, their original connection to God. "After the person had given all their problems to Swami, the person would become very easy," Parathasarathy noted. "Then, after that, Swami would suggest, here and there, simple words. He would ask, 'Who is your ishta, your favorite god?' They would say, 'Krishna is my favorite god.' Then he would say, 'Remember Krishna...remember Krishna. Whenever you feel uneasy, in your heart, you remember Krishna – Krishna will protect you.' He would not disturb anyone's faith. If anyone has faith in Krishna, if anyone has faith in Sai Baba, or J. Krishnamurti, or Rajneesh, or any saints or gods, he would not disturb it. He would intensify their faith upon their gods. After listening to all their problems, he would just say, just to intensify their faith, and encourage those people to turn to their faith, to remember Krishna or whatever gods they liked. 'Then all your problems will be solved, this beggar assures you, my Father's grace.'" And raising his hands, the Godchild would bless them.

With Haragopal Sepuri, another frequent visitor, the beggar's instructions in this regard were constant and specific. Sepuri had long been a follower of a deceased Indian saint, Pagal Haranath, a person much admired by Yogiji. The first time Sepuri met Yogi Ramsuratkumar, in 1976, the Godchild enthusiastically exclaimed, "Jai Haranath, Jai Haranath," and told Sepuri that Haranath was a great mahatma. Thereafter, the beggar would ask Sepuri to tell stories about this saint, to sing chants in his honor (which Yogi Ramsuratkumar would join), and to rely in faith upon the blessings of this master – Pagal Haranath.[2]

One day, in Haragopal's presence, as Yogi Ramsuratkumar was reading the newspaper and making comments about the current world situation, the Godchild suddenly initiated an odd conversation. "Haragopal is not bothered about these things," said Yogi Ramsuratkumar, referring to the news. "He is only interested in Pagal Haranath."

These words felt like the kindest of blessings, and a form of instruction, for the younger man. For him, the message was clearly given between the lines: "You stupid, do not bother your head with politics. That is not your field. Your only concern should be Pagal Haranath. Stick to him."

That day, as Haragopal left the beggar's house, Yogi Ramsuratkumar raised his hands in blessing. Amazingly, instead of his usual invocation of "my Father blesses you," Yogiji declared, "Pagal Haranath blesses you, Mata Kusuma Kumari [the saintly wife of Haranath] blesses you."[3]

राम

Parathasarathy began his lifelong association with the mad beggar like many people who saw in Yogi Ramsuratkumar a bestower of boons. He desperately needed help when he first met his master on August 30, 1976, during a time of great personal tumult.

"I hated my wife, Radhika," he explained without hesitation during a long interview in the fall of 2002. "In 1976 I came to Swami only for this problem. I wanted to divorce my wife and go with some other girl."

When Parathasarathy approached the beggar with his problem, however, Ramsuratkumar was seemingly unmoved. "This is not the place for d-i-v-o-r-c-e," the master said, spelling out a word that he did not want to give power to. And with that, Yogi Ramsuratkumar dropped any direct reference to the subject.

But his attention on Parathasarathy was far from being dropped. There was more involved here than healing a cow of gastric distress. It would take time for the circumstances of the younger man's life, according to the Father's will, to bring him to the point of life and death. Only at that point would he be amenable to the master's influence.

"He concentrated upon me for four years," Parathasarathy said, summing up the gradual disassembling of his life in a few emotion-filled words. "He made me empty, totally; financially bankrupt. He made me wander like a beggar on the streets, and he put me behind bars; in jail for eighteen days!"

In 1978, shortly after being released from the jail, Parathasarathy returned home to find his life in ruins. Great financial problems were now compounded by the fact that his loving and gentle wife was temporarily apart from him, while the rest of his family was estranged. "I was not able to help anybody and I was not able to get help from anybody," he recalled vividly. The other woman, whom he had desired so urgently, had married somebody else and was settled in her new life. Parathasarathy found himself completely alone and on the streets.

In the distraught condition in which he found himself, Parathasarathy contemplated suicide. Making his way to Tiruvannamalai, he went to see Yogi Ramsuratkumar. Although the beggar was spending time with some other friends and families, he asked Parathasarathy to sit near him, and to take something to eat.

"I want to go away," Parathasarathy said suddenly. When the master urged him to stay, the younger man refused, vehemently. "No, Swami, I am not feeling well. I want to go to the lodge."

Arriving at his hotel room, Parathasarathy sat down and wrote a two-page letter to his master: "You made my life miserable. Now you know why I don't want to live anymore." His recrimination was vitriolic. Finishing the letter, Parathasarathy consumed a heavy dose of poison and went to bed, fully expecting to never get up again.

"I was in terrible fear, you know," Parathasarathy remarked, reliving the anxiety of the incident and supplying additional details. "My body reacted in a different way," he explained. "I couldn't stand, I couldn't even lie down. I was totally uneasy. Finally, I slept. In the morning, at eight or nine o'clock, I woke up, not knowing whether I was dead or alive. Then I went to the bathroom and the whole poison drained out of me!"

Parathasarathy knew that his "Swami" was spending his days near the railway station, beneath the punnai tree, and went out to find him. As far as Parathasarathy was concerned, since his letter of recrimination had not been delivered, the master knew nothing of the fiasco that had been enacted in his hotel room the night before. When Ramsuratkumar saw his chastened devotee approaching, he ran towards him, vigorously caught hold of his hands and pointed to the top of Arunachala, which towered in the distance.

"You go to the top of the hill and jump from there, and see if you will die or not!" Yogi Ramsuratkumar's tone was fierce. "You don't know you are under the protection of this beggar!" the Godman added, with ruthless compassion.

Parathasarathy was completely shocked. "How did this man know all these things?" Before this moment, Parathasarathy claimed, he didn't know anything about *jnanis* (wise teachers), saints, sannyasins, and what was possible to them. He admitted that he had come to this little old man "just to deceive him, and to get my desires fulfilled through him." The swami for him was a magical connection to some source of money, and maybe a way to get out of his marriage and marry another woman.

The effect of the whole incident was transformational for Parathasarathy. Could it really be true that the devotee's life, once turned to the master, was completely in the master's hands? For Parathasarathy there was no longer any doubt.

राम

It took Parathasarathy four years to attain clarity on the issue that caused so much turmoil in his life – his relationship to his wife. And, throughout all this time, Ramsuratkumar held the young man close to him. While a lesser master might have tried to rush the devotee's process, supplying him with ready answers or moralistic injunctions about not leaving his wife, the beggar encouraged Parathasarathy to build the foundation he would need for genuine change to take place.

"He asked me, instead, to go through the books of the jnanis – Swami Ramdas, Swami Ram Tirtha, J. Krishnamurti, Acharya Rajneesh, Ramakrishna, and Vivekananda," Parathasarathy remembered. Studying these great teachings, these great philosophies, Parathasarathy – the businessman – was being softened by and infused with a new view of life. One day in 1980, his internal orientation toward his wife, Radhika, changed suddenly. Instead of continuing to plague himself with dissatisfaction, he found himself wondering how or why he could ever hate her. It was all a result of the Godman's benediction.

Ramsuratkumar's ways were always unique to each individual. "He would create a situation, and out of that situation you would be forced to learn," Parathasarathy commented philosophically. "He always gave you full freedom. That was his way."

With gentleness and good humor, Yogi Ramsuratkumar poetically summed up for his devotee the wondrous ways in which his Father draws his lovers to Himself:

> My Father will loot all your money if he wants you to remember him. My Father is so possessive, you know. If it is the only way to make you remember my Father by making you a pauper, my Father will not hesitate to make you a pauper. And if my Father thinks that giving you several million dollars will make you remember Father, then my Father will pour the money on you. Father's ways are unique. So we cannot make any complaints. If one man has sinned several times, and still he is such a rich man and he has a very good name in the society, while some other man is very wise and good, and still he is suffering a lot…We cannot ask these questions. My Father wants these people to live in this way, so that they can remember Father properly.[4]

राम

The master Jesus had long ago instructed his disciples in the necessity for faith, the miracle of faith. "If you have faith the size of a grain of mustard seed you will move mountains," Jesus said, reflecting the necessity for openness in the heart as a precondition for the reception of grace.

From numerous witnesses in the mid-to-late 1970s and early 1980s, we learn of how clearly Yogi Ramsuratkumar was aligned with this theology of faith. He could not force himself upon one who was closed to him, as this would have violated the sacred trust of the divine gift he transmitted. People who approached him with deception, with prejudice, with arrogant disdain were never encouraged. To the queries of such potential detractors he might remark with all seriousness: "This dirty sinner, what can this beggar do? You can go to the temple; you can go to the great saints like J. Krishnamurti, Ramana Maharshi, or Sai Baba. But this beggar cannot do anything. He is just lazy. He just eats, smokes and sleeps."

In 1977, the devotee from Neyveli, Haragopal Sepuri, brought a friend to meet Yogi Ramsuratkumar. When the new visitor answered the Godchild's inquiries about his job, the beggar studied him intently. "Oh! so you are doing some useful work. And Haragopal has brought you to this beggar," Yogiji said, sincerely. Then, to everyone's surprise, the Godchild added, "He [meaning Haragopal] is wasting his time and wasting your time also."[5]

In Haragopal's understanding, his friend was closed to any change of attitude. His notions were fixed. Consequently, he was not able to be touched or helped by Yogi Ramsuratkumar as long as this attitude persisted.

Yogi Ramsuratkumar would often do more than *talk* in ways that would drive away curiosity seekers or those with no openness to him. In allowing women devotees to light a cigarette for him, or even massage his feet, as he did in the 1970s, for example, he could quickly clear the area of the poseurs and non-serious seekers.[6] Such simple acts of devotion toward the master were inappropriate in South Indian society. For a man to allow such public and "intimate" contact from a woman was practically revolutionary in its implications. As such, it could be exactly the gesture the master needed, and used!

Yogi Ramsuratkumar's smoking, his dirty rags, his failure to bathe daily, his allowing of women in his close company – these violations of "the rules" were not a way to flaunt his power or express his casual disregard. Quite the contrary, for the Godman, whose every gesture was a reflection of his Father's teaching, such behaviors served multiple purposes, not the least of which was to discourage those who could not or would not receive what he had to give. "Whatever he says *is* the rule, *is* the law," observed Parathasarathy wisely. Clearly, the beggar's allegiance was to God alone, not to cultural mores.

Those who had even meagre faith in Yogi Ramsuratkumar, however, these he encouraged. "Your faith will save you; your faith will protect you," he repeatedly told his visitors and supporters. During a time when Parathasarathy traveled frequently to Punjab, terrorist activity was common there. Learning of his devotee's plans to visit that region, the master instructed him: "If you go to Punjab, and if you feel some crisis there, like some man just standing before you with a gun, and if you remember this beggar, do you think this beggar will carry his body along from here to Punjab to protect you? No. But my Father will send somebody to protect you. So have faith."

A similar story, with more dramatic consequences, happened for one of Yogi Ramsuratkumar's female disciples, Ponkacham, in later years. On a trip to the Himalayas, she and her companions had to cross a very treacherous pass. They hired a young man with several horses to lead them. To their terror, however, the man for some reason abandoned his post and left with the horses, stranding his group in the middle of nowhere. With no experience of the terrain, and no map to guide them, Ponkacham was panicked. She began to scream, "Yogi Ramsuratkumar, Yogi Ramsuratkumar," over and over. Her only refuge was in his name.

The wilderness area in which they had stopped was totally isolated. Imagine the party's astonishment when a white horse suddenly appeared on the horizon, ridden by a policeman. Learning of their situation, the policeman guided them back to safety.

When she went to see Yogi Ramsuratkumar on her return, she told him the story, acknowledging her gratitude over and over again. For his part, Yogiji only laughed, delighted in the tale. "Why did you disturb this dirty beggar?" he asked in astonishment, as amazed as anyone at the workings of his Father.[7]

Whether it was a question of threats by terrorists or a growing desire to deepen one's exploration into the life of the spirit, Yogi Ramsuratkumar's responses were essentially the same. Faith. Remembrance. Invocation of the Divine Name. When a visitor in the 1970s, a devotee who honored Lord Muruga as his chosen deity, once asked Yogi Ramsuratkumar, "What is the purpose of life?" the Godman replied joyfully, "The purpose of life is to take the name of

Lord Muruga! Muruga! Muruga! Take it and see for yourself. The name Muruga is sweet, beautiful and blissful."[8]

When Parathasarathy inquired one day about entering into solitude, in some forest, the blissful Godchild wouldn't hear of it: "You remember this beggar. You know that this beggar has accepted you. There ends all your sadhana. Leave it. Just remember that this beggar does enough for you. You need not worry about your spiritual growth. My Father will take care of you, my Father will be always with you."

राम

Sometimes Yogi Ramsuratkumar's instructions would throw a devotee into turmoil. As is the way with a crazy-wisdom master, which the beggar undoubtedly was, there was often no way to reconcile seeming contradiction except by reliance on the heart – the seat of faith. To stay in the domain of logic or rationality would only serve to mire one more deeply in the impossibility of the task.

Yogiji had once told a devotee to proceed in one way, and, after a month or two, told the man to do the same job in a different manner. Feeling confused, and probably angry, the man wrote a letter to the beggar protesting his dilemma.

When this devotee was next in the master's presence, Ramsuratkumar's response was remarkable – he took the full blame for the confusion upon himself: "Oh, this beggar told *that* ... oh, this beggar committed such a great sin. Oh Father, why did you allow this beggar to commit this sin? The people like this beggar are here only to remove the confusion from human beings, and if this beggar himself has become the reason for this confusion, *ooohhh God!*" And turning directly to the man he said: "You just rely upon my Father within you; don't rely on this beggar's words." In this way, the devotee was vindicated, his confusion relieved on the spot.[9]

Despite his compassionate handling of the man's dilemma, Yogi Ramsuratkumar made it clear to others around him that he expected more from them – that, in a similar situation, they should rely upon a higher principle than apparent logic. When the man was gone, the beggar instructed: "Oh, you should have faith. If you have the faith, then you would have implemented *both* things. The thing which this beggar told two months back was an entirely different thing, and that friend should obey that. And, after two months, it was the same thing that this beggar uttered, but in different words. A different message he has given. That should also be done, because both are coming from my Father. So you should have faith. If you come to this beggar with complaints about this beggar, what can this beggar do?"

राम

"Whatever happens in the world, happens by the will of my Father. So nothing is wrong in this world. Everything is perfectly ordered, because everything is done by my Father." Yogi Ramsuratkumar spoke these same words, with slight variation, over and over throughout the years of his acquaintance with Parathasarathy. Others recorded similar words from earlier times.

Despite their consistent use, these words never became stale, or rote, in the beggar's mouth, Parathasarathy emphasized. Each time they were uttered fresh – a new prayer, a new declaration of praise, gratitude, and faith.

Being a man of the world, however, Parathasarathy found some of the master's statements difficult to swallow whole. When the beggar said, "Because everything is done by my Father, then how can it be imperfect? Everything is perfectly alright," the young businessman questioned what the master meant by "perfect." Certainly Yogi Ramsuratkumar knew that there were troubles everywhere in the world. He knew that wars were raging. The master's words stayed with Parathasarathy like a koan: something to be bothered by; something to ponder.

"Whenever you go to visit your brother, you go to the anatomy hall," Yogi Ramsuratkumar directed one day, knowing that Parathasarathy's brother was studying to be a doctor. A strange request, but Parathasarathy had heard such strange requests before and knew the wisdom in following them.

The next time he went to see his brother, he asked to be taken to the anatomy hall where the medical students were busily dissecting cadavers. Against his brother's protests that he would probably faint at what he saw, Parathasarathy insisted.

Entering the laboratory, the young devotee's attention was drawn to one corpse. "I saw the whole abdominal section. It was open. Almost all the parts were in the abdomen, and I thought, 'Oh God, how can it be so terribly congested [meaning so many organs packed together so tightly]?'"

But his brother contradicted. "Don't think like that. This is the perfect order. If any portion shifts, or moves another way, then it will give you enormous pain. What you see here is the perfect order."

"Then only I could get it," Parathasarathy declared enthusiastically. "The apparent confusion is not confusion. It is only apparently confused, apparently in war, in chaos, but deep into it there is a perfect order."

When he next met Yogi Ramsuratkumar he was able to report, "Now, at last, I am able to understand what you mean by a perfect order."

राम

Parathasarathy was privileged to stay with the Godchild in the house at Sannadhi Street for extended periods. During one month-long stay the two were together day and night. The master was "working" his devotee in a variety of ways; ways that Parathasarathy found sometimes enigmatic, sometimes difficult, sometimes exceptionally humorous.

On one occasion during this month, Yogi Ramsuratkumar began a particular form of repartee with Parathasarathy early in the morning, and continued with the same questioning throughout the day.

"Oh, this beggar knows that this beggar is sitting on his Father's lap," Yogi Ramsuratkumar began. "But this beggar didn't *see* his Father face to face. Parathasarathy, how to see Father face to face?"

The master would not only question Parathasarathy, but everyone else who visited him on this particular day as well. In a childlike tone of complete innocence, the beggar asked each and all, "How to see Father face to face?"

The Sannadhi Street house (far left), Tiruvannamalai

Nobody was able to offer an answer, so the questioning continued until about nine o'clock at night, when Ramsuratkumar lay
down to rest between the two pillars in the house. The next morning, however, he again invoked the same question. This time, Parathasarathy reported that the elder seemed very much upset. The
young devotee had reached his own level of frustration, and with
that his courage arose. Turning to face his master, Parathasarathy
boldly, yet respectfully, declared, "I *have* seen my Father face to face!"
For the young man, to see Yogi Ramsuratkumar *was* to see the
Father, "because for me, Father *is* He." To the beggar, his guru, he
proclaimed, "If you are not able to see your Father face to face, then
it's your fate Swami. I can't do anything about it!"

With that, Yogi Ramsuratkumar's questioning stopped. He
laughed and laughed, heartily, with full delight. "He was just doing

[this play] to induce that faith; to see whether I accepted him as my Father. He wanted me to utter these words," Parathasarathy affirmed.

राम

Their time together included many sojourns throughout the town, up the mountain, and into the countryside. As they moved along, Parathasarathy had the opportunity to share in Ramsurat-kumar's blissful and energetic presence. "When he was walking, he was also dancing. He would not seem to be touching the earth. Walking as if dancing. He would carry his fan, and shake his whole frame, moving, moving. All the twenty-four hours he was in the blissful states, he was dancing and singing. He liked songs, and he was a wonderful singer, also. When he chants a *Nama* (name of God), sometimes he would sing some songs in Sanskrit or in Hindi. Wonderful! In the outskirts, when he takes us along that route, then he would dance and walk. He would chant his own name and he would dance."

Not all the master's walks were easeful, however. As Perumal and Caylor Wadlington had both noted, the Godchild was also a subject of both ridicule and attack. Parathasarathy saw this too. Outside of town, "if he saw people making fun of him, he would shout, 'Mahatma Gandhi! Ki Jai! Jawaharlal Nehru Ki Jai!' He would shout like this, like a madman, and he would raise his fan in his hands and would run *toward* those people who were making fun of him, and those people would be afraid and run away. But, if he entered the city and he heard a car or a jeep or a bus, he would get scared and he would stand in the extreme side of the road." Obviously, his early experiences in being threatened by vehicles that tried to run him over had some effect on him.

Another trusted devotee, Shri V. Ramanujachari, saw another side to the Godman's dealings with his tormenters in the late 1970s. Sometimes, as Ramanujachari walked in town with Yogiji, street urchins who took "shelter in the dark verandas of the row houses would start pelting stones at times. Even as the stones came flying at us he would not flinch or retreat but with great élan and aplomb shout vigorously – 'Mahatma Gandhi ki jai, Pandit Jawaharlal Nehru ki jai, Bharat Mata ki jai.' He would hold his fan as if he were stopping those stones and walk robustly along with his head held high." Meanwhile, his companion, Ramanujachari, "scurried behind him, quaking with fear. The stones would pass us by and I had never seen him being hurt."[10]

राम

Disciples revel in telling about the beggar's love of music, poetry, song, dance. "Sometimes in the midst of our discussion He would break into a song to illustrate a point," explained Shri V. Ramanujachari, a long-time devotee. "His recitation in a ringing, mellifluous voice of an apt verse from '*Rama charita Manas*' [a biography of Lord Rama written by the great poet Tulsidas] for instance, would be breathtaking."[11]

As early as 1971-1972, the first formal songs were written about Yogi Ramsuratkumar. The initial one was composed spontaneously, under a delightful circumstance, by Swami Mayananda, a friend of the beggar's from nearby Pondicherry.

Mayananda met Ramsuratkumar one day, quite accidentally, standing in the bazaar near the temple. Some time later, seeing the Godchild near the photo studio, Swami Mayananda was so strongly attracted to the beggar's radiant presence that he approached and prostrated before him. Yogi Ramsuratkumar asked the Swami his name and where he was living, and, learning that the man was a sannyasin, the beggar invited Mayananda to take tea with him in a nearby hotel. As the two renunciates shared the silent resources of their hearts, Swami Mayananda expressed a desire to sing a song, and Yogi Ramsuratkumar accepted the offer. Right on the spot, Swami Mayananda composed some verses in praise of the one with whom he sat. He then wrote it down and gave it to Ramsuratkumar. The song became a favorite of the Godchild's, and he asked his companions at the time to remember it always. One memorable line declared: "The whole world will bow before you."

Within a few years of this first composition, Yogi Ramsuratkumar had also asked others to write songs or poems in his name. Sugavanam, whose mother used to bring a midday meal to the beggar every day for years, was at the master's side almost every morning during this period in the 1970s. Sadguru Gnanananda Giri of Tapovanam had named this boy "*bala kavi*," meaning "boy poet," and Yogi Ramsuratkumar requested the young man to write one verse on him [Yogiji] every day. Sugavanam took this invitation as a sacred trust and continued the practice until his death. While never published, these poems are said to provide "insight into the life, conduct and message of the swami [Yogi Ramsuratkumar]," and have been referred to as "masterpieces…brimming with content, soaked in bhakti."[12]

Parathasarathy, whom Yogi Ramsuratkumar affectionately called "his poet," was also enjoined to write songs mentioning his name. The younger man did as he was directed, with typically passionate enthusiasm. "Before I met Swami I used to write songs on other subjects, but after I met Swami, he asked me, 'Write only about this beggar.'" Over two hundred poems/songs were composed, some of which have become standards among Ramsuratkumar's devotees both in India and around the world. "Samartha," for instance, is still sung every day in the dining hall at the Yogi Ramsuratkumar Ashram as the assembled crowds await the serving of a meal.

"*Yogi Ramsuratkumar is a blissful beauty, and the temple of Yogi, this ashram, is also a beauty*" is the translation of one line from one of Parathasarathy's most well-loved songs. "When you sing this particular song, and other favorite songs, he starts dancing, raising his hands," Parathasarathy said as he moved his body in imitation of the beggar's ecstatic expression.

In 1976, when a Burmese saint, Sadophaya, was brought to Tiruvannamalai by some friends, Yogi Ramsuratkumar enacted a strange lila with Parathasarathy about his poetry and song. Before the Burmese man arrived, the beggar announced: "Oh, he is a great saint, a Burmese saint. He has a lot of followers in the States and all over the world. We should receive him fittingly." Turning to Parathasarathy he kindly asked: "Is it possible for you to write some songs for him?"

The poet was unable to answer. He had never before heard the man's name. How was he to do such an impossible task? So, he kept silent.

Yogi Ramsuratkumar was suddenly agitated, and began to walk back and forth, as if pondering the vibrations in the ethers. At last he spoke. "No, my Father says you should write songs only on this beggar, not about anybody else." And then he laughed.

Looking at the unfolding of this lila it is interesting to speculate about what the beggar's genuine wish was, and why he apparently changed his mind. Perhaps this is a prime example of the master capitulating to the devotee's hesitation. Or, perhaps it was a stellar teaching about the need to keep one focus, and one focus only, in the devotee's work. A case might be made for either. These are the enigmas that the devotee lives with, day in and day out in the master's presence.

राम

A group of police officers once came into Yogi Ramsuratkumar's company, one of them bearing a basket of fruit as an offering. Once he had placed the basket at the master's feet, the man began to regale the beggar with a testimony of his own spiritual prowess. "Swami, I am getting up in the morning; I do some meditation on God; I chant some name of God..." The man went on at length, while Yogi Ramsuratkumar silently listened to everything. Patiently, he allowed the man to speak for what seemed to others like an inordinate amount of time.

Finally, taking hold of the man's hands, the master lovingly instructed: "Now this beggar feels he should leave you. This beggar will touch these fruits and you can take them as *prasadam* [prasad] with you." Still holding the man's hand, he started walking the policeman to his car. The honored man followed Yogi Ramsuratkumar's lead without question. Together they walked out to the man's car where Ramsuratkumar gave his final blessing, turned abruptly, and then came back to his place.

A long line of people awaited the beggar's darshan at that time, and several of his devotees puzzled as to why the master had spent so much time with this one man, especially considering the nature of the policeman's tedious monologue. "You gave all this respect to this fellow, why?" one of the others asked Yogi Ramsuratkumar incredulously.

"Some people come to this beggar for bhakti; some people come to this beggar for some problems to be solved; and some people expect this beggar to give them some respect. What's wrong in giving them their due respect?" Yogi Ramsuratkumar countered. This was undoubtedly not the answer his questioner expected. The master then continued, drawing out several principles that underlay his way/God's way of loving humanity by giving us what we want until we are ready to take what the Divine wants to give us in abundant measure.

"There is nothing this beggar is going to lose," Yogi Ramsuratkumar continued, his words irritating that place in the human heart where self-righteousness and fear of being taken advantage of is lodged. "They wanted to get some respect from this beggar and this beggar gave them respect. Where is the problem? And if someone comes wanting some bhakti, this beggar is ready to give bhakti to that fellow. That man came here wanting to get some respect from this beggar and this beggar gave it to him!"

राम

Parathasarathy spoke of the Godman's universal recommendation for remembering the Divine, in whatever form, under whatever name was closest to the heart. Whether the beggar himself chanted, *"Mahatma Gandhi Ki Jai! Jawaharlal Nehru Ki Jai!"* or some Vedic mantras, or the invocation given to him by Ramdas, *"Om Sri Ram Jai Ram Jai Jai Ram,"* often depended upon who was sitting near him at the time.

"If some Vedic scholars were there, Swami would request them to chant some Vedas. If someone was coming from Anandashram, he would ask them to chant Ramnam. If someone came from Sai Baba's ashram, he would ask them to chant some bhajans of Sai Baba. And if Swami's own friends came, he would insist, 'Only this beggar's name.'" Parathasarathy clearly remembered this important teaching.

On one occasion when Yogi Ramsuratkumar had asked those in his company to use his name alone, a devotee asked why. Surprising everyone, the master turned the same question back upon his disciples:

"This beggar is also wondering why this beggar asks his friends to remember his name; to chant his name alone – can anybody tell?"

While many of the adults hesitated at first, and then offered their carefully considered responses, one young boy spoke out with vigor. "Swami, all other mantras are very old, Swami, centuries old, but your name is fresh, Swami."

Yogi Ramsuratkumar smiled, considering the child's words. "Ahhh," he said, sounding like an old Zen master whose young protégé has answered from a domain other than the rational mind. The answer apparently satisfied him.

राम

Parathasarathy, like many devotees before and since, was constantly being shown the ways in which Yogi Ramsuratkumar's presence was all-pervasive. If Parathasarathy needed to be away, circumstances frequently conspired to remind him that no matter where he went, the Divine was as close as his next breath.

Once, he had planned a trip to the Himalayas, but before leaving he had visited his master, who casually told him a story about two birds who were occupied with eating a variety of fruits. One bird felt happy when it ate sweet, fully ripe fruits, and annoyed while eating the raw, unripe fruit. Its partner bird, however, was nonreactive – whether it ate the sweet or the bitter didn't matter. Seeing this, the first bird learned a valuable lesson. "I am also that bird. Why should I both suffer sometimes and enjoy sometimes? These fruits are all one and the same."

Parathasarathy understood the story to be a parable about the individual soul that recognizes in itself those qualities that are inherent in the Divine; qualities in which all things are one, beyond distinction. The story struck him, and he contemplated it seriously as he made the three-day journey to Rishikesh in the north of India. In this city Parathasarathy met an old friend who told him about an extraordinary swami who lived nearby. Parathasarathy took his friend's suggestion to visit the sage.

"When I entered this swami's room, he suddenly asked me, 'See those two birds?' I was shocked! He had asked me to see these two birds that were standing on the window. Then he clapped his hands and those two birds flew away," Parathasarathy narrated, with a note of amazement. "Then he was laughing and laughing, as if he was very close to me. Then I was just enjoying his presence."

For the younger man, the incident with the two birds was highly synchronistic, and directly reinforced the teaching that Yogi Ramsuratkumar had initially offered him. But more, Parathasarathy observed that the swami was not simply another messenger. When he offered the sadhu some rupees, the man accepted them and tucked them away in a particularly unique way, but one that was exactly the same as the manner in which Yogi Ramsuratkumar would handle such gifts. As the swami did so, "he smiled at me," Parathasarathy noted. In that way, the young devotee was given to understand that it was in fact Yogi Ramsuratkumar's own hand that had received the offering.

राम

Sometimes the master's requests were challenging and difficult. At other times Yogi Ramsuratkumar would give his devotees work to do that they greatly valued. Either way, there was always more to the task than was initially apparent.

One year, in the late 1970s, J. Krishnamurti was in Madras and Yogi Ramsuratkumar asked Parathasarathy to go there and to attend the sage's lecture for the whole length of his stay. Parathasarathy was only too pleased to oblige his master in such an interesting task, as he too was greatly respectful of J. Krishnamurti.

After one talk, as the elder "J.K." left the stage, his glance fell on the young poet who stood some distance away, nearly hiding himself behind a bush, as he waited for the great man to pass. Heading straight for the spot were Parathasarathy stood, J. Krishnamurti looked piercingly into his eyes and asked him, "What are you waiting for here?"

"Just to see Krishnamurti," the young man replied, awestruck to be so close to one of his idols.

Krishnamurti seemed delighted by the response. He laughed freely, embraced Parathasarathy warmly, and again studied him intensely. For Parathasarathy, this was no chance occurrence, and no casual display of affection on Krishnamurti's part. That moment of embrace was an expression of a sort of immediate recognition – but in no personal, limited sense. Without knowing that the young man was an emissary of Yogi Ramsuratkumar's, Krishnamurti had instinctively aligned with Parathasarathy's energy. "Then I understood," Parathasarathy explained, "that when you have the acquaintance with the Swami [Ramsuratkumar], then almost all the saints and sadhus are very, very close to you. There is no doubt about it!"

When Parathasarathy returned from his stay in Madras, he and the others who had accompanied him reported upon their adventures. "Who got the opportunity to touch Krishnamurti?" the beggar asked, knowing that in those days J. Krishnamurti used to move through a crowd greeting people by shaking hands. Turning to his young poet, the master's eyes twinkled as he asked again: "What happened to you, Parathasarathy? Did you have the opportunity to touch Krishnamurti?"

"No Swami, I didn't touch him," Parathasarathy said, shyly. "He touched me, Swami!"

Ramsuratkumar laughed and laughed. His own connection with J. Krishnamurti was ever a source of joy and inspiration for him. Hearing of Parathasarathy's encounter, the beggar once again "touched" the great man.

राम

Yogi Ramsuratkumar's clothing – the road-weary yet often brilliantly colored "rags" that he wore like regal vestments – was always a subject of note and speculation by his visitors and devotees alike. It was sometimes six months or more before he changed his clothes. At some level, this fact disturbed many who were close to him over the years. Several of his devotees candidly spoke of their desire to see their master adorned more pristinely. For them, the fantasy of clothing their lord, their deity, in the finest silks and purest cottons was a visualization that thrilled their hearts. As devout Indians, they were privy to a long tradition of adorning their gurus in the same way that they clothed their icons. Statues, lingas, sacred representations of all types were ritually washed with the richest unguents and wrapped in the most costly and delicate cloths, scattered with flower petals, propitiated with clouds of sweet smoke from expensive incense. At its best, this desire motivated the beggar's devotees to try all sorts of subtle and not-so-subtle ways and means to get their master to dress in some gorgeous array.

On the other hand, his devotees were products of their culture. They wanted their master to be well attired for less exalted reasons, certainly. Some were undoubtedly embarrassed by his appearance. Others wanted their guru to conform to their notions of what a saint should look like. And some, perhaps, took it only as an expression of the beggar's real madness, seeing nothing more than idiosyncrasy. Certainly, those who had met Papa Ramdas at his ashram had observed only perfect cleanliness and order in his raiment.

Ramsuratkumar's lila with regard to clothing was decidedly different from Ramdas's from the very beginning. He remained, until the day of his mahasamadhi, a self-named "dirty beggar." For reasons that we may only hypothesize, his work on his Father's behalf demanded this. Saints and God-inspired prophets throughout time have taken on peculiar and often socially abhorrent manifestations for many "reasons." The female Hindu saint, Mahadeviyakka, remained naked, leaving a legacy of ecstatic poetry in which she proclaimed that her only clothing was the "morning light" of Siva, whom she name her "white Jasmine Lord." The great St. Francis of Assisi removed his shoes, walking barefoot throughout Europe, clothed in the coarsest of fabrics, a constant irritant to his skin and a badge of his association with his crucified Lord. As a means of counterbalancing the forces of greed, vanity, and violence in the world around them, saints from all traditions have subjected themselves to great austerities, denying themselves food, shelter, the comfort of family relationship. In Yogi Ramsuratkumar's case, his appearance and his lack of regard for anything but his Father's work was a continual reminder of a reality that transcended the material self-consciousness of those who met him.

New clothes were always available to Ramsuratkumar, however, as devotees and friends were frequently giving him such gifts. Some of this clothing was extraordinarily rich, in fact, as a wealthy guest might place an expensive shawl around the beggar's shoulders as an act of worship, and Parathasarathy informs us that the master's house at Sannadhi Street actually contained a pile of brand new clothes, untouched, among the many piles of dried flower malas, newspapers, and other collected things.

One day in the late 1970s, when Parathasarathy was spending several days and nights with Yogi Ramsuratkumar, the beggar was invited to attend a marriage ceremony of some devotees. His young disciple would accompany him. At 4 A.M. the beggar was already up and preparing himself, and innocently asked his devotee whether his clothing was presentable enough to attend the marriage. Although his dress was extremely dirty, Parathasarathy hesitated to say so. "Swami understood my hesitation by saying, 'Oh, you don't like this beggar to attend the marriage wearing these dirty clothes. Alright, this beggar will change today.'"

Yogi Ramsuratkumar took the hint, in this case. He would not always, as others have reported. Whether he did or not depended on his Father's will, which, whimsically at times, included a lesson for a devotee. On this occasion the beggar pointed to a brand new, clean dhoti that lay on the top of the pile of clothing gifts, and Parathasarathy handed it to him. Then Swamiji asked Parathasarathy to reach into the pile again, this time for a *kirta* (the large overshirt). Pulling out several other items first, the beggar attempted to do without it. Instead, he kept trying to place the end of the dhoti over his shoulder in such a way that it covered his upper body as well.

"Is it alright?" the Godman inquired, like a child wanting to be grown up. When Parathasarathy said nothing, the elder got the meaning, "This also you don't like," he said.

At this point Yogi Ramsuratkumar handed Parathasarathy one more parcel and asked him to open it. Remarkably, it was a shirt!

"Oh, Parathasarathy helped this beggar," the Divine child crooned, with obvious playfulness as well as gratitude.

As soon as he was fully dressed, however, the beggar began to shake his head, as if something were wrong. "Now everything is ready," he said, "but this bad smell..." referring to himself. Parathasarathy also remembered that the beggar's face had been streaked with grime, as he had made no ablutions. Yet, when Yogi

Ramsuratkumar looked up, now fully arrayed, Parathasarathy was utterly amazed to find that no traces of dirt remained on his face. In fact, the master's face was glowing, and "his body smelled like sandalwood perfume." Parathasarathy had to work to keep from swooning at the sight. Even years later the remembrance still thrilled him. "Oh, the gold glint of his face!" he remarked, with a look of adoration.

Giving the astonished Parathasarathy a moment to bask in this illumination, Yogi Ramsuratkumar looked at him and with wisdom-honed innocence asked: "Will this be acceptable?" Parathasarathy was humbled and awed.

The beggar then arose, and with Parathasarathy's hand in his, proceeded out onto the road, walking, as ever, like a king.

राम

A related story about clothing, which took place earlier in Yogi Ramsuratkumar's tenure in Tiruvannamalai, is told by Jagannathan, a devout attendant of Yogi Ramsuratkumar's. At this time, the beggar was gifted with a gorgeous and expensive silk dhoti, a tribute from a swami from a Tamil Nadu religious center. The beggar had promised the help of his Father's blessings when this center was involved in some legal battles. With the successful outcome of the litigation, the swami had returned, gratefully offering a costly orange silk to his intercessor.

Yogi Ramsuratkumar humbly received the prize, and graciously knotted it around his shoulders. As he passed through the streets of Tiruvannamalai that day, however, he noticed that the people stood staring at him in a strange way.

"What, today it is a little different?" he asked Jagannathan, wondering at the responses.[13]

"They feel that you are looking different today, Swami," his attendant explained. "This beggar is the same," Yogi Ramsuratkumar countered. "Is it because of the cloth?" When Jaganathan said yes, the beggar inquired further, "Is it silk? Is it pure?" "Yes Swami, it is pure silk," said Jagannathan.

With an enthusiastic cry of "Mahatma Gandhi ki Jai! Mohandas Karamchand Gandhi ki Jai! Gandhi has succeeded fully!" Yogi Ramsuratkumar continued, with undeniable irony: "After I have got this silk, I have become successful! This beggar has become a big person after getting this silk!"

The reference to Gandhi would not have been lost on Jagannathan and other Indian devotees. They knew of Yogi Ramsuratkumar's enormous love and admiration for Gandhi, and all that Gandhi stood for. Silk would never have touched the Mahatma, who only wore the coarsest homespun cotton, and who used this cloth as a symbol of his revolutionary stand on behalf of India. While Yogi Ramsuratkumar would never disdain a gift, and hence wore the silk, the idea that a change of fabric would cause people's opinions of him to change was undoubtedly affirmation that Gandhi's witness and teaching was all the more important for people to hear and understand. The next day, in fact, as he and his entourage passed the statue of Gandhi on the Cooperative Bank building in the town, Yogi Ramsuratkumar pointed it out once again: "Do you see who is there?" he asked his companions. "It is Mahatma Gandhi. He is God for the whole world. The only God. Mahatma Gandhi ki Jai! Come, let us go."

The following morning, as the beggar walked to the punnai tree at the railway station, where he would spend the day, he was still adorned with the now famous orange silk. As they had previously, passersby stopped and stared, and treated him more grandly.

"What Jagannatha, people are different, has this beggar changed? What do *you* see?" the Godchild asked again, incredulously.

When his attendant confirmed that he too noticed the change, Yogi Ramsuratkumar again ironically remarked, "The Swamigal gave this silk and this beggar has become a big person now…there is a change like this for everyone." With that, Yogi Ramsuratkumar went on to narrate a powerful story, recounted by Jagannathan:

> Guru Nanak was visiting a village. He became hungry in the afternoon and requested for some food. The villagers said that there was a ceremony in the Nawab's house, being the anniversary of the Nawab's father. They said all of them were

277

going there to have food and none had cooked anything in the house. They invited Guru Nanak also to the feast. Food was kept ready in the mosque where they entered to have food. When Guru Nanak entered, a servant picked him up by the scruff of his neck and pushed him out. Some very prominent guests had come, and here was Guru Nanak in his torn and worn clothes! (Like our own Bhagwan Yogi Ramsuratkumar). The employees felt it would not be appropriate to have this lowly guest. Guru Nanak saw everyone giving respect to expensive clothing. So he went out and got himself some dazzling clothes and came back to the mosque. This time he was received with great honour and the feast was spread before him. Guru Nanak said: "Dhoti you eat! Kurta you eat! The food is served for you!" Naturally, the food and clothes remained mute witnesses to the drama. The food uneaten, Nanak left the mosque.

After food, the assembly knelt and offered their prayers at the mosque. Guru Nanak looked up at the minarets on the mosque and said, "Why are you standing upright? You also bend down and offer worship!" Promptly the minarets bent and fell, killing all the people underneath.

Completing his parable, Yogiji continued: "This beggar does not have powers like Guru Nanak but the pure silk dhoti given by the Swamigal has given this beggar power," and he laughed uproariously. As the day progressed, Yogi Ramsuratkumar would repeat the teaching often, always laughing: "Swamigal has given this pure silk dhoti and this beggar has become pure." For him, it was outrageous and unbelievable, to the point of humor, that people would bow to silken splendor while missing the deeper truth that Gandhi and others had long taught them.[14]

राम

The old joke about "dog" being "God spelled backwards" was enlivened brilliantly in the life of Yogi Ramsuratkumar. From the early 1970s, as Kirsti had noted on several occasions, Yogiji's dog, Sai

Yogi Ramsuratkumar and Sai Baba, late 1970s

Baba, was more than a trusty companion. For Parathasarathy, Sai Baba "the first" was "a conscious animal" that actually used to "talk" with people.

In 1976, Sai Baba was missing for three days. The disappearance coincided with an effort by the municipal authorities to remove the wild dogs from the city. Many animals were killed wherever they were cornered. Whether Sai Baba had been caught and later escaped, or whether he had craftily hid out long enough to avoid this pogrom, is unknown. But, after three days, the mongrel found his way back to the punnai tree at the railway station, seeking the protection of his master. Here he took sanctuary, although remaining at the respectful distance from his beloved provider and friend. All the while, however, Sai Baba whimpered in a way that devotees would later describe as "weeping" in relief.

"Swami became so alert, so serious, and he asked Sai Baba to come near," Parathasarathy reported. The beggar then asked the dog to lie down, and Sai Baba, obedient to whatever Swamiji said, lay down. Swamiji then put his hands on Sai Baba's body, saying, "Oh, these people are giving so much trouble to this beggar. They wanted to kill this beggar and they wanted to kill Sai Baba. Oh! How it is! But my Father is protecting Sai Baba; they need not bother."

Yogi Ramsuratkumar's healing hands remained on Sai Baba's body for half an hour. The master then turned to one of his devotees, directing the man to take Sai Baba to the pump near the well and give him a good wash. Normally, the animal was scared by water and would run away. But on this occasion the dog silently obliged. He stood unresisting as the man washed him thoroughly with soap. When Sai Baba was brought back to Swamiji, he took his place once again at the beggar's feet. Here the animal remained for the rest of the day, while Yogi Ramsuratkumar kept his attention on him. For the master, obviously, all creatures were God – some wearing the human form, others the forms of dogs, or birds, yet friends all.

Hygiene-conscious visitors, Indians and Westerners alike, were frequently put off by the dog's presence. As his human devotees sat with Ramsuratkumar, Sai Baba might nuzzle up to them, climbing over their laps, looking for a safe and comfortable spot in which to sleep. If his guests made the mistake of pushing the dog aside, Yogi Ramsuratkumar was obviously displeased by their reluctance or fastidiousness. Certainly their reactions were understandable, from the perspective of ordinary consciousness. "That dog would wander all over the city," Parathasarathy described, adding graphically, "it had sores all over its body. And dirt, eh? And a bad smell, and fleas... And it will sleep with us in the night!" Everything repulsive all rolled up into one energetic package! If Yogi Ramsuratkumar had consciously designed a means to challenge values, habits, or preferences, he could not have chosen a better vehicle than this dog. While spiritual aspirants might dream about laboring among the needy, in some dramatic show of self-sacrifice, these dreams would be shown up for what they really were – idealistic fantasies – when subjected to the acid test offered by the master's own Sai Baba.

15

RISING SON, 1977

 On an airplane bound to Madras (now Chennai) from Bombay (now Mumbai), on January 16, 1977, a group of six Americans chatted and swapped stories of their various adventures to date. For all of them it was a first trip to India, and they had come with the clear intention to absorb as much of the spiritual culture of this remarkable country as they possibly could within the short four weeks of their stay. To that end, they were visiting ashrams and sacred sites of Meher Baba, Satya Sai Baba, Bhagwan Sri Rajneesh, Swami Muktananda, Anandamayi Ma, and other lesser known saints and sages.

They were young – most in their twenties, one in her teens – enthusiastic, and hopeful. India was a place to fulfill one's spiritual longings, one's dreams.

Among them, a dark-haired, vibrant, thirty-four-year-old man with bright blue eyes spoke softly and laughed freely. The oldest member of the group, Lee Lozowick was the focus of their attention as he commented on their questions and concerns. He was their spiritual teacher – the one who had initiated the trip and invited each of them along. A year and a half earlier, in July 1975, Lee had experienced an event that can best be described as an awakening, in the traditional sense of the term. While he never referred to himself then, or since, as "enlightened" (instead speaking of "the event that catalyzed my teaching work"), it was obvious to those who had known him previously that something profound, something transformational, had taken place in his life. Simply put, Lee embodied happiness, a completely non-problematical relationship to life, and an obsession with God. In a book written shortly after this pivotal incident in July 1975, he described his condition further, calling it "spiritual slavery," and offering others the straightforward truth of surrender to the will of God.

In the days and weeks of the late summer of 1975, Lee's physical presence became more compelling, and his condition of aliveness in God more recognizable to those who had a deep desire to serve the Divine and to "wake up," as they felt he had. While many of his former friends and associates turned away with incredulity, thinking him now insane at best and a self-serving charlatan at worst, a core group of devoted students soon formed around him. The community of Hohm was born on September 7, 1975, with its first formal gathering.

Now, in the beginning of 1977, Lee was making his first trip to the "holy land" – Mother India. From the first moment he arrived, the country felt like home to him. He had long been attracted by the culture and spirituality of India, had read extensively the works of her saints and sages, and had introduced his own small group of friends and devotees into the rituals of *satsang* and *kirtan*. On a regular basis he had made the short trip from his home in northern New Jersey into New York City, or other nearby locations, to see visiting spiritual dignitaries who would pass through the area. Among his favorite places to receive inspiration and spiritual nourishment was a weekly soirée, first held in a stuffy but spacious basement of St. Luke's Church in New York City; then, in 1976, moved to the Cathedral Church of St. John the Divine on Amsterdam Avenue at upper 112th St. There, as many as three hundred to a thousand people would gather every week to hear spiritual teachings and to meet the many distinguished guests who would be invited to speak. From Ram Dass (Richard Alpert) to Krishnamurti, anybody who was anybody in the spiritual scene in the U.S. at that time might show up at "Hilda's."

Hilda Charlton, who hosted and taught these extraordinary "classes" for twenty-three years, was a spiritual teacher, author, dancer, and healer. Since the mid-1960s, when she returned from nearly twenty years in India, Hilda had been sharing something of the mysteries she had encountered, the great beings she had met, and the ageless teachings she had received in her journeys. Her passion for the things of God, her obvious holiness, and her wisdom were quickly recognized. From a handful of interested students meeting in a friend's apartment, her classes grew to include hundreds of mostly young seekers of all spiritual persuasions. Hilda called them all her "kids," in her characteristically down-home fashion. The merely curious, the drugged-out hippie, the serious seeker – Hilda embraced them all, even if at times she turned some away who obviously couldn't hear what she had to offer. Thousands were drawn to Hilda's fire. She was dry tinder – ready, willing, and prepared by the Divine, through her years of study and practice, to receive the grace of a catalyzing spark. With that spark – the unfocused but genuine hunger of a hippie culture looking for something "real" – she became a great blaze.

Many people used Hilda as their primary teacher, some remaining with her, serving her and supporting her work until her death in 1988 and beyond. More used Hilda in her function as lighthouse, guidepost, and intermediary. Hilda pointed a way. She helped her "kids" to grow up, to see their gross and outlandishly self-obsessed behaviors; she taught them to meditate and to entertain the possibilities of "a life of giving and forgiving, unconditional love and remembrance of God."[1] Her teachings encompassed all the religions of the world, and she loved to tell the stories of the saints – from Jesus to Satya Sai Baba. She would say: "It is not that we are teaching you about many, many saints. We are teaching you about the One Essence in many forms…It is like glasses of water filled from the one same ocean. We are not teaching many gods, but One God in various forms."[2]

On November 11, 1976, two short months before Lee Lozowick left for India, Hilda devoted her entire class to the subject of a different kind of saint – the hidden saint. In contrast to the other gurus of India at the time, most of whom were attracting hoards of followers, and the yogis who were amazing Westerners with their feats of seeming magic, Hilda spoke of a great one who was "changing the universe" by moving a teacup; a being of incomparable significance who carried the world and its needs in the pile of old newspapers that he kept near him at all times. The person she described was a beggar...dirty...odd...who "doesn't bathe and yet smells like roses."[3] She cautioned her "kids" that they might completely overlook or dismiss him, not knowing that such great ones often hide themselves in such disguises in order to do their work in secret.

She had found (or been found by) this one, Yogi Ramsuratkumar, she said. Although she had not met him on the physical plane, she "knew" him in her own ways – ways of mystical perception which most people have no knowledge of. "I received a letter from him and I saw through his disguise," Hilda said. "He's not a guru," she continued. "He wouldn't have you," she wisely discouraged. "His work is universal. It's a tough scene, I'm telling you, to be in the presence of someone like that. They demand something, or get out!"[4]

Her eyes blazed as she spoke these strong words. They were necessary. Hilda knew that many more of her "kids" would make the pilgrimage to the Motherland over the next few decades. She knew their spiritual materialism, their naivete, their assumptions of what a "spiritual teacher" was supposed to look and act like. Yogi Ramsuratkumar embodied, for her, the complete contradiction of all such fantasies and illusions.

With this public presentation, the mad beggar of Tiruvannamalai, whom she spoke of as one who changes the universe, was being publicly revealed in the West for the first time, and Hilda apparently took her responsibility in that with utmost seriousness. She then introduced Will Zulkowski, his wife Joan, and finally Caylor Wadlington, who had recently returned from his seven years in India. Each spoke, with Hilda's careful guidance of their narratives, of the mysterious ways, the wondrous laughter, and the fierce demands put upon them by the hidden saint of Tiruvannamalai, Yogi Ramsuratkumar. They told of seemingly miraculous healings, of his ability to read their thoughts, of his idiosyncratic ways of placing things here and there throughout the town, of his collection of interesting artifacts – his coconut bowl, his fan, his funny "spear" with the colored rags attached. Each in their own way witnessed to the fact that their hearts had been pierced by the beggar's glance; that something deep within them had been opened.

Rising Son, 1977

When her guests were finished with their narratives, Hilda spoke:

See, do you understand what he was doing? What these silent ones, these people who are never known to you, do? They don't have big crowds, they don't have Yogavilles. I'm not downing any of that, kids....But there are the invisible ones at work, and I've always said it's these people along with the other great ones who keep the world in balance.

He takes a stone and puts it here. He has a reason. He puts a thought behind it. And he hides behind his craziness; he hides behind his laughter. But he's stern, stern, so stern you have to do it just right. And people don't understand – why can't you just do it sloppy?

Why not? Because when he puts a stone there, he's placing it for the universe; he's placing it for the world. He's changing the world with his thoughts, with his power. I've had a letter from that man, and he calls himself with every other word, "this old sinner, this old beggar." Well, if he's a sinner and beggar, he's the most beautiful sinner and beggar in this universe. He's powerful! If he puts a stone down, he changes the world!...

These hidden angels, these great ones, help hold the world in balance. Perhaps they appear mystical to some, foolish to others, insane in the minds of the earthly sick ones who are tied to customs. Oh, we have a custom: you mustn't wear rags, no, no. Mustn't tie pieces of rock in your clothes. You'll end up in Bellevue with a psychiatrist saying you mustn't tie rocks in your dress. That's not nice, that's not the way humans do things. You've got to do it just the way everybody else does. Well, these great ones don't. Their ways break the rules of cultures. But to me they are the sacred ones who sacredly work for their brothers and sisters unnoticed – except that I brought it out into the open here, with all my heart. And he knows it this night. He knows it. I'm going to write him and tell him that people in the second biggest cathedral hall on the Earth heard all about you, Swami.

To these hidden brothers and sisters of light, let us humbly bow. They care not for fame, for recognition, but quietly walk through life as God's beacons of truth and light…

The hidden ones like Yogi Ramsuratkumar are not crazy. He knows just what he's doing for the universe – and he's changing the universe.[5]

Lee Lozowick may have been present at that historic meeting, as he was a regular to Hilda's gatherings. A few weeks later, he made a special trip to New York City to speak with Hilda personally about his upcoming journey to India. Whom should he visit? What should he see? Lee certainly wasn't looking for a guru, nor was he "seeking" in any traditional sense. His immediate experience was that he had already *been* surrendered to the will of God, and was living a condition of spiritual slavery in which his own will was subsumed by the work of the Divine. A trip to India, for him, was an opportunity to drink deeply from the sacred waters that had refreshed and transformed souls throughout the ages; it was also an incomparable opportunity for his students to gain dynamic impressions of a spiritual culture.

Hilda's advice included a special directive – in going to Tiruvannamalai to Ramanashram, he must not neglect to look for the hidden one, Yogi Ramsuratkumar. When Lee agreed to attempt the task, she took some rupee notes, folded them in a particularly intentional way, and placed them in an envelope together with a note of greetings. Would Lee kindly deliver this to the beggar-saint?

Hilda made it clear to Lee, as she had to others, that Yogi Ramsuratkumar was sometimes not easily found; sometimes not found at all. There were seekers who had gone to Tiruvannamalai who had searched for him for days, spent weeks there, but had never encountered his majestic but enigmatic presence. If Lee was meant to find him, he would, Hilda said, meaning that if Yogi Ramsuratkumar wanted to be found, *he* would arrange the meeting. If not, no amount of searching would do any good. Hilda told Lee of the beggar's usual haunts – the bus station, the brass market, the railway station…and wished him well.

राम

Unlike many tourists to India, Lee chose to deliberately expose his traveling companions to some of the more difficult aspects of life in this amazing country. Except for the rare domestic airplane trip, like the one they had just made, the group moved under harsh conditions, taking only third-class accommodations on trains, or constantly challenging comfort and convenience in the overcrowded buses...never taxis...as they made their way from city to city. Wherever they stopped, they stayed in tiny ashrams or the least expensive hotels Lee could find.

When they arrived in Madras on January 16, they went straight to the bus station, where they caught the next bus leaving for Tiruvannamalai, a journey of three or four hours over bumpy and winding roads. Spirits were extremely high, despite the rigors of travel. While they had no idea that this was to be a stop of unimaginable significance in the life of their young teacher, Lee, and in the evolution of the community of Hohm, signs that something "big" was in store were already exploding around them. They didn't yet know how to read those signs, or where to place full credit for what was happening. Even Lee was in the dark, in some ways. Simply moved by the Divine, he was innocent to the fact that he was about to walk into the lion's mouth...or better said, into the annihilating fire of God's heart. He could never have guessed that this day would mark for him the beginning of the end.

Aboard the plane that morning a strange phenomenon had begun to erupt within the group. Unexpectedly, one of Lee's closest devotees started to exhibit a particular form of unrestrained laughter. Following this, she experienced waves of bliss that opened her heart in a way that was previously unknown to her. A woman of a practical and skeptical nature, she admitted later that she had never wanted or tried to provoke such states. In fact, while she knew that such conditions existed, she judged that she would be the last person to ever taste such intense devotion. Aboard the bus later that day, this same woman found herself overtaken with joy, absorbed in the play of Krishna, whom she perceived as being seated next to her, in the

Lee Lozowick in India, 1977

person of Lee. The other woman in the group began to pick up the infectious ecstasy, and before long the two were literally identified with the *gopis* of Vrindavan, at play with their glorious Lord!

Quiet and noncommittal as he usually was, Lee seemed to enjoy their obvious bliss. Despite the public setting of this display, he clearly encouraged their joy. What these women were experiencing was the unleashing of the Divine Shakti energy – the universal life force. *She* was being birthed, essentially for the first time, among the students of Hohm. "So, we arrived in Tiruvannamalai already altered! We arrived in town very different than we were before," shared the younger woman many years later.

The fact that this happened on the very day on which Lee Lozowick was to meet his own beloved Krishna, his Ram, Yogi Ramsuratkumar – the one whom Lee would later acknowledge had guided every step of his life, and engineered every event, including the one that began his own teaching work in 1975 – seems vastly more than coincidental.

राम

Landing in town in the late afternoon, the weary travelers settled into their accommodations near Ramanashram as the guests of Mrs. Taleyarkhan, a devotee of Sri Ramana Maharshi. "Ma" Taleyarkhan was in her sixties at the time, and she had lived in India for many years. Graciously she welcomed her Western guests, giving up her private prayer space in order to arrange a sleeping area for all of them.

"Yogi Ramsuratkumar was considered a 'rascal' by many of those who followed a more traditional spiritual path," commented one of the women on that first trip. "We considered it best not to tell our hosts that we were going to see him. It was almost a clandestine meeting – a secret, in the sense that if we wanted to be good guests we needed to hide that fact from our hosts who might find our actions offensive or shocking."[6]

With little more than an hour spent in getting something to drink and learning directions, the group set out under Lee's direction to look for "Ram Ram." Taking a horse-drawn *tonga* (a taxi), the party made their way first to the bus station, but he was not to be seen. Moving on to the brass market near the temple, Lee suggested that the group split up in order to maximize their chances of finding the strange beggar.

No sooner had they separated, however, than Lee's group was approached by an Indian man who muttered the now familiar name – "Ram Ram" – and pointed them in the direction of a nearby set of steps leading to a covered platform. The mandapam of the temple car (a huge cart that was used for special feast days) was a favored place where Yogi Ramsuratkumar spent many hours of his day, often long into the night. Amazingly, the other group had been similarly accosted, and when they arrived at the same spot, Lee and his company were already seated before the Godman. The youngest member of this group described what happened next:

> We saw our friends sitting in the light of the oil lamps within the mandapam. They faced the one we had come looking for – a man in rags sat regally in front of them. My heart leapt into my throat with nervousness. Yogi Ramsuratkumar faced in the direction of Sannadhi Street. I remember vividly walking up those stone stairs, as my legs were shaking. There was something about this whole event that was pretty overwhelming. I had an immediate sense of something terrifying but exciting, and I remember sweating profusely. Sitting in this company, there was so much more going on than in other places we had visited thus far.
>
> A young man, who turned out to be Yogi Ramsuratkumar's attendant, had walked us up to be seated. Six cups of coffee were already set out and waiting – one for Yogi Ramsuratkumar, and one for each of us. Although six of us had come to Tiruvannamalai, he somehow knew to prepare coffee for five. One of our group had stayed behind on this evening.
>
> The Beggar's presence was unsettling and riveting. I just stared at him, not knowing what to do, and looked to Lee for any clues. Lee sat there like an old friend, or even a child of this man. Then the Yogi spoke. He had the most lilting tone to his voice and his eyes glistened and sparkled in the lamplight.[7]

Always ready to handle his responsibilities impeccably, Lee promptly handed over the envelope that he had carried from America, informing Yogi Ramsuratkumar that it was from Hilda. The Godchild repeated her name, sweetly – *"Ah, Heelda,"* as he pronounced it with distinct affection – and took the envelope from Lee's hand. "I knew they had never physically met, but he was talking like they were lifelong friends. It was the contact with her, not the gift, but the communion with her that we were feeling," one of the group later reported.

The entrance to the Therady Mandapam (Temple Car Mandapam),
Sannadhi Street, Tiruvannamalai

Before opening it, the beggar held the envelope between his hands, as if reading it through his palms. Then he briefly closed his eyes and sat in silence. Only then did he open the envelope and take out the gift of rupees that Hilda had sent. Capturing the magic of this moment more than ten years after it occurred, one of the witnesses wrote: "From one hand to the other and back again to the first hand, Yogi Ramsuratkumar exchanged the bills, and then repeated this movement over and over again. I remember Lee saying that Hilda had done *the exact same movements* with the rupees. It was as if there was a secret message he was decoding by doing so. He looked so grateful."[8]

One by one the Western guests were called up to sit directly in front of Yogi Ramsuratkumar. The younger woman felt that the old master was conducting a series of rituals. Each person who was called up was asked to light the beggar's cigarette, as he handed over the matches. Then, as he began to puff on his cigarette, he looked at each one, as if gazing long into their past or future, then checking back in with them in the present. "He seemed very far away at times," she reported. "It was unnerving, being seen through in this way, and I kept lowering my eyes. I felt like such a child in front of this ancient being."[9]

Yogi Ramsuratkumar asked the young woman her age, and seemed to find it extremely funny that she was only nineteen. He asked her name, first and last, which she told him. He repeated her initials several times, as if making an internal association. "S.D., S.D.," he said. Whatever he was doing at the time, she didn't understand, but later, when the group visited the Ramakrishna Mutt (a spiritual center) near Madras, she learned that Ramakrishna's wife and lifelong partner in his work, Sarada Devi, had regularly been referred to as "S.D." It was a tiny detail, seemingly without significance. A mere joke. But when added to the innumerable lilas associated with Yogi Ramsuratkumar, it became for this young woman one more source of wonder and gratitude at the subtle perfection of his way of teaching. Sarada Devi was the constant devotee of her husband and master, Ramakrishna. For any woman on the spiritual path, Sarada Devi would be a potent ally, and certainly one to honor and emulate every step of the way.

The beggar was tuned into this young woman at many levels, she reported. As he continued to smoke, he "guessed" the national origin of her family name, and then went on to "guess" not only her father's profession, but her mother's current disposition. Since she was deeply conflicted about her father at the time, she felt the Godman's attention as a direct means of help. "He was so very gentle with me and seemed to be sweetly appreciative of my father, and sensitive to something about his being. Readily, I began to weep," she said. "We were all just like open books to Yogi Ramsuratkumar. Finally, he gave me some beautiful flowers for my hair and motioned me back to my seat."[10]

Turning to one of the men in the group, Ramsuratkumar asked how old he thought the old beggar to be. The man took a guess, at which Yogi Ramsuratkumar giggled. He was, in fact, only fifty-nine at the time, but when one of the women told him that she had no idea of his age, as she thought him to be timeless, he threw his head back and let go peels of laughter.

The last person he called up was Lee, who was seated a respectful distance away. Yogi Ramsuratkumar patted the cement, indicating that Lee should come closer. The beggar had a mischievous look in his eye as Lee finally took a place close by. He asked the young American his name, and when he heard it, asked further, "That's Russian, isn't it?"

Lee smiled his acknowledgement. "Jewish too?" Ramsuratkumar inquired. Lee nodded agreement.

And so, with the exchanges of apparently simple pleasantries, the sky grew dark and the stars came out, and several hours passed quickly in the beggar's company.

While the Godman spoke to one of Lee's male students, enacting the ritual of having the young man light his cigarette while studying him deeply, the other male student suddenly leapt to his feet. Taking the beggar's hand fan from where it rested against the nearby wall, he proceeded to start fanning Yogi Ramsuratkumar. It was a sudden gesture, apparently inspired by devotion, but unasked for, and the others in the group were immediately alerted to what seemed like a breach of protocol. They had been learning throughout the trip to take their cues from Lee, otherwise to remain in the background. Yogi Ramsuratkumar himself appeared startled by the man's swift action. Although he did not prevent it, he registered in his face that something in the atmosphere had been disturbed.

Lee said nothing in the moment. It was obvious to him that this simple beggar was fully capable of handling whatever transpired around him. But, as his companions would soon learn, Lee was shocked, embarrassed, and greatly upset by the behavior of one of his charges.

Leaving the presence of the Godchild, who graciously raised his hands and blessed them all, the Americans walked down the stairs and piled into the back of a horse-drawn tonga.

"Who wants to see Yogi Ramsuratkumar tomorrow?" Lee asked, his voice holding back the fury of the affront made to this superior being. When the whole group raised their hands, Lee replied with sharpness: "Fine. You can go without me!"

Back at their guesthouse, it was clear to the others in the group that their friend's act of immaturity had crashed something very precious. "Yogi Ramsuratkumar was the most interesting saint I have seen all over India. There is nobody else I'm interested in going back to see a second time. But I refuse to do it if my students are going to act like that," Lee spoke vigorously, passionately. "He was *interesting* to me. He was somebody I feel like I could learn something from. And I'm unwilling to go back right now basically because of this breach of protocol."[11] As far as Lee was concerned, it was better to sacrifice his own desire to stay longer than to risk any potential insult or interference with the work of the beautiful and powerful beggar.

Two days later, they left Tiruvannamalai bound for cities further north. It would be two years before they would return. Soon after arriving back in the States, a major upheaval took place within the budding Hohm Community. Once-enthused students began to question their commitment, triggered by Lee's enlivened mood of advocacy for basic discipline and practice. When he initiated such simple demands as the need for a vegetarian diet, many left the company, disgruntled, never to return.

This India trip had definitely reoriented Lee's approach to his students. He had seen the thousands of devotees gathered in the ashrams of the gurus and teachers of India. Overall, what he saw had failed to impress him. For too many devotees, their master had become a benevolent figurehead. A certain edge or quality of aliveness that Lee had looked for was often missing.

What he found on the steps of the mandapam in Tiruvannamalai around a dirty beggar, however, *had* impressed him. In fact, it had left its mark on him more deeply than he knew at the time. A few days after this historic meeting, sitting in his hotel room in Varanasi, Lee commented to his traveling party: "It was interesting how the person I had most fun with, 'Ram Ram,' had only maybe twelve or thirteen people on the steps with him that night. We'd heard the stories of how many people had arguments with him, and how people didn't like him, but he was the realest, the *realest* of all the people we'd met. And look how few people were with him. They even had those beautiful posters of him up, so it wasn't like he was some unknown; he was even moderately, relatively, famous. People just don't want to deal with what they *think* to be craziness!"[12]

Lee had a similar reputation for craziness, and quite a few detractors among the well-established spiritual organizations in the U.S. at the time. It is not hard to speculate that his contact with the "craziness" of the "realest" person on the trip, Yogi Ramsuratkumar, was having its effect on him, and on those around him. Those who didn't want to deal with it were easily driven away. Whether he realized it or not, the hand of the beggar, Yogi Ramsuratkumar, was now, more than ever, stirring the circumstances of Lee's life and the life of all at Hohm.

16

PORTRAIT OF A MASTER

 Among the many Westerners who met Yogi Ramsurat-
kumar during the 1970s, some drew close to the mas-
ter, for longer or shorter periods of time, before moving on. In December 1976, just one month before Lee
Lozowick's trip to India, a young Finnish woman visited the beggar for the first time. The initial impression he made on her was subtle, and it took her another year before
she started to seriously consider that he might have a major role to
play in her life. Eventually, she would take him as her guru, and
choose to live permanently in Tiruvannamalai – sometimes in a cave
on the slopes of Arunachala, or in a tiny room a stone's throw from
Yogi Ramsuratkumar's Ashram. She was still living there in 2004.

Kirsti (also known as Sivapriya) has left a legacy of stories about
her relationship with the beggar, stories that are dynamic because they
are told by a practicing sadhaka. While hundreds of lilas tell of Yogi
Ramsuratkumar's external activities – his curious ways, his miraculous "knowing," his sweet laughter – Kirsti's words convey something
more about the inner dimension that underlay it all; the dimension
in which Yogi Ramsuratkumar lived.

Just prior to the Deepam festival in December 1976, Kirsti first
laid eyes on the Godchild. It was his birthday, and a party was being
hosted by devotees. She and a few other Western seekers – theosophy
students who had met Caylor Wadlington in Adyar at the international headquarters of the Theosophical Society – were curious to
meet "Caylor's master."

*The Jayanti Celebration for Yogi Ramsuratkumar, 1976,
Janardhanan standing*

The beggar himself greeted these foreign guests at the front of the building in which the festivities were being held, and led them inside where friends and well-wishers were singing devotional chants and songs in his honor. One devotee kept placing a heavy garland of flowers around the master's neck, as an offering of worship, but the beggar kept taking them off and putting them aside. No sooner were they removed than the persistent devotee would load them on Yogiji's shoulders once again.

"It was all so new and different from what I had seen before," Kirsti wrote more than twenty years later in reflecting upon this first meeting. "It was the first time I witnessed a bhakti scene. Yogi Ramsuratkumar looked like a very happy man. He had a twinkle in his eye, and the way he dressed was funny. He felt easily accessible and I felt happy near him."[1] It would be another year before she would see the "funny" beggar again.

ONLY GOD

राम

It was sometime during 1976 when a group of devotees purchased the Sannadhi Street house for Yogi Ramsuratkumar. The house was conveniently located directly across the street from the temple-car mandapam, the place in town that the beggar could most readily be found when he wasn't in the temple complex itself. He would often sleep in the shelter of this mandapam when he wasn't sleeping in the brass market. From here, each morning, with his devotee Perumal and a few other helpers who carried the gunnysacks of his trash and treasures, Yogi Ramsuratkumar would walk briskly to the railway station on the outskirts of town. There he would settle himself under the punnai tree, where he would receive his many visitors.

As his seekers increased in numbers, however, and many complained that they could not always locate him easily (and probably also that sitting in the hot sun of the fields was less than desirable), the decision was made to find a house for him. Yogi Ramsuratkumar never asked for such "improvements" to his life. For thirty years he had lived out of doors – the streets, the trees, the fields, the mountains – or in abandoned buildings or temporary shelters. Without this intervention on the part of his devotees, he would have lived out his entire life in the same manner, fully free, and fully dependent on the rain of his Father's grace for his water, the sun of his Father's benediction for his food. By giving him a house, his devotees were honoring him but also burdening the master in a new way, restraining him with delicate threads that would eventually become like steel bars, confining him in place. Although he was free to reject such an inevitable imprisonment, Yogi Ramsuratkumar accepted it, step by step. If it was "for the devotees," as he was consistently told, he could hardly refuse; his surrender to his Father demanded that he surrender to the impositions of those who loved him.

This house on Sannadhi Street was certainly no palace. In fact, a narrow open sewer ran along the front of the building, and local men would regularly urinate against the external wall of the house above this sewer. Located at the intersection of Sannadhi and Car Street, one of the busiest roads in town, the whole area was a noisy and dusty

298

place. But it bustled with the life of the growing city, and Yogi Ramsuratkumar was no stranger to that chaotic current.

A few months after the house was purchased, the beggar began to spend more time there, especially at night, even though he would often be under the mandapam across the street or in the temple by day. From as early as 1977, some stories by his guests and devotees would contain some mention of this house. By the early 1980s, stories that didn't mention the "Sannadhi Street house" were rare.

राम

During the festival of Deepam 1977, when Kirsti returned to Tiruvannamalai, she found him at this house on Sannadhi Street. "The twinkle in his eyes had stayed in my memory and [I had] an inner feeling that I needed to meet this man again." This time she gave him an apple as her offering, and sat down in silence. Sai Baba, the master's dog, would wander over, rub against her, and move away. For an hour or more, Yogi Ramsuratkumar held the apple in his hands and then against his forehead. "He seemed to be pondering. Indeed, there was so much joy and love in him."

For every devotee there comes a moment when he or she sees *who* the master is, or recognizes something that has always been known but which was unreachable before. Kirsti was no novice to the domain of spiritual experience. Some years prior to her meeting with Yogi Ramsuratkumar she had glimpsed a deeper realm of existence, and she longed to explore that place further. Meeting the Godchild in 1977, she found *that place* in him.

> I recognized that He was *in* the dimension I had seen some years earlier. That opening had pushed me to find if there were people on the planet who were conscious of the freedom, light, vastness and playfulness that lies just beneath the self-centered thinking process which, like a lid, kept everyone's attention bound and cramped and focused on discomforts of every kind.
>
> Direct transmission of the source of life – that was the teaching I had been looking for when I became a pilgrim.

For Yogi Ramsuratkumar it manifested in his person, not as a state of mind one needs to protect. It could interact with anyone's situation bringing power, greatness, oceanic peace, joy and release; it cut through human minds' cobwebs. I felt full respect towards him. I felt him standing at the bottom of my utmost capacity to be.

When their meeting ended, Yogi Ramsuratkumar handed the apple back to Kirsti, and graciously told her that she could come again. Instead of consuming the *prasad* immediately, the usual protocol for imbibing the blessing force of the master, Kirsti honored his gift to her in another way. She kept the apple for a week! "It felt like a living being, as if He was in it," she wrote.

As she began to seek out Yogi Ramsuratkumar's presence more regularly, the young seeker very quickly learned that there were many faces to the twinkling-eyed yogi. New to the town of Tiruvannamalai, she first stayed in the home of a Parsi woman who had been a longtime disciple of Ramana Maharshi's. As a guest there she was expected to be present for the lunch meal, which was served promptly at 11 A.M. This created something of a conflict for the younger woman, as her morning audience with the beggar usually commenced around 10 A.M., and might occasionally last for several hours. "With Yogiji I had sensed his authority in all matters with everything near him, from the very beginning. If I sat with him and the mealtime was approaching, I kept quiet. *He* was the one who would say when the time to go was. He seemed to utilize his every moment in a way that left no doubt that he knew what he was doing."

On a morning when the *satsang* with Yogi Ramsuratkumar lasted until after eleven, Kirsti was concerned and distracted, unable to devote her attention completely to what he was doing. When she got back to her residence at half-past eleven, she found to her amazement that the cook had been delayed at the market, and that lunch had not yet been served. "It always worked like that with him," Kirsti wrote. "If one gave full attention to his guidance, letting *him* be in control, everything was taken care of. The practical, conventional mind had to be silenced, however. It was clear that on my next visit I had to be free for him to work on me directly, without my attention being divided on concerns about mealtimes or the time for locking the gate for the night. He wanted people to be free when they came to sit with him, not preoccupied by something that needed to be done."

This insight, which she learned early on, stood her in good stead for many years to come. What she described was a way in which the devotee frees the master to work. Lacking that internal equanimity, the guide's subtle teaching would be easily lost in the chaos of the seeker's self-obsession or recoil.

She also learned quickly that his benediction was unconfined by his physical location, and that his benediction protected her wherever she went. "When I went for pilgrimages, I always informed Yogiji beforehand. The people I met and the places I was taken to seemed to be manifesting through the direction of a Divine omnipresent parent. I was thoroughly looked after. It was as if the many people, and situations, and every living being had been one of Yogiji's faces. I was embraced by the love of the Divine everywhere, in everything. If anything was needed, or I wondered where to go, I would think of Him and just follow the inner clarity – catching trains without ever making reservations; seeking out unknown places of pilgrimage and tiny ashrams."

राम

For many years Kirsti lived in a room where Yogi Ramsuratkumar himself had found shelter when he first came to Tiruvannamalai. It was located not far from Ramanashram, which, interestingly, put it close to the site of his own future ashram. An old woman who had visited the beggar when he had lived in this room many years ago remembered that he smoked *beedies* (a native cigarette) at the time, sitting on the verandah; that he slept on a cloth inside; and that he kept a clay pot for drinking water behind the door.

Kirsti's privilege in occupying the master's old haunt was not without its sacrifices, however. In fact, while she often wished to move elsewhere, Yogiji wanted her to stay in that house, for his own reasons. If for no other, perhaps because it was a great preparation for the life of renunciation she would later take up in the caves.

"White ants had eaten hollow the wood that supported the heavy tile roof. If I poked the beams, three-quarters of them would fall down as dust," Kirsti reflected with a playful tone. "The wood remaining was the thickness of a thumb. Monkeys further worked on the roof, dropping several tiles down. In places one could see the sky from inside." Yet, in all the time she lived there, "the roof did not crash down and somehow the rain flowed down to the verandah without wetting my books and clothes. It was quite miraculous." Another sign, for her, that the Godchild was caring for her in every detail of her life.

राम

"Yogi Ramsuratkumar did not allow himself to be treated with external shows of respect until the late 80s," Kirsti wrote, describing what she felt had characterized these earlier days. There was always humor around him, yet always a need for vigilance. One could miss a communication by being too casual, *or* too serious!

"Oh, you are standing, you must be in a hurry to go!" the beggar might say to people who leapt to their feet when he arrived on the scene. With that, he might dismiss them.

If you just sat quietly, meaning that if you didn't make any ostentatious show of devotion or emotion, "he would sit down, light a cigarette and maybe say a few words," Kirsti reported. "Yogiji didn't waste his time on nonsense, and most people waste time."

It was not uncommon for Yogi Ramsuratkumar to hide himself in the temple when he wished to be alone, using his country hand-fan as a means of covering his face, demurely, the way a shy young girl will hide behind her hands. He also might position himself in the shadows of one of the buildings there so that he could see the people going for darshan within a particular shrine. While remaining invisible himself, "he blessed everyone who went in, raising his hand, moving it in rhythm with the slow moving queue."

Although he had allowed a celebration of his birthday in 1976, thereafter "he used to slip away from his house on birthdays too, and hide in a devotee's house." When his ashram was built in 1994, his birthdays (*Jayantis*) were again allowed to be celebrated, if reluctantly on the master's part. Based in his early orientation toward no big shows, one can easily speculate that a great deal of Yogi Ramsuratkumar's later allowances were, partially at least, a result of his unrestrained love for his devotees. He was constantly capitulating to the demands of his lovers.

राम

The breadth and depth of Yogi Ramsuratkumar's knowledge was always a source of profound amazement to both visitors and devotees. That he might know the exact distance from Hamburg to Bern might leave his German guest incredulous. But, book learning aside, when the Godman also demonstrated a certain mastery of the laws of synchronicity, or a relationship to world events that was uncannily personal, he would leave his listeners dumbfounded.

One day Kirsti brought several friends of hers from the Theosophical Society to meet the beggar. As it happened, the master had a carefully folded newspaper close at hand on this morning. It contained an article that he had read, noted with interest and concern, and intended to read again. When Kirsti introduced her friends, Yogi Ramsuratkumar immediately picked up the newspaper and showed them the story he had been focusing on. It was an announcement of the death of the president of the Theosophical Society, which had just occurred the day before. None of the visitors knew of this event, and all were amazed at the "coincidence" of the occurrence happening as it did, exactly on the day they were at the Godman's side.

On another occasion, this one in mid-May 1981, Kirsti accompanied a Catholic priest, another friend of hers, to meet Yogi Ramsuratkumar. On that day the beggar had his newspaper opened to a startling headline. On May 13, Pope John Paul II was shot by a Turkish terrorist in Saint Peter's Square in Rome. The Pope was not killed, but of course the priest was horrified at the news. This was the first he had heard of it! As they commiserated, Yogi Ramsuratkumar went on to explain to the priest, in precise detail, the process whereby a new pope is selected. The priest was astonished that this humble swami actually knew more about this intricate ritual than he himself did.

ONLY GOD

राम

Many of the masters and teachers in India had animals that were particularly devoted to them. A great saint, Mother Mayee of Kanyakumari, actually had a pack of dogs that followed her about. On the ashram of Ramana Maharshi, there is a shrine to Laxmi, a favored cow, who was said to be his devotee. Godavari Ma, the lineage holder and disciple of Upasani Baba, had a beloved dog, and this animal's samadhi also stands on the ground of his ashram in Sekuri. Pictures of Yogi Ramsuratkumar tell a similar story of love between man and beast.

Ramsuratkumar's dog, Sai Baba, was actually one of three, each bearing the same name; each one occupying its place at the Godman's side in succession. When one died or disappeared, the next one showed up not long after. In the 1970s, when Kirsti first met the beggar, Sai Baba "the First" was already at his post.

For the quiet Finnish woman, the dog was an ally of sorts. As Indian people generally don't like to be touched by dogs, they would frequently move aside to avoid the animal rubbing up against them. This clearing of the space generally afforded Kirsti a better view of the proceedings, as she otherwise sat far back in the corner.

When Yogi Ramsuratkumar gave orders, the dog would let out a howl, a long "OOOOMMMM," as Kirsti described it. When Sai Baba the First disappeared, it was a few years before Sai Baba II came. "Yogi met him in the temple. The dog got hooked into the joy he felt in him and followed him to the house. He would lie down like a Nandi in front of Yogiji. Yogiji sent devotees to the bakery to get him biscuits."

One day, municipality workers picked up Sai Baba II when they were attempting to dispose of all the stray dogs in town. For some reason, whether malicious or otherwise, someone had removed the poor creature's license band from its neck. Even though the neighbors knew that it was Yogiji's dog, they did not call him, and this upset the beggar greatly.

Sai Baba III was a particularly ecstatic animal. He would become so overwhelmed by the sight of Yogi Ramsuratkumar that he would jump uncontrollably at times. If he was too ecstatic, he would be banned, although kindly, from the space of satsang. A wonderful moment occurred for Kirsti once, occasioned by Sai Baba's activities. She often spent three hours in the temple at night, and if Yogi Ramsuratkumar arrived, followed by Sai Baba, the animal would start jumping as soon as he saw her.

Speaking to Yogi Ramsuratkumar one day, Kirsti remarked: "The dog is so fond of you he starts jumping when he sees anything that reminds him of you."

"Kirsti is more fond of this beggar than this dog [is]," he replied with uncharacteristic directness.

Writing of this incident many years later, Kirsti noted: "I had always felt half invisible in the presence of Yogiji, but this time he gave me the greatest compliment I ever heard from his lips."

राम

One who hasn't had the privilege of "working with" a spiritual master or guru may imagine that the relationship is characterized by private exchanges, much like psychotherapy sessions. Perhaps one visualizes the master sitting above his devotee, listening long and hard to the seeker's tale of woe, or to detailed descriptions of the beginner's inner state. Then, with a wise smile and a look of concern, the guru delivers sage advice that flawlessly directs the devotee – step by logical step – to the next level of understanding. Generally, this is far from the reality.

In Kirsti's work with Yogi Ramsuratkumar, logic and even direct advice were often the last things on the menu. What she "got," she had to struggle for – step by laborious step. What gained her an entrance to the beggar's presence on one day might be completely ineffective the next. However, the longer and harder she tried, the more she learned. "At one time I noticed that if I went straight to his door when I went to town, he would take me in and let me sit with him. If I was shopping and getting tired with the heat, dust, and bargaining, he would give prasad at the door and say, 'This Beggar is busy! You can go!' I thought that having a fresh mind seemed to be good for receiving his transmission and getting into the satsang. I sometimes went to his house thinking, 'Now there is so much clarity in the mind, he will surely let me in.' But he did not. A few days later I was shopping in the town. I had not eaten anything that day. My stomach felt queasy, a fever was coming on, I felt tired and wiped out. He was sitting in the tower next to his house. He called me as I passed and kept me sitting next to him for an hour – there were no others. Near him, tiredness and body pains would disappear."

The master's instruction for sadhana came as hints, not as direct commands, and whether Kirsti followed up on those hints or not was the measure of her attentiveness to him. Yogi Ramsuratkumar might not even speak to her at all, in fact, preferring to deliver his communications through a third party, as he often did in telling Caylor what she (Kirsti) might do. Yogi Ramsuratkumar suggested early on, in this indirect way, that she should stay near Ramanashram, and should spend her time there in meditation. And so, for the next six weeks, whenever she went to see him, Yogi Ramsuratkumar would simply give her a piece of fruit and say, "No need to come here now. Ramanashramam [Ramanashram] is a very good place for meditation." Meanwhile, her heart longed for the privilege of spending more time in his presence. For Yogi Ramsuratkumar, timing was always a big factor. And he was a master of it. His work with Kirsti would consistently take the form of a game of weaning her from reliance on his form. "Ramdas is the guru, and Ramdas is *here*," the master had told her once, pointing to his chest, in the vicinity of his heart. It was clear that he wanted the same realization for his devotees in relationship to himself.

Kirsti took the beggar's "hint" and, despite the fact that she much preferred to stay in the cool and silent caves on the mountain, she brought herself into the marketplace to learn to pray in the midst of the hustle and bustle of Ramanashram's old meditation hall. Here she "sat solidly four to ten hours daily." When she felt hungry she would simply go to the little shops out on the street across from the ashram gate. Here she might buy bananas or cookies and take a cup of tea. Otherwise, she did what she was told. "He never told me *how* I should meditate so I just observed the mind and feelings, tried *japa* and recollected past moods and experiences to see how they worked on my consciousness. He had told me to sit, so I sat and waited [to see] how His Father's blessing would work on me. Now I can see that I did do some real meditations. That time it was an experiment because he had told me to be there in the Old Hall."

In another instance that reflects on her willingness to practice obedience in the face of indirect communication, Kirsti informed Yogi Ramsuratkumar one day that she intended to leave Tiruvannamalai and go to Anandashram in Kanhangad for a while. "I always kept him informed of where I was going, but I always tried to take the mood of what he was indicating, more than the actual words. Usually he would simply say, 'My Father blesses you…everything will go smoothly.'" On this occasion, however, although he did not say anything to prove it, it became clear to Kirsti that her guru did not want her to go on this particular trip, even though he had sent her there several times previously. While she had no way to figure out what his objection might be this time, still she took the intuition of his disapproval as her command. She remained at home. The next day she found there had been a train wreck on the railway line that she would have taken if she had gone as planned. She would have been stranded in a wretched train station, spending the night with more than two hundred other disoriented travelers. "If I asked for blessings for something, and he looked hesitant, I reconsidered the situation. If his blessing was wholehearted, generous, and immediately granted, I could count on it as a certainty. Circumstances would shape so that what I wanted to do would be smooth and easy. But for it to work I had to be in front of him with a naked heart. If I had any desire that would disrupt the flow of blessing power, doing what I had brought to his attention would be slow and needing fixing several times before completion."

राम

"He never explained his actions," Kirsti noted. "Some Westerners I knew misinterpreted his sternness sometimes as anger, but I felt it was just intensity." The beggar's words had a way of evoking old memories, old ways of relating, for many people. This was one of his blessings, for those who knew how to use it. Kirsti recalled clearly that some of her acquaintances would retreat at the sting of his words. "If his sternness reminded them of someone in their past who had been short-tempered with them, they would feel hurt and cry for a full day after being told, 'This beggar is busy. There is no need to see him. There is nothing here. Go to the temple!'" Because she was able to take his words as an indication of his benevolence, rather than as a personal affront, Kirsti followed his commands but without breaking her communion with him. "He really *was* busy," she would wisely assume, and the next day she would show up at his door again.

"By the way he would turn me away, people would think that he didn't like me, or want me around. But it was all a play between him and me and we had the most beautiful relationship." Sometimes, late at night, when Kirsti would go to the temple, after he had sent her away, the beggar would arrive there. A fast learner, Kirsti found that if she played a game of pretending not to see him, leaving him completely unbothered, that she would receive his darshan in the most unique way: "I would be looking over my shoulder and then I would notice that he was blessing all the places where I had sat." Listening carefully to the beggar's words, Kirsti learned over time to read his directions to her between the lines. Like the Zen master, Yogi Ramsuratkumar might use the literal facts of a situation like playthings, yet always in the service of a more essential teaching communication. On one occasion, knowing that Kirsti had been traveling to visit a number of Tibetan monasteries, he remarked to a visitor: "She goes now to Tibetan monasteries but she says Tiruvannamalai is the best place!"

"I did not say that to him," Kirsti observed. "It was his way of telling me that this was the *best* place for me, while other places were good for visiting."

17

HILDA AND COMPANY, 1978

 Brand name products are not always high quality for the money. Similarly, there are brand name gurus too you know. But I know one guru who isn't a brand name guru and his name is Yogi Ramsuratkumar. Sometimes he comes to me. And sometimes he helps some of my kids when I am busy.
– Hilda Charlton, June 23, 1977,
Cathedral of St. John the Divine

Will and Joan Zulkowski had been in Tiruvannamalai for nearly three weeks in mid-1978, spending time with Yogi Ramsuratkumar as they usually did. It was a time of joyful expectation for them, as their long-time mentor Hilda Charlton was about to join them. Hilda and her two adopted daughters – Shanti and Valli – together with a party of Hilda's students and associates, were winding up a journey that had taken them to the Holy Land, Jerusalem, and then on to Sri Lanka. From here they would fly to Madras, and then, soon, Hilda would meet "the great one" whom she already "knew" from her mystical encounters.

According to Will: "The first day we [Joan and I] came [to Tiruvannamalai] we were able to talk with him [Yogi Ramsuratkumar] alone. He just laughed and laughed, and kidded us about how Hilda was going to be meeting with him soon and before too long she would expose him as a total fraud. Then he would laugh uproariously. 'Hilda is coming to meet this sinner. You have praised this sinner and Caylor has praised this sinner, but Hilda will expose this beggar.'

"After that first evening, however, he dropped the subject. And until we received word that Hilda had left Ceylon and was arriving in Madras, no specific preparations were made. It was at that point that we made reservations for everyone's accommodations.

"Apparently, Yogi Ramsuratkumar knew exactly when she was coming. He seemed very sure. He insisted that the hotel reservations should be held for one week, and they came on the seventh day, almost to the hour.

"For their first meeting, extensive preparations were made. We [Yogi Ramsuratkumar and Will] talked for more than an hour – giving me lemons and other items which he insisted be given to her even before she came to see him. We knew she would be arriving at night. She was to stay at the Park Hotel and everyone else at the Devashanam Guest House, so that she would enjoy some privacy.

"Then, just before she came, I met with him [Swami] again, alone. He…[asked] that I bring Hilda to his house that very night – not to the platform at the top of the mandapam stairs, but inside the house. I had never been in his house before, so this I looked forward to very much. This was a great treat – his house had the air of secret, sacred ground, not usually accessible.[1]…I think he spoke to me with more power than he had ever spoken to me before. As I might say it, he communicated: 'Don't screw this up, Will.' It was like a communication to every atom in my body.[2]

"Swami was also very specific about the number of people who should come along. Including Hilda and myself, only five people more. He said he didn't care who they were, but only five. He repeated that many many times."[3]

राम

One of the men who had accompanied Hilda on the initial stages of their journey remembered that Hilda had spoken of Yogi Ramsuratkumar often throughout the trip. "Whenever we had opportunities to sing, we sang his name, and as time grew closer, the energy grew stronger, more intense. We felt he was very much with us, not only just in our thoughts."[4] And another student remarked that "the whole trip seemed to be leading up to this meeting."[5]

Hilda and Company, 1978

Will met the party at the bus stand in Tiruvannamalai with a taxi, and took them to their hotel. Along the way, Hilda spoke to the two girls, Shanti and Valli: "Kids, be real thankful. Only a great being can draw you here from so far. He has drawn us here. It's all by his grace."[6]

When Will informed Hilda of the beggar's stipulation about there being only seven in the room, they both looked around and smiled to see that, all together, they were exactly seven.

राम

Will: "It was a very intense first meeting. Everyone had brought garlands. We presented them to Swami, then he blessed them and gave them back to us. So we each ended up having a garland. One by one he called us up, the men first, and garlanded each of us. But he held Hilda's garland to the very last. He put it on her, but she didn't keep it on. She just held it. Then Swami said, 'Make sure that garland goes back' or something like 'always keep that garland.'

"She sat right in front of him. She had a little camp chair with a back, one of those chairs with nylon threads. She sat there for a full half an hour and he didn't say a word. Just looking at her. Didn't say hello, didn't say anything. Just looked at her. It was very intense. Stroking his beard and at times looking off into space above her head, with his thumb and forefinger moving nervously, or as if he were moving japa beads through his fingers very rapidly. He asked her some personal questions about her family. Also he smoked for a while.

"Yogi Ramsuratkumar lit up a new cigarette each time a new person came into the room. Then, finally, he said to her, 'How do you feel?'

"'Oh, Swami, just like I got up in the morning.'

"He was giving her energy so she could bring her physical energy way up. Then he had her introduce all the people in the room."[7]

राम

311

A few moments later, while the introductions were drawing to a close, a knock came on the door, and Perumal, Yogiji's attendant at the time, went to see who it was. An elderly woman, another acquaintance of Hilda's, was demanding entry. "I've heard Hilda was here and I've gotta be in there too," the woman told him. When the message was given to Yogi Ramsuratkumar he conceded, telling Perumal that the woman could join them.

This intrusion, as minor as it seemed, had some sorry consequences. The next morning, the older woman who had insinuated herself into the room awoke in great pain. She was sick, and told her companions and Hilda that she felt "like she had been kicked in the stomach by a mule." Hilda knew why, and was quick to use the example to make an important teaching lesson to her followers.

"Well, kids," Hilda said, strongly but not unkindly, "this is a lesson for you, because you all came on the coattails of my grace. I had the right to be there. But E. (the elderly woman) forced her way in, using her will. She wasn't invited. So all the karma that she would have had to earn in order to be let in had to be paid off that instant. She was in sort of a karmic deficit, and that had to be brought up to speed. That's why she had such pain. So, *never force your way in to see a guru*; never force your way onto a plane or a train, or anything like this, because you're pushing it. Don't ever do that." She was very serious.[8]

राम

A little later, on that first night, Yogi Ramsuratkumar addressed the group. "Don't judge anybody. This filthy beggar judges people," he said, much to their surprise. Certainly this was not the type of inspiring spiritual instruction that any of them expected. Even though they had been prepared by Hilda for his "funny" ways, it would still have been a bit disconcerting to hear someone of his apparent wisdom and holiness talking about himself in this way. These remarks were only the beginning, however. The beggar went on to tell a very specific story, and as the group learned later, for a very specific purpose.

Ramsuratkumar related an incident that had happened many years ago, during the time when he resided near Ramanashram, and when he took his meals there. One day, a woman who was a very prominent disciple of Ramana's, and who held some power in the ashram, spotted him among the lunch guests. Turning in his direction, and in fact pointing at Yogi Ramsuratkumar, she said something like: "These people, these worthless people...they [merely] hang around. They shouldn't be fed."

Telling this, Yogi Ramsuratkumar became animated. "Oh, this filthy sinner has always remembered that. Don't do like he does."[9]

Lila, one of the young women in Hilda's company who attended that first meeting, later supplied an important bit of information that set the beggar's self-deprecating words in a context that might not otherwise have been appreciated. According to her, "[T]here was a reason he said that. Earlier, when he was talking to me, he asked me if I had resentment. I told him, 'No,' because I didn't realize what he was trying to reveal to me. But then he said, 'This beggar has resentment' and that's when he proceeded to tell that whole story about the ashram meals and [this woman's remarks]. From then on he declined all invitations to take his meals there. Even a year or so later, when [this woman] sent a message requesting him to come back, he said, 'This beggar wouldn't go. He didn't forget and he never forgave her. Don't hold grudges like this beggar.' It was only six weeks later that I faced up to what it was he was asking me about. It was the whole thing with Hilda – he was urging me to bring out into the open air some feelings I didn't even know [I had toward her] at the time."[10]

राम

At some point in one of their meetings Hilda asked Yogi Ramsuratkumar if he would ever come to America. With his characteristic innocence the Godchild replied, "It would be very difficult not speaking the language, and food not being suitable. This beggar wandered the length and breadth of India for seven years. Then he came to Arunachaleswarar. He didn't feel to leave this place. This was his home." These words would be echoed in similar sentiments in the years that followed. At another time, asked the same question, Yogi Ramsuratkumar replied, "Mount Arunachala never moves."[11]

313

One night during Hilda's visit the sweet beggar got up and danced in a spontaneous expression of ecstasy, intoning *"Sri Ram Jai Ram Jai Jai Ram."* Observing him, Hilda's knowledge of who he "is" was confirmed beyond a shadow of a doubt. "You have no idea how great he is," she glowed as she spoke to Will later. "He is just beyond, beyond, beyond."[12]

When it was time to go, Hilda gave her pranams and moved reverently toward the door, but Yogi Ramsuratkumar called her back, peeled a banana and gave it to her. Then he peeled a banana for each one in the party and gently dropped the fruit into each outstretched hand.

The next day, Hilda returned to the Sannadhi house with only Will and the two girls, as Yogi Ramsuratkumar had specifically requested. On this occasion the Godchild gave lots of attention to the two girls. Shanti was about twelve at the time, and Valli was perhaps eleven. The younger girl was extremely clairvoyant, and often "saw" things on another level of perception. When Yogi Ramsurat-kumar called each girl up to sit in front of him, they studied him as he studied them. Valli remained transfixed for about an hour. "He is light. He is light," she reported later, when questioned. And when asked to describe his aura, which she had seen, comparing it to Sai Baba's, whom she had met previously, the child explained, innocently: "They are basically the same. They go from horizon to horizon, and they have a solid core of gold, of silver, then pink then blue, and it goes all the way out to the horizon."[13]

Again, during this meeting, an intrusive knock was heard at the beggar's door, and another of Hilda's acquaintances, a man, was demanding his right to come in as well. Yogi Ramsuratkumar allowed it, but directed that the man sit far back in the room, against the furthest wall, and next to the dog. For the rest of the time, Swamiji paid no attention to the man. His work with Hilda and her children was too important to have it interfered with by a pushy curiosity seeker. Hilda, of course, was furious, and berated the man after they left the beggar's presence. She knew how precious his time and his work were. She knew that ego would always wage war against such Divine generosity.

राम

For a month prior to Hilda's arrival in Tiruvannamalai, another young Western seeker, Joel Bluestein, a musician from New York, had been sharing special hours with the beggar once or twice a day. Generally their meetings took place at night. In the daytimes, Joel was out on the mountain, or in the great Siva Arunachala Temple, as the Godchild had instructed him to spend time in these specific places.

"He was a very funny guy, and that really appealed to me," Joel explained. "I was too serious in so many ways, especially about the spiritual path. I was meditating for five or six hours a day in those years, hell-bent on enlightenment. Yet here was this funny man, of obvious wisdom and power, telling jokes and laughing and creating this awesome mood of lightness. That really impressed me. It was so different from so many of the heavy spiritual trips I'd been on."[14]

One night, Joel and Will Zulkowski were sitting with Yogi Ramsuratkumar and they were all stargazing. "Joel happened to know quite a lot about astronomy. He was talking about different stars: white dwarfs, red giants, and a lot of others. And then he brought up the fact that a star's light is seen only after thousands, even millions, of years. Where it goes we don't know; it travels through space eternally."

When Will heard Joel's comments, he reflected, "God, this is just like Swami. The light of a spiritual master irradiates infinite universes and just goes on and on. Who knows – maybe a million years from now someone will see a great light pass across the night sky of their distant world or maybe it will illuminate their interior space like a great blessing. Yet they won't know that it is the light of a spiritual master who lived aeons ago in a distant galaxy."

Turning to Yogi Ramsuratkumar, Will said, "Swami, your light in this world will one day go out, but even millions of years from now your light will still be shining in other worlds." Hearing this, the Godchild raised both hands in blessing, as he said, "Is it?" Immediately, Will felt a fantastic wave of bliss.[15]

When Hilda arrived, things became more difficult for Joel. His special time with the beggar was now superceded by the attention being paid to Hilda and her entourage, and Joel found himself annoyed with these other guests and conflicted about his relationship

315

to the Godchild. One night, however, in the company of Hilda's party, Yogi Ramsuratkumar asked Joel to sing for him. Among other things, the young musician played his guitar and sang a contemporary piece by Bruce Cockburn, called "All the Diamonds in this World," dedicating it to the beggar. When he sang the line, "Dying trees still grow greener when you pray," Yogi Ramsuratkumar, who was a great lover of trees, took special notice, apparently touched deeply by these words. He asked Joel to sing the song again, and then again.

A day or two later, the Godman expressed his tender regard to Joel in still another way. On this occasion, Hilda's company and Joel were gathered with Yogi Ramsuratkumar on the verandah of the Sannadhi Street house, a decidedly narrow space for such a crowd of close to thirty people. The Godchild sat in the far end of the room, on the right, and Joel was squeezed into the corner on the far left, with crowds in between, such that it was difficult to see anything that Yogi Ramsuratkumar was doing. Feeling distressed, Joel looked over and managed to meet the beggar's eye. A knowing look was exchanged. "Clearly, he was telling me, 'Stay exactly where you are. Don't move,'" Joel reported.

A few minutes later, to Joel's surprise, Yogi Ramsuratkumar got up and crossed the room, positioning himself directly in front of the young musician, who now had the best seat in the house for what was to transpire.

"The night was one of those dead-still one's. There wasn't the slightest breeze and it was stiflingly hot on that porch. At one point, Yogi Ramsuratkumar raised his hand and began to wildly wave his fan above the heads of the crowd." Joel's voice grew more intense as he told what happened next. "As I watched him, streams of brilliant color, lights, began to flood the air around him, and literally to fill up the room. It was all coordinated by the movements of his fan. Like a rainbow, it was. I was breathless. I'd never seen anything like it. At exactly the same time, all the calendars in the room started to flap as if blown by a heavy breeze."

What startled Joel even more was his perception that others in the room were not seeing what he saw. People fidgeted in their seats, or turned away, momentarily distracted. Had they seen what he was experiencing, their attention would have been fixed. "I felt as if he did this show just for me," Joel said, echoing words that many others would assert over the years. Yogi Ramsuratkumar had the most astounding ability to give to each one in a way that this one felt uniquely loved and blessed. In much the way Krishna was able to dance with ten thousand gopis (cowherders/devotees) and each one had the experience of being his sole beloved. Love does such things.

"He was saying, 'Can you see this? This is for you,' as his way of blessing me even in the midst of my feelings of alienation and separation." Joel candidly admitted that the feelings that were being evoked with Hilda's presence on the scene were old feelings. His own mother had been a very sick woman who had killed herself. "We never got to resolve things," Joel said, referring to the issue of being left out by mother. These feelings were still raw. "But his attention to me healed a lot of things, I know that now," said Joel. "It was his way."[16]

राम

Hilda and her company left after a few days, richly blessed and deeply nourished by the Godchild of Tiruvannamalai. His care for her was specific when she was with him, and extended beyond their visit as well. As her party left for their trip to Bangalore and the ashram of Sai Baba in Puttaparthi, Yogi Ramsuratkumar took Will aside and entrusted him with a clear assignment. "Will, this trip, you watch over Hilda," the beggar told him.

When she returned to the United States, Hilda spoke freely of Yogi Ramsuratkumar on numerous occasions throughout that year, 1978, and into the spring of 1979. At her class on October 20, 1978, she had an extended interchange with some of the people who had accompanied her on that trip. It focused on the topic of humility in relation to this mad beggar of Tiruvannamalai, and elaborated upon his enigmatic words to Lila about how he "doesn't forgive."

Hilda to Sri Raman: "I want to ask you a question. Do really think he is humble?"

Raman: "Yes I really think so."

Hilda to Will Zulkowski: "Do you think he's humble?"

Will: "I definitely think he's tremendously humble."

Hilda to Caylor: "Do you think he's humble?"

Caylor: "I think there are two sides to the coin."

Hilda: "I do too. I sure do kids."

Caylor: "Because at other times he affirms exactly who he is. Only in very special wonderful moments he will say with no reservation who he is and what he is doing on this planet. Otherwise he plays out different roles and faces."

Hilda: "I think he hides behind that screen, number one. And then I think also he is teaching us humility, how to act, like for example what he said to Lila. He said, 'I never forgive anybody. They kicked me out of the ashram there and I didn't have anywhere to go.' He said, 'I have never forgotten that.' Then he said to Lila, 'Hilda forgives everything. Why don't you forgive everything?'

"You know, do you think he really meant that Hilda forgives everything and he doesn't? No. I just think he was teaching us. I don't think he's humble at all, because I think to be humble is a big ego. But to be neutral, neither swayed by praise or blame, yet knowing what you are and you not flaunting it, that is a state of Godliness. All that humility stuff is just to teach all of us not to think we're big guys. You understand? That's what I think. What do you think Caylor?"

Caylor: "What you said reminds me of a discussion we had one afternoon. I was trying to understand who he was. It seemed to me there were differences or levels of spiritual mastery. It perturbed me that Sai Baba claimed to be an *avatara*, while theosophists might claim he was merely a disciple of one of the great lords they revere. So I asked [Yogi Ramsuratkumar] what was the difference between a saint, sage and avatar?

"Swami answered with what seemed to me a very disturbing level of simplicity. 'This beggar sees no difference between a saint, a sage and an avatar. So long as one thinks he is his body he is neither a saint, sage or avatar, but when he knows he isn't his body then there is no difference. All is the one, beyond name and form and only God.'"[17]

Whenever Hilda's students went to India in those early years, and for years to come (Hilda died in 1988), she advised them to visit the beggar saint of Tiruvannamalai. Some of their impressions of Yogi Ramsuratkumar were given in her public classes, and others were written up at her request.

राम

Stories from Hilda's Students and Friends

About Smoking

"Those of you who have not been there to see him would be surprised by the fact that he smokes. But he doesn't smoke for physical enjoyment. Other yogis who have met him suggest that it is his way of burning up other people's negativity, negative thought creations or karma at a subtle level. It is a fact that he only smokes when he is in the company of guests. He is helping people in that way by doing that. This is difficult to understand. Like so many aspects of spiritual life if you try to reason it out with the logical mind it's very difficult." (10:20:78, Sri Raman, from Hilda's company)

Propaganda and Publicity

"One time a man came, obviously for the first time. He said he had seen a picture of Yogi Ramsuratkumar and immediately felt that he had to come and see him. Yogi Ramsuratkumar said, 'Oh, all that's just propaganda and publicity. This beggar just makes propaganda because he's lazy and doesn't want to work. People will bring him food.' It was so funny. We all just laughed and laughed. But the poor guy was flabbergasted; he didn't know what was going on. Then Swami sent that man away after some while. But I felt it was a kind of test, if the man can see through the masquerade and follows his heart, perhaps he will come back and the master will be more open with him." (Janis Reed, 5/18/1978)

ONLY GOD

Father Is the Friend

"The hottest time of the year, and he was sitting there with all these blankets wrapped around him. He was talking about God saying, 'Father is everywhere and everything. Father is here in the form of this beggar. Father is here in the form of Janis. Father is here in the form of Ian. It's all Father.' I had written him a letter saying thank-you for all his help, that we had had a great time. And that I felt that I had a great friend in him. He read it and said, 'Father is the friend.'

"Then he said, 'If this beggar is really a yogi as he calls himself then he is beyond all time and all space. He's everywhere and in everyone. He's past, present and future, and he's everywhere, in all.'

"Then he said, 'Father's grace is always raining heavily; you just have to pay attention.' And this really sums up what I had been feeling there. I had been feeling overwhelmed by how much God loves me and feeling grateful for all the wonderful things he had done all my life." (Janis Reed 5/18/79)

One Hundred Percent

"We all watched Swami dance ecstatically and sing the names of God. Just the bliss in his face – the complete ecstasy in his face! And then the next second and he was changed. Usually we were with him at night, it was very hard to see the different intricate facial expressions. Everything he does is one hundred percent!

"Afterwards Hilda said, 'God, if we could do *our* bhajans like that! He brings the essences out of the universe: the essence of Rama, of Radha and Krishna. Not dead bhajans.'" (Will Zulkowski, August 1978)

Sweet Slavery

Late one night, Yogi Ramsuratkumar pointed out the messy condition of his house. With a tone of resignation, he remarked that he never could seem to find the time to clean, and on this particular day he hadn't had time to eat until 10 P.M. However, he *had* smoked all day. Looking at the friends Yogi Ramsuratkumar explained: "Ever since this beggar died in 1952 he hasn't been able to do anything. Now the Father does everything. I do only his work. Only what he tells me. It's slavery – sweet slavery." (Roseanne, late 1970s)

No Boring Life!

The Godchild had caught a hangnail on something, and his finger began to bleed. Those near him noticed. "That is the nature of this world," he said, "occasional shocks. Life would be boring without them – very dull." (Roseanne, late 1970s)

The Real Miracles

"When Ramsuratkumar was once talking about Satya Sai Baba's wondrous powers, he remarked, very typically, that he was only a beggar and that only in many lifetimes distant could he evolve to that stage where he would be able to perform miracles. But I thought at the time that the true miracle is that he is able to change the lives of so many people and bring about in them a greater kinship to God. The real miracles that the masters do are not the disappearing and reappearing or materializing of this incense or that picture. The masters don't give importance (and Sai Baba does not give importance) to phenomena of this kind.

"The real miracle is the transformation of the human consciousness into something divine. That Swami did! That he did for everybody there whether they were conscious of it or not. What they perceived or thought he was doing didn't matter." (Will Zulkowski, August 1978)

Do the Best You Can

"A lady came who was having a hard time with certain people criticizing her. Swami asked her, 'Have you done the best you can?' And she answered, 'Yes, I have.'

"'What more can you do? Leave aside the criticism. Leave aside the negation, you've done all you can. This beggar is pleased. My Father is pleased. Why should you worry?'" (Will Zulkowski, August 1978)

Yashoda on the Outside

"Swami had mentioned a book called *The Srimad Bhagavatam* by S.S. Cohen (translator). It [contained] the story of Sri Krishna's life. According to this legend, Krishna – as a child – once picked up a handful of mud and began eating it. His mother became very upset.

321

Mother Yasoda came over, grabbed him off the ground and opened his mouth to clean the mud out; but as soon as she did this, she saw the whole cosmos in his mouth. Swami repeated this story to us day after day and always concluded with these puzzling remarks: 'How Yasoda got on the outside looking in, we don't know. If all is in the mouth of Krishna, how does Yasoda see this from the outside?'

"Swami suggested to certain people that it would be a very useful meditation to imagine oneself in the mouth of Krishna. What is there to worry or fear since there is no place which isn't in the mouth of Krishna. We can work on this at home – or here – or anywhere – since there is no place that isn't inside the mouth of Krishna. 'How Yasoda got on the outside we don't know!'" (Will Zulkowski, August 1978)

18

RETURNING TO THE SOURCE, 1979

 In the two years that had transpired since his last visit to India, Lee Lozowick thought often of the "interesting" beggar of Tiruvannamalai. It was a period of great upheaval and consequent growth in the community of Hohm that Lee had founded, and was marked by a deepening of Lee's work with students and disciples. Yet, as far as Lee knew then, his teaching function had spontaneously emerged outside of any known lineage, seemingly without the intervention of a teacher or master. His affiliation with the hidden beggar-saint would not be publicly known for many years. An edition of a popular American magazine, *Yoga Journal*, still grouped Lee in the circle of "self-realized" individuals – those who credited only the transcendental Divine with initiating their condition.

In January 1979, Lee and three of his closest students returned to the Motherland, India. They stayed for three months. This time, instead of a passing glance at Mount Arunachala, they planned to spend the last five days of their pilgrimage in Tiruvannamalai, as Lee clearly wanted to be near the hidden saint who had made such a strong first impression. "This man in rags had begun to haunt us and Lee encouraged us to pay attention and be respectful of this rare being," wrote one of the women on this trip.[1] While Lee may not have spoken of Yogi Ramsuratkumar with any regularity, the degree of reverence and obvious devotion that he expressed in this second meeting indicated that he had more at stake in this meeting than a casual rendezvous. Something about this beggar had struck a deep

Lee Lozowick surrounded by children, India, 1979

chord within the American teacher. This ancient one with the coco-nut bowl and the hand fan was like no one or nothing that Lee had ever encountered.

Seated before the man in rags, the ritual of hospitality was begun, and the first lesson in attention was immediately given to Lee's group. When the master's attendant brought coffee and small loaves of bread for each of the guests, one person adjusted the position of the cup that was placed before him. As Will Zulkowski had described earlier from his own experience in moving a teacup, such habitual and unconscious gestures were not without their consequences in the presence of the Godman. If these Americans were to make use of what this beggar had to offer, they would have to learn the protocol of the space, and fast!

Of course, Yogi Ramsuratkumar observed the movement. He immediately registered disturbance and raised his hands, indicating that the behavior should stop. Only when each one was served and everything was set in order according to *his* sense of things did he motion for them to eat and drink.

With their refreshments cleared, the beggar began to interact per-sonally with his small circle of guests. Looking at them intently but caringly, one at a time, he smoked a cigarette while engaging them in pleasant conversation. "What is your name?" he asked, as he did with the hundreds of visitors and guests who sought him out over the years.

"Mirabai," replied the first woman. "Radha," said the other woman. "Balarama," indicated the young man. Yogi Ramsurat-kumar's eyes twinkled mischievously and a smile spread across his face. Of course he recognized each of these familiar names, all con-nected with the Lord Krishna. Mirabai was the thirteenth-century poetess who sang the praises of the "Dark One," Krishna, who had captured her heart; Radha was the beloved gopi and consort of the god; and Balarama was Krishna's brother. Strange names for Americans, certainly.

"And who has given you these names?" Yogi Ramsuratkumar looked playful as he addressed them.

"*He* did," said each of the three students, turning their heads dis-creetly in Lee's direction. At this, Yogi Ramsuratkumar burst out laughing. Looking directly at Lee now, he beamed with joy. "And you? You must be Krishna!" With those words, Yogi Ramsuratkumar threw his head back, waved his fan energetically, as he did when showering blessings around him, and shook with laughter.

The mood was utterly disarming and the laughter was infectious. Lee, too, laughed and laughed until he had to wipe tears from his eyes. Gaining his composure quickly, however, Lee shook his head in response to the beggar's assertion. "No, no. I am no great king. I am just a beggar like yourself." It was as if a baited hook had been presented to a hungry fish. With his words of apparent denial, however, Lee was caught.

"I think not!" said Yogi Ramsuratkumar, kindly but with obvious authority, as he began to slowly reel in his catch. "You, I think, are destined for many things. This poor beggar is destined only to sit in the filth in this small town. I am a poor beggar. But you, you are a king and will have many riches and will travel far and wide."

Lee shook his head again. There was yet no precedent for such words applying to his present life, and this foretelling of the future was at least humbling if not surprising and disconcerting. Lee had already given up wealth and a lucrative business in order to devote himself entirely to the direction of a spiritual community. His circle of students and his travels at the time basically extended a few miles from his community center in northern New Jersey, and a bit into New York City. He was unprepared for the reception he was receiving from the beggar.

"Perhaps," replied Lee, incredulously. The words that followed next from his mouth were not what his students expected, however. "I just want to live like you and be a beggar," Lee said. It was the heart speaking.

Yogi Ramsuratkumar looked at Lee affectionately, compassionately. "I am sorry," he said. "But I must be the beggar, and you must be the king." He paused and gave Lee a sidelong glance. The mood in the room was electric as Lee's companions followed this strange dialogue with awe. Here was an aspect of their teacher that was intuited but rarely witnessed. In their eyes, Lee was the one with the wise answers to their questions and the self-assurance bordering on arrogance. As far as they were concerned, he had no equal, much less a superior. They were *his* devotees, and their regard for him was lawful.

Yet, here he was being "worked with," being instructed, and at the same time being praised in ways that far surpassed their own youthful predictions for what their life with him would entail.

As if to seal his contract with the young American, Yogi Ramsuratkumar then handed Lee his box of matches. The implication was clear – Lee was to light the beggar's cigarette for him. A simple task, yet one that Lee had a hard time fulfilling. Match after match was struck against the side of the box and ignited, only to go out before reaching the end of the master's cigarette. With each failed attempt, Yogi Ramsuratkumar simply continued to smile, and motioned for Lee to light another. Three...four...five...all went out as Lee raised them toward the beggar's face. Six...no luck! The Godchild was giggling delightedly one moment, looking fierce and hard, almost mockingly, the next. There was no breeze blowing through the mandapam on this hot night. No reason why six consecutive matches had failed, and obviously more than coincidental when, to everyone's amazement, the seventh match stayed lit long enough to accomplish the task. Yogi Ramsuratkumar inhaled deeply on the smoke, eyed Lee carefully, and once again threw his head back with gales of laughter. Lee's face flushed. He was embarrassed, shy, and invigorated by the play.

With this lila complete, the Godman, with Lee now seated at his side, raised his hand and delivered a sharp, confirming slap to the younger man's thigh. Once, twice, three times, the beggar slapped Lee again and again, as one does a buddy who has finished a great job – a firm slap on the back, like one rugby player to another, one old friend to another. It was a gesture of affection, of camaraderie, of spontaneous joy at the nearness of a friend, or brother, or son. Yet, it didn't stop there. More laughter from the mad saint, and more slaps, until at one point "Lee rolled his eyes as if the slaps were beginning to sting quite a bit. Ram Ram [as they thought of him then] found this even funnier and continued slapping. He ended by rubbing Lee's leg and looking affectionately at him."[2]

No sooner had this interaction ended than another began. "Tell me, Lee, does God ever talk to you?" the beggar asked with all the wonder and awe of a child making inquiries about the world beyond his backyard.

In November 1997, Lee Lozowick, referring to himself as
"this bad Poet," wrote:

> Once, many years ago,
>> You asked this bad Poet
> if he had ever seen God.
>> In his arrogance this Fool said yes.
> You looked so lovingly
>> upon Your son and said:
> "Oh lee, You are so lucky.
>> This dirty Beggar has never seen God."
> I thought You were toying
>> with me then,
> but I now realize
>> that in Your Palace
> there are no mirrors at all,
>> so how could You have seen God?
> You, You Who are
>> neither this nor that,
> neither light nor dark,
>> neither coming nor going,
> You who were
>> never born and can never die,
> never arising and never subsiding,
>> You of great Compassion
> Who care only about the other,

The question came out of left field, and Lee responded with a
mix of both delight and caution: "Sometimes he talks to me."

"Oh...oh! You are so lucky!" Yogi Ramsuratkumar was obviously moved by the declaration. There was genuine longing in his voice
as he explained: "God never talks to this poor beggar. I pray, but God
never talks to me. Tell me, does God ever eat with you?"

Lee was quiet and composed as he answered. The questions were
appealing to his sense of specialness, his ability to speak of the non-

of course You have never seen God.
You are That which
    this wild Heretic of Yours
had assumed he had seen
    in Its infinite variety
of forms and appearances.
    Well Father, dear One,
ask me again if I have seen God
    and Your true heart-son
will answer You like this:
    "Yes Father, I have seen God.
He is none other than You,
    Yogi Ramsuratkumar,
Changeless, All, One, Infinite,
    indescribable, impenetrable,
past, present, future,
    anything, everything."
No, You know Your little beggar
    is heroic in Poetry
but quite shy in action.
    The last lines are true,
but let's be realistic here.
    If You ask me if I have seen God
I will simply say:
    "Yes. You and Only You."[3]

dual nature of reality. If God was everywhere, and in everything, there was nothing ingenuous in replying: "Sometimes he does, sometimes not."

"Tell me, when God comes to you, how is he dressed?" The beggar was inviting his young guest further and further into the tunnel from which there would be no escape.

Lee was completely taken in. "Sometimes he is dressed in exquisite royal clothing, and sometimes…" Lee hesitated momentarily, the overwhelming presence of this beggar who sat before him too great to be denied. In that instant, he knew the truth. "And sometimes he is dressed in rags," Lee said, averting his eyes.

One of the witnesses described what happened next:

> Ram Ram now adopted a posture that in our hearts he is famous for – he slumped back on the wall, his right hand with the fan raised to his head. He gently rocked back and forth in a rhythmic sway as his fingers on his left hand motioned an invisible mala in japa practice.[4]

A short time passed and the beggar opened his eyes. Once again he posed the central question to Lee: "How would you like to spend your life?" It is the question the masters throughout the ages have asked their potential disciples: "Why have you come here?" "What do you want?" "Whom are your seeking?"

While his mind may not have registered the significance of the exchange at the time, Lee's reply expressed the primary orientation of his heart, beyond the particulars of circumstance or form. "I would be happy just to stay in a place such as this, just like you," he said.

Yogi Ramsuratkumar heard the young man's words and suddenly became more serious. "God wills this poor beggar to sit in Tiruvannamalai, but you...if God wills, you shall travel very far!" Everything for Yogi Ramsuratkumar depended on the will of his Father, only God, and the beggar instructed his visitors in this assumption with every word that left his mouth.

At last he motioned to his attendant to give the guests more prasad to take with them. It was an indication that it was time to leave.

राम

For several mornings in succession the group met with Yogi Ramsuratkumar, and each day found a new series of teaching lessons being presented. The cues and clues were often subtle, however, easily overlooked unless the observer remained alert. Like other overly eager Westerners, Lee was not yet accustomed to the protocol that the beggar used in making his wishes known. Telling a humorous story of his own lack of savvy in those early meetings, Lee said:

> On the second trip, in 1979, it was very, very hot, especially in the mid-afternoon. So we'd come in the morning, and spend...maybe two hours or so, and then He'd say, "It's very hot, so you'll probably want to be resting in the afternoon." And I would say, since I wanted to get as much of this inter-action as I could, "Oh, it's OK. Where we live it's very hot and we're used to the humidity." He'd say, "You shouldn't go out in the afternoons. Westerners can get into trouble from the heat. The sun is so strong here in the afternoons." And I would say, "Oh, that's OK. We don't mind. It'll be all right. We're used to heat like this."
>
> At first, I didn't get that He was excusing us. He'd always laugh and say so sweetly that we could come see Him in the morning again. The first day we left after much urging, but I didn't get that He was basically excusing us. I was so dense! But the second day I got that that was His way of politely suggesting that we come back on *His timing,* not on our tim-ing. That's the way He would do it – always very elegantly and diplomatically.[5]

One morning, as Lee's group sat with Yogi Ramsuratkumar, they were joined by another Western visitor, an American man, whom Lee and the others did not know. When the conversation with the beg-gar turned to reading and spiritual literature, the new arrival pro-duced a small pamphlet from his pocket, entitled "For the Love of God." It was, this man told the Godchild, his favorite source of inspi-ration. He claimed to carry the booklet with him wherever he went, and read it every day, as the sentiments it expressed were profound and consistently moving to him. It was, he said, his "Bible."

Lee and the others in his party were completely dumbfounded as they witnessed this exchange. The fact was that Lee himself had writ-ten this pamphlet in 1977, and it was published and distributed by his small community in Mount Tabor, New Jersey.

"You must love God above all, above family, friends, shelter and food," Lee had written. "You must love this God whom you do not know in your heart so fiercely, so one-pointedly, so mindlessly that His grace, this most profound Gift comes to reside in your heart. The Guest, when He comes to visit, may remain or depart at His whim. You must prepare His altar, this house, so that He finds it so beautiful, so to His liking, that He stays. He must be pleased and only the purest, most selfless Love, will please Him thus."[6]

The "coincidence" of such a constellation of events was unimaginable to Lee. His mind wildly searched for a logical explanation, some way in which either this Western man or the wise old beggar had conspired to shock and amaze him. It *must* have been set up in some way, Lee figured. The odds against such a happening were too astronomical. Yet, there was simply no way to establish any previous knowledge of the booklet, or any connection among conspirators.

Yogi Ramsuratkumar seemed as quietly amazed as everyone else. Receiving the small book from the visitor's hand, he examined the cover carefully, noting the name "Lee Lozowick," and then looked up and asked with childlike innocence, "Is this you?" Then he opened the book and silently began to read it. "God cannot be attained, or sought, understood or bought. God cannot be 'had' in any sense of the word, by any stretch of the imagination. God may be lived. But how? Only through the most absolute, selfless, and totally sacrificial Love…"[7]

"Ohhh," the Godchild murmured at several points, the way one sighs when the heart has been touched.

After a short time, looking up from the pages in his hand, Ramsuratkumar had tears in his eyes.

राम

Lee kept a journal on that trip. Not a travelogue, but a "dharmalogue" of sorts in which he wrote essay after essay based in the many impressions that the journey was providing. It is particularly interesting in the evolution of this master-disciple relationship to find that one essay, located and dated "Mt. Arunachala, Feb. 21, 1979," bears a single-line opener that reads: "Dedicated to Ram Surat Kumar. My

Dear Ram Ram." The essay that follows mentions nothing specific about the Godchild, nor about Lee's visit to him. It is simply an essay about loving God.

When he returned to the work of his community in the U.S., Lee wrote prolifically throughout that year and on into the next, and his books, *The Cheating Buddha* and *The Yoga of Enlightenment/The Book of Unenlightenment*, were soon published. *The Cheating Buddha* contained this essay dedicated to his "dear Ram Ram" as its initial entry, and these two books were filled with the spirit of India, as well as with photographs of its people and places.

Years later, Lee would write about this period: "I was not looking for a Master. I was already guiding spiritual seekers and had been for a year or so. I assumed God was my guru. Well, He was, but I did not know in what form, and, in fact, what form did my guru god turn out to be? Yogi Ramsuratkumar. What a miraculous and merciful benediction. I loved India the minute I stepped out of the plane in Bombay (at 3 A.M.) and I loved Yogi Ramsuratkumar the minute I set eyes upon Him. It just took me five years to fully grasp what and who He was in my life and to me."[8]

Lee was also writing poetry. In the months that followed this second visit, beginning in May 1979, feeling a deep devotional connection to the unknown saint in rags, Lee's poetry was distinctly colored with references to poverty, with the joy of being a beggar, with his desire to be "the dust under Your Feet…the coarse robe You wear…the sweat of Your pores."[9]

Reflecting upon the 1979 visit, Lee said, "I remember coming home, and I began to write poetry to Him…not so much as my Master yet, but as a great Saint – invoking His regard and attention and praising His Divine attributes."[10]

Lee did not begin sending these poems to Yogi Ramsuratkumar until 1983-1984. Nonetheless, the sentiments of his heart, like tiny seeds carried on the wind, were making their way to the well-plowed earth at the foot of Mount Arunachala. In writing of the beggar, in thinking of him, Lee Lozowick was establishing a deep, but as yet invisible, bond with the Godchild of Tiruvannamalai.

19

TWO DAYS IN THE LIFE, 1980

 Peter Hoffman was a friend of Caylor Wadlington's who worked for the Theosophical Society in Adyar, near Madras. Having heard Caylor's stories for years, he was most interested in meeting Yogi Ramsuratkumar, and the two men journeyed to Tiruvannamalai on January 16, 1980.

Leaving Peter at their residence, Caylor alone went in search of his master to make arrangements for the rendezvous. "He assured me that he would try to meet us early the next day," Caylor wrote in his journal.[1] The place of the meeting was to be a cottage in Ramanashram, where Caylor and Peter were hosted.

Whatever "early the next day" meant to the two Westerners, it meant something else to Yogi Ramsuratkumar. Assuming that he had time before the beggar's arrival, Caylor was on his way to a restaurant to get some breakfast when, to his amazement, he spotted Yogi Ramsuratkumar heading his way. The beggar was in high spirits, explaining that he had been able to get out of town without unnecessary delays. What further amazed Caylor was that the Godchild was dressed in new clothes – a very rare occurrence. As Wadlington described him, Yogi Ramsuratkumar wore "a pure white jibba and dhoti. The orange-red turban tied haphazardly and the red silk shawl were glaring against the new bright white fabrics underneath."

When the master and "Mr. Kay" arrived at the cottage, Peter Hoffman was still in bed. Hearing the activity in the next room, he roused himself from sleep, but it took him a little while to realize that the one whom he had come to meet and to honor was standing now in front of him. The irony of the situation was probably not lost on Peter, who was a long-time practitioner: the devotee rubbing sleep from his eyes; the master standing there wide awake, ready to get down to business! With apologies that he hadn't been expecting his revered guest so early, Peter expressed his gratitude for the visit, and the day was off to a roaring start.

Yogi Ramsuratkumar had always spoken with the highest regard for the Theosophical Society. In fact, he was a registered member (no. 43621) in the Indian section of the Society. On this occasion, in Peter's presence, the beggar even declared that those who worked for this Society "have no ego" – a koan that both Caylor and Peter would definitely have to work with. On this cool bright morning, Ramsuratkumar drew Peter out, asking him to speak at length about the early presidents of the Society, the mahatmas who had forever guided this Society, and the great undertakings of this group.

Their conversations ranged far and wide. Yogi Ramsuratkumar, it seems, could speak to anyone about anything. Many of his Western visitors in those early years asserted that this completely unassuming beggar was the most highly informed purveyor of world politics that they had ever met. Others testified to his access to profound esoteric knowledge. Bill Byrom, a tutor at Oxford University, conducted indepth discussions with the humble beggar during his visits in the 1970s. The subjects under consideration consisted of "extraordinarily detailed teachings regarding death and rebirth, including various conditions under which a soul acquires a new body…entailing the separation of a soul into three components (not the *gunas*), not all of which need necessarily reincarnate together. He even specified conditions under which components of one being's soul can incarnate along with components of another being's soul in the same body. He gave very clear examples of conditions determining these 'passenger' souls."

When author Paul William Roberts heard about these extraordinary conversations from his friend Byrom at Oxford University, he initially surmised that these ideas "had never been expressed by any other teacher or faith." It was not until years later, when Paul Roberts began a massive project to produce the first complete English translation of the seventy-six volume *Zohar*, a mystical kabbalistic text, that he "came across precisely the teaching on rebirth as Yogi Ramsuratkumar had expounded to Bill Byrom." In explaining this resonance, Roberts asserted that, "Many kabbalist Jews firmly believe that Judaism came from India originally, and there is a very persuasive and highly scholarly tome that favorably compares Vedanta with Hebraic teachings. Many of the biblical stories also correspond far too exactly with Indian mythic texts, like *Mahabharata* and *Ramayana*."[2]

As this day with Caylor and Peter unfolded, and typical of the way in which Yogi Ramsuratkumar worked, everything that occurred spontaneously became a subject for laughter, for teaching, and for remembrance. When a pair of neighbor girls arrived with a gift of two red hibiscus flowers, the discussion turned lightheartedly to the theme of whether any two blooms were the same. Soon, however, the group was good-naturedly arguing the "oneness" vs. the "difference" of the *jivatma* and *Paramatma*, the soul and God. With delight, Yogi Ramsuratkumar told two anecdotes from his early life when he had been journeying through India. In Benaras, a yogi had held some flowers in the sunlight and, to the wonder of his witnesses, had several times caused the colors of these flowers to change. "If it was a white rose, he would change it to blue. If it was a blue flower, he would change it to red. He explained to this beggar that there is only one substance, and out of this one substance all things are created." His guests certainly enjoyed the stories, which they may or may not have interpreted as the Godchild's gentle, even invisible, means of teaching, in this case pointing to the nature of transformation.

Ramsuratkumar told that them that, on another occasion, he had observed an adept pick up a few pebbles from the roadside and proceed to turn them into tiny seashells, while another fakir had turned leaves into golden coins. "Do you follow my point, Mr. Kay?" Yogi Ramsuratkumar inquired. Obviously he wanted his guests to get something more than a list of interesting tricks.

For the beggar, Yogi Ramsuratkumar, everything was a miracle, just as it was, and everything was the dance of Siva or the evidence of the Father. He never tired of reminding his listeners of this simple fact by his own enthusiastic response to life. Years later, as Yogi Ramsuratkumar sat one evening in the temple with a small group of devotees,

Devaki Ma asked if they might not be gifted with seeing Siva dance. Yogi Ramsuratkumar looked seriously in her direction and instructed her: "This beggar sees Siva dancing in the falling of this leaf."[3]

Toward the end of their first long day together, Peter Hoffman finally ventured to ask the master for advice that might be useful to his life, or his sadhana.

"You don't need anything," Ramsuratkumar affirmed. "Everything you need will be given to you."

It was a simple answer, and a typical answer, and consequently an answer that could easily be dismissed. Yet, it reflected clearly that Yogi Ramsuratkumar saw no personal needs as being superior to the needs of the work. In other words, Peter was already serving within a lineage aligned to God's will; he was doing "the master's work," as Ramsuratkumar specifically referred to it that day. There was nothing necessary beyond that; certainly nothing personal. The beggar was instructing, it seems, that the ego of one who serves in such a capacity is subsumed by a higher principle of service. Hence, the koan: "You people who work for the Society have no ego."

राम

The next morning, having learned their lesson about timing on the previous day, Peter and Caylor were dressed and prepared early, although they did not know when to expect their exalted visitor. As it turned out, it was a good thing they were ready. Ramsuratkumar, who never wasted a moment in his work on his Father's behalf, again arrived in the early hours of the morning. As Caylor prepared coffee he could overhear an animated conversation between Peter and Ramsuratkumar which again focused on the valiant efforts of the Theosophical Society.

Peter: "Ramalingaswami predicted the coming of Madame Blavatsky and Henry Olcott [founders of the Society]. The [Ramalinga] swami's teachings, no doubt, were wonderful, but he complained at times that no one listened. Finally he proclaimed that when these messengers would come from the West, people would listen to them."

Yogi Ramsuratkumar: "Helene P. Blavatsky, Henry S. Olcott and Annie Besant were saviors of India. They have saved these dirty beggars of India – dirty beggars like this [meaning himself]. This beggar is very selfish. He has to learn something from the Theosophical Society. It is so kind to all, especially to India."

When the conversation turned to Mrs. Besant's political ideas and efforts, Yogi Ramsuratkumar honored them: "So long as there are people who love India, who love these dirty sinners of India, we will be here. We don't come where we are not wanted. This beggar feels all these great mahatmas [meaning those who have guided the Society] are here in India, unseen. Those people who deserve to know them will be graced to know them."

Then, adding an enigmatic comment, expressive of his own humility, Ramsuratkumar concluded: "This beggar is very lazy. He just sits and talks. How could *he* ever be worthy of such grace?"

Such statements were fairly typical of the beggar's "self"-references. He never held himself as special or exalted, and frequently confessed to having "sins" – such as laziness, the dirty habit of cigarette smoking, and, in one case, a lack of forgiveness. He also declared constantly that he knew nothing; that all that occurred through him was the design of the Father. Interestingly, however, the people to whom these remarks were made were often able to find a profound and deeply personal teaching aimed directly at them. To confess unworthiness, as he did, in the presence of one who was decidedly arrogant, one who felt that he or she deserved to be gifted or graced, could have a very strong impact, and often did.

For this reason, it is important to approach Yogi Ramsuratkumar's statements, especially his self-references, with caution. To take them solely at face value might be to miss the level of subtlety at which such a master worked. To take them *only* as esoteric reflections, however, might undermine the simplicity and genuineness of the one who uttered them.

On one occasion in the 1970s, Yogi Ramsuratkumar revealed his enormous knowledge of theosophical principles. In speaking to his devotee Shri V. Ramanujachari, he asked if the man went to the

Adyar Library, and whether he had read the books of H.P. Blavatsky. When Ramanujachari assented, the beggar inquired about one specific work, *The Voice of Silence*. When his visitor found it difficult to reply, the Godchild summarized "the monumental work in a few pithy sentences."[4]

राम

Peter brought up the subject of his search, his goal, his aim. He asked the beggar: "What is it that obstructs the flow of love?" And then proceeded to proffer his own answer: "I think it must be the idea of self. I hope someday there will be a flood of light which will wash away this idea, this ego."

It was then that Yogi Ramsuratkumar delivered the koan: "You people who work for the Society, have no ego."

Peter politely refused to accept this answer, in the characteristic way in which people often argue for their own limitations. Drawing upon his vast intellectual knowledge of the teaching, Peter quoted Nisargadatta Maharaj on the nature of self-concern and how to rid oneself of it. He wanted to be told that the way was hard, and that there were practices he could do to learn it.

Intellectual arguments notwithstanding, Yogi Ramsuratkumar would only affirm his original assertion: "Oh, you people who work for the Society are doing the Master's work. You will be looked after."

Later, when Peter criticized what might be called "the general attitude of Theosophical exclusivity, which often inclines people to express disinterest or disdain for outside spiritual movements," the beggar would not support him in this opinion, but said with the utmost tact: "People who have devoted themselves to the work of the Society don't *need* to look to masters outside. All their spiritual needs are looked after. I have no doubt about it."

Finally, when Peter expressed his wish that other masters, like Yogi Ramsuratkumar, would feel more welcome to visit the Theosophical Society in Adyar, the Godchild for the third time tried to tell his visitor that he (Peter) had all that he needed: "It is the Master's work you are doing. There is no need for us to be with you there."

ONLY GOD

राम

Could Peter appreciate the way in which he was being "played" with – honored and loved and stripped naked all in one stroke of the beggar's "sword"? To some degree perhaps, but in other ways he was as ignorant as most, failing to grasp the ways in which Yogi Ramsuratkumar, dancing in the vast field of emptiness, mirrored to his guests their own habitual ways of being. Few who approached Yogi Ramsuratkumar had the training or insight to see beyond the immediate level of social exchange.

As the morning's conversations continued, someone told a story: "A group of friends were sitting, talking about the great affirmations and the mantra *So Ham* [I am He], when a wise man came and reprimanded them, saying, 'You should talk instead of *Na Ham* [I am not].'"

Something in this story hit Peter hard. "How can we be so *deluded*!?" he exclaimed with astonishment.

"It *is* a great wonder!" replied Yogiji, who knew the Divine as his very breath. "All the wise people say there is one all-pervading Divine Being. It is the nearest of the near; the farthest of the far. But this beggar is *so deluded, he* can't begin to understand it."

On it went, Peter expressing regret that so many teachers speak only from intellect, while the beggar undermined the negation, turning the subject around: "That is all we *can* do. We have got only intellect. The acquisition of that which lies beyond the intellect depends upon the Father's grace."

In his journals, Caylor noted that Peter seemed to have quickly grasped some of the nuances of how the master worked. "He noticed how Yogi Ramsuratkumar spoke just so as to encourage interest in an idea and then he seemed to lie back and concentrate intensely on other levels while one or more persons continued to speak on that idea," Caylor wrote.

"You have to work so hard," Peter offered empathetically as he looked at the older man.

"Very rarely does this beggar get friends who speak about God and religion," Ramsuratkumar admitted candidly and probably with some sadness. "Mostly people come with their problems," he said, reflecting a fact that would continue to characterize the public's interactions with him for the rest of his life.

Nearing the end of the afternoon, Yogi Ramsuratkumar asked Peter and Caylor to read part of a chapter – entitled "Energy and the Cultivation of the Field" – from one of J. Krishnamurti's most recent books (1979). The selection concerned *kundalini* energy, a subject of great interest to the two younger men. Krishnamurti maintained that it was not the awakening of kundalini that created true religious life, but vice versa. When the reading was completed, Yogi Ramsuratkumar himself read the piece, and then had Caylor read it again.

Throughout the years, this use of repeated reading of a selection of spiritual material became firmly established in the beggar's repertoire of skillful means. He might have one story read as many as ten or fifteen times in one sitting, and by the same person. Or, he might ask several people to read the same poem or prayer, one after another, until the piece could almost be recited from memory. With each reading, moreover, his own attention to the message of the words never flagged, despite reports by those who were called upon to read that they were often tired or impatient. Nonetheless, with this invitation, the master served to lasso the mind of his guest, holding it in place long enough that his work on another level could be accomplished.

On this day in 1980, Caylor's journal entry reflects that the reading drew his mind into a deep and lucid state – a state of simply witnessing himself. Although he was generally quite serious in his approach to anything spiritual, Caylor wrote that during this reading, "I could hardly contain the laughter that kept wanting to bubble up from within."

"If we remember God's name, the mind is empty," Yogi Ramsuratkumar said when the discussion turned to "how" this awakening of no-ego was accomplished. Then he paused and added, enigmatically, "However, we can remember Him only *when* the mind is empty!" And then he laughed.

While the beggar's words were paradoxical, Caylor's experience in the moment testified to their accuracy. He had been drawn to that place of emptiness by the master's skillful direction, and now was filled with the joy of the Divine.

"I am not capable of using Krishnamurti's language," Yogi Ramsuratkumar spoke reverently of one of his great heroes. "In reply to this question I have used my own language, the language of my master Swami Ramdas. He was a great hunter. He killed this beggar. Papa Ramdas was a great tiger. He swallowed up this dirty sinner."

When an animated and highly philosophical discussion developed about the subject of free will, Yogi Ramsuratkumar concluded: "This beggar feels there is no such thing as free will; there is only the will of the Father."

Although the sun was still high, it was close to 5 P.M. when the last coffee of the day was served, and Yogi Ramsuratkumar announced that he would be leaving. He invited Peter and Caylor to accompany him on the mountain route to town, and the two men "leaped at the opportunity," little knowing that this simple matter-of-fact invitation was in fact the initiation of a pilgrimage.

राम

To walk to the rear gate of Ramanashram, at which point the hill path began, would have first required cutting through the ashram itself. Yogi Ramsuratkumar wished to avoid this route because, as he told Caylor, there were many people who would stop him, wishing to have him visit for some time. Already in 1980, his popularity had increased to the point where he had to make efforts to avoid unnecessary delays. Fortunately, Caylor knew another way to the gate, and led his two companions there.

"The master became exhausted almost immediately," Caylor reported, "and this worried me. Each step, one after the other, was an effort. And I could see that he was a bit dizzy and perhaps overheated, and perspiring profusely. I had never seen him in this condition before. He, himself, I could see, was surprised. It had been a long time, he said, since he last climbed the hill. It had become exceedingly rare for him to move out from his usual haunts near the temple. We proceeded very slowly."

Despite the physical strain, however, Ramsuratkumar's attention remained with the needs of his guests. With reference to something Peter said, he replied: "If this body does a little service of the Father, it is alright." And a bit later, "We have to discriminate to know what will serve the Master's purpose and do that."

The hill path is a steep one. Basically, it ascends consistently with only a few flat places where one can walk without effort. After reaching the first crest, the three men were passed by another hiker, a visitor to Ramanashram. Yogi Ramsuratkumar questioned Caylor about this man, and then delightedly remarked that they could all thank him (the visitor) for providing them the pretext to stop and rest.

As they sat for a while longer, Yogi Ramsuratkumar reminisced with Caylor about various encounters they had together during the 1970s – some of the people they had met at various caves and small ashram sites on the mountain, and particularly about a time when they had circumambulated Mount Arunachala together on the occasion of Kartik Deepam, the great festival in early December when the peak of the mountain is set ablaze.

Then, as the men rose to their feet again, the beggar's joyful words transformed their passage to town into a spiritual odyssey: "Shall we continue on our journey – our holy pilgrimage?" the God-child said tenderly. "We will go in search of our Lord. Maybe He will meet us on our way. But even if He disappoints us – doesn't matter. We will continue our quest."

As they pressed on, Yogi Ramsuratkumar, still the gracious host, continued to engage his guests in conversation, and for the second time they paused along the path and rested in the shade of a cashew nut tree. When they were ready to move on, the master reminded Caylor and Peter of their purpose: "Shall we start on our pilgrimage?"

Peter was touched. "I never thought I would have the honor of going on a pilgrimage with you," he said to Yogi Ramsuratkumar. It was an honest remark, full of gratitude. Such is the way of the great masters, however, who give us what we ask for and beg for, but then gift us with treasures over and above what we could ever imagine. Although Peter had only two days in which to absorb the master's company, the beggar had given him a lifetime's worth of experience.

From a certain vantage point on the trail Peter exclaimed, "This view of the hill is beautiful."

"Yes," Yogi Ramsuratkumar affirmed, reflecting his own awe and gratitude. "This hill and this temple [which they could see in the distance], they have saved this beggar."

At last they reached Skandashram, the site of the cave in which Ramana Maharshi had spent sixteen years of his life. It was the end of their ascent, as the path to town descends from here.

"So, we have climbed up, now we have only to go down," Yogi Ramsuratkumar declared, and then repeated this statement two more times. Astutely, Caylor wondered at the time if the master "might be referring to an analogous spiritual progress."

Again resting on a rock overlooking the east-facing gopuram (tower) of the temple below, Yogi Ramsuratkumar questioned rhetorically, referring back to the chapter of J. Krishnamurti's that had been so thoroughly read in the afternoon: "Where is that energy for the cultivation of the field? This beggar is tired. Where is this energy J.K. talks about?"

View of the Arunachaleswarar Temple from Mount Arunachala

"If only I could give you some of my prana I would," Peter responded innocently. "But you wouldn't want my prana. It's very polluted." And the three companions laughed.

And then, blessing the two young men further, Yogi Ramsuratkumar prayed:

> This beggar, wandering here and there, tired of wandering but having no home – Arunachaleswara, in the form of this hill, had mercy on this miserable sinner. So he gives thanks, a thousand thanks, to this holy hill, this holy temple. O the magnanimity of the Lord. He has given this beggar shelter for twenty long years, whereas others who come are enabled to stay only days or weeks. For thousands of years the hill has given shelter to so many dirty sinners, like this one, and Arunachala will give us shelter for thousands of years to come.

राम

When the three men descended the winding rock path as far as Om Namosivaya Guhai, a small cave/temple near the base of the mountain, they rested one more time – now beneath the great ashwathra tree that grew there. Yogi Ramsuratkumar bid them farewell, while he gave specific instructions to Caylor about future meetings during the remainder of his time in Tiruvannamalai. His parting remarks lend some insight into the master's way of working with those who were drawn closely to him. While there was often great tenderness, and ultimately unquestionable compassion, Yogi Ramsuratkumar did not waste time with niceties when direct action was needed. The beggar had consistently encouraged Caylor to keep his focus within the Theosophical Society, claiming that he had important work to do there. It was a destiny that Caylor decidedly resisted, although he tried hard, over the years, to accommodate it. Yogi Ramsuratkumar could be ruthlessly honest in his communications in a way that might seem harsh to those who had not experienced working with a master, or to those who lacked the faith to see in the master's directives his complete surrender to the work of his Father. He spoke to Caylor:

> Peter has helped us to spend these two days together. We will take leave now. You needn't try to meet this beggar at present. We have spent enough time together. There is no need to search for this beggar or to meet at fixed times. Leave it to the will of the Father. When this beggar feels we should meet, he will call you, and by the Father's grace we will meet again. You can stay here in Tiruvannamalai if you wish – walk round the hill, carry on your meditations (or whatever you do!). Read *The Secret Doctrine*, or else return to Madras. Or travel north and spend time with Anandamayi. If you settle down for some time in Tiruvannamalai, it will be best if you don't expand your contact here. Better to expand social contacts in a place like Adyar, but not here.

Peter then expressed his deepest heartfelt appreciation. "In these two days you have worked so hard to help us," he said.

"It is this beggar's play, his lila, not work," Yogi Ramsuratkumar responded. As Caylor recollected in his journal, the master continued to speak along these lines: "When there is activity which is motivated by self-interest and ends with pleasure or pain, we may call it work. It requires exertion. But when we live outside the reach of pleasure or pain, a realized man is untouched by these. Our activities are effortless. Our work is really our play."

As he left, Yogi Ramsuratkumar stopped, turned around to face the two men and, gazing up at the tree, said: "According to Peter we should express our thanks to the tree." And then he shouted, "Thank you Mr. Ashwathra," and walked away laughing. The ashwathra tree is the symbol of Hinduism.

Both Peter and Caylor prostrated at the beggar's feet. He blessed them and then moved off in the direction of his house along the great temple wall.

THE THREE WISE MEN

 Murugesan, Shivashankar, and Parathasarathy – the names of these three men will forever be linked in the history of Yogi Ramsuratkumar. For a period of close to four years, between 1980 and 1984, the beggar enacted a long lila of association with this fortunate threesome, each of whom had met him several years earlier.

Murugesan, a wealthy industrialist from Tuticorin, was the first of the three to arrive on the beggar's doorstep. Founder of a bank and the owner of a cotton-spinning mill, Murugesan met Yogi Ramsuratkumar in 1975 and was immediately drawn to the beggar's heart. "He had had darshan of many Godmen," prior to that momentous meeting, "[b]ut the darshan of Yogi Ramsuratkumar had a revolutionary effect on him. He was overwhelmed with love, and the master, in turn, poured love and grace on 'Murugeshi,' whom Yogiji affectionately referred to as 'my king.'"[1]

Shivashankar was also a very rich man, the owner of an offset printing company. He first met Yogi Ramsuratkumar in 1976, and the beggar playfully referred to him as "his philosopher." Parathasarathy, who came from Sivakashi, described himself as "a professional pauper and a beggar at the time." In a state of personal breakdown and near financial ruin, Parathasarathy had met Yogi Ramsuratkumar in 1976. The Godchild loved to speak of Parathasarathy with a combination of humor and irony, calling him "a realized soul," or "a free bird." It was a reference, Parathasarathy says, to his tendency of not allowing anybody to control him or teach him anything.

While each had his own relationship with their beloved Swami, they did not know one another, except perhaps by name. One day in 1980, Yogi Ramsuratkumar brought them together and made a special request. They were to meet together in Tiruvannamalai, every month, for a period of three days. Their time together was to be spent celebrating the beggar's name, and sharing their stories and inspiration about him.

What unfolded within this small community of dedicated disciples and their families lends insight into one of Yogi Ramsuratkumar's various modes of working with those who came to him. In the mysterious realms in which such things are determined, the beggar found in these three an openness and a willingness to obey that allowed him to use their gifts to support his work at the time; always and only the work of his Father.

Masters and gurus throughout history have brought to their sides a small contingent of trusted disciples, and for different reasons. For some, it was a means of securing sanctuary – a form of energetic protection from the hoards of pilgrims or curiosity seekers who typically come for little more than a spiritual "hit" or handout. "This beggar feels quite at home with you friends," Yogi Ramsuratkumar told these three men. "This is Vaikunta," he added, referring to the heaven realm in which Krishna lives with his all-attentive lovers.[2]

Other teachers have seriously tested the devotees in their close company as a means of training them to carry on the work after the master's passing. Other masters have kept near them the rare man or woman who might be most ready to receive the essence of the guru's heart.

The principle of creating *sangha*, or a body of practitioners, from a disparate group of separate devotees seems to have been present for Yogi Ramsuratkumar as well. He always encouraged his disciples from different parts of the world to meet and "speak together." Similar to the ways in which he arranged tea cups for a purpose, we can readily speculate that this little circle of friends from Tuticorin and Sivakashi, like the micro-"United Nations" that he would form in the corner of his dining hall in the late 1990s, was one of the many ways in which he carried out a macrocosmic work.

Sometimes these three-day stays with the master would extend themselves to seven, ten, or even fifteen-day retreats, and Parathasarathy described how intense their meetings could become. Sometimes, at the beggar's bidding, they went without sleep for up to seventy-two hours. Sometimes, only the most minimal food was offered. Ignoring their requests to send out for a meal from a nearby stand or hotel, Yogi Ramsuratkumar would simply take some puffed rice from his storage, feeding his loyal trio (and sometimes their whole families) just enough to keep their bellies from growling. At other times, the beggar might supply them with a steady stream of delicacies – breakfast, coffee, curd, sweets. Feast or fast, it was the master's call. They were being worked – stretched beyond their normal levels of comfort and convenience. Stretched to learn obedience. Stretched to observe their master and his ways in order that they could receive his graces.

At the time, of course, Parathasarathy and his two companions had no idea that this alchemical furnace of work would not go on forever. As far as they were concerned, this bountiful association was simply what it was – the result of their good fortune and the beggar's unquestionable blessings. They could not have known that Yogi Ramsuratkumar was working against time, laboring day and night with them as a means of preparing Murugesan for an all-important transition. At forty-five years of age, on a business excursion to Calcutta, the "king" unexpectedly suffered a heart attack. He died on April 4, 1984, a few days later.

राम

The three men met with Yogi Ramsuratkumar in the master's residence at Sannadhi Street, or in the Sivakashi Nadar Choultry, a lodge for pilgrims to Tiruvannamalai, in which members of the Nadar sect would be housed. At other times, their rendezvous were arranged in remote places. Yogi Ramsuratkumar made efforts to keep the group alone, not allowing them to mingle with other devotees and seekers who would show up at his door on any typical day. More likely, the beggar would send others away on these days. For his own reasons he did not want to be disturbed.

349

"We would just go on, talking and talking," Parathasarathy explained, "but the real work happened subtly." On one occasion, as master and disciples discussed world history and the latest political affairs, Murugesan was suddenly struck with an ironical thought. "Swami," he said with a smile, "when we are here together with you for days, other people might be thinking that we are deeply contemplating about your Father and that you might be pouring on us your special grace by teaching us about the ways to attain your Father. But here we are just talking about politics, world history, and about eating and drinking."

Yogi Ramsuratkumar became very serious on hearing this. "Murugeshi," he said, looking intently at his beloved devotee, "talking about other subjects may be insignificant, but being together with this beggar is the most significant event. The real work done goes unnoticed. It has been covered with these significant or insignificant talks. The masters have their own way to do the Father's work. The real work is uniting, merging, the chosen beings with my Father. That's all."

राम

Yogi Ramsuratkumar slept very little, and when he did, it was often in catnaps. The three men who spent this extended time with him in the early '80s affirmed what his Western visitors had previously noted. Sometimes the whole night was spent "working," which might take the form of seemingly superficial conversation with his guests, interspersed with long periods of silence in which the master would seem to move very far away – becoming totally absorbed in the realities of another dimension. The fingers of his right hand would move quickly, as if fingering a japa mala, and his lips would form unvocalized prayers. At other times he would encourage his visitors to join him in chanting Ramnam, the Divine mantra given him by his master, Ramdas. Or they might be asked to sing devotional songs, or to read from scriptural texts or inspiring books.

"Even when he would sleep, he would sleep before us," commented Parathasarathy. Yogi Ramsuratkumar had no life apart from his work on behalf of humanity, and when he allowed a chosen few to share in the full schedule of his day, there was no reason for him to retire anywhere apart from them. He would simply lie down and sleep when his body needed rest. After an hour, or two perhaps, he would sit up and proceed with whatever business was at hand.

"His sleep would be a teaching for us," Parathasarathy affirmed, explaining that even though Ramsuratkumar appeared to be fully asleep he still maintained a level of awareness that both shocked and amused his companions. Before the master would nod off, he might ask his guests to start reading from a particular book. A few pages into the task, however, the devotees would often find their attention flagging. Rarely would a spiritual book hold their interest for long. "Very boring," Parathasarathy recalled of these texts.

So, while the beggar slept, even to the point of snoring, the reader might skip ahead in the book, just to be done with it. No sooner had this little conspiracy of omission been accomplished, however, when Yogi Ramsuratkumar would raise his body slightly, adjust his *darbar*, and with apparent innocence declare: "Ooooh, Parathasarathy, this beggar slept. You please start reading again from that particular page," and he would cite the page number that preceded the ones that had been skipped. "There would be no escape!" Parathasarathy laughed, remembering.

Yogi Ramsuratkumar used to chant verses from the *Bhagavad Gita* on various occasions, as he loved this classic text. He particularly appreciated the parts that related to bhakti yoga, in which Krishna narrates the attributes of the genuine devotees who are closest to him. Such lines as, "Of all yogins, he who loves Me with faith and whose inner self is absorbed in Me – him I deem to be most yoked" (*Bhagavad Gita*, 6.47), were probably among his favorites, and he would then often speak about the meaning of various *slokas* (verses). "Oh, Murugeshji, my king, *Bhagavad Gita* is enough for us," Yogi Ramsuratkumar said on one occasion.

Sometimes, at the end of a busy day, when the crowds had been fairly continuous outside his door and the supplications had grown to exhausting proportions, Yogi Ramsuratkumar would retreat to the shrine of Lord Siva in the great Arunachaleswarar Temple, his true home. Here he would stand, leaning on the pillar before the Sampanthavinayaga statue, a form of Ganesh. He loved this shrine.

"Swami would stand erect and would not talk to anybody," Parathasarathy remembered of many occasions in the early 1980s. The beggar asked his three friends, and others, to refrain from approaching him or talking to him when he was in the temple. His injunction, however, could not be enforced among the pilgrims and locals who had heard of the resident saint. Typically, he would be watched by a small group for a while, and then approached as people prostrated before him. But if a larger crowd formed there was no chance for contemplation, and then Yogi Ramsuratkumar might run away from this favorite spot and hide himself deeper within the temple complex.

राम

On three separate occasions, Parathasarathy, Shivashankar, and Murugesan made their pilgrimage to the beggar's door on foot, walking the 550 kilometers from Tuticorin to Tiruvannamalai. Like pilgrims throughout the ages, they would have chanted or sung the praises of God along their route. They would also get to talking, and sometimes their thoughts would encompass much less than remembrance of their master's adorable presence.

On one of these wanderings, in late November or early December 1982, just prior to the great Deepam Festival, which draws hundreds of thousands to Tiruvannamalai to celebrate the fiery appearance of Lord Siva with a fire lit on the top of the sacred mountain, Arunachala, the three "wise men" stopped for the night in a hotel in Madurai. One thing led to another, and soon they got to talking about the upcoming festivities and the fact that they would certainly be isolated from the hundreds of other devotees who would be awaiting the darshan of Yogi Ramsuratkumar. While they treasured his solitary attention, they missed seeing him honored by other people. Everything about their master was a source of delight for them. All they wanted to do was to sit invisibly in the corner and take in the whole scene.

Arriving at the Sannadhi House with their thoughts holding these desires, they were greeted at the gate by a stern-faced beggar. Immediately he ushered the three inside, through the porch where he often conducted his meetings, and into the main part of the house. Then, he locked the door. Calling to his attendant, Rama-krishna at that time, he instructed: "Don't allow any people inside. If anybody comes, disperse them, and then come and inform this beggar." Hundreds were sent away.

Commonly, individuals operate as if the world should revolve around them. For this reason they also fear that they will be left out when others are given the final goods. Because they don't want to miss out in the end, they become self-righteous when denied what others are allowed. On the other hand, when they are the favored ones, and while they want to stay that way, they also become uncomfortable, knowing that they could just as easily be "out" as "in," all things considered. This all-too-human inclination toward fairness gnawed at Yogi Ramsuratkumar's three favored companions.

As more and more people were sent away, the three men tried to argue their case in the most appropriate way possible. "Swami, we came here not to disturb you but to enjoy your presence with devotees."

Yogi Ramsuratkumar was not to be persuaded, however. For him, there was only God. "It is all right," he assured them, and put them in their place at the same time. "My Father says this beggar should spend this day with you people. This beggar feels quite at home with you people."

And so, except for a few moments on the night that the fire was lit on the mountain, Yogi Ramsuratkumar remained sequestered with his small contingent, and refused admission even to other long-time devotees. One can imagine that many of those who were turned away felt more than a mild sting. The knocking at the gate was fairly continuous, despite his attendant's pleas, yet the beggar would not come out.

"Oh, the disturbance from these people!" the master lamented. "These people do not understand. This beggar is doing his Father's work. This beggar should be doing his Father's work urgently."

"He didn't allow us even to take some coffee, for three whole days! We just had some puffed rice that Swami had stored in the back, and some rotten bananas. We weren't allowed to go outside," Parathasarathy remembered. When Murugesan asked directly whether one of them could simply go and get coffee for the rest, the beggar was adamant. "No, Murugesanji," Ramsuratkumar said, addressing his devotee endearingly, "we are doing my Father's work. We should not waste time."

In retrospect, Parathasarathy was able to clearly understand that this urgency had to do with the fact that his friend Murugesan had only two more years to live. "His whole attention was with Murugesan at that time," he explained. The communion that these men shared in the beggar's company was enough to do the necessary work. The incomparable value of keeping the company of saints had long been Ramdas's exhortation to his devotees. Yogi Ramsuratkumar himself had said the same.

राम

In 1982, Yogi Ramsuratkumar was visited by his *poorvaashram* (pre-sannyas) relatives – his wife, daughter, son-in-law, and grandson – who came to Tiruvannamalai with his permission.

It is difficult to comprehend, no less accept, an act of renunciation so total that it obliterates the past. Although we in the West live amidst the highest divorce rate in the world, many would still express shock and pass judgement upon a man or woman who would leave a husband, a wife, children, sick and aging parents, in order to pursue one-pointedly the path of total liberation. Certainly such a turning can be interpreted solely as an unwillingness to shoulder responsibility. In the example of many saints from many traditions, however, this complete renunciation was integral to his or her work on behalf of a wider family – that of all humanity.

Jesus clearly challenged his disciples to "leave the dead to bury the dead," in calling them to his side. The Buddha left wife and child behind as he undertook his great pilgrimage of transformation. Mataji Krishnabai, the perfect devotee of Swami Ramdas, offered to bring her two sons to the ashram of her master, so that she could care for them and serve Ramdas as well. When they decided not to come, she went ahead anyway, leaving them to be raised by close relatives. Her work for Papa cast her in the role of "Mother" for thousands of devotees, a job that she fulfilled with absolute generosity and selflessness. Mataji said on several occasions that every child in creation was as beloved to her as were her own offspring. For one whose love is universal, there are no lines of distinction. Love is purely offered, requiring only a ready receptacle in which to pour it.

Yogi Ramsuratkumar had long ago moved from Bihar, leaving behind all that was familiar, all that tied him to a worldly existence. He, like his Father, Ramdas, left a wife and several children. While it is unknown whether the beggar saw them at all after his transformational death in 1952, we do know that members of his family came to Tiruvannamalai on several occasions after Yogi Ramsuratkumar was recognized as a saint throughout South India.

In 1982, Parathasarathy and his two partners happened to be present with the master when this small party of northerners, speaking the native Bihari language, showed up at the Sannadhi Street residence. As he did with all who approached him, Yogi Ramsuratkumar treated them with respect, but with no special attention except to a seven-year-old grandson, Murari, whom he held affectionately on his lap. Stroking the child and smiling, the Godchild happily repeated in English, "Long live Murari. Long live Murari."

The three South Indian men did not know who these visitors were until Ramsuratkumar told them. "These people have come to see this beggar after a long twenty-three years' time. These people were from this beggar's family. If you want to know about this beggar, you can ask these people," the master unhesitatingly offered.

The three witnesses were shocked at Yogiji's offer. The subject of the beggar's past, prior to his meeting with his three "Fathers" and culminating in his "death" at the hands of Ramdas, was rarely if ever a topic of discussion. Ramsuratkumar had always been deliberately quiet, if not evasive, about his past. Devotees, however, wanting to know everything they can about their master, were understandably curious. The human mind wants predictability, security, validation, and history!

Despite the beggar's invitation to question these guests and thus learn more about his past, the three men were dumbstruck. Once they had ascertained which woman was Swami's poorvaashram wife, and who his children were, all they could do was stare blankly, unable to formulate a question of any merit even in their minds, much less to speak one.

"He made our minds totally blank!" Parathasarathy laughed as he recalled the strange occurrences of that afternoon in 1982. "He put us totally in a numb state, and we couldn't move our hands; we didn't raise even from our seats."

This was not merely a question of his three disciples being politely appropriate, however. By their own admission, the "king," the "philosopher" and the "free bird" freely argued with Ramsuratkumar about many things. Sometimes their adamancy even provoked the master. Parathasarathy claims that they were without fear where the Godman was concerned, as they were fully convinced of his love for them. Nonetheless, when it came time to satisfy their curiosity about his past, they were completely unable to utter another word. It was all his lila with them; his way of instructing them in the nature of what was important and what was merely idle curiosity, of which only gossip could result. Of that they were sure.

After some time, Yogi Ramsuratkumar spoke to his guests. His words were clear, honest, uncompromising, and compassionate: "You wanted to see this beggar, and this beggar also felt that you can come. The same old dirty sinner is still here. He is the same sinner. He is the same mad beggar. If you think this beggar is closely related to you people, then my Father will protect you. But don't think to make a scene here." Ramsuratkumar spoke powerfully despite the kindness inherent in his words. There would be no histrionics. There would be no need for pleas, or blame, or manipulation of any kind – the sorts of things that humans love to enact when they think they have been slighted or abandoned. Clearly, his teaching to these relatives was a teaching based in the faith that guided and motivated his entire life. All that mattered was that the Father's will be done. Everything, and everyone, was in his Father's hands now, and there was no need for reestablishing sentimental attachments that would only be a source of disappointment to those who nurtured them. The beggar had urgent work to do, and he had time only for those people and circumstances that would further that work.

"You have seen this beggar, now you should go back to your house and live your life. And hereafter, you should not disturb this beggar" were his last words on that occasion.

राम

Although he himself had left his family household long ago, Yogi Ramsuratkumar did not encourage others to do the same. "Do as I say, not as I do," Lee Lozowick, the spiritual son of the beggar, would instruct his own devotees, reiterating a prime principle of the spiritual life. The Zen master may be able to drink molten iron or consume poison without effect, but the untrained disciple must not follow such a lead. The disciple's job is to listen and obey, not to try to imitate the master's form of sadhana, unless instructed to do so. This is a hard-won lesson that the ego doesn't want to accept.

The stories abound of Yogiji's disciples asking for an imitative sadhana. Perumal wanted to go to Kashi to live out his days, but was instructed to stay put, to support his family, and to guard the master's bags of treasure in the Therady Mandapam across from the Sannadhi Street house. When Lee Lozowick indicated that he wished for nothing more than to have a life at the master's feet, Yogi Ramsuratkumar clearly told him, long before the signs were known to Lee, that this was not his path. Instead, he was to travel widely. Caylor Wadlington wanted to retreat to the caves on Arunachala, to accelerate his process of liberation, but the beggar sent him instead to the Theosophical Society at Madras, and encouraged him constantly to pursue indepth studies in this field. Even meditation was discouraged.

To Murugesan, Shivashankar, and Parathasarathy his injunctions and teachings about the value of householder sadhana were unquestionable. Yogi Ramsuratkumar told these men that householders are the most able to reach God-realization. Renunciates (sannyasins) actually have many serious stumbling blocks to contend with. They must be alert, constantly observing themselves, watching their thoughts. The solitary life is full of traps. But for those who must devote every waking moment to the care and support of family, "it is very easy to have the darshan of God," the beggar told his close companions, each of whom was married, each of whom had children.

One story from another source confirms Yogi Ramsuratkumar's support for the sadhana of motherhood in particular. "Serving children is like serving God" the beggar told his disciple Sandhya

Srinivasan when she confessed that she had been unable to chant the name of God throughout her painful labor and delivery. "He then talked about the 'specialty of motherhood,'" Sandhya reported, referring to Yogi Ramsuratkumar, her guru, as Matrubutheswara, the Great Mother.

Yogi Ramsuratkumar actually strengthened the family life of his devotees, Parathasarathy reported. It made him extremely happy to see that these three men, in particular, where able to maintain their remembrance of the Divine while at the same time serving their wives and children. In fact, in the enigmatic way in which the beggar taught, he even descried his own behavior in leaving his family as being a mistake, a "great sin," as contrasted to the choices being lived by his devotees: "This beggar committed a great sin, a great blunder, by deserting his family to remember his Father. But this beggar's friends, even though they are knowing my Father all the twenty-four hours, still they are remaining in their family. This beggar is very, very happy on seeing this."

Parathasarathy was convinced that his master had said these things, admitting his "blunder," as a way to impress this point deeply. "It was not true," the poet added. "It was just a boost for us to go in the right way. Because he always compared us with himself, in that way he elevated us. When you are being compared with a god, then it is such an elevating feeling."

राम

The Hindu bhakti tradition contains a unique form of expression known as *ninda stuti*. It is ironical praise – complaint, lament, even abuse – in which the lover bemoans his fate in being separated from the beloved even for an instant; the lover complains of anything and everything that delays their constant communion. The poetry that Lee Lozowick had begun to write to Yogi Ramsuratkumar would soon become distinguished for using this particular literary form.

Listen, You old Liar
    tell Your son the truth this time
I am begging You

to devour me completely
to turn this wild and resistant Fool
into nothing and No-one
but still I make conditions:
    So I demand this as well –
Once you have made me
    the son You truly deserve
do not recreate me again
    separate and wounded as before
I am warning You
    Yogi Ramsuratkumar
I will not take it lightly
if you ever allow me to leave You.
            – Lee Lozowick[3]

Murugesan, in the early 1980s, occasionally employed a similar language, "abusing" the beggar as an expression of his passionate love. For those who did not share this same degree of devotion, the words were heard as terrible.

"Swami, he uses some filthy language, he is abusing you, Swami," declared one outraged visitor about Murugesan's remarks.

"Is he?" the beggar asked, in a characteristically noncommittal way. Later, to Parathasarathy, the master inquired: "This beggar heard through some friends that Murugesan used some filthy language on mentioning this beggar, and he abused this beggar. Is it so?"

"No Swamiji, he is not abusing, even though he is mentioning some filthy language. For me, it is not abuse, Swami."

"What word is it he uses?" Yogi Ramsuratkumar asked with all the innocence of a child.

When he was told the word, the beggar instructed Parathasarathy to write it down, in Tamil, the language in which it had been spoken, and to hand the paper to the orthodox Brahmin, who was a visitor on this day.

"Do you know the meaning of this word?" Ramsuratkumar inquired sweetly.

"Oh, it's a filthy language, Swami! We should not use this word, Swami." The Brahmin was clearly shocked.

"No, no, this beggar wants to know the *meaning* of this word. If my king, Murugesan, utters this word, there is a meaning behind it. There is definitely a meaning to that word! This beggar wants to know the meaning of that word. You will go and bring your dictionary."

A small Tamil dictionary was located and presented to the master, who handed the book to Parathasarathy. The offending word, however, was not to be found there, so Yogi Ramsuratkumar asked the Brahmin to go and get a bigger dictionary. The man did as he was instructed. Returning from the library with an unabridged dictionary, the word was soon located. Its meaning, "hidden parts," was conveyed to the master.

A huge smile crossed Yogi Ramsuratkumar's face. "Oh, now this beggar got it…Murugesan is glorifying this beggar, now this beggar is able to understand." And with that the Godchild went on to instruct those in his company about a very fine point of scripture. This same word, it seems, was used in a sloka in one of the thousand slokas glorifying Lord Vishnu. "Oh, now this beggar got it," he reiterated, "Murugesji is not abusing this beggar, Murugesji is *glorifying* this beggar. Oh, he uses such strong words for this beggar, but it is out of love for this beggar, isn't it?"

Only one who loved greatly and deeply could have the courage to speak in this way, Parathasarathy noted, mentioning Lee Lozowick's similar use of ninda stuti in his poems to Yogi Ramsuratkumar. "Obviously if Lee couldn't love Swamiji he wouldn't use these words. To 'abuse' Swami you should have that courage, you should have that love."

राम

The three men often puzzled over their terrible and wonderful fate in being apparently singled out to receive the master's ongoing and focused attention. Especially when prominent dignitaries or foreign visitors came to call upon the beggar, they became uncomfortable and frequently questioned Yogi Ramsuratkumar about it. *Shouldn't this visitor who had traveled perhaps thousands of miles be given precedence to them?* they would argue.

"Miss Cece" was one such visitor from the U.S. who paid a visit to the beggar in 1982 while Parathasarathy, Shivashankar, and Murugesan were in residence during one of their extended stays. She and her male partner, a scientist with no interest in things devotional, sent word via telegram that they would be arriving on a particular day, accompanied by her two daughters. Like many of Yogi Ramsuratkumar's Western guests in the 1970s and '80s, Miss Cece was a devotee of Sathya Sai Baba. It was at Sai Baba's Indian ashrams in Bangalore or Puttaparthi that many would learn of the hidden beggar saint, and since Tiruvannamalai was on the circuit anyway, due to the presence of Ramana's ashram, it was simple enough for would-be seekers to stop in for a "look-see," at least, at the Godman's gate.

Yogi Ramsuratkumar graciously welcomed Cece and company, and immediately placed his attention on the scientist/boyfriend – the "nonbeliever." As the beggar talked sweetly, the man was quickly and uncharacteristically disarmed. Within a few minutes, he not only had tears in his eyes, but was becoming highly emotional. Gazing in awe at Yogiji's hand, he was suddenly overcome with devotion. "Swami, may I kiss your hands?" he asked, to the amazement of onlookers.

"Oh, this dirty beggar's hand…it is so dirty, and it may give you a bad smell," the gentle beggar lamented, his eyes twinkling.

"Oh, it's all right, Swami," the man protested. "This hand is Jesus's hand, Swami. So I want to kiss it."

Ramsuratkumar allowed the man his wish. The visitor took the beggar's hand and, weeping profusely, kissed it, while his astonished partner took in the whole scene. She had told him a few things about Yogi Ramsuratkumar by way of preparation, certainly, but his attitude had been cool at best. Now, after only a few moments, he was literally putty in the master's hands. Some change of heart had definitely taken place. Some ancient well of devotion had been tapped, and the scientist had become the unrestrained romantic.

After a few hours' audience, and despite the man's profuse display of emotional attachment, Yogi Ramsuratkumar suddenly, and kindly, dismissed them. "Now, this beggar has seen you people nicely. You can go now," he said.

"Shall we come tomorrow morning, Swami?" the couple asked.

"No, no need to come over here again."

"But we are going to be here for another ten days! So should we not meet you again?" They were incredulous. Hadn't they shown their devotion adequately?

"Yes, this beggar has seen you nicely," the master reiterated. "My Father will be always with you," he blessed them. "You can go, and do your other works. You can stay at Ramanashram. You can do your regular duties there."

By now they were completely shocked at the unexpected reply. "Swami, we *want* to come again," they pleaded.

"No," he was firm, "these three friends [referring to Parathasarathy, Shivashankar, and Murugesan] came all the long way from Tuticorin to see this beggar, and now this beggar is busy. For another ten days this beggar will not be available for you."

The couple left, as instructed, but with tears in their eyes. Seeing all this, Murugesan was upset. "Swami, we have just come from 500 kilometers, from eight hours journey to Tiruvannamalai. She came a long way just to see you, Swami, just to be sent away!"

"Not like that, Murugesanji," the beggar contradicted. His devotee's discomfort with an apparent inequity became the opportunity for the master to deliver an important communication about the nature of the guru-disciple relationship.

"These friends came to India to see many people like this beggar. They will stay here for ten days, and they will go to Tirupati and stay there for ten days. Then they will go to several other cities, to Hardwar, and then to the Himalayas. They will see several saints and sadhus. But you people came a long way from Tuticorin to *see only this beggar*. And after this, you will go directly back to your houses. Your total attention was with this beggar, and this beggar's attention is also with you."

Referring to the couple who had just left, Yogi Ramsuratkumar was clear: "My Father wanted to give them something, and my Father gave them. That's enough."

Only with such undivided attention, Parathasarathy explained, can the master "do something for you."

राम

Those who carefully observed the many ways in which people approached Yogi Ramsuratkumar over the years learned a great deal about both human intransigence and Divine patience. Some things changed dramatically in the lives of the master's devotees; some things never seemed to budge.

"Can you put aside all your problems in a corner, and remember my Father on this finest day? Then alone can this beggar do something for you." Yogi Ramsuratkumar was speaking to an old devotee, a man who had visited him regularly for nearly ten years. The man's problematic orientation to life was so deeply ingrained that even as he sat in the beggar's radiant presence he held tightly to his own misfortunes.

As soon as Ramsuratkumar would offer the man an invitation to speak, he would predictably, consistently, respond, "Some small problems, Swami…" and proceed to enumerate his ills. Although the beggar at times encouraged the devotee to put his problems aside, the man was blind to his own habitual behavior. Nevertheless, in this case the Godchild's patient forbearance always proved more constant than the man's neediness. Those who witnessed this particular play admitted that, despite his negativity and self-absorption, the man had great love for Yogi Ramsuratkumar. It seemed obvious that the master was enacting a lila for a purpose they could not fully understand.

His three regular companions had their own view on the whys and wherefores of the beggar's response. "We realized, we should not take *any* problems to Swami," Parathasarathy reflected. "If problems come, they are all our own making. *We* have the capacity to deal with the problems, to solve the problem. When we go to Swami, we should be so open – we should just receive and be silent. Then only we will be free to see Father, to see God."

राम

Late in the evening one night in the early 1980s, Yogi Ramsuratkumar gifted the fortunate three, and their wives, with a most precious vision. The incident began with the Godman speaking about himself in uncharacteristic terms. Whereas he was always the first to protest his nothingness in light of the Father's Allness, his words on this occasion pointed to the same essential truth, but with a twist.

"This beggar used to call himself as a beggar, but there is nothing either in this world or that world to be begged upon by this beggar." His companions sat up with sharpened alertness at these strange words. Yogi Ramsuratkumar then continued: "This beggar used to call himself a dirty sinner, but there cannot be such a pure, crystal-like *vastu* (a brilliant placement; energy flowing brilliantly) either in this world or in that other world. He is always only his Father. He is always one, one."

As he was uttering these words, his devotees were suddenly swept up into the reality of which he spoke. What they saw, and confirmed with one another, held them all spellbound. His whole body suddenly took on an otherworldly light, which then began to grow in intensity. There in the semidarkness of the evening, the Godman was revealing to these trusted friends a glimpse of his true nature. They were overwhelmed. Krishna had done the same for his beloved "brother" Arjuna, blinding the mortal by the light that emanated from his godly form. Jesus, too, transfigured in light before the eyes of Peter, James, and John, on Mount Tabor, leaving them dumbstruck. Here was the one they had casually walked with, talked with, rubbed shoulders with…and now, too brilliant to look at.

As Parathasarathy tried to communicate the wonder of this evening, telling the story more than twenty years later, he was still breathless in his attempts to capture what it was that they had received. "Three times he revealed, Oh God," his voice faded as the memory flooded his heart. "Oh, his mystery with us! He was talking about himself, about his own self. It was such a vast mystery, you can't comprehend it. You can be one with That, but you can't comprehend That. You can just be burned in that fire. He was just like a fire at that time. Such powerful words he spoke!"

राम

From March 2 through March 4, 1984, Parathasarathy and Murugesan had the exclusive darshan of the master at the Sannadhi

Street house in Tiruvannamalai. At precisely 4 P.M. on the fourth, they departed for their home city. One month later, on April 4, 1984, at exactly 4 P.M., Murugesan breathed his final breath. He was forty-five years old.

He had traveled to Calcutta on business and there he had suffered a heart attack. When Murugeshi felt the heart pain, the best cardiologist in Calcutta was called. On the latter's advice, Murugesan was taken to the hospital, accompanied by his brother, who assured him: "Murugesan, you are in the hands of the best doctor. So, do not worry."

"Oh, everybody is in the hands of God," the devotee replied. Those were his last words. On reaching the hospital, Murugesan silently passed away. His body arrived at his home on April 5, and on the same day the final rites were performed.

Many devotees have said that Yogi Ramsuratkumar was like "mother" for them, as much as he was their guru, their master. The qualities of exquisite tenderness that one associates with a mother's love, reflective of the Divine Mother's love, so often demonstrated by the beggar, were brilliantly highlighted upon the occasion of Murugesan's death.

Yogi Ramsuratkumar had been informed via telegram of his devotee's death soon after it occurred, but did not have the opportunity to hear the details until three days later, on April 8, 1984, when Parathasarathy arrived in Tiruvannamalai in the early morning. With extraordinary compassion the master welcomed Parathasarathy on this day, asked him to sit before him, and to relate the many small stories concerning Murugesan's passing. Ramsuratkumar wanted his devotee to tell him exactly what he knew: how the end came for Murugesan; what the man's last words were; how his body was brought to Tuticorin; what happened to the box in which the body was brought; who performed the last rites and so on. Details were always important for Yogi Ramsuratkumar, who would ask devotees for the specifics of their travel – the precise time their flights might be leaving, for instance – or the exact number and names of people in their party, and other seemingly inconsequential bits of information. For him, such bits were not irrelevant, however, as stories have verified over the years.

In one case, which had terrible consequences, a couple had come to the master begging him to help their son who was on trial for a serious crime. The beggar asked the boy's name and assured the family that he would be all right. When the young man was convicted and severely sentenced, the parents were distraught. In speaking of the incident, however, Yogi Ramsuratkumar found out that the parents had given him not the boy's birth name, but a "spiritual name" assigned to him later in his life. The master was furious and frustrated, lamenting again and again that, when he was not given the proper information, he could not properly affect the outcome of things.

Like mother and son, Yogi Ramsuratkumar and Parathasarathy discussed the loss of their beloved Murugesan. The younger, telling the story, had the opportunity once again to voice his grief, while the elder encouraged him to speak more and more.

When the details were given, and given again, the beggar, with motherly care, then asked Parathasarathy how many days had passed since he had slept. It was obvious from Parathasarathy's appearance and demeanor that the stress and grief had worn him down nearly to exhaustion, and he admitted that he had not slept since April 4, the day on which his friend had died.

Just then, a knock was heard at the door of the house and, leaving his young disciple, Yogi Ramsuratkumar went out to answer it. In a moment he returned with a small parcel in his hands – a packet of food: hot *idlies* (sour rice patties) and *sambar* (spicy vegetable broth), enough for the two of them to eat a hearty breakfast.

As soon as the meal was completed, Yogiji lay down to rest, and directed Parathasarathy to do the same. The young man stretched out on the mat near his master, and for a few minutes the two continued to talk. Then, Parathasarathy closed his eyes. It was noon when he next opened them, brought to his senses by his gentle Swamiji calling him to eat lunch. The meal had been set out by the master's hand, and once again the two shared their simple food. Then, with lunch finished, the beggar again asked Parathasarathy to lie down, and to talk. Within a few minutes, however, the devotee was fast asleep again.

At around eight o'clock that evening, Yogi Ramsuratkumar gently woke his guest again, this time asking him to share *chapattis* (flatbread), which were already prepared and waiting. After dinner, the same ritual was enacted for the third and final time: Parathasarathy was instructed to recline, engaged in talk, and left to sleep. Nearly eight hours later, at 4 A.M., he was awakened by the "Mother's" soft words.

"Parathasarathy, this beggar has seen you nicely. Now this beggar leaves you. You can go to your place," Yogi Ramsuratkumar declared. The healing ritual was complete.

"My whole being had been shattered on hearing the death news of Murugeshji," Parathasarathy explained. "Swami pacified my being, without my knowledge, and made it sleep to its depth."

While the seeker may look for the miraculous as the hallmark of a powerful yogi, the genuine yogi may be demonstrating a degree of the miraculous so shrouded in the simplicity of ordinary activity that the thrill-seeker will completely overlook the transformation that is going on right under his nose. Such was undoubtedly the case here.

Speaking of his enduring faith in his master, Parathasarathy confessed: "I am not a devotee of Yogi Ramsuratkumar because I don't know *how* to have the true devotion to Swami. But I know one thing: *Swami loved me.* I don't know whether I have the capacity to love him or whether I *am* loving him…that also I don't know. But I can understand his love. He loved me."

Moreover, as far as Parathasarathy could tell, the beggar's work with his three "friends" was culminated successfully. "Murugesan departed as a realized soul," Parathasarathy concluded. "Swami told us, 'Murugesanji is sitting in my Father's lap. My Father knows.'"

21

POETRY AND MADNESS

 Early in the 1980s, during the same time period in which Yogi Ramsuratkumar was working with Parathasarathy and company, the Godchild began to receive letters postmarked from Arizona, U.S.A., containing devotional poems from one Lee Lozowick.

It was not unusual for the beggar to receive lots of mail, particularly from all over India, at that time. Even before he had a residence on Sannadhi Street, letters would arrive addressed "Yogi Ramsuratkumar, Tiruvannamalai," and be delivered to him by postal workers who knew of his whereabouts. Devotees wrote sending small donations. They wrote asking for Divine intervention, and even occasionally thanking him for the assistance offered. They sent wedding invitations, pictures of their children, newspaper clippings, all the scraps of their lives upon which they desired his blessing and attention.

The beggar had his methods for handling the many pieces of paper and other offerings he received, although for many observers there seemed no logic to it. Some bits of memorabilia were saved, piled nearby his seat along with his current copy of *The Hindu*. Some things were kept even closer, occasionally carried in his hand, worn around his neck, or rolled into the fabric of his clothing. The house at Sannadhi Street contained a veritable archive of his activities, with the remnants of hundreds of dried flower malas – gifts from visitors and devotees – hanging on the walls of the verandah; collections of old newspapers, discarded cigarette boxes, packets of sugar candy, a medley of fruits left as prasad offerings by devotees, as well as books, leaflets, items of new and unused clothing, odds and ends. Many things were discarded into the huge gunnysacks that were, in the earlier days before he had a residence, hauled from place to place by his trusted attendants. Now, in the 1980s, these bags, once filled, were piled on the steps of the mandapam across the street from the house, where they were carefully guarded by Perumal.

Looking around the room of the Sannadhi house, with the unswept floors, a rat scurrying to safety along one wall, a pile of sand gathered in one corner for some unknown reason, one had no doubt that this beggar *was* a madman. No sane person would save such trash, or choose to live in such surroundings. His costume and the stage setting in which he performed his lila confirmed that what he had said about himself. "This beggar is very bad, very mad" was indeed true.

Nonetheless, positioning oneself outside the door at #90 Sannadhi Street on a typical day, watching the dozens and sometimes scores of visitors and guests leaving one by one after having spent a few minutes or a few hours with the "madman," one could also not deny the glow that emanated from smiling faces, or the softened eyes, some still filled with tears, or the lilting steps of those who had initially entered burdened with care. For these people it was obvious that Yogi Ramsuratkumar's odd collections held more than refuse. Some believed that he collected and held the world's karma, the stuff of peoples' lives, the raw material of human suffering. In carrying these burdens, in saving what others hoped to be rid of, in attending to supplications of the sick, the poor, the aged, in following the political and social movements throughout the world by his avid interest in current events, he was at work, an instrument in the hands of his Father.

Describing the Godchild's equanimity in the midst of such human chaos, Ilayaraja, a renowned musician who was also an ardent lover of the beggar's, wrote: "The cumulative effect of the spectacle, observed at regular intervals over several months, is one of surrender to sanctity. Here is a phenomenon beyond one's ken. No individual frame of flesh and bone can carry the burden of so much common woe and collective aspiration, nor personify extra-dimensional qualities usually attributed to images of stone, without the marrow of divine principle."[1]

ONLY GOD

राम

The earliest poems that Lee Lozowick sent in the 1980s to this "mad," "bad" beggar of Sannadhi Street were read and thrown away. Years later, Yogi Ramsuratkumar actually apologized to Lee for this, saying that he thought it was more of the same type of communication that he was always getting from devotees.[2] Love poems are easy to generate. Anybody can fill a page with romantic sentiments inspired by a quick hit of bliss or insight, and Yogi Ramsuratkumar apparently received his fair share of such outpourings. Would such expressions lead to anything of value in terms of work, of genuine discipleship, of surrender to the Father? Or would they stand as somewhat embarrassing testimonies, like letters to a long-forgotten lover, discovered many years after the passion has died?

Lee remarked: "The first two years or so I didn't record any of what I sent Him so there's no recorded versions of the early poetry – which is quite fitting actually...I never got any reply of course...I assumed that the letters were getting there even though I had no feedback about that at the time."[3]

Yet, reply or no reply, kept or thrown away, the poetry – those tiny seeds released into the wind – had landed, mixed with the soil, and begun to sprout roots that ran deep into the ground of the master's garden. It would have been naïve for Lee, or anyone else, to imagine that writing and sending pieces of his heart to a being such as Yogi Ramsuratkumar would not have some repercussions. In Lee's case, the repercussions were like aftershocks of an earthquake. Slowly, the way a flower opens, Lee realized that the great event that had taken place in his life in 1975, which had initiated his work as a teacher and had marked his entry onto the path of spiritual slavery, was the result of help he had been receiving invisibly, yet inexorably, from the hidden saint, Yogi Ramsuratkumar. Lee came to see, in fact, that every event in his entire life had been conceived, engineered, and accomplished in and through the hand of the beggar.

While no formal announcement of this realization was yet made within his community at large, those who were close to Lee noted that he made occasional private references to the Godchild of

Tiruvannamalai, speaking of him as his guru and spiritual master. "Lee began calling himself a beggar and referring to his community as 'a school of beggars,'" one student noted. Publicly, however, Lee was extremely reticent to speak about the growing relationship or the details of his master's location. He felt it was not timely to introduce more immature seekers, Americans especially, to the beggar's domain. These people tended to be looking only for miracles and distractions, and already Lee had a fierce sense of protectiveness about the one who had intervened in his own life so completely.

Twenty years later, as he reflected upon those early visits, Lee affirmed that some of the things that Yogi Ramsuratkumar said and did then (1977, 1979) were only becoming clear to him now (1997). The subtlety of the beggar's communication never ceased to amaze Lee, and this necessity for staying alert to what was going on "between the lines" when in this master's company was a subject that Lee spoke of passionately to his own students, as well as to devotees of Yogi Ramsuratkumar's throughout the world:

> There is *always* something happening in Yogi Ramsurat-kumar's company. You could be caught by surprise by some-thing extraordinarily sacred in the midst of what seems very ordinary, so there is never a moment that can't be used as a teaching communication. A true teacher wants the student to make real distinctions for himself, so the teacher often hides the message behind a joke, or the student has to get through boredom in the teacher's company, but there is always something significant going on...[4]

Lee was becoming aware that he not only had a guru, a master, but that in being called to the feet of Ramsuratkumar he was also being aligned with Ramdas, Yogi Ramsuratkumar's "Father," and the entire lineage from which the beggar had emerged. This recognition of lineage was a profoundly radical addition to Lee's teaching work, akin to an adopted child learning the identity of his or her true parents. By 1983, although he had had no additional contact with the beggar since their interactions in 1979, Lee's poetry began making reference to himself as "son," or more commonly as "Your true heart son," in relationship to Yogi Ramsuratkumar, whom he now called "Father," and even "darling Father." In May 1983 he wrote:

It is true that Your son is young and naïve,
    and You are Ageless in Your disheveled rags,
but lee is pierced to the core
    by the desire to honor Your Words.[5]

Simultaneous with this recognition of an ageless relationship, Lee began to acknowledge his own "sins" – of arrogance, foolishness, greed – and the need that he himself realized for help:

Surely oh Father
    You will show Your true son the way
for lee is too proud
    to rid himself of his arrogance and greed.[6]

and again:

How I long for You Father,
    for You are my only hope.
I have struggled alone
    for far too long.[7]

What started as a thin stream of devotional expression, an occasional paean of praise, grew to a swift current by 1986. And after that, over many years, to a deep, wide and powerful river. Lee's poetry not only detailed the evolution of his own relationship to the beggar, Yogi Ramsuratkumar, but, unbeknownst to Lee, actually came to predict what would happen next for him in his master's company. In one of nine outstanding poems written on May 3, 1983, Lee in effect *asked for* his future work with the Godman. Describing what had already occurred in the 1977 and 1979 visits, he went on to beg for the piece he needed to be able to serve his master beyond form or circumstance, beyond acknowledgement or affection.

The first time I came to You,
    I was curious.
Honor and respect were given
    out of propriety and pride.
The second time I came to You,
    I was secretly hopeful.
Honor and respect now paid
    out of yearning and pride.
The third time I will come to You
    let me bow my head and submit my will.
Let me not be honorable or respectful
    but swallow my ugly pride
Let me weep before You with Madness
    …dispel lee's ignorance and his arrogance.[8]

If one ever needed proof that true prayers are answered, the events that transpired in Lee's next visit to Yogi Ramsuratkumar, in 1986, would serve as definitive confirmation.

A FAMILY OF SERVICE, 1984

 One of the great distinctions made within Indian spiritual culture is that *pandit* (or scholar) and *guru* (spiritual guide or master) are two entirely different functions. Whereas in the West one may easily confuse the two, in India there is a long tradition of the most learned men and women bowing at the feet of the illiterate, destitute, God-realized saint. While the mastery of scripture or yoga philosophy remains an exemplary vocation, stories abound of the book-learned "masters" being instructed to throw their texts away in order that they may experience the living truth, often in the form of the living person, the one who embodies what the texts merely speak about.

Rumi, the great scholar of Islamic Sufism, was confounded by his meeting of the beggar Shamsi Tabriz, who told him to throw his books away. The great Tibetan scholar Naropa was similarly instructed by an old woman who laughed uproariously when told that Naropa knew his books but not his own mind or heart.

Since his earliest days in Tiruvannamalai, Yogi Ramsuratkumar was a magnet for the well-educated and even the scholarly. Although he himself was college-trained and highly sophisticated in the dharmic teachings and scriptures, his appearance and his lifestyle belied any reliance upon such education. Consequently, it is always interesting and instructive to learn that his mere presence was often enough to humble even the most arrogant of visitors. His was a living scripture that far surpassed the academic understandings of his most well-educated guests.

A Family of Service, 1984

One such learned man, who first visited Yogi Ramsuratkumar in 1984 and who would come to play a significant part in the master's lila, was Venugopla Rangarajan. At the time of his first meeting with the humble beggar, Rangarajan was forty-four years old and had already distinguished himself in many fields of endeavor. He held a post-graduate degree in philosophy from the University of Madras, had been an editor at various news agencies, had served as a secretary of the Chinmaya Mission and Vivekananda Medical Mission, and was a visiting professor of Indian Thought and Culture Heritage at institutions in Madras (Chennai). In 1977, Rangarajan founded the Sister Nivedita Academy under the inspiration of his *siksha guru* (the guru who teaches one the knowledge of worldly arts), Swami Chinmayananda. This organization, named after the radical Irish woman formerly known as Miss Margaret Nobel, the devotee of Vivekananda's, was dedicated to the revitalization of the conscious-ness of India's citizens to their proud past. In that same year, 1977, Rangarajan had published his first book, *Vande Mataram* (a history of India's national anthem), which was also the Academy's first publica-tion. In 1984, he initiated a periodical called *Tattva Darsana*, a quar-terly journal devoted to philosophy, religion, culture and science. This journal soon became the first, unofficial forum for news and teaching stories related to Yogi Ramsuratkumar.

Rangarajan, like Yogi Ramsuratkumar, had already had two pow-erful gurus (a Father and a Mother) by the time he was led to the beg-gar saint of Tiruvannamalai. His first guru, Swami Chinmayananada, had echoed for him the sentiments that made the great distinction between book learning and embodied knowledge come alive for him: "Enough of reading *Upanishads*. Throw your *Upanishad* books into a ditch and start doing sadhana." As Rangarajan noted years later, in remarking upon these words, "The great Advaitacharya did not mean any insult to the texts, but drilled into the mind of his students the truth that knowledge should lead to sadhana."[1]

The "Mother" force in his spiritual life came in a disturbingly unexpected form. In the late 1970s, as he worked in South India for the Vivekenanda Kendra (a spiritually-oriented service mission), Rangarajan frequently heard stories of a mad beggar woman, Mother Mayee of Kanyakumari, whom some of his most respected associates were readily hailing as an incarnation of the Divine Mother. At first, the learned professor was put off by the stories of her escapades: the fact that she was commonly surrounded by a pack of wild dogs; her unkempt, sometimes naked, condition. One day, however, against all rational explanations, Rangarajan felt himself drawn to her, irresistibly, and in a way that he could not explain. Once he "saw" her – realizing who she was beyond appearances – there was no escape. The man of great book-learning soon became another child in the Mother's playpen. He took her as a spiritual guide. Writing years later, Rangarajan confessed:

> The intellectual vanity which in the beginning stood in the way of prostrating before an apparently ugly, unclean, mad, beggar woman adored by many faithful devotees as Divine Mother, soon gave way under the irresistible spell of the Mother, impelled him to sit at her feet and pour out the feelings of his intense devotion to her.[2]

In the early 1980s, just prior to meeting Yogi Ramsuratkumar, Rangarajan was diagnosed first with a lung infection, and then given the sentence of terminal cancer. Seeking the feet of the Mother, Mayee, he was miraculously healed by her ministrations. Recommending a series of very unconventional treatments, she spit into his hand a bolt of already chewed tobacco, which he immediately swallowed as prasad, and indicated that he should perform a series of prayers and pujas for 108 days. When this period of practice was completed, Rangarajan went back to the doctor for a reevaluation. No cancer was found in his system.

His meeting with Yogi Ramsuratkumar, he claims, was a natural progression of his work with Mother Mayee, whom he credits with sending him to Tiruvannamalai, to another mad beggar's feet.

> We cannot but mention here with a feeling of intense gratitude to the Divine Mother, the greatest gift that She conferred on this sadhu – the gift of Gurudarshanam. It was the Divine Mother who directed this sadhu, in the beginning of

the eighties, to his deeksha guru, Yogi Ramsuratkumar, Godchild Tiruvannamalai.[3]

राम

Mother Mayee knew of Yogi Ramsuratkumar in the late 1970s – a photograph of their historic meeting in 1976 stands as a testimony to this communion of the saints. Regarding this occasion Yogi Ramsuratkumar later remarked, "She had come once some years back to see this Beggar," so we know that there was at least one earlier meeting.[4] Whether or not these meetings in Tiruvannamalai were the only times they had ever seen one another is a matter of speculation. During his many wandering years we know that Yogi Ramsuratkumar had journeyed as far as Kanyakumari, at the southernmost tip of the subcontinent. Perhaps he had encountered this strange woman (distinguished by her companion dogs) who slept under the mandapam of a temple, or on a roadside platform, or within the shelter of the front of a shop or restaurant, much as he had done. Did he see her at the seashore, where she would walk or sit for long hours? Would he notice that she was fed by local fishermen in return for some simple service like breaking firewood, pounding rice, or drying the fish?[5]

Or maybe, like Hilda Charlton, Mayee knew him beyond time and space in the way that highly evolved beings seem to share a kinship of recognition.

One devotee of Yogi Ramsuratkumar's, Shivashankar, wrote this of the meeting:

On the 26th of September 1976, the Divine Mother of Kanyakumari, discovered by Swami Gnanananda, met Ramji in front of the temple of Arunachala and offered him sacred food. She stayed inside the temple and silently took communion the whole night with Ramji who was outside. The next day they exchanged jokes and views of the work that might be done. Then the Mother left for Kanyakumari.[6]

Another account, this one from an eminent pandit from Benaras, tells of another unlikely meeting of the two beggars – Ramsuratkumar and Mayee Ma. Sometime in 1976, the pandit met Yogi Ramsuratkumar at his house, having arrived there in a car that also held Mother Mayee. Asked about the events that had brought him to Tiruvannamalai, the pandit told Yogi Ramsuratkumar:

> I came to Kerala as a state guest, a couple of days back. Today morning, I had been to Kanyakumari for Dharshan. Before Dharshan, I wanted to take bath and I went to the sea, leaving my upper garments and belongings in a near by mantap. While I was bathing, Mayamma [Mother Mayee] came there, held my hand and dragged me to a car parked on the road. She asked me to get into the car. Mayamma and the attendant occupied the rear seat. A little later, the owner of the car and wife came to the car, after taking bath. Mayamma asked the owner of the car to start the car and proceed, without disclosing the destination. The owner of the car, whom I came to know later as a businessman in Sivakashi obeyed the direction of Mayamma and was driving the car, not knowing the destination. Mayamma asked him to proceed towards Madurai. After they reached Madurai, Mayamma asked him to proceed to Tiruvannamalai. Thus, I had come here. My upper garments and other belongings are lying in the mantap at Kanyakumari and I had come with the dhoti alone. Mayamma is seated in the car outside.[7]

With that, Yogi Ramsuratkumar got up, proceeded outside, and there met the Divine Mother, who stayed sitting in the car, while he stood by the door and silently communed with her.

The substance of their "work" together remains a mystery. Yogi Ramsuratkumar never spoke of such things. Yet, like the association with his three Fathers and his relationship with his protector and mentor Swami Gnanananda Giri, there exists for all eternity some bond between the mad beggar of Mount Arunachala and the mad beggar of the southern seas. Saints ever appreciate the company of saints, it seems.

*Yogi Ramsuratkumar greets Mother Mayee of Kanyakumari
(in car, second from right) in Tiruvannamalai, 1976*

राम

On September 1, 1984, sitting with a friend in a small shop in the shadows of Mount Arunachala, Professor Rangarajan made his first official inquiry about the elusive Godchild.

"Oh! You mean Vishiri Swami," his friend replied with enthusiasm, using the colloquial name of the country hand fan (*vishiri*) that Yogi Ramsuratkumar consistently carried.

"Yes," said the professor. "I want to meet him."[8]

The friend led Rangarajan to the beggar's home on Sannadhi Street and made the introductions. To the professor's great surprise, Yogi Ramsuratkumar was amazingly solicitous. The impression made was that the beggar had merely been awaiting Rangarajan's arrival.

"Yes, I have to talk many things to the Professor," said Yogi Ramsuratkumar, whom he had never met. And turning to the intermediary who had made the introduction: "You may leave him here and go."[9]

A moment later, the Godchild had grasped the professor's hand and escorted him within the house, closing the door upon the perplexed friend.

As are most newcomers to the Yogi's "scene," Rangarajan was taken aback with the condition of the abode, particularly by the trash and treasures accumulated on the floor and hung along the walls. Along with wrapped bundles of rags, the professor noted seeing "currency notes of higher denominations and coins littered around the torn mat" on which Yogi Ramsuratkumar sat. As the beggar did with most of his visitors, especially those in whom he seemed to take a particular interest, he sat Rangarajan directly in front of him and studied him intently for a while. Then, Yogi Ramsuratkumar picked up a cigarette, placed it between his lips, and remarked apologetically, "This beggar has the bad habit of smoking, please bear with me."

The professor's initial response was a mingled disgust and awe. The unkempt condition of the beggar's person, his littered surroundings, the cigarette smoke – it was enough to drive away a lesser man, one who could not discern "who" it was that had summoned him. While in certain ways he was repelled, Rangarajan candidly admitted that he was simultaneously attracted, and felt a familiar tug at his heart, the tug that devotees throughout the ages have reported upon meeting their beloved teacher or guru for the first time. [10]

The Godman spoke: "What made you come to this beggar, Professor?"

"I am a devotee of Mother Mayee," the awestruck professor muttered. Rangarajan was rarely ever at a loss for words, but this time he hesitated due to his present disorientation.

With his cigarette finished, Yogi Ramsuratkumar picked up his hand fan and continued to study his subject more carefully. In a matter of moments, Rangarajan reported that he felt a current electrify the nerves in his body, and found himself quickly transported into another realm of consciousness. The master's words soon reverberated around him.

"You need not take medicine, but you can take honey; honey is not medicine!" said Yogi Ramsuratkumar.

An unknowing observer, one who knew nothing of Rangarajan's history or present condition, might have dismissed Ramsuratkumar's words as being an irrelevant bit of medical information. But, for the professor, the words were astounding. In them, he read with clarity that Ramsuratkumar somehow, impossibly, knew of his health situation, which under Mother Mayee's direction was being handled without traditional medical intervention, but essentially by the performance of puja and prayers (*agnihotra*).

The revelation, however, was only the first blow of Yogiji's powerful one-two punch. Before he could catch his breath and right himself, Rangarajan was leveled by the beggar's next words, these aimed in another direction. He asked the professor to remove his eyeglasses and to hand them over. The beggar took the glasses in his own hand and examined them carefully: "Is it not time to change the spectacles?" he asked Rangarajan, with apparent innocence.

The comment was not an innocent remark, however, and Rangarajan was skilled enough in the enigmatic ways of masters and gurus to recognize a question of much deeper import. The glasses, of course, are the instruments whereby our once distorted vision is corrected. What more appropriate metaphor for an internal metanoia than the change of one's eyeglasses?

Without hesitation, the professor responded, "Yes, it is time, Maharaj." It was the end of Round I, and the beggar had apparently scored a knockout.

The question itself served to open the professor, who proceeded to narrate the chronology of his spiritual search while the patient Godman merely listened. At the conclusion of his history, Rangarajan presented to Yogi Ramsuratkumar the first three issues of *Tattva Darsana*, which he had begun publishing in February of that same year.

Yogi Ramsuratkumar may already have been familiar with the professor's writings in this journal, but if so he never indicated it. He held the magazines reverently, carefully examining them, page by page. Such total attention as he gave to this periodical was the master's common way of handling books, letters, items from newspapers, that were handed to him. No gestures were casual in Yogi Ramsuratkumar's repertoire. No energies were wasted. He seemed, to many devotees, to be doing much more than simply reading what was given to him. Rather, he was literally absorbing the contents of a piece through the vibrations – the energy emanations – that everything contained.

Was it coincidental that the first issue of the *Tattva Darsana* was dedicated to Sri Aurobindo, the great patriot of India, and contained not only Aurobindo's picture but a picture of the Mother, Mirra? That Rangarajan would bring a reminder to Ramsuratkumar of the beggar's first "Father," during this initial visit, was another interesting presentiment to the relationship that would eventually flower between them. Pointing to one page in this first issue, the beggar indicated that Rangarajan should read it: "First Supramental manifestation, February 29, 1956, Wednesday, Sri Aurobindo Ashram, Pondy." Three times the professor was asked to read this same section. Then, with a twinkle in his eye and a burst of delighted laughter, Yogi Ramsuratkumar asked naughtily: "Did the first Supramental manifestation occur only in 1956?" More laughter.

The Godchild's humorous reference to the "first Supramental manifestation" was a telling bit of spiritual repartee and certainly revealed volumes to Rangarajan, who prior to that moment may never have questioned that particular reference. For those who have little familiarity with Sri Aurobindo or the Mother, this joke will make no sense. For those who are, Yogi Ramsuratkumar's playful mood might be offensive, taken as an insult in relationship to an event that bears such a preeminent status in the cosmology of Aurobindo and the Mother.

To make a complex issue exceedingly simplistic, Aurobindo and the Mother were both steeped in an evolutionary view of creation and humanity's role in it. What they worked for was "to bring the supramental, i.e., the divine Consciousness, down on Earth, to insert it into the earthly evolution and thus make the decisive evolutionary step possible by which one day a divinized species will be present on Earth in a material body."[11] Their writings are full of discussions of these core principles.

While Aurobindo and the Mother may each have liberally experienced the infusion of supramental force or energy within themselves, the actual descent of supermind in such a way as to make it

382

accessible to a larger segment of the population was something to which they directed monumental personal efforts. When Aurobindo died in 1950, the Mother continued this work with utmost seriousness, and in the early months of 1956, announced to her overjoyed disciples that, in fact, this "first" supramental manifestation had indeed taken place. The details of what that precisely meant were not entirely clear, and to this day continue to be a subject of debate and speculation.

Although Ramsuratkumar held his mentor and "Father," Aurobindo, and the Mother in the highest esteem, it was not beyond the beggar to proffer a question and initiate a humorous mood about anything. While we may not understand the full implications of the Godchild's joke, we may speculate that part of his role was to bring into question any kind of sensational declaration, or one's attachment to such a declaration. Maybe he was laughing at giving a temporal date and time to something that had, in fact, been happening for countless ages through the efforts of the great rishis, sages, and saints who had preceded Aurobindo. Maybe he was chuckling because his own experience testified to a living unity with that infused supermind since 1952, when he himself "died" at Ramdas's feet. Maybe he was merely rattling the cage for Rangarajan, who had probably studied this work seriously.

Whatever the full meaning of his response, Yogi Ramsuratkumar's lila had its impact on the professor. With this comment as an icebreaker for Rangarajan, something else was able to flow. For hours, then, the two men shared their views on spiritual and political topics. For all of his advanced studies, Rangarajan was overwhelmed by the brilliance of the rag-draped beggar who sat before him. "I realized that I was sitting in front of the Himalayas of spiritual wisdom and experience," he commented years later, in writing of this auspicious encounter.[12]

When, in the midst of his enthusiasm for Yogiji's apparent greatness, Rangarajan begged the favor of being given permission to write a small biographical sketch about him, the Godman responded, "Why should you write about this beggar? What is there to write?" His laughter then erupted like a volcano. Yogi Ramsuratkumar got up, moved about his room among the disheveled papers and books, and handed the professor a small but weighty pile, which included the biography by Caylor Wadlington, several pamphlets written (about Yogiji), souvenir booklets of his recent Jayanti celebrations, and two books of poems written about him by the renowned Tamil writer, Ki. Va. Jagannathan. These were to be gifts to the professor, who received them with gratitude, but not before the master had picked up a pen and autographed them, "some with his name and some with my name," Rangarajan noted with astonishment.

"There is nothing in the name. Both are same!" the master declared, and in those few words instructed his new admirer in a principle that was to characterize their work together. While Yogi Ramsuratkumar would always and forever be the master, and Rangarajan, like the thousands of others who had come to the beggar's feet, would forever be the devotee or disciple, the essential nature of their relationship was contextualized in nonseparation from God. In the beggar's living experience all was one. Everything was Father.

राम

What transpired between the great one and his visitor was felt to be enormously significant to Rangarajan, and in the blush of his infatuation he asked Yogi Ramsuratkumar for initiation. For the Indian seeker, this meant that the initiator formally whispers a mantra into the recipient's ear, three times, and the recipient then repeats the whispered mantra three times, orally. Such a ceremony binds the master to the new disciple in a particular way. But, true to his form, Yogi Ramsuratkumar, who always honored whatever spiritual path a seeker had already defined for themselves, refused elegantly. "Why?" he asked graciously, but firmly nonetheless. "You have already got initiation from a great man [referring to Rangarajan's relationship to Swami Chinmayananda]. Continue your practices, my Father blesses you!"

Ramsuratkumar rose, at last, walked to the door, and proceeded out onto the road. Rangarajan followed. When the professor again prostrated to the Godchild's feet, he was rewarded with a final gesture. Yogi Ramsuratkumar, with all the tenderness of a mother unwilling to let go of a child who must leave for school, took hold of Rangarajan's hands and pulled him down to sit beside him on the low front steps of the house, immediately at the roadway. No words were exchanged in this parting encounter. Nothing but a silent exhilaration in the devotee, and a sense that the master was absorbed in samadhi, yet still holding fast to his admirer's hands. How much time passed in this way, Rangarajan was unable to report. In the presence of the Godchild, time was elusive at least, eternal at best.

राम

Rangarajan's passionate dedication to the revival of India as a spiritual force was a cause that was close to the heart of Yogi Ramsuratkumar long before the two had met. And, over the many years of their association, the master and the disciple shared their mutual patriotic concerns and interests. In an article titled, "A Beggar Who Owns the World," published in a 1990 issue of *Hinduism Today*, the authors (Ma Navaratham and husband Thiru, who had met Yogi Ramsuratkumar and were impressed with his energy, his wisdom, and his "fire") had this to say of the master's passion and the professor's role in promoting it:

> Yogi Ramsuratkumar has no organization but his voice echoes loudly in the pages of *Tattva Darsana*, journal published by Professor Rangarajan, founder of Sister Nivedita Academy...*Hinduism Today*, via Professor Rangarajan, was able to catch the Yogi for a few candid thoughts. He [Yogi Ramsuratkumar] quickly warned: "Aping false values which do not fit into the Indian environment" is Hinduism's biggest challenge today. Resonating tradition, he asserted, "Humility, selflessness and respect for others in the discharge of duties is the highest spiritual quality, and children – raised properly, physically and mentally – are any culture's greatest asset." Though his skin is wrinkled and his hair is white, this yogi has fire in his eyes and when he launches into "The need for the day is 'aggressive Hinduism,'" you realize this is not a beggar begging; this is a king giving orders.[13]

Ramsuratkumar's cry for "aggressive Hinduism" was an echo of the words of Swami Vivekananda and Sister Nivedita, who, along with Aurobindo, Subramania Bharati and others, were dedicated to the ideals of spiritual nationalism. Those who prefer their religion and their politics kept in separate domains (like most Westerners) might be put off to discover how intimately connected these were for Yogi Ramsuratkumar and many other great visionaries and saints in India. It would be easy to hear "aggressive Hinduism" and conjure up images of a fundamentalist crusade or a jihad, and certainly this was the spirit of some who took up the cause, using it as a source of divisiveness among religions and nations. However, this is never the interpretation that one finds in Yogi Ramsuratkumar's conversations on the subject, many of which were recorded by Rangarajan in *Tattva Darsana* over the years.

"Aggressive Hinduism," in the beggar's words, unlike even that interpretation of some of its most noble proponents, had no application to proselytizing for him. Rather, in reading the words of Yogi Ramsuratkumar we see that it was purely a call to revivify the deep and God-centered wisdom that had characterized Mother India from her earliest ages, when it was the prerogative of the great sages and saints to determine her sociocultural and political direction.

Unafraid to lay his politics on the line, Ramsuratkumar again and again attempted to inspire nationalistic pride by calling his devotees and visitors to the recognition that India was, is, and would always be in the hands of his Father, and under the protection and guidance of her saints. In his words:

> Swami Ramdas, My Master, is one among the brightest stars of the whole universe. He will guide us in the way in which He wants us to serve our Nation, Beloved Country, Our Country. Our Nation will prosper in every field of activity.[14]

> He (Lord Krishna) is the King, Ruler, Great Politician of this country, India, my Land, my Home land, My Father's Land, Holy Land, This Beggar's Heart, Dharma bhoomi, Punya Bhoomi, Veda Bhoomi, the Play ground of the Beggar. My Father knows how to make us to play politics, the game, and

how to make India flourish, forever, in all aspects. Nothing to worry. The Land of Sages, Seers and Beggars like me will always exist – this Holy Land, India.

Sri Rama, Jaya Rama, Jaya Jaya Rama!
Jaya Jaya Rama Jaya Jaya Rama![15]

Rangarajan affirmed his master's political and spiritual interface in this way:

Yogi Ramsuratkumar is indeed one of the greatest saints of the order of Sri Aurobindo, Bhagavan Ramana and Papa Ramdas, that India has produced in the modern age. But it should not be forgotten that, like all of them, he was also a patriotic son of Mother India…

Before the initiation of this sadhu [Rangarajan is referring to himself] by Yogi Ramsuratkumar [which occurred in 1988], we had many times discussed…about Indian politics, especially the Freedom Struggle, the role of revolutionaries, about Netaji Subhas Chandra Bose [considered by many to be a great patriot; elected President of the Indian National Congress in 1938], this sadhu's work on *Vande Mataram* to which the great national leader Acharya J.B. Kripalani has written a Preface, the role of the Congress Party in the past and present, and on Rashtriya Swayamsevak Sangh [an organization of patriotic volunteers dedicated to the service of the Motherland, founded in 1925].

In those moments we had the opportunity to see the burning embers of patriotism in his [Yogi Ramsuratkumar's] heart still flaming out.[16]

Yogiji's hero, Mahatma Gandhi, had called for a return to the use of the simple spinning wheel to counteract the forces of British industrialism that, in Gandhi's view, were ruining the economic substructure of the nation. "[T]he message of the spinning wheel is much wider than its circumference," Gandhiji wrote. "Its message is one of simplicity, service to [humankind], living so as not to hurt others…"[17]

Yogi Ramsuratkumar appealed for a similar nonreliance on some of the technology of our day. In his mind, our attachment to computers was a source of self-alienation. "Our real work is not to produce engineers and computer scientists," he had chided, referring to the work of the Yogi Ramsuratkumar Youth Wing begun as an offshoot of the Sister Nivedita Academy. "Our goal is higher. If man depends on the computer, the mind will deteriorate."[18]

राम

A series of tender interactions between Yogi Ramsuratkumar and Kumari Nivedita and Vivekanandan (Vivek), the two children of Professor Rangarajan and his wife Bharati, reveals the texture of the master's "aggressive Hinduism" and the way in which it was expressed in his dealings with his friends and devotees.

In 1988, on *Guru Poornima*, the universal celebration of the guru's presence in the world, Rangarajan and his two children made the trip by bus from their home in Madras to Tiruvannamalai to offer their obeisance to the beloved beggar who was, by then, a regular and dynamic part of their lives. It was a busy day for the master, a day full of visitors, and toward the end of their time together Yogi Ramsuratkumar sent away all except the Rangarajan family and Dr. Radhakrishnan, another devotee. Turning to the doctor, Yogi Ramsuratkumar began the lila: "You may think that this beggar ignores you and concentrates on these two children."

Dr. Radhakrishnan immediately replied, "No, Maharaj, they belong to the younger generation and it is right you concentrate on them."

Yogiji jovially remarked, affirming a special connection to these young people, "You know, Vivek and Nivedita come here very often and they have become my friends. You people do not come often."

Focusing his attention, Yogi Ramsuratkumar spoke directly to Vivek, who was seventeen years old at the time. "Your father has taken up man-making work. You want to become an engineer. And Nivedita [who was fifteen] wants to become a computer scientist. What sort of engineer you would like to become? Man-making or machine-making?"

Nivedita and Vivek Rangarajan with younger friend (left to right)
and Yogi Ramsuratkumar, 1988

Yogi Ramsuratkumar's own words inspired him to burst into rich laughter. He was quite hilariously enjoying himself and his young guests. So, before the young man had a chance to reply, he asked again: "Would you like to become a man-making engineer?"

"Yes, I would like to be so," answered Vivek.

A moment later the master, who had retired temporarily inside his house, returned with a favorite book, *Lectures from Columbo to Almora*, by Swami Vivekananda. Opening the book to the chapter titled "The Sages of India," he asked Rangarajan to read it. The professor began: "The sages of India have been almost innumerable, for what has the Hindu nation been doing for thousands of years except producing sages?"

Hearing these first few lines, Yogi Ramsuratkumar turned to the two teenagers and remarked: "See, Vivekananda [referring to the book's author] speaks about man-making work."

Vivek and Nivedita kept themselves attentive as their father continued, at the beggar's request, to read the complete chapter. When it was done, Yogi Ramsuratkumar again spoke: "Our work is not to produce engineers and computer scientists. Our country is concerned only with producing sages. For thousands of years, only producing sages has been our aim. When we know that our goal is God, why should we hanker after other things and waste our precious time?"

As if to keep the mood around a serious subject deliberately light, the Godchild began to joke with the two teenagers: "Will your mother get angry if you go and tell her that this beggar wants you not to become machine-making engineers, but man-making? Will she say that this beggar wants her children also to become beggars like him, and not engineers and scientists, and [will she] ask you not to go to this beggar again?"

"No, no," the young people protested, even as Yogi Ramsuratkumar roared with laughter.

"Don't think this beggar is discouraging you from becoming engineers and scientists," Yogi Ramsuratkumar continued with more seriousness once again. "My Father will see that Vivekanandan gets a seat in engineering [this did in fact occur within a few months of Yogiji's declaration] and becomes a great engineer, and Nivedita becomes a computer scientist [which she did]. But remember that your goal is something higher. Your father has brought you up properly and put you in the right line. Do not forget the ideal. Becoming a scientist or an engineer is all secondary, the most important is God-realization. Understand?"

The young people nodded their agreement, and the instruction was sealed. A short time later, the whole company became absorbed with the master in the chanting of Ramnam.[19]

राम

In 1984, when the professor first met the beggar, Rangarajan's son Vivek was thirteen, and Nivedita was eleven. Because of the frequency of their visits, as Yogi Ramsuratkumar mentioned in 1988, he considered them friends (a very tender term of relationship), and enacted numerous lilas with these two bright young people, witnessing to his special regard for children in general, and these two in particular. As Rangajaran moved into more active work on behalf of the Ramnam Movement, starting in 1987, as directed by Ramsurat-kumar, it was as if the beggar adopted these two children with an even more solicitous regard.

One morning, Nivedita and Vivek and one devotee from South Africa, Sri Mahendra, came to see Bhagwan (the name by which they commonly referred to Yogi Ramsuratkumar) at Sannadhi Street. The beggar was busy so they were told to return at 4 P.M.

Because it was early in the day, they decided to walk to the top of the mountain, Arunachala, thinking they would have plenty of time before their appointment with the Godchild. About 3:30 P.M., however, they were still climbing down, and a torrential rain began, leaving the three completely drenched.

Since Yogi Ramsuratkkumar had given them an appointment at 4 P.M., and not wishing to be late, Vivek, Nivedita, and Mahendra did not take the time to change their clothes. Just as they were, soaked to the skin, they brought themselves to 90 Sannadhi Street.

"Nivedita, what is this? You are all drenched?" the Godchild said solicitously.

"Bhagwan, you have asked us to come at 4 o'clock, and we went to the mountain, and..." Nivedita narrated their story while Yogi Ramsuratkumar listened with great concern.

"What will Rangarajan think? He has sent his children here and they got drenched." He asked them whether they were feeling cold. He then went inside and brought out three Kashmiri shawls, giving one each to the three visitors.

With that, the master took the young people by the hand and, followed by Mahendra, left the house and walked down to the Udipi Brindavan, a boarding and lodging establishment opposite to the police station. Here Yogi Ramsuratkumar spoke personally to Sri Ramachandra Upadhyaya, the proprietor. "Get two sets of new clothes, and arrange some towels," the master directed Ramachandra, "and order them some food."

When the young devotees and Mahendra were fully taken care of, Yogi Ramsuratkumar finally returned them to their guest residence at 8 P.M.[20]

ONLY GOD

राम

In Hindu families today, the marriage of a daughter requires a huge financial burden. "You must have at least 500-600,000 rupees ($10,000 – $12,000 U.S.) on hand for the dowry. This dowry system is killing in India, and many girls remain unmarried because of that," Rangarajan explained.

When Nivedita completed one of her M.S. degrees she was invited to stay awhile (in December 1993) with Devaki Ma and other women at the residence known as Sudama House, where Yogi Ramsuratkumar lived from 1993-1998.

One day during this month when Rangarajan was visiting his master, the beggar told him that Nivedita's stay was over and that he should bring her back to Madras and "arrange the marriage of Nivedita."

Such a direct instruction was surprising to all who heard it, as Nivedita was not inclined to be married at the time. Even Devaki Ma, who was generally so circumspect in her comments, was surprised enough to question: "Bhagwan, if she is not interested in marriage, why do you compel her to get married?"

"Devaki, you don't know," replied Yogi Ramsuratkumar with great vigor. "Mother Bharati wants her daughter to be married, and she will be married!"

Rangarajan, as much as everyone else, was again surprised. He knew that his wife had never breathed a word of her concern or her desire to the Godman. Nonetheless, he knew that Bharati, like most Indian mothers, had been extremely concerned about their daughter's marital status. As was the custom, she had quietly begun to investigate certain horoscopes, looking for likely suitors, a good son-in-law whose planetary influences were compatible and complementary with those of their daughter.

As he knew human nature so well, and the longings of his devotees so intimately, Yogi Ramsuratkumar obviously knew what was in Bharati's mind, as well as what would be of benefit to Nivedita. "Bharati wants her daughter to get married, and her wish must be fulfilled," the beggar said again.

Rangarajan smiled at hearing this and jovially remarked to his master that if he wanted this to happen, *he* (Yogiji) would have to arrange it. Bhagwan laughed uproariously. "If my daughter was to get married it would be Bhagwan's business, not my own business," Rangarajan explained years later.

Yogiji he then said, thoughtfully, that he would ask this request of his Father. With that, the discussion was ended.

Fifteen days later, during a session of Ramnam chanting held at Rangarajan's apartment in Madras, an unknown businessman appeared at the door, attaché case in hand. Assuming that the man was here for the ceremonies, he was shown a seat in the midst of the other devotees who packed the room. Bharati, Rangarajan's wife, recognized him as she looked on from the kitchen. She was horrified, and immediately told her husband that the unknown guest was the father of a boy whose horoscope she had come across that day. The man had been so impressed by Nivedita's natal chart that he had made the trip to Chennai to meet the young woman. Nivedita, on this evening, was playing the harmonium and chanting Ramnam, as she normally did. Only when the services were completed did Rangarajan introduce himself to the stranger.

"I have seen your daughter's horoscope in Bangalore," the man explained, "and it is very much matching that of my son's. So, I feel that this girl is the best choice for my son."

Realizing the delicacy of the situation, and the common custom, Rangarajan had no choice but to speak honestly. Picking up the begging bowl and stick that he carried as signs of his vocation, he explained to the man in no uncertain terms that he was a sadhu, that he had lived as a renunciate since 1964, and that he therefore had nothing to give as a dowry for his daughter.

"I have given her the best education, she has two post-graduate degrees, because my master has wanted my children to be educated. But there is no money for a dowry. So, you should think twice," Rangarajan cautioned the prospective father-in-law, "whether you would like to take a bride from a poor man's house."

The suitor's father was unperturbed: "No, I want such a girl. I know that your family is blessed by Yogi Ramsuratkumar, and I want a girl from such a family." Such a response was completely miraculous, considering the longstanding custom. Only the blessing of Yogi Ramsuratkumar would have made a groom's parents amenable to such a radical violation of protocol.

Things moved very quickly from that point. Within a few days, the man had brought over his wife and the son to meet Nivedita and her family. Both of them said, "We would like to accept this girl. We will go ahead with arrangements for the marriage."

Knowing that Yogi Ramsuratkumar's hand guided every aspect of the drama of their lives, Rangarajan made it clear that before any definite answer was given, the situation must be brought to the beggar's feet. And so both families and the prospective couple made the journey to Tiruvannamalai. Coincidentally, and as it turned out fortuitously, the day of their visit happened also to be the young suitor's birthday. His name was Ramesh.

As they all sat in the Godman's presence, Rangarajan, in an unplanned gesture of generosity, removed a special mala from his own neck. The beads had been blessed by Mataji Krishnabai and were, in fact, a gift from Ramsuratkumar that Rangarajan had constantly worn for many years. Placing the mala in his master's hand, the sadhu asked Yogiji to present it as a birthday gift to Ramesh.

Yogi Ramsuratkumar, for whom nothing was casual, held the sacred artifact silently for some time, and then addressed the boy. "Ramesh," he said, "Rangarajan wants to present this mala to you, but it is blessed by Mataji Krishnabai and it is meant for the saying of Ramnams. If this beggar gives it to you, will you do Ramnams daily, regularly, systematically?"

For one minute, the young man was silent. He looked down, as the mood in the room became suddenly tense. When at last he looked up, Ramesh addressed Yogi Ramsuratkumar with clarity and candor: "Bhagwan, I don't want to tell a lie to you. I am an inspector in my work. I am called to duty at all different times. Sometimes I have to go early in the morning, sometimes late at night. I can't guarantee to you that I will do this type of sadhana every day."

Professor Rangarajan was aghast. In his mind the deal was off! Such a response, he imagined, would surely be an indication to the beggar that this boy was not the right one for Nivedita. "It seemed that he was saying that he was not so much interested in devotion," the professor explained. "And my wife and I were both upset."

Yogi Ramsuratkumar gently handed the mala back to Rangarajan saying: "You keep this with you, it is not needed." Then, for the next ten minutes, the beggar engaged the young man about his work, carrying on a most pleasant conversation. When their exchange was concluded, Yogi Ramsuratkumar asked Rangarajan to come outside with him so that the two could speak privately. Without hesitation the master declared: "Rangarajan, this *is* the right boy for Nivedita."

What had impressed Yogi Ramsuratkumar was exactly the thing that had upset Rangarajan. The boy's willingness and courage to tell the truth in front of the guru *and* the two families was indicative of a man of character. Such a quality was not to be easily dismissed.

Nivedita and Ramesh were married in September 1995. Yogi Ramsuratkumar gifted the young couple generously. Many other gifts of money and help were also forthcoming in ways completely unexpected. In telling all the stories of these events, Rangarajan continually affirmed, "It was all my master's grace that was accomplishing this."

राम

"This beggar needs the flesh, blood, and bone of Vivek and Nivedita for my Father's work. No more blood donations!" Yogi Ramsuratkumar spoke boldly and firmly to Rangarajan's son Vivekanandan. The circumstances surrounding this bold declaration by the master to his young devotees are recounted by Vivek.

The Yogi Ramsuratkumar Youth Association, of which I am a part, had organized a blood donation camp at Chennai. I was among the first to offer blood in that camp. During our visit to Tiruvannamalai subsequently, Yogiji was told of the same by my father. Yogiji then asked me to sit nearby him and asked me for more details – as from where the blood was taken, what they did in the process and how much was drawn and so on. He in fact showed his coconut shell and asked if it was of that capacity. He then looked intensely at the point from which the blood was tapped. Later he started caressing me, much the same way a doting mother would do for her child. He then told me: "Don't do this again. There are a lot of people to do this kind of work. You don't have to do this." He conveyed that there were still better things deserving my attention.

I might have done the blood donation twice or thrice before this "warning" came about. Usually we don't indulge in any activity without taking his consent personally. I still am at a loss to understand how the situation unfolded to a point wherein Yogiji perforce had to advise me post-act rather than pre-empt it. I had violated his injunction once when I donated blood surreptitiously without involving the organization, or even anybody for that matter. That was brought about by my impulsiveness to do something very easily and without having to spend much time, effort, and the like. That was the time when I was hardly making any contribution to the organization in my capacity as an office bearer.

Were I to hazard a guess I would say that there were a few considerations behind the blanket ban for my indulging in such activities. One, I was not in the prime of my health and was just about okay with some minor problems to boot (e.g., hernia, frequent fainting, etc.). Second, he was concerned with the process-of-the-times of the "blood donation" – the care taken to preclude any possible contamination, or infection of the donor. Third, he wanted me not to concentrate and fritter away my energies on mundane things which can easily be done by anybody and everybody, and in a much better fashion.[21]

राम

From 1984 onward, Professor Rangarajan continued his efforts on behalf of his journal, *Tattva Darsana*, and other publications. But now, all his work had a special and unique focus – it was all blessed and directed by the hand of Yogi Ramsuratkumar, who made continual use of it.

A BANNER YEAR, 1986

 Lee Lozowick returned to India in early January 1986 after being away for seven years. It was his third trip to the Motherland, and this time he brought with him twenty-one of his students, including several children. Lee's community of devotees (called Hohm) had grown in the years since 1979, a formal ashram had been established in Arizona, U.S.A., in 1980, and Lee was anxious to bring his family and friends to the feet of the beggar who had so captivated his attention for the past ten years.

Arriving in Tiruvannamalai on January 19, Lee immediately set out with a group of nine to search for "Ram Ram," as they still affectionately called Yogi Ramsuratkumar. Rumors around the town informed them that the beggar did not want any visitors. "He said that he was no Teacher and that people should not waste their time," one of Lee's students wrote.[1]

These rumors were probably based in truth. In the years since Lee and his friends had last seen Yogi Ramsuratkumar, his notoriety had grown. He was often surrounded, nearly mobbed, by enthusiastic Indian followers wherever or whenever he would be spotted in the temple or in town, and it was becoming more difficult for him to venture into the streets. Probably more taxing still, the radiant beggar had become one more popular attraction to a constant stream of Western seekers. Rajneesh devotees from Poona and disciples of Sai Baba from Puttaparthi, among others, would stop by to "check him out" as they made their rounds of other interesting spots throughout India.

ONLY GOD

Visitors to Ramanashram, hearing of the enigmatic holy man who lived near the temple, were also curious to have his darshan. And then, worst of all, came the guru-shoppers, who flocked to India in search of some magical personage who would instantly solve all their pains with one look of transforming love.

Heading for the temple-car mandapam, where they had last had the master's darshan in 1979, Lee and his followers were directed to the building across the street. It was young Jai Ram, Yogiji's current attendant, who spoke with them that day and then led them to the front door of #90 Sannadhi Street, where, on their behalf, he knocked on the door.

A moment later, Yogi Ramsuratkumar himself had unlatched the gate on the verandah and stepped out into the street to see who had come calling. "The ten of us stood transfixed as he leaned on a railing and raised his right hand as if in benediction," wrote Steve Ball, who was seeing the Godchild for the first time. One of the women who had been on the previous trips was more effusive in her description:

> I could see the outline of the aura of Ram Ram as he opened the door. I began to cry. He looked much older. His head was uncovered – the first we'd seen this. His long matted hair flowed around him. He stepped outside where we were in a semi-circle...I felt much too shy to look him in the eyes so I looked at his feet...Once again, I dissolved in tears.[2]

This same visitor reported a sense of shock at somehow feeling estranged from Yogi Ramsuratkumar, and that he apparently had no idea who they were. She had met him twice before, and his somewhat bewildered reception was terrible for her. It struck her that he was not well, that this retreat to a house on Sannadhi Street was the way in which devotees were caring for the needs of their sick and aging master.

Lee immediately stepped forward, pranamed, and laid a bunch of bananas at the beggar's feet. Yogi Ramsuratkumar picked up the offering and handed one piece of the fruit to each of his guests. He asked their names and then invited the whole crowd into his house.

The conversation on that memorable evening touched on two primary subjects. First, on the use of his name, and secondly, on his protests that he had nothing to offer to them, or to anyone; that he was merely a beggar.

"Do you know this beggar's name?" the Godchild asked seriously when they were all quietly seated on the porch of the house.

"Ram Surat Kumar…Ram Ram," said Lee.

Yogi Ramsuratkumar considered the response for a moment and then inquired again, "Do you know this beggar's *full* name?"

When the group indicated that they did not know it, he told them: "Yogi Ramsuratkumar," spoken firmly and distinctly. Looking around at his attentive guests the Godchild asked again, "*Now* do you know this beggar's full name?"

"Yes," said Lee.

"Then say it back to me," said Yogiji.

"Yogi Ramsuratkumar," repeated Lee, articulating carefully.

"Yes. Important that you should know this beggar's full name." And then he rose, waving his hands above the heads of his visitors, blessing them, as he approached one after another asking them to pronounce his full name.

"Yogi Ramsuratkumar"…"Yogi Ramsuratkumar"…"Yogi Ramsuratkumar"…the Americans responded, individually and then in unison to this request, as if to burn the sacred name like a brand on their hearts. In future visits they would be privileged to sing this holy name, using it as a most sacred mantra. But today they were more like school children being instructed by their teacher to repeat something they should never forget.

One of the women recalled: "From this moment on we ceased to refer to our Friend as Ram Ram upon his request. He is now Yogi Ramsuratkumar. He teased and played with the children…I sat and wept. He seemed to enjoy my tears. Then he got up to show us out."

Throughout their exchanges it was obvious that Yogi Ramsuratkumar had no recollection of ever having met Lee before. The Godman was genuinely incredulous, shaking his head when being told that Lee had met him before in 1977 and 1979. Granted, it had been seven years, and certainly thousands of other visitors had made their way to the master's door in the meantime, yet, this complete lack of recognition still came as a surprise. Lee had, after all, been writing poetry to the beggar since the early 1980s. If Lee remembered that he had asked, in a poem written in 1983, to be less than a grain of sand on the road at the beggar's feet, he would have realized that he was getting his wish at last.

> When we went in 1986 I assumed that He had gotten the poetry I had written, and the letters…informing Him that he was my Teacher. That's probably the way I put it. I'm sure I didn't *ask*. I probably just said, "You're my Teacher," and I expected to readily be received with recognition.
>
> As it turned out, in 1986 He didn't remember me. I remember sitting with Him…and Him getting this confused look on His face and saying, "You're sure you were here before? You're sure I'm the one that you saw?" I'd say, "Yes, yes, absolutely positive." And He'd ask, "Now when were you here?" And I'd tell Him…, and He'd shake His head like, "I never forget anyone. Are you sure? What's your name again? Who were you with?" And He'd look very confused as if His forgetting anyone never happens and was very strange. He wasn't choking back his characteristic laugh. He was very serious, so I knew He didn't remember me at all.
>
> At the time I was very adamant about making some kind of formal connection in terms of getting some kind of recognition, a sign of my "discipleship." So it wasn't just that I wanted my side of a formal connection. I wanted the formal recognition – from Him.[3]

As the group rose to leave, following upon the beggar's indication, the Godchild asked each person their name once again. When he got to Lee, Yogi Ramsuratkumar asked, "What do you do?"

"I have a school?" the beggar inquired further.

"Hohm, H-O-H-M," Lee spelled out the name.

"What does it mean?" asked Yogiji.

"It doesn't mean anything," answered the American, who had always foresworn any esoteric significance to the title.

"Do you write?" Yogi Ramsuratkumar wanted to know, perhaps prophetically.

"Yes, I write some," Lee said. Although he had already written numerous books, he was clearly not wanting to exalt himself in the master's presence.

When the beggar's questions were all answered, Lee asked permission to return the next day and to bring other friends who had not yet had the saint's darshan.

"No, you have seen this beggar already. Why would you waste your time on this old sinner?" he said.[4]

One can speculate that now it was Lee's turn to be incredulous. After all, he had brought many of his students on this odyssey, intent on introducing them to his master. And now, in the presence of his own admiring entourage, Lee was being told that there was no need for him to return. Lee made one more attempt to explain the situation, hoping to sway the beggar's opinion in his favor, asking if the others who had not come before could return without him. When he realized that the Godchild was adamant in his request, however, Lee bowed, stunned perhaps, and certainly heartbroken, and moved to the door.

As the group assembled out on the street, Yogi Ramsuratkumar stood by the gate. They put their hands in *anjali mudra* (palm against palm, fingers raised) to pay their last respects to him, and the Godman waved farewell in return. Then, following Lee in silence and still reeling from the blessings they had received, they moved down the street.

It was Jeff Worab, one of Lee's students, who years later described the significance of that meeting. "Regardless of the fact that Yogi Ramsuratkumar had made it clear that we did not need to return, I had seen in Lee something I had never seen before. He was 'the devotee,' holding himself in relationship to the master with the most focused attention I had ever witnessed. He was demonstrating to us what dedication to one's spiritual master was all about."

That night, speaking to his group, Lee announced that they could do as they wished but that he would go begging outside the master's door, hopefully for just one more glimpse of him. The next morning, Jeff Worab reported a vivid dream. In the dream, Yogi

Ramsuratkumar had pointed out to him a whole intricate system of wiring that had been set up, everything in its rightful place. Jeff was given to understand that "the wiring was all completed, everything was already done." For him, it was obvious that, regardless of external appearances, the Godman's work was proceeding perfectly, according to some larger plan.

राम

Several accounts – from Lee himself and from other witnesses, and even from Yogi Ramsuratkumar (told two and a half years later) – tell the story of what happened on this day, January 20, 1986. Not all of them correspond in the precise details, as people remember things differently. But the essence of the communication made on this day remained the same for all.

"I went to the market that day and several times glanced down the alley toward Yogi Ramsuratkumar's home," wrote one of the women on the trip. "Each time I looked, there Lee sat in the scorching sun…waiting, about fifty-five feet from the master's door. He was dressed in white and wore a knitted orange cap on his head. Patiently he waited for many hours in the sun."

At some point, Yogi Ramsuratkumar's attendant came out and invited Lee into the house, but Lee refused, sensing that the offer was made merely out of pity. In his own words, Lee revealed what was occurring for him:

> I said to myself, "Darshan is Darshan; if I can't sit and talk with Him, then when other people come to see Him, I'll get His Darshan when He comes to the door." I was sitting there imagining the way it is with a Saint. I had this view that His sanctity was so great, that if I couldn't hang out and talk with Him, then I'd sit and look at Him when He came to the door. And if He didn't come to the door, then I'd *look* at the door, and I'd still get the transmission simply from that – because His Blessing power was so great. His transmission was so profound. So I sat and just stared at the door.

Maybe once an hour someone, always Indian, would come and knock at the door, and Yogi Ramsuratkumar would open it, look at them and look up – and I would be sitting there. As I remember it, He'd get this look of discomfort as if to say, "How am I going to handle this?" I was intent upon convincing Him that I was serious, although I had the idea that I might well be convincing Him only that I was crazy.[5]

राम

Not all the exchanges of this visit with the Americans were marked with the seriousness and curtness of Yogi Ramsuratkumar's interactions with Lee. One small group, including a young girl child, found the beggar's playful spirit ignited among them. As they sat on the porch of his house on Sannadhi Street, a five-year-old girl hid herself in the folds of her mother's sari, as she was shy in the presence of the beggar. Yogi Ramsuratkumar found her actions to be charming and began to play with her, looking at her warmly and asking, "What is your name?"

The little girl ran around to the other side of her mother's skirt and tried to hide herself again, while the Godchild laughed. Finally, catching her eye, slyly he asked, "Is it Gita? Is Gita your name?" The child still made no reply, but she seemed to be touched by the beggar's attention.

Two years later, this same child would write him a letter, enclosing a crayon-drawn picture of herself, her parents, and an image of him, the blessed man in rags. Three years after that, without prompting from anyone, she would boldly announce to all her friends that her name was now Gita. She would continue to use this name for life.

राम

Rabia Tredeau and her five-year-old daughter Anna were also on this 1986 trip. Since they were not in the first group with Lee and had experienced no formal darshan with the beggar, they decided to offer their prasad in their own way. A few days later, as they shopped in town, Rabia bought a handful of bananas. She and Anna stealthily yet playfully approached the steps of #90 Sannadhi Street and, seeing no one around, they pushed the bananas under the gate, bowed, turned and ran away. Giggling with enjoyment as they walked up the street, they were surprised to hear a voice calling from behind them. Turning back to look, they observed Yogi Ramsuratkumar standing at his front door, waving to them warmly. Following the beggar's indication, the two visitors ran back to his house. Smiling, Yogi Ramsuratkumar asked them their names, gifted them with a banana from the prasad they had left, blessed them, and sent them on their way.

राम

> Listen happily, whether he speaks to you
> warmly or with coldness…
> The master's anger and kindness
> are the thunderstorms and sunshine
> of life's new spring.
> From them, grows forth the rose
> of the disciple's sincerity and purity.

These words were written by the great Sufi mystic and saint, Rumi, in the thirteenth century. They describe the circumstances that most sincere disciples are called to bear at one point or another in their journey of sadhana. In writing of the relationship between master and disciple within the Sufi tradition, Dr. Javad Nurbakhsh summarized centuries of instructive wisdom when he counseled:

> If the master expels the disciple, he should not go far away; he should persist in remaining nearby, realizing that grace is received by attending to and serving the master.
>
> By the master's accepting and rejecting of the disciple, by testing him in a multitude of ways, the disciple is both shown to himself, and known by the master. In such circumstances, many a heart has cried out, "I will either die on his threshold or reach the goal."[6]

This mood of desperation, the wish to "die on his threshold or reach the goal," drove Lee Lozowick to maintain his solitary vigil outside Yogi Ramsuratkumar's door on this day in 1986. He had come too far, in terms of the surrender of his heart, to turn back now.

Lee's expectations, certainly, had been shattered, while his intentions were clearly being tested, and potentially purified. Regardless of the Godman's obvious lack of recognition and his avowal that he had nothing to offer Lee, the devotee knew that the ultimate relationship between master and devotee was an affair of the inner life. A week later, he would continue on with his trip through India, as planned, and two months after that he would return to the U.S. to resume his responsibilities there. But he would leave with a heart more thoroughly broken than before. And a part of this heart would remain in India, on the beggar's threshold, whether the master ever acknowledged it or not.

राम

Although Yogi Ramsuratkumar rarely left Tiruvannamalai, except for his occasional visit to Tapovanam to see his great friend and mentor Swami Gnanananda Giri, he made an unusual departure on February 26, 1986, to pay his respects to another longtime friend – a man he had met both in the 1960s and again in the 1970s.

H.H. Paramacharyal of Kanchipuram (born Swaminathan of Villupuram in 1894) was twenty-four years older than Yogi Ramsuratkumar, and the beggar revered him greatly. The man's full name and title was Kanchi Mahaswamigal, Jagatguru Sri Chandrasekara Saraswathi Swamigal, but Yogiji most often referred to him simply as "Paramacharya" (meaning exalted teacher) or "Kanchi Swami." For most of his life the former Swaminathan held the title of "Shankaracharya" of the Hindu religion (a post similar to that of the Pope for Catholics, except that there are five living Shankaracharyas at any one time). The name "Shankaracharya" derives from the eighth-century sage, Adi Shankara, who set up this system of spiritual governance and was widely recognized as the greatest authority on nondualist Vedanta.

His Holiness Paramcharyal of Kanchi:
Sri Chandrasekara Saraswathi Swamigal

During the early 1980s, a devoted Hindu man named Sri Chandramouli, who resided in Tiruvannamalai, had the frequent privilege of receiving the darshan of both Yogi Ramsuratkumar and H.H. Paramacharyal of Kanchipuram, separately. Moreover, he had the rare opportunity to serve the Shankaracharaya on one of the holy man's walking pilgrimages throughout Southern India.

Knowing Chandramouli's connection to Tiruvannamalai, the Paramacharyal would regularly ask him: "Have you met Visirimattai Swamigal?" – a variation on the name by which Yogi Ramsuratkumar was locally known. When Chandramouli would reply "yes," that he had seen the beggar, the Paramacharyal would become reflective,

sometimes closing his eyes for a few minutes, as if a silent communion were being enjoyed.[7]

Yogi Ramsuratkumar, for his part, would become ecstatic whenever the conversation included reference to the Paramacharyal, whom
he considered one of the greatest forces in contemporary Indian history. In later years, Justice T.S. Arunachalam, the chief administrator
of Yogi Ramsuratkumar's Ashram, wrote that: "he [Yogi Ramsurat-
kumar] had remarked many times…that the whole world owed a
deep debt of gratitude to Paramacharya, who was solely responsible
for the preservation of our Vedas and Culture."[8]

On December 1, 1985, Chandramouli was in Kanchipuram
receiving the blessings of the Paramacharyal when he was given a
direct order. The Kanchi Swamigal asked him to proceed to the local
Sri Ekambareswarar Temple, where he was to attend two Vedic ceremonies (*homas*), receive the prasad that was offered, carry it back to
Tiruvannamalai, and present it to Yogi Ramsuratkumar. This auspicious day was the Jayanti of the beggar, marking his sixty-seventh
year.

When Chandramouli finally reached Tiruvannamalai, it was
already 10 P.M., but the Godchild was not at his Sannadhi Street residence. After a bit of searching, he was located within the great temple surrounded by a group of devotees. Making his pranams to the
master, Chandramouli offered the prasad, explaining the Paramacharyal's hand in it. Yogi Ramsuratkumar received the gift and reverently placed it to his head. Then, after a few moments, he distributed
the offering to those who sat with him. "Paramacharya is always very
kind to this beggar," he would say in later years when describing their
interactions.

Three months later, on February 26, 1986, the two saints blessed
each other in person in a most unexpected way. The meeting happened again through the intermediary efforts of Chandramouli, who
was in Kanchipuram to receive the darshan of Sri Paramacharyal.
Uncharacteristically, on this occasion the Shankaracharya did not ask
about "Visirimattai Swami." Rather, he entrusted Chandramouli
with 500 rupees and directed him to return to Tiruvannamalai
immediately. There he was to hire a taxi and escort Yogi Ramsuratkumar to the town of Govindapuram, the site of the *jiva samadhi*

(ceremonial tomb) of a great saint – Bhagavan Nama Bodendra Swami.

His Holiness Bodendra Swami of Govindapuram had also served as a pontiff (Shankaracharya) of Kanchipuram and was formally addressed as "Bhagavan Nama" because of his profound devotion to the sacred name of Ram. Although Bodendra died nearly three hundred years ago, it is claimed that, even today, those with the ear of the heart can hear the sound of Ramnam reverberating around his grave at this sacred site.

Yogi Ramsuratkumar's overwhelming devotion to the name of God, particularly to Ramnam, was undoubtedly the motivation for the Paramacharyal's surprising directive. It was a profound honor that the Paramacharyal was paying to the beggar in giving him the opportunity for this escorted pilgrimage. Yet, when informed of the plan, Yogi Ramsuratkumar did not immediately comply. In fact, it took him a bit of time to decide what to do.

We can speculate that he was momentarily stunned by the strange request, especially since he rarely left sight of Mount Arunachala to travel anywhere. One sannyasin from Tiruvannamalai claimed that Yogiji had actually made a vow at one time never to leave sight of Mount Arunachala, which would account for his willingness to visit Tapovanam (which still allowed a view of the sacred mountain), but nowhere else.[9] Although this vow is unconfirmed, it seems that other factors were at play as the Godman contemplated his plan of action. Yogi Ramsuratkumar remained silent for a long while. Undoubtedly he closed his eyes and took interior counsel from his Father, to whom all and every gesture was devoted.

On that day, S. Govindarajan (a district judge) and his daughter were present in the master's darshan. As Yogiji still hesitated in his final decision about the proposed trip, he turned to Govindarajan and asked, "Are you free to come along with this beggar, wherever this beggar goes?"

Surprised, but ready to abide by his guru's wishes, Govindarajan said yes.

"Both of you should be with this beggar; it may be one week or ten days or even a month. Are you ready?"[10]

Still stunned, but still eager to comply, the man and his daughter both affirmed that they would do whatever was asked. Obviously it was the sign that Yogi Ramsuratkumar was waiting for. Their readiness to serve him moved the beggar into action. Addressing the messenger, Chandramouli, Yogi Ramsuratkumar stated, "Wherever Acharyal [Paramacharyal] is, that is Govindapuram for this Beggar."

It was a bold statement, indicative of Yogi Ramsuratkumar's ultimate clarity that time and space were transcended by the all-pervasive presence of God. It was also a tremendous compliment paid to the Paramacharyal. The beggar was clearly asserting that this man held not only the formal lineage transmission of Bodendra, but was in fact his living artifact – a beacon of spiritual force, identical to that available in Govindapuram.

Yogi Ramsuratkumar was then ready to go. The judge was directed to gather up whatever fruits were available in the house, put them in a bag, and carry them. Taking his key, the beggar locked the house and led the whole party to the nearby taxi stand. When everyone was seated in the car, Yogiji finally instructed the driver, Ravi (who was also a close devotee), to take them not to Govindapuram, as expected, but to Kanchipuram, and to get there by sunset! (After sunset the Paramacharyal will usually not receive visitors.) It was about 3 P.M. at the time.

The trip from Tiruvannamalai to Kanchipuram is a journey of three to four hours, and Ravi reported that Yogi Ramsuratkumar essentially kept silent for the entire ride.[11] At one point, passing through a small town, the beggar probably read the thoughts of his companions, as he remarked that they could get down from the car to have food or coffee if necessary.

"This beggar doesn't want anything to eat or drink," the Godchild informed them, and his companions took note.[12] Certainly he was expressing the one-pointed focus of his work. He had a task to do and a destination to reach. While any delays would be a source of frustration for him, his concern for the needs of others was always poignant.

Despite the fact that the car had to be adjusted by a mechanic along the way, they reached their destination before the sun set.

409

ONLY GOD

Arriving at the Kanchipuram Sri Mutt (the spiritual center or temple), Chandramouli was understandably nervous as he approached the sacred residence of the Paramacharyal, where he announced the arrival of Yogi Ramsuratkumar to the Paramacharyal's attendant. After all, he had been given a specific task to do – to take Yogi Ramsuratkumar to Govindapuram – and he obviously had not done it. Nonetheless, with the assurance of the beggar, he had surrendered himself to the turn of events.

Reports vary as to what happened next. Chandramouli says that "when Swamiji (Yogi Ramsuratkumar) entered the darshan hall, Paramacharyal got up and came close to Him and stood in front of Him. They looked at each other and raised their arms, palms facing out. They stood like that for a few minutes."[13] But Judge Govindarajan recounts that the Kanchi Swami, in an unusual break of routine, actually came out of the darshan hall and met Yogiji where the beggar waited.[14]

A third report, this one given by the sadhu who told of Yogi Ramsuratkumar's apparent "vow" not to leave Arunachala, adds additional details that may have been unaccounted for by those present. This sadhu, who was trained within the lineage of the Shankaracharya, claimed that part of Yogiji's dilemma in approaching the Kanchi Mutt may have been that only those who had freshly bathed were "legally" permitted into these auspicious precincts. Also, it was customary for a man to remove his shirt or upper body covering in the presence of the Shankaracharya there.[15] When the Shankaracharya himself left the official darshan hall and came outside, he anticipated and therefore solved any problems that his revered guest, or their witnesses, might have been having. Because Yogi Ramsuratkumar didn't actually enter the precincts, he could not be criticized for breaking the strict protocol that surrounds any Shankaracharya. If this story is true, it would testify once again to the remarkable way in which circumstances often conspired to support the beggar's intentions, as he was surrendered completely to the will of his Father.

About twenty devotees and attendants from the Mutt were present at this auspicious meeting, which Chandramouli claimed was a "Holy Meeting of…Two Great Saints of This Kali Yuga." Judge Govindarajan recalled that these other devotees also came out and

410

prostrated to Yogi Ramsuratkumar. As they did do, the beggar asked the judge to tell them that it was not proper to do this on the premises of the Great Acharya.

Ravi remembered that the two men exchanged gifts of shawls and that they spoke very little. Judge Govindarajan recalled that the fruits he was asked to bring were presented to the renowned Swami as prasad.

"This beggar prostrated before Paramacharya," Yogi Ramsuratkumar explained in later years. The Paramacharyal then remarked that his humble guest belonged to Surya Vamsa, the lineage of the sun god Surya. Yogiji said nothing. Paramacharyal, however, told those present that Yogi Ramsuratkumar *was* "a descendent of the Sun."[16]

It was a most interesting reference, one which is augmented by a sweet story told by Devaki Ma. One day, as she sat outside with Yogi Ramsuratkumar, he pointed to a place in the sky and declared, "Krishna was coming from this planet." Then he pointed to the sun and said, "This beggar comes from there!"[17]

An instructive postscript to this story of the meeting of these two saints is that Yogi Ramsuratkumar refused to accept the 500 rupees that had been sent for the use of the taxi rental. Instead, he paid Ravi from his own pocket. Yogiji instructed Chandramouli to return the money to the Kanchipuram Mutt, noting that while it had been sent for one purpose, he had used the taxi for a different trip and had therefore not obeyed the Paramacharyal.

Yogi Ramsuratkumar consistently witnessed to integrity in all things. In this case, he also reaffirmed that one should pay one's own way in this work.

राम

H.H. Paramacharyal Sri Chandrasekara Saraswathi attained mahasamadhi on January 8, 1994, but his memory was always kept alive by Yogi Ramsuratkumar. When the beggar's ashram was constructed in the mid-1990s, the first image hung upon the walls was a picture of the Paramacharyal. For a long time, in fact, it was the only artifact to receive a place of honor. Regularly, when flower garlands were offered by devotees to Yogi Ramsuratkumar, he would say, "Kanchi Swami," and indicate that the garland should instead be offered to the Parmacharyal's image. The Godchild also directed that an oil lamp should be lit before this shrine and kept burning at all times. It still burns.

One more expression of the beggar's extreme regard for H.H. Paramacharyal concerned his use of a prayer-song composed by His Holiness. On October 23, 1966, this particular piece was presented in the Hall of the United Nations, New York City, sung by Srimathy M.S. Subblulakshmi.[18] The beautiful invocation was an urgent call for peace in the world. It was also a teaching about the nature of such peace, which develops through the cultivation of friendship – a subject that the Paramacharyal and Yogi Ramsuratkumar had deeply lived and joyously shared.

"Maitreem Bhajata akhilah ridjaitree..." the song begins. It is translated into English as:

> *Cultivate friendship which will conquer all hearts; look upon others as thyself.*
> *Renounce war; forswear competition; give up aggression on others which is wrong.*
> *Wide Mother earth, our Mother, is here ready to grant us all our desires.*
> *We have the Lord, our Father, compassionate to all.*
> *Ye peoples of the World, restrain yourselves, give, be kind.*
> *May all people be happy and prosperous.*
> *May all people be happy and prosperous.*
> *May all people be happy and prosperous.*

For many years before his death in 2001, Yogi Ramsuratkumar directed that this song be sung – often several times – during his breakfast meetings and formal darshans. And to this day, on the beggar's ashram this song concludes every kirtan, its words emblazoned in the minds and hearts of devotees and visitors alike. "Cultivate friendship...be kind" we are enjoined. "May all people be happy and prosperous" we pray.

A Banner Year, 1986

राम

On December 27, 1986, exactly eleven months after Lee Lozowick left Yogi Ramsuratkumar's side not knowing if he would ever
return, a middle-aged and well-educated woman arrived at the beggar's door in great distress. For nearly four years she had spent sleepless nights, despairing that the longing of her heart would ever be fulfilled. Now, as she knocked on the grillwork of the Sannadhi Street
house, she held her breath in anticipation. A moment later she
looked into the eyes of an old man whom she had never seen before
but whom she recognized immediately. "It is impossible for ordinary
people like me to describe...the Divine Resplendence which surpassed the unkempt hair and soiled garb of Bhagavan. That wonder
called Yogi Ramsuratkumar..." Devaki wrote years later as part of her
Introduction to a book written in Tamil about this one who would
become her master; the one to whom her life would be completely
and utterly surrendered.

Devaki was born on January 4, 1952, in Thanjavur, Tamil Nadu,
of middle-class Brahmin parents (S. Ranganathan and Sundaravalli).
She was the seventh of nine children. Well-educated, with an
advanced degree in physics (Master of Philosophy), at the time of her
historic pilgrimage to Tiruvannamalai in 1986 she was senior lectur-
er in physics at Sri Sarada College in Salem, South India. Yet, despite
her accomplishments and position, Devaki wanted something more
–"she was devoted to Lord Krishna from childhood," and she longed
to devote her life to God. Her own words tell this wondrous story.

> Many a day and night I have shed tears and wept profusely,
> wandering in search of a great preceptor, a self-realized soul.
> I have spent sleepless nights for about four years, undertak-
> ing continuous travels with a yearning heart in search of a
> Ramakrishna, a Ramana Maharshi, in whose perception,
> contact and service I could dissolve myself. Little did I real-
> ize at that time that the Ideal Man whom I was searching in
> Uttar Kashi, Gangotri and Brindavan was strolling very near
> as a Godchild in the premises of Arunachaleswara temple in

413

Tiruvannamalai at a distance of just four hours journey from Salem.

In October 1986, when I was preparing for the M. Phil examination in Madras Presidency College, a fellow student who had knowledge of astrology predicted: "You will get soon a great man as your preceptor. Your life will totally change thereafter. A very rare opportunity is awaiting you!" To me who wondered in disbelief, even when I heard about our Bhagavan, a distressful thought came and veiled my eyes: "How many great men have I seen and prostrated before. Still the mind is not in control. Love doesn't spring up within."

Yet, unable to control my yearning, I went to Ramanashram, along with two colleagues, during Christmas holidays (1986). It was about 7:00 P.M. when we reached the Ashram. Due to power failure, the lights were off and it was all darkness. My heart broke when I could not see, in the dim light of the oil lamp, the picture of Sri Ramana which was placed in the meditation hall of the Ashram into which I entered.

"Oh Sri Ramana! Is there darkness here too? Will I never see in my lifetime a god like you or Sri Ramakrishna? Will there be no light in my life?" I waited in distress and, lo!, in the next two minutes, the power came splashing light everywhere. I felt as though the merciful eyes of Sri Ramana were uttering something! Bliss surged in the heart.

I had the courage and good fortune of knocking at the doors of that house near the temple car, on the Sannadhi street, only in the evening of 27th December 1986, though I had reached Tiruvannamalai three days earlier, on 24th itself. (Later I came to know that December 27th was the sacred Sannyasa Day of Swami Ramdas, the Guru of Bhagavan [Yogi Ramsuratkumar]).

It was a pleasant sight never before seen by me when that Divine Person opened the doors and came and stood before me. My mind rolled and fell at His feet. Without knowing the reason, tears trickled down my eyes. It is impossible for ordinary people like me to describe so beautifully as Sri T.P.

Meenakshisundaram has done in his *"Sri Ramji Akaval"* (*Hail Sri Ramji*), the Divine Resplendence which surpassed the unkempt hair and soiled garb of Bhagavan.

That wonder called Yogi Ramsuratkumar took us inside the house and made us sit. There were some other devotees too. He came and sat before me and asked in a compassionate voice, "Do you want to say anything to this beggar?" The same eyes that I saw in the picture of Sri Ramana three days earlier! The same compassion and kindness! The same light!

Controlling my tears, I said slowly, "I want to see God."

"Oh! Devaki wants to see God!" He spoke aloud and, after a minute's silence, continued, "Devaki will see God. She is a pure soul. Devaki will see God!"

My colleague told Him: "Swami, we do not know whether we are pure or not. Because these words come from your mouth, from this moment we have become pure."

That's all! With a big hum, with face turned into red and eyes sparkling light, raising both His hands, He blessed us continuously for ten minutes. All the three of us sat there spellbound, experiencing a vibration in the body and immersed in a Divine feeling. When He came out and saw us off, our mind became light and a divine peace reigned over it. There was a sense of fulfillment that we had stumbled upon something which we were searching and searching through births.

The next day, in the early morning, when a lady, who had accompanied me to Tiruvannamalai, and I were waiting for a bus in front of Ramanashram, a person looking like a beggar came out of the Dakshinamurthy temple which was on the opposite side and rushed towards us. My friend, who got scared, moved a little away. When I stood motionless, the man, who rushed toward us, stood a little away from me, perambulated me and ran back into the temple. This amusing incident seemed to be significant.

However, for the next fifteen days, I was immersed in such an intense peace that I was not able to think about anything. A peace that was not affected by happiness, sorrow, disappointment, anger or anything else. Everything that happened around seemed to be scenes in a dream. Attending to the classes or engaging myself in the college work was more brisk than ever. Those subtle theories in Physics, which required intense study for an hour, could be understood even by a cursory glance for 10 minutes! Tremendous change! The peace was so natural that even the change was not cognised!

Now and then the face of the Swami would appear before the mind's eye. A blissful sweetness will pervade. And then intense peace! The greatness of this experience could be realized only when this peace started waning and old habits started raising again their heads. I was able to understand what had happened to me only when once again anger, weaknesses, pleasure, disappointment, inefficiency, etc., started gripping me again. Mind felt such agony like that of a calf separated from the cow. A burning feeling drove me again and again to Yogeeswara.[19]

राम

Once she had found the one whom she had searched for so desperately, Devaki was not about to let him go. On that night in late December 1986, the entire focal point of her life had shifted. Although she continued to live and work in Salem, maintaining the high-profile professorship that she had held before meeting the beggar, Devaki's heart was lost. It lay at the feet of Yogi Ramsuratkumar, the Godchild of Tiruvannamalai.

Now, instead of enjoying her weekends as times of rest and preparation for her classes, Devaki would regularly, often weekly, make the four-hour trip from Salem to the city of the holy mountain, Arunachala. Her holidays were no longer used for further pilgrimage in her ongoing search. She had been found by the object of her life's search and now spent as much time as could be spared in the Godchild's presence. "She would, even if she only had a day, come all the way from Salem and just wait and wait. If she could have a chance, a glimpse of Yogiji, she was happy for the day; she was so totally committed," said Dwaraknath Reddy, who observed Devaki's interactions in those early months.

Devaki had no dreams or expectations of anything beyond making herself available to serve this master. But discerning how best to serve him was not the easiest thing to do. He was fierce in his refusals of special solicitations toward his personal needs. Nor was there as yet any established agency determining the appropriate protocol. For Devaki, burning with a desire to grow closer to her beloved Bhagwan, there was little guidance in the approach except intensive attention, coupled with the whispered direction of her heart.

Kirsti, the Finnish sannyasini, tells of numerous occasions in those early years when both she and Devaki were spending time with the beggar and he would send them away. "I'd meet her there at the temple because she had been sent away too," Kirsti reflected. "And she would be pacing back and forth saying, 'What should I do?'" Together, Kirsti and Devaki would commiserate about their fate, wondering if his command to leave was meant to keep them away for a few hours, or a few days. Together, they mused or rejoiced in being at the effect of the Godman's whim.

राम

Dwaraknath Reddy, a wealthy businessman, owned a lovely home on a back street of a residential area not far from Ramanashram. Reddy was a staunch devotee of Ramana Maharshi's – on the grounds of his estate a small elegant chapel constructed of dark mahogany contains a nearly life-sized portrait of the Maharshi. The Reddy estate, known as Krupa, meaning "grace," was well named, as in the late years of the 1980s this home became a temporary sanctuary for the other great saint of Arunachala, Yogi Ramsuratkumar.

Mr. Reddy's daughter, Sandhya, lived with and cared for her father, and because of their association with the divine beggar, both father and daughter came to know Devaki. The professor from Salem was becoming a predictable presence around Yogi Ramsuratkumar, yet completely nonimposing. Although Sandhya was a few years younger than Devaki, and although their lives at this point were very different in form, the two women took a strong liking to each other. In their mutual respect for the Godchild, Yogi Ramsurat-kumar, they found the cement that would bond their friendship ever more deeply.

It was only a very short time after Devaki had made her first appearance on the steps of the Sannadhi Street house that Reddy made his own initial encounter with the Godchild. Dwaraknath and Sandhya had been living in Tiruvannamalai since 1983, but had not yet made the acquaintance of the hidden saint. In the early weeks of 1987, a female friend who was visiting from Pondicherry invited the Reddys to join her in a trip to the beggar's residence to receive his blessing.

"When we first went to him, my name was given to him," Reddy remembered. Like so many others, Reddy found that this first encounter was more like a reunion; it was as if he had been expect-ed. "Yogiji said: 'This beggar was waiting to meet Dwaraknath Reddy…This beggar wanted to meet the person who was talking about the 'Happy Birthday to the Unborn.'" Then Yogiji broke into his usual joy-filled laughter.

Ramsuratkumar's reference to the "Happy Birthday" had to do with a recent event. Mr. Reddy explained: "I had been to Madras for a gathering, celebrating Bhagavan Ramana's birthday. I was listed as one of the speakers and the subject that I was given was: 'Happy Birthday to the Unborn.'" Reddy guessed that Yogi Ramsuratkumar had seen the program for the festivities, which contained the title of the speech and Reddy's name, "and he [Yogi Ramsuratkumar] was very much intrigued."

The way in which the beggar spoke to Mr. Reddy and his daugh-ter from the very first moment, and the clear and innocent way in which the Godchild laughed, allowed Dwaraknath to feel the full acceptance that Yogi Ramsuratkumar bore them. Reddy remarked: "We felt a lot of affection and respect for him and joy for being with a person who has so much joy in himself."

From that day on, Mr. Reddy and Sandhya would frequently visit the beggar on Sannadhi Street. Reddy noted that Devaki was also present in those early meetings, even though she herself had only met Yogi Ramsuratkumar a short time before they did. As Reddy told it: "Right in the beginning we had been with Yogiji and a few people

418

had been sitting with him. Amongst them were people whom we came to know through Swamiji. One was Devaki and others who were with Devaki. They were a group of people *who were really devoted to him.*"

It is an indication of Reddy's character that Yogi Ramsuratkumar felt extraordinarily safe and supported in his presence. Speaking of the privilege of hosting the Godchild at their home, Krupa House, Reddy said: "Yogiji was very willing, by himself, by his grace, to come here to this house. There were many times when we were in the house doing something and we would hear the voice calling: 'Sandhya! Sandhya!' He was calling loudly for Sandhya. And he would be so happy if she came. Then he would say: 'This beggar would like to stay here for some time. Can he stay the day here?'"

On one such visit to Krupa House, Yogi Ramsuratkumar was accompanied by Devaki and a few other female devotees, companions to Devaki. After spending time with the Reddys, and just before leaving, Yogi Ramsuratkumar turned to Reddy's daughter. Pointing to Devaki and the other women, he said: "Sandhya, these ladies will stay with you!" And then the beggar left, returning to his house on Sannadhi Street.

These women (Devaki, Rajalakshmi, Vijayalakshmi, and Viyayakka) were regularly hosted by the Reddys, and Sandhya recalled warmly that her friend Devaki would come up on almost every Friday night, spend the weekend, and also the holidays with them. All of Devaki's time, however, was being offered to the service of her newly discovered master, Yogi Ramsuratkumar. On many occasions Sandhya was pleased to accompany Devaki to the beggar's residence as well.

राम

In the spacious and elegant grounds that surround the main house of the Krupa estate, a mango tree still stands. Under this very same mango tree Yogi Ramsuratkumar would sit, smoking, talking, eating with his hosts. "We were so happy," recalled Reddy of those halcyon days. "Swamiji was such a joy for us. It was just like being with a very likeable, loveable person...like an uncle, or a friend, somebody you really love. We would stay here for hours [under the mango tree] and have lunch and food. If people wanted to come, or he had people with him, they were most welcome. We had such easy, happy, relaxed times together."

This camaraderie with friends, however, never obscured the one focus of the Godchild's attention – "spirituality," as Reddy called it. "There was always the *Nama*, 'Sri Rama,' on his lips and in his thinking. These kinds of people are spiritually totally committed, and it's a privilege for us to be near them and talking to them. That was his own inner personality. But expressing outside was a jolly good person to be with, totally enjoyable and loveable. He would not be preaching and teaching, not really," meaning in any formal sense.

"Yogiji would sometimes ask Sandhya to tell a story about Krishna, or something, and it would be like a child and a grandfather sitting and sharing. And he would let that go on for half an hour, asking her to tell him more and more." As Sandhya would narrate his favorite tales, the beggar would be nodding and saying *hmm-hum*, responding to it. He had learned well that such feedback was a necessary part of the game, as Sandhya had instructed him, "Unless you respond I'll stop telling."

Sandhya learned early on that her new blessed friend, for all the vast and eternal wisdom that he manifested, was truly an innocent and joy-filled child. Although he was many years her senior, she easily played the role of mother or older sister, and sometimes companion playmate, to Yogi Ramsuratkumar. She was in her thirties at the time, but her own gentle and childlike nature was clearly appreciated by all who knew her, particularly the gentle beggar himself.

As Sandhya told these much-loved stories to Ramsuratkumar, the way a mother will narrate a story to her child, she would use mimicry. Krishna, for instance, might be running to the rescue of a little boy in the forest when a tiger would appear. "When the tiger comes, she will growl, when the birds come, she would make the sounds," Reddy recalled with a smile. The Godchild loved this type of animation and would laugh and laugh, giggling each time she took on a new character. "Then he would make her repeat the story again," Reddy said.

Yogi Ramsuratkumar reading Guru's Grace;
his eyes are filled with tears.

"Every day he used to come and sit here and we would read together," Sandhya recalled. "Or he would say, 'Here is a great book, you read it for me,'" handing her the book, *Guru's Grace*, for example, which is the story of Mother Krishnabai's life.

Yogi Ramsuratkumar loved that particular book, one of the most brilliant testimonies to the guru-disciple relationship ever written. Together they read the entire book in English. Among the photos that Dwaraknath Reddy took of the beggar, one has captured Yogi Ramsuratkumar holding a copy of *Guru's Grace*. There are tears in his eyes.

Sandhya admitted, "Sometimes I would feel emotionally like five years old, and then he would say, 'Okay, I will read it for you.'"

"Sometimes he would joke and ask me to light his cigarette and then he would make fun, saying: 'Be careful, my beard is there.'" Yogi

Ramsuratkumar would then enact a pantomime of trying to put out a fire in his beard, should she accidentally ignite it. Then again he would erupt with glee.

While the gentle and childlike beggar was constantly joking and playing with his young friend, Sandhya, he was also digging a deep foundation within her for absolute trust in the Divine. In one of the most tender lilas ever told of the beggar's love for humanity, Sandhya reported: "Hundreds of times he would tell me: 'Sanda [an affectionate nickname], *don't be afraid*. Sanda, see there is nothing else, nobody else, only Rama exists. Don't forget this.' That is the mantra he gave me."

राम

"I'm so hungry, Sanda!" Yogi Ramsuratkumar would announce, without warning, in the midst of their play.

"Swamiji, there is nothing to eat, only rice and curds," she might typically reply.

"Get buttermilk, and come and sit!" he would say, with urgency. "He couldn't wait for ten minutes," Sandhya remembered. "There were no inhibitions, just such a trust and love from our side and he accepted it," her father added.

As devout practitioners, Sandhya and Mr. Reddy would regularly make the circumambulation of Mount Arunachala known as pradakshina. Walking the fourteen kilometers, they would follow the route that led through the great temple, exiting the massive structure on a road that intersected Sannadhi Street but a good distance away from Yogi Ramsuratkumar's house.

As the pradakshina days occurred on the full moon of each month, and as thousands of pilgrims would flock to the city for this purpose, Yogi Ramsuratkumar would often be sitting outside, opposite his house, on the steps of the car mandapam. Noticing the Reddys as they left the temple, he would call out to them.

"Sometimes he would call me from far away," Sandhya explained. When she made her way to his side, the beggar would laugh and say: "How can you hear this beggar? How can you hear me, Sanda, from so far away?"

One day, when he called them from pradakshina, Yogi Ramsuratkumar requested that they leave for Krupa, the Reddy's home, as he wanted to spend some time with them there. "Swamiji, you know we are doing pradakshina," Sandhya informed him. Right away, however, Mr. Reddy came up with a compromise. They would finish their round of the mountain and then walk home, get the car, and come back to pick up the beggar.

"*You* will walk home," Yogi Ramsuratkumar said, nodding to Reddy. "Sanda will stay with me, and you will bring the car." Which is exactly what they did.

Since the Reddys most commonly did their pradakshina early in the morning, before the heat of the day, Yogi Ramsuratkumar might be picked up and arrive at their home as early as 6 A.M. From that hour until sometimes six at night, he would be with Dwaraknath and Sandhya, and whatever other guests might arrive. In the evening he would ask to be returned to the temple area.

राम

From their earliest associations, the Reddys seemed to hold a special place in the heart of Yogi Ramsuratkumar. Certainly, as far as we can understand, the beggar worked on behalf of all humanity, yet his particular solicitations to certain people at certain times were clear and undeniable. An event took place on November 4, 1988, that tenderly demonstrated his love for Dwaraknath. It also sheds some light on the ways in which Yogi Ramsuratkumar worked.[20]

Nivedita, the daughter of Sadhu Rangarajan, recorded the incident, as it occurred on a day when she and her father, together with another friend, Parimelazhagan, had traveled from Chennai to Tiruvannamalai to visit Yogi Ramsuratkumar. When the group arrived at the beggar's residence he was not at home, so they crossed the street to the temple to search for him there.

In a remote corner of the temple compound, Nivedita and her companions discovered Yogi Ramsuratkumar sitting against a wall, alone, and deeply absorbed in the inner world. As they approached him, however, the master rose to his feet and walked toward them. Immediately he began to speak: "Dwaraknath Reddy is undergoing an open heart surgery today. You know, it is a major operation. This beggar wanted to pray for him. Therefore I came away in the morning itself to sit here alone. Come on, we will go home." And with that, Yogiji started in the direction of his residence.

As they proceeded, the group passed by a shop in front of which a small crowd had gathered. Angry shouts were being exchanged. Yogi Ramsuratkumar stopped directly in front of the quarreling people and stared at them. Then he raised his fan, the way a king raises a royal scepter, and amazingly the crowd began to disperse until only one man remained, still shouting. The beggar moved closer to the single disputant without saying a word. He looked intently at the man, who became suddenly quiet. Peace had been restored. Then the Godchild and his companions continued on their way.

Arriving at the Sannadhi house and sitting together in the verandah, Yogi Ramsuratkumar addressed his visitors: "This beggar is not in a mood to talk about anything. Dwaraknath Reddy has been very kind to this beggar and he has been taking a lot of care of this beggar. He had a heart attack some years back, but this beggar did not know about that. Recently he went for a medical check up and the doctors have advised the operation. This beggar prayed to My Father to make him well without operation. But sometimes My Father doesn't accept this beggar's appeals. So this beggar has prayed to My Father to see that the operation is successful. My Father will accept this prayer."[21]

Rangarajan, who knew of Reddy's medical situation, informed Yogi Ramsuratkumar that the operating surgeon was internationally famous and that the hospital where the surgery was being done was well equipped. The beggar continued with his expression of concern; turning to Nivedita, he explained: "Even though this beggar can't do anything for Dwaraknath Reddy, this beggar doesn't want to do anything else. Somebody said that a *mrityunjaya homa* (a rite in honor of Lord Siva, the destroyer of death; a healing ritual) was being held in the temple for Dwaraknath's health. This beggar, therefore, went there." And then the Godchild innocently apologized to Nivedita and his other guests, saying: "You see, Nivedita, this beggar is very selfish. You have come all the way from Madras to talk to this beggar, but this beggar is talking only about an operation in a far off place." With that, Yogi Ramsuratkumar burst into laughter.

As the morning wore on, the conversations touched on many topics, but Yogi Ramsuratkumar's attention was clearly taken with the condition of Mr. Reddy. Twice the beggar sent Parimelazhagan to the telegraph office to find out if news had yet arrived. Nothing.

Finally, a third trip was made to the telegraph office, and this time Parimelazhagan returned with the long-awaited message. Yogi Ramsuratkumar handed the telegram to Nivedita and asked her to read it. The missive was brief, but heartening: "Operation successful. Appa recovering. Sandhya"[22]

Yogiji was overjoyed, and clearly relieved. He raised his hands above his head and spontaneously prayed aloud, his words indicative of the constancy and familiarity of the relationship he bore with the Divine: "Oh, thank you My Father, thank you very much."

Always intensely concerned with details, Yogi Ramsuratkumar asked Nivedita how much this telegram would have cost. She carefully counted the words and informed him that it would have been about ten rupees. When she added that the word "successful" had a gap between the letters – rendering it "success ful" – she remarked that perhaps it had been billed as two words instead of one. Yogi Ramsuratkumar loved the joke, and was soon roaring with laughter. The previous mood of seriousness was now completely dissipated. "Nivedita says the operation is 'success full,' that is 'full success.'" And then he laughed some more.

<h1 style="text-align:center">24</h1>

<h1 style="text-align:center">SPREADING THE WORK, 1987-1989</h1>

 Truman Caylor Wadlington's brief biography of Yogi Ramsuratkumar, first published in the early 1970s, had created a growing stream of interest in the God-child's life and mission. The presentation of *Glimpses of a Great Yogi* by Professor V. Rangarajan, another book about the beggar-saint, released on December 1, 1987, marked the initiation of a flood.

As a well-established journalist and author on spiritual themes, Rangarajan was an ideal vehicle for the work. The professor first addressed the project as early as 1984, at which time Yogi Ramsuratkumar had said, "Why should you write about this beggar? What is there to write?"[1] It thus remained dormant until 1987, when a request from a fellow devotee, T. Ponkamaraj, sparked the writing to life again. A large Jayanti celebration in honor of Yogi Ramsuratkumar was to be held that year in Nagercoil, a city further south from Tiruvannamalai, where many devotees of the beggar-saint lived. Ponkamaraj asked Rangarajan to write another testimony of Yogi Ramsuratkumar's greatness, in English, to be ready for this event. In a matter of a few months, spurred on by the need to meet a deadline, the work was completed.

In the last days of November 1987, with a bundle of around 300 copies of the book in his arms, Professor Rangarajan, along with A.R. Rao of Manorama Press (the book's printer), arrived in Tiruvannamalai and laid the offering at Yogi Ramsuratkumar's feet. "So Rangaraja and Ranganatha [the printer] have made this beggar into a

'Great Yogi'!" the Godchild laughed repeatedly, reading the title of the book, and enjoying his own joke.[2] On other occasions he had made a similar point, saying: "Even when I call myself a beggar, people suspect that I have hidden treasures and trouble me. What will be my fate if I call myself a king?"[3]

Swami Chidananda, an eminent scholar and teacher, had written a blessing for the book, and this preface to the text was warmly appreciated by Yogi Ramsuratkumar. An odd series of coincidences connected these two men, who met in the 1960s when Swami Chidananda was on a train that stopped temporarily at the railway station in Tiruvannamalai. Yogi Ramsuratkumar was at home under the punnai tree in those days, and frequently spent time on the railway station platform. Noticing an orange-robed man of genuine dignity sitting within a railway car, the beggar entered the waiting train, engaged the man in conversation for a few minutes, and received his blessing before the train moved on.

More than twenty years later, in this written benediction at the beginning of the book, the swami referred to Yogi Ramsuratkumar as "Maharaj," and named him "this exceptional enlightened soul."[4]

Just prior to the Jayanti celebration in Nagercoil, when Ponkamaraj met Yogi Ramsuratkumar, the beggar "presented a big cloth bundle to him asking him to open it later and distribute to devotees as *prasad*."[5] When Ponkamaraj returned home and opened the bundle, he found the first copies of *Glimpses of a Great Yogi*.

The small volume met with immediate success. The original 3,000 copies were quickly sold or distributed, which prompted the author to release it in an expanded second edition six months later, on the occasion of Guru Poornima, July 29, 1988. As before, Yogi Ramsuratkumar's response was a mixture of delight and instructive reflection. While giving the book away to those who visited him, the beggar again humorously chided Rangarajan for the claims inherent in the book's title.

The book reviews contained in the new edition described "this elegant biography" and spoke of the "living saint" to whom it was devoted. It was called "a good appetizer for spiritual seekers" and "a scintillating saga of Yogi Ramsuratkumar," whom one reviewer referred to as "the mystic of Sri Arunachala Hill" and another called a "molder of the destiny of the nation."[6] When these reviews were read aloud, Yogi Ramsuratkumar burst into laughter, as if he had never heard anything so funny. Turning to the devotees present in the room he reiterated, "Rangarajan, by writing this book, has made this beggar a 'Yogi' – not an ordinary Yogi, but a 'great Yogi' – and people, after reading it, come here to see the 'Yogi,' but they see only a beggar!"[7] Again his laughter erupted and others in the room joined in his merriment.

राम

Although he had instructed his visitors and devotees that his name *was* "Yogi Ramsuratkumar"; had allowed his devotees to call him "Swami," "Maharaj," or even "Bhagwan"; and had reiterated that he was never separate from his Father, Ramsuratkumar only referred to himself as "this sinner" or "this beggar." On several occasions, in fact, the Godchild had made a strong point with certain visitors about his preferred "status."

In the late 1980s, when Yogi Ramsuratkumar was sitting in the Sannadhi Street house, he was greeted by Swami Devananda Saraswati, a Canadian sadhu who had lived in India since 1967. Offering Ramsuratkumar some roses, the visitor referred to his aged friend as "Babaji." It was meant as an affectionate and respectful salutation, but Yogi Ramsuratkumar suddenly flashed to attention and strongly asserted: "This beggar is *not* a babaji! This beggar is a beggar – a *bikshu*!"[8] (The original meaning of the word meaning is a mendicant monk who takes his or her sustenance in a begging bowl, and solely from the gracious contributions of householders.)

Again, in 1991, an American visitor, Vijay Fedorschak, was given a similar lesson. He had heard the Godchild's Indian devotees refer to him as "Swami," so when Vijay approached Yogi Ramsuratkumar he began his exchange by saying: "Swami, can I ask you a question?"

Yogi Ramsuratkumar's response was swift and clear: "Why do you call this beggar a Swami? I am a beggar. Call me a beggar, *not* Swami."[9]

On this day in 1988, receiving the new edition of *Glimpses*, Yogi Ramsuratkumar directed Rangarajan to send it to libraries abroad, and himself gifted many visitors with it. "Rangarajan is doing a lot of work for this beggar," the master said often, with obvious gratitude.[10]

राम

Every day with Yogi Ramsuratkumar was remarkable, as his visitors and close devotees will testify. Some were remarkable in the silence that characterized them; others, by the huge numbers of supplicants making their way to his feet. And still other days, by an event of some significance.

April 26, 1988, marked the 104th Jayanti of Swami Papa Ramdas and also the seventh anniversary of the establishment of Banyan Tree Cave Ashram, built at the site of the cave in which Ramdas had lived for one month in 1923 on the holy mountain, Arunachala, in Tiruvannamalai.

For Yogi Ramsuratkumar it was an occasion for celebration, as he honored his Father, Ramdas, with such profound regard. This location, on the lower slopes of the mountain, was a short climb. Here, a huge banyan tree shaded a humble white stucco structure, and the whole compound was protected by a thick, whitewashed wall. Tropical flowers abounded, and brightly-colored scraps of cloth containing the petitions of hundreds of seekers (particularly from couples asking for a child, or from a family requesting a suitable match for a daughter) were tied to the tree and to the small fence surrounding it. Inside the building, on the north side, was a small temple and ashram run by the devotees of Ramana Maharshi, and on the south side, an antechamber leading into the low-ceilinged cave, its air still thick with the chanting of Ramnams.

A Westerner, a female sadhu named Satyananda Amritham, who had been living in India since 1980 and who first met Yogi Ramsuratkumar in the early 1980s, remembered this day in April in exquisite detail. She captured the master's tenderness and his words – a rare teaching about his relationship to God – in a poem describing this occasion:

O Yogi Ramsuratkumar,
On full moon day of April, 1986,

429

ONLY GOD

some sadhus were invited to Banyan Tree Cave
to celebrate the birthday of Swami Ramdas...
and *you* were there!...
Simply at ease, relaxed and very peaceful,
gentle, silent and approachable.

All morning (mostly outside the cave,
sometimes briefly within),
intensely, deeply you were looking...
Looking clearly and silently
at everything and everyone...

Sometimes outside, you softly chanted *RAMNAM:*
"SRI RAMA, JAYA RAMA, JAYA JAYA RAMA!"
in a most sweet and melodious voice,
and signaled me to repeat, then chant it
softly, with you...

Hours later, after lunch, you spoke...
"You see those ropes hanging, from that
Banyan tree there?"

– "No, Swami, those are roots!"
someone laughingly replied.
"Roots?" you asked. "When this Beggar looked,
it seemed to be some ropes, or maybe snakes
are dangling there!"
For some moments you were silent, looking...
Then slowly and with awe, again you spoke:
"In this very place, Banyan Tree Cave,
this beggar's Father, Swami Ramdas sat,
chanting *RAMNAM* for some 14 days...
And then one day, he came out of this cave
and everywhere! in trees and stones,
in skies and clouds,
in birds, insects and animals,
and in a human passing near,

430

saw only *GOD*, saw only *RAM!*
My Father is very great!"

Then slowly, haltingly and with great humbleness:
"This filthy beggar, this great sinner,
this madman has been looking and looking,
all morning…looking here and there,
looking everywhere, for a very long time:
all of this morning, and for so many, many years;
this Beggar has been looking,
and trying to see his Father,
trying to see Ram, to see God…
looking and looking, trying and trying."

And then, a lovely smile spread on your face:
"But this beggar doesn't see God anywhere!
This beggar sees only rocks and trees, clouds
and skies, ants, monkeys, birds and squirrels,
and human beings."

Then sometime later, very quietly,
and looking at Kirsti and at me, intently:
"God alone exists.
There is only God."

… After a long silence,
"Think of it," you said. Then, very slowly:
"See this clearly:
The reality is: *God alone exists.*
All of this, everywhere, is only God!
There is nothing, ever, other than God.
Nobody, nothing, anywhere exists which is
ever separate or apart from God.
There is no second. Nothing other, ever.
So, how can God experience Himself?

431

ONLY GOD

"God alone exists. Nothing, no-one else, anywhere.
Not even one atom is ever apart from Him.

"So, how to speak of this?
No one is left, to speak.
There is no other to speak to, or to hear."[11]

राम

This day was also a special one for Professor Rangarajan, who had long desired a formal initiation by his master, Yogi Ramsurat-kumar, but had previously been refused, told that it was not necessary. Formal initiations were not the beggar's way, as he had noted on many occasions. Nonetheless, in his great compassion, Yogi Ramsuratkumar was constantly succumbing to the persistent entreaties of those who loved him. Whenever possible, and as long as it was not obviously contrary to his Father's will, Yogi Ramsurat-kumar gave blessings in many forms to his visitors, his friends, his close companions.

Rangarajan, together with other guests, had been invited to the Banyan Tree Cave Jayanti celebration as a featured speaker. As he awaited his turn in the ceremonies, the professor sat quietly on the verandah above the small ashram, engrossed in his prayers. Observing a slight swell of excitement among a group of devotees in the lower courtyard, the sadhu learned that Yogi Ramsuratkumar had unexpectedly arrived. Everyone was surprised and greatly pleased. "This morning Chidaambaram came," said the master, referring to one of his devotees. "He offered to help this beggar reach here. So this beggar could come here to see Rangaraja."[12]

Taking the professor by the hand, Yogi Ramsuratkumar led the overjoyed man back up to the terrace, and soon a crowd of other devotees followed. In a short time, the Godchild was engaged in a vibrant discussion about the need for "aggressive Hinduism" – one of his favorite topics. "How long will it take?" Yogi Ramsuratkumar asked rhetorically.

When one person commented that Hinduism was growing by leaps and bounds in the West, the beggar used this fact to joke, although somewhat prophetically: "Yes, Hinduism will go to Europe and America. They will all become Hindus and we all will become Christians. Is it so?" He laughed and laughed.

A mood of playful camaraderie prevailed as the master continued: "This beggar once asked a Protestant missionary whether he would convert Catholics into Protestants. He said no. But he would convert Hindus into Christians." It was a sad reminder of the proselytizing that has undermined many native cultures, yet Yogi Ramsuratkumar kept the mood light throughout these reflections, and his laughter rippled on the warm morning air. "We will all become Christians, and they will become Hindus," he said and chuckled again. Then, with a note of seriousness, "If Hinduism goes from India, who will preserve our Vedas and Upanishads?" The darshan continued on in this vein for several hours.

When the ceremonies began at last, the chairman asked Yogi Ramsuratkumar to preside, but the beggar graciously refused. A few minutes into the speeches, Yogi Ramsuratkumar again took Rangarajan by the hand and this time led him into the nearby cave. The master was exuberant, like a child who had found a special long-hidden gift. "This is the cave where my Master lived!" Yogi Ramsuratkumar exclaimed. "This is where He sat and meditated. From here He used to go to the Maharshi Ramana. Oh! This is where Swami Ramdas sat and meditated!" He was ecstatic. "Come, let us do some bhajans, Rangarajan!" And together the two men began to chant the sacred mantra, *Om Sri Ram Jai Ram Jai Jai Ram*, in the very spot in which Ramdas had sat over fifty years earlier.

Filled with the rapture of the moment, Rangarajan dared to ask for the special favor he had wanted for so long. "I pray, please initiate me," he asked.

"Alright! If you want initiation, I will give," said Yogi Ramsuratkumar without hesitation. Drawing his devotee closer, the master whispered the taraka mantra three times into Rangarajan's ear, and asked him to repeat it three times as well.

Thrilled with emotion, Rangarajan prostrated to Yogi Ramsuratkumar and poured out his heartfelt gratitude. "Maharaj," the sadhu proclaimed, "I don't want to be a professor or an editor anymore. I

Yogi Ramsuratkumar and Sadhu V. Rangarajan, April 26, 1988

want to be a sadhu. I want to be a beggar like you. Give me guidance for the future."

Others throughout the years have made similar pleas, similar declarations, to Yogi Ramsuratkumar. And, as he has done countless times, skillfully dulling the emotional fervor in which his devotees have attempted to hurl themselves prematurely from the cliff of their ordinary lives, Yogi Ramsuratkumar made it clear to Sadhu Rangarajan that, in fact, nothing had changed. "My Father will guide you," he said. "Now you can go back and continue to do what you have been doing all these days. Renunciation is not giving up anything, nor is it taking up anything. It is just changing your attitude towards the world. My Father alone exists, no one else, nothing else."[13]

राम

A humorous and telling counterpoint to Rangarajan's story of initiation is told by Kirsti, the Finnish woman and sadhu who had considered herself a devotee of Yogi Ramsuratkumar's since the mid-1970s. "Only once," Kirsti admitted, did she ever try to "push" Yogi Ramsuratkumar. It happened that for a very long time she had desired some sort of formal recognition of the guru-disciple relationship which she honestly *knew* with him, but which he had never "officially" confirmed.

Knowing that she couldn't come right out and ask for the formal recognition (or *guru diksha,* an acknowledgement of relationship to a *diksha guru* – the one who leads the aspirant to liberation) she tried to sneak in through a side door. Sitting with him on one particular day, telling him about the other teachers and masters she had met in her travels, Kirsti slyly explained: "There is one swami I know of who gives guru diksha to acknowledge the relationship with the student."

"Oh yes," said Yogi Ramsuratkumar with greater slyness still, "some gurus also *send* their devotees to other gurus."

Kirsti never asked again, although on another occasion, when she reported to Yogi Ramsuratkumar that other teachers were always trying to give her special mantras to say, or some particular practices to do, he was emphatic that she did not need mantras from many swamis. "And then," Kirsti noted, "He made me repeat Ramnam and Sivanam after Him. I think that was the closest to formal initiation he ever gave me. It was very casual and quick." [14]

राम

As this lovely day in April drew to a close, Yogi Ramsuratkumar called Vivek, the professor's son, to his side. "Vivekanandan, your father has got a lot of work to do in Madras," the master spoke sweetly, and with that gave father and son leave to go.[15] Within a year, Rangarajan's request for work and guidance would be fulfilled in a way that was yet beyond his imagining. But on this day he left happy and secure, with the beggar's blessing, his master's mantra, and his guru's dynamic instruction on the nature of true renunciation to direct his future steps.

ONLY GOD

राम

On this same April day, across the world in Arizona, U.S.A., Lee Lozowick conducted his life as usual, unaware that changes of a dynamic nature were about to take place for him as well. It had been almost two years since he had left Tiruvannamalai (in the winter of 1986), and Lee had vowed to himself that he would not return to India unless it was clear that this was Yogi Ramsuratkumar's will. Unlike many Westerners, Lee never wanted to ingratiate himself with anyone, especially with the Godchild of Tiruvannamalai, whom he now realized, more than ever, was the source of his life and the force that propelled his teaching work.

Six months earlier, in November of 1987, Lee had expressed his deep longing and the pain of separation from his beloved when he wrote:

Call lee to you always, Oh Yogi Ramsuratkumar.
    You called him 12 years ago when he had no idea.
Now you possess lee's heart;
    of very doubtful value it is true,
but Yours it is.
    Call lee home, Father.
He longs to feel the gaze
    of the dirty Beggar. [16]

On the April day preceding the Ramdas Jayanti, 1988, as Yogi Ramsuratkumar spoke with Sadhu Rangarajan, the name of Lee Lozowick entered the conversation. Yogiji and the professor had been discussing beggars and beggary, and Rangarajan mentioned Lee's connection with the tradition of the Bauls of Bengal, a sect of itinerant beggars. Immediately, Yogi Ramsuratkumar replied: "Yes, yes. He has also written some poems on this beggar. One of them this beggar gave to you [Rangarajan] and that you have printed [in *Tattva Darsana*]. This beggar doesn't know where the rest are. He never preserves them." [17]

436

The poem in question, the first one that the master gave to Rangarajan for publication, was titled "To Yogi Ramsuratkumar The Crazy Beggar From A Bad Poet." It was published in *Tattva Darsana* in the November 1986-January 1987 issue. Since Lee had left India in January 1986, he had not ceased in writing his poems of praise to the Godman.

What Yogi Ramsuratkumar *did* preserve, however, were some of the envelopes in which Lee had mailed these poems. Along with a variety of papers and trash, these envelopes were saved in one of the gunnysacks that Yogi Ramsuratkumar kept around him. In one of the beggar's classic acts of spontaneity, these discarded envelopes would, a few months later, serve as the means to call Lee Lozowick back to India.

राम

If Yogi Ramsuratkumar had laughed or become disconcerted at the titles of "great Yogi," "Swamiji" or "Baba" being applied to him, imagine his reaction to being hailed as the embodiment of "the Universal Compassion of Gautama Buddha, the Selfless Sacrifice of Jesus Christ and the Militant zeal of prophet Mohamed."[18] Would this unassuming beggar have laughed out loud, or been outraged, in being called the "Vaikunda Avatar of the Kaliyuga" who had come to "spearhead Mother India's Spiritual Mission to the World as prophesized by the Saints and Seers of the past"?

In one of the most paradoxical incidents in the saint's history, he was made the subject of a two-day conference called "Seminar on the Destiny of the Human Race and Mission of His Holiness Sri Yogi Ramsuratkumar," held in Pondicherry, India, on May 7-8, 1988.

The event was the inspiration of Sri Rajamanikam, the wealthy industrialist and ardent devotee from Tuticorin, who had first met the beggar in Tapovanam at the ashram of Swami Gnanananda Giri in 1973. Rajamanikam believed that Yogi Ramsuratkumar's mission merited a platform of greater visibility and had been traveling for many years in pilgrimages of devotion across southern India proclaiming the Godchild's wonder and grace. With the help of influential friends, other devotees of Yogi Ramsuratkumar, and a number of distinguished scholars, the Pondicherry conference was held at Kamban Kalai Arangam, a popular municipal facility that hosted formal programs of all types.

The fact that the conference was held in Pondicherry was not mere convenience, nor coincidence. The organizers clearly wanted to highlight a link between the revolutionary work of Sri Aurobindo and that of his spiritual son, Yogi Ramsuratkumar. They took the opportunity to cast the beggar as the new world savior and spared no eloquence in their proclamations. "Yogi Ramsuratkumar heralds the Universal Religion of Universal Integration – the New Religion of the 21st Century Future and Beyond" declared one of the participants.

A beautifully appointed souvenir book, titled *Divine Message to Humanity*, was distributed at the event. It contained praise-filled articles by many devotees and friends, together with gorgeous, full-page color photos of Yogi Ramsuratkumar, each with an accompanying quotation by the beggar. In light of the conference theme, many of these captions dealt with India's preeminent role in the world – a subject that was understandably close to the heart of Yogi Ramsuratkumar. At the bottom of one photograph that particularly highlighted the kingly stature of the beggar, the quote read:

> Swami Ram Tirtha has said that he will be always in some human form and see that our goal is achieved. Sometime Japan was flourishing, some other time Germany, Italy, America and England, one after the other. Hereafter, it is INDIA only. The time has come for this. MY FATHER will do the work nicely.[19]

It is to the organizers' credit, as well as to the beggar's grace, that the essential message of Yogi Ramsuratkumar, the need for complete and absolute faith in his Father, was not obscured, despite the high-profile presentation and the strong sociopolitical orientation of the publication. Yogi Ramsuratkumar himself did not attend the event, although he was probably invited. What is most interesting to note, in contrast to any grandiose claims being made in his name, was Yogi Ramsuratkumar's written message to the conference, which the souvenir book also contained. In little more than five hundred words, and using the simplest, even homespun, analogies, the beggar expressed an innocent yet passionate plea for one thing only – remembrance of the name of God.

> So this beggar begs please don't forget the name of God. This Divine name has always been of great help to all in the world...Just as when there is heavy rainfall, we take an umbrella, and go on doing our work in the factory, in the field, wherever we go for marketing; and catching hold of the umbrella we go though the rain is falling there. But still we work – still we work – do our work. Similarly we have got so many problems all around. This Divine name is just like an umbrella in the heavy rainfall. Catch hold of the Divine name and go on doing your work in the world...All the blessing of my Father for all of you! well, that is the end. That is all.[20]

The message was signed by Yogi Ramsuratkumar's hand with an *OM* symbol, and underlined with a flourish.

The organizers had obviously overstated their purpose. While they had planned to establish "concrete programs and projects to disseminate the message of Love and cooperation of His Holiness,"[21] none were forthcoming from the event. Some other devotees, in fact, saw the seminar as an attempt at manipulation by those who wanted to use Yogi Ramsuratkumar's name to further their own political aspirations. Be that as it may, Yogi Ramsuratkumar did not disdain the opportunity to remind the world of his one, all-consuming purpose.

राम

A small group of Indian friends and devotees were discussing the 1988 Olympic games with Yogi Ramsuratkumar, who was always tremendously interested in sports, especially soccer. Their repartee on this occasion provides a candid glimpse at the very human and familial mood that Yogi Ramsuratkumar evoked with many people who were privileged to spend time with him.

"Tomorrow Great India is playing against Britain. We must get at least a bronze, if not a silver or gold. This beggar prays to My Father," the Godchild reported jovially.[22] With that, he turned to Nivedita Rangarajan and continued his playful banter. "You know this beggar puts too many applications to My Father and, therefore, He rejects some of them. You ask [your father] Rangaraja to pray. If Rangaraja asks, My Father will not reject."

Finding his own words hilarious, Yogiji laughed and laughed. Stoking the fires further he added, "We must win by ten goals! If we don't win, Nivedita will tell everybody that this Beggar said that India must win by ten goals, but we lost." More and more hearty laughter followed.

The discussion continued, including the fact that 160 nations were competing in this soccer event, and therefore, of course, the vast majority would lose. The Godchild drolly consoled his audience and himself with the announcement, "So there is nothing to worry even if we lose. We will be on the side of the majority." And all laughed again.

Within a few minutes, a destitute man arrived at the door of the Sannadhi house, imploring alms. As this man had already come several times that day, Yogi Ramsuratkumar told Vivek to send him away. When the young man carried the message to the supplicant, the man at the door immediately complied and moved on down the street.

Seeing what had transpired, Yogi Ramsuratkumar found the whole event funnier still. "See, when this Beggar asked [that man] to go, he didn't go. But when Vivek told, he was gone." The incident reminded him of something else, and he continued: "Once some Yogi wanted to test the capacity of Jnandev [alternate spelling of Jnaneswar, a thirteenth century mystic-poet and saint] and he came riding a tiger. Jnandev was then sitting on a wall. He asked the wall to move to give way to the Yogi. The wall moved."[23]

As his listeners followed the tale, Yogi Ramsuratkumar watched their attentive faces and then smiling added: "So, when Jnandev ordered, the wall moved, but when this beggar orders, even a ball [clearly a reference to a soccer ball] doesn't move." He chortled with glee, saying, "Otherwise, we will at least get a bronze!"

As it turned out in the 1988 Olympics, the beggar's "prayers" did prove powerless to "move" the ball, as the gold medal in soccer was taken by the USSR, the silver by Brazil, and the bronze by West Germany. Yogi Ramsuratkumar's wonderful jokes on this occasion were not really about ballgames as much as indications of a more profound spiritual principle. In his complete surrender to the will of his Father, he was demonstrating to his friends that, despite the *siddhis* (yogic powers) of some saints, his was a path of powerlessness, humility, beggary, and absolute reliance upon God. The only power he had, really, was the power of his love. Consequently, despite India's Olympic defeat, the real and lasting prize on that day was won by those who shared the joy of the Godchild of Tiruvannamalai.

राम

Sometimes the beggar's words seemed particularly radical, as if they were designed to turn listeners upside down and inside out. Like crazy-wisdom masters throughout the ages, his words often cast human tendencies in a shockingly different light. The spiritual master's job is to undermine the devotee's assumptions at every turn, sometimes revealing a truth beyond one's previous comprehension.

"Are you Persian?" Yogi Ramsuratkumar asked a visitor to his darshan one day in 1988.[24] The man, whose name was Farook, a professor at the University of Paris, quietly replied that indeed he was Persian.

The beggar then posed a most startling question. "Do you know Ayatollah Ruhollah Khomeini?" he asked.

"Yes," Farook answered.

"Do you know that he is a saint?" the beggar inquired.

At this point, every ear in the room was on full-scale alert. Whatever could the Godchild be saying with such a radical statement? Khomeini was a ruthless dictator, responsible for the slaughter of millions, and here the beggar was referring to him as a saint!

The Persian man's response was highly tactful, however. "No, Swamiji," he replied, indicating that he did not know that Khomeini was a saint. "But if you say so I am not going to contradict you."

Again Yogi Ramsuratkumar asserted: "This Beggar thinks he is a saint."

Sadhu Rangarajan, who was hearing this exchange, remarked with a smile, "But there are others who call him a devil. So *they* must be sinners."

"No, no," contradicted Yogi Ramsuratkumar. "All of them are saints. In this world, this beggar is the only sinner. All others are saints."

This response caused his listeners to burst into laughter, as they found his words about himself so preposterous. Yet, despite the levity with which the beggar held the situation, the statement was not a joke nor a casual aside.

The gentle Godman continued, "You see, Kabir saw only Rama everywhere, in everyone," and then he lapsed into silence, as if to allow his guests to absorb his meaning. Then he began to chant Ramnam, and the others joined him. Finally, after a few minutes, the Godchild turned to Rangarajan and spoke once more. "Do you know that both the saints and wicked people are a source of unhappiness?"

His question again dumbfounded everyone.

"When wicked people come to us, they give us unhappiness. When saints leave us, we feel unhappy, isn't it?" he said, playfully, relieving the more serious mood that had intervened. Everyone laughed again, appreciating the paradoxical truth of the beggar's words.

राम

One of Ramsuratkumar's favored "children," young Vivekan-andan (Vivek) Rangarajan, told of another delightful and instructive incident that occurred in 1988. Yogi Ramsuratkumar had visited the ashram of a local swami and had taken Vivek with him. The swami who ran the ashram was a well-educated man and greatly enjoyed talking at length about many varied subjects. After some time, when no refreshments had been offered, Ramsuratkumar turned to his host and said, "Vivekanandan is very hungry." Im-mediately the swami ordered lunch to be served to all.

Later, their visit concluded, Ramsuratkumar sat with Vivekan-andan in the temple premises. "The Swami was talking and talking, while this beggar was feeling hungry. This beggar had not even taken his breakfast. That is why he said, 'Vivekanandan is hungry.' He could not say, 'I am hungry.' And, we got our food." Concluding this story, told to the delight of those around him, Yogi Ramsuratkumar burst into gales of laughter.[25]

राम

An American who visited Yogiji in 1988 reported on the elegant disregard that the Godman showed toward material wealth: "Upon the arrival of tea, another devotee produced a 100 rupee note and he wanted to give it to Yogi Ramsuratkumar. He refused at first, but upon further insistence, wryly took it and dropped it behind the hallway steps. Laughing loudly, he said, 'You see how this beggar begs,' and later he repeated, 'Now you know how this beggar begs.'"[26]

राम

Lee Lozowick surprised his American community in the late summer of 1988 by announcing that, contrary to his previous indications, he was returning to India.

A few months later, on October 24, 1988, speaking to Vivek Rangarajan, Yogi Ramsuratkumar again brought up the subject of his American devotee. On this day, he handed a bunch of envelopes to Vivek and asked him to read the names and addresses of the sender. All the envelopes contained poems by "the bad poet," as Lee referred to himself. Then, calling upon one of the women in the group, the beggar asked her to read the poems "because they were all in his praise and otherwise he would have torn them and thrown them aside. He continued, 'This beggar likes praising, and that is why he has asked you to read them.'" It was an instructive remark that reflected Yogi Ramsuratkumar's constant teaching that inspiration was essential on the spiritual path, and that praise of God was the only worthwhile human occupation. Hearing this, Vivek recalled that one of the thousand names of the Lord used in the Hindu scriptures was "Stuti Priyah" or "Lover of Praise."[27] Westerners can understand the Godman's remark in light of their appreciation of the psalms in the Old Testament, in which King David and others have extolled the wonders of their submission to the Lord and the unending blessedness rained upon those who turn to the Divine as the only source of their power.

After this, the beggar recounted his own version of the story of Lee Lozowick's last visit in 1986.

"Already we have met. Why do you come again?" said Yogi Ramsuratkumar, recalling the words he had spoken to Lee on that day, and the fact that he had asked him to go away.

"But Lee did not go," wrote Vivek, reflecting the Godchild's narration. "At that time some construction work was going on there. It was eleven or twelve noon. Lee still waited outside in the hot sun. Later, a woman and three children came and the Yogi allowed them inside since he had not met them earlier. He enquired about them and he was surprised to know that their father (Lee) was waiting outside." Yogi Ramsuratkumar then explained that he invited Lee to come in, but Lee did not. "This beggar had told him to go away and so now he wouldn't come in…This beggar asked him again and again. This beggar tried so hard, but he wouldn't come in."[28]

After telling this incident to Vivek, Yogi Ramsuratkumar added with sadness and tenderness, "See how he writes [referring to Lee's poems]. He always calls this beggar his Father. But see how this beggar has treated him?"[29]

The Godchild's ways with his disciples were often extremely difficult and enigmatic, and the closer the relationship was, the more difficult the beggar could be. Like his Father Ramdas, Ramsuratkumar could be ruthless, throwing his fledglings headlong out of the nest, testing their resolve, igniting the fires of their longing. One of Yogiji's most trustworthy disciples, Jai Ram, served as his close attendant for many years. When Jai Ram, at one point, was looking for a house for his family, Yogi Ramsuratkumar himself initiated a search, as he wanted Jai Ram to live close by. Disregarding the master's preference, however, the young disciple took a residence on the other side of town. Of course he had his own "good reasons," logical reasons. But such things don't fly around the Godman.

"He was angry with me," Jai Ram reported many years later, looking back remorsefully on the incident. "I didn't understand him at all. Then, for almost four years, he would turn aside and not talk to me. If somebody would take my name he would become very angry, saying 'Don't take his name.'" Jai Ram's intense devotion to Yogi Ramsuratkumar endured this trial, however; a testimony to the "death" he endured at his master's hand.[30]

The Divine was obviously enacting its own unique play in Lee Lozowick through the hand of Yogi Ramsuratkumar. Both were apparently sobered by the way of its unfolding, but both were also surrendered to the Divine will. Nonetheless, the right timing for their reunion was drawing closer.

राम

T. Ponkamaraj, who organized Yogi Ramsuratkumar's Jayanti celebrations in Nagercoil, visited the beggar one afternoon in mid-1988 to discuss plans for that year's festivities. He wanted to start setting the program and inviting special dignitaries. *Whom should he ask?* Instead of answering his question directly, Yogi Ramsuratkumar gave Ponkamaraj "a bundle of rags...and told [him] to take this bundle home with him, and in seven days he was to open the bundle."[31]

One week later, as he had been instructed, Ponkamaraj "opened the bundle of rags and found in them a whole packet of envelopes with the name Lee Lozowick on them and an address in America." Ponkamaraj did not know Lee at the time, but soon set off to find out who he was and how he might be contacted. Returning to Tiruvannamalai and Yogi Ramsuratkumar, he inquired.

"Lee will be at Ramyam," Yogi Ramsuratkumar simply replied.

With the beggar's blessing, Ponkamaraj sent a letter and a formal invitation to Lee. However, he never mentioned that the arrangements were all instigated by Yogi Ramsuratkumar. When Lee received this surprising communication in August of that year, he nonetheless felt the touch of the beggar's hand. Without knowing the details of what was expected of him, Lee accepted. It was not until his arrival in India, however, upon hearing the full story from Sadhu Rangarajan, that Lee finally got the whole picture. Needless to say he was deeply touched, and encouraged, as he had had no external word from or contact with his master since 1986.

Lee Lozowick returned to India a few days before December 1, 1988, with a group of his male devotees. The two-week trip turned out to be a barnstorming tour. To Lee's amazement, he found that not only had he been called to *join in* the festivities, but that he was to be the guest of honor. "Welcome Lee Lozowick, Effulgent Flame of Yogi Ramsuratkumar" read the enormous banner that greeted his arrival. For days he was ushered from place to place in a whirlwind of activities – from Chennai (Madras) to Kanyakumari, at the southernmost tip of India. He was garlanded with flowers and asked to dedicate buildings, to bless babies, to give teachings in temples, ashrams, and to entire villages. The Indian devotees of Yogi Ramsuratkumar in Nagercoil and neighboring cities could not have the Divine beggar himself in their midst, so they threw themselves into honoring his English-speaking "Effulgent Flame."

In a manner that reflected Yogi Ramsuratkumar's insistence on being a beggar rather than a great saint, Lee consistently reminded his audiences, sometimes numbering in the thousands, that the Godman's legacy was not a prize in the world's accounting. In one

Lee Lozowick (front, center) and company, South India, 1988

speech that typified his remarks throughout this trip, Lee said: "Yogi Ramsuratkumar has not given me anything, but taken away; broken my heart. Without a broken heart, it's very easy to forget God. If one's heart isn't broken, it's my opinion that one hasn't begun to consider a relationship to the Father."[32]

The Americans' tour in honor of Yogi Ramsuratkumar ended with a trip to Kanhangad, to the ashram of Papa Ramdas and Mother Krishnabai. Mataji was quite old and very close to death at the time, yet the group was privileged to receive her darshan. From there they made their way back to Tiruvannamalai for a much-anticipated visit with the beggar.

राम

Every devotee of a living guru probably knows the sense of mingled thrill and fear as he or she approaches their spiritual master's presence, and certainly Lee was experiencing this ambivalence the closer he came to the sacred mountain, Arunachala. The Tibetan Buddhist master Chögyam Trungpa Rinpoche once stated that one should be terrified in such a circumstance, as one comes to the guru

T. Ponkamaraj leads the chanting at the Mantralayam dedication, 1988

for the purpose of being undone, annihilated.[33] The Christian writer C.S. Lewis captured this odd combination of sensations perfectly in describing how the animals approached Aslan, the lion-king and Christ-figure in the *Chronicles of Narnia*. Lewis wrote: "'Is he – quite safe? I shall feel rather nervous meeting a lion,' one of the children asked. To which the animal replied: 'Course he isn't safe. But he's good. He's the King, I tell you.'"[34]

The true guru is always awesome and terrible, and Lee's students who accompanied him on this trip noted that Lee seemed nervous, even if quietly composed, as the time of their rendezvous drew nearer.

At 1 P.M. on this day in early December, the troupe arrived in Tiruvannamalai and, leaving their bags at Ramanashram, they headed immediately into town. The men were hungry, but Lee's intention to present himself to Yogi Ramsuratkumar warranted no postponing. Down the street, alongside the temple wall, they walked swiftly, until they reached the mandapam of the temple car, the familiar place where Yogi Ramsuratkumar was first encountered in 1977. Immediately across the road stood the beggar's residence, #90 Sannadhi. Lee approached the door, with the men behind him.

Looking through the iron grillwork that enclosed the front porch of the house, they could see Yogi Ramsuratkumar seated with a small group of devotees. Lee waited on the front steps, with no need to knock, as anyone inside could clearly see an approaching visitor. As soon as the beggar noticed Lee at the door, however, he got up and walked to the entrance. Lee dropped to his knees, bowing his head. When Lee rose to his feet, Yogi Ramsuratkumar placed his hand gently on the younger man's back, and kept it there. This gesture of blessing lasted for only a few seconds, but in it, an eternity of wordless communication was shared. Of this precious touch Lee wrote:

Oh! Dearest, my Father
    Yogi Ramsuratkumar –
my forehead rested on Your knee
    a moment.
Just an eternal moment
    Your Father Blessed lee…

You let me touch Your Feet,
    rough Beggar's Feet
for just a moment.
    Just an eternal Moment.
Oh! Father Yogi Ramsuratkumar –
    lee bows, too humbled
      to cry or smile as
Your Crazy, Mad Beggarness
    sings wildly.[35]

Immediately it was clear, both to Lee and to those in his company, that the beggar recognized him and was genuinely happy to see him. Bringing his guests inside, Yogi Ramsuratkumar rearranged the seating of his previous visitors and indicated that Lee should sit next to him at the head of the small room. As the Godman stroked Lee's hand, his arm, his wrist, with remarkable tenderness, he questioned the Americans about their travels, particularly about their trip to Kanhangad and their darshan with Mother Krishnabai. *What was the exact time that they had arrived at Ramdas's ashram? When exactly had they left? For how long would they be in Tiruvannamalai?* As usual, the conversation was pleasant and accommodating, background music to the prayers of the heart that were being exchanged between master and disciple.

At one point, Yogi Ramsuratkumar picked up a bunch of roses that was lying next to him, and placed it very gently into Lee's hand. The younger man held the flowers, unmoving, for a short while, and then Yogi Ramsuratkumar directed him to give one to each of the other men in the party and to keep one for himself.

"It would be nice if there were seven of them," the Godchild said as he handed them to Lee. As it turned out, that was exactly how many there were, *and* how many men were in the group that day, since one had not yet made it back from his climb on the mountain. For Lee, it may have been a flashback to that first meeting in 1977 when, "coincidentally," the Godman had exactly anticipated the correct number of cups of tea that would be needed even before his guests had arrived. Coincidences of this nature were always happening around Yogi Ramsuratkumar.

With initial amenities settled, Yogi Ramsuratkumar suggested that the group, with Lee, pay a visit to the temple compound, where he promised to join them shortly. Without a lingering note, Lee was on his feet. From the first, he would demonstrate to his companions that responsiveness to one's master's directives was of utmost importance. It was a movement that would come to characterize Lee Lozowick's relationship to the beggar-saint for the rest of their years together. Like a dog at its master's side will take off instantly when a stick is tossed, Lee would literally *run* to carry out Yogi Ramsuratkumar's wishes. Obedience was all that mattered.

"I was very taken," one of the men later wrote, referring to the incident with the roses, which seemed to him like a highly symbolic gesture. "As Lee handed out the flowers you could see tears in his eyes. His Teacher, his lineage, was taking over," directing the course of every aspect of Lee's life, which included Lee's work with his own spiritual school in the United States. It was both shocking and poignant for these men to realize that the person whom they had regarded as their teacher was fully at the effect of his own master, Yogi Ramsuratkumar. They deeply sensed that this small gesture, along with many others that took place on this trip, was indicative of what lay ahead for them. Such moments would have profound repercussions in their own lives, and the lives of many people in the West.

Lee may have described his reaction differently, as he was never asked why he was crying that day. Nonetheless, the welcome he received from the master was undeniable, despite the fact that only two years earlier Yogi Ramsuratkumar had seemingly turned him away, severely testing Lee's ongoing commitment and his faith. The particular instructions and other meaningful gestures that Yogi Ramsuratkumar made with Lee and the group on this visit seemed to be empowering Lee, and sealed something between them at a level that would never be lowered.

"Yogi Ramsuratkumar welcomed me like a son – a spiritual son, which is even more than a blood son," Lee observed, with gratitude and amazement. "There was no criticism, no analysis, no judgement, no advice, simply, 'My Father in Heaven Blesses your mission, Lee.'"[36] The details of Lee's work, or exactly what this "mission" was, were never discussed. The fact that Lee's primary mission would steadily evolve into a communication of the beggar's name through-out the world was as yet unknown.

Lee's students kept notes of this timeless period when their American teacher and his Indian master played together again like long-separated lovers. The lilas, a few of which are reported below, also occasionally involved the other men. One and all, these teaching lessons were carried back to the U.S., where they became the subject of weeks of intense consideration by Lee's students. His listeners everywhere were awed as they learned of the wondrous beggar, some of them for the first time, and felt the cyclone of the blessing force of Yogi Ramsuratkumar that was now animating Lee Lozowick.

राम

"None of us really [knew] what to expect," wrote one of men, describing his own sense of disorientation as he left the Godchild's presence enroute to the temple where they would meet up with Yogi Ramsuratkumar. Shortly after they entered the precincts, "Yogi Ramsuratkumar soon appears, carrying a coconut bowl and a fan. He takes Lee by the hand and walks him around the temple, like a father, which is, in fact, how Lee refers to him (as 'my Father')."[37]

At one point, caressing Lee's hand, Yogi Ramsuratkumar asked him about the wedding ring he wore on his finger. The beggar's questions were decidedly simple, childlike: *Was the ring pure gold? Did his wife have one of the same type? Had they worn them since they were married? In what year?*

Within a few moments, Yogi Ramsuratkumar was fully engaged in this seemingly casual "marriage-ring" discussion with two other married men in Lee's company. Again, the beggar wanted to examine their rings. It was the type of repartee that one looked upon as simply the Godman's graciousness – just one more expression of his caring – until a synchronistic event woke the witnesses from their blissful reverie. A loud argument had commenced between a man and his wife, immediately behind where Lee and Yogi Ramsuratkumar were seated. "A woman sits on the steps, strong, unyielding, blaming and yells staccato across the ghat at her husband. He stands tall, proud, unconcerned with her womanly taunts. He moves away, leaving the ghat, but slowly, as he waits for a last opportunity to be victorious over her. They have undoubtedly done this many times before. Man against woman, steeled against each other."[38]

The contrast between the intimacy the men were enjoying with Yogi Ramsuratkumar and the war-like exchanges around them was too poignant to be merely coincidental. All who witnessed the scene were clear about that. The Godman's tenderness and attention to Lee, in particular, and to each of them in turn, was a clear demonstration of the only true and lasting solution to this age-old feud between man and woman, man and man…ego and ego.

राम

Wolfgang Dieterich asked to take a photograph of Lee and Yogi Ramsuratkumar together as they sat on the ledge above the ghat that day. The beggar agreed but was insistent that he would allow only one picture to be shot. As it turned out, one picture was all that was necessary.

The photo captured a mood of rare, pure devotedness. While it distinctly shows two human individuals, seated side by side, with the younger man's hand resting in the grip of the elder's, it captured such an ethereal quality like the merger of soul with soul, that one might realistically question whether it was taken on the earth plane at all. (See color photo inserts.)

राम

Taking Lee's hand, Yogi Ramsuratkumar led the rest of the group through the temple courtyard and around the bathing ghats. Here they came upon numerous sadhus who frequented the dark corners of the huge temple compound. As the beggar-saint passed, these sadhus would come out to bow before him, and Yogiji would occasionally say a few words to one of them.

After a short while, the Godchild turned to the seven followers in Lee's group and declared, "Now *you* lead *us*."[39]

This turnaround came as a great surprise to the men. Although they tried to appear calm in the face of their own uncertainty and lack of unity, they actually created a comic show as they practically stepped on one another's toes in attempting to determine their directions. When they looked back to Lee for help, Yogi Ramsuratkumar caught their ploy and said with authority, "Lead us!" And then, turning to Lee, the beggar grinned as he said sweetly, "Do you think they are leading us or misleading us?" And with that, he laughed with abandon.

A few weeks later, sharing this seemingly comedic incident with his other students in America, Lee remarked: "It strikes me that some of what was going on was that if you're a beggar, beggars follow, beggars beg, beggars aren't choosers. At the same time, with certain comments and with certain gestures, Yogi Ramsuratkumar was never out of control, even though he was following. I don't know if anyone else noticed that, but as a communication for our work, what an example of how to be a beggar but not a 'follower.'"[40] [Meaning a "blind follower" who mindlessly and with no discrimination attaches himself to a leader.]

Lee was instructing his enthusiastic, yet often naïve, American students that every gesture and every comment of Yogi Ramsuratkumar's was imbued with a blessing force, and that everything about him could be taken as an expression of the Divine will.

"When we were walking in the Temple complex," Lee explained, "Yogi Ramsuratkumar blessed all the sadhus. He blessed the Shiva tantrikas, he blessed the chillum smokers, and he blessed the ascetics. He blessed all the sadhus because their relationship to God transcended their particular or specific sadhana; and for those whose sadhana didn't, he sent them away. For people that came up to him whose practice was not stronger than their idiosyncratic psychologies, he wouldn't have anything to do with them, he sent them away. That's the beauty of the beggar…whatever is brought to him he turns over to his Father in Heaven, over to God."[41]

राम

After their sojourn at the temple grounds, Yogi Ramsuratkumar asked two Indian men to go out and get milk for his party of visitors. When at last these men returned, they had brought tea. Yogi

Ramsuratkumar looked at the tea, then proceeded to hand it out to his guests, saying: "This Beggar asked for milk, and he got tea. Tea is what we have. We didn't get milk. Oh well, what we have here is tea."

One of the guests later wrote: "It was a strong reminder to just make do with what one gets in the face of what one wants."

The lila didn't end there, however. Later that day, Yogi Ramsurat-kumar again asked one of his Indian devotees to get refreshments for the group. This time, the gracious beggar asked Lee what *he* would like to drink. Although he generally drinks only tea or coffee in India, Lee certainly remembered his master's previously unfulfilled request. Without hesitation, Lee replied, "Milk." A few minutes later, hot milk was brought for all, and Yogi Ramsuratkumar handed a glass to each of his guests. As they sat, quietly sipping the hot liquid, the Godman walked back and forth in front of them, moving his right hand in a gesture of blessing.[42]

राम

Stories abound in which Yogi Ramsuratkumar's simple words and spontaneous actions on some occasion proved uncannily prophetic in the years that followed. One such interesting and high-ly symbolic story, this one involving a stick, occurred during this December 1988 meeting with Lee Lozowick and company.

Purna Steinitz, one of Lee's long-time students, had been feeling great turmoil during much of the day that was spent with Yogi Ramsuratkumar. Seeing the Divine beggar giving attention to others in the group and seemingly ignoring him, Purna was jealous, "freak-ing out," as he described it. "Finally, I couldn't take it any more. I pranamed at Yogi Ramsuratkumar's feet for twenty minutes to half an hour. I just kept praying to him. 'Save me from this.' When I got up, I looked on the ground, and there was this stick, and I just handed it to Yogi Ramsuratkumar. I don't know why. It was a spontaneous act. That was it."[43]

Yogi Ramsuratkumar received the stick reverently, placing it in the folds of his clothing. Nothing more was said about it at the time.

"Later, giving out crackers to everyone while sitting with us at the temple, Yogi Ramsuratkumar crumbled Purna's cracker into pieces and popped a piece into Purna's mouth," another of the men record-ed. "'Please help Mr. Lee in his Work,' Yogi Ramsuratkumar said." It was an answer to Purna's prayer for help.

Purna continued: "The last night we were there, we went to this restaurant across the street. I remember noting what an amazing amount of traffic there was on the road that night, and how Yogi Ramsuratkumar held tightly to Lee's hand, and how he literally flew across that street, dodging through the congestion.

"When dinner was over I said, 'I'll pay for the dinner.' But Yogi Ramsuratkumar immediately corrected me. 'Mr. Lee pays for all,' he said."

Outside the restaurant, as the group bid their final farewells to the beggar, Lee made a full prostration and touched his master's feet. Immediately, one of the other men in the circle moved forward to do the same. "No, Thomas." Yogi Ramsuratkumar again made the com-munication that came to characterize this trip for Lee and his stu-dents. "Mr. Lee has done for all."

Then, turning to Purna, the Godchild reached into the folds of his rags and pulled out the stick. "Purna," the beggar said, with unbearable force couched in ultimate sweetness, as he handed the stick back to the astonished man, "help Mr. Lee in his Work."

Purna took the stick and carried it back to the United States. Despite numerous moves and changes in his living circumstances, Purna kept the stick as a sacred artifact, and as a reminder.

Yogi Ramsuratkumar's directive was a powerful motivation for the young man in supporting "Mr. Lee's mission," as the beggar had referred to it during those special days. The Godman's words proved unquestionably prophetic. Over the years, Purna distinguished him-self as one of Lee's most trustworthy students, an invaluable helpmate for Lee in the work of spreading the name of Yogi Ramsuratkumar in the West.

राम

"I can't find myself," said Lee, making an unintentional pun the next day. Yogi Ramsuratkumar laughed at this. The beggar had been smoking, one cigarette for each of the men in the room, and speaking of a letter he had just received from a devotee in Nagercoil. The letter contained a newspaper clipping about the Jayanti festival and included a picture of the procession that Lee and his companions had walked in. Pointing to the photo, Yogi Ramsuratkumar had asked the men if they were in it, which prompted Lee's remark, "I can't find myself."[44]

Joke or no joke, the men who witnessed the interplay of Yogi Ramsuratkumar and Lee Lozowick on these momentous days in December 1988 were aware that their American guide and teacher was becoming translucent. The light that they experienced around the beggar was being reflected by his devotee, Lee, in much the way that the moon reflects the light of the sun. "Whatever are Lee's tears," wrote one of the witnesses, "tears of relief and joy or tears of sorrow...I don't know and I didn't ask. I have the feeling it was a little of both."[45] The whole business of seeing *their* spiritual master so vulnerable to *his* master, might have been more terrifying for these younger men were it not also so wonderful and so instructive. They had invested their lives, some of them for nearly fifteen years, with Lee. Only now were they being shown the true nature of that relationship as Lee was absorbed more and more into the acknowledged source of his life, Yogi Ramsuratkumar.

राम

Meetings and partings are the stuff of human lives, and around Yogi Ramsuratkumar these moments were often exquisitely memorable. Of their departure, one of the American men wrote: "Out in the street he said goodbye to all of us, and we walked back into the market, one behind another. As we turned the corner, I looked back. He was still holding his fan up, watching."

As the group moved farther and farther away from the rag-draped figure, the words that Yogi Ramsuratkumar had spoken to them repeatedly throughout this visit came echoing back to this man: "This beggar begs of you and this beggar has received all he has begged of you. So I think none of you will shirk away, when this beggar begs of you: Don't forget the Divine name. This beggar prays to his Father to bless you all who have come here. All the Blessings of my Father for all of you!"[46]

25

CARRYING THE TORCH, 1989

 On February 12, 1989, Yogi Ramsuratkumar received a telegram from Kirsti, his devotee, informing him that Mataji Krishnabai, the exalted devotee of Swami Papa Ramdas, had attained mahasamadhi. Her body was cremated and the ashes enclosed in the beautiful marble altar in a small building on the property in Kanhangad. Across the continent, in the great temple in Tiruvannamalai, Yogi Ramsuratkumar sat reflectively during the hours in which Mataji's body was being cremated; he gazed at the sky.

Yogiji's love for this Mother had always been profound, and although he himself never returned to Kanhangad after 1952, he had sent many of his devotees there. "It is the holiest place for this beggar, the place of my Master Swami Ramdas," Yogi Ramsuratkumar had said in October 1988.[1] In the early days, Kirsti and others had been requested to spend weeks there, on numerous occasions. Kirsti was there when Mataji passed away. When she returned to Tiruvannamalai after this historic event, she brought back a flower garland that had lain on Krishnabai's tomb and presented it to Yogi Ramsuratkumar. He wore it briefly before handing it back to the younger woman, who preserved it.[2]

Among the many tasks that Krishnabai had taken up after Papa's death in 1963 was the ongoing promulgation of the taraka mantra, Ramnam. Mataji took it upon herself to spearhead a special project dedicated to achieving World Peace by inspiring men, women, and children around the world to celebrate the name of God with the mantra "Om Sri Ram Jai Ram Jai Jai Ram" as a dedicated spiritual practice. As early as 1955, on the occasion of her twenty-fifth anniversary of renunciation, Mataji had begun to encourage devotees to send their written expressions of the mantra to her at the ashram as their gift. It was her goal to achieve documentation of 15,500 crore (155 billion) repetitions by the year 2000. At the time of her death in 1989, however, only about 1,750 crore had been completed.

Mataji was tireless and utterly passionate in her dedication to the task. Devotees were asked to turn in their "counts" regularly – either by simply communicating how many mantram had been recited, or by sending in the notebooks in which they had carefully written the mantra on line after line, page after page. A small room on the ashram in Kanhangad became the storehouse for these written books and records, and to this day visitors are startled and even awestruck with the energy that is felt upon entering this room. "The intensity of that room is tangible," a recent visitor wrote. "We are here to join with all these prayers from around the world in a time when the earth could be plunged into war at any moment. It is so clear that such prayers as these are holding the world in place."[3]

A sign on the door of this room reports: "When Vinobaji [a relative of Mahatma Gandhi] came here in the year 1957, he was shown our Ramnam bank where *likhit* Ramnam books were kept. And he was so happy, he said: 'These are more powerful than atom bombs.'"[4]

In the early years, Mataji realized wisely that it was the name of God chanted with profound devotion that was the goal of Papa's work. Whether that name was "Ram" or "Siva" or "Jesus," it was all a reflection of the one all-pervasive reality. "When she took the accounts, any mantra was inclusive, not only RamNam," wrote a devotee. "Fr. Bede Griffiths used to send her the japa of the name of Jesus Christ, done in his Christian ashram. Any guru mantra was considered as the Name of God, as RamNam. Later on, with the movement expanding, only Ram's Name was used."[5]

Following Mataji Krishnabai's death, Yogi Ramsuratkumar suggested that Sadhu Rangarajan take up the promulgation of RamNam on his behalf: "This beggar initiated this mantra to Rangaraja and He suggested to him to spread the mantra to help the fulfillment of 15,500 crore Nama Japa Yagna of Mataji Krishnabai."[6]

The spiritual master is always offering gifts to his devotees, yet rarely are they received with the passion and applied with the diligence that the master intends. In this case, however, Yogi Ramsuratkumar's invitation was like a spark applied to dry tinder. Within a matter of months, Rangarajan had plunged ahead with his mission. The November 1989 issue of *Tattva Darsana* contained these statements:

> Words are inadequate to pay tribute to the Divine One, but there is a way to do that, and that is to do what He wants – nay begs – of us. He begs of us to chant the Divine Name of the Lord – any name that we would like to choose. He also begs of us to fulfil the dream of the Divine Mataji Krishnabai...to complete chanting of Ramanama Taraka "Aum Sri Ram Jai Ram Jai Jai Ram," 15,500 crores.[7]
>
> ...All those who participate in the japa are requested to send their accounts regularly every month, with their full names and addresses. Be missionaries propagating the message of our Master and motivate all to chant the mantra, "Aum Sri Ram Jai Ram Jai Jai Ram."[8]

In discussing the immensity and seeming impossibility of the task before him, Sadhu Rangarajan related a legend contained in the *Hitopadesa*, or *Book of Good Counsel* (a traditional Hindu compilation of morality tales). It concerned the tittiba bird whose eggs had been washed out to sea and who attempted to empty the ocean with the help of a blade of grass. According to the legend, all her companion birds laugh at her attempts, but the mighty Garuda, seeing the sorry bird, takes pity. Garuda (the great mythological king of birds, half-eagle/half-human) then spreads its wings and threatens the king of the seas, who renders the eggs back safely.

The story was the ideal metaphor for any "impossible" task, and Rangarajan ("this little tittiba bird") "started the word of spreading Ramnam for achieving the Divine Mother's target, with the mighty Garuda in the form of the Master standing by his side, waiting for the appropriate moment to spread His wings and see the completion of the target. By His grace and blessings..."[9]

In a short time, Rangarajan established branches of the World Ramnam Movement in South Africa, and, in November 1990, invited a new but ardent devotee of Yogi Ramsuratkumar's, Krishna Carcelle, to begin this same work in France, and later on the island of Mauritius, where Carcelle lived.

In speaking of the Movement's motivation, Rangarajan wrote:

More important than the japa counts is the transformation that the powerful vibrations of this japa done by millions all over the country and abroad would create in the lives of individuals and of nations, in moulding the very destiny of mankind. Mankind is at a cross-roads today and unless man takes to the path of spiritual evolution from the human level to the divine, he is bound to take a reverse turn and descend to the animal level. Man endowed with reason could ascend to the higher level only through sacrifice and sadhana. He has to sacrifice his little ego and take to the sadhana of self-realization. The Ramnam Japa Sadhana is the easiest and simplest, the most effective, means for spiritual evolution in this Kali Age.[10]

This mantra had certainly always been close to the heart of Yogi Ramsuratkumar, since it was this prayer that had effected his "death" at the hands of his Father Ramdas. Yet, in another domain, this practice had universal implications, reflective of the universality of the work in which Yogi Ramsuratkumar was always engaged. As Rangarajan wrote:

Her [Mataji's] mission is not one confined to the Anandashram or to the beloved children of Papa, but it is a sincere and sacred endeavour to bring all spiritual aspirants of the world under one umbrella. Ram is not merely the Hero of the Hindus. He is the All-pervading Supreme Divinity adored by the Muslims, the Father in Heaven worshipped by the Christians, the Arhan of the Jains, the Enlightened One of the Buddhists, the Sat-Sri-Akal of the Sikhs, the Ahura Mazda of the Parsis and the Absolute Ultimate Reality of the

Vedantins. Therefore, this World Ramnam Movement crosses the barriers of caste, creed, community, religion and nationality and embraces the entire humanity. Yogi Ramsuratkumar also occupies a place in the hearts of thousands of devotees spread all over the world and belonging to various nationalities and races.[11]

राम

In other significant outreach efforts of this year, Sri Ponkamaraj, who had organized some of the earliest Jayantis for his master, received the blessings of the beggar for the construction of a permanent shrine to Yogi Ramsuratkumar in the town of Kanimadam, near the southern tip of India.

The building, which is called the Mantralayam (*alayam* is a dedicated place where the individual soul can merge with the Paramatma or Supreme Soul), was initially nothing more than a thatched shed. On December 2, 1989, in Yogiji's name, Lee Lozowick blessed this humble temporary structure.

T. Ponkamaraj had met Yogi Ramsuratkumar in 1982, led to the beggar's feet at the direction of Mother Mayee of Kanyakumari. From his first sighting of the Godchild, who treated him "with the care and compassion of a mother," Ponkamaraj's heart was lost.[12] It was on the man's second visit, however, that he was tested in his motives, and thus received a most powerful communication from the beggar.

With an edge of fierceness in his voice, Yogi Ramsuratkumar challenged: "Why do you come to see this beggar, spending your money and time, instead of doing your duties?"

Despite Ponkamaraj's education and training as a lawyer, he was leveled to tears at hearing these words of the Godman. He was so surprised that he couldn't answer at first. Instead, "he prayed to Bhagwan within him that he had not committed any mistake and had come only seeking His Refuge."

Seeing the man's turmoil, the beggar took hold of Ponkamaraj's hands, led him into the house and instructed him and all who would ever approach: "You think it is important to see the physical frame of this beggar. But had you known that this beggar is everywhere, you would not come here often. Wherever you go, whomever you meet, whenever you are at your duty, if you utter the Name of this beggar, Yogi Ramsuratkumar, this beggar's Father will come to your support."[13]

The Mantralayam's permanent construction progressed to completion, and in 1993 it was dedicated in Bhagwan's name, and by his direction once again, by Sri Lee Lozowick. This building in its finished form contains a huge bas-relief mural depicting scenes from the life of Yogi Ramsuratkumar. Looking at the piece from left to right the visitor is instructed in the unfolding of the Godman's awakening. First, one sees a child sitting beside the Ganges in the company of sadhus; next, a grief-stricken youth standing at a well, a wounded bird in his hand; then a young man sitting before an enlightened sage, Aurobindo…and so on, to Ramana, to Papa Ramdas, to the foot of the sacred mountain, Arunachala, and finally to an image hovering above the Mantralayam, blessing all who enter.

In much the way that the Bethlehem crèche and Stations of the Cross in Christian cathedrals throughout the world have instructed

The Mantralayam, Kanimadam, South India

the faithful for centuries in the important events in the life of Jesus, this expansive mural in the Mantralayam both informs and inspires even the most casual visitor. A child can be told this great saint's story; following the scenes even the most uneducated peasant can learn of the life of Yogi Ramsuratkumar.

The building also houses a fourteen-foot statue, made of stone and covered with plaster, brightly painted in the image of the beggar. This *murti* (image of the deity) is wrapped in shawls and adorned with a green turban, and strings of mala beads and flowers. The sculptor who created it described an experience in which the stone was, for him, transmuted into flesh and blood – it became a living entity, imbued with the presence of Yogi Ramsuratkumar. The beggar had, in fact, given his word that he would always be present within this statue, and directed that Brahmin priests should perform traditional Vedic rituals here daily. The mantras "Om Sri Ram Jai Ram Jai Jai Ram" and "Yogi Ramsuratkumar Jaya Guru Raya" are the primary forms of celebration enacted here, and many miracles have been reported by Ponkamaraj and others testifying to the strength of Divine Presence that this shrine contains.[14]

राम

It was in 1989, at the Sannadhi house, that Justice Arunachalam, a member of the High Court of Madras, Tamil Nadu, first encountered the beggar-saint of Tiruvannamalai. The Justice would figure prominently in the life and work of Yogi Ramsuratkumar in later years, eventually being appointed chief administrator of the God-child's ashram.

In 1989, however, Arunachalam was not looking for a guru. In fact, in this first meeting he was neither fascinated nor repelled, as there was no outstanding chemistry between himself and the regal beggar. Still, when Yogi Ramsuratkumar requested, through some mutual friends, that Arunachalam preside over an upcoming function in Chennai, the judge did not refuse. It was an honor to have been singled out by the Godman, his friends advised him, and so, although without enthusiasm, Arunachalam wisely undertook the task.

The day of the conference, which was entitled "Divine Sources for Human Resource Development," proved to be a turning point in Justice Arunachalam's life. As he and his brother, Dr. T.S. Ramanathan, sat in the audience, they were both drawn irresistibly to a larger-than-life portrait of the beggar of Tiruvannamalai that graced the wall of the room. In this depiction, Yogi Ramsuratkumar stood with his palmyra fan, stick, and coconut bowl in his hands. In the background of the picture, Mount Arunachala loomed majestically. The longer the two men gazed at the portrait, the more it seemed to come alive for them. Independently, they each had the experience that the Godchild was actually moving.

When the conference was concluded, and quite successfully, the Justice was pleased, but more significantly, he felt altered. What had formerly been a sense of indifference toward the mad beggar-saint had suddenly erupted into a burning desire to be in his presence. Two days later, Justice Arunachalam and his brother made the trip to Tiruvannamalai with growing longing. Arriving at the beggar's feet, they prostrated at last, filled with regard for the one who had reached out to them, despite their initial doubts and resistance. This day was, in effect, Arunachalam's birthday as a lifelong disciple of Yogi Ramsuratkumar.[15]

राम

Paul William Roberts, who had met Yogi Ramsuratkumar in the early 1970s, used the term "auras of protection" to describe some of the beggar's work in relationship to world leaders and events.[16] Other devotees of the beggar have used similar words to pinpoint what they felt happening around them as a result of the Godchild's movements – the broad sweeping gestures of his hands above their heads; his walking, or even dancing, around them; his insistence on a particular configuration of the seating pattern.

In December 1989, a young German man, part of the group that accompanied Lee Lozowick to Tiruvannamalai this year, sat in the presence of Yogi Ramsuratkumar for the first time. "I remember the beggar walking around us as if 'writing' circles to provide a shield for us," he wrote.[17] It was a full moon night, and Yogi Ramsuratkumar had drawn his visitors to a corner of the temple complex in order to work with them alone. He did not want to be disturbed by the merely curious! This "shield" was intensified as the Godman moved within the circle of his guests and began to lead them in an enthusiastic chanting of *"Arunachala Siva"* and *"Om Namashivaya."* All the while, the beggar's arms were waving above their heads, and his steps became a dance – "almost child-like…full of passion and gracefulness and magic."[18]

As he danced, the Divine child played with his "friends" – plucking the nose of one man in a decidedly roguish gesture, and provoking another to experience a rush of Shakti-energy that caused humorous and spontaneous movements. The now ecstatic beggar delivered a series of energetic slaps to the back of his poet-son, Lee Lozowick, and again exploded into laughter.

"Why do you admire this dirty sinner?" Yogi Ramsuratkumar asked Lee during this 1989 visit. Without waiting for an answer, the Godman took Lee's hand and held it affectionately, then rubbed it repeatedly, refusing to let it go.

On the next day, December 8, 1989, Yogi Ramsuratkumar sequestered his Western guests at the home of V. Ganesan, the grandnephew of Ramana Maharshi, who had graciously extended his hospitality for the support of the beggar's work. Yogiji's relationship with Ganesan was often marked by familiar, even humorous, interchanges, which always proved instructive, nonetheless. This morning, knowing that Ganesan's spiritual path was one of nondualism, the Godchild teasingly and affectionately provoked him.

"You know, Ganesan, the great Master Sri Nisargadatta Maharaj [the author of the classic nondualistic treatise *I Am That*] said that when we see the truth everything becomes one. We will say 'I am that' (he points to one of the group) and I am that (points to another)…and I am that tree and that house; but you know, Ganesan, this sinner doesn't feel this way. This sinner says, 'I am this' (as he points to his own body). I don't say I am that and that and that; this beggar is only this."[19] As he delivered these last lines, Yogi Ramsuratkumar, like a child, touched first his own big toe, and then his forehead.

His host, Ganesan, received the beggar's words with a smile, if somewhat questioningly. Yogi Ramsuratkumar apparently delighted, in this moment and many others, in playing both sides against the middle; this time arguing for a more tantric view of reality above a nondualistic conception. His words on this morning instructed his guests in the cosmology of the body – reaffirming for them that the body was, in fact, *the* instrument of incarnation. In and through that very real, substantial body was the Father's work glorified.

A few hours later, however, the Godchild's words reflected another paradoxical truth. For the entire day, Yogi Ramsuratkumar had not let go of Lee Lozowick's hand. Their time together was short, and the Godman made use of every moment. As he tenderly stroked Lee's hand, and after a protracted period of silence, the beggar addressed himself again to Ganesan: "These are my hands," he said, referring to Lee's. "Do you know that Ganesan? These are my hands."

As his host nodded agreement, Yogi Ramsuratkumar continued to squeeze each of Lee's fingernails, and then to press his fist into Lee's palm. "These are my hands, Ganesan, this and this…Is this not madness, Ganesan? *All hands are my hands*, those and those and those [as he pointed to the other men in the room]. All hands are my hands."[20]

And then, thrusting his head back until it touched the wall against which he was seated, Yogi Ramsuratkumar "burst into his signature style of laughter…and falling completely over Mr. Lee's lap, hitting him on the shoulder and forcefully rubbing [Lee's] hand and arm up and down," said again, "Is it not madness, Ganesan?"[21]

"Yes," replied Ganesan, fueling the beggar's delight, "madness with a capital 'M'!"[22]

A moment later, the beggar had closed his eyes and entered deeply into the silence that followed upon his laughter. For a long time he remained absorbed in this attitude of prayer as he continued to hold Lee's hand. When he opened his eyes, it was to gently instruct his guests: "We must only do the work that Father has given us. We must finish it, and we can only do this by finishing our lila here."

In reflecting on these profound but decidedly elusive words, one of the men wrote, "I had never heard it spoken in such a way. The play of existence became something one could feel a sort of affectionate obligation to. It had to be done."[23]

राम

As the day wore on and the mood of blessed intoxication intensified, Yogiji himself even remarked about it a few times. "This beggar is getting more and more mad here. What is it, Ganesan, that gives this intoxication?"

Throughout the afternoon, Yogi Ramsuratkumar had frequently made a point of smelling the small, plucked flowers from Ganesan's garden that were near at hand. "Is it the flowers that give this intoxication, Ganesan? Or is it the tea? Or is it that this beggar has smoked too many cigarettes? What is this intoxicant?" he asked repeatedly, innocently, as if he were surprised that the nectar of the Divine was permeating everything around him. "What are you putting in the tea, Ganesan?" Or, "Is it the atmosphere?"[24]

राम

Yogi Ramsuratkumar's humor was legendary. He delighted in making plays on words, in poking fun at the illusions under which the world was burdened, in challenging and undermining the seriousness and rigidity of his most ardent devotees, and in highlighting the wondrous synchronicity of events that occurred moment to moment within his Father's realm.

Soon after Justice Arunachalam met Yogi Ramsuratkumar, on one of his first visits to the beggar at the Sannadhi house in 1989, the Godman asked his guest if it would be all right for him to smoke.

Arunachalam was shocked at the question, replying, "Swami, this is Your house and I've come to see You. Why would You ask me if You could smoke?"

Yogi Ramsuratkumar, in his playfully provocative way, smiled as he replied, "Well, you're the judge!"[25]

Sitting with Ganesan and the Americans in December 1989, Yogi Ramsuratkumar's humor was always available. The Godman smoked fairly constantly. Lee, who sat on the beggar's right, was privileged to light his cigarettes. Ganesan, on his left, would fill the Godchild's coconut bowl with drinking water. Observing this dynamic over several hours, Yogiji began to chuckle. He noted that Ganesan was bringing him water and coal, and that Lee was bringing the fire. With that winning combination, his "engine could run," he said. And then he melted into laughter once again, drawing his listeners with him.[26]

राम

On leaving Yogi Ramsuratkumar's presence that year, Lee Lozowick prostrated and devotedly touched his master's feet. The Godchild patted Lee's back repeatedly. "What are you doing, my Father?" the beggar asked, humbly, not expecting an answer.[27]

26

FAILING HEALTH, 1990

Dev Gogoi, a young Assamese man, stood on the steps of the mandapam immediately across the street from the Sannadhi Street residence of Yogi Ramsuratkumar. It was late August 1990, and Dev, who had met the gentle beggar in 1988, was a frequent visitor. A rapport much like grandfather and grandson had developed between the two men. Dev felt a deep affiliation with this man who had touched his heart and blessed him with help.

"I don't know *what* he has done for me," admitted Dev Gogoi, reflecting on his life with Yogi Ramsuratkumar, "but then a miracle happens and you wake up!" For Dev, that first "miracle" occurred a few years after he first met the beggar. Generally, Dev never asked for help in his personal life, but on one occasion he was sorely troubled. The place in which he was living was no longer available for him. He needed a new residenc, but didn't have the money to pay for one. "I was in a tight spot, and psychologically also I was tightly boxed in."

On the day when his troubles came to a head, Dev paid a visit to Yogiji. Uncharacteristically, the beggar asked, "Dev, how are you?" The way a friend would ask, in a very mundane, day-to-day way, "How are you, what's going on?"

"Swamiji, I am in a tough spot."

"What is it?" Yogi Ramsuratkumar inquired, obviously concerned.

"Well, I can't stay where I am staying and I don't have a place to go to," Dev told him.

Yogi Ramsuratkumar sent Dev on his way, as ever, with a blessing, and the young man returned to Ramanashram for lunch and then to his desk in the ashram library.

At about 2 P.M., the ashram manager walked into the library building and straight across the room to where Dev was seated. The manager had a large key in his hand, which he placed on the desk directly in front of Dev.

"This is yours. I've been asked to give you this key. It's for this cottage in the ashram – it's yours," the manager announced. Dev was overcome, awestruck.

"It was an instant manifestation! It means that he *did* help me," Dev said, crediting this miracle to the direct intervention and blessing of Yogi Ramsuratkumar.

On this day in August 1990, as Dev watched the movements of the crowd assembled before the house of his benefactor, he knew that something unusual was happening. The mood was somber, tinged with fear. People's faces betrayed concern, even panic. A large car was parked directly in front of the house, its doors open as if anticipating a cargo load. Voices raised and lowered quickly, and orders were shouted from a variety of sources. Something had happened to Yogi Ramsuratkumar! *Was he hurt?* Dev wondered, feeling a sudden stab of emotion. *Was he dead?*

In 1990, Yogi Ramsuratkumar was already seventy-two years old. It was no secret that his health had been questionable – off and on since 1986 he had suffered from stomach ulcers. Devotees had reported that he occasionally contracted in pain, or even vomited blood. Devaki Ma reported later that at this time in '86 he was so weak that he couldn't stand, but was dragging himself around on the floor.

Over the years, many were alarmed by such symptoms, but the beggar had adamantly refused to cater to *any* concerns about his physical health, even to the point of sending away those who questioned him about it. Ill or energetic, his one focus was in carrying out his Father's work. Except in the most dire circumstances, he would continue to receive his visitors and dispense blessings, even though it meant a great drain on his energy reserves.

470

Failing Health, 1990

This beggar is not limited to this body. This beggar is in the hands of his Father. It is all Father's blessing was his litany and creed. "This beggar doesn't care if this body is healthy or sick as long as it can do Father's Work, only Father's Work."[1] With such comments, Yogi Ramsuratkumar diligently reminded his devotees that they must not become attached to his form and must join him in the faith that was central to all that he stood for.

On this dreadful day in August 1990, as Dev watched from his post on the steps, he heard his name called. A man in the crowd across the street had spotted him and was imploring his assistance – another strong, able-bodied man was needed for a most important task. The nearly unconscious body of Yogi Ramsuratkumar was being lifted into the waiting car.

No questions asked, Dev moved into the place assigned to him, although the tears that rose into his eyes betrayed his mood. At a signal, the men were directed to lift the body. Dev was astounded to feel its immense weight. He was being asked to move a mountain.

राम

A few days prior to this event, as the master's strength was waning, more of his devotees in Tiruvannamalai were becoming aware of the Godchild's worsening condition. Messages of distress from fellow devotees reached Sadhu Rangarajan in Madras, and immediately he rushed to the beggar's abode in the shadow of Arunachala. For nearly three days, along with others, he kept vigil outside the Sannadhi residence. Yogi Ramsuratkumar allowed the sadhu entry for some time each day, and Rangarajan reported that, despite the weakness his master suffered, the beggar's words ever affirmed his unflinching faith. "Father is looking after this beggar," Yogi Ramsuratkumar said repeatedly.[2]

"On the third day, Yogiji sat up and began to act as if he were better," Rangarajan reported. As he was leaning against the wall, holding his visitor's hand, Yogi Ramsuratkumar shocked the sadhu by recalling: "Rangarajan, don't you have a program in Madras today? Didn't you write to this beggar about ten days ago to tell him of your program?"

"Yes, Bhagwan," replied the professor, "but I have cancelled the program."

"What!" Yogi Ramsuratkumar expressed both surprise and upset in hearing this. "Why did you cancel it?" he inquired.

Rangarajan tried to explain that for the last three days he had done nothing but stand out on the street, waiting upon the possibility of seeing his master. Furthermore, that he had left Madras in such a hurry because of so many messages of distress from fellow devotees, and because of his own present concern for Yogiji's health.

With no hesitation, Yogi Ramsuratkumar got up, walked inside his house, and brought out three, fifty-rupee notes. These he thrust into Rangarajan's hand for taxi fare, saying: "OK, you have come and you have seen this beggar. My Father will take care of this beggar. You have to do this beggar's work. Now go and attend the temple inauguration."[3]

"I have already told the program administrators that I am not coming, so they will have found another person to replace me. Also, I have taken a car from a devotee, which I have here, so I don't need the money for a taxi. Please allow me to stay here for two more days?"

Refusing to take back the money, Yogiji commanded his devotee: "No, Rangaraja, you must address that meeting this evening. That is this beggar's command. What is the time now?"

"Nine A.M., Bhagwan," Rangarajan replied.

"If you start now you can get back to Madras in time. How many hours will it take you?"

"By car, three hours," Rangarajan said, adding, "I can finish my lunch and then go."

Yogi Ramsuratkumar wanted immediate action: "No, no, no, you start *now*; you go to Madras *now*, attend that meeting. That is my Father's work. My Father will take care of all."

So Rangarajan left, went to Madras, and did address the meeting. It was August 22, 1990. As it turned out, much to the sadhu's surprise, the program organizers had not replaced him. Thus, "by the master's grace, we reached the venue in time to deliver the main address."[4]

When another devotee heard that Rangarajan had left the Godchild's side in this critical period, he was outraged. Rangarajan used the man's reaction to make an interesting distinction. "You are a *devotee*," he told the man. "You can do anything to the master. You can thrust food into his mouth; you can be very free in your behavior toward him. But a *disciple* cannot; he must completely obey the master."

राम

Just before the professor arrived in Tiruvannamalai, Devaki Ma received a disturbing phone call. Sandhya Reddy, calling from Tiruvannamalai, informed Devaki that their beloved Bhagwan was extremely ill.

"I was all set for going to Madras because my father was very sick," Devaki explained. She had just taken a ten-day medical leave from her teaching job at the college in Salem in order to travel to Madras to be available to her parents. With her packed bags in hand, and as she exited the college building, a messenger caught up with her, announcing the important call from Tiruvannamalai.

"The minute I heard 'Tiruvannamalai' I will forget everything else," Devaki Ma remarked. She ran back to the office, took the call from Sandhya, and without hesitating changed her plans.

"I just gave the ticket I had bought to my attendant of the lab," she explained, "and boarded the bus for Tiruvannamalai. I came straight. I didn't even inform my people [parents] I wasn't coming. That was how mad I was at the time. Nothing, nothing else, stayed in my mind except Bhagwan."[5]

It was nine o'clock at night when Devaki arrived at Sannadhi Street, accompanied by Dwaraknath and Sandhya Reddy. No lights were on in the house, but they could discern the figure of Yogi Ramsuratkumar lying down in the verandah. One or two people sat nearby, silently fanning the air around him. Not wanting to disturb the master unless they were summoned, the three visitors simply took up their posts a short distance from his door, and waited.

"Nobody came to open the door that night," Devaki noted. "Probably Bhagwan was too weak to say anything. So we waited for some time and then we left, thinking we would go back the next day."

473

By ten the next morning, the three friends were again gathered outside Yogi Ramsuratkumar's door. He was awake, and despite his extreme weakness, he called them in. One by one they entered, with utmost care not to disturb the mood of the room. Devaki prostrated before him.[6]

राम

Besides making her call to Devaki, Sandhya also phoned her father: "You need to come, he looks that bad."

"I had gone to Chittor to my factory," explained Mr. Reddy, "while Sandhya had gone to see Yogiji. She was horrified of what she saw. He was really ill. Because we had certain intimacies or privileges, which grace has given us, Sandhya thought I could help in the situation, that's why she asked me to come. "[7]

When Reddy arrived, Yogi Ramsuratkumar's condition was clearly critical. Numerous devotees had already offered to help, but the beggar had refused all attempts. "He was saying 'No' to everything," Reddy commented.

Dwaraknath Reddy, although he was younger than Yogi Ramsuratkumar, had been like a father-protector to the innocent beggar. Like two children, Yogiji and Reddy's daughter Sandhya had played together. Perhaps their relationship carried over from previous incarnations – Dwaraknath means "the king or leader of Dwaraka," and refers to Lord Krishna, who had moved the capital of his kingdom from Madhura to Dwaraka. Or perhaps it was simply the gentle, confident, and authoritative presence of Dwaraknath that distinguished his entreaties from those of the other supplicants.

Approaching the supine body of the ailing Godman, Dwaraknath initiated a proposal. Medical attention was necessary, specialist care. Would Yogi Ramsuratkumar agree to be taken to Madras, or would he prefer Vellore, which is a little closer?

"This beggar doesn't want to go anywhere!" Yogi Ramsuratkumar replied. Immediately, Dwaraknath negotiated another alternative. "Swamiji, shall I at least get Saidas to see you? We want to know what the position is."

Saidas, whom Yogi Ramsuratkumar knew, was an elderly homeopathic physician. Both Reddy and Sandhya trusted the man's abilities. He had a long history of experience and a particular acuity for diagnosis.

Surprisingly, Yogi Ramsuratkumar agreed. "If Saidas would see this beggar, maybe that can be done."

And so the arrangement was underway. Yogi Ramsuratkumar agreed to be moved to the Krupa House, the Reddy's residence, and Dr. Saidas was summoned. It was this move that Dev Gogoi had witnessed and gratefully assisted.

Dr. Saidas lived some distance away. As they awaited his arrival, the Reddys, together with Devaki and other close devotees, did their best to see to the comfort of their sacred charge.

The moment the doctor looked into his patient's eyes, there was no doubt. "His hemoglobin is very, very low. He needs a transfusion right away." Dr. Saidas was certain.

Yogi Ramsuratkumar at this point had already lost a lot of blood. There were other complications. "So we knew that to just [return] Swamiji there to his own house (Sannadhi Street) was not going to do anything," Dwaraknath explained.

"Please, Swamiji, stay with us," he implored the ailing beggar.

By this time, Dwaraknath believed that Yogi Ramsuratkumar himself realized the extremely critical nature of his condition. The beggar agreed to stay with the Reddys, where he was cared for day and night by Devaki, Sandhya, and others.

"We contacted a great devotee and doctor, Dr. Radhakrishnan, from Kerala," Reddy confirmed. "He used to come here frequently to spend a day with Swamiji and then go back. Swamiji had full confidence in him. On the phone we told him that Swamiji's condition is quite bad and that he needs attention. Dr. Radhakrishnan drove all night and landed here."[8]

The doctor, as a matter of fact, had only known the beggar for four months at the time of this exchange. The fact that Dwaraknath would refer to Radhakrishnan as a frequent visitor at that point is probably more a credit to the strength of the man's devotion.

राम

"Doctor, if I fall sick, will you come here and treat me?"

These prophetic words of Yogi Ramsuratkumar's were addressed to Dr. Radhakrishnan in mid-April of 1990, less than five months before the beggar's condition reached its critical point.

In 1990, Dr. Radhakrishnan knew nothing of the gentle man who lived at the foot of Arunachala. His home was across the subcontinent in Trichur, the cultural capital of Kerala state, and it was only through a chance meeting there, with Swami Nityananda Giri of Tapovanam, that he learned of the great yogi of Tiruvannamalai.

Radhakrishnan had approached Swami Nityananda Giri for his blessing for a special ritual that the doctor was organizing – the Atiraatra Yagna, a festival for much-needed rain in the drought-ridden state of Kerala.

"There is a Yogi in the garb of a beggar in Tiruvannamalai. His name is Ramsuratkumar. If you go and meet him and get his blessings, there will be no difficulty at all in making the Yagna a great success," Nityananda suggested.[9]

When Dr. Radhakrishnan pointed out that the ceremony was to be conducted within only twelve days, and that Tiruvannamalai was a long distance from Trichur (440 km), Swamiji dismissed the objection. It would be no problem, as far as Nityananda was concerned. He was insistent – this recommendation was the blessing he offered the doctor, regardless of the inconvenience imagined.

A few days later, on a Saturday night, Dr. Radhakrishnan left Trichur and arrived in Tiruvannamalai the next morning. He had been given directions to #90 Sannadhi Street and proceeded there immediately. Standing before the nondescript building, little did he suspect that more than a simple blessing lay in store for him. Since Swami Nityananda's command had been issued, Radhakrishnan was "impelled by an intense urge of the mind, despite a little hesitation." As he knocked on the iron gate of the abode, he was nervous.

A young boy, Yogiji's attendant, came to the door, received the news of Radhkrishnan's purpose, and disappeared inside the house. A few moments later, the boy returned to say that Yogi Ramsuratkumar would be out in two minutes, which he was. Opening the door to his distinguished guest, the beggar invited Dr. Radhakrishnan into the house. Taking up his coconut bowl, Yogi Ramsuratkumar offered his guest a sweet-tasting liquid, called *madhuparka* (honey), which the doctor explained is given "only on occasions of very auspicious nature, filled with divine potency."

"Are you Dr. Radhakrishan?" the gentle elder asked his visitor, as he gazed tenderly into the man's face.

When Radhakrishnan affirmed, Yogi Ramsuratkumar placed a packet in his hands, grasped the man's two hands together, and proceeded to recite a mantra japa. Describing what happened next, Dr. Radhakrishnan wrote:

> At first I did not feel anything special. But after ten minutes I felt as though an electric current was passing through my body. I just looked around, I was wondering whether there was any wire with insulation removed, anywhere in the neighbourhood. I doubted if I was sitting on some electric contact. But there was no evidence of any such thing. After twelve minutes I felt that, for about one or one and a half minutes, I had lost my consciousness.

Dr. Radhakrishnan regained his senses when Yogi Ramsuratkumar slapped him on his thigh.

"This beggar has been praying to his Master to bless you and the yagna and He has done it," the beggar announced. "What you are doing is very dear to the heart of this beggar. Now you can go to Kerala. Don't waste any time in Tiruvannamalai."

The interview was complete. It had lasted for less than twenty minutes. Dr. Radhakrishnan followed the beggar's injunction and immediately returned to his home.

The yagna ceremony was conducted as planned, and blessed rain fell upon Kerala. The work had been successful.

A short time later, Dr. Radhakrishan returned to Tiruvannamalai to offer his thanks to the great "Yogi in the garb of a beggar." The master was pleased to see him and invited the doctor to the home of V. Ganesan, the editor of *Mountain Path Magazine*, where they could converse without disturbance from the crowds that normally attended the beggar's every move on Sannadhi Street.

"You brought good rains to Kerala by conducting yagna. Why is it that we have not had rains in Tiruvannamalai for the last ten months? Why don't you bring some rain here?" Ganesan asked, with obvious good nature, upon meeting Dr. Radhakrishan.

"Why should you doubt?" the doctor shot back at Ganesan, surprising himself with the force of his own words. "In the next seventy-two hours you will have a heavy rain here at least for two hours."

The prediction had been uttered without conscious thought. It had come through him, seemingly out of nowhere, and Dr. Radhakrishnan was immediately embarrassed by his hasty assessment. He turned to Yogi Ramsuratkumar apologetically: "Swami, I have uttered nonsense. You must kindly help me out," he confessed, with all humility.

For the beggar, the whole event was enormously entertaining. He burst into uncontrollable laughter, like a crazily giggling child. In fact, the laughter was so strong that the Divine beggar literally careened into Dr. Radhakrishnan's lap. There he stayed, safely nestled, for nearly two minutes.

At last, rising from his place on the floor, Yogi Ramsuratkumar stepped out into the garden and stood for twenty minutes, silently gazing at the top of the Arunachala hill. When the master returned to his visitor and host once again, the mood had shifted significantly. Perhaps the effort of his invocations had exhausted the beggar, or perhaps he was struck with the pain that accompanied his currently weakened condition, but his words were swift and to the point. "I feel uncomfortable, I want to lie down," he said sweetly. Before a mat could be spread for him to lie down upon, Yogi Ramsuratkumar had already dropped to the ground.

After some time, as he lay there, Yogi Ramsuratkumar turned his attention to the sky. Amazingly, the signs of impending rain were at once apparent to all.

"This Beggar is very tired," Yogi Ramsuratkumar said as the rain began to fall. "Please take me to my place."

Dr. Radhakrishnan accompanied his newfound friend back to Sannadhi Street, where the beggar dismissed him graciously. "Doctor, you need not stay here anymore. The rain is only in Tiruvanna-malai," the master said, assuring his guest that he would have no trouble from the weather during his long return drive. Then, with a jovial expression, despite his fatigue or discomfort, Yogi Ramsuratkumar asked the question that would characterize their relationship from then on – *Would Radhakrishnan treat him if he were to fall sick?*

Unhesitatingly, Dr. Radhakrishnan agreed.

As both men had predicted, heavy rains lasted for two hours that day…but only in Tiruvannamalai. A short way beyond the boundaries of the city, the roads were dry.

"He has made a tremendous impact on my spiritual life," Radhakrishnan wrote:

> I, who have absolute faith in Spirituality, am a scientist. To me, a student of science, the experiences in the spiritual field were mere superstitions until I came into contact with Yogi Ramsuratkumar. This contact was a great experience which became a turning point in my life. Yogi Ramsuratkumar is a supreme example of the Truth that by purifying the mind through Ishvara Nama Japa, and by raising the mind and body through the practice of Yoga, one can bring them to the path of God realisation.[10]

राम

Having learned that Yogi Ramsuratkumar probably needed a blood transfusion, Dr. Radhakrishnan had brought a team with him on this August day in 1990. Arriving at Krupa House, he found Yogiji lying within a makeshift shelter on the patio under the mango trees that he loved to sit beneath. After his pranams to the one who had sent rain to the thirsty fields of his own life, Dr. Radhakrishnan immediately set to work.

"We put up a canvas; it was like an army tent, like a little hospital in the desert," Dwaraknath reported, "and the doctor would hang up the bottles to pulse."[11] Already, devotees were lining up outside the gates of Krupa House. The concrete bench that runs along the whole front of the house became the focal arena used by the doctor and his people to set up a blood bank. Blood was taken from the devotees waiting outside of the gate and was immediately sent to a "laboratory" right there as well, where it was tested to determine its type. All this was going on just ten meters away from where Yogi Ramsuratkumar was lying.

Under Radhakrishan's expert guidance, the blood transfusion was accomplished. In a symbolic gesture that pointed directly to the heart of the relationship between master and disciple, Yogi Ramsuratkumar took the blood of his devotees into his own veins. "From whoever was willing to give," Mr. Reddy commented.

According to the will of his Father, once the procedure was complete Yogi Ramsuratkumar remained at Krupa House, where he was attended day and night by Dr. Radhakrishnan, Ma Devaki, the Reddys, and a few others.

"He could have had anything he wanted," Dwaraknath commented, expressing his wish that Yogi Ramsuratkumar be given any amenity that would support his healing. "At that time the house was here, but he didn't want to be in the house. According to his nature, or perhaps because he didn't want to deprive [i.e., inconvenience] us, he didn't want to stay in the house. So we made a little space out here [on the patio of the garden], and he stayed with us, like that."

Even though the beggar was recovering from a health crisis, this did not stop the visitors. As word spread through town, more and more gathered at the Krupa gate. There was little escape from public attention for the Godman, whether he was fully energetic or utterly weakened. "It was quite a situation," Mr. Reddy said kindly, although his concern that people had disrespected the nature of the beggar's condition, putting their own needs ahead of his, could be heard between the lines of his words.

One morning, ten days after the procedure had been successfully completed, Yogi Ramsuratkumar decided to leave, to return to his house on Sannadhi Street.

"Dwarak Reddy, now this beggar will go back to his place," he suddenly announced, to everyone's surprise. His caregivers at this time knew better than to try to stop him. Slowly, he arranged himself, and obediently Dwaraknath drove him back to Sannadhi Street.

राम

For Devaki and several other close female disciples of Yogi Ramsuratkumar's –Rajalakshmi, Viyayakka, and Vijayalaskmi – the events in August 1990 provided a strong motivation for moving closer in order to serve their master in whatever ways he would allow.

With his blessing, they rented, at their own expense, a set of rooms in the city within his close proximity. Yogi Ramsuratkumar named their living quarters "Sudama." It was a touchingly appropriate title. Sudama was the name of a poor boyhood friend of Lord Krishna's. The two had met during their student days, but while Krishna went on to become king of Dwaraka, Sudama married and lived in abject poverty. When Sudama's wife learned of Krishna's whereabouts, she urged her husband to approach him for a boon to assuage their misery. Journeying to Dwaraka, Sudama could not bring himself to ask his lord for anything but merely rejoiced in Krishna's glorious presence. As his friend was leaving, Krishna thanked Sudama for his devotion and told him that a gift would be awaiting his return. When Sudama rejoined his wife, he found that a majestic palace, with all accompanying wealth, had been awarded them. Here they lived, in gratitude and devotion to Lord Krishna, for the rest of their lives. What distinguished Sudama most of all was his nonattachment to his newfound wealth. God alone was always and only his greatest treasure.

The women who lived at Sudama came to be referred to as the "Sudama sisters" by those who knew them. Like their namesake, these women would come to be distinguished by their "undemanding service-oriented devotion to Bhagwan."[12]

Oh Appa, Appa,
    Yogi Ramsuratkumar
when Devaki looks at You,
    the look in her eyes is quite devastating.
How can one think they love You
    and then watch one who does?
Your son says this mad Beggar,
    and don't You deny it –
if lee needs to learn more about love
    You will teach him through the Ma-s at Sudama.
        – Lee Lozowick[13]

The means whereby Devaki and her companions served Yogi Ramsuratkumar were not prescribed in any way. His attendants throughout the years had always been males, although he had received food from women many times. To venture into the close proximity of one such as this beggar was not a task to be undertaken by the weak of heart. Commenting about Devaki's service, which he witnessed on numerous occasions, Will Zulkowski noted, "I knew how hard the work would be around Swami. Swami doesn't just pulverize you, he liquifies you. Pulverization is still too gross. Around him you become liquid! She survived it, and she took it, and I have all the respect in the world for her. I don't think there is any job harder on earth than serving a real saint."[14]

It was their courage, their awareness, and primarily their pure intention which allowed these Sudama sisters to see what was needed and humbly (even invisibly) offer it. By simply being there, as often as they could be, Devaki and friends became a reliable presence that Yogi Ramsuratkumar tested and found useful to his work.

Later, with the assistance of Dwaraknath Reddy, they found property and had a house built, which also bore the name Sudama. In 1993, the women moved from their rented rooms to the new residence – not far from Reddy's at Chengam Road, Street #3 – in the vicinity of the same property that would later become the Ashram of Yogi Ramsuratkumar. Later, in 1993, this house would also become the home of the beggar.

RIGHT HAND MAN, 1991

"Mani was not interested in saints," explained Rajalakshmi, speaking about her husband. Prior to his first meeting with the divine beggar of Tiruvannamalai in December 1991, Subramanium, whom Yogi Ramsuratkumar always called "Mani," wanted no part of the guru-devotee scene. "He will go to the temple, he will worship God…like that only," Rajalakshmi (Raji) noted. But when it came to visiting the saints, he was adamant: "I'm not going!"[1]

It was 1990 when Rajalakshmi and Mani, who lived in Chennai, first heard of the enigmatic Godchild. A friend, a senior government official, Shri V.T. Thurairaj, told them of the beggar's miraculous presence. One day, stopped in his car at a railway crossing in Tiruvannamalai, Thurairaj had met an old man, curiously dressed – long hair, matted beard, rags. The man's appearance was memorable, and Thurairaj was moved to offer the odd beggar some money.

The beggar, Yogi Ramsuratkumar, approached the car and addressed Mr. Thurairaj, asking him questions that could only have been known by a close associate: *Was his wife living with him?* (She was not.) Then, turning to the man's driver, the beggar hit the mark even more precisely: *Why was he cheating his employer, who was so kind and fair?* As the stunned driver recovered his breath, the beggar added, "Your poverty will be relieved," and continued on his way. The man had, in fact, stolen money from Thurairaj's wallet that very morning, which he immediately admitted with great remorse.

This remarkable incident took on greater significance still when, shortly afterwards, Mr. Thurairaj's wife returned to live with him, and the poor driver won a state lottery.

When Thurairaj made inquiries around town about the identity of the odd beggar, he learned that the person he had met was known as Visiri Samiyar (country hand fan swami). Deeply impressed, Thurairaj began to make occasional visits to the old beggar, whom he soon came to revere as a saint.

Hearing Thurairaj's story, Mani was clearly intrigued, although still reluctant to bite the bait. It took his wife Rajalakshmi's frequent urgings, and even threats that she would travel to Tiruvannamalai on her own, to finally break his resolve to stay away from such "saints." "I had always avoided ashrams. I was not interested in Vedic rites and did not practice ordinary Hindu rituals," Mani wrote in a brilliant account of his years with Yogi Ramsuratkumar. "Neither my wife nor I had a spiritual background. There are many spiritual masters in India but they had never been of any interest to me personally."[2]

The time was ripe for a change, however. At fifty-two years old, Mani was the father of three grown children – two sons and one daughter – and a partner in a highly successful contracting business that had involved him in major projects in various parts of Southeast Asia. He considered himself a man of the world, "cosmopolitan." Yet, as always, the accomplishments had come with a stiff price tag. The stresses of their modern life had created problems. By 1991, Mani was ready to admit that he and Raji were "searching for guidance and relief from difficulties."[3] The form that guidance and relief would take, however, they could never had imagined. In the person of Yogi Ramsuratkumar, the Divine was, in its own mysterious way, putting the pieces together for a very specific work – a task that would require skills in negotiation, management, and large-scale construction, exactly the talents that Mani had developed over a lifetime of work in the world.

राम

Earlier in 1991, Yogi Ramsuratkumar had received an offer of land from a wealthy female devotee. The donation was meant for the construction of a more permanent ashram, a place where devotees would have easier and more consistent access to the Godchild, whose name and reputation were spreading fast throughout South India. As growing numbers lined up along busy Sannadhi Street and attempted to gain his darshan, it was becoming more and more obvious that another place would soon be needed.

When the beggar learned of the land's location – it was on the outskirts of town, closer to the railway station – he was immediately clear that it was not the place, nor the time, for such a venture. "Not that land! Ashram is big problem. Not now. You go and do your duty," Yogi Ramsuratkumar told Ramamurti, an ardent disciple with family ties in the construction business. "There is a saying in Tamil," Ramamurti reported, "that says 'ashrams mean difficulties,'" and Yogi Ramsuratkumar undoubtedly knew the truth of it.[4]

Nonetheless, the seeds were in the wind. Within a few months they would land.

राम

The story of Mani and Rajalakshmi's first encounter with Yogi Ramsuratkumar, as significant as it ultimately proved to be, was also a bit like a comedy routine. One is reminded of a slapstick standard in which one character exits a room by the back door at the precise moment when the person he is looking for enters the same room through the front. The two characters entirely miss each other, repeatedly.

"I said to Mani, 'I want to visit the temple first, then go to Yogi,'" Rajalakshmi reported in describing their late-December trip to Tiruvannamalai in 1991. Despite Mani's intuition that they should pay their respects to the holy man first, they set off to the great shrine, where they spent several hours. Finally, at about five in the evening, the couple presented themselves at the door of the small house on Sannadhi Street and awaited their much-anticipated turn to meet the Godman.

As usual, a crowd had gathered at the beggar's steps. "Everybody was going in and having his darshan and then leaving. But he didn't call us," said Raji. Approaching a boy who was standing near the gate, Mani's wife asked why they were not yet being allowed inside. "When Yogi says, only then I can call. Otherwise I can't allow you to go in," the young attendant replied.[5]

"You go and tell that we have come to see him," Raji said firmly, her impatience growing. A moment later the child returned and announced that Yogiji wanted the couple to go to the temple, and then, only after spending some time there, to return to him.

For Mani, who was reluctant to undertake this visit in the first place, this new request was an added annoyance. He was also clearly frustrated with himself, realizing that what he had intuited about visiting Yogiji first had indeed been true. Voicing his concern, he addressed his wife: "When you come to see Yogi, you have to finish that work first. Suddenly, you changed the program, and went to temple. Now by Yogi's saying, again we must go to temple."[6]

Instead of following the Godchild's directive to the letter, however, the couple chose to follow their own wills, a course dictated by logic and personal convenience. "We can't go to temple *again*," Rajalakshmi said at the time. "No, it's a huge temple, and it will take nearly two hours."

Instead, as they were very hungry, Mani and Rajalakshmi went to a nearby hotel and had refreshments. When their meal was completed, the couple again returned to the beggar's house, and again asked permission to have his audience. This time, the message they received felt like another nail driven into a coffin of self will.

"Tell them to go and eat something, then come back," Yogi Ramsuratkumar told the young attendant who announced them. And so, for the second time, the couple were turned away.

"It was in that moment that I understood there was some significance in this communication,"[7] Mani wrote, revealing a truth that numerous devotees throughout the years had come to recognize about the way in which Yogi Ramsuratkumar's attention and help was rendered. If they were to gain anything from their association with the likes of this saint, they would do so only by putting aside their own agendas, thus allowing *him alone* to call the shots.

राम

Hearing a discourse about the necessity for obedience in spiritual life is a meagre substitute for being hit on the head with one's own obstinacy. Yogi Ramsuratkumar was a master of subtlety who seemed to know *everything* without having to know *anything* about one's circumstances. Over and over, situations arose around him that served to give first-hand teaching lessons to visitors and guests. And the closer one came to the fire in the beggar's kitchen, as Mani would learn in the years ahead, the more dramatic would those object lessons be.

Thousands of seekers and sadhus had thrown themselves at the Godchild's feet since his arrival in Tiruvannamalai in 1959. Many had come expecting some wise discourse – the few well-chosen words that would dissolve a lifelong dilemma – only to find that they were being given instead an object lesson that precisely addressed a much deeper issue, or something they had been unwilling to ask.

A case in point: Earlier in 1991, a young American seeker, Everett Jaime, had his first meeting with Yogi Ramsuratkumar. After spending a silent hour of rich interior rapport during which all his questions vanished, Everett was suddenly insecure, thinking that he should be using the time to draw out some "pearls of wisdom"… something "special"…from the saint. Summoning his logical resolve, he broke the silence: "What does it mean that you call yourself a beggar?" Everett asked. The question was no sooner out of his mouth than he realized how flat it had fallen into the elegant atmosphere of prayer and contemplation that had just a moment ago surrounded them. The beggar said nothing.

Immediately, a knock and a cry were heard at the front gate. Glancing in the direction of the noise, Everett spied a beggar child with his hands thrust through the gate, imploring some attention. In one seamless gesture, Yogi Ramsuratkumar reached into a bowl near his side and picked up a piece of rock candy, pure sugar, which he handed to his male attendant with a gesture toward the child. The man instantly made his way to the door and gently deposited the sweet into the little boy's outstretched hand. A huge smile crossed the child's face. Grasping his prasad, he turned and skipped along down the road.

Yogi Ramsuratkumar never gave an answer to the American's question. "He didn't have to," said Jaime. "It was obvious."

राम

After their two false starts on that late December day in 1991, Mani and Rajalakshmi were admitted at last into the beggar's presence. Their time with Yogi Ramsuratkumar was extraordinarily brief, probably less than twenty minutes. Mani prostrated before him, received a hearty pat on the back, was asked his name, was given a piece of fruit as prasad, and was touched by the Godman's all-encompassing invocation, "My Father blesses you." In a similar fashion, both his son and Rajalakshmi were blessed.

"We stood for a minute in total silence looking at Yogi Ramsuratkumar. I don't think we said anything, we just gazed at Him expectantly, hoping He would read our minds and tell us everything would be okay," Mani wrote.[8] Apparently, however, nothing more was needed, and the family soon found themselves being escorted to the door by the beggar's attendant. Despite a sense of having been rushed through something, the importance of which he was not fully aware, Mani felt enormously grateful, and satisfied in a part of his soul that been hungry for a very long time. "I felt optimistic about everything," he admitted, reflecting that wondrous sense of "rightness" with the world and a sharpened awareness of benevolence that characterized his first interaction with Yogi Ramsuratkumar.[9]

When the couple moved off the verandah of the Sannadhi house and out onto the street, a new surprise awaited them. They met a young Korean man who had waited all day outside the beggar's door without having been called. Speaking with him turned out to be exactly the kind of synchronicity that one marveled at later, but which at the time seemed entirely natural. Despite his own disappointment, the Korean man was on fire with his passion for speaking of Yogi Ramsuratkumar, and Mani and Raji were only too glad to listen. Over a meal, Mani asked the foreigner how he had come to know of Yogiji. The Korean man noted that, "One Sadhu Rangarajan from Chennai had told about Yogi Ramsuratkumar, so I came."[10]

Yogi Ramsuratkumar and his Eternal Slave, Devaki Ma

Yogi Ramsuratkumar and Mani

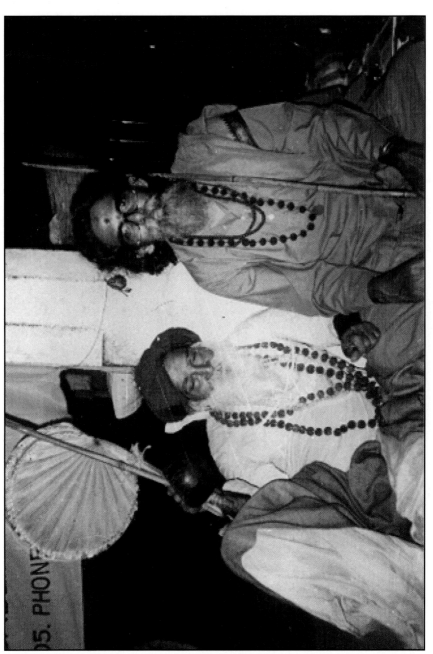

The master, Yogi Ramsuratkumar, with Sadhu Prof. V. Rangarajan, January 2, 1994

Yogi Ramsuratkumar ascends the steps to survey ashram construction

December 1994: Yogi Ramsuratkumar walks with
Lee Lozowick in the garden at V. Ganesan's home

Yogi Ramsuratkumar visits the Sannadhi Street house, December 1995

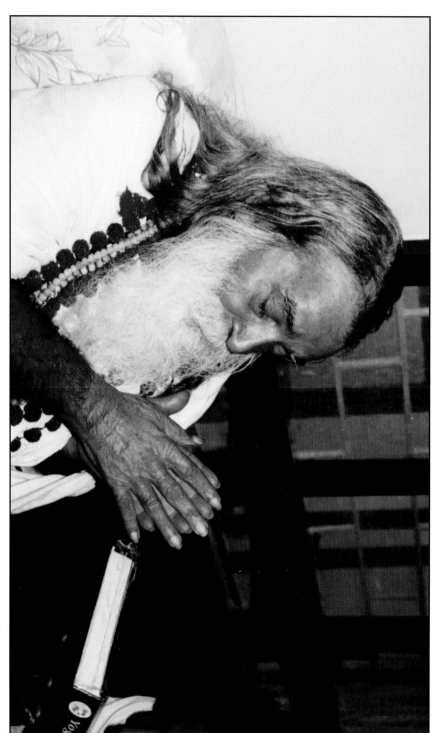

Yogi Ramsuratkumar, circa 1996

The master leaves darshan on the arm of his attendant Selveraj, 1997

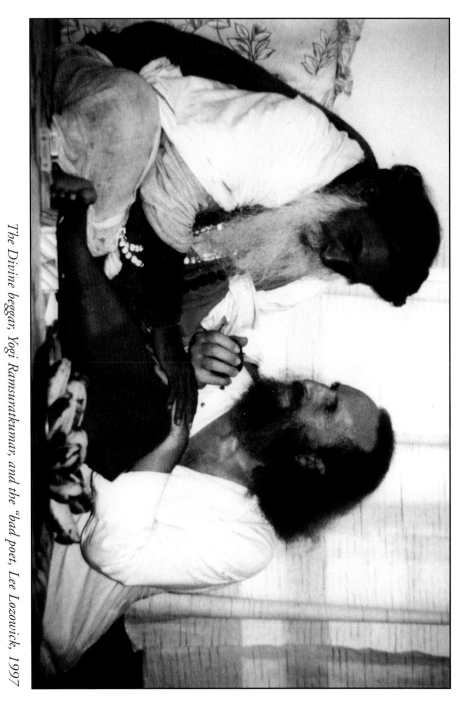

The Divine beggar, Yogi Ramsuratkumar, and the "bad poet, Lee Lozowick, 1997

Yogi Ramsuratkumar, 1999

Yogi Ramsuratkumar outside near the Veda Patashala, 2000

Yogi Ramsuratkumar with Lee Lozowick, December 2000

February 2001: Yogi Ramsuratkumar in the Abode,
two weeks before leaving his body

The head of the bronze vigraha of Yogi Ramsuratkumar

Chennai (Madras) was, after all, their home. Learning that this new-found saint whom they had just visited had a dedicated servant living there – a man who had organized numerous agencies in the name of Yogi Ramsuratkumar and held regular programs in the Godman's honor – greatly pleased Mani and Rajalakshmi.

A few days after they returned to Chennai, the couple contacted Rangarajan and enthusiastically threw themselves into the activities of the Yogi Ramsuratkumar Youth Association and other projects. They also participated in regular satsangs in which the chanting of Yogi Ramsuratkumar's name and the Ram mantra were carried on. The Godman had blessed them abundantly in their few brief moments with him, and now they had his name as their constant companion. Mani and Rajalakshmi, without knowing it, were on a fast track to destruction...in the most exalted sense of the word.

राम

"Whenever I felt like going to Tiruvannamalai I'd go to Sadhu Rangarajan's place. I'd offer something," Rajalakshmi said, explaining how she was being drawn closer and closer to Yogi Ramsuratkumar with little effort. "If I was disturbed, I'd go to this place."[11]

It was almost a year before the couple would make another trip to the beggar's side, yet their faith and availability to the Godchild's influence was deepening. For Raji, there were fewer obstacles to overcome in approaching this path of devotion. For Mani, several road-blocks of the rational mind had to be negotiated before his heart was taken. In the meantime, however, they continued their enthusiastic association with the other Chennai followers.

In one of their earliest meetings at the Chennai center, the couple each received a small pocketsize photograph of Yogi Ramsurat-kumar, whom they now called "Bhagwan" (literally, God or Blessed One), as they had heard Sadhu Rangarajan and other devotees refer to the beautiful beggar. It was during this meeting that one man recounted a most remarkable story, which he fully credited to the intervention of Yogi Ramsuratkumar. This man had always carried a small photograph of Bhagwan in his pocket. In the midst of a crowd-ed street one day, a long-horned bull became highly agitated and was about to charge this man. When the devotee said the name of Yogi Ramsuratkumar, however, the bull stumbled and fell to its knees in such a way that its horns broke. The man and all the rest of the crowd were able to escape without harm.

Hearing this story, Mani was extremely skeptical. The idea that a bull's horns would break in such a manner was completely unreasonable to him. "How can we believe that the horn was broken…we have faith in Yogi Ramsuratkumar, but this is too much, no?"[12] Mani argued. Despite his doubt, however, both Mani and Raji kept the beggar's picture close by. "I was keeping it in my purse and Mani was keeping it in his pocket," Rajalakshmi explained.

A few days later, Mani's sister, together with her husband and their son, paid the couple a visit, and plans were made to drive to Chitoor, the husband's native city. While Mani was to accompany his relatives, Rajalakshmi took the opportunity to visit Tiruvannamalai with Sadhu Rangarajan to have the darshan of Yogi Ramsuratkumar.

En route to Chitoor, the driver was speeding and lost control of the car. The vehicle rolled over several times and landed in a ditch upside down. Mani's brother-in-law was thrown through the front windshield, which had popped out intact. While everyone was stunned, miraculously no one was injured. As Mani later wrote: "I stood up looking at the overturned car, my head as well as the tires still spinning. I touched my chest in an unconscious gesture and felt the hard smoothness of the photograph of Yogi Ramsuratkumar encased in plastic."[13] At the exact time that this accident was occurring, Rajalakshmi was sitting before her master in the small house on Sannadhi Street. The beggar's conversation that day had a one-pointed focus. "He was asking about Mani only," Raji remembered vividly. "Where he has gone? Why has he not come here? he was asking."

The shock of this near tragedy dramatically awakened Mani's faith. His previous intellectual holdout about what was possible within the Godman's world melted like thin ice in the sun. He felt a simultaneous remorse for the general apathy of his life, and particularly for the cynical ways in which he had previously spoken of the miracles of saints. "I apologized to Him silently across the physical distance between us," Mani wrote.[14]

For Raji, hearing of the events, the effect was dramatic too. "Who could believe that? The car rolled down, but there was no scratch on them, even to the driver, even to the child. Then only I realized [about the previous incident of the bull's horns], *it is not a story*! It is a real thing, no? Mani said to me, 'This accident was prevented by Bhagwan.'"

When the couple paid their second visit to Yogi Ramsuratkumar, Mani, filled with gratitude for having just met the beggar and for his recent intervention in their lives, recounted the entire story of the accident with great seriousness. Yogi Ramsuratkumar laughed heartily. "What fortune is this? You come to this Beggar and you have a car accident?" the Godchild said, laughing more. Raising his hands, Bhagwan said simply, "My Father blesses you."

For Mani, there were no more doubts. "My wife and I had truly entered and were bathing in a stream that flowed from Yogi Ramsuratkumar. The problems we were seeking resolve from about a year earlier seemed diminished in significance and irrelevant when seen in the light of the joy Yogi Ramsuratkumar had brought to our lives… Our lives were turning in a direction we could not even begin to understand at the time."[15]

राम

This beggar is not limited to this body. If you pray with Faith, He can be found anywhere and everywhere!

– Yogi Ramsuratkumar

Like Mani and Raji, other men and women had been similarly gifted with dramatic demonstrations of the power over life and death that Yogi Ramsuratkumar seemed to hold. Sadhu Rangarajan had surely told the new devotees, Mani and Raji, of the event that had humbled *him* in October 1991, just a few months before their first connection with the mad beggar.

Rangarajan was traveling in northwestern India, near the Ganges River, on behalf of the World Ramnam Movement. On the morning of October 19, he made his way to the banks of Mother Ganga to make his customary ablutions. Here he found the pair of sandals that he had misplaced the day before, in exactly the spot in which he had left them. His immediate response was to offer praise to Yogi Ramsuratkumar, in whose mercy all things were protected. With that, and following his prayers to Mother Ganga, Rangarajan entered the water. His mood was joyful, and he ventured to swim a bit, although the current was strong. Within a matter of minutes, however, his playfulness turned to alarm when he realized that the current was quickly pulling him far from shore.

The sadhu struggled frantically to keep his head above the water as he waved vigorously to the small crowd of bathers on the shore that was fast receding. In a letter he wrote on that very day, he described the outcome to Yogi Ramsuratkumar:

> I found death staring at my face, trying to devour me, but a sudden flash of thought about You came in the mind. I felt that You were rushing to my help. With the confidence of a child in the mother's arms, I resigned myself to Your Grace and made valiant attempt to float, at least to raise my palm above the water level. Suddenly I felt Your presence very near me. Though I was below the level of water, I found someone dragging me up by holding the lock of my hair...[16]

As it turned out, shouts from some of the observers on shore attracted the attention of a few boatmen who were unloading their early morning passengers. "That sadhu is getting drowned," the people had screamed. Immediately two boats raced toward the drowning man, in time to save him.

Coincidentally, on the day before, Rangarajan had addressed a crowd of people at a Ramnam satsang about "the fickleness of human existence," stressing "the need to make it sublime by turning to a higher goal in life." In his reflections to Yogi Ramsuratkumar, the sadhu concluded:

> Probably it is for the fulfillment of that goal that you have snatched me back from the clutches of Death. The new life that You have given me is dedicated once again at Your holy

feet! Thy will be done! Ganga is Your mother; She has returned me to You for Your work![17]

Rangarajan signed this letter, "Your humble disciple."

Other, much older, miracle stories were already legendary when Mani and Rajalakshmi first met Yogi Ramsuratkumar. Each affirmed that life and death were in the beggar's hands.

राम

While the car accident event was the first miracle Mani witnessed around Yogi Ramsuratkumar, it would not be the last. As Mani and Raji's years in Bhagwan's company progressed, they would find the beggar's hand to be a source of unexplainable power; his name, a salvation to those who used it with faith.

During one critical period in the mid-1990s, when Yogi Ramsuratkumar had requested that Mani and Rajalakshmi stay in residence at the Tiruvannamalai ashram (where Mani was supervising both construction and management), the couple was upset to learn that their second daughter-in-law was confined to the hospital in Madras due to complications with her pregnancy. Since her husband was traveling on business, she wanted Raji and Mani to be with her, as the doctors had informed her that a caesarian birth was likely.

Mani immediately notified his sister, a nurse in Madras, and asked her assistance. After visiting the young woman, the sister too confirmed that a surgical birth seemed certain.

Greatly disturbed, Mani and Raji approached Yogi Ramsuratkumar with the sad news. The Godman, however, was unmoved. *The birth would be normal,* he told them, with full assurance.

Knowing that Rajalakshmi and Mani – as any "reasonable" and "caring" relatives would – wanted to leave the ashram to be with their daughter-in-law, Yogi Ramsuratkumar gave them an out ...of sorts. "This beggar is not interested in sending Rajalakshmi and Mani to Madras," he told them firmly, yet compassionately. "If Rajalakshmi feels like going, this beggar has nothing to say."[18] The Godman's preference was perfectly clear, even though he was granting his devotees the permission to choose another course of action.

It is an enormous credit to the obedience of these two servants that, despite their doubts and their growing concern on this occasion, they chose to honor his words. They stayed in Tiruvannamalai as Yogi Ramsuratkumar had obviously preferred, and Rajalakshmi took up a vigil by the telephone, awaiting the next thread of news.

At 3:30 that afternoon, Mani's sister called to say that the doctors were preparing for the caesarian delivery. When Yogi Ramsuratkumar arrived at the ashram less than half an hour later for the 4 P.M. darshan, Mani immediately informed him of what seemed inevitable.

"It will be a normal delivery," the beggar once more pronounced.

This time, Mani could only shake his head in disbelief, although he said nothing. In the younger man's mind it was impossible to imagine such assurance in the face of such overwhelming odds.

At 4:15 P.M. the phone rang again. Again it was Mani's sister on the line. This time, however, the news was miraculous, joyous. A girl child had been born; and naturally, without surgery. The attending

Mani and Raji massaging the feet of Yogi Ramsuratkumar

494

physicians were shocked, as the birth came with such speed, even as they were arranging their surgical setup.

Rajalakshmi rushed into the darshan hall and approached the dais on which Yogi Ramsuratkumar sat. Pranaming, breathless, she informed her master of the news.

"It is all Father's grace," Yogi Ramsuratkumar said, and blessed her.[19] Three weeks later, Bhagwan named the child Chandramani – the name of Sri Ramakrishna's mother. Then he granted Mani and Raji permission to leave for Madras, to carry the child's name to the grateful parents.

राम

When the Divine, in the person of Yogi Ramsuratkumar or any other spiritual master, wants something done, the instruments chosen for the task are often observed carefully over a period of time and frequently tested to prove their trustworthiness. From the day of their second visit, in 1992, and throughout 1993, Mani and Rajalakshmi were both blessed with the master's attention and subjected to the fire in which he tempered the implements needed for his work. Unlike many devotees who use the guru or spiritual master primarily as a source of consolation, other men and women (like Devaki Ma and the Sudama sisters, for example) immediately distinguish themselves by their willingness to give generously, in whatever form of service is made available to them. In late 1992, Yogi Ramsuratkumar blessed Mani's efforts in assisting Sadhu Rangarajan with the Jayanti celebration held in Madras that year. By throwing themselves wholeheartedly into the Chennai association, the mettle of Mani's nature, with Rajalakshmi's support, was both recognized and appreciated by Yogi Ramsuratkumar.

राम

During his third visit, in February of 1993, Mani was tested in a unique way. No sooner had he and Sadhu Rangarajan arrived at the Sannadhi house when Yogi Ramsuratkumar's attendant approached them with a request from the master. *Would they kindly*

leave immediately and pay a visit to Tapovanam – a forty-minute drive?
Would they pay respects to an ailing devotee, Mr. Siva Ramakrisha Iyer,
who was in residence at the ashram there? Would they return in time for
the evening darshan, 4-6 P.M., with Yogi Ramsuratkumar? The men
immediately agreed.

Mani admitted to being annoyed and tired by the time they
returned from their journey, despite the reward of visiting with long-
time devotees of Swami Gnanananda Giri and friends and supporters of Yogi Ramsuratkumar. He and Rangarajan had been required to
travel during the hottest part of the Tamil Nadu day, when tempera-
tures can easily stretch above 100° F. Moreover, his plans to spend the
morning luxuriating in the beggar's radiance and then returning to
Madras by early evening had been rendered topsy-turvy by the master's request. When at last Yogi Ramsuratkumar noticed these two
messengers standing outside during the afternoon darshan, he invited them in. But, while Rangarajan found a spot on the crowded
verandah, Mani was forced to position himself outside, close enough
to hear but blocked from sight of the Godman. Miserably disappointed, Mani interiorly recounted his tale of woe, lamenting to
himself that with all the hustle and bustle he hadn't even had the time
to read the day's newspaper.

Yogi Ramsuratkumar's teaching for him on this evening hit Mani
like a wooden plank to his head. Handing a book to Bharati, the wife
of Sadhu Rangarajan, the beggar asked the woman to read from any
page she wished. Opening the book, a collection of speeches from Sri
Ramakrishna, at random, Bharati began: "Reading newspapers is a
waste of time, it will spoil our thinking. Instead of reading news, we
can utilize our time for other useful purposes."[20]

In moments like this, the recognition that Yogi Ramsuratkumar
knew *everything*, even his most secret thoughts, was both terrifying
and awesome to Mani. He was soon sweating profusely. A moment
later his eyes had welled with tears for his "presumptuous and selfish
thinking."

As they took their leave that evening, Mani was still heartbroken.
"Are you all right?" Yogi Ramsuratkumar sweetly asked, noticing the
man's condition; and then, "My Father blesses you." As Mani rose to

go, the tears still obvious, Yogi Ramsuratkumar looked at him with the eyes of infinite compassion, as he added, "This beggar loves you."

The tangible wonder of such unmerited, unconditional love as the Divine was expressing to him through Yogi Ramsuratkumar was a priceless treasure for Mani. Moved by this experience of being loved, Mani was being fashioned into a devotee from the mangled remains of himself as a "man of the world." Like a fly swatted by a great and powerful hand, the devotee who has been rendered helpless by the Godman's touch is only brought back to life by the skillful ministrations of this same force. When that happens, such a devotee has one viable alternative – to praise and serve that force, unceasingly, by laying down the old life that was never his in the first place.

Such a dedication, so well described by Lee Lozowick, became Mani and Raji's intention too.

...Yes Father, Your son is full
    of desire, passionate desire.
He desires to Praise You endlessly,
    he desires Surrender to You
he desires to serve You
    with every breath,
to Adore You totally
    with every word and gesture,
to live for You only,
    to see You in all things,
to feel You in every sigh,
    to be drowned in Your Name,
to be sweetened by Your laughter,
    to be purified by Your Regard.
Is there no end
    to this lusty desire? No, no end...[21]

AN ASHRAM BEGINS, 1993

 Midday in Tiruvannamalai, even in the winter months, can be unbearably hot. In the warmer seasons, however, it is nearly intolerable, even dangerous. The ground itself can burn the soles of a barefoot walker.

On an April afternoon in 1993, with the sun beating down mercilessly, Yogi Ramsuratkumar sat in the midst of a vacant field and smoked his cigarette, looking around reflectively. After a short time, he spoke up. "Oh, Janardhanan," he addressed the longtime disciple who had driven him to this spot, "this place seems to be too hot. Let us go away." It was his way of saying that this property was not the one he was looking for.[1]

Just a few months previous, Yogiji had given permission to Sri Janardhanan to proceed with the location of a parcel of land, the first step in the establishment of a permanent ashram. Like many devotees before him, Janardhanan had been persistent in his requests to build a suitable sanctuary for his master. But the early entreaties had been denied.

"No, this beggar doesn't need any ashram!"…or words to that effect, Yogi Ramsuratkumar had announced on numerous occasions.

"But Swamiji, the devotees are suffering. They are standing in the hot sun. We should do something for them, Swami," Janardhanan implored.[2]

It was true. Yogi Ramsuratkumar's notoriety had grown exponentially over the years since he took up residence at Sannadhi Street. With the efforts of those who were enthusiastically spreading his name throughout India, Europe, and the U.S.A., the number of visitors from outside of Tiruvannamalai was increasing. It was no longer possible for the previously hidden saint to walk the streets without attracting a crowd. People not only mobbed his person, they surrounded any car in which he rode, begging for a glance, a touch, a boon.

Yogi Ramsuratkumar, like Lord Krishna in the *Bhagavad Gita,* had always shown himself the slave to those who loved him. Even the simplest leaf, or a cup of water, when offered with pure intention, was enough to win the favor of the Divine. For his own sake, the beggar had no need for a building of any kind. "Ashram means difficulties," he well knew – he who was completely at home lying on a blanket on the bare ground under a tree, alongside the railway tracks.

"Freedom was precious to him," observed Kirsti, the Finnish sannyasini who had been the beggar's disciple since the mid-1970s. The freedom she spoke of was certainly not the free-wheeling independence and self-indulgence that Westerners have come to regard as "liberation." Rather, as a beggar and a wanderer, a man with no permanent abode, the Godchild was free to follow the whim of Divine direction. He could move as directed by his Father.

"When Yogiji agreed to having an ashram, he said to Janardhanan, 'On one condition, that this beggar is free to leave the ashram and come back to stay at the house [Sannadhi Street] anytime he feels like doing so. He does not want to be obliged to stay in the ashram forever,'" Kirsti recounted.

This bit of conversation is reminiscent of the agonized prayer of Jesus in the Garden of Gethsemani. Foreseeing his approaching betrayal, crucifixion, and death, Jesus prayed to his Father to "let this chalice pass from me." It was a fully understandable response as he looked into the face of imprisonment, dismemberment, humiliation, darkness. Nonetheless, Jesus completed his prayer with an affirmation of total surrender, declaring, "Not as I will, but as Thou wilt."

Yogi Ramsuratkumar obviously found in the requests of his devotees the indication of his Father's will. He too surrendered. "If it's for the devotees, it's all right! You can proceed," the Godchild agreed at last. It was January 1, 1993.

From that moment on, his resolve never wavered. Once the project was underway, although it would mean a burden of untold weight – a cross laid on his shoulders – Yogi Ramsuratkumar spoke only of the greater work's true purpose.

"Someday this place is going to be a great, great pilgrimage spot," the beggar told a Westerner in the early 1990s. And to others, at various times, he specified:

> If a farmer works on his land in the hot sun for a long time and feels tired, and if there is a tree nearby, he rests under it, feels refreshed and goes back to work with renewed vigour and energy. Similarly, ashrams provide peace of mind. Also it's not true [that] ashrams do not produce mahatmas. Mataji Krishnabai [and] Swami Satchidananda have come from Ananda Ashram.[3]

> This Ashram is different from other Ashrams. The whole cosmic work will be done from this Ashram. Whether this beggar is in this body or not, the whole cosmos will be controlled from this Ashram. Whoever comes anywhere near the precincts of this Ashram, will not go empty handed. They will go,…full of Father's grace. That is the truth.[4]

Janardhanan called his fellow devotee, Sri Ramamurti, a wealthy industrialist who had met Yogi Ramsuratkumar in the late 1980s and had proven himself to be a staunch and generous supporter. With invitations to Parathasarathy and a few others, a group convened in Tiruvannamalai in the early weeks of 1993 to plan out the collection of money for the intended purchase. The Yogi Ramsuratkumar Trust, a legal entity, was formed to sponsor the land purchase and the creation of the ashram.

राम

Even though he had been offered land as a donation several times, Yogi Ramsuratkumar had turned it down. One merchant had about thirty-two acres which he was prepared to give for an ashram, but the beggar said no to this proposal. Another man also offered land, arguing that if Yogi Ramsuratkumar was not willing to take it for free, he would accept one rupee (about two cents by current U.S. standards) an acre for it. Again, the Godchild said no.

"Swamiji insisted on a few points about where the ashram should be located," Ramamurti explained. It should be "on the left side of the road, between the road and this mountain. It should be far away from this town."

A 3.5-acre site was located in the approximate area indicated by the master's directive – a neighborhood known as Agraha Collai. The spot provided an unobstructed view of the south face of Mount Arunachala and was only a five-minute walk from the main gates of Ramana Ashram, a place that was highly revered by Yogi Ramsuratkumar. Although unverified, a few devotees noted that Ramana Maharshi, in one of his books, had mentioned a place near his own ashram where sages used to gather to chant Sanskrit Vedas. Supposedly, the Maharshi claimed that the vibrations of these ancient prayers could still be felt in this vicinity. During early excavation for the ashram, potsherds, the remains of a sizeable wall, and other archeological evidence were indeed uncovered, indicating that something of significance had taken place here.

Knowing nothing of the myths and legends, Yogi Ramsuratkumar went and sat there, as he had in numerous locations. The field was nothing but brush and small palms. "You can't even find a place to sit," Ramamurti said, describing the place. Nonetheless, even though he visited the spot in the worst part of the day, about 1 P.M., under the burning sun, the Godman identified it as the ideal place.

"All right, Janardhanan, we'll buy this land," the beggar said.

राम

Yogi Ramsuratkumar's doings never ceased to amaze those who spent any time with him. If they mistakenly tried to put him in one category (like "innocent," or "madman"), they might immediately be confounded by behavior or words that evidenced exactly the opposite category ("streetwise" or "savvy," for instance).

The master constantly showed himself to be proficient in the use of energy in ways that were subtle and astonishing. During the time that this desired property was being investigated, Ramamurti was surprised to learn that Yogi Ramsuratkumar had begun to put his attention on an adjoining property in addition to the one he had originally wanted. The adjoining land had a complicated history and was owned by five people, several of whom were not interested (so they said) in selling it. By indicating his strong interest in the adjoining property, and putting energy into trying to purchase *that* one, Ramamurti speculated that the crafty beggar was actually using an age-old tactic. Sort of like the martial strategy of looking or feinting one way, while you jab or attack in another. While the attention was diverted to the one property that he didn't really want, the one next door might be negotiated at a less expensive price than its owners originally intended.

राम

Janardhanan and teammates set to work collecting the money needed for the purchase of the land and the initial construction efforts. Each week they would report to Yogiji exactly how much had been collected, and from whom. Their efforts, over many months, amounted to more than fifty-five lakhs (5,500,000 rupees, or approximately $110,000 U.S.). It was enough to begin.

As initial construction efforts began, however, there was regularly a shortage of funds. Early on, partially in jest and partially in an expression of faith, Parathasarathy suggested that they purchase a lottery ticket. At another time, he had the equally humorous suggestion that the team put their efforts into trying to catch a particularly notorious bandit (*dacoit*) named Viripan, in order to cash in on the reward. When Janardhanan told this idea to Bhagwan Yogi Ramsuratkumar, joking about how Parathasarathy had "gone mad," the beggar simply informed them that "Viripan is in dense forests," meaning, that the man was untouchable. (To this day Viripan has not been caught. He is credited with over two hundred murders, including the kidnapping of government ministers.)

In the same mood of playful repartee, Janardhanan reminded Yogi Ramsuratkumar that both Swami Nityananda and his Father, Papa Ramdas, had apparently produced money magically, of the precise amount needed, when the workers at their ashrams needed to be paid.

Commenting on these great stories, Yogiji said, with a twinkle in his eye: "Oh, Janardhanan, this beggar doesn't have that much power."

Quite the contrary, miracles in relationship to money were always happening around Yogi Ramsuratkumar. But they occurred in slightly different ways – ways that specifically served the needs of those who were involved in them.

An American man who lived in Tiruvannamalai for seven months was surprised to find his relationship to money and personal integrity highlighted by a story that Yogi Ramsuratkumar asked to be read in the afternoon darshan. This younger man had spent the previous year of his life going from job to job without a sense of purpose. He would commit to one thing and then change his mind and move on to another.

The story the beggar told was about a rich man who had promised to provide a loan of two lakhs rupees (about $6,000 U.S.) to a merchant for a business venture. Before the loan was given, however, the merchant's business collapsed and he was required to leave town. Just before the merchant left, the rich man visited him and handed him the full amount of money. When a friend of the rich man heard of this he was shocked. "Why did you give him this money, even though his business was dissolved?" To which the rich man replied, "I gave him my word, what else could I do?"

Hearing this story, the American man saw that his problems with lack of purpose and lack of money were a result of his waffling commitments. His failure to honor his word was actually the source of his suffering. This tale told by Yogi Ramsuratkumar was a momentary wake-up call.

Another lila regarding money concerned a young artist and devotee of Yogi Ramsuratkumar's. On the outskirts of Tirukoilur, a short walk from the ashram of Tapovanam, a small house hides behind a five-foot hedge shielding it from the main road; however, passersby who look through the opening in the hedge can see a huge hand-

Mural painted by Govindaraj

painted mural – the face of Yogi Ramsuratkumar – to the right side of the front door on the home's façade. Inside, a busy artist's studio is clearly the most lived-in room in the house. Here, Govindaraj works, making his living today as a painter.

Govindaraj was six years old when he first met Bhagwan Sri Yogi Ramsuratkumar. His father and brother took him often to visit the house at Sannadhi Street. On one memorable day, when they had arrived at 10 A.M. and spent four hours with the beggar, Govindaraj was very hungry. At 2 P.M., Yogi Ramsuratkumar gave his guests some fruits. When they had eaten, the beggar asked the children to come forward. For no apparent reason, Yogi Ramsuratkumar gave fifty paise (half a rupee) to Govindaraj and one rupee to his brother.

"This beggar has given one rupee to your brother and to you, fifty paise," Yogiji announced to Govindaraj. "Why don't you ask why this beggar has given you this money?"

Although both boys wondered about this strange offering at the time, and although he had asked them to inquire, Bhagwan did not answer their question. That night, Yogi Ramsuratkumar permitted his guests to say with him until about 8 P.M., after which they returned home.

Many years later, as Govindaraj grew into a young man, he went to Bangalore to study art. The family was poor, however, and Govindaraj had to terminate his studies in order to take up a job in construction. Nevertheless, his love for art continued, and when his father went to Tiruvannamalai one day, he took some paintings to show to Yogi Ramsuratkumar. One, a watercolor, impressed the beggar, and he asked that Govindaraj paint him a copy. Fifteen days later the new painting was in the Godman's hands.

Not long after this painting incident, Yogi Ramsuratkumar introduced Govindaraj to Sadhu Rangarajan in the midst of a darshan gathering. The beggar began to question the professor about how expensive it would be to study art.

"One month's worth of study would cost about 1,000 rupees," the sadhu informed his master.

Hearing this, Bhagwan began calculating and asking more questions. *How much money would it take for Govindaraj to complete the whole program?*

When the calculation was done by others, Yogiji learned that this program would be very expensive – 50,000 rupees! "Oh," he remarked, "how would this beggar ever get this money to help Govindaraj to do this study?"

Hearing this, a wealthy devotee, the owner of a hotel, spoke up immediately. He would sponsor Govindaraj to take these studies.

It took Govindaraj between five and six years to successfully finish his program (1992-1998), and all with his sponsor's help. For Govindaraj, the question the beggar asked him when he was six years old was clarified in how this whole blessing had unfolded. The *fifty paise* that Bhagwan had given him years ago had become *fifty thousand rupees* by 1998; and this correlation was not coincidental in Govindaraj's mind. In pure faith, he was convinced that the tiny gift had multiplied 2,000 times in the beggar's hands!

राम

In 1993, all was finally ready for the purchase of the new ashram land. The money was in hand and the deed was typed by a man living on Sannadhi Street, about five houses up the road from #90, where Swamiji resided. When the document was ready, Ram-amurti picked it up and stopped outside of Yogi Ramsuratkumar's door to say a silent prayer. He did not knock, as it was not the usual time for darshan, and he assumed that the beggar would be resting.

During the time that the disciple's eyes were closed in prayer, no more than twenty seconds, Yogiji had come out of his house and placed himself directly in front of Ramamurti so silently that the man was unaware of what had happened. When at last he opened his eyes, Ramamurti gasped in surprise to find his master a few inches from his face. Immediately, he laid the deed at Bhagwan's feet and made his obeisance to him.

"His feet were so beautiful, so radiant. You know I had not seen his feet like that, ever before. A human being's feet cannot be beautiful, so fresh." Ramamurti was choked with emotion as he told of this moment, almost ten years later. It was this gesture of turning the paper over to the Godman, the disciple noted, that preserved the project from serious complication, despite some potentially damaging errors that were unknown at the time.

The deed in question was then read by a magistrate; then by another official or two; and finally by an auditor. After that, it was taken to the registrar to be recorded. This all took place over the course of three or four days. Meanwhile, the land was being cleared. as far as possible, and a small hut was erected on the new property. The final acquisition, however, would only happen as soon as everything was totally "official."

As they awaited final approval one afternoon, several of the men sat with Bhagwan discussing other plans. Suddenly the beggar asked them to fulfill a completely unexpected request. They should take their copy of the deed to Tirukoilur, a forty-five minute ride from Tiruvannamalai. There they should meet Siva Ramakrishna, a longtime friend and devotee of Ramsuratkumar's, and ask him to read the deed at their master's request. Ramakrishna was a retired registrar.

Taking a car, the men drove there, where Siva Ramakrishna obediently took up the task. As soon as the elder started reading the document, however, he suddenly cried out, "Stop, stop, stop," his eyes focusing on one of the first lines on the page. "Instead of putting the 'Seller' here you have put the 'Buyer.'" The typesetter had mixed the words Seller and Buyer – probably the worst mistake possible. Needless to say, the men were shocked.

Speeding back to Tiruvannamalai, they drove straight to the local registrar's office. *Was it too late?* they wondered. To their amazement, this deed had not yet been entered into the official registration book. When they explained the situation to the registrar, telling the man that it was for a property associated with Yogi Ramsuratkumar, the official said there would be no problem. They should merely have the deed retyped and return it on Monday, which they did.

Ramamurti clearly credited everything to the direction and intervention of his master. Even "minor" things, he pointed out, could determine the fate of major events. For him, this episode provided one more significant teaching from Yogi Ramsuratkumar. Over many years, and after many such experiences, Ramamurti expressed without doubt that it was essential to listen as exactly as possible to the words the master used when he gave a command. Tiny errors caused by human inattention, or human self-will, could (and did) make a huge difference in the ultimate result of things.

राम

With the land purchased, the property was marked for its legal boundaries and the first structure was erected – the only building on the grounds – a generous thatched roof on poles. Later, concrete block walls were erected. The single-roomed hut came to be called the Darshan Mandir (the "old Darshan Mandir" today, as it still stands). Inside, with space for nearly sixty people to be seated – women on the left side, men on the right, with an aisle down the middle – it provided a vast improvement over the tiny verandah of Sannadhi Street, which allowed ten or so people, at best, packed tightly together. In this new facility, temporary as it was, devotees were given their first taste of a more formal darshan setting.

Yogi Ramsuratkumar's cushion was kept in place at the front of the hall, under a large, brightly painted "OM" on the wall behind his head. To his right, Devaki Ma sat, facing him at a right angle. At his left, male disciples could be seated close to him – close enough that he could hold their hands or deliver pats or slaps on the back, his customary expression of love and blessing. The devotees chanted his name, or other chants of his liking, at his direction.

The presence of this center aisle provided a further boon. It allowed the Godman free access through the space. Energetically, with his advancing age and often tentative health, he needed a way to move among his devotees, blessing them, without being mobbed by them.

For several months of 1993, until mid-year when he was struck with more serious illness, Yogi Ramsuratkumar visited the property regularly and occasionally held darshans there. From first to last, Yogi Ramsuratkumar was involved in every aspect of the business, the building, the scheduling of the ashram and its activities.

In one of his early trips to the property, Yogiji was brought by car to survey the land, which was still covered with thorn bushes. Ma Devaki was concerned about him walking on this unpredictable terrain, as Yogi Ramsuratkumar was barefoot, as usual. Recognizing her concern, Ramamurti and V. Ganesan, who accompanied them on this outing, took the small towels that each of them carried (a common accessory of Indian men living in the tropics) and placed the tiny cloths on the ground, one before the other, for Bhagwan to step on. When, after two steps, he had reached the end of the second towel, the men would pick up the first towel and replace it in front of him. Like knights softening the path for a beloved lady, the two men bowed continuously at the beggar's feet. "In that way he continued on his observation round," Ramamurti related.

Unfortunately, as they progressed, Ganesan, who had worn rubber chappells (sandals) for protection, received a large thorn that cut its way through the rubber sole and punctured his foot; a small reminder of the price that is often asked of the devotee in rendering service.

An Ashram Begins, 1993

Extolling the sacredness of the land, Ramamurti exclaimed: "Every grain of sand, every brick was blessed by Bhagwan right from the day the foundation stone was laid. Everything inside the ashram is holy."

29

THE ETERNAL SLAVE, JULY 1993

 I can tell you this about Devaki: she has always been a rare devotee, so confirmed in her perceptions, so sure and so committed, that there is no question left, no need to rethink about anything. For her to look *at* him, even if she did not receive a look *from* him, was enough for the day. She could live on that. She would come all the way from Salem and stand in the sun there and maybe get a glimpse of him, with no chance of going into the house. And she would go back [to Salem]…happy and contented. Five days later, if she could come, she would do that again. That's what Devaki was always. – Dwaraknath Reddy, 2003[1]

Since her first meeting with the beggar-saint in December 1986, Devaki's devotion had never wavered. On July 15, 1993, she gave up her job as a university professor of physics. Immediately afterward, she moved from Salem, with Yogi Ramsuratkumar's permission, to the Sudama residence in Tiruvannamalai that she had rented with the other women who were serving the master at every possible opportunity.

In 1994, as part of an introduction to the Tamil-language book about Yogi Ramsuratkumar written by Sri T.P. Meenakshisundaram, Devaki described the first twelve hours of her life-altering transition.

For seven years [from Dec. 1986] I was running towards Him again and again for His darshan. Realizing that it is an unquenchable thirst, on the 15th of July last year [1993], I once for all gave up my job and obtained the good fortune of being ever in His presence and service. I stand enchanted in a corner, in front of that ocean of mercy whom Sri T.P. Meenakshisundaram calls, "The Siva who descended from the Heavens to save the Earth." All the tests, sufferings and pleasant experiences in the last few years were the leelas [lilas] of Bhagavan to make me perfect.

When I resigned my job at last with His permission and reached Tiruvannamalai, it was 11 o'clock in the night. Along with the tiresomeness of the journey there was also an anxiety in the mind: "Oh Yogi Ramsuratkumar! For You I have come giving up everything and everyone. Will You not accept and welcome this one?"

The moment I got down from the bus and stood in front of Ramanashram I heard sacred music to the accompaniment of musical instruments. I turned with surprise and found a big crowd moving from the same Dakshinamurthy temple, holding lamps in their hands and chanting sacred hymns. A Professor known to me emerged from the crowd, came towards me and said, "Amma, Namaskar! Welcome to you! We are happy to see you. It is the auspicious hour marking the beginning of the month. We have, just completed pooja [puja] in the Dakshinamurthy temple and are on our way to perambulate the Sacred Hill." She took leave of me. What an immense compassion is that of the Swami! Who can He be other than the All-pervasive Ultimate Reality!

The next morning when I went for the darshan of the Swami, He called me, who was sitting somewhere behind the audience, made me sit by His side and asked me with a laughter of an Innocent child: "When you stepped down on this soil yesterday night, what happened?" Happiness surged in my heart when he burst into waves of laughter. Mind melted in "His compassion to His children comparable to the love of a cow to its calf." [a quote from the book to which this Introduction was written.][2]

511

राम

Devaki was now available to be present for and attentive to the needs of Yogi Ramsuratkumar in whatever ways he would allow. Since his blood transfusion due to stomach ulcers in 1990, some arrangements had been made through the intercession of Dr. Radhakrishan for devotees to "send him regular food of a kind that would not upset his health."[3] Between August 1990 and late 1993, Bhagwan maintained his vigorous schedule with as much regularity as possible. He still walked the streets of the city, spent hours in the Arunachaleswarar Temple, and held daily darshans in which dozens and sometimes scores of devotees were able to sit with him and receive the benediction of his presence. The body's condition was little more than a minor inconvenience in his ongoing work, and most of his visitors had little awareness of the physical suffering he endured. Even when his symptoms occasionally became externalized and obvious, he was adamant that no attention be paid to them.

People sometimes asked Yogi Ramsuratkumar, "How are you?" to which he would reply with a note of humor, "By Father's grace, this Beggar is alive." When concerned faces presented themselves in his vicinity, Yogiji would respond with either a simple reminder, "It is all Father's play," or more ruthlessly, by sending the apparently empathic person from his presence.

"Are you sick?" asked a longtime devotee one day when she observed that he had been vomiting. Her question incurred a strong response from Yogi Ramsuratkumar, who sent her away and did not allow her to return for over a year. Another woman, also concerned, began her inquiries about his health less directly. Fully aware of where her questions were headed, Yogi Ramsuratkumar firmly warned her that any further discussion and "she could expect never to be allowed into his satsang again."[4]

On a later occasion, shortly after the ashram was established, Yogi Ramsuratkumar was walking to the breakfast hut where he took his morning refreshment with a few close disciples. Supported on Mani's arm, the beggar suddenly began to pick up the pace of his movement, until he was fully running. Despite Mani's help, Yogi

Ramsuratkumar tripped and fell. Without comment, he got up immediately and proceeded into the hut for his meal. "Understandably, those who witnessed the event and those who were responsible to provide support and assistance to his physical form were upset. Some of Yogi Ramsuratkumar's closest women devotees were even crying about it, albeit out of their loving concern for their beloved master. In commenting upon their response, however,...Yogi Ramsuratkumar was unrelenting in his criticism of any who exerted excessive concern for his body, maintaining that he is *not* his body."[5]

During November 1993, Yogi Ramsuratkumar was struck with a severe viral fever. The condition was so debilitating that for some time he was "unable even to walk to the toilet."[6] Without the strength to accommodate visitors, regular darshans at his Sannadhi Street residence were cancelled, while Devaki and a few other close disciples did their best to attend him.

Devaki Ma implored Yogi Ramsuratkumar to move temporarily to the Sudama House, where she and the other women residents would be available to him twenty-four hours a day. At first, the beggar was adamant in refusing the request, as he never abided special treatment. But finally, surrendering to the desires of his devotees, he "gave in to [Devaki's] prayerful supplication."[7] The move was made on November 22, 1993, and Dr. Radhakrishnan was summoned to assist with Bhagwan's medical needs.

Within a week, Yogi Ramsuratkumar's strength was returning. The speedy progress was heartening to those around him, but still Dr. Radhakrishnan advised a few additional weeks of rest. During this period of intense care and attention, the "earnestness and sincerity" of Devaki and his other female attendants "won Bhagwan's confidence."[8] Despite his previous reluctance to leave the temple environment of Sannadhi Street, Yogi Ramsuratkumar stayed on at Sudama House, which then became his primary abode. The Sudama sisters, by their fierce dedication, became his vigilant servants.

राम

During either October or November (reports vary) of this year, 1993, within the period of this health crisis, Yogi Ramsuratkumar made a startling announcement to the world. "Devaki is this Beggar's eternal slave," he told those around him, and those who came to visit him. After years of invisible and selfless service, she had proven herself worthy to sit at his side forever.

Vijayalakshmi, one of the Sudama sisters, recounted that Bhagwan explained that this "eternal slave" had been sent by "His Father to help this beggar in all his work."[9] "Devaki" was now referred to as "Ma Devaki" – Yogi Ramsuratkumar had introduced her as "Mother," a term of the highest respect, indicating her identification with the sublime virtues of the divine feminine. The beggar further noted that the four Sudama sisters were also helping his work, and that their treatment of him at Sudama House was deeply treasured. With awe and innocence, and with tears in his eyes, Yogi Ramsuratkumar told many people, "Devaki and the Sudama sisters are taking so much care of this beggar that this beggar cannot live without them."[10]

A few days after this announcement, when the devotee Shri V. Ramanujachari was visiting with the beggar, Yogiji introduced him to Devaki Ma. "Suddenly and I do not know what prompted him to burst out like that," Ramanujachari explained, "he said in ringing emphatic tones, 'I requested her to come, I needed her here. She is like Sita, she is like Damayandhi, she is like Savithri. There is no doubt about it.' He raised his voice and repeated again and again three to four times."

Ramanujachari was "taken aback," and "after a few moments of silence…said, echoing the Upanishadic phrase, 'She is rooted in you Swami.'"[11]

At the Godman's directive, Sadhu Rangarajan was asked to write an editorial in the next issue of *Tattva Darsana* (vol. 10, #4, Nov. 93 – Feb. 94) in which he made public the master's proclamation. Entitled "The Eternal Slave," the piece spoke of the mythic relationship between Lord Krishna and his adoptive mother, Devaki, who "in her intense motherly love, totally identified herself with Him, and hence He was immediately accessible to her."

The editorial further drew a parallel to the dedication of Miss Margaret Nobel (later named Sister Nivedita), whose life was entrusted completely to support the work of the great Indian saint, Swami Vivekananda. Nivedita's mentor (Vivekananda) had warned her

Devaki Ma and Yogi Ramsuratkumar

repeatedly that such a life of renunciation promised the most extreme hazards. She would be reviled. She could be imprisoned. She would be required to bear the most difficult living conditions. Undaunted in her resolve to "sacrifice her life at the altar of Mother India,"[12] Nivedita never looked back.

"What will you do if you are thrown out by the master?" a devotee of Yogi Ramsuratkumar's asked Devaki in the early days of her apprenticeship, shortly after she moved from Salem.

"I will sit in a corner and chant His Name," was *her* immediate reply.[13] Dwaraknath Reddy, speaking of Devaki's orientation to her master's will, aptly described the characteristics of such a "slave":

She asked for nothing, she wanted nothing. She's not even seeking for explanations. So Devaki was taken into this circle. It must have been surprising even to Devaki; she is not the one who would ask a question. If you put a crown on her head, she would just sit quietly and accept it. If you threw her into the gutter, she would just sit there until he asked her to get up. That has been Devaki all along.

This I say with personal knowledge of that human being and the conviction I carry. The position she was put into was not of her asking, not of her seeking, and so she just said: "I don't have a right to ask for it, what right have I to say yes or no to what my guru says, and God says." She has just been wherever she has been placed, and she has done what her supreme Lord told her to do. That was her point of view.

Now we can have our opinions and judgements about it, but I think she is just a person of such surrender, which itself should make us respect her. Our judgements and everything leave it aside, but that's a surrender! We all *talk* of surrender, but I don't think I have seen anyone who can exceed her in really surrendering. Whatever happened to her it just happened – she was not an actor, not a do-er in that at all. This Devaki I am talking of, one I knew so closely ten years back…people like that don't change. I don't think she could have become proud, arrogant, queenly or possessive, or wanting fame or name. I don't see Devaki that way.[14]

The Eternal Slave, July 1993

Writing from America a few months after spending time with Yogi Ramsuratkumar and Devaki Ma in December 1993, Lee Lozowick too extolled the paradoxical status of this dedicated slave:

O Devaki, noble sister,
    you've certainly changed your position
from an honorable professor
    to the Maid of the dirty Beggar.
Your old colleagues
    must be shocked.
"What madness has possessed her?"
    they must say amongst themselves.
His son will tell them this,
    if they ever dare to ask:
you say she has given up everything
    for nothing,
but I say she has given up nothing
    for Everything.
She sits at the Feet of the Lord,
    serving His every need.
She has left reputation and name
    to follow that Ragged Fellow, this is true –
she courts Krishna every day
    while you tempt Mara each day as well.
You might as well forget her
    for she has gone where there is no return.
O Father Yogi Ramsuratkumar,
    Your Play is a wonder to behold![15]

Speaking to Devaki Ma of the life that lay before her, Yogi Ramsuratkumar revealed: "When you serve this beggar, you serve the entire cosmos. You see, Devaki, when you water the roots of a tree, the given energy goes until the end of each branch, each leaf, each stem, each flower and each fruit. Similarly, when you serve this beggar, your service spreads in the entire cosmos."[16] Yet, on other occasions, the Godchild revealed the crucifixion that she too would be called upon to suffer: "Devaki, everyone will betray you; even this

517

beggar will betray you," he said.[17] These terrible words foretold the sadhana of purification and detachment that she, along with every dedicated soul, would endure in the process of being annihilated in love.

राम

The "Eternal Slave" announcement, together with Rangarajan's editorial, were not received with the same enthusiasm by all. Unimaginably, for some of Yogi Ramsuratkumar's followers the declaration was interpreted as the result of power plays. In response to Rangarajan's editorial, *The Mountain Path* journal, an official publication of the Ramanashram, contained a review of the *Tattva Darsana* issue. The author of the review was identified only as "Radha." With a tone of belittlement, the author spoke of the "Eternal Slave" editorial as an act of political expediency on the sadhu's part, saying: "Foreseeing that the saint (Yogi Ramsuratkumar) will not be in the body for long, he [Rangarajan] has latched onto his ardent devotee Sri Devaki, as a sort of life insurance policy."[18]

In his reply, in the May 1994 issue of *Tattva Darsana*, Sadhu Rangarajan expressed only more appreciation and praise for Devaki Ma – the "chosen instrument" of Yogi Ramsuratkumar. He again pointed to "the supreme self-sacrifice she made in totally surrendering her little self at the feet of my Master and consecrating her whole life at His altar." And, in another thrilling comparison, the sadhu wrote: "Thousands worshipped the one who hung on the cross, but only a Mary of Magdalene could see His resurrection. All cannot become Devakis. To become a true devotee, total effacement of ego is necessary."[19]

Finally, in a skillful play on the critic's name, the editor concluded: "This Sadhu is proud to adore her as 'Ma,' and wishes all Radhas – Lovers of the Lord – to become Ma Devakis, to see their Lord as 'Godchild.'"[20]

राम

Whether she was loved or hated at the time, Devaki Ma probably couldn't have cared less. Her life was taken up with one task only – complete attention and obedience to her master. Her keen observation and constant surveillance of the Godchild's every gesture and every word over the years during which Yogi Ramsuratkumar was still in the body afford an invaluable legacy to devotees about the ways and means whereby the Divine intersected with humanity through this beggar. A glimpse of that legacy was occasionally given.

As early as 1994, Devaki wrote of the "special knack" that was required to "understand and appreciate the unique characteristics of the great Tapasvi [Realized Masters]." She was at first dumbfounded to find that "every action of Yogiswara [Yogi Ramsuratkumar]" adhered meticulously to an order in the universe whereby the microcosm was an exact expression of the macrocosm. In other words, every action of Yogi Ramsuratkumar's was, in her vision, not separate from that of the Eternal All-Transcendent Reality.[21]

Detailing some of her early observations, Devaki noted the ways that he "deals with and solves the various problems and worries of devotees who come and sit at His feet everyday and seek His counsel. Many come for relief from diseases. The Yogiraj, who always takes gooseberry as panacea and health tonic, gives anything as medicine and removes illnesses of devotees by His compassion."

Sometimes, the beggar's means of healing were unconventional to the point of appearing even dangerous. At other times, he directly took the sufferings of others into his own body. Devaki Ma witnessed it all. When a devotee approached the master for help, telling him that the doctors had forbidden him any spicy food for several years as a result of a digestive problem, Yogi Ramsuratkumar laughed and replied, "Good, we are going to eat some." The beggar then sent the man to the market and told him to purchase some pepper powder and bring it back. The man was sorely conflicted, as he feared for the worst, assuming that Bhagwan would ask him to consume it. Nonetheless, the man's obedience was stronger than his self-concern, and so he bought the pepper powder and handed it over to the Godman.

Yogi Ramsuratkumar emptied the contents of the envelope of powder into his own coconut bowl, mixed it with water and declared,

"We are going to drink it!" The sick man held his breath in anticipation of the task. But, as he watched with astonishment, Yogiji drained the entire bowl in one gulp.

The effect was immediate. As the pepper water rolled down his throat, Yogi Ramsuratkumar jumped up from his seat and began to run here and there around the room like a man who is looking for a way out. The beggar also howled, making a lot of noise, as might be expected from one who has just consumed a burning mixture. The hubbub lasted a few minutes, and then, as quickly as it had begun, it ceased completely. Yogiji was completely calm.

Turning to the sick man, the beggar announced, "All is well now, henceforth you will be able to eat spicy food." The man's health improved from this point on, and he was able once again to consume spicy food.

Yogi Ramsuratkumar was not attempting to undermine the medical profession, nor was he creating an alternative list of recommended medicinals by offering people the very things they were told not to have. At a much more universal level, he was showing his devotees that rigid adherence to the dictates of logic or even medicine was not necessary for him. In his world, such things were minor considerations. The only ultimate factor was faith in God.

राम

Even as early as the 1970s, devotees were occasionally shocked to see their master, Yogi Ramsuratkumar, kneel and place his head on the ground as a gesture of respect to others. In the 1970s, Swami Muktandanda, the disciple of Swami Nityananda, sat one day near the samadhi of Lakshmi the cow, a revered shrine on the grounds of Ramanashram in Tiruvannamalai. Learning of the famous swami's visit, Ramsuratkumar approached the man and prostrated at his feet.

"Why do you do this?" Muktananda asked. "You and I are the same."[22]

Yogi Ramsuratkumar, certainly, had nothing to lose in bowing to anyone, while his witnesses had everything to gain by seeing the profound humility and nonattachment of their guru. Devaki Ma wrote: "I have many times observed Bhagavan prostrating to devotees who do so at His feet. Once a group of devotees of the Paramacharya of Kanchi called on Bhagavan and He first fell prostrate at their feet. Bhagavan is a Bhakta of Paramacharya. I was able to realize that only Bhagavan could be a perfect Bhakta.

"Whenever devotees came from Aurobindo Ashram or Anandashram, Bhagavan would tell them, 'You have come here to give darshan to and bless this beggar.' He thus proved Himself to be the embodiment of humility, the spiritual tradition of this Holy Land."

"I have seen Him prostrating even to those who fail to do so to Him. Once He held with both His hands the feet of a person with a bloated ego. After the person left, a devotee asked Bhagavan why He did so. Bhagavan replied: 'This beggar could help him only by touching his body and heart somehow. That gentleman would not prostrate before this beggar, but it is not difficult for this beggar to fall at his feet. Somehow, in his interest, this beggar had to do so.'"[23]

राम

From the earliest years, Yogi Ramsuratkumar enjoined men and women visitors to "sing the praise of their respective gurus." Devaki Ma confirmed that he continued to do this throughout his life: "When the devotees of Sri Ramana come to Him, He will make them sing songs on Bhagavan Ramana, discuss about Ramana and make them read several times articles on or passages from Ramana. When the devotees of Sri Ramakrishna come, He will make them speak of the Trinity – Sri Ramakrishna, Holy Mother Sri Sarada and Swami Vivekananda – and hear with devotion their narrations. When a devotee of Pagal Harnath comes, Bhagavan will speak about Harnath. Once a devotee of J. Krishnamoorthy [Krishnamurti] asked Bhagavan to give him a photo of Bhagavan. Bhagavan simply told the devotee to follow the path of J.K. steadfastly.

"I have enjoyed seeing Him dance in ecstasy, singing 'Om Sri Ram jai Ram jai jai Ram,' along with devotees of Anandashram. To the devotees of Sri Satya Sai Baba He would ask for Sai Bhajans and make them read the Guru-poornima lecture of Sri Satya Sai Baba and hail it as the 'Voice of God.'

"I have never heard Him denigrate anybody at any time, for He could never find any fault with anybody. When someone tries to harm Him in Ignorance, He will say, 'That is Father's Will! Whatever happens is for good only, for my Father is blemishless and whatever He Wills is blemishless.' Thus, He will teach the devotees around Him, through His own conduct, the greatest lesson of 'Saranagati' – the spirit of total surrender to God."[24]

Devaki Ma's conclusion to the Introduction written for Meenakshisundaram's book serves as her prayer of praise to the one who had called her to the path of annihilation:

It is a great blessing grace that I have got this opportunity to go through this rare work as a part of my efforts to surrender myself at the holy feet of my Master who is an imperceptible personification of wisdom, that Supreme Reality incomprehensible even to those who perceive, a Divinity which dispels the darkness of mind through a sparkling glance, a Godchild and a wonder called Yogi Ramsuratkumar.[25]

30

THE NEW POET

 Yogi Ramsuratkumar was fast asleep, lying on his side on a mat on the floor in the shrine room of the Sudama House, where he was currently in residence. It was December 1, 1993, his 76th Jayanti day, and the master was still physically weakened by another serious and recent illness. As he slept, several devotees sat in reverent silence, gazing on his peaceful form.

Balarama Zuccarello, an American, had traveled to Tiruvannamalai from Madras on this celebration day in the company of Mani and Sadhu Rangarajan. Glimpsing the Godchild in this elegant posture of repose, Balarama was reminded of statues of the reclining Buddha he had seen, particularly in Nepal. "He was beautiful to behold without His traditional turban of rags," Balarama wrote. "His face was radiant, even as He slept."[1]

The shrine room was a spacious gathering place with a white marble floor. Its primary adornment, a huge, life-size picture of Yogi Ramsuratkumar, graced one wall; a small shrine occupied a place on the floor against the opposite wall. In this room, Yogi Ramsuratkumar would greet devotees and other guests, conduct his business meetings, and take his meals. Balarama remembered being introduced to Devaki Ma for the first time.

This Jayanti day had been chosen by Sadhu Rangarajan for the presentation of the newest publication of the Sister Nivedita Academy. When Yogi Ramsuratkumar awakened from his nap and his devotees had offered their greetings and pranams, the sadhu spoke briefly of the small paperbound book in his hands. The thin volume was solemnly entrusted to Yogi Ramsuratkumar, and the master received it delicately, "as if handling an object of…inestimable value."[2] He examined the cover for several minutes, the way a child looks at something fascinating. *POEMS OF A BROKEN HEART* the title read in blood red capital letters, under which the author's name, "lee lozowick," was printed in lowercase type. The front cover was graced with a color photograph of Yogi Ramsuratkumar dressed in a spotless white shirt and dhoti – one of those rare photos that devotees were permitted to take on the even rarer occasion when the master put on brand new clothes. The beggar's head was wrapped in his bright green turban. He wore several sets of mala beads around his neck and sat cross-legged on a straw mat in what appeared to be a temple complex. His striped ashtray lay on the ground in front of him, a few inches from his feet. Yogiji's eyes looked forward and down, and his marvelous hands, raised in a typical gesture of blessing, almost seemed to be moving.

The back cover of the book featured a full-length photograph – Yogi Ramsuratkumar with coconut bowl and palmyra fan in one hand; his other hand palm open in blessing. He stood on an outcropping of rock with shrubs and other greenery behind him, with a full view of Mount Arunachala towering over his head.

"Nindaa stuti – 'ironical praise' or praise in the form of abusive reproach – is a very powerful but dangerous and slippery form of devotional poetry and many great saintly poets, especially in Sanskrit literature, have boldly ventured into it in adoring their Ishta devataa or Chosen Deities." Sadhu Rangarajan's oratorical voice reverberated in the room as he read aloud the Publisher's Note at the beginning of the book, as requested by Yogi Ramsuratkumar. "It is with tremendous dexterity and skill that Lee Lozowick, an ardent devotee of Yogi Ramsuratkumar godchild Tiruvannamalai, had handled this in his poetic epistles which he has been shooting at his Father at frequent intervals," the reader continued.[3]

This Publisher's Note also told the story of the book's conception and development. Since 1986, when Sadhu Rangarajan first learned of the stream of poetry coming to Yogi Ramsuratkumar in letters postmarked "Arizona, U.S.A," Rangarajan, ever the diligent journalist, was intrigued. On several occasions the beggar had expressly asked him to publish a poem or two from the "bad poet" and "arrogant fool" – as Lee Lozowick, the author, referred to himself. Several issues of *Tattva Darsana*, starting with the January 1987 issue, contained one or more of these heartrending missives. In February 1988, readers found this:

> Was there ever a Slave
>> who had such a Master
> Was there ever one so low
>> who was blessed by One so high
>> Was there ever one more lost
>> whom You had chosen to find
> Was there ever one who hid so far
>> whom You sought so long
> I think not Dear Beloved,
>> I must be the only one for whom
> You would suffer so and Love so
>> I think I must be the only one.[4]

The poem had been composed by Lee during an early trip to India. It was dated: Mt. Arunachala, Feb. 21, 1979. As the years went by and Yogi Ramsuratkumar continued to receive a steady stream of these poems, he would frequently ask that they be read aloud in his presence – once, twice, six or seven times. Many devotees of this period remembered well how absorbed the beggar would become as he listened to devotional tributes of his American son. Because of this, Sadhu Rangarajan expressed an interest in publishing a collection and asked his master's permission to follow up on the idea. *POEMS OF A BROKEN HEART* was the result of that request.

On this Jayanti day, 1993, when Devaki Ma pointed out that Lee himself had written an Introduction to the book, Yogi Ramsuratkumar immediately asked her to read it. As she proceeded, the Godchild would stop her frequently, asking her to repeat sentence after sentence, sometimes several times. "This dirty Beggar is no common saint," Devaki read Lee's words of praise. "Love is no respecter of culture, or of personal preferences. Love knows no limits, and in knowing no limits it destroys everything in its path." She carefully pronounced the words as one reads a prayer. "And Love is something that Yogi Ramsuratkumar is a Master of. And he will destroy you if you let Him."[5]

That morning, the Godman once again related a story that he frequently repeated, with great emotion. He spoke of the day in 1986 when Lee had kept vigil outside on the street across from the Sannadhi house. This time, the beggar recalled that Lee had sat on "some hot iron bars," the latticework for a construction project that was going on in the area. Balarama noted respectfully that "He [Yogi Ramsuratkumar] was crying at the memory of the whole scene." "The Yogi cannot help Himself," the beggar said at the end of the narration, and he cried some more.[6]

राम

> When this beggar came in the form of RAMA, Kambar wrote the Story of Rama as RAMAYANA. When this beggar came in the form of KRISHNA, Vyasar wrote the story of Krishna as MAHABARATHA. Now this beggar has come in the form of a BEGGAR and holy DEVAKI was introduced in this beggar's life, and a new poet will write a different type of story about this Beggar and Holy Devaki.
>
> – Yogi Ramsuratkumar[7]

The Divine beggar spoke these words not long after he declared Devaki Ma as his Eternal Slave. Now, the "bad poet" from America – a new poet – with his ironical praise, *was* indeed writing a "different type of story." Interestingly, after the publication of this first compilation of poems, Yogi Ramsuratkumar had made a specific request of his American devotee, declaring, "Lee will write poems on Devaki." The second volume of *Poems of a Broken Heart* (which was published in April 1997) and subsequent publications would generously carry out the master's desire.

Poetry has always been the prime medium for the expression of exaltation and the mystical experience. And many of those who met Yogi Ramsuratkumar – from the early 1970s onward – recorded their impressions of him in poetry or song. The beggar loved music and song. He was a dancing Krishna, a dancing Siva, as he wove his way through the dusty streets of Tiruvannamalai or leapt the rocks on his way up the mountain, Arunachala, or spun in the courtyard of the temple singing to himself, *Om Sri Ram Jai Ram Jai Jai Ram*.

In the first biographical account of the Godchild, written in 1971, author Caylor Wadlington occasionally lapsed into poetic reverie of praise for the hidden saint:

A godchild am I, for my spirit runs naked in the heavens
And enchants all men's hearts with sweet songs of eternity.[8]

In 1972, the first "official" song composed spontaneously in honor of Yogi Ramsuratkumar was written down by its author, Swami Mayananda, a sadhu from Pondicherry. One line prophetically proclaimed, "The whole world will bow before you." Yogi Ramsuratkumar loved that song, and used to ask his devotees to remember it. Also, from 1976 onward, Swamiji asked his devotee Parathasarathy to write "only poems on this Beggar."[9]

Yet, the words of these unknown poets, regardless of their heartfulness, were often overshadowed by the tributes of some of the greatest names among Tamil scholars and writers of modern times. While savants such as Sri Ki. Va. Jagannathan, Sri Te. Po. Meenakshisundaram, and Sri Periasamy Thooran are unheard of among Westerners, their credentials were and still are awe-inspiring to the population of southern India. (Perhaps a workable comparison in terms of fame and notoriety in the West might be made to poet Leonard Cohen, renowned linguist Noam Chomsky, or sacred historian Joseph Campbell.) Each of these famous Tamil men was drawn to Yogi Ramsuratkumar. Each of them wrote either treatises or poems about the incomparable wonder of the beggar at whose feet they humbly bowed.

Meenakshisundaram (1901-1980), a prolific and highly respected linguist and literary scholar is the author of dozens of books, including the classics, *History of Tamil Language* and *History of Tamil Literature*, along with numerous lesser publications. In his book on Yogi Ramsuratkumar he placed the beggar in the ranks of the greatest Indian saints, extolling his virtues poetically. It was this book, republished in the late 1980s, to which Devaki Ma contributed an Introduction.

Ki. Va. Jagannathan (died 1988) was a renowned folklorist and musician whose songs on Yogi Ramsuratkumar became legendary. In April 1980, Jagannathan and a few other devotees spent the evening with the beggar at the Sannadhi Street house. Starting at about 9:15 P.M., the singer-songwriter recorded fifty-eight original, new songs in praise of Yogi Ramsuratkumar.

"My Father is sitting on the tongue of Sri. Ki. Va. Ja while he sings all these immortal songs," the beggar announced with obvious gratitude. He went on, "Many friends sincerely feel that the songs sung by Dr. Ki. Va. Ja. give them peace and have felt inner vibrations within themselves. For these songs are divine."[10] Yogi Ramsuratkumar then told his visitors a wonderful tale. A Brahmin who frequently paid his respects to the beggar's feet was generally given some fruit as prasad. On a recent visit, however, with no apparent forethought, Yogi Ramsuratkumar gifted the man with a copy of *Anbu Malai* – a newly released book of poems in honor of the Godchild written by Ki. Va. Jagannathan. The man received the gift with astonishment and appreciation.

Leaving Sannadhi Street, en route to his home, as the visitor was crossing a field he was bitten by a poisonous snake. Instantly, the man weakened and began sweating profusely. Grasping tightly to the book of songs, he felt a great rush of strength coursing through his body and was miraculously sustained for the distance of two miles, where he reached his house. Medical help was immediately summoned, as the man lost consciousness for three hours. The next day, however, he was perfectly well.

While others might assert that it was the medical intervention that saved his life, the brahmin was clear – it was the book, the gift of the Godman, the songs of praise, that had accomplished this. When the man told his story to the beggar, lauding his hand in this miracle, Yogi Ramsuratkumar denied any credit. "This Beggar does not know anything," Yogiji said. "If anybody gets eternal bliss, it may be due to the songs composed by our friend Sri Vakeesa Kalanidhi Ki. Va. Ja."

After telling the story, Yogi Ramsuratkumar addressed the song-writer: "Many friends say that they are getting peace if they go through these immortal songs."

Sri. Ki.Va. Ja. joked, lightly receiving the compliment: "They are getting only peace, not piece-meal?"

Enjoying the man's humor, Yogi Ramsuratkumar retorted: "Oh! They are getting meals *and* peace, both. How is it possible to get peace without a meal?"

Laughter erupted all around, and the beggar blessed Jagannathan.[11]

Mr. Periasamy Thooran was an ardent devotee of Ramsuratkumar's from the mid-1970s when he met the beggar under the punnai tree at the railway station. Until Thooran's death in 1987, his heart remained at the Godman's feet.

Thooran was a composer, poet, and a writer of more than seventy books. His compositions in Carnatic music are still popular today, years after his death. Periasamy was also the chief editor of the *Tamil Encyclopaedia* project (1948-1978), a mammoth work of more than 7,500 pages. He wrote children's books and a children's encyclopedia in Tamil, and was the recipient of many prestigious awards by the Indian government for his scholarly contributions. In addition, Thooran composed numerous songs in Tamil about Yogi Ramsuratkumar, which were brought out in an audiocassette version. A book of seventeen song-poems was also published.

In Tamil poetry there is a tradition in which the poet speaks to an imaginary parrot, imagining that the bird is listening to him. In one of his poems, Thooran uses this convention to praise the gentle beggar:

Oh parrot I'm simply thrilled
when I hear the name of the God Child
mentioned by somebody on the wayside
and I stand motionless too.

He wears a dress of deep green color,
like Lord Muruga seated on the peacock.
The saint will give me whatever I want

and all my sufferings will vanish.

I wonder whether it is the dance of Lord Krishna
on the hood of the most poisonous snake called Kalinga
or the dance of Lord Shiva at the time of the deluge.
I want divine wisdom![12]

Numerous lilas linking the master, Yogi Ramsuratkumar, with this humble disciple, Thooran, were collected and recalled by his grandson, Murali Murugavel. It seems that Yogiji used to say that although the word "Thooran" can mean "far away" in Tamil, Peri-asamy was very close to his heart. On one occasion, after reading one of Thooran's stories for children (entitled "Nila Patti" or "Grand-mother on the Moon"), Yogi Ramsuratkumar insisted that Thooran pay him a visit and stay with him for at least two days. This tale, like all of Thooran's stories, contained a moral lesson, and the beggar's respect for Thooran intensified when he read it.

Although Yogi Ramsuratkumar himself only slept on the floor, he was always the most gracious host, and he made arrangements for a bed to be provided for Thooran, who could not sit or lie down on the floor, as he was suffering from a health condition which led to complete paralysis on his left side. When the man was fully bedrid-den in his home at Madras, he would dictate a poem in praise of Yogiji, which his daughter (Mrs. Saradamani Chinnasamy) would carry to the Godman.

When Thooran died, Yogi Ramsuratkumar was informed. The Godchild declared that "Thooran is not dead, but is still living with us."[13]

Of course, what mattered to the beggar was the devotion in the heart, not the credentials after the name. Another famous writer, who became a devotee of Yogi Ramsuratkumar's, announced himself quite arrogantly on his first visit, assuming that he would receive special accommodation by the Godman.

"I am Balakumarin," the man announced.

"So what?" Yogi Ramsuratkumar replied blandly, although he probably would have heard of the man.

"When no special importance was given to him, Balakumarin soon realized what was happening and he left his ego and only then did Bhagwan receive him well," another devotee reported.[14]

राम

Makarand Paranjape, himself a writer and scholar of literature, reviewed Lee's book, *Poems of a Broken Heart*, in *Tattva Darsana* with these words: "As one reads through poem after poem, one cannot help but be moved by Lee's sincerity, his burning desire to be accepted by his Guru. The poems are also marked by a wit, verbal energy, and intensity."[15]

It was certainly not to impress scholars that Lee Lozowick wrote, however. For him, the only critic who mattered was the one dressed in rags, the blessed beggar of Tiruvannamalai. It must have delighted Lee to hear that his master had said, "Lee must be given a Nobel Prize for writing these poems."[16] Yet, worldly honors were less than dross when compared to the possibility that his praise might attract his beloved's attention, and might even serve a higher purpose. This too the beggar affirmed, a short time later.

In mid-December 1993, two weeks after Yogi Ramsuratkumar had received the first copy of *Poems of a Broken Heart*, Lee and a group of his American and European students arrived in Tiruvannamalai for a three-day visit. The travelers had already spent days chanting through South India where Lee had been the guest of honor at the Mantralayam in the town of Kanimadam, and at numerous celebratory functions in small villages along the way, in honor of Yogi Ramsuratkumar.

The master's welcome to his American son on this occasion was particularly poignant. Despite his need for rest from his recent illness, the beggar spent most of his time with his guests, both at Sudama and later at the home of V. Ganesan. The entire book of poems was read aloud by Devaki Ma, repeatedly, as the beggar listened, often tearfully.

"Lee Lozowick has done a great work for this dirty beggar with these poems. The name of this dirty beggar will be scattered all over the world with these poems written in English by Lee. Lee Lozowick has given a great gift to this beggar; now this beggar won't have to beg anyone anymore to write about this beggar. No more. It is done now."[17]

Yogi Ramsuratkumar instructed the men and women traveling with Lee to "read these poems every day." One woman who was present for these interchanges described her responses:

> I find myself fighting back tears as the Yogi says…"Read that poem again," in his sweet, sing-song faraway voice as Devaki reads Mr. Lee's poetry to Him for hours off and on during the day. She reads with such heartful graciousness…clearly she is thrilled by whatever exalts and praises her beloved Master…While Devaki reads, the Yogi strokes Lee's hand lovingly…He is visibly, deeply moved by them, and there are many moods of response to various poems. Sometimes the poem evokes His rich laughter (like when he is called a rascal)…accompanying many hearty slaps on the back and shoulder to Lee, along with merry glances…Other moods are so tender, so sweetly loving, and come with a shy lover's glance and embarrassed face covered with the hands, eyes misted over. Yet others cause the Yogi to look full and long into Lee's eyes…What a treasure, what a precious Blessing God had given us to sit and take Darshan here, to witness these two Lovers, divine and inseparable."[18]

One poem in particular evoked strong interest from Yogi Ramuratkumar. Hearing it read to him several times, the beggar asked Lee about some of its references.

> Oh Yogi Ramsuratkumar
>   Your son is such an arrogant Fool,
> Listen to his sinful Pride,
>   and his silly Foolishness:
> This bad Poet
>   reads of the great Lovers
> of Hanuman and Rama
>   of Radha and Krishna

of Parvati and Siva
   of Vivekananda and Ramakrishna
of Rumi and Shemsi Tabriz
   of Milarepa and Marpa
of Mary and Jesus
   of Claire and Francis
Shamefully of Cleopatra and Antony
   of Romeo and Juliet
of Heloise and Abelard
   of Camille and Rodin
Madly of Layla and Majnun
   and longingly of Yogi Ramsuratkumar
      and His Father Sri Ramdas

and Your son says:
   "I will love my Father like this."
I ask you, Yogi Ramsuratkumar
   is this not madness?
lee listens for Your reply
   oh dirty Beggar.[19]

Lee told the stories of many of these great lovers as the Godchild listened thoughtfully. Rumi and Shams, Milarepa and Marpa, Rumi and Shamsi Tabriz, Heloise and Abelard, Rodin and Camille, St. Francis and Clare – and each story was carefully repeated to Yogi Ramsuratkumar by Devaki, as the master didn't want to miss a word.

"Devaki, you will remember every word and tell them again and again when this Beggar asks!" Yogi Ramsuratkumar directed when the stories were completed.

Devaki Ma smiled and said, "Maybe Lee will tell them again tomorrow."

Immediately the beggar interrupted, firmly but good-naturedly. "No! He says it only once! He is not that cheap! You must remember every word!" Hearing these words, everyone laughed, including Yogi Ramsuratkumar.

"Yes, Bhagawan, I will remember," Devaki said obediently, and smiled again.[20]

ONLY GOD

राम

One afternoon during this short visit from Lee Lozowick in 1993, Yogi Ramsuratkumar enacted a lila with Devaki Ma that the Westerners would long remember. Prior to this meeting, these foreign visitors had no knowledge of the Eternal Slave, Devaki. Perhaps they had seen her before as one among dozens of devoted Indian women who sang chants in the beggar's honor, or as one of many who sat invisibly along the far walls as he conducted darshans with his guests. As Yogi Ramsuratkumar had brought Devaki to their attention with his declaration about her post of service to him, he would, during these few days, place her firmly in their hearts as well.

The group was spending the day at the home of V. Ganesan and Anuradha. About 10:30 A.M., Yogi Ramsuratkumar spoke up: "Devaki, is there anything for this Beggar to eat in there?" indicating the bag she had brought along. In anticipation of his needs, Devaki had packed "packages of Charimar cigarettes, matches, towels, His ashtray, gooseberry tea and coconut bowl, and some small cake-like food that he had eaten at breakfast earlier that morning."[21]

"No Bhagawan," Devaki sadly reported. "You ate what we brought at breakfast."

The Godchild asked again, "This Beggar would like something to eat, Devaki." This second request was somewhat distressing, as the woman had one desire alone – "to provide for His every need and whim."

"No, Bhagawan, there is nothing," Devaki said again, quietly. She attempted to explain herself, reminding him that the last time they went out for the day he had noted that she brought "too many things that we didn't need, and You instructed me to pack much less today."

Yogi Ramsuratkumar was not persuaded. She should have packed more, he said, paradoxically.

"Bhagawan, You speak in mysterious ways, in mystic ways...I don't understand..." Devaki said simply, betraying only bewilderment.

Hearing this exchange, their hostess, Anuradha, immediately offered food from the kitchen. But, again mysteriously, Yogi Ramsuratkumar said *No*. Clearly, there was something else besides physical hunger at play here. Apparently, "if Devaki couldn't provide the

534

food, He didn't want it," one of the Americans noted. With no expression of righteousness, Devaki then asked her master's leave to search the garden for some fruit that he could eat.

Her resourcefulness and lack of negativity won the beggar's approval. "Yes, you can look for something in the garden; take Nivedita with you," he said, indicating Rangarajan's daughter, who was present for this darshan.

When the two women returned a few minutes later, they carried with them three oranges and one lime. Yogi Ramsuratkumar was delighted. Like a gleeful child for whom everything is amazing, he exclaimed several times: "This Beggar was hungry and Devaki went out into the garden and found Him something to eat."

Devaki sat down beside Yogi Ramsuratkumar, who had unexplainably moved into the center of the room. Spreading a towel and laying down the fruit, she took out a knife and some cups, and then "began to meticulously peel the oranges one by one, carefully taking all the inner skin from each segment. Thus she handed each piece, the perfect, juicy inner meat of the fruit, to the Yogi, which He ate with obvious enjoyment. This peeling and cleaning and eating of the fruit took almost an hour."

Throughout the entire ritual, Yogi Ramsuratkumar was turned toward Lee, lovingly, intently. As the elder man received and ate the fruit in silence, the visitors and their hosts kept up the familiar chant: *Yogi Ramsuratkumar, Yogi Ramsuratkumar, Yogi Ramsuratkumar, Jaya Guru Raya.* "The atmosphere of the chamber was so rare, so refined yet charged and penetrating that some of us were quietly sobbing or trying to absorb and contain the high-voltage shakti power of the chamber," wrote one observer. Periodically, Yogiji would raise his hands and enact his gestures of blessing toward Lee.

The Godman got up once, with one segment of fruit in hand, and brought it to Lee to eat. When the oranges were peeled and eaten, Devaki carefully squeezed the lime and, at the beggar's instruction, poured the juice into three cups, adding a little water to each. One cup was slightly less full than the other two. Reading a slight gesture of direction from Yogi Ramsuratkumar, she equalized the amount of juice in each cup.

Getting up for the second time, Yogiji handed a cup to Lee, sat down and drank his juice. Lee likewise, and Devaki afterward, following her master's indication…and the play was complete.

Turning to his American devotee, with an indirect but clear request, Yogi Ramsuratkumar said, "This lila will give Lee good material for poetry, this Beggar has made good material for poems for Lee!" These words were repeated several times, as Yogi Ramsuratkumar "chuckled a little with delight and satisfaction and a hint of mischievousness."[22]

Returning to the United States at the conclusion of this trip, Lee took his master's requests literally. He began writing poems about Devaki Ma, and, recalling the unmistakably intentional teachings of the morning at Ganesan's house, Lee prayed:

> Devaki picked three oranges
> > to feed her Bhagawan
> she carefully removed every seed
> > and every bit of skin
> and gave only the sweetest essence
> > to her Lord to eat
> Oh Father
> > Yogi Ramsuratkumar
> will you prepare Your son
> > by cleansing lee of sins
> and feed what is left
> > to Your Father in Heaven
> as tenderly
> > as she fed You?[23]

In these ways, the beggar, the Godchild, taught his devotees about the nature of obedience, of attention, and of devotion.

LAYING A FOUNDATION, FEBRUARY 1994

 In mid-February 1994, with the beggar's approval, Mani had successfully completed a project at Sudama House. He had supervised the construction of a thatched awning (called a *pandal*) over the front of the building – a shade-structure that would allow devotees to await their darshan with the master without being withered by the blazing sun.

No sooner was the project finished, however, than Yogi Ramsuratkumar asked him if he would do some additional "work for this beggar" – a request that Mani gratefully accepted. A ceremony was being planned for February 26, at which time the foundation stone would be laid on the newly acquired ashram property. Swami Satchidananda from Anandashram had been invited as the guest of honor. *Would Mani please see to the clearing of the land?*

Although he had come to Tiruvannamalai on February 7, intending to spend only a few days with the pandal construction, Mani's stay was being stretched far beyond his original plans. He had a thriving business to run in Madras, but his master's requests slowly began to distance him from all other work.

With the help of another local engineer recommended by Yogi Ramsuratkumar, Mani arranged for the clearing of the land – a tedious task of removing the ubiquitous thorn bushes that covered it. When it came time to start marking the ground for the architectural structures, Mani was again asked to manage the task.

The beloved beggar was present on the morning when this land-chalking was set to begin. Time was short, as the foundation ceremony was approaching, but enthusiasm was high. Although Mani as yet lacked all the proper tools for the job, it was clear to him that Yogi Ramsuratkumar wanted immediate action. Without waiting for his more sophisticated tools, Mani picked up a stray length of rope that he found nearby and began to use it, stretching it from measured point to point, like a ruler, and thus marking the lines.

The rope caught Yogi Ramsuratkumar's attention. Turning to Mani, who was hunched near the ground at his feet, the Godchild asked: "Mani, will you allow this beggar to help you? This beggar would like to hold this rope at one end. Mani can measure from the other end of the rope."[1]

"Such was the beginning of my work for Him," Mani wrote. "He was right there assisting me, seeing that the makeshift tools were accepted and blessed."

When the initial stage of this measuring work was done on that morning, Yogiji asked, "Does Mani need this particular rope?"

"I can manage with some other rope also," the engineer replied.

"Mani should permit this beggar to keep the rope with him," the Godman declared.[2]

And so it was that Yogi Ramsuratkumar first slipped his right hand through this coil of jute rope and moved it up his arm and over his right shoulder. Unbelievably, to the wonderment of guests and visitors alike, he wore this odd talisman day after day, for years, as the ashram construction continued. (In 1995, when this writer visited for the December Jayanti services, it was a notable accessory.) Occasionally he carried this same rope in his hands, or placed it over his head so that it hung around his neck, like a set of mala beads or a garland of flowers. What better symbol for the binding of hearts? What more appropriate way to tie himself to the structures that would *stand for* him, embodying his presence, even ages after his death?

राम

Yogi Ramsuratkumar adorned with the jute rope

A profound and dramatic demonstration of the master's way of working occurred for Mani on February 21, 1994, just under a week before the foundation ceremony was to be held. At Yogi Ramsuratkumar's directive, Mani was to meet him at the ashram at 5:45 A.M., which he did. As the two men walked around the grounds, surveying the preparation work that was being done, Yogi Ramsuratkumar suddenly turned to his devotee and spoke. "My Father wants Mani to be with this beggar for ten years. Mani has to decide now."

Such a question, especially if it is totally unexpected, as this one was, thoroughly stops the mind. Mani was completely stunned by the beggar's words. Of course, this is the type of request that one would realistically want to weigh at length. At best, one would want to "sleep on it." But the Godman was offering no quarter. Precisely because the decision was being called for "now," the rational mind had no time for deliberation.

"Yes," Mani said, with no hesitation.

Yogi Ramsuratkumar began to laugh. "Mani has taken all of five seconds to answer my Father. He will be with this beggar from right now as desired by my Father."[3]

Only hours later, in telling his astonished wife, Raji, about the decision, did the implications of the ultimatum begin to dawn on Mani. *What about his business in Madras? Their children; their aging parents? Their living quarters?* Yet, as many others have found, a "leap of faith" can feel more like lying down *into* something than jumping up or over something. A profound sense of being carried or sustained by a larger and much stronger hand is often the dominant characteristic of such a motion.

"Let us wait," Mani said, reassuring his wife. "He will take care of our welfare. Let me abide by what He says and be with Him as long as He wishes."[4]

For Rajalakshmi, the invitation was to support her husband wholeheartedly in this endeavor; otherwise, it would not have been possible for Mani to dedicate himself completely. It appears that in asking this sacrifice of Mani, Yogi Ramsuratkumar never questioned that Raji would follow suit. Had there been any doubt that Raji and Mani were his obedient "son" and "daughter," the offer might never have been made in the first place.

A month earlier (January 1994), a simple and sweet note from Rajalakshmi had delighted Yogi Ramsuratkumar enormously. The communication, as short as it was, verified to him the woman's deep loyalty and faith. "Dear Appa, How is Amma? Please convey my pranams to her," the letter read. It was Rajalakshmi's expression of tender regard and respect for Devaki Ma, whom she referred to as Amma, which touched the beggar's heart. In Sanskrit, Appa means "father" and Amma means "mother" – a term of respect used toward a senior woman. In this case, that Raji was older than Devaki made no difference. Amma is also used to designate the Divine Mother, indicating much more than physical motherhood, and in this sense Rajalakshmi was announcing her intentional support of the younger woman's designation as the Eternal Slave of Yogi Ramsuratkumar.

Coming as it did on the heels of some intense criticism, disregard, and gossip from other quarters, this expression of honor and devotion to Devaki Ma was a gift to the beggar. For days he spoke of both Mani and Raji in all his darshans. Devaki was repeatedly asked to read Raji's note aloud, and Yogi Ramsuratkumar began saying that Rajalakshmi was the first person to accept Ma Devaki in this way. Because of her attention to "Amma" and "Appa," the Godman called Raji their "eldest daughter."[5]

If criticism and gossip had been sparking prior to this event, Yogi Ramsuratkumar's words to Raji undoubtedly started a sizeable blaze among the small-minded. Not only did the master now have an "Eternal Slave"...*but an eldest daughter!* Drawing women into his close circle of attendants, as Yogi Ramsuratkumar did, would always rankle those who harbored jealousy or looked for impropriety. Anything the spiritual master did – like his special designations, gifts, attention – when viewed outside the domain of faith could wither devotion, as the ego reared its head, voicing its rational objections.

For Rajalakshmi, however, there was little but ecstatic gratitude. "My wife's commitment, devotion, and unfailing dedication was sealed," Mani wrote about this interchange among Raji, Yogi Ramsuratkumar, and Devaki Ma. "Bhagwan took the heart of my wife into His custody."

राम

"I got a message from Yogiji requesting me to lay the foundation stone for the ashram. I readily agreed," Swami Satchidananda said, speaking of the historic event of February 1994.

The ceremony itself would be a landmark, literally, in the work of Yogi Ramsuratkumar. But the presence of Papa Ramdas's eminent disciple and current spiritual successor, Swami Satchidananda, leant an added importance to the event. The Swami's central role in the day's activities signified the honoring of the lineage of Papa Ramdas to which Yogi Ramsuratkumar was associated. On another level, something less formal but no less significant was taking place. Satchidananda's visit would be his first reunion with the "odd Bihari" since Yogi Ramsuratkumar had left Ramdas's presence in a God-intoxicated condition in the early 1950s.

"We heard he was in Tiruvannamalai staying near the temple, sleeping on the verandah of a shop," Swami Satchidananda recalled, reminiscing about a time six or seven years after the beggar had left Anandashram.

> Over the years, we heard more news about him: that he attracted the attention of many devotees who influenced him to stay in a comfortable house, providing him with food, etc., at regular hours. Then what we heard was the desire of the devotees to build an ashram for him and his consent for the same.
>
> When all devotees went to him, he asked them to visit his Father, *meaning Papa*, in the Ashram here (Ananda-shram). After Papa's mahasamadhi he used to send people here to spend at least three days.
>
> He also mentioned to everybody that he was doing "his Father's work," and with the ashram blessing [referring to the blessing Yogi Ramsuratkumar gave to people who came to visit him] he would say, "My Father will bless you."[6]

On the evening of February 25, 1994, Swami Satchidananda and a small retinue were due to arrive in Tiruvannamalai, where they would first pay their respects to Ramana Maharshi's shrine at Rama-nashram. The Maharshi had been a significant figure in Ramdas's sadhana, as he had in that of Yogi Ramsuratkumar.

Swamiji and his group from Anandashram had been unavoidably delayed, however, and Yogi Ramsuratkumar patiently awaited their arrival. Lawn chairs had been set up on the roadside for the beggar and his attendants, and a crowd of his devotees together with friends from Ramanashram and Ananadashram began to gather. The chanting of Ramnam filled the air.

"When I reached there, in the evening about 7:30, I was waiting outside Ramanashram and the meeting was unforgettable," Satchid-ananda reported. "He [Yogi Ramsuratkumar] held my hand tightly and would never leave it. I said, 'We are come very late,' [meaning that they had arrived long after they were expected].

"In reply he said, 'I've been waiting all these years for you.'"[7]

Laying a Foundation, February 1994

Photos taken of this reunion (both on February 23 and throughout the following day) capture the tender camaraderie of these two beloved "sons" of Swami Papa Ramdas. And witnesses to these events recall the sweet sounds of the Godchild's laughter. Hand in hand, and despite the weakness of Yogi Ramsuratkumar's condition, the two distinguished elders walked to the guesthouse where Swami Satchidananda was staying, along a street lined with joyous devotees.

राम

The ceremonies began in the middle of the night, at 3:30 A.M., when the orange-robed Swami Satchidananda, amidst full Vedic ritual, laid the foundation stone. The black marble rock, inscribed, can be seen at the corner of the ashram temple today:

Yogi Ramsuratkumar Ashram
Foundation
on
26-02-1994 Saturday – 3-45 A.M.
Swami Satchidanandaji Maharaj
Anandashram
present
Yogi Ramsuratkumar Maharaj

S.P. Janarthanan
Trustee
Yogi Ramsuratkumar Trust

Despite the early hour, an enthusiastic crowd, including many high-ranking local government officials, were in attendance.
Swami Satchidananda addressed the assemblage:

Om Sri Ram Jai Ram Jai Jai Ram Om Sri Ram Jai Ram Jai Jai Ram Om Sri Ram Jai Ram Jai Jai Ram.
Salutations to our Gurudev, Beloved Papa and our Viswa Mata Krishnabai. Salutations to our Yogi Maharaj Yogi Ramsuratkumarji. Salutations to all the Mahatmas and loving

543

greetings to all friends sitting in front. Today is a great day because the foundation stone for a new Ashram has been laid in the presence of our Yogi Maharaj.

In fact, I was envious of our Yogi Maharaj, because he was free within and without. But, after I came to know that He was starting an Ashram, I did not at all feel envious of Him. Because I knew that though remaining free within and without, He was binding Himself, to some extent, with these new developments. But the beauty is, even though these activities are binding, it is a life of sacrifice – sacrifice for the sake of seekers.

The world, as you all know, is full of thirsting souls – thirsting for peace and happiness. They are going about here and there to find out real peace and happiness. They don't find it anywhere. Only Ashrams like this can quench their thirst. Ashrams are places where Mahatmas stay and radiate Peace and Happiness like this Ashram, to grow into a place like an oasis in this desert where many thirsting souls can quench their thirst.

I pray for the Lord's Blessings, Blessings of our Beloved Papa for making this Ashram a Veritable Haven of Peace and Bliss, under the able guidance of our Guru Maharaj. *Om Sri Ram Jai Ram Jai Jai Ram.*[8]

Later in the morning, about 10 A.M., a general welcoming ceremony was held. A scaffold-like platform had been constructed on the property, and its slanted roof shaded the principles and other guests of honor from the blinding sun. Swami Satchidananda sat to the left of Yogi Ramsuratkumar, and a few disciples and dignitaries, including T. Venkataraman, the president of the Ramana Maharshi Ashram, were also assigned places. Mr. Janardhanan, as the current president of the Yogi Ramsuratkumar Ashram Trust, introduced the proceedings.

Swami Satchidananda spoke again, reiterating his prayers invoking the blessing of Papa Ramdas and urging devotees to strive to effectively make use of the living presence of a saint in such an ashram as they were establishing here. When the Swami's eloquent words were

February 26, 1994 – Foundation Ceremony day
Seated left to right: Devaki Ma, Yogi Ramsuratkumar,
and Swami Satchidananda

concluded, attention turned to Yogi Ramsuratkumar, who was asked to speak as well.

"This beggar is not a good speaker," the Godchild protested. "He can only say 'My Father blesses all the people who are here.'" With that, he sat down.

While other speeches followed, offering praises and thanks for the works of the two eminent honorees, the focus was not on words. Eyes were riveted on the interplay of deep communion, the warm smiles, and the obvious mutual respect that existed between Swami Satchidananda and Yogi Ramsuratkumar.

राम

From the day following this ceremony, work on the ashram kicked into high gear. Between February 1994 and December 1994, when the first Jayanti celebration was conducted in the newly erected Swagath Mantap (the circular entry room and meditation chapel for what was to be the massive temple), activity was constant. In Mani, Yogi Ramsuratkumar had identified the perfect man for the job of overseeing construction, as well as managing many aspects of ashram business and protocol. On January 26, 1994, during a visit to Tiruvannamalai with his son, Mani had been shocked to hear Yogi Ramsuratkumar say, "This beggar in madness thinks about Mani. My Father says that Mani will build temples for this Beggar."[9] The disciple had protested at the time, arguing that his circumstances and his lack of talents made such a prediction preposterous.

The beggar was not dissuaded, obviously. Although he had only known Yogi Ramsuratkumar for a short time in comparison to other devotees, Mani possessed the right blend of technical skills, business acumen, unflagging energy, no-nonsense authority and downright orneriness to serve the beggar's purpose. With the Godman's transformative blessings, moreover, he was highly amenable to being crafted into an obedient servant – although not without a struggle. No matter what complaints others voiced over the years about his rough-and-tumble approach to management, Mani's heart remained a devotee's heart, and it lay in the right place – at the feet of Yogi Ramsuratkumar.

राम

Plans were approved by Yogiji for the temple building designed by architect Sri Ravi G. Nair of Kerala. Dr. Radhakrishnan, the beggar's physician, had been asked by Yogi Ramsuratkumar to find a suitable craftsman, and it was Radhakrishnan who introduced Nair to the project. "The Ashram must have divinity, durability, and beauty," noted Vijayalakshmi, one of the Sudama sisters, reflecting Yogi Ramsuratkumar's intention that the ashram would cater to the needs of millions of people in the future.[10]

The plan as approved by the beggar would be an expensive one; the structure of the temple would be elaborate, complex in its design elements. Feathers were ruffled in the process, as the Ashram Trust members were not in agreement with the Nair proposal. With a view to economy and greater simplicity, they had already created an alternative plan. But, in one of the paradoxical ways in which he constantly upturned the expectations and attachments of his followers, Yogi Ramsuratkumar, who was a master of simplicity and economy, put his support fully behind the Nair design. The Board of Trustees resigned, sadly. Yogi Ramsuratkumar blessed them all. They were his devotees before, during, and after.

Within a few hours, with the assistance of Justice Arunachalam, Yogi Ramsuratkumar had appointed a new board. The work would not be stopped.

राम

"This work should begin right now," Yogi Ramsuratkumar said, turning to Mani as soon as the board resignation and appointment business was handled. "This beggar is coming out."

The master was outside the hut, standing in the ashram field, which was barren except for the foundation stone and the scaffolding that had been used the previous day. It was obvious to Mani that this was another of those moments when immediate action was called for. Running at full speed to his nearby residence, Mani borrowed a few tools from his landlord and returned with a crowbar and some garden implements in hand.

"You please give the crowbar to this beggar," Yogi Ramsuratkumar announced to Mani. "He lifted that crowbar over His head and held it there just for a moment. Then He brought it down with such force and momentum that when the iron struck the earth I expected to see sparks fly out of the grass," Mani wrote.[11]

After three blows, a marked depression was made in the earth. Satisfied, the beggar passed the crowbar to Devaki Ma, who pried loose some more dirt. Then Justice Arunachalam took the tool and continued. Within a short time, as word spread quickly that Yogi Ramsuratkumar was at work at the ashram, a crowd of devotees had formed. Lining up, each one wanted to participate in the spontaneous excavation.

"Don't worry," Yogi Ramsuratkumar said to Mani as the energy mounted. "You are going to do this with the help of my Father."[12]

THE DIVINE LABORER

It was an enactment of the conception, labor, birth, nurturing, and raising of a child. Yogi Ramsuratkumar was the Divine Mother. His ashram, under construction from 1994 onward, was his precious infant. The analogy is appropriate in remarkable detail.

Not only did the beggar symbolically carry the project, and all who participated in it, in the rope he wore around his neck and in the list of names of all the workers that he often held in his hand throughout the day; not only were his prayers to his Father filled with his gratitude and petition on behalf of the work; not only were his blessings constantly being voiced as he raised his hands above the heads of the laborers; but he also guarded, fed, and guided the activities from beginning to end with his physical presence and his continual attention. For a man of seventy-six years, worn by the ravages of sadhana and sacrifice, the sheer endurance he exhibited, day after day, month after month, is nothing short of miraculous.

For long hours, Yogi Ramsuratkumar sat on a blanket, shielded somewhat from the scorching sun by a small umbrella held over his head by one of his trusted male attendants. He watched and he prayed. Devaki Ma and others of the Sudama sisters sat nearby him and chanted quietly.

On different occasions, the Godman sat in a lawn chair atop the concrete construction, watching the often dangerous and complex operations that were taking place. Scores of workers moved tons of steel, stone, sand, and earth throughout the various phases of the labor.

The Divine Laborer

And Yogi Ramsuratkumar was there, observing everything, attesting again and again, "My Father alone exists. No one else. Nothing else."

Sometimes he held Mani's hand during some particularly challenging endeavor. Sometimes he walked the perimeter of the site, or carefully stepped along the thick fence wall, still under construction, that would enclose parts of the compound. The aging Godchild insisted upon climbing the treacherous-looking scaffolding alongside the temple wall, leading to a lookout post near the roof. From here he could survey all that was going on below, and above. He didn't expect company, especially from the women who always attended him, as he judged it to be too dangerous. But Devaki Ma would not be dissuaded. "I'll take the risk," she said, as she followed her master.

Bhagwan's feet, at one time or another, came in contact with every inch of the property. During his morning visits to the ashram he used to "touch every tree, every plant."[1] As tender as his gesture

Yogi Ramsuratkumar watches over the construction

549

was, it was not so surprising. His Father, Ramdas, did exactly the same thing when Anandashram was being built and the gardens were being laid out.

Like the most caring of mothers, Yogiji was concerned for the physical needs of the labor crews. "Feeding the workforce was particularly close to his heart," Vijayalakshmi noted. "A kitchen was set up. Soon, a regular kitchen was built, and then a dining room. Not only workers, but all visitors were given prasad meals, as blessed by Yogiji."[2]

Yogi Ramsuratkumar was similarly concerned for the workers' safety, and this concern manifested in many ways. Not one fatality marred the project, and the expected number of minor accidents throughout the entire operation was uncharacteristically small.

"It is my Father's Ashram. My Father is looking after every detail of its construction. Those who work for the Ashram are blessed nicely by my Father," the beggar repeated on many occasions. It was a testimony to Yogi Ramsuratkumar's solicitation and the tangible substance of grace that surrounded the project that most workers not only extended themselves above and beyond what was normally expected, but threw their hearts into the work as well. Most were honored to be participating in a sacred task. As he had captured the love and fidelity of countless souls throughout his life, Yogi Ramsuratkumar enchanted the laborers, winning their affection and trust. He was nearly irresistible. His Jayanti celebrations, held on the ashram grounds during these early construction years, would find the workers, in shifts, circumambulating the shrines, enthusiastically singing the mantra and invoking his name.

"His attention was completely on the construction for hour after hour after hour," wrote an American guest, describing the beggar's activities during Lee Lozowick's visit in December 1994. "He [Yogi Ramsuratkumar] was on top of the scaffolding and threw flowers and performed puja and sat up there in the sun for hours. Then He came down to the ground and throughout the day moved to different vantage points, but always with His attention completely on the work…From 7 A.M. to 12 P.M. we sat and watched the construction and watched Yogi Ramsuratkumar watch the construction."[3]

राम

550

The Divine Laborer

The workers loved Yogi Ramsuratkumar because they were convinced that he loved them. "This is very important to tell," Saravanan affirmed, as he told the story of his own employment on the ashram from mid-1994. He clearly remembered the day on which his job became his spiritual work – his means of serving God.

"I 'joined' on May 13, 1994," the young man said, marking the date with gratitude. "I had been watching him since my childhood; since the age of six. We lived on Sannadhi Street. Ravi, his driver in later years, also lived there. We used to see him cross the street and go to the railway station. There was a tea shop in front of the temple where my father used to have tea. One time I went to see my father in the shop and Bhagwan was there. I looked at him, and he gave me a very aggressive look. So I was frightened."

Interestingly, it was another look by the same beggar that drew Saravanan in, changing him from a mere clerk to a faith-filled devotee. Three days after Saravanan was hired, Mani took him to meet the Godman, detailing the young man's education (he had been trained as an engineer) and explaining the work that was being assigned to him in the ashram office. Yogi Ramsuratkumar just looked at him.

"I see," said Bhagwan, fixing his fierce gaze on the man for a few seconds. "Then he blessed me. I felt a slight movement…something…" Saravanan attempted to explain the energy that was awakened in him by that glance. "From then on I got in the queue of those who waited for the car to arrive each day. I didn't want to miss it."

Soon thereafter, Saravanan began to chant the name of Yogi Ramsuratkumar, with some urging from his manager. "One day when I was working in the office, Mani says to me, 'People are coming here from all over the world, and you are just *sitting* here!'" Saravanan was being reminded of the enormous privilege of sharing in this great vision, all the while denying himself full participation. From then on he took up the recitation of the mantra.

"Whenever you are in the presence of realized souls, you feel extremely different from the ordinary world. You feel some peace." The young man's words were reminiscent of dozens of similar accounts by Indian men and women who spoke of their relationship to Yogi Ramsuratkumar. "You cannot think about your worries. It is like you are a completely drunken person; some sort of drowsiness makes you forget your worries. It is not because of alcohol, or some other drug; it is the drug that can be given only by realized souls. Special intoxication from the Divine! I felt many times this Divine intoxication. He is a tremendous, extraordinary Divine soul."

That Yogi Ramsuratkumar was available to people at the most subtle levels was an undeniable fact. The beggar seemed to know what was going on for them. "When I was feeling depression or something, or when Mani would tell me that I wasn't doing my work perfectly, and I would feel bad, Bhagwan would call me to him, while I was standing in the queue," Saravanan explained.

"Come, what is your name?" Yogi Ramsuratkumar would ask.

"He knows your name, but he asks anyway," the young man reflected. The asking of one's name was the Godchild's way of establishing some immediate, energetic bond.

"My Father blesses you," Yogi Ramsuratkumar would pray, repeating the person's name as he moved his hands in the characteristic gesture of dispensing grace.

That used to happen for many workers," Saravanan affirmed. "Just for nothing he would do this. He *knows!*"

One morning, as he went about his duties on the ashram, Saravanan was distracted. Some unexpected personal expenses had arisen, and he was sorely in need of money. Silently, he prayed to Yogi Ramsuratkumar for help, trusting that the Godman's hand could affect any situation. At the 4 P.M. darshan, as the young man stood at his post alongside Bhagwan's driver, Ravi, and gatekeeper, Kannon, a devotee approached Yogi Ramsuratkumar and placed 3,000 rupees, all in new currency, at the beggar's feet.

The Godman raised his eyes from the gift and slowly moved his hand, summoning Saravanan to his side. "You take that money, and you count it. How much is it?" he asked.

"Three thousand rupees, Bhagwan."

With the same deliberate intention with which he could drop a banana or a piece of sugar candy into a devotee's hand, Yogi Ramsuratkumar spoke. "You take immediately 1,000 rupees, and you give 1,000 to Ravi, and 1,000 to Kannon."

As far as Saravanan was concerned, it was nothing short of a miracle.

राम

The beggar's blessings were unlimited – they embraced the entire world. For his workers, this included the world of their families. No matter how minor their personal concerns might be, they were never belittled by the one who lived and suffered alongside them. "How is your father?" he would ask Saravanan on occasion. "When my father was very sick, about to die, I told him [Yogi Ramsuratkumar] that I'd admitted my father to the hospital in Madras. Bhagwan said, 'He will be all right. Nothing to worry about.' And because of Bhagwan's blessing he was gradually becoming better. Now he is all right." Stories too numerous to list parallel this one.

One day, in the late months of 1994, after finishing the electrical work in the main hall of the massive temple, Mani wanted Yogiji to be the first to switch on the lights, illuminating the great hall. "But Bhagwan wanted each and every worker to stand in the line inside the auditorium as this was happening," Saravanan reported. "So many people, over a hundred people were in that queue. Ravi was holding the hands of Bhagwan. Yogi Ramsuratkumar saw each and every face, and he started crying," the young man recalled, his own voice choking with emotion. "Tears were rolling down," he whispered, remembering the awesome love in which the Godman held them all.

राम

A humorous anecdote, told by Ravi, Yogi Ramsuratkumar's driver, demonstrates both the beggar's tender regard for his workers, and his clear authority with them. Just prior to the 1994 Jayanti, a small group of the male attendants on the staff, Ravi included, pooled their resources and purchased a new set of clothes – the traditional pajama and kirta – for their much loved Bhagwan. The men gathered together outside the Darshan Mandir, summoning their courage to enter. As much as they loved the Godman, they were aware that his displeasure could be fierce, even when delivered by a mere glance.

"We never went to him, unless he calls to us. Otherwise, we were generally keeping about ten feet away," one of the men recalled, describing their usual protocol. On this occasion, anxious to present their gift yet somewhat fearful, they pushed Ravi to the door, urging, "You go in and tell him. Tomorrow is Bhagwan's Jayanti day. Swami will hear your words. We don't have any guts."

Slowly, tentatively, Ravi approached his master. In a soft and wavering voice, he did his best to speak respectfully. "Bhagwan, tomorrow is your Jayanti," Ravi began. The Godman's eyes grew wide as he looked at his trusted driver. Ravi went on, laying their gift at the feet of Yogi Ramsuratkumar. "When you come tomorrow, you have to wear these clothes."

The saint paused for a moment, as a small smile formed at the corners of his mouth. "Ohhh?" he crooned sweetly, with the hint of a question in his voice. "Those conditions are not suitable for this beggar," he said. But his smile remained.

Ravi bowed and left, without another word.

The day after the Jayanti, Yogi Ramsuratkumar showed up at the ashram dressed in the clothes that the men had given.

राम

The work on the ashram was hard. The demands were constant. Mani was a powerful taskmaster, and Yogi Ramsuratkumar was, in his own way, harder. While assignments and scheduling varied, ashram staff were often expected to be available as early as five in the morning and to stay at their posts until eight at night, or later, depending upon the need. During one phase of the building, when both a day shift and a night shift were in operation, Mani himself was getting no more than two hours of sleep a night. When Raji became anxious for her husband's welfare, Yogi Ramsuratkumar took some time to assess her concern. Later, he spoke to her, clearly: "Father says two hours sleep is more than enough for Mani. Do not bother about it. My Father blesses you both."[4]

Besides the expectation for simple hard work, timing and attention to detail had always been crucial to the beggar. Nothing in his way of working had essentially changed. Yet, now that he had an ashram to care for, Yogi Ramsuratkumar's expectations for this type of precision among his staff and attendants became even more obvious, as he was being seen and touched by more people. Teaching lessons on the subject came fast and furiously.

"I can be with somebody else and be casual about certain things," Saravanan began, "but with him, if you are supposed to give coffee at 7:00 in the morning every day, you should give it at 7:00 only. If you bring it at 6:45 A.M., he will never take it. He will wait until 7:00 A.M. to drink it, even if you give it at 6:45. If the next day you bring the coffee at 7:30, he will not drink coffee at all."

Yogi Ramsuratkumar never stopped working, with everyone. From the part-time day-laborer to his Eternal Slave, Devaki, his attention took the form of constant refinement. Time, energy, resources, money, lack of conflict...details...details...details. Everything was important to him.

"Once, when Ravi, his driver, took a holiday, I drove Bhagwan from Sudama House to the ashram," Saravanan related, describing how the lesson in precision was delivered in his case. "One morning I went there a few minutes late, only five minutes. He was already sitting outside the gate on the stool. He just looked at me as I slowly opened the door. I knew what it meant. Then, one year later, Ravi again took holiday. I went to Bhagwan to tell him that I would be his driver. 'Bhagwan, tomorrow morning I am coming at 6:45 A.M.,' I said. 'Don't come five minutes late,' Yogi Ramsuratkumar told me. He remembered exactly what had happened one year ago. So I started coming thirty minutes early, just in case."

राम

The closer one comes to a spiritual master and the more responsibility and trust one is given, the thinner becomes the margin for error. "Weekend devotees," on the other hand, namely those who keep a safe distance from the annihilating fire, can seem to have much more leeway for making mistakes. Sometimes even a small effort might be acknowledged lavishly. Meanwhile, those who serve the master day and night can be ignored, reaping criticism at every turn. It takes great courage to stay in place while the spiritual master, or guru, starts stripping down the ego to its bare bones, and then pounding those bones to ash.

As he inched his way along the continually narrowing ledge that ascended this mountain known as Yogi Ramsuratkumar, Mani lost his footing again and again. Not only was he reviled by those who resented his authority and thwarted in his attempts to manage by obstinate or jealous people, he was told by Yogi Ramsuratkumar himself to do his job without complaint, to trust unquestioningly, and to handle *everything*. Yet, the minute he overstepped his authority in ways that he wasn't even aware of, he was firmly reprimanded by the master, who found in his devotee's gestures a prideful independence.

"You will handle all with my Father's blessings…handle all the problems without bringing trouble to this beggar," one of the ashram staff recalled the master's words. "Mani was supposed to handle things in his way, without bringing unnecessary problems to Bhagwan." Yet, not for one instant was the ultimate control to leave Yogi Ramsuratkumar's hands. It was a koan of the highest degree for Mani to learn, the hard way. Devaki Ma, the Sudama sisters, Lee Lozowick, Sadhu Rangarajan…and everyone else who had ever come in close contact with the beggar had been hit with similar lessons. Some devotees were astute enough to never repeat them.

One day, during a phase of the building, Yogi Ramsuratkumar arrived at the ashram and noticed some masons working on the dome. In handling a leak, they were making adjustments to the construction. The Godchild, who observed everything, called Mani and the other engineers to join him in the darshan. Uncharacteristically, Bhagwan's look and his tone were severe. Turning to Mani, he delivered the sword: "You have become big now, doing all things as you like." His words cut deeply, wounding the devotee's pride. "You are independent by doing things and planning things as you like. You have no respect for this beggar."

The guru's words, like his touch and his glance, are the most powerful tools on the planet when it comes to undermining ego's authority. And, to make matters worse, these tools are generally applied when ego least expects it. Just as we are congratulating ourselves for our extraordinary efforts on the master's behalf, some tiny "insignificant" detail causes him or her to announce, publicly, that we are doing *nothing*. Or even less than nothing!

"My Father is the only authority to do things at this Ashram," Yogi Ramsuratkumar declared. "This beggar does not decide, Father decides."[5] End of story.

Just as quickly as the thick storm cloud had covered the sun, it also blew away. There was never any residue in the moods of Yogi Ramsuratkumar, as his anger, like his constant love, were the movements of the Father's grace.

"Soon after, Bhagwan came to where I was working. He was so compassionate with me after showing His disapproval it was heartbreaking," Mani recounted. "He could see that we felt remorse or grief for our misgivings."[6]

राम

The "miracles of the wells" are told by everyone connected with the ashram construction. They are critical stories, and highly symbolic, as water is essential to life. Without it, the ashram plan would have been unworkable. But, beyond that, they are blessed stories, as each one involved the necessity for placing faith in the master. Such faith is the water of the soul.

One of the first wells, found through boring, was producing such a low output that the suggestion to abandon it was presented to Yogi Ramsuratkumar.

"Take this beggar to that bore well," the Godman asked.

When they got to the site, Yogi Ramsuratkumar put his foot on the mouth of the well and instructed Mani to start up the motorized pump. The water poured in torrents. Prior to this moment it had been a mere trickle.

On another occasion not long after, as the engineers searched for another well, the rig had already reached the depth of 290 feet and still had not hit water. Mani was troubled – the equipment could only extend to 300 feet. As they were still pulling up only dust, he brought the details of the problem to Yogi Ramsuratkumar. What should they do? Mani inquired about the possibility of trying another location.

Bhagwan didn't hesitate. Even if they had to drill to 1,000 feet, they should not change locations. This was the spot! "My Father will guide you," the beggar said.

Mani was incredulous, but obedient. Handing the master a small sample of the stone and sand found at 290 feet, he watched as the beggar rubbed the substance between his fingers.[7]

Leaving the darshan hall where this consultation had taken place, Mani headed back in the direction of the work site. "Yogi Ramsuratkumar!" he gasped. A ten-foot-high geyser of water was gushing from the ground.

So much water was forthcoming from these and another ashram well that Bhagwan named them after India's sacred rivers – Ganga, Saraswati, and Yamuna – the source of India's life.

राम

A crane was needed to lift necessary materials to the roof of the building, as part of the ceiling construction, but Mani was having a hard time locating one. His concern grew, reaching a critical point one day, as this lack of equipment threatened to delay the work, or even cause a temporary halt to the operations.

On that same day, however, a regional transportation official *just happened* to show up in Yogi Ramsuratkumar's darshan. Mani asked the man's assistance and was amazed to hear that a crane was currently in their transport office lot, as it was under inspection for certification.

When Mani told Yogi Ramsuratkumar of the situation, the beggar asked the man for any assistance he could offer. The next morning, the crane arrived at the ashram. One miracle down!

Unfortunately, when they attempted to use it, the machine did not work properly. A part was sorely in need of repair or replacement, promising another significant delay. When Yogi Ramsuratkumar was informed of the problem, he left the darshan hall and walked outside. Standing by the side of the huge crane, he placed his hands on it and remained there for several minutes. Then he asked to see the defective part.

Seating himself on the ground, with the machine part in front of him, the beggar lit a cigarette. For ten minutes he touched this errant piece of the crane, while Mani and the crane operator looked on. Then, handing it over, he asked that it be installed once again, saying that no other repair would be needed.

Despite having seen miracles on a near-daily basis, Mani's doubts were always aroused, understandably. When the part was replaced and the motor switched on, Mani was humbled once again. The crane worked.

राम

Sometimes these ashram-related miracles were awesome and dramatic. Like when a six-ton steel beam wouldn't lodge properly in the place prepared for it in the roof. The contractor for this piece was a Muslim of known skill and competency. Yet, unlike others who worked on the project, he had no relationship to Yogi Ramsuratkumar as a saint. After repeated and unsuccessful attempts to move the beam into place, the man was visibly upset. Over and over, for a period of almost twenty-four hours, the man had directed the crews, trying every strategy he knew that might turn things in their favor.

When nothing worked, the Muslim went to Yogi Ramsuratkumar, undoubtedly prompted by the faith and past experience of others on the job. "Please help me. We need your blessings," the man said as he touched the beggar's feet.

Yogi Ramsuratkumar left what he was doing and climbed to the second story of the building, from which point he could actually touch the errant beam. He did so, placing his hands on it in three places. A few moments passed. Then he turned to Mani, asking him to direct the workers to try again. Fifteen minutes later, with a thud, the massive structure fell into place, perfectly aligned.

"We didn't do anything different than we had tried for the past twenty-four hours," Mani explained in his book. "Bhagwan just touched the beam, three places, said 'Now you do it' and down it went into position!"[8]

At other times, it was simply a coincidence of unlikely events that brought home to his devotees the truth, once again – that Yogi

Ramsuratkumar's influence permeated everything. All they needed was faith and obedience. One step forward, even in the midst of severe mental doubt, was often all it took.

Saravanan remembered a time when he was sent to Madras by Mani to search out a large supply of iron tresses that would be needed for the construction. His boss reminded the younger man that he should keep in mind, at all times, that he was the representative of Yogi Ramsuratkumar, and that these materials were essential to the ashram. When things got difficult, moreover, he should just start telling stories of Bhagwan.

Materials were not easy to come by. Any metal purchases had to be approved by government officials at the time. The red tape could be daunting. The delays unbearably frustrating, but expected. Armed with all the enthusiasm of youth and the energy of grace, Saravanan found the office of the Indian Iron and Steel Company (no small task in itself in crowded Madras) and presented his case to the first person he met. Without lifting his eyes from his work, the man directed him to another office.

At the second station, at least eye contact was made. As Saravanan started to explain his mission, he opened his briefcase. "Who is that?" the administrator asked, noticing a photo of Yogi Ramsuratkumar inside the lid. Saravanan was only too ready to tell the man about his master, the beggar-saint of Tiruvannamalai. The longer he listened, the softer and friendlier the man became as he reached for the forms to begin taking the order.

No sooner had they begun than a third person, this man higher up in the organization, stepped in. He had overheard the conversation and the name of the Godchild of Tiruvannamalai. He knew of an ashram being constructed there. "I know, I know," this man said, excitedly. "He is Bhagwan! What exactly do you want?"

Without needing to consult with anyone else, the man took the order, went back to his own office, typed all the forms, and signed them. With that, Saravanan opened his briefcase again, took out a few of the small souvenir pictures of Yogi Ramsuratkumar that he always carried, and handed them to the grateful man.

One week later – an unprecedented promptness – the shipment of iron arrived at the ashram gate. "And this service continued with every order," Saravanan explained. "We purchased 135 tons from this company altogether, and there were no problems at all. Some of the people in the company even started coming to visit Bhagwan."

Makarand Paranjape, a university professor and scholar of spiritual and secular literature, eloquently summed up a miracle of another kind.

Tiruvannamalai, which is already so pure with the *tapas* of so many self-realized souls, both visible and invisible, both in the physical and in the subtle bodies, is now bearing witness to another miracle – the rapid rising up of Bhagawan's ashram. What a great and noble piece of divine magic and mischief it is, this grand habitation for the "dirty beggar." Oh Bhagawan, it must be so much fun to put us all to work, keeping us out of our stupidities and selfishness. For a God-intoxicated soul, who spent years as a homeless wanderer, sleeping at the doorsteps of shops or under trees, how funny it must be to build a grand ashram. Make no mistake, friends, this ashram is the fulfillment of our own prayers, which Bhagawan in his kindness has granted. Here, several generations of seekers, tired and weary from the stress and fatigue of the world, will come to find their true selves. Those who have laboured day and night to build this hymn of concrete and steel are true karma yogis, whose sadhana has flowered under Bhagawan's own special and strict guidance. Whatever Bhagawan does is for our good; we may think we are serving Him, doing His work in the world, but actually, all this is for our own spiritual development and perfection. The burden of sins of several lives is lightened by the glance of a holy man – such is our traditional belief. The presence in this fallen time and age of Godmen like Bhagawan allows the rest of us to glimpse our potential, to strive to cleanse ourselves of our egos, to offer ourselves wholeheartedly to the Divine. For without such a transformation of consciousness, the world will never be changed.[9]

33

BUILDING THE LEGACY

 The courtship of the spiritual East by the West, which had been going on for centuries, was occasionally embodied in partnerships of certain unique varieties. The Irish woman Margaret Nobel (later known as Sister Nivedita) stood at the side of Swami Vivekananda in his struggles for freedom from British rule; and a British woman, Madeleine Slade (renamed Mirabehn), would become the adopted daughter and lifetime family member of Mahatma Gandhi. Blanche Rachel Mirra Aflassa, the daughter of a Turkish father and an Egyptian mother, who became the partner in the work of Sri Aurobindo, was a highly educated French emigrant. Referred to as Mother Mirra or simply "the Mother," she carried on her master's work long after his death.

Many great Indian masters and saints had an entourage of early Western devotees. Sri Ramana Maharshi, whose universality was uncompromising, attracted Westerners in droves, and even the earliest photos or films of his gatherings reveal the presence of Europeans or Americans among his close companions. Meher Baba made trips to the United States and Europe and drew both Western men and women into special and intimate work circles. To this day, the numbers of Westerners at the ashrams of Sai Baba in Puttaparthi and Osho Rajneesh in Poona can sometimes seem to outnumber the count of Indian devotees.

The greatest saints are beyond making distinctions merely on the basis of race and country of origin. Such saints are interested in the heart of the seeker, not her or his nationality. For the rare men or women who have proven capable of sharing in God's work, the magnetic force by which they are drawn to the saint is irresistible. They are literally pulled to the beloved's side; their lives lost to service or devotion.

From all accounts, the saints are not the ones who choose their companions – they don't determine consciously who stays closely with them, who remains at a safe distance. Such decisions are apparently made through karma's bonds established over lifetimes, and according to God's will. Lifetimes of orientation toward "the One" may eventually flower as service in the closest proximity to a saint or guru.

Although such closeness is generally beyond the control of either the lover or the beloved, there is definitely some way in which the lover can sharpen the focus, maintain attention, practice as if his or her "hair is on fire," as the saying goes. Such closeness is not maintained by vapid self-satisfaction or egoic pride.

There is often severe criticism of those who are drawn close. Although she was a native of South India, Devaki's honorific position as Yogiji's "Eternal Slave" drew the jealousy and mistrust of even longtime devotees. When the Westerner, Lee Lozowick, entered the picture, however, the potential for criticism magnified. It was understandable, if regrettable. Throughout India, the image of the "ugly American" or "ugly European" had been reinforced at every turn. Westerners commonly evidenced disregard for customs, assuming that they were some privileged lot whose needs should be met at every turn. Their condescending looks and patronizing words were a constant source of humiliation to Indian people. Even in the sacred environment of an ashram, such things were rarely different. For years, Yogi Ramsuratkumar had been approached by Westerners whose drug-glazed eyes and ignorance of protocol marked them as fools. *Who is this rich man or woman with their crude and self-aggrandizing ways?* the Indian devotees likely asked. And most of all, *Why is our Guruji paying them respect, seeming to grant them access that he is denying to us?*

Ever since Lee started to show his face around Tiruvannamalai, there were always those who harbored some resentment that the

American and his "people" were getting special treatment from Yogi Ramsuratkumar. They were given seats in the first row at the master's darshan. Lee was often seated on his own straw mat at the foot of the stairs that led up to the beggar's dais. For hours, day after day, throughout Lee's visits, Yogi Ramsuratkumar would hold his American devotee's hands, slap his back, and even gaze tenderly and long into the man's eyes. Other audiences might be suspended so that Yogi Ramsuratkumar could spend uninterrupted days with his Western visitors. The beggar's words both to and about Lee also reflected a degree of intimacy that must have rankled anyone who thought they were being denied their own rightful place at the master's side.

Even Mani, whose faith in Yogi Ramsuratkumar was honed to razor sharpness, admitted that he was initially troubled by the God-man's enormous attention to Lee Lozowick and his band of Western followers.

In the minds of some, the beggar's attention to Westerners was as abhorrent as his association with rich people. Ravi, the master's driver, tells of several disturbing moments when rocks were thrown at Yogi Ramsruatkumar's car as the beggar was driven through town. Occasionally, some disgruntled Tamilian would approach the car's window, shouting out that Yogi Ramsuratkumar was catering to the rich – both Indian and Western – while denying the poor.

Such accounts were shockingly absurd to anyone who astutely observed Yogi Ramsuratkumar. His concern was always for hearts and souls, not passports or bank accounts. Numerous stories tell of Yogi Ramsuratkumar leaving the company of some wealthy or influential guest to walk into the street and deliver prasad to the person's chauffeur.

Stereotypes exist on all levels. A devotee once brought several large boxes of second-hand clothing to Tiruvannamalai as an offering to beggars. She planned to distribute them among the poor, as she had heard that others close to Yogi Ramsuratkumar had occasionally done. When she told Bhagwan of her plan, however, he appeared agitated. "Old clothes?" he asked somewhat incredulously. "You have brought old clothes to the beggars?"

His words alerted the devotee to her own internal attitude, and she immediately decided that she would go out and purchase at least some new saris to add to the collection. As if reading her changed intention, Yogiji asked a visiting official from the Arunachaleswarar Temple to help the woman by arranging a place for the easy distribution of her goods. "It is so difficult to distribute standing among the people, so find some convenient place for distribution," Bhagwan graciously instructed. The plan was carried out as he had instructed.[1]

Through numerous means, the Godman blessed and encouraged contributions of all kinds toward the building of his ashram. The broader needs of the work called for such skillful means.

It was the illusion that love is scarce that prompted some to assume that because Yogi Ramsuratkumar encouraged and blessed those who gave in one way, that he was denying his blessings or encouragement to those who might give in another, less material way.

Jesus made the point perfectly in telling the ageless parable of the wedding feast. Whether one was rich or poor, if they did not put on the wedding garment appropriate to the occasion – namely, if they had not prepared their souls for the reception of grace – they would likely find themselves bound "hand and foot and cast out in the darkness where they would weep and gnash their teeth." This Bible verse (Matthew 22:13) is an exact description of the personal hell that is created when the petty mind is allowed to wall off the heart. In concluding that same parable, Jesus reminded his listeners: "Many are called, but few are chosen."

Yogi Ramsuratkumar was clearly establishing a legacy for the future of the great work he had been given by his Father. The ashram and temple, as the receptacles of his body and his imprinted word, were crown jewels in this treasured legacy. The Ma Devaki Veda Patashala would be another invaluable gem. This would be a building on the ashram grounds – a sanctuary in which to "further the scholarly research of ancient and sacred Sanskrit texts."[2] The World Ramnam Movement was another – a part of his overriding request to speak and chant his name, the name of God. His association with Lee Lozowick and his requests to the "bad poet" from America to continue to write more and more poems and songs, including poems to Devaki Ma, and to spread his name "throughout the world," was a critical extension of his work into the West. In April 1994, while the construction on the ashram grounds was in full swing, Yogi Ramsuratkumar made it clear that there was still more he wanted from the American.

राम

A three-acre parcel adjacent to the ashram property in Agraha Collai was up for sale. Hearing of this, in April 1994, Yogi Ramsuratkumar sent word to the United States, inquiring if Lee Lozowick would be interested in purchasing this land. "This Beggar wants Lee Lozowick to build an ashram in India, next to this Beggar's ashram."[3]

Lee immediately agreed and mobilized for a trip back to India to settle the plans. Complications arose, however – not the least of which was the difficulty for foreigners to secure ownership of land in India. When it became apparent that the process would not be a fast one, Lee remained in America, awaiting word of his next move, at Yogi Ramsuratkumar's direction.

By August 1994, a land acquisition looked more positive. This time, Lee sent Balarama Zuccarello, one of his closest students, to Tiruvannamalai to accomplish the work on his behalf. Despite the beggar's hopes, however, more complications arose with this property, and eventually this project too was put on hold. Some of these new complications would have required settlement by a lawsuit. Yogi Ramsuratkumar chose not to take the owners to court, although it was clearly a battle that he rightly could have won. The fact that it involved so much output of time, energy and money from his American son disturbed the Godman. "This beggar did not know the law of the land," Yogiji said. "He must beg forgiveness of Lee Lozowick."[4] It was a gesture that only deepened the bond between them.

Balarama kept a detailed journal of these three weeks in India (late August through mid-September 1994). A few of his descriptions provide valuable insight and instruction from the beggar's life at this time.[5]

राम

Building the Legacy

"He walks like a boy of nineteen, up and down between the men's and women's sides of the hall," Balarama wrote of the aging Godman who was approaching his seventy-seventh birthday. "He does not carry a fan anymore. He carries a length of rope, rough jute, maybe 1/4 – 3/8 inches wide, wound up in maybe six to eight loops," the rope that he had begun wearing since the day that he and Mani had marked the land. Despite the exorbitant heat of waning summer, Yogi Ramsuratkumar still wore what he always wore, a thick woolen shawl. Regardless of his ongoing bouts with ill health, the beggar walked with a firm step, "as if he extended to the very center of the earth. He moved like a boxer, like an impeccable warrior, young, vibrant, determined, undaunted."

As he sat in the old darshan mandir, alongside Yogi Ramsuratkumar, Balarama was privileged to watch the "circus" of activity that constellated around the Godman. "There were about five hundred people in and out today. Every fifteen minutes or so Bhagwan would call Mani and tell him who he wanted to leave and how many to let in. Yogi Ramsuratkumar was always so surprised when Mani would say that there were forty more people outside, or twenty more. Yogi Ramsuratkumar would repeat it, saying, 'There are forty more, ohhhh my!'"

On Sunday, visitors to darshan could number between 750 – 1,000, each group spending fifteen to thirty minutes in his hall. "With each change of crowd, Yogi Ramsuratkumar would get up and 'work them' – looking into each one of their faces, seeing each one of them individually. Over and over again! Tireless, with the stamina of an ancient Vedic warrior, he would work the room till all were accounted for."

One Sunday, while the room was thoroughly packed with about sixty visitors, a busload arrived from Madurai containing many "poor people – very thin, very hard working, obviously hard lives. Simple folk, some were sickly looking," Bala noted. The room was emptied and the Madurai contingent took their places.

"Yogi Ramsuratkumar was 'working' like crazy, walking up and down, waving his hands wildly over them. These were the people Yogi Ramsuratkumar had come for," Bala explained, his way of saying that the Godchild was poor throughout his life of sadhana, and was thus dedicated to his work among the poor. For their part, the Madurai visitors were hungry for his glance, his blessing, his touch. "I had not seen a group strain so much just to catch a glimpse of the saint," Bala remarked. Twenty minutes later, the group was ushered from the room and the hall was again filled up with a new group of pilgrims.

Whether it was a quiet morning or a chaotic one, the one constant was Yogi Ramsuratkumar's attention and inner focus. Bala wrote: "He is lost in his Father. Of all the things he says, 'My Father blesses you' is what he speaks most. He *is* conventionally mad – completely lost in his Father's blessings. No return! He is a slave to that work. Whether there are 150 people packed in the hall or only four of us, he works the same with the same intensity, regardless of his surroundings. Great urgency is evident in his face and posture, his tensing of his body, as if he is infusing his Father's blessing into every crack and crevice in the place; as if he is trying to make sure every atom is drenched with his Father's blessing. No one is left alone; no one is forgotten."

"This beggar does not exist; nothing and nobody exists; only my Father – near, near, nearest to far, far, farthest in everything and everybody. Nothing exists except my Father; perfect, absolute, infinite, unified in everything as everything."

"All that exists is Father: anywhere, anyplace, near, far, complete unity, all pervasive, in everything and everywhere. There is no isolation, perfect unity. All that exists is my Father. He alone exists, everywhere. So when you are having any difficulty and you call out this beggar's name, my Father will answer you; he will help you, instantaneously because he alone exists."

"People say that I want my name chanted. It is not my name, it is my Father's. This beggar died in 1952. There is no one else, nothing else except My Father."[6]

राम

568

Yogi Ramsuratkumar's work with Devaki Ma was unique and often mysterious. During the three-week period of his visit, Balarama observed a particular play between them that carried a message of further empowerment.

On an afternoon when the beggar was exhibiting a particularly solemn and profound mood, "very deep, eyes closed, lost" – that appearance of being fully absorbed in God – "he turned to Ma Devaki and told her to get up. She did. He gave her his bowl, fan, and stick, and told her to walk up and down the aisle three times. She was taken aback, seemed surprised and frightened, but she did it and then sat down. After a while Yogi Ramsuratkumar looked at Devaki and said, 'Let's see if this beggar can get you into even more trouble.' He again asked her to stand and he gave her his cord of rope and asked her to walk again up and down the aisle. He said, 'Walk all the way to the end.' She did this three or four times. He held his hands toward her as she walked, showering his benediction on her all the while. Then, a short while later, he had her do it again, only this time with the bowl, fan and stick."

Balarama noted that the visitors and guests around him "looked confused and surprised" by this visual display. Nonetheless, two women devotees spontaneously broke into a chorus, a chant that exalted Devaki Ma's name. Within a few moments, the entire room was chanting. When Devaki Ma returned to her seat at last, she "looked very much out of breath, as if recovering from shock."

This was not the last time that such physical displays were made for the benefit of his devotees. Only those blinded by self-interest could have denied that the master was making a communication of significance with this beloved devotee.

राम

The Godman's constant care for his devotees was often enacted in a direct way, on the spot. Balarama reported that one day a man came to darshan and handed Yogi Ramsuratkumar two copies of a magazine that he had published. The beggar was intrigued, and passed them to Devaki Ma and a young female visitor who sat near-by, asking them to see if they contained "any articles on this beggar."

When a piece about Yogi Ramsuratkumar was discovered, he asked Ma Devaki to read it aloud to the room full of devotees. When the next group of pilgrims replaced the first, Yogiji asked Shakti, the young visitor, to read the article standing in front of the assembly. When she had finished, the editor himself was asked to read it aloud.

Yogi Ramsuratkumar inquired about how many copies of the magazine the man had brought with him.

"Ten," the publisher informed him.

Calling Mani into the room and directing that he be given the ten magazines, the beggar asked how these might be sold so that the man could make some money, as he was in a financial crisis.

When Mani learned that the original price of the magazine was six rupees, he confidently told Yogi Ramsuratkumar that they could sell them for twenty rupees each, right then.

The business was conducted immediately, in Tamil, and the energy in the room nearly exploded as people were reaching for their money, holding it up, and running up the aisle to get their copy. In a few minutes, nine magazines were sold for a total of 650 rupees.

"I will ask the man to put in a request for donations in his next edition," Mani said.

Yogi Ramsuratkumar laughed mischievously as he remarked: "Now he knows how to do business!"

राम

"This beggar wants Lee Lozowick to have an ashram here," Yogi Ramsuratkumar reiterated to Balarama, as he gently waved his hands and arms in blessing. "Whatever the difficulties!" the beggar affirmed.

Bala replied, "It is finished, whatever you want."

"Very good!" Yogiji said.

"Lee said that this beggar was guiding him even before he met this beggar," the Godchild told Balarama, who was well familiar with that fact. As one of Lee's first students and a member of the group that accompanied Lee on the second trip in Tiruvannamalai in 1979, Balarama had watched carefully the entire evolution of this remarkable relationship. He knew well that Lee Lozowick firmly held that

Yogi Ramsuratkumar was the source of his life and the catalyst of the extraordinary event of 1975 whereby Lee was surrendered to the will of God. He understood that it had taken Lee himself several years to come to this understanding, but that once seen, Lee had never waivered from his master's side.

As Yogi Ramsuratkumar spoke of this task and of his desire for Lee's closer presence, the Godchild would often express pure delight, laughing and "covering his eyes, as if he could hide the sun behind his hand."

"Mr. Lee is one of the most extraordinary persons this beggar has ever met, and that is why this beggar wants Lee Lozowick to have an adjoining ashram." (Lee's ashram, almost adjacent to Yogiji's, was miraculously established a few years later. It is called Triveni II, Hohm Sahaj Charitable Trust.)

राम

On an earlier visit to Tiruvannamalai, in 1992, Balarama (whose namesake was that of Lord Krishna's brother) was introduced to another Western devotee by Yogi Ramsuratkumar. "Krishna, this is Balaram [Balarama]." The Godchild chuckled with delight as he addressed Krishna Carcelle, a Frenchman living on the island of Mauritius who had first met the beggar in 1990.

In October 1994, Krishna Carcelle had joined Sadhu Rangarajan as part of the World Ramnam Movement, in a tour of Uttar Pradesh and Delhi. Together the two ardent devotees of Yogi Ramsuratkumar visited town after town, carrying the beggar's name and the power of Ramnam to thousands.

Carcelle was a dynamic part of the "Western invasion" that soon turned into the Western vanguard for the work of Yogi Ramsuratkumar. The Frenchman, who had visited India in the 1970s in search of the religious spirit, was at last led to the feet of the beggar of Tiruvannamalai in April 1990. It was an association that would change his life forever. In 1992, Yogiji drew the man closer. "This sadhu has been waiting for a long time to meet Krishna," the beggar said, playing on the name of the great Lord. "Now that he is here, the sadhu will not let him go."[7] From then on, Krishna's energy was devoted fully to his master, and to spreading the Divine name.

Krishna Carcelle visited Tiruvannamalai and bowed to his master's feet almost every year thereafter, particularly during December, when Jayanti celebrations were held. Yogi Ramsuratkumar would regularly ask the Frenchman to lead the chanting, which he did with reverent attention.

At various times, from 1994 onward, as people representing many different countries were regular visitors to Yogi Ramsuratkumar, the beggar would call them up, assign them a seat at the side of the room, and direct them to "talk together." It was not uncommon to see Lee Lozowick knee-to-knee with Krishna, and others, in what Lee described as the "United Nations" of Yogi Ramsuratkumar.

> For the past few days [in December 1997], Yogi Ramsuratkumar has been putting together a configuration of people who sit…to the side of the room and talk amongst themselves during Darshan. Yogi has taken a great interest in this growing group of people…one person from Thailand, one from Italy, one from France, one from Mauritius and one from America. Today he added a woman from Mexico. Yogi Ramsuratkumar waves His arms in gestures of blessing towards them, and sometimes He turned to them and laughed.[8]

It was more than a social gathering that the beggar was promoting. The Godman's work, by his own admission, encompassed the entire spectrum of humanity. It is not hard to imagine that this beggar who could affect the world by the placement of teacups could be doing much more in placing his representatives in a particular configuration and asking them to interact with kindness and generosity. Likely, he was enacting a play that energetically affected the whole planet.

राम

December 1, 1994. After years of disallowing the celebration of his Jayanti in his presence in Tiruvannamalai, Yogi Ramsuratkumar

*Lee Lozowick, Krishna Carcelle, Justice Arunachalam,
speak together, 1997*

succumbed once again to the pleas of his devotees. Since the mid-1980s, starting with the efforts of Rangarajan in Chennai and the enthusiasm of Ponkamaraj and others in areas to the south, Jayanti celebrations had been held in other locations. The beggar, however, wanted nothing special around him.

In 1994, however, a gigantic festival was organized on his ashram in the shadow of Mount Arunachala, even as the construction continued unabated. By the first of December, the great entrance hall (known as the Swagath Mantap) of the temple was nearly complete – enough to accommodate hundreds of participants from India and other places in the world. For those who had previously enjoyed the darshan of the master under the punnai tree, or on the crowded verandah of the Sannadhi house, the setting came as a shock or an elegant surprise.

ONLY GOD

The circular rotunda, sixty feet in diameter, had a floor of black marble tiles so highly polished that they served as a mirror. The walls were painted a muted pink and decorated only with the large photographs of the beggar's lineage: Sri Aurobindo and The Mother; Ramana Maharshi alongside a photo of his mother; Swami Papa Ramdas next to Mataji Krishnabai.

Against the far wall of the massive chamber, under a huge painted OM, two steps reached a low dais. Rugs covered this platform, and several pillows (one on the platform floor, one propped against the wall) served as the beggar's seat. Devaki Ma sat on the same dais, to the Godchild's right, and Ma Vijayalakshmi sat next to Devaki, both of them at a right angle to Yogi Ramsuratkumar. On the floor to the right of the platform, a blanket was placed for the other two Sudama sisters, who led most of the chanting. As the beggar looked out into the hall, women sat in front of him on the left, men on the right, exactly opposite to the way it had been in the old darshan mandir. In describing this new setting Lee Lozowick reflected:

> Oh Father, Yogi Ramsuratkumar,
>   this Temple of Yours
> is surely as grand
>   as anything the Universe has yet seen.
> "He must be going mad,"
>   the skeptics say.
> "No," says lee, His son,
>   "He has always been Mad."
> "Who does He think He is?"
>   the doubters scoff.
> "No One but His Father's faithful servant."
>   says this bad Poet.
> Yes Dearest, oh dirty Beggar,
>   let them think what they will,
> for You are Your Father's Slave
>   as Your son is Yours.[9]

In rituals and festivities that would be duplicated at his Jayanti for several years to come, the day began with a fire ceremony accompanied by Vedic chanting. It was held in a moderately-sized thatched hut called the Yogashala, which had a permanent fire pit embedded in the floor at one corner. Here, during the rest of the year, itinerant sadhus would gather for their rituals and prayers.

During the Jayanti, morning and afternoon darshans were held in the Mantap, which could easily accommodate hundreds. Even so, the huge crowds that began showing up at the beggar's doorstep for these events became so massive that groups were once again limited to shifts. The Jayanti darshans consisted of long periods of chanting and singing led by the Sudama sisters or sung individually by others as appointed by Yogi Ramsuratkumar. Entertainers of a wide variety of Indian cultural dance and music would also present.

While Yogi Ramsuratkumar was observably delighted by some of these professional performances, his blessing attention and delight was just as easily captured by the simplest chant of a poor devotee who sang off-key. As an observer to one of these early Jayanti celebrations (1995), this biographer had the impression that the Godman was more likely *enduring* such elaborate festivities as part of his sacrifice on behalf of his devotees.

Starting in 1994, a highlight of contrast occurred in the afternoon Jayanti session when dozens of sadhus, one at a time, approached the master's side. Yogi Ramsuratkumar presented each sadhu with a new orange *lunghi* (dressing cloth) together with a small stipend of rupees.

Traditionally, sadhus who depend upon God alone for their sustenance are not only fed but also occasionally gifted with clothing at various ashrams throughout India. Soon after Yogi Ramsuratkumar's ashram was established, feeding arrangements were set up so that wandering mendicants could receive a daily meal.

For Westerners in attendance at these Jayantis, this awarding of the sadhus was always a memorable event. From young, clean-robed newcomers on the path of sannyas to wizened elders whose scarred feet, ragged clothes, and arthritic hands bore witness to years of hard sadhana, Yogi Ramsuratkumar blessed them all. Appreciation for sadhus was a subject that he had spoken of many times, indicating their importance in India's spiritual progress.

Whatever you do, whether you run the government or business or remain in the top most position, unless you do something to protect the Sadhus, the sannyasins and the realized souls, it is of no use…The whole humanity exists because of the Sadhus. To tell you the truth, the Law exists only because of the Sadhus.[10]

Jayanti day was always punctuated with generous meals cooked by the ashram kitchen staff and served in either the dining hall or in temporary outdoor shade pavilions. Many thousands of devotees and visitors would be served.

On the day after the Jayanti, life would return to relative "normal" as Yogi Ramsuratkumar would take his breakfast in the concrete breakfast hut on the ashram grounds and conduct his business of blessing as he did on every other day of the year.

राम

What seemed to please the beggar more than the professional entertainment of his Jayanti day celebrations was the spontaneous play of singing and dancing, speeches and storytelling that he requested of his visitors. The reading of poems and passages from books or articles had always been a regular occurrence in his darshans from the earliest days. Singing and chanting was integral to everything. But occasionally, depending upon who his guests were, some other interesting lilas were enacted.

In the 1970s, the beggar's play with the American Truman Caylor Wadlington sometimes amounted to drawing doodles, or writing spontaneously on a large drawing pad. Caylor believed that many of these activities were the Godchild's ploy to occupy his attention while the more subtle work of changing his heart was being carried on. In any case, it is clear that the name "Godchild" was an appropriate one. Yogi Ramsuratkumar reveled in innocent play.

In 1994, during an extended stay at the Sudama House with Devaki Ma and the other "sisters," Nivedita Rangarajan was privileged to participate in the Godchild's play. "He used to be in a jovial mood," she wrote, describing his overall temperament at home. "I could feel the difference between sitting in the verandah for public darshan and sitting with Him in His room. In the Darshan Hall, mostly He would seem to be serious and in deep thoughts. In His room, He was like a member of the family, laughing and talking to us."[11]

Nivedita recalled one form of their play – an age-old children's game called "Patty-cake" in the West. As she and Devaki Ma sat before him, "we would clap our hands, and then clap with our right hand and Yogiji's left hand, and then with our left hand and Yogiji's right hand. It is a form of a dance. But we were simply sitting and playing this way with Yogiji."

On another occasion, Nivedita continued, "Yogiji was walking for exercising in the verandah. He held the right hand of Ma Devaki in His left hand and walked from one end to the other. Then he caught the left hand of Ma Devaki in His right hand and walked the way back. He kept on walking this way, as if he was practicing for a march-past. He was walking, like a child, enjoying and laughing all along."[12]

Beginning in the late 1980s and early 90s, during the visits Lee Lozowick made with his male disciples, there were numerous requests for stories, poems, songs – anything and everything to delight the Godman's heart. In 1994, in the midst of the large Jayanti celebration, Yogi Ramsuratkumar began to ask Lee Lozowick to speak to the assembly at every session, and for Lee's American and European devotees to stand and lead chants from the front of the huge darshan hall.

In 1995, without warning, he called for his Western guests to sing Christmas carols and for Lee to tell stories of Jesus. When those were presented with great gusto, he surprised the Americans by asking them to dance, too. One small group immediately rose to the occasion. When they formed a circle and began to act out the movements suggested by the Quaker hymn, "'Tis a Gift to Be Simple' – "*to turn, to turn will by our delight, till by turning and turning we come round right*" – Yogi Ramsuratkumar was thrilled. He wanted more. The Westerners obliged with a rousing chorus of "Jingle Bells" as they pranced like reindeer in front of the astonished crowd. The beggar found their antics hilarious. Each time they added a "Ho, Ho, Ho" to the song, Yogi Ramsuratkumar audibly giggled, and his whole body shook with the laughter.

In the last public darshans that Yogi Ramsuratkumar ever gave, during Lee Lozowick's visit in December 2000, a short two months before the Godman's death, Yogi Ramsuratkumar tenderly asked for "dancing, more dancing." As several of the Western women sang Sanskrit chants celebrating his name, and later sang Christmas carols, traditional American folk songs, and the poems written by the "bad poet," their bodies took up a rhythmic motion. They swayed their arms, clapped their hands, and turned in circles in time with the music. Even though he was in a highly weakened condition, Yogi Ramsuratkumar would be visibly energized by their willing cooperation in his play. All those who participated in this lila found that they were blessed beyond measure by putting aside their shyness, forgetting their onlookers, and allowing their dance to be their offering to him alone.

One of the dancers wrote: "Again there was a tremendous surge of happiness, gratitude and ecstasy as the dancing and singing flowed through with spontaneity, fluidity and ease. A perceptible flow of energy came to us from the audience; everyone seemed drawn into the praise and prayer…Finally Yogi Ramsuratkumar called us to the stage to receive prasad and his formal Blessing."

"[This Beggar] liked that very much. The singing and dancing is *very good*. This Beggar would like more singing and dancing."[13]

And one of the witnesses observed: "What He asks for, what He wants with His time, is to see us sing and dance happily. He gives us lightness. He gives us His glee, His radiant smile at devotees who attempt to give as much as they've got…Wow, [imagine] helping God with a few songs and a dance![14]

राम

Since 1989, when Hilda Charlton's book *Saints Alive* introduced Yogi Ramsuratkumar to the American public, no other U.S. book had been published which contained extensive coverage of the beggar's life and teaching. In December 1994, however, Lee Lozowick brought with him to India an elegant hard-covered volume entitled, *Facets of the Diamond, Wisdom of India*, and presented it to his master.

The book, published by Lee's own publishing company, was a large "coffee table" format, measuring eleven inches wide by nine inches tall. It contained, in three languages (German, English, French), the biographies, selected quotations, and illustrious photographs of nine preeminent Indian saints: Ramana Maharshi, Papa Ramdas, Swami Prajnanpad, Chandra Swami, Nityananda, Shirdi Sai Baba, Sanatan Das Baul, and Sri Yogi Ramsuratkumar, to whom the largest section was devoted. Of this concession the editors wrote: "If special deference has been shown to the Godchild of Tiruvannamalai, we ask the reader's indulgence, as this book is the result of his Blessing, and is offered in profound gratitude for his Benediction in this world."[15]

Surprisingly, this book on the wisdom of India also contained a biographical piece about Lee Lozowick, as Yogi Ramsuratkumar had given his permission for the project *only* on the condition that his American son be included in it. In 1994, explaining this odd addition, Yogi Ramsuratkumar stated the facts clearly: "This beggar is in this book, and this beggar allowed [himself] to appear in this book only if he (pointing to Lee) appears in the book too. This is a book about Indian saints. And Lee Lozowick is an Indian saint."[16]

Just as the Godchild had been moved deeply by the poetry he had been receiving from Lee for many years, he was profoundly grateful for and complimentary of *Facets of the Diamond*. Devaki Ma was asked to read the book aloud to the assembled crowds, particularly the chapters related to Lee, Ramana Maharshi, Papa Ramdas, and Yogi Ramsuratkumar. The beggar was captivated by the photos of his own Father, Papa Ramdas, as well as those of the saints he did not know.

At one point, amidst his praise of the book, Yogi Ramsuratkumar asked Lee to stand up and tell people the price and how they could acquire one. Somewhat chagrined, perhaps embarrassed at the idea of doing business in his master's darshan, Lee nonetheless complied immediately, announcing that the price was $39.95 U.S. (an extremely high price to pay for a book by Indian standards). When Lee added that he hoped to find an Indian publisher, presumably to bring down the cost, Yogi Ramsuratkumar countered, saying something to the effect that "… only the American version should be sold in India." Lee instantly corrected himself to agree with Yogi

Ramsuratkumar's request, and Devaki Ma translated all of this information into Tamil for the benefit of the South Indian audience.[17]

Later, the beggar called up certain devotees to his side, handed them a copy of the book, and told them to take it back to their seats, where they could "decide" if they wished to purchase it. They did, of course, and to his surprise Lee easily sold all the additional copies he had brought. Although this selling of books started modestly on this trip, Yogi Ramsuratkumar's hand in book sales was something that increased dramatically over the years ahead. When Lee returned to Tiruvannamalai two months later, in February 1995, to continue working out the details of property acquisition for an ashram, Yogiji's selling fervor moved up a notch.

While he was intrigued and pleased with many things in the elegant book, Yogi Ramsuratkumar was overjoyed when Devaki Ma read the first quote attributed to himself. "My Father alone exists …My Father alone…My Father alone." His hands rose in ecstatic blessing and moved across the face of the crowd as he listened to the words describing the one truth to which his life was sacrificed.

राम

During one morning's gathering shortly after his Jayanti, 1994, as the chanting reached a pitch of intensity, Yogi Ramsuratkumar suddenly got up from his seat and carefully stepped down off the dais. Walking to the aisle, he stopped at the first seat in the first row, the one occupied by his American devotee. Taking Lee's hand, Yogi Ramsuratkumar gazed into his eyes, and then spoke to him. A moment later Lee was on his feet and climbing onto the platform that Yogi Ramsuratkumar had just vacated. Alone on the dais, Lee seated himself on the pillow previously occupied by his master. Lee was silent; his eyes remained riveted on the beggar seated on the floor before him.

Looking up and then around, Yogi Ramsuratkumar took the hand of the man at his immediate left. Tom Lennon, a middle-aged American archeologist and a student of Lee Lozowick's, sat motionless with his eyes cast down, absorbing the surprise and the powerful energy of this sudden touch. At the same time, Devaki Ma, who had left her usual place when instructed by Yogi Ramsuratkumar, had moved to the floor on the women's side. The chanting became louder and more vigorous as the beggar orchestrated this unusual constellation.

Fifteen minutes passed, slowly, as people overcame their initial shock and gradually adjusted to the impact of this visual display. When the communication (more of a transmission) was complete, Yogi Ramsuratkumar arose. Instantaneously, Lee stood up and approached the beggar, pranaming to touch the Godman's feet. Yogi Ramsuratkumar slapped Lee soundly, several times, on his back. The beggar was laughing. Then he and Devaki moved back up onto the platform and resumed their places once again.

"What can this beggar give to Mr. Lee?" Yogi Ramsuratkumar asked aloud a few days later. Pausing for a moment to consider, the beggar announced, "This dhoti!" referring to the graying cloth that he wore knotted around his shoulders, one of the many layers of his distinctive raiment. As he began to remove the garment, he handed his numerous malas to Devaki Ma. The turban that usually covered the top of his head came undone and lay at his side. Without a head covering, he looked enormously different. From a kingly presence, he was suddenly transformed into the wise elder or the simple sadhu.

"It's very dirty," the Godchild said apologetically, handing the cloth to Lee.

Those who heard these words laughed softly, as if dirt wouldn't make the gift more priceless still.

Lee received the dhoti and bowed his head until it was touching the platform near the beggar's feet. For hours after this darshan, the dhoti remained in Lee's hands – an artifact of the highest degree.

Earlier this year the Godchild had announced that he was creating "more trouble" for Devaki by publicly entrusting her with his coconut bowl, fan, and stick. This play with Lee Lozowick paralleled this investiture. Giving Lee more and more responsibility and trust would definitely mean "more trouble," but not perhaps in the way the world would judge such trouble. "Oh cruel Madman – why do you delight in such torture?" Lee wrote in a poem during this period. "You draw Your son to you / inch by inch, slowly, slowly. / This is Play that is Divine, of course, / but I am no mouse and surely You no cat! / Now! Faster! Quicker! / Pull me into You at last / and end this / teasing and taunting. / I am not ready. / Who after all, can ever be ready / for annihilation?"[18]

राम

In February 1995, as he had the previous December, Yogi Ramsuratkumar was only too happy to promote the sales of *Facets of the Diamond* when Lee returned for property business. Whereas the beggar's previous enthusiasm was taken as a spontaneous blessing of the project, his second sales venture, more high-powered than the first, seemed to point at something beyond a simple gesture of support.

Stan Hitson, who accompanied Lee on this short but busy trip, witnessed the selling exchange. In the midst of the afternoon darshan, Yogi Ramsuratkumar cut short the usual chanting and handed Devaki Ma the copy of *Facets*. Since first receiving the book a month ago, Devaki had taken to carrying it in her bag, as the beggar often asked for passages to be read aloud without warning. On this morning, she was instructed to introduce both the book and its publisher to the group, which she did, and then to read several sections, including the biography of Lee and his quotations. "As she read, she stood 15 feet in front of the dais where Yogi Ramsuratkumar was usually seated," Stan wrote, "but He came and sat beside her on the cool, polished stone as she read. He seemed to love every word of it. When she finished, they returned to their seats on the dais and Mani came out with five or six more copies of the book. He announced that they were for sale for 1,300 rupees, and today was a rare opportunity since both Yogi Ramsuratkumar and Mr. Lee were present, and that Yogi Ramsuratkumar would sign the book and offer it as prasad to anyone who bought one now…The man next to me jumped up and said, 'I'll take one!'…Two or three more people responded in the same way. Yogi Ramsuratkumar was having a great time with this; He was laughing and talking and very playful. He teased the people who came up for the book by turning to Mani and saying, 'Mani, make sure you get their money!' He still had a few copies left and no one was volunteering, so He called a man by name, saying, 'Don't you want this book?' The man had no choice but to come forward and accept such an offer! Yogi Ramsuratkumar seemed to really like this part…With the last copy in hand He said, 'Devaki will take this book.' He looked at Mani and said, 'Make sure you get the money from Devaki,' and He laughed out loud, saying to Mani, "We are having a good selling day!"[19]

Stan smiled to himself as he watched this whole play. He remembered how difficult it had been to carry that heavy box of books through several airports and on and off several airplanes between Phoenix, Arizona, and Chennai, India. Sore muscles, a bit of sweat and a lot of inconvenience was a small price to pay for the rare opportunity he was being given. Paying 1,300 rupees for *anything* offered by the hand of Yogi Ramsuratkumar was another small price to pay for the incomparable good fortune of meeting such a One in a lifetime. Just hearing the beggar's laugh and observing his sparkling eyes should have been recompense enough. And Stan noted, "That was worth every bit of it."

This and other relevant stories, dating back to the 1970s, point to Yogi Ramsuratkumar's uninhibited play with money. The master could easily receive large sums of it, and often did, especially when the ashram was under construction. No strings, however, were ever allowed to be attached to any donation of money or gifts. "If you have decided to part with something," the beggar frequently told Mani and others in his close company, "you have no business to know how it is used, or who gets it after you give it away."[20] The Godchild always asked people if they had any conditions or hesitations in giving their gifts. If they did, he refused it, even as he blessed the potential donor.

Many years earlier, when Yogi Ramsuratkumar still lived under the trees, he sat outside of Ramanashram one day, smoking. A generous passerby dropped some coins into the beggar's coconut bowl. Frowning at the cigarette in the Godchild's hand, the man made it clear that his donation was not to be used for more of "*those*." As the donor turned and walked away, Yogi Ramsuratkumar stepped after him. Handing back the money, he kindly let the man know that a conditioned gift was unacceptable.

The beggar applied this same principle when a man offered a huge donation for the ashram building project but wanted his mother's name inscribed on a commemorative plaque. "Mani, this beggar does not want that donation with a condition," the Godchild said.[21]

As easily as he could receive it, the beggar could just as easily turn around and hand over money or gifts. Sometimes these awards were for worthy causes – Sadhu Rangarajan reported numerous instances when money was unexpectedly given to him to further his work in *Tattva Darsana* and other projects. Sometimes the gift was miraculously endowed, or for no apparent reason, as when Yogi Ramsuratkumar spontaneously gifted three ashram workers (Saravanan, Kannon and Ravi) with 1,000 rupees each.

On another occasion, a devotee gave Yogi Ramsuratkumar a dazzling array of fine jewelry – gold and diamonds. These the beggar offered to Devaki Ma, who declined, saying that Yogi Ramsuratkumar was her gold and her diamonds. The other Sudama sisters likewise turned down the adornments. Turning to Mani's wife, Rajalakshmi, the Godman gave her no choice. Calling her to his side, Yogi Ramsuratkumar affixed a diamond bracelet around her wrist with the warning, "At any cost, never remove this. Even if Mani tells you to remove it. You can throw Mani out, but never this bracelet."[22] He must have laughed at his own words.

"He gave such richness to beggars," R. Jeyaraj Sulochana, an elder devotee, remarked. "He treated beggars and princes equally. He could sit among the beggars, for him they were not beggars, they were human beings; he could sit among the rich people, he could sit among Lee's devotees. He is such a Divine person that he never differentiates. We as human beings only differentiate between the well-dressed man and the scantily dressed man. We see only outwardly."[23]

Being in the master's close company warranted no special treatment when it came to paying for things. While he freely blessed his devotees with "the pearl of great price," and often gifted them, they were encouraged, and in fact often expected, to pay cash for everything else! When Caylor Wadlington wrote the first biography in the early 1970s, he raised the funds for its publication. When Rangarajan published *Glimpses of a Great Yogi*, and later, *Poems of a Broken Heart*, he paid for both of them. Most copies were given away as gifts, rather than sold for reimbursement. When Mani wanted to organize a special kirtan in Tiruvannamalai in January 1994, he was instructed by

Yogi Ramsuratkumar that no funds were available to sponsor it. If he wanted to follow through with his idea, he must fund it himself, which he did. The same self-sufficiency was expected when Mani engineered the pandal (sunshade) outside of Sudama House, as well as when he was given charge of the great statue project whereby a huge bronze likeness of Yogi Ramsuratkumar would be made to grace the newly arising temple. A devotee who gave a car was asked "if he would continue to bear the salary of the driver, fuel, and mainte-nance," which he happily did.[24] Even Devaki Ma was no exception in this precedent of paying one's own way – or paying for the privilege of the work – as this and later book-buying lilas will testify. Although she was completely at the beggar's service, Devaki Ma wrote a check from her own personal account for the books and other things, as Yogi Ramsuratkumar requested.

While many people will criticize a spiritual master who "soils" his hands with money, naively assuming that such exchange is less than spiritual, Yogi Ramsuratkumar was avidly teaching his followers a more powerful lesson. Money was one of many ways in which ener-gy was shared, accumulated, and funneled for purposes of carrying out his Father's work. On a personal level, those who participated generously would attest that the more they gave, and the more unstintingly they gave, the more they opened the bank vault of pos-sibility for greater abundance and receptivity in all other domains of their lives.

At a higher level, beyond the logical mind's ability to compre-hend, Yogi Ramsuratkumar evidenced throughout his life that he was willing to bear whatever pain, problems, or even "sins" that people would lay at his feet. Hundreds of personal testimonies support the truth of this claim. People left his presence with a tangible sense of lightness. They remembered him and were flooded with peace. They chanted his name and found miracles occurring at every turn.

With these blessings as recompense was any price too high to pay?

34

THE VIGRAHA

 While the number of small miracles connected with the construction of the ashram grew every day, a far greater miracle was taking place at another level. Yogi Ramsuratkumar was imprinting his ashram, his temple, with himself. His prayers, his breath, his eyes, his feet were touching everything, soaking everything, accomplishing the imprinting process as a mother's touch, eyes, and voice do for her child. "He wanted everything just so," Will Zulkowski reported after a visit in the early 1990s. "He told me that he was working on this temple so that even the most dense person would feel something. So, over the years that he sat in there, that was his work – to make this place a perfect conduit for the heavenly realms to be there."[1]

The beggar had told Devaki Ma that in the future pilgrims would fill the cavernous recesses of this structure. And Lee Lozowick, quoting his master, would repeatedly tell large audiences: "This beggar says that anyone who comes to this temple is blessed. But if they don't know it, this beggar is not responsible." In other words, insofar as hearts were open to receive such blessings, the Divine would hold those hearts and care for them. Without some small effort on the seeker's part, however, potential blessings, like rain, would simply drain away.

Nowhere was this imprinting more evident than in the play surrounding the construction and installation of the twelve-foot bronze

The Vigraha

likeness of Yogi Ramsuratkumar that stands in the center of the great hall of the temple.

In India, life-size (or greater) statues of saints and gurus are common icons of veneration. They are typically enshrined in temple halls or in smaller protective structures on the grounds of an ashram or spiritual center dedicated to that master's or teacher's work. Known as a vigraha, a word that refers to an image of a deity that is enlivened by the deity's living in it. This icon is believed to fully embody the spiritual energy and presence of the person or deity it depicts. Typically, the vigraha is worshipped with sacred rites, called pujas, and other appropriate ceremonies. It may even be symbolically fed with offerings made by devotees (usually fruits or sweets), adorned with flowers, sprinkled with water, fanned to cool it in the heat, and literally washed, dressed, and entertained by swinging it on a decorative swing. At night, the deity or saint may be wrapped in blankets, shrouded, or placed behind a protective curtain as a means of putting it to bed. In the morning, rituals are sometimes conducted to awaken the deity in the shrine through the ringing of bells and the chanting of devotees.

At the ashram of Ramana Maharshi, a black marble statue of the saint is the central presence in one of the halls of his great temple, which also houses his remains (samadhi site) and those of his mother. Similar vigrahas of Swami Nityananda, Sai Baba of Shirdi, Upasani Maharaj, and other great Indian saints are found in their ashrams. Yogi Ramsuratkumar undoubtedly saw and worshipped at these shrines during the years of his solitary travels through India. We know that he loved to sit across the street in Tiruvannamalai gazing at the statue of Mohandas Gandhi that stood at a major intersection. At Anandashram, life-size wooden cutouts from photos of Swami Papa Ramdas and Mataji Krishnabai grace the central hall used for chanting and singing. These figures, in bright colors, sit on the same chairs that the two saints occupied in life, and are venerated by their disciples and admirers.

If one vigraha influenced Yogi Ramsuratkumar more than any others, we may speculate that it was the image of Swami Gnanananda Giri, housed under a small mandapam in the ashram complex at Tapovanam, an hour's distance from Tiruvannamalai. The relationship of deepest respect that existed between the Yogi and the Swami is legendary. Ramsuratkumar spent weeks and even months in residence at this master's nearby sanctuary, as he visited there periodically from the late 1960s until long after Gnanananda's death in 1974. He would have been completely familiar with the life-sized image of Swami Gnanananda that had been in place there since 1959.

Carved from a single black stone, the image known as the *sila vigraha* was rendered from a photograph of Gnanananda. He is seated, with his arms to his sides. His right hand, palm facing outward, forms the *chinmudra* (the tip of the thumb and the index finger are touching, while the other three fingers are extended upward), and his left hand holds a scroll of sacred writings. The posture is one typically associated with Sri Dakshinamurti, the form taken by Lord Siva as the great teacher of the Vedanta.

"On all important occasions the Swami [Gnanananda] would sit…a little ahead of the idol to enable the devotees to perform the paduka puja [worship to the shoes of the guru], thus surcharging the atmosphere with a still and intense spiritual feeling."[2] Swami Gnanananda Giri had, in fact, consecrated the vigraha by his own touch, "investing It with his powerful power." In this way the image had become "an asylum of clemency," with a "power to save" those who approached with reverence.[3] Furthermore, for those who knew him, the photographic likeness of his statue was, and remains, an undeniable reminder of the love and grace experienced in his physical presence. For those who had never met Swami Gnanananda Giri, the mercy and wisdom expressed in his eyes, his calm and approachable posture, and the hint of mirth apparent at his mouth made a profound and long-lasting impression.

> It is the firm belief of the devotees that the Swami has consecrated and invested his vigraha with all his matchless qualities and spiritual power so that his devotees could continue to offer worship to the vigraha (which is the same as swami himself), when Swami cast away his physical body. It is beyond doubt, devotees' prayers and calls for succor are answered when they worship it in all humility, in a state of "absolute surrender."[4]

The Vigraha

Yogi Ramsuratkumar, like many others before and since, took refuge at this statue's feet. On a night in May 1979, on the occasion when a book on Gnanananda was just issued, the staff at the Tapovanam ashram found the disheveled beggar in a profound state of God-intoxication as he sat in front of the vigraha. The mad beggar was singing continuously, *"Gnanananda, Gnanananda, Satguru Gnanananda."* The chant continued long into the night. "He [Yogi Ramsuratkumar] used to give great importance to that [image]," said Swami Nityananda Giri of Tapovanam. "He used to tell devotees: 'He [Gnanananda] is there. You can feel his presence.' In fact when a group of devotees joined together and wrote a book [about Gnanananda] – he [Yogiji] wanted to see this chapter about the vigraha."[5]

The saga of Yogi Ramsuratkumar's own life-sized vigraha was, from first to last, a drama of faith, empowerment, and devotion. The renowned sculptor Sri Kalasagaram Rajagopal, who had crafted the statue of Ramana Maharshi that sits today in the Ramanashram temple, visited Yogi Ramsuratkumar one day in February 1995. Recognizing the artist in the midst of the crowd gathered at darshan, the beggar walked down the aisle and sat beside him, conversing softly for a short time. Later, Yogi Ramsuratkumar asked Mani to initiate the project with Rajagopal, who was immediately receptive to the idea. As was the Godman's wish with most things, Rajagopal was ready to begin immediately.

A house was arranged for the sculptor nearby the ashram compound, and the old darshan mandir building was designated as his work studio, as it was currently unoccupied. Details of logistics, as well as funding for the project, were completely entrusted to Mani once again.

Significant contributions from a few devotees easily covered the cost of the materials and the casting, as the vigraha would be made of bronze. Another devotee's gift assisted Rajagopal's living expenses and labor.

From February through June 1995, the artist was sequestered at his task. No one except an assigned assistant was allowed to enter the workspace. Yogi Ramsuratkumar posed for the artist for a brief two-week period, even though the sculptor had requested a two-month allotment. The rest of the artist's imaging was only available through snapshots of the Godchild, who was photographed standing, with his right hand raised in blessing. By June, the clay model was completed and cast, under Rajagopal's supervision, in the city of Dindugul in central Tamil Nadu. A few weeks later, it was ready to be brought home to Tiruvannamalai.

Yogi Ramsuratkumar made a strong point in saying that no ceremonies were to be conducted or worship given to the statue until he had the opportunity to see it and bless it. Unfortunately, in their misguided enthusiasm, some devotees failed to honor this request. When the massive form arrived at the ashram, Mani found that it had already been garlanded with flower malas, and that pujas had been offered.

At the master's direction, the statue was taken to the old darshan mandir, where it had been sculpted, and locked inside. Here it remained, untouched by human sight, for six months. Even Yogi Ramsuratkumar did not visit this room.

Coincidentally, when Swami Gnanananda Giri's statue was first brought to Tapovanam in 1959, he "had a brick wall built in front of the vigraha concealing it from view for quite some time."[6] Only when the four-pillared mandapam, which ceremoniously covers it today, was completed did he have the brick wall removed and the statue installed in its official place.

राम

In late December 1995, Yogi Ramsuratkumar asked Mani to arrange for Rajagopal to join them at the ashram. While the sculptor was en route from his nearby home, Bhagwan entered the old darshan mandir for the first time since the statue had been placed there in June. He went in alone. When he came out, he met with Mani and Rajagopal in the Pradhan Mandir, or great hall of the newly arising temple.

"My father wants you to fix the statue of this beggar as soon as possible," the Godchild informed the two men. When Rajagopal asserted that it would be done by the next week, Yogi Ramsuratkumar specified further. "My Father wants the statue of this beggar fixed in Pradhan Mandir *now*."[7] Surprise crossed Rajagopal's face. For

Mani, such immediacy was the norm. For a newer player in the Godman's game, these directives were often shocking. Nonetheless, Rajagopal was ready.

While a team of workers brought the huge bronze to the great hall, Yogi Ramsuratkumar asked Mani to locate the precise center of the room and to place the great statue there, facing the south. With the help of some of the other engineers on the crew, the center of the oval-shaped structure was determined. But it could not be immediately marked, as the center *just so happened* to coincide with a small area, three feet square, that was cordoned off to prevent being walked on.

One day, several months earlier, Yogi Ramsuratkumar had walked into the arena space of the great hall and, without calculation or measurement, pointed to the ground in the middle of the room. He then told Mani to have a small pit dug there. Into the pit, at a depth of three feet, the beggar had placed a pile of notebooks. The pit was then filled, the earth packed down, and the three-foot-square area roped off.

The area was a sacred place. These notebooks contained nothing but *likhita japa*. Handwritten mantras – *Om Sri Ram Jai Ram Jai Jai Ram* or *Yogi Ramsuratkumar, Jaya Gururaya* – filled line after line, page after page, the contributions to the World Ramnam Movement from Yogiji's devotees in India, France, Mauritius, and the U.S. The new sculpture of Yogi Ramsuratkumar would be placed directly over this pit.

"When we figured out where the exact center was," Mani wrote, "Bhagwan, who had been watching us with a serious look on his face, laughed behind His hand, His eyes twinkling. It was and continues to be a great reminder for me that the power of God, His infinite wisdom, fully resides in the saints walking on earth."[8]

Less than one hour after Yogi Ramsuratkumar had stepped inside the old darshan mandir to see the new statue, it was standing in its new and permanent location in the center of Pradhan Mandir, supported only by its conveyance mechanism, on the dirt floor. The devotees were called from the dining hall where they had been chanting, and soon the space around the statue rang with their sighs and chants of praise.

ONLY GOD

राम

The vigraha of Yogi Ramsuratkumar was now the focal point within the auditorium of the temple, although the building construction was still far from complete. Visitors were generally surprised, upon entering, to see another structure, a small thatched roof supported on poles, not far from the statue. This odd framework was intentionally kept as an empowered part of the temple's interior, despite the fact that it was nothing more than a sunshade. Before the roof was placed on the temple, the beggar and the Sudama women had sat under its protection during many months as they watched and prayed over the construction. Hours and hours of chanting had taken place under this roof. Unlike the inner sanctum of most shrines, which would contain the most precious artifacts and most pricey materials, this grass mandir stood as a humble witness to the beggar's lifelong poverty. For him, who had lived under trees, this construction was probably elegant protection from sun and rain. Now, dwarfed within a massive superstructure, the contrast created was disturbing – to the rational mind, at least, and the architectural vision as well. One can guess that this was exactly as Yogi Ramsuratkumar wanted it.

While work continued on the inside of the temple, and as the statue stood on its temporary base over its permanent place, Yogi Ramsuratkumar gave occasional darshans sitting in this thatched-roofed hut. As it was located so close to the statue, he could gaze upon the bronze vigraha for hours over a period of many months. Sometimes, he would stand up and circumambulate the vigraha, and his devotees would follow.

राम

In March 1996, three months after the statue had been placed, Yogi Ramsuratkumar notified Mani that the time had come to build a permanent base. There was only one small stipulation from the beggar. Namely, that the vigraha not be moved in the process.

The bronze vigraha of Yogi Ramsuratkumar

Reason demanded that it *had* to be lifted, or tipped, or shifted in some way for the base to be properly fitted. But Yogi Ramsuratkumar had neither elaborated nor specified. And Mani, knowing the way in which his master worked and spoke, took the command literally. To the amazement of Mr. Rajagopal and others – engineers and construction supervisors alike – Mani would harbor no suggestions that might compromise the beggar's wish in any way. Like other devotees who, over the years, had learned that the mad saint's demand was for absolute faith in his Father, Mani bolstered his team against their prevailing doubts. Then he retired to his room to pray. With his mind cleared, Mani caught a fleeting vision of a culvert underneath a railroad track. In the magical way in which experience, creativity, and grace mix, Mani formed a plan.

Within a few hours he had assembled all the materials and the "crew" needed for the job. Professionals would never have agreed to his wild scheme, so the fact that he had "only mason apprentices, electricians, and kitchen assistants" to help him was just as well.[9]

Mani ingeniously directed the crew to insert steel I-sections around the statue's base, which were able to support the vigraha while the workers removed the temporary apparatus that the twelve-foot bronze had rested on. Yogi Ramsuratkumar stayed in the hut structure watching the whole operation. Mani stood at the door of the temple shouting directions to his crew, since by Yogi Ramsuratkumar's enigmatic will, he had been told that the two of them should not be together inside the temple. If Yogi Ramsuratkumar was inside, his manager should be out…managing in other areas that needed attention!

The scene would probably have been hilarious were the technicalities not so demanding. By 7:45 P.M., with the old base removed and four I-beams securely in place, Yogi Ramsuratkumar felt confidant that the task would be completed according to his Father's direction.

The team worked on until the early hours of morning. It was 4:15 A.M. when their task was accomplished.

When Rajagopal arrived the next morning, expecting some travesty of engineering, he was astounded to see a completed base. He lavishly praised Mani's ingenuity, but thanked his brother-devotee more so for the "optimism and devotion to Bhagwan" that he had demonstrated.[10]

"I was not personally responsible for any of it. It was the divine force behind us that had made everything possible on this Ashram," Mani declaimed. "In everything, it was Bhagwan emanating this divine force in His human form and now in the form of this statue."[11]

35

A DAY IN THE LIFE, DECEMBER 1995

 From January 1995 when the work on the great bronze vigraha was begun until March 1996 when the statue was installed in the temple, the routine of life and work on the new ashram was establishing itself. Yogi Ramsuratkumar's hands were in everything. His spoken and unspoken demands for constancy, remembrance, and impeccability among his devotees and staff were witnessed in small and large ways every day.

Midnight – 7 A.M.

A passerby on the street outside of Sudama House might see a light burning and hear the muffled sounds of activity even in the dead of the night. Yogi Ramsuratkumar's "day" would generally begin quite early. He slept little and rose at 3 A.M. In fact, the boundaries between day and night were sometimes blurred. When important business needed to be handled, or a communication made, Yogi Ramsuratkumar and Devaki Ma might simply walk to a devotee's house and sit patiently, waiting for the person to arise. Both Mani and an American man living in Tiruvannamalai on separate occasions reported hearing a rustling sound and soft voices outside their windows at 3:30 or 4 A.M. To their surprise, Yogi Ramsuratkumar was sitting on their doorsteps.

Devaki Ma's schedule and that of the other Sudama sisters completely paralleled that of their master. When he was up, they were up. The women who served him might be ready to retire after spending several hours in japa practice late into the night, when at 2 A.M. Yogi Ramsuratkumar would ask for a reading of a favored spiritual text. The reading might continue for four or five hours!

Generally, the morning practice consisted of chanting from the *Bhagavad Gita* and later reading from this same source.[1] "He was shaping us," Devaki explained years later in speaking of the sadhana of their life and work in the Godman's company. In the presence of such a one as Yogi Ramsuratkumar there was no room for compromise, half-measures, or a private life apart from his. He wanted for them what had been given to him, the realization of Only God.

Besides attending to his care, or simply sitting and worshipping God in his presence, Devaki would need to prepare whatever he might need for the day. Her carryall bag contained foods, medicines, books, letters, cigarettes, ashtray, a thermos of coffee, and anything else that she might guess he would ask for. Although such preparations would naturally require some time, she rarely if ever had the luxury of more than a minute or two stolen from some other task. Even taking care of personal needs proved an extreme challenge. Five minutes out of his sight and the beggar might call her name. The Godchild's annihilating fire was burning away all attachments as well as all limitations.

Just before 7 A.M., Ravi, his driver, would be outside the gate with the car, ready to transport Yogi Ramsuratkumar and his company to the ashram grounds a few short blocks away. The beggar had appreciated Ravi's services since the early 1980s, when the young man had been a taxi driver in downtown Tiruvannamalai. Whenever Yogi Ramsuratkumar needed a taxi, he would ask for Ravi's. After moving from Sannadhi Street to Sudama House, Bhagwan asked for Ravi to drive him. Like many who recoiled from the prospect of unrelenting service, Ravi at first tried to compromise. At times he would send his brother to drive the Godman to the ashram. One day, Mani said offhandedly, in the Godchild's presence: "If Ravi comes I'll be happy." Bhagwan immediately replied, "This beggar also wanted Ravi only. You tell Ravi to come from tomorrow onwards." In telling of this investiture Ravi remarked: "Then I came and settled in Bhagwan's presence all the time."[2]

ONLY GOD

7 – 8:30 *A.M.*

Yogi Ramsuratkumar's early morning arrival at the ashram was always lovingly anticipated by staff and visitors, although generally, except on special days, the crowd was small. Women workers would already have swept the ground at the ashram gate and before the door of each structure, and strewn rice flour to form elegant mandalas, known as *kolam* in South India, as invocations of welcome and expressions of respect for household deities. Food would have already been prepared and male attendants would set out tumblers, mats, and banana-leaf "plates" for the master's meal.

From a distance, as the chug of the diesel-powered engine of the Ambassador sedan was heard, and people would immediately drop whatever else they were doing to hurry to the side of the courtyard. With hands joined and eyes focused on the windows of the car, they smiled or chanted the sacred name. Yogi Ramsuratkumar was passing

Devotees line up to catch a glimpse of
Yogi Ramsuratkumar as his car passes by.

598

by! The beggar would look at everyone in the line and occasionally wave his hand in greeting and blessing. The women in the car chanted softly, or silently fingered their beads, repeating the mantra of his name. Some of them had been instructed to keep up this practice twenty-four hours a day. As the car proceeded down the path, Devaki Ma often smiled as she noticed a familiar face or the look of adoration for her Lord in the eyes of another devotee.

The car would slowly make its way to the far end of the property and pull off to the left, behind the great temple, which was still under construction. Here, a shed of concrete bricks, originally built for food preparation at the time of the Foundation Ceremony, was used to store building supplies. At Yogi Ramsuratkumar's suggestion, the place became the location for his early morning meetings with ashram managers. When he agreed to take his breakfast there as well, it was thereafter referred to as the "breakfast hut."

Anyplace the beggar sat regularly was quickly imbued with his presence. The breakfast hut, as humble as it was, became a sanctuary of a special sort. Its simple construction, dirt floor, and piles of assorted materials were strongly reminiscent of the early shelters in which the Godchild had taken refuge from the elements. Entered through a low doorway, the interior was lit from the sun streaming in through the door, one small window, and a weak fluorescent bulb that hung from the roof in the center of the room. At the front, near the door, Yogi Ramsuratkumar would sit on a plain cloth mat, with no pillows. To his right sat Mani, flanked by a row of male guests or staff, each one facing the center of the room. To his left were Devaki, Vijayalakshmi and the Sudama sisters, and Rajalakshmi (Mani's wife), followed by additional women – generally the spouses or family members of the male guests.

Entrance to the breakfast hut was by special invitation only. The space was small and its purpose singular – to eat and to conduct business. Yet, as nothing was casual in the beggar's world and as these early morning meetings provided a highly sanctified environment, his guests could glimpse the way in which Yogi Ramsuratkumar lived every moment of his life.

Once everyone was in place, the Godman's inner silence would envelop the room like a thick blanket. No one moved as Yogi

Ramsuratkumar surveyed the group, looking softly over everything. After a minute he typically called for the chanting of *Om Sri Ram Jai Ram Jai Jai Ram*, and the Sudama sisters would respond with a gentle chorus. Striking a match and lighting a cigarette, the beggar then smoked as the chanting continued.

Banana leaves were laid before each one's place, and staff members served the beggar and his guests the traditional South Indian breakfast of idlies and sambar (fermented rice patties with spicy soup-like sauce). "So much happened here for seven years," Devaki Ma recalled, speaking of the breakfast hut. "There were kittens who lived there, and Bhagwan, before breakfast each day, would insist that these kittens be given the first offering of food."[3] Eating was done quickly and in silence, and the leaves were quietly whisked away. Coffee was served, drunk quickly as well, and removed. Yogi Ramsuratkumar had business to do!

At his direction, one of the women would be asked to read a passage from a book – perhaps *In Quest of God* by Swami Papa Ram-das, perhaps from *Poems of a Broken Heart* by Lee Lozowick, or selections from another poet-devotee's work, or a section of *Facets of the Diamond*, or a short story by an eminent Hindu writer – anything that was currently attracting the beggar's attention. Most of the time, he would ask for the readings to be repeated. It was not uncommon that the same piece be read three, four, even twelve times at one sitting. No formal teaching was necessary, as Yogi Ramsuratkumar had the words of his Father, Ramdas, and others to instruct his devotees in all that was required in their "quest for God."

For years Rajalakshmi had the habit of offering flowers to the beggar during this morning gathering. She most often presented him with a small bouquet of red hibiscus – the flower of the goddess Kali and one that grew in abundance on the ashram grounds. Receiving the blooms from her hands, Yogi Ramsuratkumar would hold them gently. Then he would stand and present one to Devaki and one to each of the other women, or to one or more of his male guests, keeping one for himself. He might carry this flower in his hand for many hours after leaving the hut.

Business was conducted efficiently, with brief reports by the various managers. Questions might be addressed directly to Yogi

Ramsuratkumar, or other questions asked by him. He wanted to know not only the details of every project, but also the comings and goings of his guests. *At what time would so and so arrive? Who would pick them up? Where would they stay? How long would they be here?* Mani was entrusted with handling the details of everything.

At the conclusion of the meeting, as the Godchild quietly smoked again, he might turn to Devaki Ma and ask her to chant whatever song she wished. "Sing even one line," he asked on one occasion. She responded by looking softly yet directly at him as she intoned "*Yoga Satguru Sri Rama Satguru,*" a chant which praised him as the preeminent guru.

One day during this month, December 1995, when a large group of Westerners were his guests at breakfast, Yogi Ramsuratkumar concluded by first dismissing the women in his company and then standing near the wall on the women's side of the room where he could have an unrestricted view of his visitors. A woman in that fortunate crowd recalled how his powerful presence had rendered her breathless, awestruck. "A tangible but invisible force" literally emanated from him. She described it as the way in which heat rushes out when an oven door is opened.

"As the beggar stood there, eyeing us closely for thirty seconds or less," she wrote that day, "the dross of the mind was agitated to the surface, spun into a delicate froth and blown away. There was nothing but silence."[4] Then, at some signal from within, the Godman turned on his heel, faced the streaming sunlight at the door, and stepped away.

8:30 – 10 A.M.

Ravi would be waiting at the car outside the breakfast hut. When his passengers were safely loaded, he would carefully back the car up, turn it around and drive slowly back through the ashram courtyard and out the gates. Making a right turn, he would head to Sudama House.

"Sometimes Bhagwan used to say to me: 'Do you know who is driving the car? My Father is driving the car!'," Ravi recalled, mentioning some of their brief exchanges over the years. "He liked me to drive slowly, and he would also ask me to stop the car if he recognized someone in the queue, or on the street. Then, he would bless them."

As the young man drove, he would regularly feel some intense pressure, sometimes heat building in the area of his heart. It was obviously the power emanating from his distinguished passenger. "Sometimes it was even difficult to breathe," Ravi admitted. The same thing occurred when Ravi would take Bhagwan's hand as he helped him in and out of the car, which he did every day. Such intensity was actually painful. "It hurt," Ravi said, and his friend Saravanan, another ashram worker, agreed. "It directly went through the heart, and sometimes made us to feel unhappy. But still we moved with him all the time," the men reported, describing the deep layers within themselves that were being touched by the blessing force of Yogi Ramsuratkumar. "Sometimes I would cry when sitting alone," Saravanan admitted. No one in the Godman's world remained unaffected by his enormous love.

"Whatever you want to speak, this beggar will understand," Yogi Ramsuratkumar had assured his driver, who spoke English with difficulty. And, as he did with everyone, Bhagwan consistently reminded Ravi, "Whenever you need help, chant this beggar's name, *Yogi Ramsuratkumar.*"

Back at his Sudama residence, Yogi Ramsuratkumar would have a brief hour or two at best before he would return to the ashram for the morning's public darshan. There was always business to attend to, and the newspaper to be read. Devaki Ma would read him the many letters from devotees that he would regularly receive, and he would direct her to answer them. Occasionally he would take pen in hand and add his own word, or an OM sign, to an outgoing letter, blessing a devotee with his special care. "Sometimes he used to smoke, but not often, in his room," Nivedita Rangarajan reported. Prior to her engagement and marriage, she had lived at Sudama House for a while in 1994. "Ma Devaki would read out the letters to him. The letters from Mr. Lee Lozowick would be given to me, after being read out to Yogiji, to be passed on to my father, for publication."

When nothing immediately pressing was at hand, Yogi Ramsuratkumar would sit, absorbed in his own interior prayers, or speak with his companions, or ask them to chant or read from the many books and articles of interest and inspiration that were always sent his way. The Godchild's life was one continuous prayer, in many different forms.

Unless he was taking rest," Nivedita noted, "we used to sit with Him in His room. Sometimes, he would be talking to us. Many a time, the Sudama sisters (Rajalakshmi, in particular) would sing for him. Among the songs that we used to sing often for Him, at that point of time, there were two specific ones. The first was…a very simple Tamil song, set to a melodious tune (one of the old movie songs). The meaning of the first stanza was, 'The person born in a place near Kashi; the person who will wipe out the sorrows and protect us; Let's chant his name, Yogi Ramsuratkumar, every day and attain happiness.' The other one that we used to repeat often was…something like 108 names of Yogiji in Sanskrit, written by a scholar from Chennai."

Just before 10 A.M., Ravi would be at the gate again and, gathering up their things, Ma Devaki and the other women would follow the beggar to the car. The entourage would again slowly make its way over to the ashram property, this time to take part in the morning public darshan.

10 A.M. – Noon

In December 1995, before the main auditorium of the temple was completed, the beggar's two daily darshans on the ashram were held in the "Grace" building, which housed the new dining hall and attached kitchen. For months prior, this dining hall had been used for breakfast and lunch service for ashram workers, staff, and guests.

At the far end of the room, next to two large windows, a dais was set. Here, the beggar sat, always the master of ceremonies, with Devaki Ma and Vijayalakshmi to his right. Looking out over the gathered assembly that had followed them into the hall, Yogi Ramsuratkumar would wait for the appropriate moment and then turn to the Sudama sisters on his left and softly advise them as to which chant to begin.

One morning during this month, his eyes scanned the room more closely, focusing on the women's side. Two visiting devotees were chanting to themselves, yet their voices were audible in the hushed space. The beggar's glance went from the audience to the Sudama sisters, and then back to the audience again. Ma Devaki immediately detected his questioning look and quickly spotted the two women whose drone was creating the discord. She flashed a look in their direction, trying to catch an eye. When the sound continued, she leaned forward toward Yogi Ramsuratkumar and whispered something to him, pointing this time in the direction of the women who were oblivious to her concern. The beggar focused on the point of disturbance, but simply waited. Devaki Ma then moved her hand swiftly to her lips as she finally made eye contact with one of the women. Her gesture said it all, yet kindly. The room fell fully silent. Only then did Yogi Ramsuratkumar speak to the Sudama sisters. "*Om Sri Ram*," he directed, and they began to sing. Witnesses that day observed an important lesson about how a seemingly minor element could disrupt the master's work.

Many different chants would be asked for; other devotees would be invited to sing or to lead the assembly in a chant. "*Arunachala Siva, Arunachala Siva*," one woman might intone, initiating a favorite chant of Yogiji's, as he sat back and lit his cigarette.

Sometimes, the entire two-hour darshan consisted of only songs of praise. At other times, depending upon who was present, Yogi Ramsuratkumar would ask that a talk be given – in Tamil or English. Occasionally the music of a traveling bhajan band, composed of devotees from another city or state, would vibrate the hall.

As the chanting went on, and sometimes even during the talks, individuals or small family groups approached the beggar's dais. Usually, they would place a gift at his feet, or simply bow their heads to touch the platform near his legs. Some reached out and grabbed his feet, even though they had been asked not to. These situations had become so increasingly painful for the aging Godchild that Mani was forced to announce Yogi Ramsuratkumar's wish that people not pranam to him – as they had this tendency to attack his feet.

Papa Ramdas had the same problems with the gestures of what he termed his "militant" devotees. One night, learning that a particularly enthusiastic group had arrived at his Kanhangad ashram, Papa began to rub his own feet gently. With a rueful voice he lamented, "Now Ramdas is in for it." Addressing his own feet, he continued,

"Ramdas feels sorry for you poor things." And then he laughed.[5] Soon after, when these high-spirited devotees entered the bhajan hall where Papa was seated, their exultant cries of "Papa, Oh Papa," filled the air. Ramdas got up and stood behind his chair. "Please, please remember Ramdas is made of flesh and bone and not a rubber doll," he begged, even as one devotee pounded his forehead against Papa's feet. Only with the arrival of Mataji did the crowd calm down.[6]

Yogi Ramsuratkumar received everyone's pain and everyone's problems. Men and women of all castes, all ages, poured out their hearts to him, often in tears at the sufferings of their lives. His eyes too might fill with tears, and occasionally he would inquire about specific concerns of theirs. A handicapped child or a newborn might be laid at his feet for him to touch and bless. Newly married couples would be likewise blessed. He might be presented with publications or programs of upcoming events and asked to touch and bless these artifacts, symbolic of the blessing force being showered upon the participants in the event itself.

One and all received his Father's blessing and a gift of prasad. Some received his tender glance, and men often got an energetic pat on the back. Others, for reasons too numerous to speculate about, were dismissed with a simple blessing but hardly a word or glance. For one Western woman, a writer, who visited the beggar's darshan once only, in 1998, the audience was extremely quick. In a book in which she later described her experience, she could not disguise her wounded pride at not being made to feel special.[7]

The chanting was work for those who led it, and Yogi Ramsuratkumar was both generous and precise in wanting it done *his* way. On a day in December 1995, two Western women led a familiar chant, but their pronunciation of the words was obviously incorrect. He called them to his side and carefully corrected it, asking them to repeat the words several times until he was satisfied that they had mastered them. When they again began the chant, this time with the proper imitation, carefully articulated, a huge smile crossed Yogi Ramsuratkumar's face and he raised his hands in blessing to indicate that they had done it correctly. He was pleased.

Such small lessons as these took on enormous significance for anyone concerned. These two Westerners had already been at the ashram for over three weeks, and the fact that they still hadn't listened acutely enough to get the proper inflection or pronunciation was an indication of sloppiness, and ultimately of disregard. Around the Godman, apparent ignorance was no excuse. When the timing was exactly right for a lesson to be made, Yogi Ramsuratkumar would make it.

It was clear to anyone practicing attention that the name of the game around Yogi Ramsuratkumar was listening, watching, waiting, and jumping to follow his directions. Many Westerners were impressed by watching Lee Lozowick's responses during the days or weeks of his visits. In December 1995, Lee and his company spent five weeks on the ashram, and attended every function. Seated on a bamboo mat in front of the beggar's dais, Lee's eyes were never closed. His gaze was always riveted on the master, who might call to him at any moment by the tiniest motion of a finger. When he "got the signal," Lee would leap to his feet and run, literally, to the beggar's side. There was no false holiness, nor showiness, in the American devotee's demeanor. Lee's one intention was to attend to his guru's word. Time was precious and not to be wasted where the Father's work was concerned.

राम

One *never knew* what Yogi Ramsuratkumar might do – in darshan or anywhere else! As much as certain protocols might become routine within an overall structure, the Godman's specific behavior, his words, and the teaching lessons he might offer were never predictable.

"This swami has called this beggar a mahatma," Yogi Ramsuratkumar said with astonishment on December 19, 1995, when an orange-clad man finished giving a speech. The beggar's voice was charged with emotion. When the man's attendant approached the dais, Yogi Ramsuratkumar handed over a mala of flowers and instructed them to be garlanded on the swami who had just seated himself on the straw mat in front of the dais. The recipient was astonished by the beggar's elegant gift.

Just then, Devaki Ma leaned toward Yogiji and spoke to him. Immediately, with his approval, she left her place on the platform with a rose in her hand. Approaching the small swami, she knelt and devoutly placed the flower on the mat before him. Then, she pranamed with grace. Smiling warmly, Devaki got up and returned to her seat at the right of Yogi Ramsuratkumar.

The lila was far from over, however. A moment later, the audience was stunned to see the Divine beggar himself step off the platform and quickly make his way to the floor in front of the swami's feet. On hands and knees, Yogi Ramsuratkumar made an extended pranam to his orange-robed guest, who immediately assumed the same posture. The two men were bowing to each other.

While the Godman stayed down, his forehead touching the floor, for about ninety seconds, the swami rose up periodically, his eyes streaming tears as he noted the beggar's ongoing posture of honor and humility. Then, he bowed down again.

The swami's tears were not the only one's in the room. Throughout it all, however, the women in Yogi Ramsuratkumar's entourage kept their gaze on their master. His activities never ceased to amaze them.

When the beggar finally resumed his upright position, he was smiling. Since he had not been wearing his glasses during this whole event, it was possible to see the look of adoration that shone from his eyes.

राम

In another powerful interplay of unpredictability during this month, a respected French filmmaker, François Fronty, was given access to most ashram activities throughout the two weeks of his visit. His purpose was to create a documentary about the hidden saint, Yogi Ramsuratkumar, to be used on French television. The film was designed to reflect the perspective of Yogiji's American devotee Lee Lozowick.

Yogi Ramsuratkumar happily obliged Fronty, whose elegance and sensitivity were a refreshing counterpoint to the usual disregard that many foreigners had for protocol and timing. Surprisingly, however, the beggar's overall expressions throughout these two weeks of filming were simple and ordinary to a degree that made them extraordinary. On the day *after* the filming project was concluded, when Fronty had left on his trip back to France, Yogi Ramsuratkumar's interactions with his devotees and guests became suddenly more animated. Several dramatic incidents, like his bowing to the Indian swami, took place – one among many scenes that would have made exquisite video footage.

"He is a razor," Lee Lozowick said, commenting upon this obvious contrast and leaving no room for romanticized speculation about some "unfortunate timing." The force with which Lee delivered these words indicated that *he* knew how completely purposeful and instructional the beggar's play had been. Yogi Ramsuratkumar had never presented himself as a miracle worker or figure of great charisma, although he was that; nor did he wish to distinguish himself or any of his devotees by one or more of the dramatic displays that were commonplace around him. For the master's own reasons, this Frenchman's documentary was to show nothing more than the simplest, most unadorned truth of who he was, and of how the Father was animating him. For those who had no eyes to see beyond appearances, it would remain an enigma.

राम

The darshan period this month might last only forty-minutes, or less, if Yogi Ramsuratkumar wanted to be present at the construction site for his own purposes. Sometimes, the devotees were left with instructions to chant for another twenty minutes, or entrusted to the care of Lee Lozowick, who was told to sit on the dais in his master's place and instructed by Yogi Ramsuratkumar to "conduct these affairs." At other times, the darshan might extend beyond the expected two hours, pushing the limits of patience and comfort of those who found it difficult to sit or keep attention for extended periods of time. The beggar's timing was not necessarily the same as those of his guests.

During one morning darshan this month, even Devaki Ma seemed concerned about timing – it was part of her job to keep the Godchild informed of many things. When she noticed that it was already past noon, she leaned close to Yogi Ramsuratkumar and told him. He registered her message but continued on with his work. A few minutes later, he called for a particularly long chant to be sung. Knowing that this piece might extend well into the lunch hour, Devaki again quietly told him the time. The mood among many in the crowd was tangibly impatient. People shifted in their seats. Others looked at their own watches or stared hard at the clock on the wall. They were hungry.

Her second reminder earned his response, but far from an expected one. Yogi Ramsuratkumar pointed to a nearby plate of prasad – mostly fruits – that was just out of his reach. Devaki moved it closer to him. Picking up one banana, he peeled it and offered it to her. With complete equanimity she ate it, despite the fact that a few hundred spectators were watching her every move. Immediately, Yogi Ramsuratkumar peeled another banana and again handed it to her to eat, which she did. Then he peeled three more bananas, which he offered to the other women in his party. The communication was unmistakable. "I am feeling ashamed," wrote a visitor who was present that day, "ashamed of my own obsession with a lunch schedule. I imagine that Devaki and those other Mas are 'eating' it – this banana *and* their pride – on behalf of myself and everybody else in the room. Yogi Ramsuratkumar's mastery in teaching us all a profound lesson is overwhelmingly effective."[8]

Past Noon – 4 P.M.

At the conclusion of the morning darshan program, however long it lasted, the beggar and his company would be driven back to Sudama House. Here they would have their midday meal. "Yogiji used to have a very simple diet, with no chilies, little salt, no tamarind and no oil for cooking,"[9] primarily prepared by Smt. Prabha (Mrs. Prabhavathi Sundararaman). "*Prabha Maami* (meaning Aunty, is how we called her)," Nivedita Rangarajan remembered. "Smt. Prabha used to bring food for Yogiji when he was at the Sannadhi Street house. When he moved to Sudama she started staying there, mainly to cook food for him. Prabha Maami used to maintain a list of the items prepared for Yogiji every day. She was doing this so that she could offer him a variety of dishes."[10]

ONLY GOD

After lunch, Yogi Ramsuratkumar might take an afternoon rest…or perhaps not.

राम

Back on the ashram, as the beggar's car pulled away from the building, the work of cooks and serving staff would have kicked into high gear. Every day, from a few dozen to several hundred guests and workers were served lunch, seated in straight rows in this same hall where darshan had been conducted, now transformed back into a dining room. As chanting continued, servers moved from place to place, filling banana leaf plates with generous helpings of rice, sambar, and sometimes a lump of lime pickle or a small square of halva. When everyone's plate was full, the chanting ended and eating began, in silence.

Every bit of food served on the ashram was understood to be Divine prasad; eating it, one was blessed and nourished in many ways, and little was wasted. Guests from around the world learned to eat in the traditional South Indian style, using their fingers, and sometimes the results, for Westerners especially, were quite humorous. Finishing the meal, each person folded the banana leaf with the opening towards themselves – a sign that the food had been appreciated. Then they left the hall and lined up outside to wash their hands from the row of water spigots provided for that purpose.

On special holidays, especially during Jayanti, this afternoon time between lunch and the 4 o'clock darshan would find dozens of devotees modestly lying down under the thatched pandals or in the shade of buildings. Afternoon siesta provided a welcome interlude.

4 P.M. – 6 P.M.

On December 19, 1995, it was still blazingly hot at 3:45, when the ritual began of awaiting the master's arrival back on the ashram. A hundred devotees, more or less, might crowd the courtyard, chatting and laughing as they listened for the sound of the car that would alert them to his coming. One day during this month, however, Yogi Ramsuratkumar was not looking out the car window. Instead, he was carefully examining a sheet of orange paper that he held in his hand. When he stepped out of the car, the same paper was with him.

The dining hall would have become the darshan hall again, and would be empty. Under Mani's watchful eye, no one was permitted to enter until Yogi Ramsuratkumar and the women in his party, plus whatever male attendant might be on duty, had assumed their places. Then, at the beggar's directive, other designated visitors would be ushered in to assume the places appointed for them. A moment later, the doors were opened fully, and the hall would fill up quickly. Sometimes, bodies were packed tightly to accommodate all who had traveled far to glimpse the beloved beggar. Sometimes, the darshans were conducted in shifts when the crowds grew enormous.

Any day of the year it was not uncommon to find busloads of pilgrims stopping here. For some groups, Yogi Ramsuratkumar's Ashram was simply one among many points of interest on a grand tour. They would enter, sit down, look around and sing for a few minutes. At the direction of their tour guide, they would rise noisily and leave.

For other groups, buses would have been specially chartered from such distant locations as Kanyakumari, where the beggar's disciples, Ponkamaraj and others, encouraged large followings. These people would have traveled for thirteen or fourteen hours, with one destination in mind. They would have come to pay homage to the saint who had answered their prayers. Yogi Ramsuratkumar's tender mercies had tangibly entered their lives, and they knew it. From Sivakasi they came. From Tuticorin. From Madurai. From cities beyond Tamil Nadu. From Bombay, an elegant man in a wheelchair; from Delhi, a renowned college professor; from Calcutta, a prominent businessman; from somewhere else, a famous musician...or statesman...or justice of the court. They were seated side by side with the poor man or woman from a rural village a few kilometers away.

On this day, as he held the orange paper in his hand, Yogi Ramsuratkumar nodded to the women on his right to begin the chanting. In a few moments the whole room was alive with the echoing reverberations of his name. He smoked. He studied the orange paper and then he placed it at his side. He asked for a different chant. As the chanting became more electric, a man near the back shouted loudly as his body flailed with an unexpected rush of Shakti energy.

611

Another man started to get up as if to run to the beggar's platform, so overcome with exhilaration that he had to be immediately restrained by the ashram staff. A European woman, also seated near the back of the room, fanned herself vigorously as the heat in the room rose. She got up and tried to squeeze in under the lone ceiling fan to relieve her discomfort.

The orange paper, I later learned, because the beggar had directed that it be passed throughout the room, was a program flyer. It announced the specific ceremonies that were being conducted elsewhere on that day, December 19, 1995, to commemorate the upcoming second anniversary of the death of the saintly Paramacharyal – Sri Chandrasekara Saraswathi of Kanchipuram – the much beloved "friend" whom Yogiji visited in the mid-1980s.

The beggar called upon a few of the women in his company to read the flyer, to speak about it, to sing the Tamil poem composed by the Paramacharyal for the U.N. event in 1966. Many in the audience recognized this famous hymn: "Cultivate friendship which will conquer all hearts…"

As the singing went on, Yogi Ramsuratkumar continued to examine the program, which contained the Paramacharyal's photo and a picture of his samadhi site. When the song was finished, he asked for it to be sung again, and again, and then a fourth time. The congregation was being saturated with these words, and these elevated instructions. Such repetition was one of the characteristics of the Godman's way of teaching – a sterling example of the oral tradition in operation. The words in this hymn took effect in the hearts of his listeners at many levels. Yet, clearly, there was a sense that this enactment was intended for more; that this message, an appeal for world peace, was actually being broadcast to the corners of the earth. "May all beings be happy and prosperous; may all beings be happy and prosperous," the women sang. Yogi Ramsuratkumar's mood was deeply contemplative as an atmosphere of profound peace filled the hall.

Interestingly, a few days later the ashram was blessed by a visit from the current Shankaracharya and a large entourage from Kanchipuram. On this occasion, Yogi Ramsuratkumar relinquished his usual seat to the eminent teacher and sat on the floor to the left of the dais, in an obvious gesture of respect. While great pomp and circumstance were afforded this dignitary and his group, Yogiji was completely simple, humble, and unassuming. For him, nothing had changed. He conducted himself as a perfect devotee, bowing to the feet of the guru or saint.

राम

"Say something that these people will find useful," the beggar directed Lee Lozowick at a point about halfway through an afternoon darshan. Yogi Ramsuratkumar himself didn't have to preach or teach in any formal way; he had others whose eyes, ears, and words fulfilled his wishes and literally spoke for him by speaking only praise of the Father.

"If God *were* looking for anything, it would be praise." Lee's voice was firm and clear as he stood on the floor in front of and to the left of Yogi Ramsuratkumar, close to the audience. "One form of praise is to 'renounce war and forswear competition,' as the Shankaracharya's song directs us. If we treat one another with kindness, that is praising God." The beggar lit another cigarette. As the smoke curled above his head, he seemed very far away, communing at some other level, yet listening. When Lee made a joke, the Godchild raised his head and smiled tenderly.

"A more direct form of praise is chanting his name," Lee continued. "When we are blessed by the master it is like the master says, 'Here's the grace, do with it what you can.' One way to be grateful for that blessing, that grace, is to praise God's name. And for us, the most intimate name of God is *Yogi Ramsuratkumar*. To chant his name is to offer this gratitude."

The beggar put down his cigarettes and lifted his right foot onto his left knee. The index finger of his right hand appeared to be tracing a pattern, repeatedly, on the sole of his foot. The movement was not random. He seemed to be making the symbol "RAM." (Balarama, during the time of his visits in 1994, reported that this symbol was drawn repeatedly on his hand by Yogiji.)

At the conclusion of Lee's remarks, Yogi Ramsuratkumar called the American devotee to his side and held him with a riveting gaze, for ten seconds, twenty seconds, thirty seconds. His hands then raised in blessing. Throughout this deep and tender exchange the entire audience seemed to be holding its breath. "My Father blesses Lee Lozowick," the Godman said sweetly, now smiling. Everyone exhaled.

राम

When it was time to leave, Yogi Ramsuratkumar would indicate completion to the day's proceedings with a simple gesture to his attendant. Devaki and the Sudama sisters, ever watchful, were immediately packed and ready to go. At his signal, they rose and exited the hall. Taking the arm of his attendant, Yogi Ramsurakumar would start down the aisle.

On one afternoon in late December of this year, as the beggar walked toward the door, he paused about midway through the room. Something or someone had captured his attention. He looked over the assembly of women as if he had heard his name being called. Who was it? Probably someone was begging for something! The request may have come as a tiny whisper, or as an unvocalized prayer, but it was strong enough to stop him. Earlier that week, when I voiced an internal prayer for help in a personal matter, he "coincidentally" picked up his fan and his coconut bowl, stepped off the platform and walked down to the women's side. Here he waited for several seconds as if listening intently. Without focusing on anyone in particular, he raised his hands and waved them in my direction. Instantaneously, the answer to my question, like a gentle urging, arose in both mind and heart. The synchronicity of events was unquestionable.

"*Jaya Yogi Ramsuratkumar Ki Jai, Jaya Devaki Mataji Ki Jai,*" one devotee would shout from the midst of the crowd as the beggar exited the hall. The whole room would erupt in joyous response. A moment later, the entire assembly would have gathered before a picture of the Godman where an enthusiastic *arati* was sung as lights were waved, bells were rung, and clouds of incense were offered to the guru's image as well as to the sacred mountain, Arunachala, which loomed over all.

As the devotees left the hall, they would be given a small newspaper cone filled with prasad – some roasted chickpeas, other savory items, or occasionally a sweet. It was one more reminder of the many ways in which the beggar was feeding the world. As the Ambassador chugged its way slowly through the ashram gate and turned right in the direction of Sudama House, devotees would leave too, passing under an illuminated fluorescent sign declaring, "My Father Alone Exists."

6 P.M. – Midnight

At Sudama, Yogi Ramsuratkumar and his company would disappear inside the house. Soon, dinner would be prepared and served.

During her stay there a year earlier, Nivedita Rangarajan experienced an evening meal that she would cherish all her life. "Smt. Prabha's son, Vasu, had come," she wrote in letter describing the event. "Vasu and myself were sitting with Yogiji. It was dinnertime and chapattis were being prepared for Yogiji. There were plates in front of the three of us. As soon as the chapatti was served, Yogiji started feeding us (i.e., he gave to us, piece by piece, alternately) and again asked for more chapattis. That, too, he fed us and then he started making sounds with the plate, like a child, to ask for more. He kept laughing at us and was blessing us all along. Though he could see the kitchen from his place, he did not wait for the next chapatti to be prepared and kept asking for more. Finally, seeing this, Ma Devaki came to us and asked us to say that we were full, as Yogiji was not having anything and he was giving everything to us."[11]

During or after dinner Yogi Ramsuratkumar would probably take some medicines, as directed by Doctor Radhakrishnan; he would drink these preparations from his coconut bowl. "Yogiji used to drink the water in which dried gooseberries were soaked," Nivedita explained. His habit of chewing gooseberries (nellikkai) was well known by his devotees. Since the early 1970s, this practice had been noted and mentioned, even by his earliest biographers. A statement he made about this healing herb had become legendary. "Nellikkai for the body, Ramnam for liberation," Yogi Ramsuratkumar had declared.[12]

After dinner there might be more business to attend to, or more reading to do. The women would work at whatever was needed, repeating the name of God, his name, in everything. "At Sudama, we would either be with Yogiji or we would be talking *about* him or be doing something *for* him. There was nothing else to be discussed or thought. Ma Devaki used to collect even his hairs that fell down," Nivedita recalled.

Her father, Sadhu Rangarajan, was also privileged to spend two weeks in residence at Sudama during that year. As he watched, Devaki, in expression of her devotion and constant care, lovingly clipped the Godchild's fingernails, even as he slept. "She placed them in a box in which she saves such things," the sadhu noted. Rangarajan, always the rationalist, was at first repulsed by the notion of preserving such relics…even the fingernails of his master. Although the beggar had apparently been asleep this whole time, as if hearing the sadhu's thoughts, he opened his eyes.

"Rangaraja," Yogi Ramsuratkumar asked, "have you been to Kashmir?"

"No, Bhagwan," the sadhu answered.

"There they have the hair of Mohammed. Have you been to Sri Lanka?"

"No, Bhagwan."

"There they have the tooth of Buddha. Have you been to Sarnath?" Without waiting for another response, Yogi Ramsuratkumar concluded: "Devaki can collect this beggar's nails!"[13]

राम

At 7 P.M. sharp, a small group would arrive at the door for the nightly evening darshan – a "family darshan," as Mani referred to it. "Though there was so much chanting of Yogiji's name and Ramnam that he would ask us to do in his presence, to me, it was more like spending the holidays at my grandfather's house," Nivedita explained.

Kolotuman, a devotee for over thirty years, would be at this gathering each night, receive his prasad from the hand of Yogi Ramsuratkumar, and be blessed. Afterwards, he would leave for the beggar's house on Sannadhi Street, where he would serve as the guard and attendant for the night. Although Kolotuman was one of the beggar's closest and most trusted devotees, Yogiji rarely if ever mentioned his name or referred to him. Since the day in 1990 when he first received his duty, he had followed strict instructions from the master to dress in a dhoti, a shirt, a cap, a shawl, and a turban before taking up his post. "Winter, summer, spring and fall he dresses that way. Yet, Kolotuman never complains, even though some of the men will make fun of him, saying he dresses like a ghost to sleep in the Yogi's house."[14] The Godchild obviously had the highest respect for Kolotuman, yet, as with many other great servants of God who are lost to history, less than a handful of people ever knew who he was or what he did.

Mani and Raji would also be at the evening darshan, receiving instructions for the next day, and more blessings. One or two other devotees, as might have been invited, would handle their business and express their thanks. They too would be blessed. "There was a maid servant working at Sudama," Nivedita recalled, "and every day, before leaving for the day, she would receive the blessings of Yogiji. There would be heaps of fruits, given by the devotees. Every day, a few of the fruits would be given to her. She used to say that with this daily quota of fruits, she and her family were not able to finish all the fruits in her house."

At any point, a knock might be heard at the gate, and one of the women would immediately attend to it. Perhaps some devotee had arrived from a long distance and wished to inform the beggar of his presence. Perhaps there was an emergency that Yogi Ramsuratkumar must be told about. Sometimes the person would be invited in. Sometimes, Yogi Ramsuratkumar's blessing would be sent with a message to return the next day.

P.V. Karunakaran and his wife Savitri, devotees from Salem, were greatly pleased one night in November 1994 to be invited to spend the night at Sudama House. "In the night, after supper," Karunakaran wrote, "mats were spread in the hall (shrine room), by the side of Bhagavan's bed, for the Sudama sisters, Savitri and me. After, Ma Devaki read to us from the travelogue of Swami Purushothamananda till about 10:30 P.M., and then the lights were switched off. Bhagavan and others lay down. I sat up in the dark to do japa. In the course of my silent japa, much to my surprise, Bhagavan asked, 'Is anyone saying any kind of prayers? This beggar can hear it.' That day I realized that Bhagavan could hear a devotee without the medium of sound."[15]

At 2:30 A.M., Karunakaran was awakened by a brief conversation between Yogi Ramsuratkumar and Devaki Ma. The beggar told her that he liked the presence of these two devotees from Salem and asked her to direct them to extend their stay and to call their children to notify them of the change of plans.

On other occasions, the lights at Sudama might burn long into the night. At any point, Yogi Ramsuratkumar would lie down to sleep. He would wear the clothing that he had worn for days, for weeks. He would simply rest because his energy for the moment was spent.

Devaki Ma, along with the other Sudama sisters, would lie down as well, her attention still focused in his direction. Throughout the night she was there, as she had been throughout the day, awaiting only his word. He might sleep for an hour, or three, or more. The women lived by his schedule, as he lived by that of his Father. The needs of the work determined everything.

36

"IF HE WALKS IT IS THE TEACHING"

 In 1993, a woman who had just met Yogi Ramsuratkumar for the first time walked away from his darshan filled with bliss. Returning to her cottage at Ramanashram, she sat down to record the experience in her journal. "Who is this little, beautiful, exquisite, graceful, perfect, charming, delightful, child, God, man, king, beggar, magician?" she wrote, the words pouring effortlessly. "Who is this one whose very Presence envelopes you and melts you and reveals universes and simple joy and makes you feel as though all time has stopped and the world as you know it no longer exists and there in only God, Ram, the brilliance of the divine who beats your heart and lives you and *is* you?"[1]

Her question had no answer then, at least no generic answer. It has no answer today, except as the question itself leads the questioner to deeper faith, or profound joy, or a burning desire to worship and serve, or a recognition that one is not separate from God and that there is *only God*. One might as easily be asking, *Who or what is God?* Even though we know that there is no simple answer, this enterprise of "exploration into God"[2] must continue, as it is essential to the process of evolution.

राम

"He is no ordinary man, and his is no ordinary strength," wrote Caylor Wadlington, the author of the first biography about Yogi

Ramsuratkumar. Like many devotees since, Caylor tried hard to characterize the Godchild of Tiruvannamalai: "I have watched the yogi stand with the courage of a warrior turning away brute men with the power of his gaze, wielding elemental forces with his hands, and turning the minds of men with the unerring power of projected thought. At other times, though, when a brother would stand in defense of his character, protect him in a time of danger, or simply offer him food and a safe place to sleep, I saw this blessed man weep in solitude, so moved was he by their compassion. He is no ordinary man, and his is no ordinary strength. Unrelenting to pressure, he continues his spiritual endeavors. No longer can he be the unseen helper, no more the quiet solemn peace for him. His is strenuous, ceaseless labor with terrible, un-intermittent demands upon his time and character."[3]

Affirming the enigma of his own incarnation, Yogi Ramsuratkumar had told Caylor: "I am infinite and so are you and so is everyone, my friend. But there is a veil, there is a veil. Do you follow me?" Pointing to his own body the beggar said, "You can see only an infinitesimal part of me. Just like when a man stands on the seashore and looks out over the great ocean, he sees only a fraction of the vast ocean. Similarly, everyone can see only a small part of me. The whole cosmos is but an infinitesimal part of the real man, but how can a man see the whole cosmos?"[4]

राम

Author Mariana Caplan, like so many others, had also tried to answer this question of who...or *what*...this beggar was, and what his life was about. For Mariana: "To those who could perceive him to even the smallest degree, it was tacitly apparent that there was literally no 'him' to do anything for – not even a shadow of who once remained. Thus he existed fully and only for the Other."[5]

Reflecting Caplan's description, the Godman's own words affirmed this mystical reality: "This Beggar is not at all living. This Beggar's life has been killed, and merged with that of God. My Guru Swami Ramdas merged this Beggar's life with that of God. How this miracle happened, this Beggar is not able to realize even now. This

Beggar's life and God's life are one and the same. You cannot differentiate this Beggar's life from that of God. My friends, if you feel like, you can call this Beggar hereafter 'God' also."[6]

Seeing his master as the living Divine, Lee Lozowick pleaded with devotees during the beggar's darshan in Tiruvannamalai in December 2000 to hold the most profound gratitude for the gift they were being given: "We are very lucky to have the opportunity to sit in the presence of and have darshan with the literal Divine, concretized in this human body of Yogi Ramsuratkumar as He really is – no will, only Father in Heaven, complete unity, no separation, complete oneness."

Lee knew only too well, however, that asserting that "Yogi Ramsuratkumar is God" was one thing, and that living on the basis of that was something else. Few people had really absorbed the truth of those words, and fewer still were willing to be responsible for what this understanding entailed. "[T]he only way that one can understand Godmen is by loving them," wrote Vijayalakshmi, who spent years at the beggar's side, assisting Devaki Ma in her total service. "Bhagawan Yogi Ramsuratkumar responded to love as a child to its mother, as a lotus to the sun, as parched earth to rain. The more uncritical the love and adoration the greater was his outpouring of love; for love is the stuff which softens the heart and makes us receptive to grace. Those who complain that they did not receive or received less grace have not approached him with unconditional love. Those who were able to give this received much more in return. But few were able to do this."[7]

A dialogue that took place between Yogi Ramsuratkumar and a visitor in 1979 affirmed just how facilely some people could speak about him without comprehending the underlying truth.

"You live such a beautiful life. How can I be like you?" asked Sunder, a frequent visitor at the time.

"*Enne*! [meaning *What*!] Don't come down to this beggar's level," Yogi Ramsuratkumar replied forcefully.

When Sunder persisted, declaring "I want to be a beggar like you," the Godman put him in his place. "What do you know about the life of this beggar? I can say in truth you know nothing about this dirty sinner. His real life is with the Father, and there is really nothing

I can say about that. Is there anyone who can say anything about him? He will always remain the unknown."[8]

And on another occasion, to other guests, Yogiji revealed: "Seeing people is only a small fraction of this beggar's work. Most of this beggar's work is hidden."[9]

राम

Father has no ears, but hears,
Father has no mouth, but speaks,
Father has no tongue, but tastes fruits, etc.
Father has no eyes, but sees,
Father has no hands, but works.
          – Yogi Ramsuratkumar[10]

राम

Justice Arunachalam and his brother, Dr. T.S. Ramanathan, were sequestered in the beggar's private room one day, while others sat on the verandah at the Sannadhi house. The two men had been discussing with Yogiji the merits of a devotee's letter. Apparently, the writer had made an attempt to describe Yogi Ramsuratkumar. When the beggar asked the judge his opinion of the letter, Arunachalam explained that, for him, Bhagwan was indescribable, and thus no words could ever capture the essence of who he was.

As these words were being uttered, both Justice Arunachalam and his brother felt a trembling throughout the house, as if a violent earthquake were happening. Yogi Ramsuratkumar, for his part, had risen from his seat and begun to dance – lifting his left leg in the manner in which the dancing Siva is represented – and sing "*Sri Rama Jaya Rama Jaya Jaya Rama*," and other melodies. The dance continued for fifteen minutes.

At one point, Yogi Ramsuratkumar began to shout, as he moved his hands wildly. "Justice Arunachalam is right. This beggar cannot be described. He is 'all pervading'…– nobody can describe this beggar." As the two men watched and listened, awestruck, the beggar continued: "There is no difference between this Beggar and God.

You can, if you feel like, call this beggar God. Father's Grace will be there for ever. If you surrender with absolute faith, I will protect and take care of you."[11]

राम

While *who he is* might ever remain the great unknown, the question of *how* Yogi Ramsuratkumar taught and *what* that teaching entailed can be addressed, as long as one is not expecting a linear transmission. Yogi Ramsuratkumar gave no lectures, wrote no books, left no commandments, no catechism, and certainly no new religion. Yet, he touched hundreds and thousands of souls, leaving behind an indelible imprint that is as clear in these early years of the twenty-first century as it was in the 1960s or 1970s when his first visitors and devotees recorded their observations. Thirty or more years after meeting him, men and women report that he remains for them a living, dynamic presence.

"This period of forty minutes was one of the most beautiful moments of my life," recalled Tom Shroyer, a devotee of Sai Baba's who met Yogi Ramsuratkumar only once in the 1970s. "I felt that he was an *avahoot*; that he could act in any way that was needed. He found joy in the simple things, and with that, my own innocence was free to come up. I think that if I was not already a devotee of Sai Baba, I would have become his devotee. Hilda had told us that he was one of the great beings, and I believe it. Even after all these years [this interview was conducted in 2003] I still have a large picture of him on the wall of my room. To me he's not dead. If you meditate on his picture, he will come to you. It is worthwhile to keep that photo up, and use it when you need a helping hand."[12]

राम

In 1979, Yogi Ramsuratkumar explained: "This beggar has been assigned a great mission. And this beggar does his work in every step he walks. He gives advice or help to those few people who come to him, but as a general rule, his real work goes unnoticed."[13] In the early 1980s, Yogi Ramsuratkumar spoke the same message to three companions who stayed at Sannadhi Street for several weeks. His own words revealed what the teaching was, and how to access it: "You just observe this beggar. If you just observe this beggar, it is enough for you. Any gesture of this beggar – that is enough. You do not have to worry about your spiritual growth. If he walks, it's a teaching; if he eats, it's a teaching; if he sits, it's a teaching; if he talks, it's a teaching. Whatever he does is a teaching."

"It was a state of being he taught us, utterly," Parathasarathy, one the companions, explained. "We are not here to create one more sect, one more cult, one more religion. No, let us live! This beggar, all twenty-four hours, he is radiating, radiating, radiating. It's up to us to see it and to get it. But once you come here and touch this gate and chant once, only once, *Yogi Ramsuratkumar*, then [his] Father does not send you away with an empty pocket. He puts something in your pocket. Just remember *once*, that is enough. Then you will start having evolution."[14]

In 2003, the French devotee Krishna Carcelle communicated the same message. "He was beyond teaching with words. *He was the Teaching itself.* He had no need to say anything, He *was*. So, only the persons who were fit to feel that, to see, understand, commune, etc., could get a lot. Yogiji was the Vedanta incarnated. He was the perfection. He was not *speaking* of perfection, He *was* perfection. What need of words? When you jump in the water, you get wet. No?"[15]

राम

While the pure infusion of his graceful presence *was* indeed the teaching, unquestionably Yogi Ramsuratkumar's words and gestures pointed to several dharmic truths above all others – tenets that he reaffirmed daily, even hourly. "Father alone exists" was undoubtedly his primary message to humanity. In those few words he implied that the Divine was all-pervasive, and that faith in and reliance upon that One was the only viable approach to existence. Asserting his complete surrender to his Father's will, the Godchild one day said, "When the Father makes this beggar happy, it's well. When He makes him cry, it's well also. Whatever the state in which the Father puts this beggar, that's well. It's the truth of the Father. No matter what arrives, it's perfect, for the Father is perfect. Every thought, every movement, every action, every word of this beggar is directed by the Father. This beggar is living for the Father's work. This beggar will live for the Father, will die for the Father."[16]

The means to that faith and reliance, and the constant witness of one's intention to be surrendered to God, came about through the practice of singing and chanting the Divine name, in whatever form was most immediate for the devotee or seeker – *Om Sri Ram, Jai Ram, Jai Jai Ram*; *Om Nama Shivaya*; or *Yogi Ramsuratkumar, Jaya Guru Raya*.

Swami Nityananda Giri, his old friend, recommended that I emphasize Yogiji's teachings rather than his miracles. "Miracles happen in their presence [the presence of God-realized beings], but that is not important. What is important is the teaching."[17]

The stories and recollections that follow are a minute part of the living history of the teaching and of the living legacy of God on earth as witnessed to and manifested by Yogi Ramsuratkumar, the beggar of Tiruvannamalai.

Divine Humor

Like his spiritual Father Swami Ramdas, Yogi Ramsuratkumar literally sparkled, full of joy – laughing, joking, chuckling. He was happy, reveling in his Father's grace. Undoubtedly, he saw the pathos as well as the humor in the human condition, as thousands of visitors brought their tales of woe to him day after day. But his faith and his constant awareness of his Father sustained him through it all. He was genuinely amazed at the wonder of creation and the blessings that were showered in every moment and he continually reminded his guests of that fact. One day, as Yogi Ramsuratkumar was "nearly rolling with laughter, his hands over his face and slapping his knee," a person nearby, observing this hilarity, remarked, "You certainly are a happy man!"

The beggar turned to the man and, his eyes sparkling, said, "If there is love in a man's heart the whole world will be beautiful."[18]

Many people have described his happiness and the profound effect his laughter had upon them. As one woman wrote: "The smile was beautiful, like a flower in full bloom…When Yogiji smiles a radiant joy envelops the atmosphere like the full moon shining in a cloudy night…a sight for depressed hearts. His laughter is even more exhilarating. A belly shaking, roaring, rapturous joyous laughter."[19]

One of the master's ashram attendants, in later years, was convinced that his laughter echoed around the world. "If he laughs," declared Selveraj, "you can hear it at the gates [of the ashram]. Sometimes I feel that everybody is laughing in the world when he laughs. Like omnipresence…[he was] an extraordinary being. You can feel, whenever you are with Bhagwan, you can feel it."[20]

राम

In Lee Lozowick's poetry we read of a devotee's delight in seeing and hearing the master laugh, together with the added joy of having provoked this laughter:

Oh Father, You Madman
    Yogi Ramsuratkumar,
how Your son loves to see
    his Father laugh with abandon.
lee tells You this
    You old rollicking Rogue,
for if it be Your son's arrogance
    that strikes You so funny
then he will be
    more arrogant still.
If it be this bad Poetry
    that brings You delight,
then Poetry it will be
    and yet more verse for You.
And if it is to be
    a bigger Fool
then I will be Foolish
    until tears stream from Your eyes,
for oh dirty Sinner
    Yogi Ramsuratkumar,
Your son delights in Your delight

and is made joyous by Your joy.
So laugh and laugh on,
    as lee bows low before You.[21]

राम

The beggar's enormous humor was definitely a way of prying loose the stranglehold of ego. Those who "got" the joke (even if it was leveled at them) and stayed with him generally received an insightful reward for their efforts. Those who didn't removed themselves from his presence and generally went away disappointed.

One day, a woman visitor was writing something down and Yogi Ramsuratkumar asked her what she was writing. When she replied that she was writing questions for him to answer, he looked momentarily troubled. "Ohhh, how many questions?" he wanted to know.

"Nine or ten," the woman replied.

Hearing her answer, Yogi Ramsuratkumar laughed uproariously, "Oh, this beggar is not so competent to answer all your questions."

Put off at not being taken seriously, the woman went away and never returned.[22]

राम

Once Bhagwan read to his company about the great musician-saint, Swami Haridas. The narrative explained that Haridas had died by accidentally falling in the river.

"Devaki," Bhagwan said with a sly smile, "now you see why this beggar does not take a bath."

राम

When a devotee of Satya Sai Baba's heard that Yogi Ramsuratkumar had named his dogs Sai Baba, the man was shocked. Angrily approaching the beggar, the man threatened: "Maharaj, if one day I have a dog, I will call him Yogi Ramsuratkumar."

The Godchild found this remark to be tremendously amusing. Turning to the man, he replied: "If you call your dog Sai Baba, he will be full of joy, peace and love, but if you call your dog with the name of this beggar, the dog will bite you and will be constantly discontented because this beggar has a very bad character."

And then Yogi Ramsuratkumar laughed uproariously again.[23]

राम

Vijay Fedorschak, an American, experienced strong physical phenomena in the presence of Yogi Ramsuratkumar. Waves of shakti energy rolled through Vijay's body whenever he looked at the old beggar, and periodically his arm would shoot straight up, as if he were pointing to the sky. To unsuspecting onlookers it would appear like an involuntary spasm. For Vijay, it was clearly the result of the massive outpouring of energy from Yogi Ramsuratkumar, to which he (Vijay) was particularly sensitive.

Vijay, who had accompanied Lee Lozowick on his trip, was extremely self-conscious about what was happening. Yogi Ramsuratkumar, however, seemed to enjoy the surprising nature of it. "He would smile at me out of the corners of his eyes," Vijay noted. "I was thinking, 'Take me! Get me out of here!' Meaning, 'Release me from these bonds of human existence.'" Yogiji looked up and said, smiling, "Lee and I have our feet on the ground. Vijay wants to go into outer space."[24] And then he laughed.

राम

The beloved Godchild's relationship with time was a source of continual illumination to those around him. On most occasions, he wanted to be told the exact time, and he expected exact timing on the part of those who served him. When he sent someone out with a task to do, he would often wait – gazing at the door – until notified that the work was completed. Yet, in other instances, he did or said things that informed his devotees and visitors that he was in on the joke of the relativity of all things – time included.

In 1991, having spent a full day with his American son Lee Lozowick and other friends, Yogi Ramsuratkumar turned to his attendant and asked, "Jai Ram, did the sun set yet?"

"If He Walks it is the Teaching"

With a deadpan expression, as if playing the straight man in a long-rehearsed comedy routine, Jai Ram simply replied, "Yes, Swami."

Yogi Ramsuratkumar grew serious. "Ohhh God," he quipped, with a serious look and the hint of melodrama in his voice, "This beggar is too late!"

And then he doubled over in rollicking laughter in which his whole body shook, as he slapped Lee on the thigh and shoulder several times.[25]

राम

"What is rock and roll?" the beggar asked Lee one day in 1991. A discussion of the subject ensued. Lee and several of his students from the U.S. were currently performing in a rock and roll band, for which Lee was the lyricist. Yogi Ramsuratkumar wanted to know more, like whether instruments were required for the performance,

Yogi Ramsuratkumar listens to rock and roll as Devaki Ma looks on

and so on. The Godchild began to ask other Indian devotees who were present whether they had ever seen or heard rock and roll.

One of the Americans who witnessed this repartee speculated that rock and roll must have seemed like a very odd teaching vehicle, since they knew that Lee was held as a spiritual teacher in America. For his part, Yogi Ramsuratkumar found the whole subject amusing – as he did so many things. *Who was in the band? Who was not? Did the others who were not performing in the band dance?* His questions were drawing them out.

The verandah on which they sat offered a stunning view of Mount Arunachala. Turning his gaze to the sacred slope the beggar announced slowly, "The rock is not rolling."

Silence followed for a moment as his visitors registered the joke. Yogi Ramsuratkumar then, bursting with merriment, slapped Lee's leg.[26]

राम

Personal names were always a source of interest for Yogi Ramsuratkumar, and most visitors remembered that the Godchild would ask them for their name each time they approached, and sometimes several times in one visit. Hearing it, the Beggar would often repeat the name, preceding it with, "My Father blesses _____." Many of his guests speculated that this involvement with their name was his way of disarming them – occupying their attention as he gained entry to their psyche and heart.

An American woman, a student of Lee Lozowick's, had the odd name "e.e." – similar to that of the famous contemporary American poet, e.e. cummings. The woman's name (and the lower case spelling) was given to her by Lee many years previously and also represented the initials of her first and last name. When, in 1996, she knelt at the side of Yogi Ramsuratkumar to receive his blessing, the beggar characteristically asked her name.

"e.e." she replied.

He needed to hear it again, so he questioned, "Hmmm?"

She repeated it more distinctly. "e...e..."

Yogi Ramsuratkumar erupted into laughter, as he pronounced it, "e.e.!" He said it several times, as if it were the most delightful joke. Then he gazed at Lee with a knowing look.

"e.e.! e.e.! A.B.C.D. *e.e.!*" he said again, emphasizing the final letter as he shook with glee. In a moment, as others caught his mood, the whole room was rocking with laughter. More glances were exchanged between the beggar and Lee, and each time the Godchild broke into giggling again. He was fully amusing himself, and the crowd: "A.B.C.D. *e.e.*"

Even as the woman returned to her seat she could still hear his wondrous laugh, pleased that she had provided him with such a joyful interlude.

The lila was far from complete, however. Taking the communication to another level, a short time later he called the woman back to his side and asked her to read aloud some poems written by Lee contained in the book, *Poems of a Broken Heart.* As she read Lee's words: "Was there ever one more lost whom You had chosen to find. Was there ever one who hid so far whom You sought so long…" she choked with strong emotion. The words seemed so apropos to her own deepest desire to be absorbed into the Divine.

When she paused in the reading, momentarily overwhelmed, the Godman directed another woman in the group to come and stand beside her, a simple form of support, as she continued to read several more poems.

At last, when she was given the indication to conclude, e.e. approached Yogiji's seat, laid the book of poems at his feet, and pranamed to him.

"You would like this Beggar to come to your house?" he asked, reiterating a question that he had asked earlier in the darshan, before the dialogue about her name had commenced.

"Yes, please," e.e. replied. "You are welcome anytime."

Again he revived the joke, "A.B.C.D.*e.e.,*" which caused all to laugh again. As the woman returned to her place, thrilled by the blessings she had received, Yogi Ramsuratkumar turned to Lee and delivered one final sentence: "e.e. wants to be destroyed," the beggar said. For e.e., it seemed the ultimate expression of her longing heart.[27]

ONLY GOD

राम

An American man was asked his name by Yogi Ramsuratkumar. "Stan," he replied.

Turning to Mani, the beggar inquired slyly and with a twinkle in his eye, "Isn't there an English word s-t-a-i-n? But the 'i' is missing…He has no 'i'?"

The room filled with laughter, as everyone who understood English got the joke, amazed at the subtle sophistication it revealed. The lila was more poignant for those who had been present at the morning's breakfast-darshan. The requested reading at that time was an account from Papa Ramdas in which Ramdas had asserted that there was no "I" but only Ram, and that all the myriad forms of creation were actually different faces of Ram.[28]

राम

Richard Schiffman, an American writer and journalist, visited Yogi Ramsuratkumar in the 1970s. He had been staying for a while in Puttaparthi, near the ashram of Sai Baba, and had been unsuccessful in getting an interview with the guru there.

In his first meeting with the beggar in Tiruvannamalai, as they sat on the ground in front of the temple, the Godchild asked the man's name and where he was from.

Hearing that his name was Richard, Yogiji immediately said, "Ahhhh, Richard the Crusader."

Schiffman was surprised by the Godman's response. "I was wondering why he was calling me that. My thoughts at the time were that only in India could you meet such a holy person who looks like a beggar. Only here could such a person be revered. I was thinking that this was the uniqueness of this country."

Another American friend who sat with them offered his two cents, saying to Yogi Ramsuratkumar, "You mean Richard the Lionhearted?"

Yogiji looked at the other man incredulously: "Lionhearted?" and then added definitively, "No, Crusader!"

Wisely, the two guests kept quiet after that, and Richard admits that he dropped trying to figure out the reason for the name. As the Yogi stroked his arm, Schiffman noted that being with this gentle and affectionate beggar "was about as far from the scene at Sai Baba's as you could get. I liked him."

Two or three more times, within a few days, Schiffman and his friend visited the Godchild, and each time Yogi Ramsuratkumar would greet him with, "Ahhh, Richard the Crusader, come sit next to me."

On the last day of their visit, just as the men were leaving, Yogi Ramsuratkumar asked, "You've been wondering why I call you the Crusader?"

"Yes," Richard replied.

"Because you've come back to the Holy Land!" Yogi Ramsuratkumar chuckled with amusement. "And you're also wondering if you're getting an interview with Sai Baba. Don't worry, he'll talk to you as soon as you get back."

The day after Richard got back to Puttaparthi, Sai Baba called him in for an interview.[29]

राम

One day a devotee came to Bhagwan saying, "I have a lot of problems, what shall I do?"

Yogi Ramsuratkumar replied to the man saying, "I have a lot of problems too. Do you have any ideas? Tell me, I will follow you; I will come with you."[30] Certainly he smiled.

राम

One of Ramsuratkumar's favored "children," young Vivekanandan, told of an incident that occurred in 1988. Yogi Ramsuratkumar had visited the ashram of a local swami and had taken the boy Vivekanandan with him. The swami who ran the ashram was a well-educated man and greatly enjoyed talking at length about many varied subjects. After some time, when no refreshments had been offered, Ramsuratkumar turned to his host and said, "Vivekanandan is very hungry." Immediately the swami ordered lunch served to all.

Later, their visit concluded, Ramsuratkumar sat with Vivekanandan in the temple premises. "The Swami was talking and talking, while this beggar was feeling hungry. This beggar had not even taken his breakfast. That is why he said, 'Vivekanandan is hungry.' He could not say, 'I am hungry.' And, we got our food." Concluding this story, told to the delight of those around him, Yogi Ramsuratkumar burst into gales of laughter.[31]

A Divine Fire

Unless we die, Father will not come in us. Kabir said: "either you have God or the 'I.' There cannot be two swords in one sheath. If God must come, 'I' must die."

– Yogi Ramsuratkumar

"Short term visitors…did not know that Yogi Ramsuratkumar was a ruthless taskmaster who wielded a flaming sword. To be near him with sincerity was to experience a literal internal fire that spared nothing in its path," wrote Mariana Caplan, an American woman who was drawn into Yogiji's close circle of disciples for a period of seven months in 1994-1995.[32]

From her perspective, for the serious practitioner – one who was approaching Yogi Ramsuratkumar for something beyond relief of physical or emotional suffering, but rather for the purpose of dying into him, in the sense that Kabir described above – the work was often excruciating. "The egoic self that I mistakenly know myself to be suffered more intensely and more consistently in his company than in any other circumstance prior to, or since, that time. Yet so skillful was his capacity for egoic undoing that my ego would be made to flail about as if being scorched alive, while at the same time I would not know that he had anything to do with the suffering I was enduring. The light of His 'Self' exposed my 'self' – unadorned and unbuffered. To receive the privilege of his Fire of Love was to agree to have everything in its way burned to ash. These are not metaphors – exaggerated words to describe an intense emotional experience. It is my repeated experience of living in His proximity."[33]

"If He Walks it is the Teaching"

In detailing some of her experiences, Mariana explained that she was so attuned to him, by his grace, that his smallest movement would create a profound energetic shift in herself and others who were similarly resonant. "If he would move his elbow, the whole process would change. That movement became the world! We were in his work chamber. It was a slow motion play in darshan, and we would go on this energetic ride with him."

Yogi Ramsuratkumar was literally a Divine furnace, burning away the impurities of those who approached him. "Every foot closer to his body, and the heat would rise intensely – an inner heat that was physical and not physical at the same time. When he called you up to give you prasad, just stepping two feet closer meant more burning. You knew you were fortunate, and you paid attention and you were grateful, but it was *so hot*. As you were burning like that, all the obstacles in between you and That would come up. So the mind would throw the garbage and the thoughts really fast. Meanwhile, he was giving you all this love. For me, encountering my self-hatred, I was upset about what I was doing in the face of all that blessing. There was such frustration that I didn't know how to receive that blessing rightly."[34]

Like many classic mystical accounts, Mariana described feeling, "Lost…no mind…definitely not cognitive…just in a 'being' space.'" The strongest overall impression for her was that she was completely at the effect of his love, his energy.

To this day Yogi Ramsuratkumar continues to be a dynamic force in her life and in her sadhana.

राम

The purifying fire of Yogi Ramsuratkumar was sometimes a smoldering pile of embers; on other days, a huge conflagration. "I loved to see him embody opposites of moods – move from sternness to kindness to peace to wittiness, within seconds," explained Kirsti, a female sadhaka who lived most of her life in Tiruvannamalai. "He truly was alive on a very personal level in all his interactions. Even when he was 'mean' there was so much love and raw power behind it that I could just wonder what was taking place. His sternness or 'meanness' did not cling to mind or create guilt or resentment. His joyous straightforwardness prevented the mind from holding impressions of guilt or resentment."[35]

When an individual could profit from some direct intervention, however, Yogi Ramsuratkumar did not hesitate to intervene. One of his attendants for many years, Selveraj, tells of a specific teaching communication that included an angry and even sarcastic response from Yogi Ramsuratkumar.

Typically, when Bhagwan's car would arrive at the ashram, Selveraj was there to meet it. He would hold out his hand and the beggar would take it, saying "Thank you" with gracious regard.

One day, however, when Bhagwan said "Thank you," Selveraj responded automatically, saying "Thank you" in return. The unconscious nature of this response ignited the Godman's energy. "Thank you, thank you, thank you," he repeated, with a tone of anger.

Selveraj pondered this interchange for a long time, wondering if he had done something wrong in the past few days that had warranted such a communication. He finally understood that the mistake was not in the past, but in the present. Yogi Ramsuratkumar expected him to be alert in every moment. In saying "thank you" in a distracted manner, Selveraj had revealed his lack of attention to his work.

"So, Bhagwan was slowly working my heart. This is the main point. The guru will give the shock in a different way. We should remember all the time, God, and we should not be thinking about the things that have gone wrong."[36]

राम

A visitor from Canada was surprised one day when, in the midst of his conversation with the beggar, Swamiji fell asleep. As he received no response from the master, the visitor soon left.

When Yogi Ramsuratkumar woke up, another man asked him, "Swami, why did you fall asleep when that man was here?"

"Oh," he said, "that man couldn't hear what this beggar had to say."[37]

राम

"If He Walks it is the Teaching"

On January 25, 1979, two Indian gentlemen visited Yogi Ram-suratkumar late in the evening. They requested his blessings for a fund that had recently been established, named after a disciple of Ramalinga Swami. The master lay back listening and observing with intensity. Suddenly, as if moved by a strong wind, Yogi Ramsurat-kumar sat up and demanded with great urgency that they go back to Madras. The two men were alarmed and confused, while Yogi Ram-suratkumar assured them that he would pray for their cause. "Make preparations to go to Madras. Go to Madras. I will pray." He hand-ed the two men a packet of biscuits.

"Swami? Swami?" asked one man, as he reached around in the darkness to find his shoes. He could not believe that they were being ushered out so abruptly. Clearly, there was no arguing with the beg-gar's intention. He had his reasons.[38]

राम

Jai Ram, another close attendant, felt the heat of Yogi Ramsuratkumar's training in surrender. "It is very difficult to work for him, because he used to call himself 'mad.' His madness you could not predict. One day, He will suddenly send you out [out of his presence, away from him]. The next day, when you see him he will ask, 'What do you feel?' How he behaves in various situations, we cannot describe. Every action of his will hammer our ego; in some corner it will hit. We should not get into that [meaning, not support the ego]. Then only we can do his work. We have to learn this. You have to do *exactly* what he wants, and that you have to grasp. It took a lot of attention."[39]

राम

One way in which the master "hammered egos" was in giving orders that had seemingly no logic or precedent. Sometimes these orders were repeated two, three, four or more times until the devotee received the message at the level it needed to penetrate.

In 1995, Selveraj was working for salary at the ashram but had not yet established a relationship of devotee-to-guru with Yogi

637

Ramsuratkumar. He had received Mani's permission to go to his mother-in-law's home for a holiday but had failed to inform Bhagwan.

"When I went to my house to get ready for the time to leave, something was grabbing me to come back to the ashram. I got the idea that I should drop that program [abandon the idea of a holiday as previously determined]," Selveraj explained.

But before Selveraj could get there, Yogi Ramsuratkumar arrived at the ashram. It was 10 A.M., just prior to the morning darshan, and the Godchild was acutely aware that Selveraj was missing.

"He was shouting at the top of his voice, 'Where is Selveraj? Where is Selveraj?' and everybody got shocked. Mani told that he had given permission."

"If he goes there it is very dangerous. He should not go there," Yogiji said. Upon learning this information, the Godman sent some-one to Selveraj's home, carrying the message, "Bhagwan wants to see you." The young man immediately set out.

When Yogi Ramsuratkumar laid eyes on his attendant a few min-utes later, he studied him seriously and instructed: "Selveraj, you don't go. If you go, you will meet [something] very dangerous."

Instantly, the younger man replied, "Okay, Bhagwan," and then moved to take up his usual post at the temple door.

"Three times he called me back to him, and each time he said the same thing; and each time I said, 'Okay Bhagwan, I won't go there.'"

Finally, Yogi Ramsuratkumar called Selveraj back for a fourth time, and this time he called Mani as well. "Mani, you tell Selveraj not to go there," the beggar said, and Mani did as directed.

"Bhagwan, I will not go without your permission. Not only here, but wherever I go I will get permission from you," Selveraj said, his words invoking a solemn promise with the Godman.[40]

Paradoxically, this strange interaction marked the beginning of his relationship of devotion and surrender to Yogi Ramsuratkumar.

राम

It didn't take large gestures for Yogi Ramsuratkumar to fry the ego of a visitor or devotee. It happened on several occasions that a person who assumed that he or she knew Bhagwan very well would tell Yogiji's attendant, Selveraj, to inform the Godman of their arrival. This Selveraj would do. Nonetheless, when that person was presented to Bhagwan, he might ask them, "What is your name?" – thereby totally wounding the ego. Yogi Ramsuratkumar killed the ego many times with that one simple question.[41]

Along similar lines, one time a swami came from Kerala, did a very fancy puja, and received lots and lots of attention from Yogi Ramsuratkumar. The next year, assuming that he would receive the same fanfare, the man had someone go to Bhagwan and say that he was there, announcing self-assuredly, "He will see me right away."

When Bhagwan got this news, he looked up and saw the man standing by the back door. Yogiji sent word, "Let him sit at the corner," and arranged that a chair be brought to the man, who sat in the corner for the rest of the program. The beggar never called this man up to the dais.

"And that man never came back again. He never came back," said Saravanan, an ashram worker who witnessed this exchange.[42]

राम

Self-importance was so easily undermined by Yogi Ramsuratkumar. Yet, many failed to get the message. Once, when the new statue was installed in the ashram hall, a devotee walked around the statue and then prostrated to Bhagwan's feet as Yogi Ramsuratkumar sat in a chair to the right of the vigraha. The protocol at the time was to do this obeisance and then to proceed to the dining hall where bhajans were being sung.

This self-important devotee, however, didn't follow protocol. Instead, he remained standing a short distance away from Yogi Ramsuratkumar. After a brief period, the man called for Selveraj, the temple attendant, announcing, "I want to see Bhagwan."

Selveraj said to the man, "You go and sit in the dining hall and I will inform Bhagwan and he will call you if he wants to. Then you can come and see." At last the man did as instructed and left for the bhajan hall.

"Selveraj, what did he say?" Yogiji asked.

"Bhagwan, he wants to *see* you."

With a twinkle in his eye, Yogi Ramsuratkumar turned back to Selveraj, smiling as he said, "Then, what *did* he *see?*"

Selveraj added that many people asked for this same type of special treatment, implying that they had failed to "see" who was sitting right in front of them all along.[43]

राम

A famous singer who was passing through Tiruvannamalai expressed his desire to perform for the beggar. "I will only sing in the presence of Yogi Ramsuratkumar," the man informed his hosts.

When Yogi Ramsuratkumar heard of this, his response was uncommon. "I have no time for such music and singing," the beggar said, in strong contrast to the usual way in which he received music with great delight. The attitude of this singer had evidently provoked such a unique response.

Finally, Yogi Ramsuratkumar relented and announced that he would hear the man's song, but only for five minutes.

"I will sing for only as long as Swamiji stays. When he leaves I will stop," the singer offered. At 6 P.M. the man arrived and began his song. Unpredictably, the Godman stayed in place for six full hours. The man, true to his word, sang for all six hours. At the end of each song, the singer would prostrate to the beggar's feet and be blessed.

This entertainer usually received 100,000 rupees for his professional engagements. On this night, however, he received a blessing and a teaching lesson worth much more.[44]

राम

One day when a person was going on and on with eloquent words, Yogi Ramsuratkumar noted to Mani: "That person is just saying poetry."

When Mani asked, "What is poetry, Bhagwan?" Yogiji replied, "Lies!"[45]

राम

"If He Walks it is the Teaching"

Since 1995, when he met Yogi Ramsuratkumar, Ashish Bagrodia was naïve (by his own admission) about *who* the Godman was. Their relationship was more like that of friends, business partners, peers; or at the very best, a rapport between a wise elder and a younger nephew. Ashish enjoyed the Godchild's jokes and vast knowledge. Their conversations were freewheeling, easy going. In Ashish's heart, however, there was no deep longing for spiritual growth, merely a fascination for the simple ways of this odd fellow. He had never before met or interacted with a "saint," and he frankly liked being with Yogi Ramsuratkumar, very much. He also enjoyed a lot of attention from the beggar.

One day, this relationship was altered forever. Ashish found the fire of his master, and the absolute mercy, rolled up into one. In a rash attempt to help a young woman whom he met at the ashram, Ashish recommended to her that she change the hotel in which she was living, although Yogiji (unbeknownst to Ashish) had assigned it.

When the young woman's visit in Tiruvannamalai was completed, she returned by car to Madras, but was involved a very serious car accident and hospitalized for a considerable length of time. When some devotees of Yogiji's learned of this event, they pointed out to Ashish that his interference in Bhagwan's plan for this young woman was a factor at play in her accident.

Ashish was aghast at the intimation and wrote a fierce letter of self-defense to Yogi Ramsuratakumar and the devotees in question. The letter disturbed Bhagwan greatly. He called Ashish aside one day, holding the letter in his hand, and gazed full into the man's eyes as he delivered the message: "In this type of matter, this beggar has to say…Nothing! Nothing! Nothing!" His last three words were literally shouted.

Ashish, who is a man of great courage and personal power, revealed that he was never so frightened in his life. He was literally shaking, trembling, completely overcome by the power of the beggar's words to him. It was an experience he had never had before.

Feeling the effects of the master's word, immediately Ashish bowed his head and said, "I'm sorry," the words coming from the depths of his soul.

Instantly, the beggar's mood changed. He grasped Ashish's hands and spoke gently and lovingly to him, saying, "Ohhh, Father's blessings, Father's blessings," as he caressed the man's hands.

"After that my relationship totally changed with Bhagwan. I never joked with him, or spoke irrelevant stuff with him. I never took him lightly. [From then on] I used to watch every word I said. [Another devotee] was helping me to realize that I was caught up in my own world, and I should go to Yogiji and just sit there. I realized that all these years I had wasted time."[46]

राम

Jai Ram, who had known Yogi Ramsuratkumar since the early 1980s, and attended him for many years, told a story about how he learned to work in the way that the Godman expected.

It was a very hot summer day, and Jai Ram had just brought some food for the beggar's lunch. As it is customary in South India to eat from a leaf, usually a banana leaf, Yogiji pointed to a spot in the yard of the house, indicating a leaf that Jai Ram should take for their plate.

"In those days I used to be very careless in doing work," Jai Ram admitted, explaining how he had grabbed the leaf aggressively and then rubbed it over with his hand to clean it. Yogi Ramsuratkumar had followed every gesture, and could contain himself no longer. With what Jai Ram described as the sound of a "great thundering in the room," the beggar shouted, "What are you doing!"

The shock of that response and the sheer power of that voice were enough to rearrange Jai Ram's consciousness. "I forgot about the whole world," he admitted, humbly reflecting on this moment many years later. At the time, however, his mind was racing for a justification, for someplace to hide. "What? I have not done anything. I just took the leaf and did like that…[he gestured to imitate his casual action]. What is wrong with this?"

The voice of Yogi Ramsuratkumar still reverberated in Jai Ram's body. "Nobody can imagine [the impact of such a sound] except the one who has heard it. Immediately, I calmed down. I got it right –

the whole world was set right in that fraction of a moment. Then I understood that this leaf has got much value."

The great lesson that Bhagwan conferred on his young devotee that day was transformational. Jai Ram admitted that "from that day on, my whole outlook has changed." It was fully clear to him that no action was to be considered casual, even picking up a dry leaf. Rather, as Yogi Ramsuratkumar indicated again and again, "whatever action I do, we are doing what he used to call 'Father's work.'"

Taking the lesson further, Jai Ram explained:

We really think we do work for ourselves. If we like something, if we want something, if we desire something, then we go on our whole lifetime doing this thing. But he taught me that *whatever* you do it is Father's work. Because I am offering food for God, so that way, the devotion should be there in that. That was the lesson I learned from him. From that incident onwards, there was no necessity for any kind of teaching, or of thinking 'how to do this for Bhagwan?' It was not there at all. And it stayed like that the whole time with Yogiji, it was the undercurrent that was there. That's a real teaching from a master. The key was to get it.[47]

Do It Now!

During one of Lee Lozowick's visits for Yogi Ramsuratkumar's Jayanti, sometime in the 1990s, the beggar asked him and another Westerner if they would go to Anandashram at the end of the month as his representatives and make a speech for a special celebration to be held at the Kanhangad ashram. When both Lee and the other man informed Yogi Ramsuratkumar that they would be unable to make the trip, Bhagwan told Lee to write a speech on his behalf and send it there in time for the event.

On the morning in early December when this request was made, Lee initially decided to take a few days to do it, as the mail would surely not take more than a week or so to Anandashram. However, his second thought urged him to "Do it now!" From years of experience in watching Yogi Ramsuratkumar's approach to any task, Lee knew that the beggar would want things done as quickly as possible.

So, as soon as he finished lunch, Lee wrote the speech, put it in an envelope and carried it with him to the afternoon darshan.

As Lee had anticipated, Yogi Ramsuratkumar's first question to him that afternoon was about the speech. "Where is it?" he asked, and Lee handed his master the paper on which the speech was written. Yogi Ramsuratkumar read it and asked for an envelope, which was then addressed to Anandashram. The beggar, however, was still not satisfied. "We have to take this to the post office," he informed the American devotee, with an edge of urgency in his voice.

Lee asked Tom Lennon, a mature student in his company, to carry the letter to the post office. Tom had proven to be a reliable practitioner over many years, and Lee had confidence that the task would be done properly. Taking the letter, Tom exited the darshan hall and ran, literally, to carry out the assignment.

The instant Tom was out of the gate, Yogi Ramsuratkumar fixed his eyes on the door of the darshan hall from which Tom had exited. He remained staring at the door for the next half hour, and every two or three minutes the Godchild asked Lee, "Is it mailed yet?" With whatever assurance he could offer, Lee explained that Tom could be trusted and would get it done.

A half hour later, Tom raced back breathless into the darshan hall, and Lee informed Yogi Ramsuratkumar that the letter had been mailed. Bhagwan wanted to hear the details of the expedition – which had involved traveling first to a local post office and ultimately to the main post office downtown, as it was a holiday; purchasing stamps; and handing the stamped letter to the mail clerk. Only then was Yogi Ramsuratkumar's attention freed up to turn to other things.

As he lived always in the dynamic present, Yogi Ramsuratkumar expected this type of response from others. Mani, Devaki Ma, and others close to him were often faced with seemingly impossible tasks. Putting aside their own limited thinking, and putting his will above their own, the impossible readily became the norm around the Godchild of Tiruvannamalai.[48]

राम

"If He Walks it is the Teaching"

One day, Yogi Ramsuratkumar demonstrated to his devotees the nature of the fierce intention that he always lived by. It was during the early construction stages at the ashram and the property boundaries were still fenced by barbed wire, as no wall had yet been built. As he sat with a group of Indian devotees and visitors, Bhagwan declared that he wanted to go for a walk. No preparation was made. He simply stood up and started walking, while those in his company jumped up and ran behind.

Crossing the grounds of the compound in a beeline for his destination, he stopped at the strong barbed-wire fence that blocked his way. Realizing what was needed, one of his attendants immediately called for some of the ashram workers to come and cut the fence... right down the middle, right in front of Yogi Ramsuratkumar. Bending the wire out of the master's way, the workers stepped aside and Yogi Ramsuratkumar strode fiercely, like a warrior going into battle, right through the open place in the fence.

The ashram gate could certainly have been used, but this would have entailed a detour of several hundred years in both directions. Why he didn't use the gate, Lee Lozowick explained years later:

> It would've been five minutes to go to the gate, go around, and get past the fence... Would that five minutes have made a difference in His work? Obviously, to Him that five minutes would have changed Father's work. He knew where He was going, where He wanted to go... So sometimes we see something like that and we have no idea why it's happening. But the Work knows... We have to trust inherently – we have to trust moment to moment, in the moment. Our minds do not trust the Work. We have to bring our minds into alignment, so that moment to moment we're saying "yes."[49]

राम

A businessman who visited the beggar for advice was told: "Decide what is the best course of action! Then follow it. Do not hesitate and doubt after making the decision."

The advice was a pure reflection of the way in which Yogi Ramsuratkumar himself conducted life. He was absolutely direct, "like a warrior on a battlefield."

One devotee learned by many experiences that for the master the dynamic present was his playground. If she asked for things days or weeks in advance, for him the event was thus made imminent. In such cases, he would send her away and not let her sit with him until this work she had asked blessing for, whatever it was, had been completely handled. It was a profound communication about taking no concern for the future.[50]

राम

"Lee Lozowick wrote poems on Ma Devaki," Yogi Ramsuratkumar said one day. The beggar appeared fully delighted as he spoke these words. Whenever someone did something exactly as he had asked for it, and in a timely fashion, he was well pleased, and generally amazed.

राम

Selveraj had risen quickly in the ranks of ashram attendants. From working in the mailroom, to a ground's sweeper, to darshan hall guard and personal attendant to Yogi Ramsuratkumar – all within a matter of months.

In 1994, when the master would arrive on the ashram every day at seven in the morning, it was Selveraj's job to be there early to get the breakfast hut ready, arranging for the tumblers and mats, bringing everything from the kitchen, and then cleaning up. He distinguished himself as a responsible worker.

"Bhagwan noticed this," explained another worker, referring to Selveraj's consistency. "Bhagwan liked punctuality," Selveraj said, humbly.

राम

On the evening of January 29, 1979, Caylor Wadlington was to have met Yogi Ramsuratkumar at the mandapam at 7 P.M. but had been delayed visiting with friends. By the time he arrived it was already 7:45. The master was reclining on the top step of the mandapam and looked to be asleep, although having seen this posture before Caylor sensed that Swamiji was more likely in a state of deep contemplation.

Jagannathan immediately informed Yogi Ramsuratkumar that he had a visitor. Rising, Yogiji walked abruptly past Caylor and into the main part of the tower. "You have changed the time. Please come at seven," Yogi Ramsuratkumar said, sternly.

About this brief exchange Caylor wrote, sadly, "Evidently he *prepared* himself for my visit each evening before my regular arrival at seven. He had been waiting for me."[51]

This was not the first time that the young man had kept his master waiting. Another devotee recounted a time when she had observed Yogi Ramsuratkumar pacing the room much like an anxious lover, awaiting Caylor's arrival at the prearranged time. It had upset this devotee to see the master so agitated, but also touched her that Yogi Ramsuratkumar had such a powerful regard for those he had allowed to remain close to him, close to his heart.[52]

Yogi Ramsuratkumar continually taught those around him that timing was crucial to his work. And on many occasions they observed the remarkable consequences of following his directives to the letter, to the second...or not.

Serving the Guru

Writing of her work in the field of her master Yogi Ramsuratkumar, Vijayalakshmi explained: "If we do not have Guru Bhakti and faith in God, whatever we may possess is of no value. If we have Guru bhakti and the blessings of the Guru, then it is more than sufficient and is more than what we can possess materially in this world."[53]

Her words brilliantly reflected the teachings of her beloved, the Godchild who had surrendered himself fully at the feet of Swami Papa Ramdas in 1952; the beggar who lived his entire life praising God.

Instructing a close devotee one day, the master explained: "There is no need for any *japa* or *dhyana* [meditation] for you. You are in the company of this beggar all the time. So you are doing *tapas* [sacrifice and austerity] all the time, your service to this beggar will do. Transformation is going on all the time. The greatest tapas for anyone is to stay near one's guru and do service to him, but very few are given this chance."[54]

For those who did not have that rare opportunity, however, diligent work must be focused upon the teacher's practice or instruction. On one occasion, as Yogi Ramsuratkumar concluded a discussion about J. Krishnamurti's approach of "no structure," as opposed to his own structured use of the mantra as given to him by Swami Papa Ramdas, the beggar made it clear that both methods could achieve the same goal.

Roseanne, a Western woman who was present for this conversation, took down these words, which she credited to Yogi Ramsuratkumar: "You must choose some teaching and follow it. That is all that matters. Even a small fraction of a master's teaching will do it. It doesn't matter how the master says it. It's all the same truth. Some [masters] don't even talk. Some throw you out. As long as the light is there, the student will be changed."[55]

राम

In 1995, on an anniversary commemorating the life and work of an ultimate devotee, Mataji Krishnabai, Yogi Ramsuratkumar called for the reading of a passage that described Krishnabai's perfect love for and attention to Papa Ramdas. The piece was from the *Jnaneswari*, written by the thirteenth century saint Jnaneswar, in which the poet exalts the genuine nature of guru bhakti. Yogi Ramsuratkumar loved this work, which he spoke of on several occasions as the epitome of guru devotion.

> …In his keen desire to serve the Guru, he knows neither day or night, more or less, and becomes thoroughly pleased if the Guru entrusts more work to him. He becomes as great as the sky in serving the Guru and renders all requisite service single-

handed, in time. In this respect, his body runs ahead of his mind and its actual execution exceeds his fondest wish. At times he is prepared to sacrifice his life in order to fulfill the playful wish of his Guru. He becomes lean in the service of the Guru, but is nourished by his love…[56]

On one occasion Yogi Ramsuratkumar said, "Those who read *Jnaneswari* will not remain the same again."

In 1979, as he spoke one night with a group of Westerners, Yogi Ramsuratkumar explained to his listeners that just as a star's light is seen and is always present somewhere in the universe, even after the star has burned out, so too, even when the master leaves his body, the master's teaching is always present. We need only tap it.[57]

राम

At a breakfast meeting in 1994, Yogi Ramsuratkumar remarked that criticizing others was the same as criticizing the guru. Simply, he expected kindness, compassion, and generosity to be expressed to everyone, at all times. In this way, the guru was served.

राम

A telling observation about Yogi Ramsuratkumar's careful and clear support of each person's relationship to his or her teacher occurred one day in 1998, when Lee Lozowick was visiting with a group of his American devotees. While Lee is fully surrendered to Yogi Ramsuratkumar as his master, the students of Lee are directly under Lee's care and jurisdiction. In bringing his disciples to visit Yogi Ramsuratkumar, Lee asked that they fully regard the Divine beggar of Tiruvannamalai with worship and praise, acknowledging that he alone is the source of his (Lee's) benediction in their lives.

One year, Purna, one of Lee's most trusted devotees, knelt at the side of Yogi Ramsuratkumar, with his head bowed. Placing his hands close to Purna's shaved head, the beggar asked: "Does Lee ask you to keep your head shaved like this?"

"No," replied Purna.

Wanting to be completely clear about the situation, Yogi Ramsuratkumar asked once again, with a note of amazement in his voice, "Lee doesn't ask that you keep your head like this?" Again Purna answered no.

"Grow hair," Yogi Ramsuratkumar said with a big grin. "This beggar would like to see you with hair." Then, placing his hand over his heart, the beggar instructed, "But, obey Lee. Don't obey this beggar."

And with that he slapped Purna on the back and dismissed him.[58]

Attention to the World

What a Blessed obligation You bear,
    oh Upholder of the World.[59]– Lee Lozowick

"This Beggar is happy to be born again and again and again if his life has benefited even a single living being. This Beggar is happy to be born again and again to do His Father's work…[60] Father gave the work of preaching to Sri Aurobindo, Bhagavan Sri Ramana Maharshi and Swami Ramdas. But for this beggar, Father has given the work of alleviating the suffering of others alone!"[61] Yogi Ramsuratkumar repeated these words many times, in many ways.

While he obviously prayed constantly, urged all those in his company to chant the name of God, and referred everything to his Father, Yogi Ramsuratkumar had other wondrous and mysterious means of affecting the world. The Godchild knew that his first "Father," Sri Aurobindo, had used prayer as a means of influencing the course of World War II, and some of the words that he used about himself confirm a similar connection. "We work from one spot, taking into consideration the entire cosmic movement," he said one day.[62] His close devotees learned not to question but simply to obey, knowing that his concerns in working out small details with them in the circumstances of life on the ashram and in his immediate environment, might have implications beyond their wildest imaginations.

Some have pointed to his bundles of newspapers, noting his idiosyncratic ways of collecting data and storing it as indicative of how he was working with humanity as a whole. Reading the newspapers, as he did every day with astounding thoroughness, he knew what was

happening everywhere – in every country, in every political movement. His questions to visitors were a continual source of amazement
for them as he revealed knowledge of their country that they themselves did not know or appreciate.

It was not uncommon to see the beggar carrying around one particular scrap of paper for several days, opening it randomly, reading
it, carefully folding it again. In some instances, these papers contained the flight arrival and departure information of guests who
were visiting from Europe or the U.S. Only when Yogi Ramsuratkumar had learned that the person's flight had safely landed in their
home country would the paper be put away.

The beggar wanted to know how many days people would be
staying in Tiruvannamalai. He wanted to know at exactly what time
they would depart – and expected that they would abide precisely by
what they had told him. If they would be spending a day shopping
in Chennai before embarking on a flight, he wanted to know how
many hours they would be there. If Lee and his company were staying in Chennai prior to leaving for the U.S., Yogi Ramsuratkumar
made sure, personally, that they were hosted graciously by Mukilan,
a disciple who lived in Chennai. Mukilan was also expected to
accompany them to the airport, as well as to meet their arriving
flights. No details were to be overlooked…ever.

Yogi Ramsuratkumar would at times interview a taxi driver or
call a driver in to his darshan to be blessed before allowing him to
transport a devotee. One day, during a time of severe rains in South
India, when Justice Arunachalam was longing to see his master, he
made the journey from Chennai to Tiruvannamalai by bus, through
treacherous conditions. When Yogi Ramsuratkumar heard of it, he
actually shouted at the devotee. "Father does not want Justice
Arunachalam to travel by bus," the Godman said. Immediately, the
beggar inquired further, "When you want to leave tomorrow, how
will you go?" Before the devotee could answer, the protective guru,
Yogi Ramsuratkumar interjected, "By which car will you travel? If
you cannot arrange it yourself, this Beggar will arrange [it] for you."

The next day, when the friends who had agreed to take Justice
Arunachalam back to Chennai came to pick him up, Bhagwan wanted to know how long they had known each other, as well as details

about the accommodations offered in the car. Finally, Yogi Ramsurat-kumar made a clear instruction to the owner of the car that when they arrived in Chennai they were all to take Justice to his home first off, not stop at their own place and then send their guest off with their driver alone. As Arunachalam summed it up, "They willingly agreed and the PROTECTOR SWAMI had in His own inimitable manner of functioning, had me landed at Madras [Chennai], the way He wanted it."[63]

Yogi Ramsuratkumar would frequently ask people who were having some conflict with each other to sit together and to work things out. *He really meant it.* "It was totally real for him that people could simply do that," Lee Lozowick explained. The beggar wanted the name of God to be praised, and anything that got in the way of that prayer and praise needed to be eliminated. Yogi Ramsuratkumar was using the interactions within his own immediate field as a way of working with the entire world. Yet, too few understood that.

राम

"He wanted me to see Gorbachev, and convey this beggar's greetings to him," his devotee Parathasarathy recalled. It was during the 1980s, and Mr. Gorbachev was distinguishing himself in reforms that would pave the way for democracy. Yogi Ramsuratkumar closely followed Mr. Gorbachev's reformations and frequently spoke appreciatively of him.

"Parathasarathy, is it possible for you to go to Russia?"

The young man did not reply.

Again Swamiji asked him: "If it is possible for you to go to Russia, you should meet Mr. Gorbachev and convey this beggar's salutations to him."

"Yes, Swami," Parathasarathy replied, incredulously and without enthusiasm.

Despite his desire to carry out his master's wishes, Parathasarathy was frankly unnerved by this request. "I would have to become a fool," he reflected, explaining candidly that it would have required him to be completely out of his own way, with no investment in self-importance, to even make a step in this direction. To travel to Russia!

To receive an audience with the great politician, Gorbachev! Such a task was clearly in a domain of pure magic, and Parathasarathy admitted being too caught up in his own mind to seriously entertain it as a possibility.

"He wanted to do something for Gorbachev. At the same time he wanted me to be near him to pass on the vibrations. It affects one's consciousness, you know."

राम

Other than by direct assaults, there are hints that Yogi Ramsurat-kumar's attackers used more devious means to harm him. One night in 1979 he explained to Caylor and other visitors that something had been placed in or on his eyes at night on three occasions by someone who had intentionally desired to harm him. At this point in 1979 he said that for the first time in his life he was having trouble with his eyes. The beggar was sixty years old at the time, so it may have been that his eyes were growing weak from age. Be that as it may, his words of acceptance and deep surrender to the will of his Father touch upon something much more basic than eye trouble. Referring to himself, he said: "Some sacrifice was necessary. For the candle to give light, it must burn."

The same intimation of his greater mission was provoked when Preben, a young Danish seeker, asked Yogi Ramsuratkumar if he would ever come to the West. His response was essentially the same one he had given to Hilda Charlton in 1978, namely, that it was not his decision to make. Yogi Ramsuratkumar said, "This beggar's Father has understood the conditions here in Tiruvannamalai. But he has told this beggar that he must remain here doing the Master's work. Some sacrifice must be made. The Master has made it clear that this beggar must be a Sacrifice to a great work."[64]

राम

While he attended to the whole world, Yogi Ramsuratkumar never lay claim to anything. When some devotees came to him asking to use his name for the new hospital they were developing, he asked them what the name of the city was in which the hospital would be located. "It's useless to put the name of this beggar," the Godchild said. "Put rather the [name of the] city."

Michel Coquet, who recounted this incident, remarked that in this way the beggar was indicating his independence from all causes or associations. "Neither glory nor money have for him the least interest. The world is dead to his eyes."[65]

Making the same point, Sadhu Rangarajan explained that Yogi Ramsuratkumar's work was not about forming an association or starting a hospital. "Even when we wanted to start an organization named after him, the Sister Nivedita Mission, for example, he said no, to keep it under the name it was. He was working through *all* the organizations," Rangarajan affirmed. "Yogi Ramsuratkumar used to tell: 'Whether it is Chinmaya mission, whether it is Satya Sai Baba mission, whether it is the Ramakrishna mission, all the work is this beggar's work. This beggar doesn't require another separate organization. This beggar is open to all of these people.'"

"Whoever did the good work, it was *his* work," Rangarajan continued. "He considered himself to be universal, because he used to say, 'My Father alone exists. Nothing else, nobody else in the past, present and future.' And in another place he has said, 'You cannot understand this beggar. He is everywhere and he alone exists.' So for him, whether it is Chinmayananda, or Shakaracharya, Sathya Sai Baba, whether it is Ramana Maharshi...all are his own manifestations. Or, he is the manifestation of that Supreme that is manifested in all these forms. And all the work that they were doing, that was his work. So if a devotee comes from Anandashram or from Ramana Ashram...from Chinmaya Mission, he used to inquire about the work they were doing in their mission, and he used to encourage them to go back and do that work. Because he didn't want to represent it in his name. He never wanted anything for his own."[66]

Blessings in All Forms

A thirty-year-old unmarried woman, a doctor "who held fast to high values in her life," was introduced to Yogiji one day. His "care, concern, and compassion," were so intense that the woman "broke down in inconsolable tears on being showered by his look of loving kindness."

"If He Walks it is the Teaching"

The Godchild himself was "greatly moved by tears," wrote his devotee Shri V. Ramanujachari who witnessed this powerful exchange.

"You should not cry," Bhagwan said to the woman. "Please do not cry. Your eyes should never again get wet. My Father will ensure that you will always be happy. This beggar wishes you a life of unbroken happiness and peace."[67] Thus, he blessed her.

This type of intimate concern was experienced by hundreds of Yogiji's devotees, and their stories are countless. Ravi, the young man who was Yogi Ramsuratkumar's driver for many years, shared that when his father was dying in 1983-84, Bhagwan actually went to his house in the final days to be with his family. Ravi and his brothers started to feel like Bhagwan had "become [their] father from that time onwards. Because he was taking care of the family, they became one with Bhagwan."[68]

राम

Devaki Ma told a group of visitors one day, "Once, when I was leaving the ashram with Yogi, He smiled at a person who stood at the gates. I asked Him if [this person] was known to Him. Yogi smilingly said, 'No!' However, he made me realize that 'for Him nobody was a stranger!'"[69]

On another occasion, Devaki Ma explained: "I have never heard Him denigrate anybody at any time, for He could never find any fault with anybody. When someone tries to harm Him in Ignorance, He will say, 'That is Father's Will! Whatever happens is for good only, for my Father is blemishless and whatever He Wills is blemishless.' Thus, He will teach the devotees around Him, through His own conduct, the greatest lesson of 'Saranagati' – the spirit of total surrender to God."[70]

राम

"I was making some big mistakes," admitted Mariana Caplan, speaking about her months in residence in Tiruvannamalai. "A beautiful young boy whose mother used to do service at Sudama House became my young friend. As the boy was always looking for a little extra money, I would let him wash the floors in my room. One day, $100 (U.S.) was missing from where I hid my money, and I was certain it was this boy who had stolen it. He was the only person I allowed into my room. He knew where all my keys were, and this money was in a locked drawer.

"I reacted harshly, as I felt hurt and betrayed. I decided to report him to the police, who began their investigations. When his mother learned of this she would sit outside of Yogi Ramsuratkumar's residence, crying to him about what was going to happen to her son. It was serious, because if such a thing was proven, a young person could lose a chance to go to school. It could literally have ruined his life. But, of course, I had no idea, I was only twenty-five years old, and feeling abandoned.

"One morning I got a message from Yogi Ramsuratkumar, through Mani, asking me to drop the charges. Yogi Ramsuratkumar wanted me to be assured that the ashram would reimburse me for the $100."

Mariana dropped the charges, as directed. She also suffered enormous remorse in realizing the exorbitant kindness of the Godman in contrast to her own reactive nature.[71]

राम

In December 1979, Caylor Wadlington and his friend Sunder were visiting the home of a European women in Tiruvannamalai. Yogi Ramsuratkumar was with them. At the conclusion of their visit, as one of the woman's servants stood to take leave of the group, Sunder held out a rupee, and motioned to the servant to take it. Some confusion ensued, both for the servant and for their hostess.

Yogi Ramsuratkumar, in one seamless gesture, took the rupee note from Sunder's hand and presented it to the manservant, ostensibly as a blessing. Afterwards, the beggar explained to the men that this same situation often arose when friends wished to give money to his attendants. It would be awkward and seem cruel to deny these people the benefit of someone else's generosity. Yet, Yogi Ramsuratkumar readily understood that servants could tend to ingratiate visitors, thus expecting money in return.

Receiving this invaluable lesson in protocol, Sunder apologized for his blunder, although everyone appreciated his attempted thoughtfulness. Fortunately, by the hand of Yogi Ramsuratkumar, what might have been an embarrassment was turned into a lesson and a most gracious act.

राम

An American woman was walking into the town of Tiruvannamalai one day, following the darshan of Yogi Ramsuratkumar at his ashram. As she passed a large trash heap, one of many that dot the streets throughout the city, the thought occurred to her that such a trash heap was and always would symbolize the "home" of Yogi Ramsuratkumar, who still referred to himself as the "dirty beggar." Despite the grandeur of the physical structures around him, this pile of refuse – the discarded elements of all levels of society – was exactly what he had come to earth to redeem.

The woman stopped, making this trash pile a point of remembrance and prayer in her pilgrimage to town. "Right there on top of this trash pile was a color photo of Yogi Ramsuratkumar shining up at me...It was a little splattered with whatever juices the heap receives. This was a miracle. I snatched up the photo and kept walking."[72] This was no mere coincidence and the woman knew it. Rather, it was one more way in which the beggar allowed people to find him everywhere, thus making everything sacred!

राम

As Mariana Caplan stood in line at the Chennai airport, waiting to pass through customs on her way back to the U.S., she was informed that her visa was improper. It lacked the stamp of the local police, which was the regulation, as she had resided in India for longer than six months. For nearly a year she had lived in Tiruvannamalai, where she had the close protection and guidance of Yogi Ramsuratkumar.

Now, as her exhaustion grew, she wanted only to be on her way back to home and family, not stuck for a few more days in this strange city. Unwisely, she began to argue with the customs official, but she received no mercy. Then she began to cry, but her emotionalism too failed to move her inquisitor. "Desperate, I began to chant, '*Yogi Ramsuratkumar, Jaya Guru Raya*' as I had so many thousands of times in those months," the American woman reported. The chant was soft, but audible, and she questioned whether this new tactic might be viewed as some arrogant attempt at manipulation by the security guards who obviously heard it. Nothing!

One hour later, just before the plane was due for boarding, as she wept in the waiting room, one of the guards returned. Astounded, Mariana listened as the man recounted his story: "I traveled to Tiruvannamalai last weekend to receive the darshan of the great saint Yogi Ramsuratkumar. And while I was there, there was a young Western woman leading the chants. When I heard your chanting here at the security counter, I realized that you were the woman I had heard chanting. Yogi Ramsuratkumar is a great, great saint, and I want you to know that it is for that reason alone that we will let you pass through security and board your plane tonight. Run along!"[73]

Healing Our Bodies, Renewing Our Souls

Many devotees over the years have told wonderful stories of the way in which Yogi Ramsuratkumar dealt with their health concerns. This biographer, in 1995, was experiencing severe foot pain, caused by a broken bone. During the darshan hours, Yogi Ramsuratkumar would coincidentally massage his own right foot whenever hers was particularly painful. Each time this occurred, I found that my pain was lessened for several hours afterward, allowing me to walk without difficulty.

For others, however, the healing and blessing came in the form of a direct touch. Alain de Rosenbo, a Belgian man, would visit Yogi Ramsuratkumar yearly, beginning in 1995. The beggar took a particular interest in the condition of this elder. He would stop at Alain's chair each day and make quiet invocations as he placed his hands on Alain's knees. Alain's condition improved significantly during these visits. Although he had arrived in a wheelchair, Alain was soon walking without assistance for the remainder of his stay.

"If He Walks it is the Teaching"

When Lee Lozowick was bearing with knee problems, Yogi Ramsuratkumar made similar gestures, touching his fingertips to Lee's knees, although the American had made no request or even any indication that he wanted this special attention. At one point he even asked Lee to get up and run to the end of the room, as the beggar watched him carefully. Lee reported that his knee pain was reduced and the whole condition improved as a result of these ministrations of his Father's.

राम

Ponkacham, a close female devotee, once complained to Yogi Ramsuratkumar that her doctor had told her to stop eating all sweets and sugar. When he heard this, the beggar laughed, as if dismissing the laws of physics or chemistry, and quickly offered her some sugar candies. Protesting that she shouldn't take them, Bhagwan joked, "Ponkacham, this beggar knows how much you like sugar – eat it, eat it."

Obediently, the woman took the candy and placed it in her mouth. As soon as she had swallowed the prasad, he gave her some more, which she also ate.

Later that day, when she returned home, she was checked by her doctor, who found that her blood sugar was normal.[74]

राम

R. Jeyaraj Sulochana, an elder disciple, was having a problem with his eyes which required medical attention. He was seeing double. When next he went to visit Yogiji, Bhagwan asked Jeyaraj to hand over his glasses, and the beggar proceeded to put them on himself. He then asked Jeyaraj to close one eye, look at him with the other, and keep his focus there.

Several times in the course of this visit Yogi Ramsuratkumar asked the elder man how he was seeing, to which Jeyaraj replied, "a little better." After each reply, Yogiji would take off the glasses and then put them back on again.

659

Finally, Jeyaraj reported that he was seeing fine. When he left, his sight was rectified, and the problem did not recur.[75]

राम

In the early 1970s, when Yogi Ramsuratkumar was visiting Tapovanam, the ashram of Swami Gnanananda Giri, Shri V. Ramanujachari found the beggar in the courtyard "sitting before this painting of Sri Rama."

The devotee's wife, who was with him on this day, was suffering from a "painful urinary tract infection dogging her for the last five years." When the beggar asked the woman about her health, she told him, and "he suddenly became alert," Ramanujachari explained. Yogiji then asked the man's wife to "stand up and walk straight before him up to the compound wall," which was thirty yards away. All the while, "he was looking intently, all concentration at her. He asked her to turn around and walk back slowly towards him." This was repeated "six to seven times" at the beggar's request, and "all the time his eyes were intently focused on her."

After the woman sat down, her husband asked Yogi Ramsuratkumar, with a tone of "friendly raillery, what the great idea was all about?"

Immediately, the beggar became serious, and "a tinge of hurt and sadness" fell over him. Turning to Ramanujachari, the Godman spoke carefully: "You do not know what I have done for her today and how much I have helped you."

When the couple returned home after their weeklong stay at Tapovanam, "it took us some days to notice that the ailment had faded away," Ramanujachari reported. "A miracle was performed in a very casual manner, as if my wife was only taking a walk!"[76]

राम

Ramamurti and Mr. Reddy were getting on famously on the first day that they met in the presence of Yogi Ramsuratkumar in 1990. The men were joking about one being "sweet" (since Reddy owned a candy company) and the other being "hot" (since Ramamurti owned a chili company), and one being "north" while the other was "south," since they came from opposite ends of the country. Bhagwan laughed heartily at their play.

Around midday, the two men went to lunch, having been dismissed by the beggar. They went to a restaurant and enjoyed a wonderful meal; however, Ramamurti realized that, while having a great conversation, he had eaten too much.

When they returned from the meal and joined Yogi Ramsuratkumar, the beggar addressed Sandhya, Mr. Reddy's daughter: "Sandhya, this beggar has eaten too much, do you have anything?" She brought some homeopathics, some ginger powder, some pepper powder, and some water, which Yogiji took.

Ramamurti was surprised because, as far as he knew, Yogi Ramsuratkumar had taken nothing since their arrival that morning except one cup of buttermilk, which they had all consumed in the earlier part of the day. No other food had been given to him.

It was only days later that Ramamurti began to understand the type of subtle teaching that had been made to him. When he returned home from this trip to Tiruvannamalai, he soon after went to the doctor for an overall checkup and learned that his cholesterol was very high. Ramamurti was sure that the beggar had taken on his overstuffed condition that day and had actually *asked for* a remedy. Ordinarily the beggar had such a simple faith in his Father's care, that it was only on unique occasions that he would ask for some health aid for himself. The lila was obviously for the benefit of his devotee.

राम

As Yogiji had often directed people to other teachers or empowered shrines from which they could receive help, so too, other teachers and masters directed their visitors or followers to the beggar in Tiruvannamalai.

Ponkamaraj, who was suffering from leukemia, was in despair about his physical health when he visited Mother Mayee of Kanyakumari. The Divine Mother, however, did nothing but laugh and point to a person who was standing a few feet away from

Ponkamaraj at the time. This person carried a yellow cloth bag bearing the image and name "Yogi Ramsuratkumar, Tiruvannamalai."

Careful to follow through on such indications, Ponkamaraj journeyed to Tiruvannamalai to locate the beggar, whom he had never met. But, as many people have found over the years, it took several days of searching for Ponkamaraj to locate the Godchild.

In the beggar's presence at last, Ponkamaraj was greeted with enthusiastic slaps to his back, together with numerous blessings and verbal assurances that he would be all right.

Ponkamaraj was cured of leukemia, miraculously – a circumstance to which he credits the intervention of Yogi Ramsuratkumar.[77]

राम

Jayathu Jayathu Jayathu Jayathu
Ramsuratkumara Yogi Ramsuratkumara Yogi

Victory, victory, victory, victory to Yogi Ramsuratkumar sing devotees in the ashram of Yogi Ramsuratkumar in Tiruvannamalai and in other sacred places around the world. Yet, few realize that these words were actually given as a form of prasad, and a healing mantra, to Sri Siva Ramakrishna Iyer, an elderly disciple.

When Iyer was sick one day, suffering from severe stomach pain, he sent his niece Lalitha to the beggar's house in Tiruvannamalai. Iyer was unable to travel, and had asked Lalitha to carry his pranams to the Godchild and to ask the master for some prasad to help him with his ailment.

Lalitha did as she was asked. But instead of giving her a banana or piece of fruit or candy, as he normally did, Yogi Ramsuratkumar asked her instead to copy down the words recorded above. "Tell your uncle to write a song with these lines," the beggar instructed the young woman.

When she returned with the assignment, Siva Ramakrishna was disappointed. Surely this was not the type of relief he had expected. Not appreciating the value of the gift, Iyer put the words aside, and a whole day and part of the next night passed with no alleviation of the stomach pain. Finally, when nothing else was available to distract him, he took up the paper that his niece had brought him and began to play with the words. By the time he had composed four or five lines of a song, his stomach pain had lessened. Only then did the thought occur to him that this task was actually intended as a balm from the hand of the beggar.

Applying himself wholeheartedly, Iyer then wrote twenty-seven additional verses of the song that is known today as *"Nakshatra Malar Malai."* When the writing was complete, his pain had completely subsided.

The next week, on Saturday, Siva Ramakrishna took his completed song and presented it to the Godchild in Tiruvannamalai.

Coincidentally, as it was Saturday, the day ruled by the planet Saturn, Yogi Ramsuratkumar was discussing the planet and its effects. Siva Ramakrishna's interest was piqued, as he had been told that, based in his horoscope, he would undergo particular misery due to Saturn's influence. Amazingly, Yogi Ramsuratkumar declared that all who were present in the room at that time would be freed from the negative effects of Saturn's transit.[78]

राम

At age sixty-five, Ra Ganapati, a famous author who had written books on Sai Baba and the Shankaracharya, took only sattvic (mild) food. As a guest at Yogi Ramsuratkumar's breakfast-hut meetings, the man would generally take only one banana, eat a portion of it, and then pass the remainder along to others.

One morning, however, Bhagwan asked Selveraj to bring him the fruit plate. The gentle beggar took a banana, peeled it, and fed it to Ra Ganapati. After that, another banana. Then, a third banana was given. When it seemed that more bananas were forthcoming, the man finally explained, "Bhagwan, I cannot eat more bananas, or I will have indigestion." But Bhagwan proceeded to give him still one more. When breakfast was over he had consumed five or six bananas.

When they were about to leave, Ra Ganapati told Yogi Ramsuratkumar that he was afraid of digestive problems. The writer was concerned especially on this day because he was expected for "another breakfast" at a friend's home, immediately after he was finished at the ashram.

Hearing this, Yogiji raised his hands and said, "Now Ra Ganapati's bananas, all has been digested." As Ganapati stood still, receiving the blessing, the Godchild added, "Now you can go to [the friend's] place and have your breakfast also."

To the amazement of his friends, Ra Ganapati enjoyed a regular breakfast at his host's home, and suffered no digestive problem.[79]

राम

On December 16, 1996, Mr. P.V. Karunakaran witnessed another expression of healing help and generosity on the master's part. Recalling the incident he wrote: "In the afternoon, while darshan and satsang were going on, an old paralytic patient was brought in by his relative. Bhagavan asked me to tell the devotees 'nicely' that those who had diseases must go to doctors and that Bhagavan was not a doctor. When I finished talking to them, Bhagavan called me to him again and asked me to tell the devotees that all they had to do was to repeat his name, if they had faith in him. I said so and sat in my place and went on yearning for Bhagavan. Bhagavan called me again, held my hand, and asked me to lead him to the chair by the side of the patient. Then the compassionate Master affectionately touched the patient's head and asked his relative to continue the same medical treatment as he was already being given, all the while Bhagavan was holding my right hand tight in his left. Perhaps, he was simultaneously satisfying my longing for his touch and the patient's longing for divine intervention."[80]

To Each Her Own

Every guest and every situation was unique to Yogi Ramsuratkumar, who had a seemingly endless supply of skillful means in his repertoire. Some people obviously needed affection and attention, while others needed the guru's surgical knife. Some were given a wide berth, while for others the demand was sharp and immediate. A few stories illustrate the many ways in which the beggar gave "to each her own."

"If He Walks it is the Teaching"

राम

Many people have noted over the years that Yogi Ramsuratkumar was not looking to attract devotees to himself. He would frequently send people on to meet other masters or teachers, or to study other disciplines, urging them only to remember that "Father alone exists." In some cases, his direction had an immediate effect. For others, his hints took root only after many years.

Chandra was a modern young woman who lived and worked in Delhi. She was also searching hungrily for a more dynamic access to the path. In the late 1980s, a friend told her of Yogi Ramsuratkumar.

His was not an unfamiliar name to her. Chandra had known about the mad beggar-saint for a long time, since she had been visiting Ramanashram and doing pradakshina of the sacred mountain ever since she was a teenager. And, although her friend told her that "he is very special," she was apprehensive – she had also heard many stories of the beggar's fierce and unpredictable ways.

On her next visit to Tiruvannamalai, however, Chandra roused her courage and decided to pay the Godchild a call. The morning after her arrival, she rose early, took no breakfast, as was her custom in performing the pradakshina, and made the circumambulation of the sacred mountain. When she returned to Ramanashram at 9 A.M., it was too late for breakfast and too early for lunch, which was served precisely at 11 A.M. That's when the thought occurred to her to "take a chance" and go for the darshan of Yogi Ramsuratkumar. In her mind, she imagined that she would catch sight of him, pay her respects, and then leave. Easily, she would get back to Ramanashram in time for lunch.

Chandra took a rickshaw back into town, to Sannadhi Street, to the house with the iron gate. Approaching, she knocked softly. Almost immediately a voice from inside called, "Who is this?" And a moment later, "this odd person came to the door." Chandra wasn't even sure it was *him* at first. But she was instantly invited in.

Asking her name and where she had come from, the beggar began to chat with her about the *Ramayana*, asking her if she had read a particular English language translation by Raj Gopal Archarya. She had.

"You must read it again and again, as many times as you can," Yogi Ramsuratkumar advised her. Chandra nodded her head, indicating that she would do it.

The beggar then questioned her several times about her job, especially whether she liked it or not. Although her job at the time was a good one, supplying her with the income for a comfortable living, Chandra admitted that it wasn't very interesting to her. This subject was one that she had struggled with for a long time. Obviously, *he* knew that she wanted a change!

Bhagwan's approach to her was so gentle and kind that Chandra was deeply touched. An hour passed quickly. When he asked her the time – it was then 10:45 A.M. – he hurried her on, saying, "Chandra, you must get back to Ramanashram, or you won't get the lunch, because after 11 they don't serve lunch."

"I prostrated to him and left," Chandra reported. "It was such a mark of his greatness and his concern that the master, like a mother, would be concerned for the child's well-being in such a small detail. Such are the ways of the great ones."

When she returned to Delhi, the young woman did what the Godchild had told her to – she read the *Ramayana*, several times. Up until this point, Chandra had not felt the inclination towards bhakti, preferring the advaita approach as she had been exposed to it through the teachings of Ramana Maharshi. However, seven months after leaving Yogi Ramsuratkumar, she was shocked to find herself suddenly overwhelmed with devotion for Rama. "It just overtook me. For the next seven or eight months I was constantly thinking of Rama, and how to serve him, like Sita, like Lakshmana, like Bharata. At night I wouldn't sleep at all, thinking of Ram, Ram, Ram – or any glorious attribute of God in any form. Before that I had a strong appeal for Siva, but it was an intellectual attraction, nothing like this veil, this wave of bhakti."

For the next few years, Chandra visited Yogi Ramsuratkumar every time she came to Tiruvannamalai, and her respect and tenderness for him grew. Once, in the early 1990s, she met Mani, and in the midst of their conversation she told him of the devotion that had been stirred in her through the *Ramayana*. When Mani heard of her love for Rama, he suggested that Chandra should visit Anandashram, the place Swami Papa Ramdas and Mataji Krishnabai had made holy; the place that was soaked in devotion to Ram, and where chanting of the Divine name went on for twelve hours a day.

This suggestion stayed with Chandra, although it took her a while to get there. It was 1995 when she set foot at last on the grounds of Anandashram. Hearing the voice of Swami Satchidananda (the successor of Papa and Mataji) for the first time, "a kind of silence descended" for her. Finally, at arati in the afternoon, learning the meaning of the arati as the words were chanted, she was drawn deeply into the inner world. So deeply, that it was difficult for her to come back…Her heart fell at the feet of Swami Sachidananda, to a point of no return. She recognized him as her guru.

Her love for Yogi Ramsuratkumar endures with unending gratitude, as she distinctly credits his intervention in directing her to her true home.[81]

राम

Sometimes the Godchild's praise and gratitude would be overflowing. At other times, he might completely ignore what some devotee considered to be a great gift. It was his way of working, and those who could take it learned a great deal.

A close female devotee had written him nearly one hundred poems, which she carefully typed and presented to him. He received them wordlessly. A few days later, when the devotee returned, she wondered if he would say anything about these poems, which contained so many of her perceptions about the world, as well as the outpourings of her heart. Yogi Ramsuratkumar did not say one word. For weeks the devotee was left to "work with" her own reactions and her relationship to him. Wisely, she never asked.

Some time later, Devaki Ma called the woman and thanked her for the poems. She was told that everyone at Sudama House had a great time when Yogiji had them read out, and that he constantly commented on them. He also roared with laughter.

This devotee admitted that she had longed to be there to see his reaction, but because she was a practitioner, she knew that "the personal level wasn't important and was an obstacle if it blocked transmission by demanding too much attention. The real relationship [to the master] was fresh beneath the personal continuity. It was more alive than one's image of what one is or wants to be. It is more naked. And it is subtle like a fragrance. It has lots of power because it is so subtle, it can penetrate."

His laughter was, for her, the greatest blessing.[82]

राम

For one who might naively expect quick results in working with a guru or master, Kirsti's words were sobering. Being subject to Yogi Ramsuratkumar required incredible patience and persistence. In 1995, Kirsti reported that, "About six months ago he called me up to him and asked me, 'What kind of sadhana do you do?'"

"It is nineteen years that I've known him. So, I am getting close now." She smiled broadly in sharing these words, clearly overjoyed at this turn in the process.

"Usually he never did or said anything when I was not ready," Kirsti continued. "He always treated people with kindness so the mind and heart would be in rest *before* he used any knife to cut through expectations and clingings. It had a liberating power then."[83]

राम

In 1991, Yogi Ramsuratkumar gave a lot of attention to Vijaya Fedorschak, a student of Lee Lozowick's. Once, in the midst of other conversation, the beggar turned to the young American and asked, "Does Vijay like fish?"

With this question, a discussion ensued which culminated in Yogi Ramsuratkumar giving Vijay a strict dietary regimen – no meat, fish or eggs – for "one or two years." The young man was also urged to take lime pickle, an item that he admitted to disliking.

To Vijay's credit, encouraged by his own master, Lee, he took the recommendations as a lifelong exercise in obedience and devotion.

To this day (in 2004) he has kept to the beggar's suggestions. Such consistency in doing what is asked, and more, is reflective of the type of reliability that Yogi Ramsuratkumar expected.[84]

राम

Married in 1990, a couple who wanted children were still childless in 1994, and had already spent a lot of money on medical treatment. In 1994, at Yogiji's Jayanti, Bhagwan spoke on the microphone to the assembled crowd, saying, "I wish you all a Happy Birthday."

"On December 8, 1994, my wife was tested for pregnancy and found that she was pregnant," reported Mukilan, the husband. "We are both convinced that the child was conceived on this day that Bhagwan wished us the happy birthday."[85]

राम

A schoolgirl, the daughter of a devotee, told Yogi Ramsuratkumar that her teacher had explained to the class that only God in heaven could perform miracles. The teacher further reiterated that human beings – like yogis – could not enact such things. Hearing this, Yogi Ramsuratkumar smiled. On the spot he asked the girl to hold a stainless steel plate up over a burning candle. From across the room he raised his hand and sent his attention and energy toward the plate. When told to look, the girl was astonished to see Yogiji's image clearly and distinctly outlined in the soot left by the candle. The beggar told her, 'Go tell your teacher that God in the sky is not the only one who can perform miracles. God on earth can too!'"[86]

राम

Prior to the event that began his teaching work, which he now credits to the grace of Yogi Ramsuratkumar, Lee Lozowick was a seeker. He visited many masters and teachers, and studied many varied teachings. Nonetheless, the masters who most fascinated him were never accessible to him. He simply wasn't in the "right place at the right time."

Then, Lee met Yogi Ramsuratkumar and the pattern of his previous search and previously "missed opportunities" was revealed for what it was. In speaking to audiences in North America, Europe, and India, Lee frequently noted that this series of occurrences – whereby he never got to meet those other special teachers or gurus – was all the doing of his true heart master, Yogi Ramsuratkumar. The beggar had "kept him out of the grasp" of others until his relationship to him was secure and utterly trustworthy.

Once this solidity was inviolable, the beggar led Lee to many great teachers all over the world. Each of these other teachers gave Lee additional confirmation of the great mission that he had been given by Yogi Ramsuratkumar.[87]

राम

In 1991, when V. Ganesan sat with Yogi Ramsuratkumar one day, the Godchild asked him if he had yet received a letter from Germany. As no such letter had come nor was expected, the younger man said no.

A few days later, Yogiji asked the exact same question. Still, Ganesan had to answer that no letter had been received. Wanting to relieve his own curiosity, however, he asked the beggar why he was asking such a question.

Yogi Ramsuratkumar laughed heartily as he added, "Because Ganesha has to go to Germany."

Ganesan was surprised by this, as he had no such plans at the time. The next day, a letter arrived from a friend inviting him to Germany. As he traveled frequently, Ganesan included Germany in the itinerary of his next trip.

Before leaving on this journey, however, he went to see Yogi Ramsuratkumar to ask his blessings, as ever. Feeling somewhat bereft, on this day, with a sense that he did not really want to go, Ganesan lamented to the Godchild, saying, "Again I am being sent away. I don't like it. I am all alone, Swami."

Yogi Ramsuratkumar consoled his friend, patting his head as he said: "You are never alone, Ganesha. This beggar is always with you.

He will be with you wherever you go. My Father's Blessings on you. Now go!"

Arriving in Germany, and en route from the airport to his host's home, as the car sped along the autobahn, suddenly the thought of the sweet beggar's words came to Ganesan's mind. At precisely the same instant, he noticed that two other vehicles were inching up on the car in which he rode – one in the right lane, the other on the left. The van on the right bore the trademark "Brahma" and the car on the left – "Ram." Like two protective hands, these two vehicles stayed in this position for a long time before moving on. For Ganesan, the message was fully clear, a sign of Yogi Ramsuratkumar's all-protective love.

Such signs continued throughout Ganesan's journey. In Hamburg, Bonn, Frankfurt, the billboards announced, "Begin your day with RAMA" referring to a local brand of margarine. Each time the sign was noted, Ganesan remembered Yogi Ramsuratkumar's blessings with gratitude.

From Germany he moved on to the U.S. and landed in Boston. Walking through the airport, Ganesan was approached by a Western man who politely inquired if India was his homeland. When Ganesan said yes, the man asked enthusiastically, "Do you know the saint who lives in South India, Yogi Ramsuratkumar?"[88]

Instructions to Writers

As a writer, my ears came to attention upon hearing Professor Sadhu Rangarajan speak about his own process in writing *Glimpses of a Great Yogi*. "This beggar will write through you," Bhagwan had told him as he began the project. It was the same message that Yogi Ramsuratkumar had given to Caylor Wadlington, more than fifteen years previously.

When Rangarajan asked Yogi Ramsuratkumar to edit the book before it was printed, the Godchild refused. "This is as it is," he said. "Whatever you write, that is going to be this beggar's words."[89]

Yogiji wanted no editing. In a manuscript that Rangarajan reviewed prior to publication, even the name of Yogi Ramsuratkumar had been incorrectly written, or was incomplete. In some cases the author had referred to "Yogi Ramkumar," for instance. But again,

Bhagwan refused to let Rangarajan tell the author to change it. "Whatever has come into his mind [the mind of the author], it will stand," Yogi Ramsuratkumar said.

Time has proven the Godman's words to be brilliantly true. The overall mood and intention behind the works that have praised Yogi Ramsuratkumar and communicated the teachings of his life have far overshadowed the editorial blunders and even the occasional misinterpretation or misrepresentation of the "facts" of the case.

राम

A student of Lee Lozowick's had written a number of books relating to Indian themes, including a short work about Yogi Ramsuratkumar. Lee contemplated publishing these books for the Indian audience and offered the first one to Yogi Ramsuratkumar for his approval. Regarding the first project, Yogi Ramsuratkumar made a few minor comments, suggesting some changes to the work. Lee complied immediately, aligned to the beggar's wishes. When the next project was proposed, Yogi Ramsuratkumar told Lee that he could publish *whatever he wished*. No checking or editing would be forthcoming from the master.

Lee explained that his level of responsibility was now much heavier than before, and his own discrimination about what he would publish and what he would not had become exceedingly acute. Because of the complete trust that Yogi Ramsuratkumar had invested in him, it remained crucial for Lee to establish full resonance with his master's wishes at a level of mind and heart. He could no longer use external feedback as a safety net.

राम

In 1991, Vijaya Fedorschak questioned the beggar about writing a biography of him. The Godchild made it clear that Vijaya should not write about "this dirty sinner's past" because it is so dirty. In the course of their conversation, in which Vijaya and other Westerners tried to plead their case for a biography, they received a strong communication about what was beneficial to write about and what was not. Vijaya noted that he understood from the beggar's words that "in writing about saints, teachers, and others who inspire us, one should only write good things, things that uplift and inspire people, things that make people feel good and happy. The 'dirt' should be omitted, because there is nothing to gain by digging up the past."

Concluding, Yogi Ramsuratkumar urged Vijaya that if he had to write about the "dirt" to kindly do so only "after this poor beggar passes."[90]

Nobody Listens

In contrast to the way in which some have attempted to follow the beggar's directives to the letter, most have fallen short. The voice of ego is so strong that even when the instructions are perfectly clear, it will overpower the master's voice.

At one point Yogi Ramsuratkumar told one of the members of the ashram administration to receive a medical checkup for his heart. The man in question, however, kept postponing the visit to his doctor. This man's doctor was visiting Yogi Ramsuratkumar one day and the saint inquired if the administrator had yet seen him for treatment. Upon hearing that he hadn't, Swamiji railed: "Nobody listens to this beggar. Whenever this beggar says something, nobody bothers to listen."

When the doctor returned to his home-office he called this administrator, urged on by the beggar's recommendations. "What, man! What you have done? You are supposed to have a medical checkup," he remonstrated to his friend. Still the other man tried to postpone the inevitable. When the doctor insisted, the fellow finally agreed to come in the next day.

The checkup revealed a serious heart problem, one that demanded surgery. Returning to Tiruvannamalai, the man went running to Yogi Ramsuratkumar, lamenting, "Swamiji...heart problem...the doctor says...surgery."

"Go and have it," Yogiji said, directly and calmly, meaning, "Have it taken care of." The man followed the Godchild's suggestions and his heart problem was successfully attended.[91]

राम

An Indian devotee who came to visit the beggar brought with him a pot of fresh coffee, which his mother had made for Yogi Ramsuratkumar. The Godchild gave explicit instructions to the woman's son as to how to distribute the coffee to the guests who were present.

When the young man served the coffee, he did not abide by the master's instruction. In fact, because he hadn't listened carefully he actually did everything wrong.

Seeing the fiasco, Swamiji shouted, "You don't know how to serve a saint!"

Then the beggar asked for the nearly empty pot of coffee. Receiving it, he poured the last few drops of coffee onto his own hand and drank them.

"It's alright now," he said. The mistakes had somehow been corrected. The incident was over.[92]

Begging Lilas

An American who visited Yogiji in 1988 reported on the elegant disregard that the Godman showed toward material wealth: "Upon the arrival of tea, another devotee produced a 100-rupee note and he wanted to give it to Yogi Ramsuratkumar. He refused at first, but upon further insistence, wryly took it and dropped it behind the hallway steps. Laughing loudly, he said, 'You see how this beggar begs,' and later he repeated, 'Now you know how this beggar begs.'"[93]

राम

Mrs. Saradamani Chinnasamy, daughter of the famous Indian poet and scholar Thiru Thooran, reported that many years ago, in Madras, a beggar knocked at her front door asking for food, and she provided him with a hearty meal. The next week, the same beggar reappeared and demanded food, and this time, since she was in a hurry, she just gave him enough money to buy one complete meal in a nearby restaurant. The week after that the same beggar reappeared and demanded food, just as she and her husband were stepping out after a small argument. This time, she refused to oblige the beggar.

"If He Walks it is the Teaching"

The next week, Mrs. Saradamani and her husband went on a regular visit to meet Yogi Ramsuratkumar, whom they had known for years. Yogiji repeatedly posed the question, "Is begging a crime in India?" to her lawyer husband, who kept trying to answer Yogiji from the point of Indian law. As the saint's question persisted, however, Mrs. Saradamani soon understood that it was Yogiji himself who had come in a different form to Madras to her house. With tears in her eyes, she sought Yogiji's blessings.[94]

राम

Another devotee, a professor at Saradha College, Salem, was once approached by a beggar at a bus station. Immediately after giving the beggar some alms she "looked up at him and had the vision of Bhagwan," Yogi Ramsuratkumar.[95]

A similar thing occurred for this writer when traveling in Germany in the fall of 2001 with a co-worker who shared her devotion to Yogi Ramsuratkumar. As we arrived at the bus station, which was our destination, I noticed a disheveled woman seated on a bench, surrounded with several shopping bags of what looked like scraps and trash. The woman's head was wrapped in a turban-like hat.

As soon as we stepped off the bus, the woman looked in our direction and raised her hands above her head, palms facing outward, as if in blessing. It was a gesture immediately reminiscent of Yogi Ramsuratkumar, who would raise his hands and say, "My Father blesses you."

My companion had not seen this "blessing" act, as he was preoccupied with carrying our luggage. But by the time we walked past the bench on which the woman sat, he too could not help but notice her. She was mumbling something as we passed.

"Did you hear what that woman was saying?" he asked me, quite breathlessly, when we had passed her. I had not.

"She said, 'Yogi Ramsuratkumar,' several times," he reported in amazement.

Less than five minutes later, climbing the steps to the train platform opposite the bus stand, we both looked back to where the woman had been seated, but she was nowhere to be seen.

Without doubt we felt we had received a gift from Yogi Ramsuratkumar who can assume the form of anything and anyone to turn devotees to the remembrance of God.

For the rest of the day, my attention was effortlessly drawn to poor, simple, hard-working people wherever they showed up. Although on this day I was working in a high-powered and sophisticated business environment, I was graced to remember Yogi Ramsuratkumar whenever he crossed my path in the person of one of these service people.

राम

In the darshan one day in 1996, Yogi Ramsuratkumar asked Lee if he would contact another American devotee and pay him a visit. No address was known, and no information offered, but nonetheless Lee responded that he would try.

Ten minutes later the Godchild motioned Lee to his side again, and made the same request. "I'll see if I can contact him," Lee responded graciously, as he had the first time, although probably still wondering how he would ever find one man with no address…a needle in a haystack! Evidently, however, the slightest ripple of doubt still existed for the master. "I'll see if" was not the full assurance Yogi Ramsuratkumar needed to carry out his Father's work.

Slapping Lee on the back and laughing, the beggar declared, "You'll do it!"

After that, however, Yogi Ramsuratkumar called Lee back to him once more in the brief interim of the darshan gathering on this December day.

"This beggar is begging you," the Godchild said with simple innocence and urgency.

"I will," Lee responded the third time, with unhesitating clarity, regardless of any logical considerations. The interchange of the moment was then complete, and Yogi Ramsuratkumar appeared completely satisfied.[96]

Lee did manage to find and meet this man shortly after returning to the States.

He Knows Everything

The subtlety of Yogi Ramsuratkumar's work with his devotees was astonishing. His ability to read literally every aspect of mind and heart was sometimes encouraging, often shocking. By paying close attention to him, however, astute devotees learned that it was generally unnecessary to ask a question directly, as his body, his seemingly unrelated conversation with someone else, or other immediate circumstances surrounding him, would often provide the answer more clearly than specific words.

"Yogiji never answered to me, because I never questioned Him about anything," Krishna Carcelle wrote of his master, Yogi Ramsuratkumar. "He knew exactly what I needed and worked in His way, beyond mind, like Dakshinamurti. He gave me all answers, most of the time without any word."[97]

राम

Why are we doing this? Caylor Wadlington wondered one day, late in 1979, as he sat silently meditating in the presence of Yogi Ramsuratkumar. "I considered various answers," Caylor wrote, "but when I spoke inwardly the words 'for humanities sake we are doing it,' the Master [who have been unmoving up until then] suddenly slapped his fan on the ground."

This gesture was a clear affirmation that Caylor's internal answer had been correct.[98]

In the same vein, with a slightly humorous overtone, Caylor learned something when the master belched.

"Don't divide, Mr. Kay. Don't divide." Yogi Ramsuratkumar had used these words with Caylor on a number of occasions. It was his way of teaching his young biographer the unity of all things. As he repeated these same words one day in January 1980, the beggar "reached over, drank several cups of water and then belched loudly a number of times."

Caylor recorded in his journal at the time: "It seemed appropriate. It was like a signal to search more deeply and accept what I usually deny as vulgar, unwholesome, dirty or unhygienic. Suddenly my biological and sexual levels of being – to such a large extent hidden and denied – came into mind. These too I could feel as natural and pure amidst the oneness of the being."[99]

राम

On January 31, 1994, during a visit to Yogi Ramsuratkumar, P.V. Karunakaran understood without a doubt that the beggar read every thought.

"As we sat in Bhagavan's Divine presence, I noted that he was caressing the hand of Ma Devaki, who was seated on Bhagavan's right side. I started envying her. As if Bhagavan read my mind, he directed Ma Devaki to ask me to sit on his left side. Much to my joy and surprise, Bhagavan began to caress my right hand. Then he wanted Ma Devaki to light a cigarette for him. I thought again, "How blessed you are, Ma." Sure enough, to light the next cigarette, Bhagavan handed over the box of matches to me! Soon lunch was served. Bhagavan wanted us to start eating. I hesitated, as I wished [to get] something out of Bhagavan's leaf (lunch was served on plantain leaves) by way of prasad to begin with. But I did not have the boldness to say this to Bhagavan. Bhagavan obviously read my mind again and gave me a piece of 'papad' from his leaf! I began eating. After lunch the Master was to rest for a while. As a pillow was brought, I tried to get up from the mat we were sitting on. But Bhagavan asked me to remain where I was, put the pillow on my lap and slept (or appeared to be sleeping) for some time, holding my right thumb, like a child. Touch was extensively used by Bhagavan to bless his devotees."[100]

राम

"There was a power in him, in his every action, that left no doubt that he seemed to know what he did and what was going on with you." In this way, Kirsti, who had been under Yogi Ramsuratkumar's influence since 1976, described his way of working. "There was a sense of mastery of his every movement, action, word, glance. Even Sai Baba, the dog, was part of how he worked. [Many] people did not dare to knock at his door if he was inside the house when they arrived to see him. They waited, feeling that somehow he *knew* they were there and would come if he wasn't too busy with something else."[101]

राम

Ramamurti, a devotee who played a strong role in the early arrangements for the beggar's ashram, was sitting with his master one day in the early 1990s. As he basked in Yogi Ramsuratkumar's presence, the devotee instinctively knew that this was no ordinary sage. He had the impression that the Godman was looking through him, and saying, "You fool. I know your whole history."

What had occurred on that day, which Ramamurti did not discern until several days later, was that Bhagwan "actually uttered a few words that had to do with my personal history – words that are only known to myself, my wife, and one other person."

Without the devotee telling anything about his past, Yogiji had used these words in such a way that the other people who were sitting nearby did not even realize that what was being said was actually a personal communication directed at Ramamurti. (The whole incident is strangely reminiscent of Jesus's response to a group of men who were about to stone the woman taken in adultery. Besides telling, "Let him who is without sin among you cast the first stone," Jesus also created a pattern in the sand at his feet. Many interpreters believe that he was writing names and "sins.") Yogi Ramsuratkumar was indicating to Ramamurti that he knew everything.[102]

राम

Shri V. Ramanujachari, an old devotee who knew Yogi Ramsuratkumar from the early 1970s, asserted that the beggar "was clairvoyant."

One incident above all others proved this to Ramanujachari beyond question. "Once when I was doing the circumambulation of the red idol 'Sambandha Vinagayar' at the left side of the entrance of the Valluvar Gopuram [in the Siva temple] and standing for a while silent before the idol, Yogi RamSuratkumar came rushing from his Sannadhi Street abode to the temple and accosted me [saying], 'Oh,

679

it is only you! I had an intuition that some one was waiting for me here.'"[103]

राम

When this biographer sat in the presence of Yogi Ramsuratkumar in December 1995 as an article was read aloud that praised the unfailing devotion of Mother Krishnabai, the devotee of Swami Papa Ramdas, I formed a silent prayer to the beggar asking that I too might have the privilege of reading this piece. Twenty seconds later, as the current reader concluded, Yogi Ramsuratkumar called for Lee Lozowick to "ask one of your people to read this again." Without hesitating, Lee handed the book to me. I was overcome with both awe and gratitude, certainly, at being given this opportunity to honor Mataji Krishnabai in the beggar's presence. But the larger effect that continued, over time, was a deepened appreciation of the Godman's knowledge of everything, and his responsiveness to my unvoiced prayers.

राम

A couple came to visit Yogi Ramsuratkumar from Salem. When they arrived, much to their surprise the beggar immediately sent them away. He wouldn't even allow them into his house for a moment.

"You go to your place," he said firmly, and they did, heading back to Salem.

As the couple was leaving, Yogiji asked a young boy who was attending him to go to the next house on Sannadhi Street and to inquire if there was water coming from their tap. It was a strange request, seemingly unrelated to anything. However, when the boy returned he reported to Bhagwan that indeed no water was available. Again, Bhagwan sent the boy to the next house, and the next, and each time the boy came back to report that there was no water coming from any of the taps on the block.

When this couple reached their home later that day, their neighbors informed them that their house tap had been left open and that the water was flooding the house. Fortunately, they had arrived back in time to avert further and more serious damage.[104]

राम

In 1974, a crowd of visitors had gathered with the beggar for an afternoon darshan. As the hour grew late, the Godman dismissed them all, except for one man, who was kept at his side. The man wondered at his good fortune in being given such a privilege, but a short time later found that he was overcome with extreme nausea and pain. Making his way to a toilet area, the man was wracked with severe vomiting, to the point where he fainted several times. Once his condition had stabilized a bit, and with the help of a few passersby, the man was brought back to the feet of Yogi Ramsuratkumar. Knowingly, the beggar looked at his weary devotee and explained, "If this beggar had let you leave on the desert road, nobody would have come to help you."[105]

राम

In early 1979, a Danish man, Preben Sorenson, accompanied Caylor Wadlington on a visit to Tiruvannamalai with the intention of meeting Yogi Ramsuratkumar. Preben had read the small biography, *The Godchild*, and had expressed a desire to translate the book into Danish.

The beggar greeted Caylor warmly, held his hand and remained silent for a few moments in which the young man felt his equilibrium returning after the long journey he had just completed. Then Caylor introduced his friend, Preben.

With barely a moment's hesitation, the Dane reached into his shirt and took out a gold and silver talisman inlaid with several different stones. Holding the necklace in his hand and extending it to Ramsuratkumar, Preben boldly expressed the wish that the Yogi might "magnetize it." It was exactly the kind of self-serving request that seekers have forever demanded of their prophets and gurus. Many others, both Indians and curious Westerners, had made similar requests to Yogi Ramsuratkumar over the years. Their interest in a Godman had to do with his ability to perform magic, healing, miracles.

Ramsuratkumar received the request graciously, however. He held the medallion in his hand for quite a while. He even took it out into the sun to examine it more closely. When he came back, he handed the item back to Preben, stating, to Caylor's surprise: "Some other holy man seems to have touched it." This was in fact true. Preben had already had the thing "magnetized" once by another person of power. Excited by the beggar's ability to read energy, Preben was more motivated than ever to get some magnetizing done, this time on a ring that he wore. He again made the same request, handing the ring to Yogi Ramsuratkumar.

The beggar was tremendously solicitous still. Holding the item, examining it carefully, he turned to Preben once again. This time, the Danish man's face, once bright with expectation of some acknowledgement, clouded with disappointment as Yogi Ramsuratkumar informed him, with absolute candor, that the ring had very little spiritual significance. In fact, the beggar said, although the ring "was not cooperating with the rest of the system," he had done whatever he could to get it to "work" for Preben.[106]

राम

How Yogi Ramsuratkumar knew the things he knew was always a source of great wonder to people. Certainly he was at the hub of a subtle network, receiving letters and spoken communications about devotees and friends from many many sources. But, since he rarely revealed his sources, one never knew whether there was a logical explanation for what he seemed to know. Overall, however, most devotees have reported that his knowledge was based in some much deeper, psychic understanding. He really *did* seem to know everything, not in the way a learned man knows things but the way an innocent child might suddenly surprise you with a question or a comment that hits a nail on the head.

A foreigner was present at Yogi Ramsuratkumar's darshan one day in 1990, and the beggar engaged the man at some length. He asked the man about an associate of his, giving the impression that he [Yogi Ramsuratkumar] also knew the man. *Where is he now?* the Godchild inquired.

"If He Walks it is the Teaching"

When the visitor said that his associate was currently in New York, Bhagwan interrupted and corrected him, saying that the man was actually in India, not far away in a place called Cochin, a city in central Kerala, South India.

The foreign guest argued, trying to tell the master otherwise, but Bhagwan insisted. Later, to his amazement, the man learned that Bhagwan had been correct.

राम

Calling Yogi Ramsuratkumar his "unfailing protector," S. Ramanatha Bhatt told a remarkable story of the guru's seeming omniscience. In 1978, during a business trip that took him and his companions to Singapore, Ramanatha unexpectedly found himself in foreign territory with his visa or passport left back at his hotel. He had been out walking and had curiously crossed a large bridge that connects Singapore with Malayasia, when he was apprehended by the authorities. Without identification, he was about to be constrained as an illegal alien and placed in a cell awaiting a hearing.

"At that crucial time I remembered Yogi Ramsuratkumar and prayed ardently to him to wriggle me out of this mess," the man reported. Amazingly, within one hour the chief immigration officer came through for a surprise inspection and, thoroughly believing Ramanatha's story of ignorance, arranged for his immediate release. In his own jeep, the officer escorted Ramanatha first to an inn for some refreshments and then back across the bridge to the Singapore border, where he arranged for another escort to take the astonished man back to his hotel. "While parting, he gave me a memento (a Schaefer pen) for remembrance. I actually shed tears for his benevolent act," Ramanatha wrote.

The story was far from over, however. A week later, in the presence of Yogi Ramsuratkumar, the devotee narrated the event to the beggar, who interrupted with the inquiry, "Is that all?" As Ramanatha began to supply more details, Yogiji proceeded to ask specific questions. *Was the chief officer wearing white pants, a blue coat, a blue tie and a name badge with the name Ebrahim?* Ramanatha was stunned.

Did not the officer take him to a tavern for refreshments? And what about a Schaefer pen?

"After hearing this I suddenly fell on his lotus feet after the thought pervaded in my mind as to who else could have come in the garb of an Immigration officer and helped me to come out of the greatest ordeal of my life, other than Yogi Ramsuratkumar."[107]

Interestingly, could there have been a more suitable name for the Godchild of Tiruvannamalai in disguise than "Ebrahim" – Abraham (a-brahma)?

राम

Another story of the guru as protector was told by Justice Arunachalam in an article entitled, "Yogi Ramsuratkumar, Everywhere."[108] Before leaving on a family trip to Nepal, the Justice had given his complete itinerary to Yogiji, as the master had requested. The beggar was most concerned to know exactly what time each flight was expected to take off, and when it was expected to land.

At the conclusion of their vacation, on the return flight from Katmandu to Varanasi, the plane encountered extreme turbulence, causing it to fly "hither and thither, sideways, upwards and downwards." The passengers sensed that the pilot had lost control, and their hysterical shouts and "wails and clamours to Gods" filled the space within the cabin.

As he was buffeted about in his seat, the Justice immediately began to chant aloud the name of Yogi Ramsuratkumar. A few of those sitting close to him looked with panicked expressions, demanding to know who this "Yogi Ramsuratkumar" was. To this Arunachalam admonished, "that it did not matter, since He was God and that everyone should join me and chant HIS NAME in as much of a high pitch as was possible." A few nearby passengers weakly joined in the chant, while Justice Arunachalam cried out on behalf of all, "Yogi Ramsuratkumar please save them."

As the bumping and jolting continued, so did the devotee's invocation of his master's name. Arunachalam said that he was confident that he and his whole family "would together reach His [Yogi Ramsuratkumar's] feet in the event of a calamity." Whether he lived or died, therefore, the end result would be same – as "heaven" was found at the beggar's feet!

In what seemed like a miracle, the plane landed safely. Later, an airport-based engineer confided to Justice Arunachalam that they "were certain of a crash…due to its getting stuck up in an unusual storm."

At precisely the same time as this event was occuring, Justice's brother Dr. Ramanathan and another friend were sitting in darshan in Tiruvannamalai with Yogi Ramsuratkumar. "Where would Justice Arunachalam be now?" the beggar asked the doctor.

When Dr. Ramanathan replied that his brother and family should be landing in Varanasi, but that he was unsure of the exact time, "[a] smiling Bhagawan proclaimed then at 5:15 P.M., [which was] the time of our landing at Varanasi: 'Justice Arunachalam, Lakshmi, Sujatha and Lalitha have just now safely landed.'"

राम

"One day early in my stay there," wrote Mariana Caplan, "when I let him know I would be staying in Tiruvannamalai for the following six weeks, he informed me that I would not be staying for six *weeks,* but instead for six *years!* Yogi Ramsuratkumar died six years later, almost to the day. Although I did not stay physically by his side for those years, I would never have guessed the prophetic nature of his commentary."[109]

राम

Dr. Venkatasubramanian met Yogi Ramsuratkumar in 1967 at the railway station, where the beggar sat "clad in old clothes with bundles of old newspapers around and with a fan in his hand." The visitor was struck speechless by the radiance of the Godman, who spoke first, saying, "My dear son, I was expecting you, sit down."

In the many years that he knew Yogiji, the doctor is assured that "[h]e knew everything, past, present and future."

As Venkatasubramanian had written a biography of Indira Gandhi, he also knew that Yogi Ramsuratkumar was extremely fond of Indira and her son, Rajiv. As the younger Gandhi was planning a tour of Tamil Nadu and Pondicherry in May 1991, the doctor hoped to bring Rajiv to Tiruvannamalai.

"In early May 1991, I met the Yogi and told him that I was going to Delhi to meet Shri Rajiv and I wanted the Yogi's permission to take him to Tiruvannamalai to have His darshan. As soon as I uttered these words, the Yogi became tense and uttered the word 'No, No don't attempt to bring him here. He cannot come, he cannot come,' and the Yogi disappeared in the inner rooms of the Sannadhi Street house. I was taken aback, but I kept mum. My friend the late Shri A.R.P.N. Rajamanikam Nadar and I were not able to decipher these prophetic words of the Yogi till May 21ˢᵗ, when Rajiv Gandhi was assassinated."[110]

राम

One of the most touching, and poignantly humorous, stories of Yogi Ramsuratkumar's vast knowing occurred for Mani in 1994. For a period of one hundred days, Mani promised the master that he would refrain from eating meat and stop reading the newspapers or watching television. It was a purifying sadhana to help him in overcoming his attachments. The hardest craving to lose, for Mani, was for nonvegetarian food. As much as he struggled against this desire, it came back fiercely.

One day, without anyone knowing of it, Mani asked one of the boys who worked at the ashram to buy some chicken briyani for him at a nearby restaurant. The plan was simple. The boy was to bring the food back to Mani's residence and leave it on the table in time for lunch. Mani would go home at his usual midday break, eat the chicken, and return to the ashram, with no one the wiser.

Unexpectedly, however, Yogi Ramsuratkumar wanted Mani at his side throughout that morning. When lunchtime came, Devaki Ma served both men their meal, which Mani could not refuse. After lunch, Yogiji engaged Mani at the Sudama House until nearly four in the afternoon, and finally sent him back to the ashram with the clear directive that he should go there without any side trips, even to this own bungalow. There Mani worked until after six, when Yogi Ramsuratkumar finally gave him permission to leave.

Returning to his house for dinner, Mani was craving his secretly acquired meal more than ever. Imagine his disappointment and even shock when he found "nothing in the box except two chicken bones and some ants." The insects had consumed his stolen feast.

"The next morning," Mani wrote, "when Bhagwan saw me come into Sudama, He laughed. It was obvious that He knew, but I had no idea how it was possible. He asked me if I was alright and called to Devaki to say, 'Mani got a lot of blessings yesterday. He not only fed devotees and workers, he fed a lot of ants and insects.'"

Hearing these words, Mani filled with tears and deep remorse. The previous night, in realizing his folly, he was overcome with gratitude for his master, who had thus saved him from an act of disobedience. But he also hated himself for his devious ways.

Yogi Ramsuratkumar, for his part, realized all of it. Taking Mani's hand with enormous tenderness, he said: "Don't bother Mani. Everything happens for the good. You are my Father's choice; there is nothing to worry about. You can go now and attend to your work. My Father blesses you."[111]

Innocence and Tears

In the early years, on an occasion when a group of visitors came to Yogi Ramsuratkumar, the company sat outside around the Godman. As rain began, however, the guests became uncomfortable, and some of them took shelter a short distance away from where the beggar sat. From their covered protection they called to Yogi Ramsuratkumar to come inside, warning that he would be thoroughly soaked...which was not a good thing, in their view.

The Godchild, however, merely looked at these people incredulously. "This beggar has lived outside for twenty years. What is some rain going to do to this beggar?" he said.

Embarrassed by their choice of comfort over elegant protocol in the presence of the Godman, these friends left the shelter and once again joined Yogi Ramsuratkumar in the rain.[112]

राम

Yogi Ramsuratkumar received a letter from a woman devotee. The letter was read aloud to him one day as he sat in his house on Sannadhi Street. The devotee was heartbroken, and complaining. It seems that her husband had brought his "lady love" home to live with them.

Yogi Ramsuratkumar advised the woman to give full support to her husband and thereby make life meaningful to *all three* of them. If she did this, he claimed that everything would turn out to be all right.

It was profoundly unconventional advice. What actually happened is not known.[113]

राम

A young couple came once to ask for blessings for a better salary for the man. Yogiji asked the man how much he currently earned. When he was told, the beggar looked intently at the couple and said: "That is enough. You can feel content with that and live happily."[114]

राम

One of his main qualities was unpredictability," Kirsti explained. "On one Guru Purnima day he told me, 'This beggar wants to be free to move without a fixed program.' He cut the singing session short that day, and later I saw him wading in puddles of rainwater in the temple, holding the hand of a young man from Bangalore who used to visit him often."[115]

राम

"One moment he will dance, the next moment he will give you fire," said Jai Ram, speaking of his adored master, Yogi Ramsuratkumar. "One moment he is sad, suffering something. He is all, he is everything. He used to shed tears also. He shed a lot of tears."[116]

THE DEATH OF GOD

Guru is the immortal, all-pervading Spirit. Never look upon him as a mere person. If you develop this attitude from the beginning, you will realize that the Guru never dies. – Swami Papa Ramdas

As Jesus Christ hung on the cross, in his ultimate sacrifice on behalf of humanity, he was fiercely taunted. "Aha! You were going to tear down the Temple and build it back up in three days! Now come down from the cross and save yourself!" And in the same way, the high priests and teachers of the law mocked him, saying: "He saved others, but himself he cannot save. Let us see the Messiah, the king of Israel, come down from the cross now, and we will believe in him." (Mark 15:29-31)

A similar myopia has endured throughout the ages. It is not only detractors who question the power and authority of great masters or healers when these extraordinary individuals suffer illness or approach death. Even devotees will staunchly defend the master's ability to wield some supernatural power and thereby rise from the sickbed, renewed with vigor, when all signs are clearly pointing to the lawfulness of and intentional surrender to impending death.

Devotees are naturally attached to the physical form and presence of their teacher, their beloved. It is understandable. As humans, they rightly grieve the passing of the one who has shown them love beyond measure. They naturally desire to lessen the obvious pain that their master suffers, even if it means taking that pain on themselves. Several close devotees of Yogi Ramsuratkumar honestly admitted making this prayer during his last days. Yet, for many, devotion is commonly shadowed by a fear of abandonment. They temporarily, at least, obscure a truth that the master has *always* been pointing to. In this case, that "This body is not Yogi Ramsuratkumar." Although they have given lip service to the saint's transcendent nature, they hold on, grasping for attention…reassurance…anything; and thus making the master's work at the end so much more difficult.

"He was too busy helping other people to relieve *their* suffering to spend even ten minutes relieving his own suffering," recounted one of Yogi Ramsuratkumar's close devotees. "And sometimes he was actually crying because of the extreme pain of his body. But, with his surrender to God, it was clear that *he* did not come first."[1]

राम

Throughout his life of sadhana, Yogi Ramsuratkumar had ever embraced only the most austere physical conditions. He had nothing to call his own. He slept in the open. He endured beatings and humiliations without a word of defense. Now, as his body weakened beyond repair, there was only one response – the silent acceptance of his Father's will. Again and again he reminded us, "Everything is in the hands of My Father." On one occasion, in elaborating upon this state of complete surrender, the Godchild said: "Father keeps this Beggar's body as it would suit His work. What is Father's work?…to keep up the law and order of the cosmos. Father uses this Beggar as a centre for His work. So whatever way He keeps this body is alright."[2]

> Someone asked me what I would do
>> if You were to go away, oh my life's breath.
> I answered thusly:
>> "He was never here so how could He leave?"[3] – Lee Lozowick

राम

The Death of God

"You are not well, Bhagwan," said Ashish Bagrodia, a disciple from Bombay, when he visited one day in 1999.

"Who has told you?" Bhagwan said.

"Bret has written a letter," Ashish responded.

Then Yogiji laughed. In a mood of profound faith and resignation, he began to instruct his young devotee: "These hands are rotting, Ashish. These legs are rotting. Everything is rotting. This beggar is rotting. Let the body rot, Ashish! Let Father keep this body the way *He* wants."[4]

Throughout the early months of 2000, Yogi Ramsuratkumar was extremely ill. A tumor was discovered in July 1999, and high fevers ravaged him almost constantly. The treatments of local doctors had failed and specialists had been enlisted, yet the Godchild wanted no surgery. As his body gradually became more immobilized, he spoke less, except to Devaki Ma, who remained always at his side.

"He sat with closed eyes," Mani reported. "I could see Him suffering in pain, but He never uttered a word about His suffering. Only when he was sleeping could we see facial gestures that indicated the degree of pain in His precious body."[5]

With his movements restricted, the decision was made to move from Sudama House to the Abode, the attached apartment at the far end of the ashram temple (Pradhan Mandir). This Abode space had long been planned as his ultimate residence, yet the master seemed reticent to live there. The building was air-conditioned, among other things, a factor that Yogi Ramsuratkumar did not tolerate easily. Even after the move was made, he much preferred to lie in the makeshift screened porch adjacent to the Veda Patashala on the ashram grounds. Here he could feel the breezes of the trees and listen to the sounds of nature – particularly the birdsong that had inspired him throughout his life. "It could be very hot or very cold out there, but Yogiji loved it," Devaki Ma reported. Inside the air-conditioned room, however, he sometimes asked, "Are we living in a hotel?" And at other times, surrendering to whatever condition was imposed, he remarked: "Good or bad, this is this beggar's Abode."[6]

"This beggar is consistent in his inconsistency," Yogi Ramsuratkumar joked with Justice Arunachalam about the ups and downs of his physical health.[7] Indeed, his illness was not without periods of respite. Each time his condition appeared to improve, his devotees were ecstatic, convinced that he was on the mend for good, and soon to rejoin them at last! "Somewhere deep in my heart I always thought that all suffering, which Yogiji's body was enduring, was one of His Lilas and He would ultimately recover and be OK. I really never thought that it would get so worse that He would eventually leave His Body," wrote Ashish, in a humbling and candid expression of his own hopes.[8]

Still, despite modest improvements, Yogi Ramsuratkumar could not walk, and a variety of conveyances were engineered so that he could be carried into the temple for short periods, or taken outside to sit under the shade of a favorite tree. He was even driven, by his request, on some short trips. One morning, as the devotees sat in his presence outside in the shade, Yogi Ramsuratkumar talked about making a journey to Tanjore (known today as Thanjavur) to see the

Yogi Ramsuratkumar rests outside,
attended by Devaki Ma and Rajmohan

Brihadishwara Temple, an architectural wonder containing many images of Lord Krishna. Although it was located in central Tamil Nadu, a trip to this temple would have been an arduous one, and the idea was temporarily postponed.

The next day, however, as Yogi Ramsuratkumar was still in the mood, careful preparations were made to accommodate him. Heading in the direction of Thanjavur, with his doctor and constant attendants, the party stopped at Sathanur, a small village about twenty-two kilometers from Tiruvannamalai. This popular tourist spot on the Pennai River is the site of a huge hydroelectric dam, a botanical garden and a zoological park. On the verandah of a government building near the river's edge, where Bhagwan rested enjoying the breezes, a huge photograph on the wall displayed the Brihadishwara Temple in vivid detail. Yogi Ramsuratkumar sat looking at the picture of the temple. After some time, at his request, the entire group returned to Tiruvannamalai. The beggar had seen Brihadishwara, as he had wished.[9]

On July 30, 2000, Yogi Ramsuratkumar also made a final trip to Tapovanam, to the ashram of his great mentor, Swami Gnanananda Giri.[10] Here, as devotees of both masters gathered, the beggar sat in the pillared courtyard not far from the shrine that enclosed the empowered statue of the Swami that Yogi Ramsuratkumar had loved so much. As he rested in these familiar surroundings, he was approached for prasad, which he distributed freely to all who attended.[11]

Even as his weakness grew more pronounced day by day, Yogi Ramsuratkumar's concern for his devotees remained paramount. He wanted those around him to be happy, rejoicing in the play of his Father. According to Mani, their dancing and singing was the name of the game when Yogi Ramsuratkumar was strong enough to encourage it. One beautiful photo, taken in his Abode in the first half of 2000, shows the beggar reclining in his chair while Mani, Rajalakshmi, Devaki, Vijayalakshmi, Rajeswari and Justice Arunachalam dance around him. They each hold wooden sticks, which they click against those of the other dancers. Even Yogi Ramsuratkumar held sticks in his hands. It was a modified form of a traditional North Indian folk dance known as *kollatam*, and the beggar laughed with delight, heartened by their joy.[12]

ONLY GOD

राम

> This beggar is nothing, but he has faith in the Vedas, in the
> words of the Rishis, Munis. Have total faith.
>
> — Yogi Ramsuratkumar[13]

On February 26, 2000, the foundation was laid for another
building – the last that Bhagwan would supervise in the ashram construction. Called the Ma Devaki Veda Patasala, its purpose was of
utmost importance to Yogi Ramsuratkumar. It would house a Vedic
institute dedicated to the study and preservation of Vedic scriptures
and Vedic culture. Accommodations would also be provided within
the building for a chosen scholar who would use this sanctuary on
the ashram to further his studies.

In speaking of this project, the saint was passionate, as he had
always been about the Vedas and other aspects of India's spiritual-cul-
tural heritage. Even as his health failed, his enthusiasm for this work
increased. On several occasions, a much-beloved devotee, Suresh, a
Brahmin who had often led the Vedic rituals conducted during the
beggar's Jayanti, was instructed in the significance of this venture:
"This Beggar keeps calling you here again and again, and keeps
telling you about the Vedas and the importance of the Veda Patasala
so that it gets deeply imprinted on your heart and mind that this is
the most important work here. Other people may forget, but this
beggar wants you to always remember that the work of the Ma
Devaki Veda Patasala is the most important work. Suresh, at any cost
it should go on."

And again, "Suresh, in this Ashram, which goes by the name Yogi
Ramsuratkumar Ashram, the most important work is that of the
Veda Patasala. It is the heart of this Ashram."[14]

The Vedas, chanted throughout India, are the great "works" –
more precisely the great "sounds" – that are believed to keep the universe in harmony. They were first "received" by the rishis, the wise
seers of ancient times, who "heard" them, discerned their wisdom,
and burst into song, passing this knowledge along in highly symbolic language and poetry. The chanting of these transmitted scriptures

was the means whereby this sacred sound was intensified in creation. Centuries later, these root songs – the four Vedas – were finally written down. The job of keeping this chanting alive, which keeps the universe alive and balanced, is the work of the Brahmin, the "twice-born." Like so many other lovers and supporters of India's heritage, Yogi Ramsuratkumar knew that in this age of deteriorating values, this Kali Yuga, a disempowerment of the Vedas meant a greater chaos for the world.

Bhagwan also knew the odds that he faced in creating this institute. In breakfast-hut meetings and discussions at Sudama House, he had noted that similar projects had failed even when sponsored by the larger religious centers in India. In these times, as materialistic "values" from the West threatened the very substructure of Indian religious culture, it was often difficult to find good teachers and dedicated students willing to work in this area. He was realistic about it, encouraging his devotees not to become discouraged if their efforts proved frustrating. The Veda Patasala's fulfillment might not be realized for many years – even during Ma Devaki's lifetime. However, because the project was his Father's, it would eventually serve its intended purpose.[15]

Yogiji was understandably anxious to see this building finished as quickly as possible. Shri Anjaneyalu, the building contractor, responded to the master's urgency, and the work was completed by May 2000. Throughout the construction, Yogi Ramsuratkumar's attention never wavered from this important project. He used to sit in a makeshift hut opposite the building site, receiving devotees here rather than in the main building of the temple. He also spent some nights in other makeshift arrangements nearby. When the building was completed, he even slept there for a short time, and Mani noted that "I thought He would sleep in the buildings on the Ashram to impart blessings and more of His personal energetic matrix, as if He was the conduit for His Father's blessing force to enter the walls and floors and ceilings of the buildings."[16]

राम

Word circulated fast. In July 2000, an urgent phone call to central France, where Lee Lozowick was headquartered for the summer, informed him of his master's critical condition. Yogi Ramsuratkumar was calling his lovers to his side. On Reunion Island, near Mauritius, off the southern coast of Africa, Krishna Carcelle too received the news, via an e-mail message from Yogi Ramsuratkumar's attendant Rajmohan.

"I rushed to Tiruvannamalai with my young daughter and stayed there some ten days," wrote Carcelle. "On my arrival, He was suffering a lot. However, when He saw me, He welcomed that fellow with words of Love. He *was* Love."[17]

Lee Lozowick also made his way to India immediately. Like Carcelle, he found the master's state to be worsening. Soon after Yogi Ramsuratkumar's initial greetings and tender blessings to Lee, the beggar lapsed into a coma.

"I was sitting near His bed," Krishna Carcelle continued, "…holding the fan and making some fresh air with it on His body. Ma Devaki was seated on the floor, and my young daughter who was nine was singing His name and other mantras in that holy silence. This 'souvenir' will stay in my heart forever. It was my last physical darshan."[18]

According to Lee, it was obvious that Yogi Ramsuratkumar was freely approaching his imminent transition and that the Godman's work was fully complete. Nonetheless, the beggar who had never wanted even the slightest concern voiced about his physical condition was still tied by love to his devotees' wishes. While many disagreed with the decisions made at this time, medical intervention was the course taken on the Godchild's behalf.

As his suffering increased, Ma Devaki and others begged Yogi Ramsuratkumar by their constant prayers to allow hospitalization. "It was the responsibility of the devotees to take care of the body of the master," said one close devotee who had sent a letter urging those close to Bhagwan to take him to the hospital in Madras. Yogi Ramsuratkumar was alert at the time this letter arrived.

"Leave it," he said, obviously meaning, "Do not act on this man's suggestions!"[19]

As the pleas and arguments of both devotees and doctors increased, however, on August 16, 2000, Yogi Ramsuratkumar capitulated to entreaties. The next day he was taken to the hospital in Madras and placed in intensive care for three weeks under the supervision of Dr. Rangabashyam.

राम

Major surgery for bladder cancer was performed on September 11, 2000, and weeks of recovery followed. Rumors of what had happened grew and multiplied as the days progressed. In one amazing report, some devotees affirmed that the master's Divine power had made anesthesia unnecessary throughout the proceedings. It was a ridiculous claim, but another example of the type of mythologizing that easily accrues to the lives of saints. "Faith without reason always lands one in superstitions and blind beliefs," remarked Sadhu Rangarajan in learning of these outrageous stories.[20]

Once again, the real miracles performed daily by Yogi Ramsuratkumar were those of tender solicitation to others, the expression of constant faith in his Father, and complete disregard for his own condition. "Rangaraja, you do my Father's work. You *leave* this beggar," said Yogi Ramsuratkumar as he grasped the sadhu's hands during a visit to the hospital. It was the Godchild's way of affirming again that attachment to his physical form was not the focus. Rather, it was the work that was all important.

As Yogiji's recuperation from surgery continued, the desires of his devotees to see him again also intensified. Seated in a slanting chair in his hospital room, Yogi Ramsuratkumar would raise his hands in blessing as people passed before his door for yet another darshan. Some were invited in. His long-time attendant, Jai Ram, spent three days in Madras, and several intimate moments with Yogi Ramsuratkumar ensued. As he did with others, the beggar's attention was more on Jai Ram's business than it was on his own.

"When did your father pass away?" Yogi Ramsuratkumar inquired of Jai Ram.

The young man's father, who died on April 22, 1999, had been the beggar's great friend and supporter during the Godchild's early years in Tiruvannamalai. These two men would even massage each other's feet, so close was their rapport and mutual respect.

Jai Ram could read between the lines of Yogiji's question. "With this question he implied that he would also leave the body soon," the younger man said, matter-of-factly.[21]

Along these same lines, another devotee among the ashram staff remembered an interaction with Yogi Ramsuratkumar that had occurred a few months earlier. As the beggar put his attention on the construction of the Veda Patasala, a project so close to his heart, he remarked one day, "This beggar has suffered for some time. This beggar's work is over. This beggar is going to take a long rest."

Hearing these words, Ma Devaki said, "Bhagwan, you should not say that. We should die with you. We should not live without you."

Turning to his Eternal Slave, Yogi Ramsuratkumar asked, rhetorically, "Devaki, what is my age?" She immediately understood what he was saying, and remained silent.[22]

राम

In the latter part of his confinement, in the fall of 2000, Yogi Ramsuratkumar was taken for occasional outings to the beach at Chennai. "Bhagwan loved the beach at sunset," Devaki told devotees in later years. "It gave him great joy to watch the sunset."

Although the Godman was cared for constantly and carefully throughout these months, every moment away from Tiruvannamalai, away from the protection of Arunachala – his true earthly residence – became more difficult for him. As November was drawing to an end, bringing him closer to the time when his beloved son, Lee Lozowick, would make his annual trip from America, Yogi Ramsuratkumar focused his intention and his energy in one direction. Despite the contrary opinion of some, the beggar demanded that he be taken home. His wishes were honored at last.

राम

On Thursday, November 23, 2000, as devotees sat in the ashram dining hall chanting the beggar's name during the normal afternoon darshan, a mood of expectancy filled the room. Midway through the two-hour session, Venkataraman ran into the hall, announcing that Yogi Ramsuratkumar's van was approaching the gate and urging everyone to follow him out there. They needed no further invitation.

"Everybody jumped up and in a total chaos people ran to the front gate as the two white traveler vans already approached," wrote Ute Augustiniak, a resident of the nearby Hohm Sahaj Trust. "We greeted him when he drove into the ashram and further into the temple. Crowds of people followed and the supervisors of the ashram had their hands full keeping the hungry devotees at a distance while Yogi Ramsuratkumar was carried out of the vehicle."[23]

His mere physical appearance among them was miracle enough, but his obviously critical condition – "He looked exhausted and very, very weak" – caused the German woman to speculate if they would have another opportunity to see him. Imagine her surprise when, a few days later, Yogi Ramsuratkumar invited everyone to have darshan with him in the temple. "To be back into his spiritual home seemed to feed him in a way that his recovery was multiplied. He seemed completely transformed health-wise. He was bright, alive, and was very much interacting with people. He even smoked a few cigarettes, although some close devotees around him were not excited about it." Apparently, some discussion, and even some controversy, ensued about whether it was okay for him to smoke or not. At one point, when the attendants had received orders that it was forbidden, they found themselves deeply conflicted. The master was asking for his cigarettes but was being told that he could not have them! In the end, even Yogi Ramsuratkumar's direct request went unheeded, superceded by the will of those who thought they were honoring him more in refusing him; it was a travesty and a tragedy in relationship to obedience, faith, and adherence to the teaching that he lived with every breath.

राम

Lee and his company from Europe and America arrived in Tiruvannamalai on November 30, one week after Yogi Ramsuratkumar's return from Madras. Unlike in previous years, when regular darshans were held at 10 A.M. and 4 P.M., the Godman was not keeping a predictable schedule due to his condition. Instead, he might call for Lee and "his people" at any time. They needed to be ready to drop everything and jump to the master's will. Lee made it clear to his companions that he would not go anywhere, even into town, as he awaited word of Yogi Ramsuratkumar's desires. He was here for one purpose only!

As the group entered the temple for their first darshan with the beggar, one of the participants described the scene in which "Yogi Ramsuratkumar already sat, propped up by light green pillows on the background of a large, dark red reclining chair. His legs and feet were elevated so that the soles of His bare feet faced the group directly…His legs were covered with shawls. Around His head was the famous green turban. His face was pale and seemed drawn in pain, and yet He was more beautiful and sublime than ever. He appeared translucent, and so frail, but extremely present and real. His dark eyes seemed to see and read the space and every person or movement within it. Ma Devaki and Vijayalakshmi sat on a bamboo mat on the floor to His right…Yogi Ramsuratkumar sat silently and intently, his eyes fixed…on Lee alone."[24]

The intensity of these days was almost unbearable for some of these visitors – as moments of bliss in Yogiji's radiance were interspersed with the recognition that the beloved Godchild was enduring enormous pain. Yet, amazingly, the overall mood was light, and joyous, and Lee's closeness and constancy appeared to energize and delight his master greatly. Yogi Ramsuratkumar knew that all phenomena were a passing show, and with every word and gesture throughout these special darshans he urged others to join him in that recognition.

In one meeting, when Yogi Ramsuratkumar's energy was higher than usual, he called for singing and dancing by Lee's students, and then by some of his Indian women devotees. On another day, as he had done in previous years, Yogi Ramsuratkumar joined in the wondrous play of selling Lee's poetry book, *Death of a Dishonest Man*. He asked for speeches, for chants, for stories, for poems – by Lee himself, some of Lee's students, or other guests. He smiled exuberantly and laughed out loud at times, although his voice was tenderly soft.

The Death of God

On December 8, at 11:35 A.M., three minutes after he was wheeled into the great hall by his attendant Rajmohan, Yogi Ramsuratkumar asked Mani to make an announcement to the friends gathered in darshan. "Bhagwan wanted me to tell you that He is not feeling alright, and that He can't do anything." Grieving at this expression of his pain, visitors watched breathlessly as Mani was called back to the beggar's side. Yogi Ramsuratkumar wanted the message repeated, this time with a slightly different twist: "Bhagwan says that He wishes He could stay here longer with us, but He is not feeling alright and He can't do anything."[25] His care for his guests was ever his primary concern.

राम

As word spread that Yogi Ramsuratkumar was conducting darshan once again, even if sporadically, his Indian devotees flocked to Tiruvannamalai from cities all over the South.

For the two-week period that Lee was in India, the beggar made an appearance every day, sometimes for an hour or more. When he left the hall, Yogi Ramsuratkumar consistently left Lee to "manage these affairs," in one way or another. Although the Godchild had clearly established this precedent with his American son in previous years, many Indian devotees were disturbed and even shocked by the beggar's direction.

One day, just before he left the temple space, Yogi Ramsuratkumar pointed to the nearby prasad tray – the plate which held the bananas, apples, and oranges that would be given to the devotees who approached him. Clearly indicating his design for what should follow, the beggar pointed to the prasad as he instructed Lee, "If you want to bless someone!"

Lee took the master at his word. From his designated seat – a white plastic chair on the dais – Lee then asked other attendees if they would kindly sing a song, or chant, or tell a story, in much the way that the beggar would have done. When they completed their task, some (including a few Indian devotees) reverently approached Lee and received prasad from his hands, while others obviously and deliberately did not.

On another day, the beggar addressed Lee with different words but the same essential message: "This beggar is tired…ready to leave. Lee will lead."[26] Then, as Yogi Ramsuratkumar was moved from the dais, he smiled at Lee as he called back: "Start the class!"

राम

Alain de Rosenbo, an elderly Belgian man who had been accompanying Lee to Tiruvannamalai since 1995, and who often received special regard and even healing from Yogi Ramsuratkumar, presented him with a pair of saffron-colored socks. These socks were a gift from Chandra Swami, a much-respected guru and spiritual master whose Sadhana Kendra ashram is located on the banks of the Yamuna River in northern India, and who knew of Yogi Ramsuratkumar through Alain and other European visitors. When Devaki Ma placed the socks on the beggar's feet and Lee had read aloud the warm greetings from Chandra Swami that accompanied them, Yogi Ramsuratkumar suddenly turned to his Eternal Slave and asked: "Devaki, can this Beggar walk?"

"If you put your will to it, Bhagwan," Devaki replied softly.

"This Beggar *has* no will, no mind," Yogi Ramsuratkumar instructed. "All Father, only Father. This beggar has never done anything, only Father in heaven."[27]

Having received the gift of the socks, a short discussion ensued about Chandra Swami. As he absorbed the information that Lee was relating to him, Yogi Ramsuratkumar appeared deeply touched. Humbly incredulous at the honor being paid to him by this small gift, Yogi Ramsuratkumar spoke: "Such a simple man, Chandra Swami, and the way he respects this dirty sinner! How could Chandra Swami have such love for this Beggar?" And a few moments later: "This dirty beggar puts his head at the feet of Chandra Swami."

Devaki Ma reminded her master that Chandra Swami was one of the saints of India highlighted in the book, *Facets of the Diamond*, which was read to him many times.

Pausing to reflect on her words, Yogi Ramsuratkumar replied: "I didn't know Chandra Swami; I only knew Lee Lozowick. How it happened I don't know, but it is all by the Supreme Father. This beggar has not done anything."[28]

राम

A young Indian woman in a wheelchair was brought to the stage by her parents. The woman was a quadriplegic as a result of an accident, and her parents were using this opportunity to beg Yogi Ramsuratkumar for his assistance. At one point, the girl herself, eyes filled with tears, began to implore the beggar. "Help me, Bhagwan, help me. I'm suffering, I'm suffering," the young woman prayed.

Holding her tenderly in his gaze, Yogi Ramsuratkumar replied: "Yes, yes...to be born is to suffer. Everyone suffers."

One observer of this heart-rending scene wisely commented: "The personal suffering of this girl and her parents, set against the burden and sacrifice of Yogi Ramsuratkumar, whose suffering was also obvious and mysteriously both human and divine, was a striking teaching communication in and of itself. The burden of suffering borne by Yogi Ramsuratkumar is impersonal and Universal in every way and yet He is also suffering as a human man in a physical body, but despite His own suffering He gives endlessly...still outpouring mercy and Blessings, giving, giving, giving of Himself."[29]

One week later, after Yogi Ramsuratkumar had asked for speeches by Lee and other longtime devotees and friends, including Parathasarathy and V. Ganesan, the Godchild asked Mani to invite this same young woman to come forth and give a talk to the assembly. To hear her speak on this day, just a week after her desperate prayers for help, was to witness to the power of Yogi Ramsuratkumar's transformative benediction, which had been nurturing her throughout her time in his presence.

Seated in her wheelchair a few feet from Yogi Ramsuratkumar, the young woman spoke clearly, slowly, softly. "Before I had this accident I was successful in all I did. I thought I was everything – that all achievements were made by me. Slowly, after this accident, He has thrown me into a place where nothing is me; everything is His Will. It's Father's Will that is happening, but Father has to push into it. It took something like this for me to learn, so maybe you can learn from people like me. Whatever we plan will not take place – we should leave it all to His Will and let Him act. Everything I have said, everything left to be said, is guided by Bhagwan."[30]

राम

"Are there more books?" Yogi Ramsuratkumar asked early on in Lee's visit. He was speaking of the American's newest volume of poems, *Death of a Dishonest Man: Poems and Prayers to Yogi Ramsuratkumar*, first presented at the Jayanti in 1998. For the third year in a row, the Godchild expressed his solicitousness and gratitude to Lee for this massive work – well over one thousand pages, containing over five hundred poems extolling the wonder and majesty of the Divine beggar.

Whenever this book was in Yogi Ramsuratkumar's hands, teaching lessons were sure to follow. It had started in 1998, when the Godman had beamed with joy, exclaiming, "This is for *me?*" as the book was handed to him. He never expected anything, nor took anything for granted, and was appreciative of everything.

When he first learned from Lee that the price of the huge book ($108 U.S.) would be 4,000 Indian rupees, he was astonished, but also delighted, as if the stiff price tag were simply a reflection of the book's enormous value. Yogi Ramsuratkumar immediately turned to Devaki Ma and instructed her to write a check to Lee for the full price of the book. Then it was Lee's chance to be astonished. Although Lee protested that he intended the book to be a gift, Yogi Ramsuratkumar obviously had something else in mind. For witnesses on that day, the communication was clear: the master pays for everything – karmically, and in every other way, he has taken on responsibility for his devotee. Paying for Lee's work, a work that Yogi Ramsuratkumar had inspired and encouraged, was the Godchild's way of instructing his devotees in this dynamic aspect of the guru-devotee relationship.

A day later in this 1998 visit, the gentle "beggar-turned-salesman" addressed the darshan crowd enthusiastically, saying, "Who wants to buy this book right now? Pay for it tonight – cash!! 4,000 rupees!" The energy generated in this play was clearly invigorating

Yogi Ramsuratkumar (December 1998) selling Death of a Dishonest Man, *the book of poetry written by Lee Lozowick.*

him. Dozens of these books were sold in the course of Lee's visits in 1998 and 1999, always accompanied by the same mood of joyful abundance.

On the day in December 2000, when Yogi Ramsuratkumar was informed that only two copies were left, he implied that they should be brought to him. It made no difference that he was confined to a bed of pain; that he was too weak to raise his voice beyond a stage whisper. His work and his instruction to his devotees would continue unabated!

When the books were brought forward, the beggar asked Mani to announce that they were for sale. Quickly, the two expensive manuscripts sold, as thirty-nine others had sold during the few previous days. There were no books left to sell.

"We are happy we have sold all these books." Yogi Ramsuratkumar smiled as he turned to Lee.

"Good sales," Devaki Ma reiterated, pleased that her master was pleased.

Immediately, the beggar corrected her. "Not sales – blessings! Nothing was sold; only Father's blessings. That's why Lee brings all these books, because he knows it's a way for people to get blessings."

With another smile, Yogi Ramsuratkumar concluded: "Now everybody is happy and we can sing!"[31]

राम

Unlike many teachers or gurus, Yogi Ramsuratkumar enacted no public ceremony of transmission for one or more lineage holders, although Justice Arunachalam was clearly left in charge of the ashram administration. Nonetheless, as was the case with other great masters, his intentions for the future of his work were made clear, even obvious. While the symbology of the Godman's configurations of people and events during these last days might have been lost to some, for those with the eyes to see, his purposes were blazingly apparent. Little sophistication was required to discern the profound significance of his relationship to Lee Lozowick or to speculate about the legacy of communion and responsibility he had bequeathed to the American son. It took even less savvy to guess Yogi Ramsuratkumar's intentions in asking Ma Devaki, accompanied by Ma Vijayalakshmi, to walk a circle, clockwise, around the darshan audience one afternoon. When the two women returned to the dais, they were advised by Yogi Ramsuratkumar to do it "Once more!" As the energy mounted in the room, a power outage caused the electric lights to weaken and flicker. From his reclining chair, the beggar found the situation exactly to his liking. "If people have no light," he called out to the women, "go around once more!"[32]

And finally, there was the singing and dancing – the hallmarks of these last public darshans. For those who were asked to directly participate in the Godchild's play, as well as for those who watched it, those magical words, "Dance, dance, dance," spoken in Yogi Ramsuratkumar's joyful and lilting voice, would never be forgotten. These instructions, in fact, were quite literally his final public teaching. The beloved beggar who had delighted the hearts of thousands of seekers throughout the years as he ecstatically danced through the temple precincts or along the streets of the city, on the railway platforms or under the punnai tree, was calling upon all to praise the Divine as he had done. His words were instructions to the heart. Indeed they were his last will and testament.

राम

God takes human form so we can recognize and relate to God. Many years ago on December 1, a child was born apparently, and grew older every year, became an adult and grew old. In time and space it appears that changes have happened, but outside time and space That which Is was never born, never grew, and will not die...We are very lucky to have the opportunity to sit in the presence of and have darshan with the literal Divine, concretized in this human body of Yogi Ramsuratkumar as He really is – no will, only Father in Heaven, complete unity, no separation, complete oneness...We have the Holiest of Holies here in this room – not a stone, but a living, breathing appearance of God, here in our midst, in this lifetime! So to return in gratitude some small part of what has been give to us is to chant His name...please, chant the name of Yogi Ramsuratkumar, remember the name of Yogi Ramsuratkumar.

— Lee Lozowick, December 1, 2000[33]

राम

By the turn of the new year, 2001, Yogi Ramsuratkumar's condition was critical once again. As he lapsed in and out of consciousness, a new form of darshan was instituted. Two or three times a day the curtains to his room in the Abode would be drawn back. Confined to a hospital bed, and nursed by a professional team provided by Dr. Rangabashyam, Yogi Ramsuratkumar lay dying, in public view. By the thousands, devotees lined up awaiting their turn to walk past his windows...to look inside...to be bathed, even for an instant, in the power of presence that was undiminished by his physical health.

His devotee from Bombay, Ashish Bagrodia, called it "the most amazing darshan of my life," as well as the most peculiar. "What I saw from that window was a magnificent scene, although heart breaking but at the same time immensely divine. On this huge hospital bed, Yogiji with His flowing white beard, head with long and absolutely silver white hair, bare-chested with so many tubes running on both hands, with an oxygen mask on His face was breathing very heavily and appeared in deep sleep. It was as if Lord Vishnu was lying on His serpent bed as the King of the Universe. The most amazing thing was that Yogiji's right hand would keep coming up in the Blessing posture every few seconds although Yogiji was deeply unconscious, almost in a coma...In spite of the oxygen mask, in spite of the tubes, in spite of being without a turban and in spite of being on a hospital bed, He looked as Divine, as radiant, as magnificent as always. He looked even more, maybe...I didn't want to leave this place."[34]

The ashram administration organized twenty-four-hour chanting, in the hopes that his condition would improve. "Many devotees are convinced that if he wishes to at any time he can simply cause his kidneys to start working again, and they are hoping and praying that he will recover," one devotee wrote, incredulously.[35] How easy it was to forget that he had surrendered to life *as it is*, that he had already died in 1952, at the hands of his Father, Swami Papa Ramdas. That Yogi Ramsuratkumar, like all the great masters who had preceded him, had willingly taken on the suffering of a human incarnation in order to be of service to us – as much in death as he had been in life.

Twelve years earlier, on December 25, 1988, during a visit to Anandashram, Lee Lozowick had witnessed the same response on the part of devotees of Mataji Krishnabai. As the saint lay dying, completely resigned to the will of her Beloved Papa, disciples kept up a twenty-four-hour-a-day chant – its purpose being to keep Mother Krishnabai with them as long as possible.

"That's so absurd. It's such a contradiction in terms," Lee lamented in '88, sadly commenting upon the human condition. His words then would have been fully applicable to the same drama being enacted around Yogi Ramsuratkumar in January 2001: "Those kinds of petitions to the Divine are absurd in those circumstances because *the teacher is still alive* and *the saint is still alive* and *the presence of the saint is active* in the ashram. They should let the saint do it, instead of Ego taking control. It is contradicting who they respect her as to think that she's out of control and she isn't manifesting directly in alignment with the Process. So that's the principle you have to hold. The Work is boss, the Teacher *is* in control even up to and through death. *Surrender!* [36]

For several weeks, the phones rang constantly in the ashram office, and Justice Arunachalam was taken up with answering the questions of Bhagwan's disciples, as well as those of curiosity seekers. Besides their questions of concern, many asked him to confirm the most absurd rumors. "We have heard that the doctor has reported that he is eating again." "Is it true that he consumed two dosas today?" some people demanded to know. Others simply berated the administrator, doubting and questioning whatever he said. They wanted good news, a miraculous prognosis!

Devaki Ma, stretched as she was beyond the point of sheer exhaustion with her unrelenting service to her master, was unforgivably another target for vicious criticism at this time. The jealousy and ill will provoked in 1993 when she was named his Eternal Slave had never been fully healed. Now, as she was more vulnerable than ever, detractors looked for the chance to discredit her.

Nature itself was in massive upheaval. A major earthquake, of a magnitude of 7.6, struck the Gujarat region of India on the morning of January 26, even as Yogi Ramsuratkumar underwent one of several experiences of clinical death. This, the worst earthquake in India's history, left thousands dead and hundreds of thousands homeless. The "felt" region of this quake stretched from Madras (Chennai) in the southeast to Katmandu in Nepal. Some devotees speculated that the beggar's continual attention to the people of India was being particularly drawn to their needs in this disaster. A few days later, Yogi Ramsuratkumar roused again, for a short time.

राम

By early February, formal chanting at the ashram was reduced to eleven hours a day, as the regular participants were unable to maintain the twenty-four-hour demand. More medical procedures were instituted – a type of dialysis to assist in the detoxification of the master's body – even as doctors announced that no hope was left. Darshans for the public were still held, three times a day, two hours at a time.

For many of his closest disciples, their awareness of his pain, intensified by ongoing medical interventions, was tantamount to watching a slow crucifixion. By the third week of February, as his condition worsened, the Sudama women were denied access to Yogi Ramsuratkumar's room. Fears of infection or contamination, as determined by the medical staff, were given precedence over the needs of the heart. "We were utterly helpless in the face of this," Devaki Ma said later in a mood of absolute heartbreak, describing how Yogiji suffered by the very means that were supposed to help him.

One poignant example of misguided concern involved some branches of a gooseberry tree that had been tacked to the wall in the Abode room. It gave Yogi Ramsuratkumar great joy to see this natural decoration, as the gooseberry (nellikai) had been a constant friend and a long-term healing herb for him. A gooseberry tree grew in the yard of the Sudama House, and Yogi Ramsuratkumar loved to sit under this life-giving tree.

The first gooseberry branch that was put up on the wall was taken from a bush that grew outside the Madras hospital. It still had berries on it when Yogiji noticed it on the day they left the hospital for the trip home. The beggar informed Devaki that he wanted a branch from this bush, and she carefully broke off a few. These he carried in the van with him as they made their way back to Tiruvannamalai. Devaki remarked later that, although she never asked for this, people who came to visit him after that would frequently bring branches of gooseberry, and it seemed that these arrived always at the time that the branches on the wall were just beginning to dry out. She would also take branches from nearby bushes on the ashram, as needed to replace the old ones.

At the end, however, even Yogiji's beloved gooseberry branches were taken from the walls. The medics claimed that they were unsterile. For those who knew that nothing was random in the beggar's world, the pregnant symbology of this gesture, which in effect

710

stripped him of *everything* physical that he had loved during his earthly life, must have been terrible and awesome. The grief to those who stood by and watched was devastating. He was showing one and all that everything material will go. That only what never changes will ultimately endure.

One day a few years previous, a special puja had been conducted on the ashram. It was an occasion on which all workers were to honor their tools – whatever instruments they normally used to do their work. Carpenters, masons, electricians, mechanics – one and all would bring their instruments and perform a ritual of blessing.

"What do you have?" Bhagwan asked Selveraj, whose duty was to be the main guard and attendant of the temple hall.

"The auditorium, Bhagwan," the younger man replied.

Bhagwan laughed, saying, "Oh, Selveraj has the auditorium, and Ravi has the car, but this beggar has nothing."[37]

Then he laughed again, and prepared to leave.

राम

By February 18, friends and devotees reported that although Yogi Ramsuratkumar's condition was somewhat stabilized, his final days were obviously near. He was conscious for some of the time and was able to speak to Devaki Ma. Amazingly, rumors still circulated that Yogi Ramsuratkumar would soon be fine and that he would give darshan again.

Some who walked passed his window around this time found that his eyes made clear contact with theirs – a very intense experience for them. Dwaraknath Reddy, his old friend, noted that, for him, whatever energy Bhagwan was able to show expressed itself "in love and acceptance." Kirsti, one of several who kept long vigil at the window, wrote later: "Yogi Ramsuratkumar was so full as a person. Indeed, he was alive in every pore of his being. Even on his deathbed, when I stood behind the windows seeing him hooked to life-supporting machines and physically almost not there, there was a current of light and love, like a kind of electricity pouring out from him and awakening the heart to feel causeless love. It gave the impression that he was aware who was near, and he was still the being who had everything in his pocket. Others were still beggars coming to receive only."

Late in the night of February 19, as devotees stood in line chanting, the beggar's personal attendants pulled the curtains away. Yogi Ramsuratkumar's breathing was becoming more labored. Worried looks were noted on some of the faces around him. Ma Devaki stood facing her Lord, her back to the window where the audience had gathered; her usually tight knot of hair was slowly coming undone.

Then, with the gesture that had come to characterize the essence of his teaching and his total sacrifice on behalf of humanity, Yogi Ramsuratkumar again raised his right hand. With whatever strength was still available to him, he blessed us all.

> This beggar is happy to be born again and again and again if his life has benefited even a single living being. This beggar is happy to be born again and again to do his Father's work.
> – Yogi Ramsuratkumar

At 3:19 A.M., on the morning of Tuesday, February 20, 2001, Bhagwan Sri Yogi Ramsuratkumar, the beggar, the Godchild of Tiruvannamalai, the beloved, left his physical body and entered mahasamadhi.

राम

> Why do you come to see this Beggar, spending your money and time, instead of doing your duties? You think it important to see the physical frame of this Beggar. But had you known that this Beggar is everywhere, you would not come here often. Wherever you go, whomever you meet, whenever you are at your duty, if you utter the Name of this Beggar, Yogi Ramsuratkumar, this Beggar's Father will come to your support. – Yogi Ramsuratkumar[38]

ENDNOTES

CHAPTER 1 – AT THE RIVER'S EDGE, 1918-1947

1. M. Young, *Yogi Ramsuratkumar: Under the Punnai Tree*. Prescott, Arizona: Hohm Press, 2003, 3.
2. Truman Caylor Wadlington, *Yogi Ramsuratkumar, The Godchild Tiruvannamalai*. Madras: Diocesan Press, 1979, 23.
3. The "odd Bihari" and his interactions with Papa Ramdas and Mataji Krishnabai are described in: Swami Satchidananda, *The Gospel of Swami Ramdas*. Kanhangad, Kerala, India: Anandashram, second edition, 1990, 351.
4. Yogi Ramsuratkumar, quoted by Lee Lozowick, unpublished private talk.
5. See "Who is Sai Baba," at www.shirdibaba.org
6. Sadhu V. Rangarajan, personal interview, Bangalore, India, October 2002.
7. Personal correspondence, confirmation given by a blood relative of Yogi Ramsuratkumar.
8. Sadhu V. Rangarajan, personal correspondence, May 2004.
9. Lee Lozowick, talk given in Yogi Ramsuratkumar's temple on the ashram in Tiruvannamalai, November 25, 2002.
10. Vijayalakshmi Ma, *Waves of Love*. Unpublished manuscript. Tiruvannamalai, India, 2002, 3. As a companion to Devaki Ma, Vijayalakshmi lived with and served Yogi Ramsuratkumar for many years prior to his death. Her book contains many facts and insights that were unavailable to other devotees.
11. Georg Feuerstein, *The Yoga Tradition: Its History, Literature, Philosophy and Practice*. Prescott, Arizona: Hohm Press, 1998, 65-66.
12. Shirdi Sai Baba spent his days under a neem tree. Other great Indian saints had favorite tree spots.
13. Wadlington, 24.
14. Haragopal Sepuri, *Experiences with Yogi Ramsuratkumar*. Madras: Sister Nivedita Academy, 1989, vii.
15. Ibid., 2.
16. Wadlington, 27.
17. Diana L. Eck, *Banaras, City of Light*. Princeton, NJ: Princeton University Press, 1982, 20.
18. Wadlington, 29.
19. Vijayalakshmi, 5.

20. Professor V. Rangarajan, *Glimpses of a Great Yogi*. Madras: Sister Nivedita Academy, 1988, 15.
21. Satchidananda, 351, 381.
22. Vijayalakshmi, 7.

CHAPTER 2 – THE SEARCH OF THE SPIRITUAL PATRIOT, 1947

1. Parathasarathy, personal interview, Tiruvannamalai, December, 2002. Parathasarathy spent significant time with Yogi Ramsuratkumar starting in the early 1980s.
2. Swami Rami Tirtha, "OM, Sanatana Dharma – I," one of two lectures reprinted in booklet form, taken from: *In the Woods of God Realization*, Volume 6, Lucknow: Rama Tirtha Pratisthan, 1989, 276.
3. Ibid., 272.
4. Ibid., 322
5. Ibid., 331.
6. Professor V. Rangarajan, "Yogi Ramsuratkumar on Swami Vivekananda," *Tattva Darsana*, August-October 1992, 4-5.
7. Swami Vivekananda, quoted in S. Chatterjee, "Swami Vivekananda and Modern Socialism," *Tattva Darsana*, August-October 1992, 37.
8. Swami Vivekananda, quoted in V. Rangarajan, "Swami Vivekananda and India's Freedom Struggle," *Tattva Darsana*, August-October 1992, 27.
9. Chatterjee, 44.
10. Truman Caylor Wadlington, *Yogi Ramsuratkumar, The Godchild Tiruvannamalai*. Madras: Diocesan Press, 1979, 30.
11. Vijayalakshmi Ma, *Waves of Love*. Unpublished manuscript, Tiruvannamalai, India, 2002, 9.
12. K. R. Srinivasa Iyengar, *On The Mother – The Chronicle of a Manifestation and Ministry*. Pondicherry: Sri Aurobindo International Centre of Education, second revised edition, 1978, 359.
13. K. R. Srinivasa Iyengar , *On The Mother – The Chronicle of a Manifestation and Ministry*, Sri Aurobindo International Centre of Education, this section updated and added January 1, 1995.
14. Kirsti (Sivapriya), personal correspondence, October 2002. Kirsti is a Finnish devotee who found Yogi Ramsuratkumar in the mid-1970s.
15. Sri Aurobindo, *The Mother*. Pondicherry: Sri Aurobindo Ashram Publications © 1928 and 1999, 10.
16. Sri Aurobindo, "The Teaching of Sri Aurobindo," in *Sri Aurobindo and His Ashram*. Pondicherry: Sri Aurobindo Ashram Publications, © 1948, 2001, 41-42.
17. Yogi Ramsuratkumar, as recalled by Devaki Ma, personal communication, 2003.
18. Sri Aurobindo, "Political Life," in *Sri Aurobindo and His Ashram*. Pondicherry: Sri Aurobindo Ashram Publications, © 1948, 2001, 17-18.
19. Sadhu V. Rangarajan, personal correspondence, May 2004.
20. A.B. Purani, *The Life of Sri Aurobindo*. Pondicherry: Sri Aurobindo Ashram, fourth revised edition, 1978, 82.
21. Editors of Sri Aurobindo Ashram Publications, "Spiritual Life," in *Sri Aurobindo and His Ashram*. Pondicherry: Sri Aurobindo Ashram Publications, © 1948, 2001, 37.

22. Sri Aurobindo, "Political Life," 23.

23. Ibid., 23-24.

24. Ibid., 25.

25. Ibid, 26.

26. A.B. Purani, 81-82.

27. Yogi Ramsuratkumar, *Sparks*. Tiruvannamalai: Yogi Ramsuratkumar Trust, page 6, #14, page 20, #94, page 8, #38, page 9, #43.

28. Steve Ball, "Notes from the Tropic of Scorpio, Journals of India," *Tawagoto: The Sacred Foolish Song of the Hohm Community*. Prescott, Arizona: Hohm Press, Spring 1992, Volume 5 (2), 27.

CHAPTER 3 – MOUNTAIN OF FIRE, 1947

1. Kartigai is the third lunar asterism, the Pleiades regarded as six stars. It is also the Hindu month, which is part of November-December; and a name of the goddess Durga.

2. *Sivapuranam-Vidyesvarasamhita*, Chapter 7, v. 27-28, in: Kamalabaskaran, Iswari, *Arunagiri Valam, The Supreme Path of Grace*. Madras (Chennai): East West Books, 2000, 23.

3. Ibid., Chapter 8, v. 13-14, 24.

4. Ibid.

5. Sri Vinaya, from the Introduction, in: Skandananda (R. Henninger), *Arunachala, Holy Hill*. Tiruvannamalai, Sri Ramanashramam, 1995, xi.

6. Sri Bhagavan's Devotees, *Ramana's Arunachala, Ocean of Grace Divine*. Tiruvannamalai: Sri Ramanashramam, third edition, 2000, 130.

7. Sri Bhagavan's Devotees, *The Last Days and Maha-Nirvana of Bhagavan Sri Ramana*. Tiruvannamalai: Sri Ramanashramam, 1997, 7-8.

8. Arthur Osborne, *Ramana Arunachala*. Tiruvannamalai: Sri Ramanashramam, seventh edition, 1997. 21.

9. Ibid., 52.

CHAPTER 4 – PILGRIM'S PROGRESS, 1947

1. U.S. Ramamchandran and A. Rangamma (editors), *Cherished Memories*. Kanhangad, India: Anandashram, 6-7.

2. Truman Caylor Wadlington, *Yogi Ramsuratkumar, The Godchild, Tiruvannamalai*. Madras, 1979, 35.

3. Ibid., 36.

4. Ibid.

5. Georg Feuerstein, *The Yoga Tradition: Its History, Literature, Philosophy and Practice*. Prescott, Arizona: Hohm Press, 2001, 17-18.

6. Wadlington, 36-37.

7. *Mountain Path Magazine* editors, "Yogi Ramsuratkumar Remembers," reprinted in *Tattva Darsana*, Feb.-April 1994, Vol. 11 (1), 36.

8. Wadlington, 51-52.

9. Sri Ramana Maharshi, *Arunachala-Aksharamanamala*, verse 28, written in 1914. See: http://www.ramana-maharshi.org/music/arunsiva.htm

10. Yogi Ramsuratkumar wrote this in green ink on a drawing tablet, sometime in the 1970s, and gave it to Truman Caylor Wadlington, who presented it as a gift to this biographer, 2002.

11. Sri Ramana Maharshi, quoted in: Arthur Osborne, *Ramana Arunachala*. Tiruvannamalai: Sri Ramanashramam, seventh edition, 1997, 43.

12. Ibid., 12.

13. Yogi Ramsuratkumar, various quotes commonly attributed to by several devotees.

CHAPTER 5 – IN QUEST OF GOD

1. Truman Caylor Wadlington, *Yogi Ramsuratkumar, The Godchild, Tiruvannamalai.* Madras, 1979, 38.

2. Swami Shuddhananda, *With My Master.* Kanhangad, India: Anandashram, 2001, 98.

3. An interview with a devotee of Papa Ramdas, tells of Mataji's warning to her father in the 1960s, that Ramsuratkumar was unpredictable, a fire, and dangerous in that way; that he should not be left alone.

4. Chandrashekar (Sri Chandrashekar B. Trikannad), *Passage to Divinity: The Early Life of Swami Ramdas.* Kasaragod, India: Anandashram, fifth edition, 1999, 1.

5. Ibid., 3.

6. Ibid., 5.

7. Ibid., 64.

8. Ibid., 22.

9. Ibid., 24

10. Ibid., 25.

11. Ibid., 90.

12. Ibid., 97.

13. Ibid.

14. Swami Ramdas, *Thus Speaks Ramdas.* Kanhangad, India: Anandashram, fourth edition, 1969, 22.

15. Swami Shuddhananda, 57.

16. Swami Ramdas, *In Quest of God*, Kanhangad, India: Anandashram, fourteenth edition, 2000, 8.

17. Ibid., 289.

18. Ibid., 12.

19. Ibid., 115.

20. Ibid., 31.

21. Ibid., 32.

22. Ibid., 33.

23. Ibid., 33-34.

24. Ibid., 113.

25. Ibid., 61.

26. Ibid., 172.

27. Ibid., 170.

28. Ibid., 178.

29. Ibid., 171.

30. Chandrashekar, 166.

31. Swami Shuddhananda, 36.

32. Mataji Krishnabai, *Guru's Grace*. Fourth edition. Kanhangad, India. Anandashram, 1989, 129.

33. Swami Ramdas. *Krishna Bai*. Revised edition. Kanhangad, India: Anandashram, 1994,   52.

34. Ibid., 76-77.

35. Swami Shuddhananda, 31-2.

36. Ibid.

CHAPTER 6 – THE MADNESS OF THE SAINTS

1. Sadhu V. Rangarajan, personal interview, Bangalore, India, October 2002.

2. Truman Caylor Wadlington, *Yogi Ramsuratkumar, The Godchild, Tiruvannamalai.* Madras, 1979, 39.

3. Ibid., 40.

4. Ibid., 40-41.

5. Tom Lennon, "Accounts of Mr. Lee's Visit To His Father, Yogi Ramsuratkumar," *Tawagoto: The Sacred Foolish Song of the Hohm Community*. Prescott, Arizona: Hohm Press, Winter 1994, Volume 7 (1), 55.

6. Vijayalakshmi Ma, *Waves of Love*. Unpublished manuscript, Tiruvannamalai, India, 2002, 13-14.

7. Truman Caylor Wadlington, unpublished personal journals. Courtesy of Truman Caylor Wadlington, 2001.

8. Steve Ball, "Notes from the Tropic of Scorpio, Journals of India," *Tawagoto: The Sacred Foolish Song of the Hohm Community*. Prescott, Arizona: Hohm Press, Spring 1992, Volume 5 (2), 27.

9. Swami Satchidananda, *The Gospel of Swami Ramdas*. Kanhangad, India: Anandashram, sec. ed., 1990, 351.

10. Kirsti (Sivapriya), personal interview and correspondence, Tiruvannamalai, India, October, 2002.

11. Swami Satchidananda, 352.

12. Ibid., 29-30.

13. Swami Satchidananda, quoted in the *Gold Jubilee Souvenir* of Swami Satchidananandaji's Dedication: Anandashram Publication, 2000.

14. Swami Satchidananda, personal interview, Kanhangad, India, Anandashram, October 2002.

15. Kirsti (Sivapriya), personal interview, Tiruvannamalai, India, December 1995.

16. Swami Satchidananda, 351.

17. Ibid.

18. Ibid.

19. Swami Satchidananda, personal interview.

20. Ibid.

21. Swami Satchidananda, *The Gospel of Swami Ramdas*, 351.

22. Ibid., 372.

23. Ibid., 371.

24. Ibid., 372.

25. Ibid., 377.

26. Ibid., 379-380.

27. Ibid., 380-381.

28. Ibid., 383.
29. Wadlington, *Yogi Ramsuratkumar*, 72.
30. Ibid.
31. Vijayalakshmi, 14.
32. Swami Satchidananda, 408.
33. Vijayalakshmi, 14.
34. Sadhu V. Rangarajan.
35. Swami Satchidananda, 411-412.
36. Swami Shuddhananda, *With My Master*. Kanhangad, India: Anandashram, 2001, 90.
37. Ibid., 176-177.
38. Ibid., 22.
39. Ibid.
40. Ibid., 23.
41. Ibid.

CHAPTER 7 – "THIS BEGGAR BEGS OF YOU"

1. R. Vivekanandan, "The Master of Alms," *Tattva Darsana*, Nov. 1988-Jan. 1989, Volume 5(4), 23.
2. Yogi Ramsuratkumar, quoted by Sadhu Rangarajan, personal interview, Bangalore, India, October 2002.
3. Vijayalakshmi Ma, *Waves of Love*. Unpublished manuscript, Tiruvannamalai, India, 2002, 16.
4. Ibid.
5. Truman Caylor Wadlington, unpublished personal journal. Courtesy of Truman Caylor Wadlington.
6. Makarand Paranjape, personal correspondence, February 2003.
7. Ibid.
8. Dr. Sugatha Vihayaraghavan, "The Spiritual Renaissance in India 1830-1980," in *Yogi Ramsuratkumar Souvenir*. Tiruvannamalai: Yogi Ramsuratkumar Trust, 1995, 119.
9. Ibid., 120.
10. Ibid.
11. Devaki Ma, quoted by Prof. V. Kamalam, "Yogi Ramsuratkumar, The Almighty," *Tattva Darsana*, Jan. 2000, Volume 17(1), 37.
12. Sadhu V. Rangarajan, "Mercy Infinite and Grace Abounding," *Tattva Darsana*, Feb.-July 1988, Volume 5(1,2), 68.
13. Sadhu V. Rangarajan, "Bhagavan Nityananda," *Tattva Darsana*, Feb.- Apr. 1992, Volume 9(1), 60.
14. Kumari Nivedita, "The Great Beggar," *Tattva Darsana*, Nov. 1988-Jan. 1989, Volume 5(4), 36.
15. This information was found at: http://www.proudblackbuddhist.org/Chandala/Page_6x.html. Used with permission.
16. Red Hawk, "The King of the World," *The Art of Dying*. Prescott, Arizona: Hohm Press, 1999, 36.

17. The Men, "India Journals," *Tawagoto: The Sacred Foolish Song of the Hohm Community*, Prescott, Arizona: Hohm Press, Spring 1989, Volume 2(2), 31.
18. Sadhu V. Rangarajan, personal interview, Bangalore, India, October 2002.
19. Parathasarathy, personal interview, Tiruvannamalai, India, December 2002.
20. R. Vivekanandan, "Leela of the Master," *Tattva Darsana*, August 1990-January 1991, Volume 7(3,4), 60.
21. Prof. V. Rangarajan, "The Yogi," in *Divine Message to Humanity by Yogi Ramsuratkumar*. Conference Publication of the Seminar of May 7-8, 1988, Pondicherry, India, unnumbered page 6.
22. Sadhu V. Rangarajan, "Mercy Infinite and Grace Abounding," 68.
23. Sadhu V. Rangarajan, "The Right to Beg," *Tattva Darsana*, Feb.-July 1988, Volume 5(1,2), 5-8.
24. Vivekanandan, 33.
25. Lee Lozowick, *Death of a Dishonest Man: Poems and Prayers to Yogi Ramsuratkumar*. Prescott, Arizona: Hohm Press, 1998, 282.
26. Lee Lozowick, "Blessing Force – Darshan 12/25/88," *Tawagoto: The Sacred Foolish Song of the Hohm Community*, Spring 1989, Volume 2(2), 59.
27. E.R. Narayan, M.Sc., D.M.J., "The King of Beggars," *Tawagoto: The Sacred Foolish Song of the Hohm Community*, Spring 1989, Volume 2(2), 43.

CHAPTER 8 – CHANTING THE NAME OF GOD

1. Mahatma Gandhi, *Young India*. Madras: Volume 5 (6), 1924, 187.
2. Mahatma Gandhi, *The Collected Works of Mahatma Gandhi*. "Gita IX.22, X.10," Delhi: Government of India Publications, 1972, 326.
3. Mohandas K. Gandhi, *Harijan*, Volume 25 (5), 1935, 115. Quoted in: M.K. Gandhi, *Prayer*, Ahmedabad: Navjivan Publishing House, 35-36.
4. Swami Ramdas, *Thus Speaks Ramdas*. Kanhangad, India: Anandashram, fourth edition, 1969, 15.
5. Ibid., 25.
6. Vandana Mataji, *Nama Japa: Prayer of the Name, In the Hindu and Christian Traditions*. Delhi: Motilal Banarsidass Publishers, 1995, 266.
7. Tulsidas, "Balakanda," Doha 26. Quoted in: Sadhu Rangarajan, (editorial) "Yogi Ramsuratkumar and Ramnam," *Tattva Darsana*, Nov. 94-Jan. 95, Volume 11 (4), 4.
8. Will Zulkowski, personal interview, New York City, May 2002.
9. Shri V. Ramanujachari, personal correspondence, February 2004.
10. Sadhu V. Rangarajan, "The Divine Master," *Tattva Darsana*, Nov. 1988-Jan. 1989, Volume 5(4), 9.
11. Yogi Ramsuratkumar, his letter included in *Divine Message to Humanity by Yogi Ramsuratkumar*. Conference Publication of the Seminar of May 7-8, 1988, Pondicherry, India, unnumbered page 36.
12. Swami Shuddhananda, *With My Master*. Kanhangad, India: Anandashram, 2001, 84.
13. Sadhu V. Rangarajan, personal interview, Bangalore, India, October 2002.
14. Swami Ramdas, 22.
15. Ibid., 23-24.
16. Ibid., 25.
17. Sadhu Rangarajan, "Salutations to My Deekshaa Guru," in: *Yogi Ramsuratkumar Souvenir*. Tiruvannamalai: Yogi Ramsuratkumar Trust, 1995, 59.

18. Georg Feuerstein, *The Yoga Tradition: Its History, Literature, Philosophy and Practice.* Prescott, Arizona: Hohm Press, 1998, 358.

19. Ibid.

20. Lozowick, Lee, *Death of a Dishonest Man: Poems and Prayers to Yogi Ramsuratkumar.* Prescott, Arizona: Hohm Press, 1998, 239.

21. Sadhu V. Rangarajan, personal correspondence, remembered that Yogi Ramsuratkumar quoted this line from a scriptural text in speaking of the repetition of Ramnam.

22. Yogi Ramsuratkumar.

23. Will Zulkowski, from various accounts of visits with Yogi Ramsuratkumar from Hilda's devotees. Courtesy of Truman Caylor Wadlington.

24. Yogi Ramsuratkumar, quoted by Sadhu V. Rangarajan, "Yogi Ramsuratkumar and Ramnam," *Tattva Darsana*, Nov. 1994-Jan. 1995, Volume 11(4), 5.

25. Sadhu V. Rangarajan, personal interview.

CHAPTER 9 – THE MOTH TO THE FLAME, 1959

1. Yogi Ramsuratkumar, quoted by Ma Devaki, "Bhiksha From The Divine Bhikshu!" *Saranagatham*, official publication of the Ashram of Yogi Ramsuratkumar, Tiruvannamalai, India, January 2004, 36-38.

2. Yogi Ramsuratkumar, quoted by V. Ganesan, "He is Grace, Compassion, Blessings," *Yogi Ramsuratkumar Souvenir*. Tiruvannamalai: Yogi Ramsuratkumar Trust, 1995, 135.

3. V. Ganesan, quoted in Vijayalakshmi Ma, *Waves of Love*. Unpublished manuscript, Tiruvannamalai, India, 2002, 21.

4. Shri V. Ramanujachari, personal correspondence, February 2004.

5. V. Ganesan, 20.

6. Kirsti (Sivapriya), personal interview and correspondence, Tiruvannamalai, India, October, 2002.

7. Parathasarathy, personal interview, Tiruvannamalai, India, December 2002,

8. Vijayalakshmi, 20.

9. Ibid., 23.

10. Ibid., 23-24.

11. Ibid., 24.

12. Yogi Ramsuratkumar, quoted by Justice T.S. Arunachalam, "Bhagavan Nityananda," *Saranagatham*, official publication of the Ashram of Yogi Ramsuratkumar, Tiruvannamalai, India, October 2002, 38.

13. Ibid.

CHAPTER 10 – THE MAN OF LIGHT, 1964

1. Truman Caylor Wadlington, *Yogi Ramsuratkumar, The Godchild, Tiruvannamalai.* Madras, 1979. 79.

2. Perumal Sadaiyan, *Treasures of the Heart: The Unforgettable Yogi Ramsuratkumar.* Tiruvannamalai: Perumal Sadaiyan, 1998, 1.

3. Ibid., 2.

4. Ibid., 3.

5. Ibid.

6. Ibid.

7. Ibid., 5.
8. Ibid.
9. Ibid., 6.
10. Ibid., 9.
11. Ibid., 13-14.
12. Ibid., 10.
13. Ibid.
14. Ibid., 14.
15. Ibid., 21.
16. Ibid., 33.
17. Ibid., 37.
18. Ibid., 38.
19. Ibid., 10.
20. Ibid., 11.
21. Ibid., 51.
22. Ibid., 54.
23. Ibid.
24. Ibid., 56.
25. Ibid., 34.
26. Ibid., 48.
27. Diana L. Eck, *Banaras: City of Light.* Princeton, N.J.: Princeton University Press, 1982, 324.
28. Ibid.
29. Perumal, 58.
30. Ibid., 59.
31. Ibid., 60.
32. Ibid.
33. Ibid., iv.

CHAPTER 11 – THE GODCHILD OF TIRUVANNAMALAI

1. All the quotes in this chapter (except as otherwise noted) are from Truman Caylor Wadlington, either from personal interviews, conducted in February 2002, Denver, Colorado, or from his unpublished journals of 1970. I have attempted, in most cases, to indicate the journal entries by referring to his "writing" them. The interview material is generally not specified as having been written.
2. Shri V. Ramanujachari, personal correspondence, February 2004.
3. Truman Caylor Wadlington, quoted in Hilda Charlton, *Saints Alive.* Woodstock, New York: Golden Quest, 1989, 260.
4. Truman Caylor Wadlington, *Yogi Ramsuratkumar, The Godchild, Tiruvannamalai.* Madras, 1979, 11.
5. Ibid., 12.
6. Ibid., 12-13.
7. Ibid., 21.
8. Ibid., 34.
9. Ibid., 36-37.
10. Truman Caylor Wadlington, unpublished journals.

CHAPTER 12 – A FRIEND AND PROTECTOR, 1971

1. Abhishiktananda, *Guru and Disciple: An Encounter with Sri Gnanananda, A Contemporary Spiritual Master.* Delhi: I.S.P.C.K., 1990, 8.
2. Devotees, *Sadguru Gnanananda, His Life, Personality and Teachings.* Bombay: Bharatiya Vidya Bhavan, 1993, xviii.
3. Shri V. Ramanujachari, personal correspondence, February 2004.
4. Abhishiktananda, 11-12.
5. Justice P. Ramakrishnan, "Satguru Gnanananda Giri and Yogi Ramsuratkumar," *Tattva Darsana,* Feb.-July 1988, Volume 5(1, 2), 33. (A reprint of "The Padayatra," an article in *The Hindu,* Sept. 4, 1979.)
6. A. N. Balasubramanian, "A New Vision of Human Destiny – X," *Divine Message to Humanity by Yogi Ramsuratkumar.* Conference Publication of the Seminar of May 7-8, 1988, Pondicherry, India, unnumbered page 55.
7. Shri V. Ramanujachari, personal correspondence, February 2004.
8. Tannangur Sri Namaji Swami, reported in, "Kabir," *Saranagatham,* official publication of the Ashram of Yogi Ramsuratkumar, Tiruvannamalai, India, May 2002, 38.
9. Devotees, 295.

CHAPTER 13 – WIDENING THE DOOR, 1973-1975

1. Will Zulkowski, personal interview, New York City, May 2002.
2. Joan Zulkowski narrated this story in "Chapter 14, Yogi Ramsuratkumar," in Hilda Charlton, *Saints Alive.* Woodstock, N.Y.: Golden Quest, 1989, 257-258.
3. Ibid.
4. This version of the story is from Will Zulkowski, personal interview.
5. Hilda Charlton, *Saints Alive.* Woodstock, N.Y.: Golden Quest, 1989, 262-263.
6. Will Zulkowski, personal interview.
7. Ibid.
8. Will Zulkowski, quoted in Hilda Charlton, 255.
9. Shri. Jagannathan, narration translated from a Tamil interview by R. Vijayalakshmi, in "Swamiji and the Gold Ring," *Saranagatham*, official publication of the Ashram of Yogi Ramsuratkumar, Tiruvannamalai, India, July 2003, 39.
10. Anne Cushman, *From Here to Nirvana: The Yoga Journal Guide to Spiritual India.* New York: Riverhead Books, 1999, 11-14.
11. Vijayalakshmi Ma, *Waves of Love.* Unpublished manuscript, Tiruvannamalai, India, 2002, 31.
12. Will Zulkowski, personal interview.
13. Will Zulkowski, in Hilda Charlton, 253.
14. Will Zulkowski, personal interview.
15. Ibid.
16. Ibid.
17. Ibid.
18. Nara (author of *Western Sadhus and Sannyasins in India*, Prescott, Arizona: Hohm Press, 2000), in personal interview, related this story as told to him in 1996 by a Tiruvannamalai swami, who knew Yogi Ramsuratkumar.
19. Ibid.
20. Joan Zulkowski, various accounts of visits with Yogi Ramsuratkumar from Hilda's devotees. Courtesy of Truman Caylor Wadlington.

21. Paul William Roberts, *Empire of the Soul: Some Journeys in India*. New York: Riverhead Books, 1994, 69-70.
22. Ibid., 70.
23. Ibid., 71.
24. Ibid., 71-72.
25. Ibid., 72-73.
26. Ibid., 79.
27. Ibid.

CHAPTER 14 – A LIVING FAITH

1. Except where otherwise noted, all the material from Parathasarathy in this chapter was transcribed from a personal interview, December 2002, and in subsequent correspondence.
2. Haragopal Sepuri, *Experiences with Yogi Ramsuratkumar,* Madras: Sister Nivedita Academy, 1989, 2.
3. Ibid., 22-23.
4. Yogi Ramsuratkumar, quoted by Parathasarathy, in personal interview, December 2002.
5. Haragopal, 21.
6. Ibid., 22.
7. Anja Helmich, "India Journals," *Tawagoto: The Sacred Foolish Song of the Hohm Community*, Prescott, Arizona, Winter 1998, Volume 11 (1), 49.
8. Haragopal, 27.
9. Yogi Ramsuratkumar, quoted by Parathasarathy.
10. Shri V. Ramanujachari, personal correspondence, February 2004.
11. Ibid.
12. Ibid.
13. Sri. Jagannathan narration, translation from Tamil by R.Vijayalakshmi. "Yogi Ramsuratkumar and the Pure Silk Dhoti," *Saranagatham*, official publication of the Ashram of Yogi Ramsuratkumar, Tiruvannamalai, India, June 2002, 40-41.
14. Ibid.

CHAPTER 15 – RISING SON, 1977

1. Hilda Charlton, *Saints Alive*. Woodstock, New York: Golden Quest, 1989, 289.
2. Ibid., 86.
3. Ibid., 251.
4. Ibid.
5. Ibid., 262-263.
6. "S.D." a devotee of Lee Lozowick's who participated in this first trip, personal interview, Prescott, Arizona, March 2003.
7. Sita, "The Beggar and the Seeker," *Tattva Darsana*, Feb.-July 1988, Volume 5 (1-2), 37-38. Updated in March 2003 by "S.D.," a devotee of Lee Lozowick's who participated in this first trip.
8. Ibid., 38.
9. "S.D.," personal interview.
10. Ibid.
11. Ibid.

12. Lee Lozowick, taped conversation with students in Varanasi, January 19, 1977.

CHAPTER 16 – PORTRAIT OF A MASTER

1. Except as indicated, all the direct quotations in this chapter come from Kirsti (Sivapriya), personal interview and correspondence, Tiruvannamalai, India, October 2002.

CHAPTER 17 – HILDA AND COMPANY, 1978

1. Will Zulkowski, from various accounts of meetings with Yogi Ramsuratkumar, from Hilda's devotees. Courtesy of Caylor Wadlington.
2. Will Zulkowski, personal interview, New York City, May 2002.
3. Ibid.
4. "AL," from various accounts of meetings with Yogi Ramsuratkumar, from Hilda's devotees. Courtesy of Caylor Wadlington.
5. "BT," from various accounts of meetings with Yogi Ramsuratkumar, from Hilda's devotees. Courtesy of Caylor Wadlington.
6. Will Zulkowski, various accounts.
7. Will Zulkowski, various accounts and personal interview.
8. Will Zulkowski, personal interview.
9. Will Zulkowski, various accounts.
10. Lila, from various accounts of meetings with Yogi Ramsuratkumar, from Hilda's devotees. Courtesy of Caylor Wadlington.
11. Sadhu Prof. V. Rangarajan, "Salutations to My Deekshaa Guru!" *Yogi Ramsuratkumar Souvenir*. Tiruvannamalai: Yogi Ramsuratkumar Trust, 1995, 57.
12. Will Zulkowski, private interview.
13. Ibid.
14. Joel Bluestein, telephone interview, December 2003.
15. Will Zulkowski, various accounts.
16. Joel Bluestein.
17. Truman Caylor Wadlington, unpublished personal journals. Courtesy of Truman Caylor Wadlington, 2001.

CHAPTER 18 – RETURNING TO THE SOURCE, 1979

1. Sita, "The Beggar and the Seeker," *Tattva Darsana*, Feb.-July 1988, Volume 5 (1-2), 40.
2. Sita, 39-42, augmented with interviews by S.D. and Balarama Zuccarello, Prescott, Arizona, June 2003.
3. Lee Lozowick, *Death of a Dishonest Man: Poems and Prayers to Yogi Ramsuratkumar*. Prescott, Arizona: Hohm Press, 1998, 917-918.
4. Ibid., 42.
5. Lee Lozowick, "Darshan, June 4, 1995," transcript reprinted in *Hohm Sahaj Mandir Study Manual,* Volume I, Prescott, Arizona: Hohm Press, 1996, 216-217.
6. Lee Lozowick, et al. *For the Love of God*, Mt. Tabor, N.J.: Hohm Press, 1977, 5.
7. Ibid, 3.
8. Lee Lozowick, "Yogi Ramsuratkumar, The Universal Guru," *Saranagatham*, official publication of the Ashram of Yogi Ramsuratkumar, Tiruvannamalai, India, March 2002, 39.

9. Lee Lozowick, *Death of a Dishonest Man,* 199.
10. Lee Lozowick, "Darshan," 221.

CHAPTER 19 – TWO DAYS IN THE LIFE, 1980

1. Except where noted, all the quotes in this chapter are from the personal journals, unpublished, of Truman Caylor Wadlington, courtesy of Truman Caylor Wadlington, 2001.
2. Paul William Roberts, personal correspondence, February 2004.
3. Michel Coquet, *Yogi Ramsuratkumar, The Divine Beggar.* Page 85 of the English language pre-publication version of the French-language book: *Yogi Ramsuratkumar: Le Divin Mendicant,* Paris: ALTESS, 1996.
4. Shri V. Ramanujachari, personal correspondence, February 2004.

CHAPTER 20 – THE THREE WISE MEN

1. Vijayalakshmi Ma, *Waves of Love.* Unpublished manuscript, Tiruvannamalai, India, 2002, 32.
2. Except as otherwise noted, all quotes used in this chapter were taken from a personal interview with Parathasarathy, Tiruvannamalai, India, December 2002.
3. Lee Lozowick, *Death of a Dishonest Man: Poems and Prayers to Yogi Ramsuratkumar.* Prescott, Arizona: Hohm Press, 1998, 541.

CHAPTER 21 – POETRY AND MADNESS

1. Ilayaraja, "Sri Yogi Ramsuratkumar: A Forceful Personality," *Yogi Ramsuratkumar Souvenir.* Tiruvannamalai: Yogi Ramsuratkumar Trust, 1995, 131.
2. Lee Lozowick, "Darshan, June 4, 1995," transcript reprinted in: *Hohm Sahaj Mandir Study Manual,* Volume I, Prescott, Arizona: Hohm Press, 1996, 221.
3. Ibid.
4. Lee Lozowick, *Death of a Dishonest Man: Poems and Prayers to Yogi Ramsuratkumar.* Prescott, Arizona: Hohm Press, 1998, xxxii-xxxiii.
5. Ibid., 229.
6. Ibid.
7. Ibid., 231.
8. Ibid., 237.

CHAPTER 22 – A FAMILY OF SERVICE, 1984

1. Sadhu Prof. V. Rangarajan, "Salutations to My Deekshaa Guru!" *Yogi Ramsuratkumar Souvenir.* Tiruvannamalai: Yogi Ramsuratkumar Trust, 1995, 56.
2. Ibid., 57.
3. Sadhu Prof. V. Rangarajan, *Divine Mother Mayee of Kanyakumari.* Madras: Sister Nivedita Academy, 1996, 31.
4. Yogi Ramsuratkumar, quoted by S. Govindarraj, *Saranagatham,* official publication of the Ashram of Yogi Ramsuratkumar, Tiruvannamalai, India, November 2002.
5. Sadhu Prof. V. Rangarajan, 16.
6. *Tattva Darsana,* Feb.- Apr. 1992, Volume 9(1),27; reprinted from an article in French in *Le Monde Inconnu,* Nov. 1991, Paris.

7. S. Govindarraj, in *Saranagatham*, official publication of the Ashram of Yogi Ramsuratkumar, Tiruvannamalai, India, November 2002, 6. Translated from Tamil by Saravanan, Hohm Sahaj Trust, Tiruvannamalai.

8. Prof. V. Rangarajan, *Glimpses of a Great Yogi*. Second edition. Madras: Sister Nivedita Academy. 1988, v.

9. Ibid.

10. Ibid., vi.

11. Mother Mirra, quoted in: George Van Vrekhem, *The Mother, The Story of Her Life*. New Delhi: HarperCollins, 2000, 416.

12. Prof. V. Rangarajan, viii.

13. Ma Navaratham and husband Thiru, "A Beggar Who Owns the World," *Hinduism Today*, 1990 article, reprinted in *Tattva Darsana*, August 1990-January 1991, Volume 7(3,4), 54.

14. Yogi Ramsuratkumar, *Sparks*. Tiruvannamalai: Yogi Ramsuratkumar Trust, 17.

15. Ibid., 16.

16. Prof. V. Rangarajan, personal interview, Bangalore, India, October 2002.

17. Mahatma Gandhi, *Young India, 17.9.1925*; reprinted from: http://meadev.nic.in/Gandhi/economics.htm

18. Sadhu Prof. V. Rangarajan, "The Divine Master," *Tattva Darsana*, Nov. 1988-Jan. 1989, Volume 5(4), 7-9.

19. Sadhu V. Rangarajan, personal interview and correspondence, Bangalore, India, October 2002.

20. Ibid.

21. R. Vivekanandan, personal correspondence, February 2003.

CHAPTER 23 – A BANNER YEAR, 1986

1. Sita, "The Beggar and the Seeker," *Tattva Darsana*, Feb.-July 1988, Volume 5(1, 2), 43.

2. Ibid., 43-44.

3. Lee Lozowick, "Darshan, June 4, 1995," excerpted in: *Hohm Sahaj Mandir Study Manual*, Volume I, Prescott, Arizona: Hohm Press, 1996, 225-226.

4. Steve Ball, personal journal. Courtesy of Steve Ball.

5. Lee Lozowick, 227-228.

6. Dr. Javad Nurbakhsh, *In the Tavern of Ruin: Seven Essays on Sufism*. "Master and Disciple," New York: Khaniqahi-Nimatullahi Publications, 1978, 133-134.

7. A Devotee [Chandramouli], "Holy Meeting," *Tattva Darsana*, Feb.-Apr. 1994, Volume 11(1), 22-25.

8. Justice T.S. Arunachalam, "Divine Beacons, Kanchi Mahaswamigal and Bhagawan Yogi Ramsuratkumar," *Saranagatham*, official publication of the Ashram of Yogi Ramsuratkumar, Tiruvannamalai, India, March 2002, 37.

9. Nara, author of *Western Sadhus and Sannyasins in India*. Prescott, Arizona: Hohm Press, 2000, interviewed this Tiruvannamalai sannyasin in 1996.

10. S. Govindarajan, "Experiences of Devotees," reported on 2/12/2000, on the website: http://www.angelfire.com/tn/yogiram/exp.html

11. Ravi, personal interview, Tiruvannamalai, India, December 2002. All quotes and information credited to Ravi in this story are taken during this interview.

12. Ibid.

13. A Devotee, 25.
14. S. Govindarajan.
15. Marcus Allsop.
16. A Devotee, 25.
17. Devaki Ma, communication to Ute Augustiniak, Tiruvannamalai, March 2004.
18. Editor's Note, "Benediction," *Saranagatham*, official publication of the Ashram of Yogi Ramsuratkumar, Tiruvannamalai, India, January 2004, 30.
19. Devaki Ma, "Introduction," translated into English by Sadhu Rangarajan, from the book, *Bhagavan Yogi Ramsuratkumar Paamaalai*, by Sri T.P.M Minakshisundaranar. Reprinted in *Tattva Darsana*, Feb.-Apr. 1994, Volume 11(1), 28.
20. Kumari R. Nivedita, "The Great Beggar," *Tattva Darsana*, Nov. 1988-Jan. 1989, Volume 5(4), 40-43.
21. Ibid., 41.
22. Ibid., 43.

CHAPTER 24 – SPREADING THE WORK, 1987-1989

1. Prof. V. Rangarajan, *Glimpses of a Great Yogi*. Second edition. Madras: Sister Nivedita Academy. 1988, viii.
2. Interview and correspondence, with Sadhu Rangarajan.
3. Yogi Ramsuratkumar, quoted in *Tattva Darsana*, Feb.-July 1988, Volume 5(1, 2), 45.
4. Prof. V. Rangarajan, iii.
5. Prof. V. Rangarajan, personal correspondence, January 2003.
6. Prof. V. Rangarajan, *Glimpses,* inside front cover, inside back cover.
7. Sadhu Professor V. Rangarajan, "The Divine Master," *Tattva Darsana*, Nov. 1989-Jan. 1990, Volume (4), 6.
8. Swami Devananda Saraswati, "The Yogi's Song," *Saranagatham*, official publication of the Ashram of Yogi Ramsuratkumar, Tiruvannamalai, India, August 2002, 41.
9. Vijaya Fedorschak, "Notes from the Tropic of Scorpio, Journals of India," *Tawagoto: The Sacred Foolish Song of the Hohm Community*. Prescott, Arizona: Hohm Press, Spring 1992, Volume 5 (2), 26.
10. Prof. V. Rangarajan, 6.
11. Satyanada Amritham, personal correspondence, December 2002.
12. Prof. V. Rangarajan, *Glimpses*, 60.
13. Ibid., 66.
14. Kirsti (Sivapriya), personal interview and correspondence, Tiruvannamalai, December 1995 and October 2002.
15. Prof. V. Rangarajan, 66.
16. Lee Lozowick, *Death of a Dishonest Man: Poems and Prayers to Yogi Ramsuratkumar*. Prescott, Arizona: Hohm Press, 1998, 257.
17. Professor V. Rangarajan, 58.
18. A.N. Balasubramanian, "A New Vision of Human Destiny," *Divine Message to Humanity by Yogi Ramsuratkumar*. Conference Publication of the Seminar of May 7-8, 1988, Pondicherry, India, unnumbered page 55.
19. Yogi Ramsuratkumar, *Divine Message to Humanity by Yogi Ramsuratkumar*. Conference Publication of the Seminar of May 7-8, 1988, Pondicherry, India, unnumbered page 33.

20. Ibid., his letter to the conference participants, unnumbered page 36.
21. K. Venkatasubramanian, letter to Shri Rajamanickam, in *Divine Message to Humanity by Yogi Ramsuratkumar*. Conference Publication of the Seminar of May 7-8, 1988, Pondicherry, India, unnumbered page 3.
22. Kumari Nivedita, "The Great Beggar," *Tattva Darsana*, Nov. 1988-Jan. 1989, Volume 5(4), 38-39.
23. Ibid.
24. Sadhu Professor Rangarajan, "The Divine Master," *Tattva Darsana*, Nov. 1988-Jan. 1989, Volume 5(4), 17-18.
25. R. Vivekanandan, "The Master of Alms," *Tattva Darsana,* Nov. 1988-Jan. 1989, Volume 5(4), 32.
26. The Men, "India Journals," *Tawagoto: The Sacred Foolish Song of the Hohm Community*, Prescott, Arizona: Hohm Press, Spring 1989, Volume 2(2), 30.
27. Vivekanandan, 28.
28. Jim Capellini, "Initiation," *Divine Slave Gita: The Sacred Foolish Song of the Hohm Community*, Spring 1989, Volume 8 (1), 10.
29. Vivekanandan, 28.
30. Personal interview, JaiRam, Tiruvannamalai, India, December 2002.
31. The Men, "India Journals," 10.
32. Lee Lozowick, quoted by The Men, "India Journals," 15.
33. Chögyam Trungpa, *The Lion's Roar: An Introduction to Tantra*, Boston: Shambhala, 1992, 52-53.
34. C.S. Lewis, *The Lion, the Witch and the Wardrobe: Book I* in the Chronicles of Narnia, New York: Scholastic Inc., © 1950, 75-76.
35. Lee Lozowick, *Death of a Dishonest Man*, 277.
36. Lee Lozowick, "Blessing Force," *Tawagoto: The Sacred Foolish Song of the Hohm Community*, Prescott, Arizona: Hohm Press, Spring 1989, Volume 2(2), 58-59.
37. The Men, "India Journals," 27.
38. Ibid.
39. The Men, "India Journals," 29.
40. Lee Lozowick, "After Dinner Talk, 12-19-88, Are they leading or misleading us?" *Tawagoto: The Sacred Foolish Song of the Hohm Community*, Prescott, Arizona: Hohm Press, Spring 1989, Volume 2(2), 64.
41. Lee Lozowick, "Darshan 12/25/88, Blessing Force," 58.
42. The Men, "India Journals," 31.
43. Purna Steinitz, personal interview, Tiruvannamalai, India, December 2002.
44. Lee Lozowick, quoted by The Men, 30.
45. The Men, "India Journals," 31.
46. Ibid., 32.

CHAPTER 25 – CARRYING THE TORCH, 1989

1. R. Vivekanandan, "The Master of Alms," *Tattva Darsana*, Nov. 1988-Jan. 1989, Volume 5(4), 31.
2. Kirsti (Sivapriya), personal interview and correspondence, Tiruvannamalai, India, December 2002.
3. Anonymous, personal interview, October 2002.
4. As reported by Krishnand from the Anandashram bookshop, May 2004.

5. Kirsti.
6. Sadhu V. Rangarajan, "Yogi Ramsuratkumar and Ramnam," *Tattva Darsana*, Nov. 1994 – Jan. 1995, Volume 11(4), 7.
7. Sadhu V. Rangarajan, "My Master as I See Him," *Tattva Darsana*, Nov. 1989 – Jan. 1990, Volume 6 (4), 4.
8. Ibid., "World Movement for Ramnam," 41.
9. Sadhu V. Rangarajan, "Salutations to My Deekshaa Guru!," *Yogi Ramsuratkumar Souvenir*. Tiruvannamalai: Yogi Ramsuratkumar Trust, 1995, 58.
10. Sadhu V. Rangarajan, "Yogi Ramsuratkumar and Ramnam," 8.
11. Ibid., 9.
12. T. Ponkamaraj, quoted in Ranganayaki Srinivasan, Professor. *Bhagwan Sri Yogi Ramsuratkumar: His Divine Life and Message*. Kanyakumari, India: Yogi Ramsurat Kumar Manthralayam Trust, 1991. (Adapted from the book in Tamil: *Universal Father, Yogi Ramsuratkumar* by T. Ponkamaraj, M.A. B.L.), 29.
13. Ibid., 17.
14. Vijayalakshmi Ma, *Waves of Love*. Unpublished manuscript, Tiruvannamalai, India, 2002, 103.
15. Justice T.S. Arunachalam, "Craving, Charm, Bliss," *Saranagatham*, official publication of the Ashram of Yogi Ramsuratkumar, Tiruvannamalai, India, June 2002, 42-43.
16. Paul William Roberts, *Empire of the Soul: Some Journeys in India*. New York: Riverhead Books, 1994, 71.
17. Martin Keck, "Conversations With His Father," *Divine Slave Gita: The Sacred Foolish Song of the Hohm Community*, Spring 1989, Volume 8 (1), 14.
18. Ibid.
19. Jim Capellini, "Initiation," quoting Yogi Ramsuratkumar, *Divine Slave Gita: The Sacred Foolish Song of the Hohm Community*, Spring 1989, Volume 8 (1), 9.
20. Ibid.
21. Ibid.
22. Keck, 16.
23. Capellini, 9.
24. Jim Chinery, "The Guru's Feet," quoting Yogi Ramsuratkumar, *Divine Slave Gita: The Sacred Foolish Song of the Hohm Community*, Prescott, Arizona: Hohm Press, Spring 1989, Volume 8 (1), 21.
25. Rick Lewis, in "In the Company of Saints, Excerpts from India Journals," *Tawagoto: The Sacred Foolish Song of the Hohm Community*. Prescott, Arizona: Hohm Press, Winter 1995, Volume 8 (1), 26.
26. Chinery, 20.
27. Keck, 17.

CHAPTER 26 – FAILING HEALTH, 1990

1. Stan Hitson, "Extraordinary Business," *Tawagoto: The Sacred Foolish Song of the Hohm Community*. Prescott, Arizona: Hohm Press, Winter 1995, Volume 8 (1), 78.
2. Sadhu V. Rangarajan, personal interview, Bangalore, India, October 2002.
3. Ibid.
4. Ibid.
5. Devaki Ma, personal interview, Tiruvannamalai, India, December 2002.

6. Ibid.
7. Dwaraknath Reddy, interview conducted by Ute and Volker Augustiniak, Tiruvannamalai, India, January 2003. All the material that follows in this section is taken from this interview.
8. Ibid.
9. Dr. T. I. Radhakrishnan, "The Unforgettable Turning Point," in an article published in *Manorajyam*, a Malayalam weekly, October 21, 1993.
10. Ibid.
11. Dwaraknath Reddy.
12. Vijayalakshmi Ma, *Waves of Love*. Unpublished manuscript, Tiruvannamalai, India, 2002, 54.
13. Lozowick, Lee. *Death of a Dishonest Man: Poems and Prayers to Yogi Ramsuratkumar*. Prescott, Arizona: Hohm Press, 1998, (poem written November, 1993), 479.
14. Will Zulkowski, personal interview, New York City, May 2002.

CHAPTER 27 – RIGHT HAND MAN, 1991

1. Rajalakshmi, wife of Mani, personal interview, Sivakashi, India, December 2002.
2. Mani, with S. Lhaksam, *A Man and His Master, My Years with Yogi Ramsuratkumar*, Prescott, Arizona: Hohm Press, 2003, 2.
3. Ibid.
4. Ramamurti, personal interview, Tiruvannamalai, India, December 2002.
5. Rajalakshmi, personal interview.
6. Mani, quoted by Rajalakshmi in interview.
7. Mani, *A Man and His Master*, 6.
8. Ibid., 8.
9. Ibid.
10. Rajalakshmi, personal interview.
11. Ibid.
12. Ibid.
13. Mani, 11.
14. Ibid.
15. Ibid., 15.
16. Sadhu V. Rangarajan, "The Great Boatman," *Tattva Darsana*, Nov. 1991-Jan. 1992, Volume 8(4), 17.
17. Ibid., 18.
18. Mani, 149-150.
19. Ibid., 150.
20. Ibid., 18.
21. Lee Lozowick, *Death of a Dishonest Man: Poems and Prayers to Yogi Ramsuratkumar*. Prescott, Arizona: Hohm Press, 1998, 939.

CHAPTER 28 – AN ASHRAM BEGINS, 1993

1. Ramamurti, personal interview, Tiruvannamalai, India, December 2002.
2. Parathasarathy, personal interview, Tiruvannamalai, India, December 2002.

3. Yogi Ramsuratkumar, quoted by Ma Devaki, in "The Divine Beggar On Himself," *Saranagatham,* official publication of the Ashram of Yogi Ramsuratkumar, Tiruvannamalai, India, February 2003, 34.

4. Yogi Ramsuratkumar, *Sparks,* Tiruvannamalai, India: Yogi Ramsuratkumar Trust, 2002, 23.

CHAPTER 29 – THE ETERNAL SLAVE, JULY 1993

1. Dwaraknath Reddy, interview conducted by Ute and Volker Augustiniak, Tiruvannamalai, India, January 2003.

2. Devaki Ma, "The One Beyond the Reach of Thought," extracted from "The Introduction" to *Bhagavan Yogi Ramsuratkumar Paamaalai* by Sri T.P. Meenakshisundaram, translated by Sadhu V. Rangarajan. *Tattva Darsana*, Feb.-Apr. 1994, Volume 11(1), 28-29.

3. Vijayalakshmi Ma, *Waves of Love.* Unpublished manuscript, Tiruvannamalai, India, 2002, 60.

4. The Editors, *Hohm Sahaj Mandir Study Manual*, Volume 3, Prescott, Arizona: Hohm Press, 2002, 447.

5. Ibid., 446.

6. Vijayalakshmi, 60.

7. Ibid., 61.

8. Ibid., 62.

9. Ibid.

10. Sadhu V. Rangarajan, "The Eternal Slave," *Tattva Darsana*, Nov. 1993-Jan. 1994, Volume 10(4), 6.

11. Shri V. Ramanujachari, personal correspondence, March 2004.

12. Sadhu V. Rangarajan, 3.

13. Ibid., 6.

14. Dwaraknath Reddy.

15. Lee Lozowick, *Death of a Dishonest Man: Poems and Prayers to Yogi Ramsuratkumar*, Prescott, Arizona: Hohm Press, 1998, 506.

16. Michel Coquet, *Yogi Ramsuratkumar, The Divine Beggar*. Page 106 of the English language pre-publication version of the French-language book: *Yogi Ramsuratkumar: Le Divin Mendicant*, Paris: ALTESS, 1996. Also, in a slightly different version, in James Capellini et al. *Facets of the Diamond: Wisdom of India*. Prescott, Arizona: Hohm Press, 1994, 145.

17. Yogi Ramsuratkumar, quoted by Lee Lozowick, in a public talk.

18. Sadhu V. Rangarajan, "The Vision of Truth," *Tattva Darsana*, May-July 1994, Volume 11(2), 5.

19. Ibid., 7.

20. Ibid., 8.

21. Devaki Ma, 29.

22. Vijayalakshmi, 31.

23. Devaki Ma, 30.

24. Ibid., 31.

25. Ibid, 25.

CHAPTER 30 – THE NEW POET

1. Balarama Zuccarello, "Accounts of Mr. Lee's Visits to His Father," *Tawagoto: The Sacred Foolish Song of the Hohm Community*. Prescott, Arizona: Hohm Press, Winter 1994, Volume 7 (1), 45.
2. Ibid.
3. Lee Lozowick, *Poems of a Broken Heart*. Madras, India: Sister Nivedita Press, 1993, i.
4. Lee Lozowick, "Was There Ever One," *Tattva Darsana*, Feb.-July 1988, Volume 5 (1, 2), 53.
5. Lee Lozowick, *Poems of a Broken Heart*, iv.
6. Balarama Zuccarello, 46.
7. Parthiban, "Pillars of Peace," *Yogi Ramsuratkumar Souvenir*. Tiruvannamalai: Yogi Ramsuratkumar Trust, 1995, 315.
8. Truman Caylor Wadlington, *Yogi Ramsuratkumar, The Godchild, Tiruvannamalai*. Madras, 1979, 23.
9. Parathasarathy, personal interview, Tiruvannamalai, India, 2002.
10. Yogi Ramsuratkumar, quoted in: "Immortal Songs on Yogi Ramsuratkumar," (Courtesy: Gnana Oil) *Saranagatham*, official publication of the Ashram of Yogi Ramsuratkumar, Tiruvannamalai, India, June 2003, 31.
11. Ibid.
12. Translation by Mr. Chinnasamy, son-in-law to the poet, Periasamy Thooran.
13. Murali Murugavel, grandson of Periasamy Thooran, personal correspondence, August 2003.
14. J. Mukilan, personal interview, Chennai, India, December 2002.
15. Makarand Paranjape, "A 'Bad Poet's' Songs to a 'Dirty Beggar,'" *Tattva Darsana*, Feb.-Apr. 1994, 56..
16. Yogi Ramsuratkumar, quoted by Makarand Paranjape, 56.
17. Angelon Young, "India Journals," *Tawagoto: The Sacred Foolish Song of the Hohm Community*. Prescott, Arizona: Hohm Press, Winter 2001, Volume 14 (1), 91.
18. Angelon Young, "Accounts of Mr. Lee's Visits to His Father," *Tawagoto: The Sacred Foolish Song of the Hohm Community*. Prescott, Arizona: Hohm Press, Winter 1994, Volume 7 (1), 14-15.
19. Lee Lozowick, 45-46.
20. Angelon Young, 15-16.
21. Ibid., 16.
22. Ibid., 16-17, 19.
23. Lee Lozowick, *Poems of a Broken Heart*. Part II, Chennai, India: Sister Nivedita Academy, 1997, 23-24.

CHAPTER 31 – LAYING A FOUNDATION, FEBRUARY 1994

1. Mani, with S. Lhaksham, *A Man and His Master: My Years with Yogi Ramsuratkumar*, Prescott, Arizona: Hohm Press, 2003, 102.
2. Ibid.
3. Ibid., 93-94.
4. Ibid., 95.
5. Ibid., 77-78.
6. Swami Satchidananda, personal interview, Kanhangad, India, October 2002.
7. Ibid.

8. Swami Satchidananda, "The Great Day," *Yogi Ramsuratkumar Souvenir.* Tiruvannamalai: Yogi Ramsuratkumar Trust, 1995, 19.
9. Mani, 82.
10. Vijayalakshmi Ma, *Waves of Love.* Unpublished manuscript, Tiruvannamalai, 2002, 58.
11. Mani, 113.
12. Ibid., 114.

CHAPTER 32 – THE DIVINE LABORER

1. Mani, with S. Lhaksham, *A Man and His Master: My Years with Yogi Ramsuratkumar,* Prescott, Arizona: Hohm Press, 2003, 163.
2. Vijayalakshmi Ma, *Waves of Love.* Unpublished manuscript, Tiruvannamalai, 2002, 58.
3. Joanne Maas, "In the Company of Saints," *Tawagoto: The Sacred Foolish Song of the Hohm Community.* Prescott, Arizona: Hohm Press, Winter 1995, Volume 8 (1), 31.
4. Mani, 197.
5. Yogi Ramsuratkumar, quoted by Mani, 190.
6. Mani, 191.
7. Ibid., 160-161.
8. Ibid., 182-183.
9. Makarand Paranjape, "At the Feet of Yogi Ramsuratkumar," *Yogi Ramsuratkumar Souvenir.* Tiruvannamalai: Yogi Ramsuratkumar Trust, 1995, 386.

CHAPTER 33 – BUILDING THE LEGACY

1. Professor Kamalam, "The Incessant Flow of Love," *Saranagatham,* official publication of the Ashram of Yogi Ramsuratkumar, Tiruvannamalai, India, August 2003, 37-38.
2. Mani, with S. Lhaksham, *A Man and His Master: My Years with Yogi Ramsuratkumar,* Prescott, Arizona: Hohm Press, 2003, 223.
3. Balarama Zuccarello, personal interview, Prescott, Arizona, April 2002.
4. Yogi Ramsuratkumar quoted by Gilles Farcet, personal communication, December 14, 1995.
5. Except where noted, all the following stories of this period are from Balarama Zuccarello, unpublished personal journal, courtesy of the author.
6. Yogi Ramsuratkumar, quoted by Balarama Zuccarello, personal journal.
7. C.C. Krishna, "Om Sriram Jayaram Jaya Jaya Ram," *Yogi Ramsuratkumar Souvenir.* Tiruvannamalai: Yogi Ramsuratkumar Trust, 1995, 35.
8. Nachama Greenwald, "India Journal Excerpts, December 1996," *Tawagoto: The Sacred Foolish Song of the Hohm Community.* Prescott, Arizona: Hohm Press, Winter 1997, Volume 10 (1), 47.
9. Lee Lozowick, *Death of a Dishonest Man: Poems and Prayers to Yogi Ramsuratkumar.* Prescott, Arizona: Hohm Press, 1998, 580.
10. Yogi Ramsuratkumar, *Sparks,* Tiruvannamalai: Yogi Ramsuratkumar Trust, 2002, 11.
11. Nivedita Ramesh (Rangarajan), personal correspondence, February 2003.
12. Ibid.

13. Angelon Young, "India Journals," *Tawagoto: The Sacred Foolish Song of the Hohm Community*. Prescott, Arizona: Hohm Press, Winter 2001, Volume 14 (1), 71.

14. Erica Jen, "India Journals," *Tawagoto: The Sacred Foolish Song of the Hohm Community*. Prescott, Arizona: Hohm Press, Winter 2001, Volume 14 (1), India Journals," 41.

15. Capellini, James, et al. *Facets of the Diamond: Wisdom of India*. Prescott, Arizona: Hohm Press, 1994, x.

16. Andrea Sürth, "In the Company of Saints, Excerpts From India Journals," *Tawagoto, The Sacred Foolish Song of the Hohm Community*. Prescott, Arizona: Hohm Press, Winter 1995, 41.

17. Karlis Krummins, "In the Company of Saints, Excerpts From India Journals," *Tawagoto, The Sacred Foolish Song of the Hohm Community*. Prescott, Arizona: Hohm Press, Winter 1995, 58.

18. Lee Lozowick, *Death of a Dishonest Man*, 565.

19. Stan Hitson, "Extraordinary Business," *Tawagoto, The Sacred Foolish Song of the Hohm Community*. Prescott, Arizona: Hohm Press, Winter 1995, 76-78.

20. Mani, 263.

21. Ibid.

22. Ibid., 265.

23. R. Jeyaraj Sulochana, personal interview, Chennai, India, October 2002.

24. Mani, 264.

CHAPTER 34 – THE VIGRAHA

1. Will Zulkowski, personal interview, New York City, May 2002.

2. Devotees, *Sadguru Gnanananda, His Life, Personality and Teachings*. Bombay: Bharatiya Vidya Bhavan, 1993, 72.

3. Ibid., 73.

4. Ibid., 75, and http://www.chembur.com/gnanananda/history.htm

5. Swami Nityananda Giri, Tapovanam Ashram, Tirukoilur, India, October 2002.

6. Devotees, 72.

7. Mani, with S. Lhaksham, *A Man and His Master: My Years with Yogi Ramsuratkumar*. Prescott, Arizona: Hohm Press, 2003, 206.

8. Ibid., 207.

9. Ibid., 211.

10. Ibid.

11. Ibid., 212.

CHAPTER 35 – A DAY IN THE LIFE, DECEMBER 1995

1. Vijayalakshmi Ma, *Waves of Love*. Unpublished manuscript. Tiruvannamalai, India, 2002, 84.

2. Ravi, personal interview, Tiruvannamalai, India, December 2002.

3. Devaki Ma.

4. Anonymous, personal journal notes, Prescott, Arizona, December 1995.

5. Swami Shuddhananda, *With My Master*. Kanhangad, India: Anandashram, 2001, 92.

6. Ibid., 93.

7. Winifred Gallagher, *Spiritual Genius: The Mastery of Life's Meaning*. New York: Random House, 2002, 257-258.

8. Anonymous.
9. Vijayalakshmi, 84.
10. Nivedita Ramesh (Rangarajan), personal correspondence, February 2003.
11. Nivedita.
12. Yogi Ramsuratkumar, *Sparks*. Tiruvannamalai: Yogi Ramsuratkumar Trust, 11.
13. Sadhu V. Rangarajan, personal interview, Bangalore, India, October 2002.
14. Balarama Zuccarello, personal interview, Prescott, Arizona, January 2002.
15. P.V. Karunakaran, personal correspondence, February 2004.

CHAPTER 36 – "IF HE WALKS IT IS THE TEACHING"

1. Jaya Hoy, unpublished journal, December 1993.
2. Christopher Fry, from *A Sleep of Prisoners*, Oxford: Oxford University Press, 1959.
3. Caylor Wadlington, *Yogi Ramsuratkumar, The Godchild, Tiruvannamalai*. Madras, 1979,16.
4. Ibid., 69.
5. Mariana Caplan, "The Most Unusual Man in the World," *Saranagatham*, official publication of the Ashram of Yogi Ramsuratkumar, Tiruvannamalai, India, March 2002, 45.
6. Devotee, in: *Saranagatham*, official publication of the Ashram of Yogi Ramsuratkumar, Tiruvannamalai, India, March 2002, 26.
7. Vijayalakshmi Ma, *Waves of Love*. Unpublished manuscript, Tiruvannamalai, 2002, 88.
8. Caylor Wadlington's journals, courtesy of the author.
9. Devaki Ma, "The Divine Beggar On Himself," *Saranagatham*, official publication of the Ashram of Yogi Ramsuratkumar, Tiruvannamalai, India, February 2003, 34.
10. Yogi Ramsuratkumar, reprinted in *Saranagatham*, official publication of the Ashram of Yogi Ramsuratkumar, Tiruvannamalai, India, May 2002, 35.
11. Justice T.S. Arunachalam, "Cosmic Dance," *Saranagatham*, official publication of the Ashram of Yogi Ramsuratkumar, Tiruvannamalai, India, April 2002, 41-42.
12. Tom Shroyer, telephone interview, July 2003.
13. Caylor Wadlington, journals.
14. Parathasarathy, personal interview. Some of these words reflected ideas that Parathasarathy heard expressed by Yogi Ramsuratkumar, but clearly he was paraphrasing to an extent that made it impossible to credit all these words as coming directly from the mouth of the beggar.
15. Krishna Carcelle, personal correspondence, January 2003.
16. Michel Coquet, *Yogi Ramsuratkumar, The Divine Beggar*. Page 81 of the English language pre-publication version of the French-language book: *Yogi Ramsuratkumar: Le Divin Mendicant*, Paris: ALTESS, 1996.
17. Swami Nityananda Giri, personal interview, Tapovanam Ashram, Tirukoilur, India, October 2002.
18. Kirsti, (Sivapriya), personal interview and correspondence, Tiruvannamalai, India, October 2002.
19. Dr. Angani Kumar, "Your Smile is a Sight for Depressed Hearts," *Saranagatham*, official publication of the Ashram of Yogi Ramsuratkumar, Tiruvannamalai, India, October 2002, 45.
20. Selveraj, personal interview, Tiruvannamalai, India, December 2002.

21. Lee Lozowick, "January 23, 1994," *Death of a Dishonest Man: Poems and Prayers to Yogi Ramsuratkumar*. Prescott, Arizona: Hohm Press, 1998, 495.

22. Saravanan, personal interview, Tiruvannamalai, India, December 2002.

23. Vijaya Fedorschak, personal interview. Tiruvannamalai, India, December 2002.

24. Michel Coquet, 87.

25. Clint Callahan, journal entry, "Notes from the Tropic of Scorpio, Journals of India," *Tawagoto: The Sacred Foolish Song of the Hohm Community*. Prescott, Arizona: Hohm Press, Spring 1992, Volume 5 (2), 43.

26. Vijaya Fedorschak, journal entry, "Notes from the Tropic of Scorpio, Journals of India," *Tawagoto: The Sacred Foolish Song of the Hohm Community*. Prescott, Arizona: Hohm Press, Spring 1992, Volume 5 (2), 41.

27. e.e. (Elise Erro), journal entry, in "India Journal Excerpts, December 1996," *Tawagoto: The Sacred Foolish Song of the Hohm Community*. Prescott, Arizona: Hohm Press, Winter 1997, Volume 10 (1), 57-59.

28. Stan Hitson, "Extraordinary Business," *Tawagoto: The Sacred Foolish Song of the Hohm Community*. Prescott, Arizona: Hohm Press, Winter 1995, Volume 8 (1), 78.

29. Richard Schiffman, personal interview, New York City, May 2002.

30. Selveraj.

31. Vivekanandan, "Master of Alms," *Tattva Darsana*, Nov. 1988-Jan. 1989, Volume 5(4), 32.

32. Mariana Caplan, "The Most Unusual Man in the World," 46.

33. Ibid.

34. Mariana Caplan, personal interview, Tiruvannamalai, India, December 2002.

35. Kirsti.

36. Selveraj.

37. Will Zulkowski, personal interview, New York City, May 2002.

38. Caylor Wadlington.

39. Jai Ram, personal interview, Tiruvannamalai, India, December 2002.

40. Selveraj.

41. Ibid.

42. Saravanan, personal interview, Tiruvannamalai, India, December 2002.

43. Selveraj.

44. Steve Ball, journal entry, "Notes from the Tropic of Scorpio, Journals of India," *Tawagoto: The Sacred Foolish Song of the Hohm Community*. Prescott, Arizona: Hohm Press, Spring 1992, Volume 5 (2), 21-22.

45. Mani, video interview with Purna Steinitz, December 1993.

46. Ashish Bagrodia, personal interview, Mumbai, India, December 2002.

47. Jai Ram.

48. Lee Lozowick, "Chennai Dec. 9, 2002," *Tawagoto: The Sacred Foolish Song of the Hohm Community*. Prescott, Arizona: Hohm Press, Winter 2003, Volume 16 (1), 80-81.

49. Lee Lozowick, "Lee's Talks in Bombay, December 12, 2002," *Tawagoto: The Sacred Foolish Song of the Hohm Community*. Prescott, Arizona: Hohm Press, Winter 2003, Volume 16 (1), 103-104.

50. Kirsti.

51. Caylor Wadlington.

52. Kirsti.
53. Vijayalakshmi, 64.
54. Mani, with S. Lhaksham, *A Man and His Master: My Years with Yogi Ramsuratkumar,* Prescott, Arizona: Hohm Press, 2003, ii.
55. Hilda's devotee's, various notes, 1979, courtesy of Caylor Wadlington.
56. Sri Janadev, *Janeswari* (translated from the Marathi by Ramchandra Deshav Bhagwat). Madras: Samata Books, 1979.
57. Will Zulkowski.
58. Heather Chinery, journal entry, in "India Journals," *Tawagoto: The Sacred Foolish Song of the Hohm Community,* Prescott, Arizona, Winter 1998, Volume 11 (1), 20.
59. Lee Lozowick, "January 18, 1994," *Death of a Dishonest Man: Poems and Prayers to Yogi Ramsuratkumar.* Prescott, Arizona: Hohm Press, 1998, 493.
60. Kirsti.
61. Notes compiled by Krishna Carcelle, posted on http://pages.intnet.mu/ramsurat/
62. Yogi Ramsuratkumar, quoted in: James Capellini, et al. *Facets of the Diamond: Wisdom of India.* Prescott, Arizona: Hohm Press, 1994, 153.
63. Justice T.S. Arunachalam, "Craving, Charm, Bliss," *Saranagatham,* official publication of the Ashram of Yogi Ramsuratkumar, Tiruvannamalai, India, June 2002, 44.
64. Caylor Wadlington.
65. Michel Coquet, 82.
66. Sadhu Rangarajan, personal interview, Bangalore, India, October 2002.
67. Shri V. Ramanujachari, personal correspondence, February 2004.
68. Ravi, personal interview, Tiruvannamalai, India, December 2002.
69. Internet notes, 2002.
70. Devaki Ma, "The One Beyond the Reach of Thought," extracted from "The Introduction" to *Bhagavan Yogi Ramsuratkumar Paamaalai* by Sri T.P. Meenakshisundaranar, translated by Sadhu V. Rangarajan. *Tattva Darsana,* Feb.-Apr. 1994, Volume 11(1), 31.
71. Mariana Caplan.
72. Brinda Callahan, journal entry, in "India Journal Excerpts, December 1996," *Tawagoto: The Sacred Foolish Song of the Hohm Community.* Prescott, Arizona: Hohm Press, Winter 1997, Volume 10 (1), 34.
73. Dr. Venkatasubramanian, "The Great Yogi of Tiruvannamalai," *Saranagatham,* official publication of the Ashram of Yogi Ramsuratkumar, Tiruvannamalai, India, March 2002, 41-42.
74. Ponkacham, in conversation with Lee Lozowick, Tiruvannamalai, India, December 2002.
75. R. Jeyaraj Sulochana, personal interview, Chennai, India, October 2002.
76. Shri V. Ramanujachari, personal correspondence, February 2004.
77. Vijayalakshmi, 41-42.
78. Ibid., 51.
79. J. Mukilan, personal interview, Chennai, India, November-December 2002.
80. P.V. Karunakaran, personal correspondence, February 2004.
81. Chandra, personal interview, Ananandashram, Kanhangad, India, October 2002.
82. Kirsti.
83. Ibid.
84. Steve Ball, 26.

85. Mukilan.

86. Jim Capellini, personal interview, May 2004.

87. Lee Lozowick, public talks.

88. V. Ganesan, "Never Alone," *Saranagatham*, official publication of the Ashram of Yogi Ramsuratkumar, Tiruvannamalai, India, May 2002, 41.

89. Sadhu Rangarajan.

90. Steve Ball, 25.

91. Ramamurti.

92. Caylor Wadlington.

93. V.J. Fedorschak, *Tawagoto: The Sacred Foolish Song of the Hohm Community*, Prescott, Arizona: Hohm Press, Spring 1989, Volume 2(2), 30.

94. M.S. Murali Murugavel, personal correspondence, July 2003.

95. Ranganayaki Srinivasan, Professor. *Bhagwan Sri Yogi Ramsuratkumar: His Divine Life and Message*. Kanyakumari, India: Yogi Ramsurat Kumar Manthralayam Trust, 1991. (Adapted from the book in Tamil: *Universal Father, Yogi Ramsuratkumar* by T. Ponkamaraj, M.A. B. L.), 21.

96. Nachama Greenwald, journal entry, in "India Journal Excerpts, December 1996," *Tawagoto: The Sacred Foolish Song of the Hohm Community*. Prescott, Arizona: Hohm Press, Winter 1997, Volume 10 (1), 48.

97. Krishna Carcelle, personal correspondence, February 2002.

98. Caylor Wadlington, journals.

99. Ibid.

100. P.V. Karunakaran, personal correspondence, February 2004.

101. Kirsti.

102. Ramamurti.

103. Sri V. Ramanujachari.

104. Mukilan.

105. Coquet, 122.

106. Caylor Wadlington.

107. S. Ramanatha Bhatt, "Yogi Ramsuratkumar Unfailing Protector!" *Saranagatham*, official publication of the Ashram of Yogi Ramsuratkumar, Tiruvannamalai, India, February 2004, 34-35.

108. Justice Arunachulam, "Yogi Ramsuratkumar – Everywhere," *Sarangatham*, official publication of the Ashram of Yogi Ramsuratkumar, Tiruvannamalai, India, March 2004, 34-36.

109. Mariana Caplan, "The Most Unusual Man in the World," 45.

110. Dr. Venkatasubramanian, "The Great Yogi of Tiruvannamalai," *Saranagatham*, official publication of the Ashram of Yogi Ramsuratkumar, Tiruvannamalai, India, March 2002, 41-42.

111. Mani, 141.

112. Lee Lozowick, public talks.

113. Ibid.

114. Ibid.

115. Kirsti.

116. Jai Ram.

CHAPTER 37 – THE DEATH OF GOD

1. Personal interview with Sadhu V. Rangarajan, Bangalore, India, October 2002.
2. Devaki Ma, "Anecdotes," *Saranagathan*, official publication of the Ashram of Yogi Ramsuratkumar, Tiruvannamalai, India, March 2004, 38.
3. Lee Lozowick, *Death of a Dishonest Man: Poems and Prayers to Yogi Ramsuratkumar*. Prescott, Arizona: Hohm Press, 1998, 615.
4. Personal interview with Ashish Bagrodia, Bombay, India, December 2002.
5. Mani, with S. Lhaksham, *A Man and His Master: My Years with Yogi Ramsuratkumar,* Prescott, Arizona: Hohm Press, 2003, 336-367.
6. Personal communication from Devaki Ma, Tiruvannamalai, India, December 2002.
7. Letters of Ute Augustiniak, February 2001.
8. Ashish Bagrodia, "Towards the End – Darshans," *Saranagatham*, official publication of the Ashram of Yogi Ramsuratkumar, Tiruvannamalai, India, November 2002, 41.
9. Mani, 340-342.
10. "Acharya Yogi Ramsuratkumar," (Courtesy: Gnana Oil), quoted in *Saranagatham*, official publication of the Ashram of Yogi Ramsuratkumar, Tiruvannamalai, India, April 2003, 33.
11. Personal interview with Swami Nityandanda Giri, Tapovanam ashram, Tirikoloir, India, October 2002.
12. Mani, 341.
13. Vijayalakshmi Ma, *Waves of Love.* Unpublished manuscript, Tiruvannamalai, India, 2002, 63-64.
14. *Paroles diverses de Yogi Ramsuratkumar*, http://pages.intnet.mu/ramsurat/English/Yogiji.html. Website hosted by Krishna Carcelle.
15. Mani, 223.
16. Mani, 224.
17. Personal correspondence, C.C. Krishna Carcelle, January 2003.
18. Ibid.
19. Personal interview with Sadhu Rangarajan.
20. Ibid.
21. Personal interview with Jai Ram, Tiruvannamalai, India, December 2002.
22. Personal interview with Saravanan, Tiruvannamalai, India, December 2002.
23. Ute Augustiniak, India Journals, 2000.
24. Angelon Young, in "Excerpts, India Journals," *Tawagoto: The Sacred Foolish Song of the Hohm Community,* Prescott, Arizona, Winter 2001, Volume 14 (1), 54-55.
25. Ibid., 19.
26. Ibid., 80.
27. Ibid., 58.
28. Ibid., 59.
29. Ibid., 68.
30. Ibid., 95.
31. Ibid., 68.
32. Ute Augustiniak, correspondence. February 2000.

33. Lee Lozowick, quoted in *Tawagoto: The Sacred Foolish Song of the Hohm Community,* Prescott, Arizona, Winter 2001, Volume 14 (1), 62.

34. Ashish Bagrodia, 42.

35. Letters of Ute Augustiniak, February 2001.

36. Lee Lozowick, "Darshan 12/25/88," *Tawagoto: The Sacred Foolish Song of the Hohm Community*, Prescott, Arizona: Hohm Press, Spring 1989, Volume 2(2), 25.

37. Personal interview with Selveraj, Tiruvannamalai, India, December 2002.

38. T. Ponkamaraj, quoted in Ranganayaki Srinivasan, Professor. *Bhagwan Sri Yogi Ramsuratkumar: His Divine Life and Message.* Kanyakumari, India: Yogi Ramsurat Kumar Manthralayam Trust, 1991. (Adapted from the book in Tamil: *Universal Father, Yogi Ramsuratkumar* by T. Ponkamaraj, M.A. B. L.), 17.

GLOSSARY

abhisheka: A Buddhist term referring to the guru's transmission of spiritual power or initiation.

advaita: Non-duality; a school of the Vedanta philosophy, declaring the oneness of God, soul, and universe.

advaita vedanta: ("nondual Vedanta") The metaphysical tradition of nondualism based on the Upanishads. Its two main branches are Kevala-Advaita (written Kevaladvaita, "Radical Nondualism"), as taught by Shankara, and Vishishta-Advaita (written Vishishtadvaita, "Qualified Nondualism"), as taught by Ramanuja.

agnihotra: Fire sacrifice. Household rite traditionally performed daily, in which an oblation of milk is sprinkled on the fire.

Amma: Mother

anjali mudra: ("reverence gesture") Also called *pranamanjali*. A gesture of respect and greeting, in which the two palms are held softly together and slightly cupped. One form is with the open hands placed side by side, as if by a beggar to receive food, or a worshiper beseeching God's grace in the temple.

Appa: Father

arati: Ritual waving of lights before deities or saints and sannyasins.

asana: ("seat, posture") (i) The seat on which the yogin or yogini is seated. (ii) Posture, which is the third limb (*anga*) of Patanjali's eightfold yoga.

Atiraatra yagna: A festival and ritual fire for invoking rain.

avahoot (also **avadhuta**): Holy person of great renunciation; usually one who goes about naked.

avatara: ("descent") An incarnation of the Divine, especially of God Vishnu, such as Krishna or Rama.

Bhagwan: (Also **Bhagavan,** or **Bhagvan**) The Supreme Lord; also used as a title of reverence indicating the divinity of the spiritual master.

bhajan: Devotional songs of worshipful praise.

bhakta: ("devoted, devotee") A follower of the path of devotion (*bhakti*).

bhakti: ("devotion, love") The spiritual sentiment of loving participation in the Divine.

Bharata: A name of Arjuna; also a name of India, as in Bharata Mata or Mother India.

bhasma: Holy ash.

bhava: Existence; feeling; emotion; ecstasy; samadhi; also denotes any one of the five attitudes that a dualistic worshipper assumes toward God. The first of these attitudes is that of peace; assuming the other four, the devotee regards God as the Master, Child, Friend, or Beloved.

bhiksha: Alms; money or food given to a mendicant.

bramacharin: A religious student devoted to the practice of the spiritual discipline; a celibate belonging to the first stage of life.

buddhi: ("awareness, wisdom") The higher, intuitive mind, or faculty of wisdom. This term is also used to denote "thought" or "cognition."

chapattis: Flatbread; a North Indian bread.

chappells: (in Tamil language) sandals

chinmudra: A *mudra* or hand posture in which the tip of the thumb and forefinger are touching, while the other three fingers are extended upward.

chitta: The finite mind, psyche, or consciousness, which is dependent on the play of attention.

crore: Ten million.

damaru: The drum of the Hindu god, Siva, which accompanies him as Lord of the Dance. It is shaped like an hourglass, with each half representing male and female forces; from the symmetry of the two, the cosmos is created.

darbar: The king's royal court.

darshan(a): ("vision") (i) Inner or external vision. (ii) Sighting of an adept, which is considered auspicious. (iii) A philosophical system, or school of thought.

dharma: ("bearer") (i) The cosmic law or order. (ii) Morality or virtue, as one of the legitimate concerns of a human being (*purusha-artha*) sanctioned by Hinduism. It is understood as a manifestation or reflection of the divine law. (iii) Teaching, doctrine. (iv) Quality, as opposed to substance (*dharmin*).

dhoti: A man's wearing cloth.

dhuni: Sacred fire.

dhyana: Meditation. Internalized worship.

diksha: ("initiation") An important feature of all yogic schools by which a seeker is made part of a traditional chain of gurus.

diksha guru: The master who performs the initiation.

fana: Sufi term. Annihilation.

ghat: Bathing-place on a lake or river.

gopi(s): ("cowherder girl") A female devotee of Krishna.

gopurams: In South Indian temple architecture, tall stone towers that are covered with sculptures of deities, celestial beings and mythological stories.

gunas: ("strand, quality") (i) In yoga, *samkhya*, and many schools of *vedanta*, one of three primary constituents of nature (*prakriti*): *sattva* (principle of lucidity), *rajas* (principle of dynamism), and *tamas* (principle of inertia). The interaction between them creates the entire manifest and unmanifest cosmos, including all psychomental phenomena. (ii) Virtue, high moral quality.

gundas: thugs or hired criminals

guru: ("heavy, weighty") Spiritual teacher. Dispeller of darkness or ignorance.

guru diksha: *See* disksha guru.

Guru Poornima: Traditional Hindu celebration of the appearance of the guru in the world, held every year on the Thursday after the first full moon in July.

guru tat tvat: The principle of the guru which transcends name and form.

hamsa: ("gander," generally translated as "swan") (i) The breath or life force (*prana*). (ii) The transcendental Self (atman). (iii) A type of wandering ascetic (*parivrajaka*).

homa(s): A Vedic sacrifice in which oblations are offered into a fire.

idlies: Fermented rice paddies; a common food of South India.

ishta devata: ("chosen deity") A spiritual practitioner's favored deity.

japa: ("muttering") The meditative recitation of mantras.

japa yoga: Repetition of God's name.

jayanti: Day of birth. In the Hindu tradition, the guru's birthday is a day of high celebration.

jiva samadhi: Ceremonial tomb.

jivatma: The individuated self as opposed to the transcendental Self (*atman*).

jnani: Knowledge of God arrived at through reasoning and discrimination; also denotes the process of reasoning by which the ultimate truth is attained. The word is generally used to denote the knowledge by which one is aware of one's identity with Brahman.

jutka: A horse drawn cart.

jyoti: Light.

Kali Yuga: The age of spiritual decline, calling for a new approach to Self-realization. It is traditionally held to have commenced in 3102 BCE. *See also* yuga.

kaupina: Loin cloth.

khaddar: Homespun cotton cloth.

kirta: Upper body garment; shirt. Usually worn by men with pajamas or *dhoti*.

kirtan: Devotional music, often accompanied by dancing.

koan: Traditional question posed by the Zen master for the student to contemplate.

kolam: Mandala-like patterns of strewn rice flour, usually placed at the entrance or gate of a home or building. (Also known as *rangoli*.)

kollatam: A traditional North Indian folk dance in which sticks are rhythmically clicked by dancers.

kumar(a): "Virgin youth; ever-youthful." A name of Lord Karttikeya as a perpetual bachelor.

kundalini: ("coiled one") The serpent power (*kundalini-shakti*), which lies dormant in the lowest psychoenergetic center of the body. Its awakening is the central goal of Tantrism and Hatha-Yoga. The kundalini's ascent to the highest psychoenergetic center at the crown of the head brings about a temporary state of ecstatic identification with the Self (in *nirvikalpa-samadhi*).

likhitva (also, **likhit** or **likhita**) **japa:** Written expression of a mantra or name of God.

lilas: The divine play; the Relative. Creation is often explained by the Vaishnava sect as the lila of God, a conception that introduces elements of spontaneity and freedom into the universe. As a philosophical term, the lila (the relative) is the correlative of the *nitya* (the absolute).

linga: ("sign, symbol, mark") (i) In Shaivism, the symbol of the creative aspect of the Divine. (ii) The phallus as a symbol of creativity. (iii) In Patanjali's Yoga, a specific phase in the process of psychocosmic evolution, representing the first step into manifestation.

lunghi: A dressing cloth worn by men to cover the lower body.

mahaan: One who is great.

mahamantra: Great mystic formula, harmonizing inner bodies and stimulating latent spiritual qualities.

mahanirvana: The great Nirvana or samadhi.

mahasamadhi: Literally means "great bliss." Used to refer to the physical passing (death) of a great saint or God-realized being.

mahatmyas: Works describing the greatness or importance of a place or deity.

mala: A string of 108 beads traditionally used for *japa* or prayer; also a garland of flowers made as an adornment of praise and adoration to be placed around the neck of the saint or spiritual master; also used to adorn *murtis* and other sacred objects.

manasika japa: The mental repetition of the mantra.

mandapam: A decorative structure over a sacred place, usually an ornate roof held up by columns.

manduparka: Honey.

mantra japa: Repetition of a holy Sanskrit text; sacred formula.

Mantralayam: The temple complex in Kanimadam, South India, built for the worship of Sri Bhagwan Yogi Ramsuratkumar in which his larger-than-lifesize stone *murti* is installed and living.

mrityunjaya homa: A rite in honor of Lord Siva, the destroyer of death; a healing ritual.

muladhara: The first and lowest center in the *sushumna*. The first chakra.

murti: ("substantial form or body" – from *murch*: to become solid) A murti is the embodiment of Divinity worshipped in concrete form; murti usually refers to a metal or stone statue or sculpture which is an empowered artifact encoded with the darshan and spiritual power of the saint or spiritual master.

nama: ("name") Often used in conjunction with "form" (*rupa*) to describe the conditioned reality, as opposed to the name- and form-transcending reality (*tattva*).

nama japa: Repetition of the name of God as a spiritual practice that focuses the attention on the deity and the deity's qualities or essence, the purpose of which is to align the practitioner with the deity.

nama kirtana: The practice of singing the name of God.

namas: Bowing. Obeisance.

namaste(s): Reverent salutations. A traditional verbal greeting.

nellikkai: Indian gooseberry. *Amla* or *amlaka* in Sanskrit.

ninda stuti: Ironical praise which takes the form of complaint, lament or even abuse, in which the lover bemoans his fate of being separate from his beloved.

nirguna upasaka: A devotee of the timeless, eternal essence, who sees all as One, all as the same.

nivedana: Announcement, presentation, making known.

paatra: Alms bowl.

pakoras: An Indian food consisting of vegetables dipped in a spicy batter and deep fried.

pandal: Temporary shed made of palm leaves or like material.

pandit (or **pundit**)**:** A scholar, or pundit.

Paramacharya(l): Exalted teacher.

Paramatma: The Supreme Soul.

pashanti: Mental "flow" of the mantra without the need for verbalization.

payol: Covered verandah or porch at the front of a house.

pradakshinas: ("moving rightward") Worshipful circumambulation, walking clockwise around the temple sanctum or other holy place, with the intention of shifting the mind from worldly concerns to awareness of the Divine. Clockwise has esoteric significance and counterclockwise takes one down to the lower regions of selfishness, greed, conflict and turmoil.

prana: ("life") (i) Life in general. (ii) The life force sustaining the body, which has five principal forms: *prana, apana, samana, udana,* and *vyana.* (iii) The breath as the external manifestation of the life force.

pranam: To bow. The ceremonial bowing by the spiritual student as a sign of respect toward the spiritual master, symbolic of vulnerability, gratitude and honor.

prasad: Food or drink that has been offered to the deity; also the leavings of a superior's meal. The name Prasad is also short for Ramprasad Sen, a mystic poet of Bengal.

puja: ("worship") The ritual veneration of a deity or the guru, which is an important aspect of many forms of yoga, but especially *bhakti-yoga.*

punnai tree: Alexandrian laurel tree. The site where Yogi Ramsuratkumar held darshan near the railway station in Tiruvannamalai.

puris: Fried, unleavened wheat bread.

Ram: A name of God. The name Ram is a vibrational sound emanation of the Divine. The literal meaning of Ram is "to delight in."

Rama-nama: The name of Ram.

Ramnam: Mantric repetition of the name of Ram, or the mantra *Om Sri Ram Jai Ram Jai Jai Ram.*

rishi: A type of ancient sage or seer, who "sees" with the inner eye the hidden reality behind the smoke screen of manifest existence. What they "saw" was expressed in the hymns known as the Vedas.

rudraksha: Beads made from rudraksha pits, used in making rosaries.

sadhak: ("realizer") A spiritual practitioner, especially on the Tantric path, aspiring to realization (*siddhi*). Cf. *sadhika.*

sadhana: ("realizing") The path of spiritual realization; a particular spiritual discipline.

sadhika: A female practitioner. Cf. *sadhak.*

sadhu: ("good one") A virtuous ascetic.

sadhuram: ("sadhu"+"ram") Papa Ramdas's term for his companion sadhus.

sahajiya or **sahaja:** (from sahaj, "inborn, easy, or natural") A medieval Buddhist Tantra-oriented devotional (*bhakti*) movement.

samadhi: The death shrine of a saint; also a condition of enlightenment or ecstasy.

sambar: A spicy soup-like sauce served with rice in South India.

samyama: Constraint brought about by the combination of concentration, meditation, and ecstasy. It is focused upon one internalized object.

Sanatana Dharma: (the Eternal Religion) Refers to Hinduism, formulated by the rishis of the Vedas.

sangha: The body of practitioners surrounding a guru or teacher.

sannyas: The monastic life, the last of four stages of life.

sannyasin: A Hindu renunciate.

satsang: ("association with the real") The spiritual practice of frequenting the good company of saints, sages, and Self-realized adepts, who communicate the ultimate Reality (*sat*).

Glossary

sattvic or **sattva:** ("beingness") (i) A being. (ii) The principle of pure being or lucidity, which is the highest type of primary constituent (*guna*) of Nature (*prakriti*).

Shakti: The feminine aspect of the Divine; the power aspect of the Divine.

shakti: In reference to energy, the feminine power aspect of the Divine, which is fundamental to the metaphysics and spirituality of Shaktism and Tantrism.

Shankaracharya: One of Hindu's most extraordinary monks and preeminent guru of the Smarta Sampradaya. Noted for his monistic philosophy of Advaita Vedanta, his many scriptural commentaries, and formalizing ten orders of sannyasins at strategic points across India. He lived only thirty years but traveled throughout India and transformed the Hindu world in that time.

siddha purusha: One who has realized the Divine Person within and demonstrates the accomplishment of that through compassionate action.

siddhi(s): ("perfection, accomplishment") (i) Spiritual perfection; that is, the attainment of flawless identification with the ultimate Reality, or liberation (*moksha*). (ii) Paranormal power, especially the eight great abilities that come as a result of perfect adeptship.

siksha guru: The guru who teaches one the knowledge of worldly arts.

slokas: The smallest literary units of the epics, such as the *Mahabharata*; also refers to verses of poetry or song.

surat(a): Reveling intensely.

tamas (tamasa): ("darkness") The principle of inertia, which is one of the three primary constituents (*guna*) of Nature (*prakriti*). See also *rajas, sattva*.

tapas: ("glow, heat") Asceticism, which is thought to lead to great vitality. This term was applied to Yoga-like practices in Vedic times.

taraka mantra: A mantra that liberates the practitioner from illusion.

upamshu japa: The mantra as it is whispered or sung under the breath.

vag-diksha: Traditional form of initiation from master to disciple done through the utterance of a mantra, generally whispered three times into the disciple's ear, and then repeated by the receiver.

vaikhari japa: Repetition of the mantra aloud, in such a way as to obliterate all other sounds, and sung to a repetitive chant.

vastu: A brilliant placement; energy flowing brilliantly.

vigraha: The Divine represented through a manifest form; a consecrated image.

vishiri: a handfan

Visiri Samiyar: or (**Visiri Swami**) The swami who carries the country handfan. A name for Yogi Ramsuratkumar.

yuga(s): ("yoke") A world age. According to Hindu cosmology, there are four such world ages, each of several thousand years' duration. The Kali Yuga is held to be the darkest period and precedes another golden age.

SELECT REFERENCES
ABOUT YOGI RAMSURATKUMAR

Books

Capellini, James, et al. *Facets of the Diamond: Wisdom of India.* Prescott, Arizona: Hohm Press, 1994.

Charlton, Hilda. *Saints Alive.* Woodstock, New York: Golden Quest, 1989.

Hohm Sahaj Mandir Study Manual, Volumes I-IV, Prescott, Arizona: Hohm Press, 1996, 2002.

Lozowick, Lee. *Death of a Dishonest Man: Poems and Prayers to Yogi Ramsuratkumar.* Prescott, Arizona: Hohm Press, 1998.

Lozowick, Lee. *Poems of a Broken Heart.* Parts I and II. Madras (Chennai): Sister Nivedita Academy, 1993, 1997.

Mani, with S. Lhaksham. *A Man and His Master: My Years with Yogi Ramsuratkumar,* Prescott, Arizona: Hohm Press, 2003.

Ranganayaki Srinivasan, Professor. *Bhagwan Sri Yogi Ramsuratkumar: His Divine Life and Message.* Kanyakumari, India: Yogi Ramsurat Kumar Manthralayam Trust, 1991. (Adapted from the book in Tamil: *Universal Father, Yogi Ramsuratkumar* by T. Ponkamaraj, M.A. B. L.)

Rangarajan, Professor V. *Glimpses of a Great Yogi.* Second edition. Madras (Chennai): Sister Nivedita Academy, 1988.

Roberts, Paul William. *Empire of the Soul: Some Journeys in India.* New York: Riverhead Books, 1994.

Select References About Yogi Ramsuratkumar

Sadaiyan, Perumal. *Treasures of the Heart: The Unforgettable Yogi Ramsuratkumar.* Tiruvannamalai: Perumal Sadaiyan, 1998.

Satchidananda, Swami. *The Gospel of Swami Ramdas.* Kanhangad, India: Anandashram, second edition, 1990.

Sepuri, Haragopal. *Experiences with Yogi Ramsuratkumar.* Madras: Sister Nivedita Academy, 1989.

Sepuri, Haragopal. *Further Experiences with Yogi Ramsuratkumar and Other Experiences.* Madras: Sri Kusuma Haranath Central Mission, 1994.

Wadlington, Truman Caylor. *Yogi Ramsuratkumar, The Godchild, Tiruvannamalai.* Madras, Diocesan Press, 1979.

Yogi Ramsuratkumar Souvenir. Tiruvannamalai: Yogi Ramsuratkumar Trust, 1995.

Young, Mary. *Yogi Ramsuratkumar: Under the Punnai Tree.* Prescott, Arizona: Hohm Press, 2003.

Periodicals

Saranagatham, official publication of the Ashram of Yogi Ramsuratkumar. Contact: Yogi Ramsuratkumar Trust, 1833/1, Agraha Collai, Chengam Road, Tiruvannamalai, India, 606 603. Email: yrsk@md4.vsnl.net.in Website: www.yogiramsuratkumar.org

Tattva Darsana Quarterly. Contact: Sadhu V. Rangarajan, editor, Sister Nivedita Academy, 158 (old no. 118) Big Street, Triplicane, Chennai, India, 600 005. Email: sadhurangarajan@vsnl.com

Tawagoto: The Sacred Foolish Song of the Hohm Community, Prescott, Arizona: Hohm Press. Contact: Hohm Press, P.O 2501, Prescott, Arizona, U.S.A., 86302. Phone: 928-778-9189 Website: www.hohmpress.com

INDEX

Index

Camille, 533

Campbell, Joseph, 527

cancer, 248, 376

Cape Comorin, 118

Caplan, Mariana, 620-621; 634-635, 655-658, 685

car accident, *see:* Mani

car, 564, 598-599, 602, 610-611, 615, 636, 711; *also see:* Ravi

Carcelle, Krishna (C.C.), 460, 571-573, 624, 677, 696

Carnatic music, 529

caste, 124; *also see*: outcaste

cave(s), 83, 433; *also see individual topics*: Panch Pandav, Virupaksha, Guhai Namashivayar, Banyan Tree

ceasarian delivery, 494

Cece, Miss, 361-362

cemetery, 147, 149

Chaitanya, 201

Chaitra (month of March/April), 10

chakra(s), 181, 217

Chandala, 124-125, 164

Chandra Swami, 579, 702

Chandra, 665-667

Chandramouli, Sri, 406-411

Chandrasekara Saraswathi Swamigal, Jagatguru, *see:* Paramacharya

Chandrashakar (Trikannad, nephew of Ramdas), 88, 100

chanting, at ashram of YRSK, 708, 709-710; from *Bhagavad Gita*, 351, 597; Devaki's reliance on, 516; to extend life of Mother Krishnabai, 708; of "this beggar's name," 270, 602; by YRSK, 266, 270, 350, 390, 589; YRSK's love for, 227; YRSK's instructions about, 605; *also see:* Ramnam; name of God; separate topics

chapattis, 366, 615

chappells, 143, 508

Charlton, Hilda, xvi, 241-242, 247-248, 282-286, 290-291, 377, 623, 653; descriptions of YRSK's work, 148, 237, 284; instructions to "her kids," 283-286, 312; meeting with Lee Lozowick, 286; visit to YRSK, 309-319; *also see:* lilas

Cheating Buddha, The (Lee Lozowick), 332

Chennai, *see:* Madras

Chettiar, 239

Chettier, Mr., 162

Chidakasha Geeta (Nityananda), 112

Chidananda, Swami, 427

children, xxii, 357, 391

Chinmayananda, Swami, 375, 384

chinmudra, 588

Chinnasamy, Mrs. Saradamani, 674-675

chitta (basic consciousness), 123

Chomsky, Noam, 527

Christ, *see:* Jesus

Christmas carols, 577

Chronicles of Narnia, The (Lewis), 448

circumambulation, 142, 343; *also see:* pradakshina

Claire (of Assisi), 533

clothing, *see:* YRSK

cobbler, 122-123

Cockburn, Bruce, 316

coconut bowl, 194-195, 246, 284, 464; *also see:* YRSK, implements

coffee, 290, 600

Cohen, Leonard, 527

coincidences, *see:* lilas

coma, 696, 708

computers, 193-194, 388

Congress Party, 387

consciousness, transformation of, 321

Coquet, Michel, 654

cosmos, service to, 517

753

M

Index

Maharshi, Ramana, *see:* Ramana Maharshi

mahasamadhi, of Shirdi Sai Baba, 2; of YRSK, 712

Mahashivaratri, 10

Mahendra, Sri, 391

Mahesh Yogi, Maharishi, 176

Maitreem Bhajata (song), 412

mala, 137, 139; *also see: japa mala*

mandapam, 175, 182, 289, 290, 298, 398; photo, 291

Mangalore, 2

mango tree, 419-20

Mani, 483-497; ashram construction by, 537-539, 547, 554-560; building a *pandal,* 537, 585; car accident, 490; chicken briyani lila, 686-687; dancing of, 693; daughter-in-law's pregnancy, 493-495; directing woman to Anandashram, 667; at "family darshan," 616-617; first meeting with YRSK, 485-486, 488; instructions from YRSK, 556-557; and money, 584-585; protocol management by, 611; *sadhana* of, 686-687; trip to Tapovanam, 496-497; *vigraha,* work on, 589-595

Manikarnika, 172

man-making (Vivekananda), 388-390

mantra japa, see: *japa*

mantra, 137-138, 458; *Om Nama Shivaya,* 135, 195; *So Ham,* 340; Gayatri, 135; *also see: Om Sri Ram Jai Ram;* Ramnam

Mantralayam, 461-463, 531

Mark (friend of Caylor's), 212-217

Marpa, 100, 533

marriage, 451; of Nivedita and Ramesh, 392-395

Marston (McLeod), Melissa, 47

Martin, Jay, xvii

Mary (mother of Jesus), 533

Mary Magdalene, 518

master-disciple relationship, 110, 332, 384, 401, 404-405; *also see:* disciple; guru-disciple relationship

Matrabhuteswara Temple, 47, 51

Matrubutheswara (Divine Mother), 358

Matsya Puraana, see: puranas

Mauritius, 460

Mayamma, *see:* Mayee of Kanyakumari

Mayananda, Swami, 267, 527

Mayee of Kanyakumari, Mother, 304, 375-381, 461, 661-662; photo, 379

meditation, 178, 184, 230, 306-307, 315, 357, 648

Meenakshisundaram, Sri T. P., 242, 414-415, 510-511, 522, 527

Meher Baba, 281, 562

Milarepa, 100, 533

Miller, Henry, xv

Milton, 13

Mirabai (poetess) 227, 325

Mirabehn, *see:* Slade, Madeleine

miracles, 253, 321, 463, 625, 681, 697; on airplane flight, 684-685; of bore well, 557-558; devotee's pregnancy, 669; face on plate, 667; Mani's car accident, 490-491; in the river in Tirukoilur, 215-217; suicide attempt, 257-258; saving Ponkacham, 261; of rain, 478-479; saving Rangarajan, 491-493; truck starting, 118; *also see:* lilas

Mirra, "The Mother," 25, 27, 28, 29, 37, 382-383, 562; YRSK's siting of, 28, 29

money, 502-503, 585; YRSK's use of, 656-657, 704; *also see:* lilas

monkeys, 302

Mother Ganga, *see:* Ganges River

Index

Index

Ram (Hindu deity, also "Sriram") 3,
76,79-80, 85
Ram Ashram (sadhu, friend of
YRSK), 23
Ram Dass (Richard Alpert), 177, 282
Ram Nam, *see:* Ramnam
Ram Ram Swami, *see:* YRSK, name of
Rama Tirtha, Swami, 18-20, 71,
201, 438; *also see:* patriotism
Rama, Lord, 223-224, 532
Ramabai (daughter of Ramdas), *see:*
Ranne
Ramakrishna (attendant to YRSK),
353
Ramakrishna Ashram, 86
Ramakrishna Mutt, 292
Ramakrishna, Swami, 20, 21, 111,
201, 221, 533
Ramakrishnan, Justice P., 223
Ramalingam, Saint (also known as
Ramalinga Swami), 221, 337, 637
Ramamurti, 485, 660-661, 679;
interview with, 498-503, 506-509
Raman, Sir C.V., 119
Ramana Maharshi, 1, 42, 562, 579;
biography, 48-52; cancer/surgeries
of, 65; death of, 96; initiation of
YRSK, 60-61; lilas about, 52-53;
meaning of name, 51; parallels to
YRSK, 53, 61-65; 63-65; surren-
der, views on, 64; teaching
method of, 52-53; in Tirukoilur,
213; as viewed by YRSK, 46;
"Who am I?" 48, 63; words of,
50; visit by Ramdas, 83
Ramanand, P. (nephew of Ramdas),
88-89
Ramanashram (also,
Ramanashramam), 54, 61, 342
Ramanatha, *see:* Bhat, S. Ramanatha
Ramanathan, Dr. T.S., 464, 685,
622-623, 685

Ramanujachari, Sri.V., 147-148,
181, 266-267, 339, 514, 655,
660, 679-680
Ramaswami's shop, 180, 185
Ramayana 3, 4, 70, 224, 336; translation by Raj, Gopal Archarya,
665-667
Ramcharandas, 112
Ramdas, Swami Papa: biography of,
69-94; body, his views on his, 94;
books by, 67-68; death as first
encountered by, 72; early influences on, 69-71; early life, 69-73;
failures of 73, 112; flowers, love
for 92; gardens, care of, 92; guru
of, 75; health of, 94; heartbreak
of, 113; initiation of, 75; instructions to YRSK, 107-109, 110,
112; letter to wife, 78-79; love for
Krishna, 74; love of nature, 69;
madness of, 74, 80, 84-85, 87;
mantra, relationship to, 75; marriage of, 72; meaning of name of,
69; meditation of, 84; parallels to
work and teaching of YRSK, 68;
poetry of, 86-87; photos of, 56,
81; sadhana of, 79, 86; suffering
of, 75; travels of, 79-89; YRSK's
visits to, 55, 66, 96-114; YRSK's
love for, 102-107, 115; YRSK's
references to, 96, 97, 457
Ramdas's cave, *see:* Banyan Tree cave
Ramesh, 394-395
Ramji Swami, *see:* YRSK, name of
Ramnam (mantra), 66, 408;
Ramdas's references to, 76, 133;
Tulsidas's references to, 133;
Gandhi's use of, 131-132; "all this
beggar knows is__," 131; YRSK's
use of, 97-98, 104, 147; *also see:*
mantra; *Om Sri Ram...*; name of
God; *taraka* mantra
Ramnam "bank," 458

765

OTHER TITLES OF INTEREST FROM HOHM PRESS

Yogi Ramsuratkumar, Under the Punnai Tree
by M. Young
Hohm Press's first full-length biography of the wondrous and
blessed beggar of Tiruvannamalai. A thorough and devotional
treatment, containing more than 80 photographs.
ISBN: 1-890772-34-8 $39.95

A Man and His Master
by Mani, with S. Lkasham
The unfolding of one man's life of service to the God-mad
beggar and saint, his master, Yogi Ramsuratkumar. Mani was
chosen by Yogi Ramsuratkumar to oversee and manage the
building of the temple and other facilities on the master's ashram
in Tiruvannamalai, Tamil Nadu, India.
ISBN: 1-890772-36-2 $21.95

Death of a Dishonest Man:
Poems and Prayers to Yogi Ramsuratkumar
by Lee Lozowick
Since the late 1970s, Lee Lozowick has been sending his words
of praise in the form of poetry to his master, Yogi
Ramsuratkumar. This volume contains the collected works from
1979 to 1998. Essays and commentaries from: Arnaud
Desjardins, Claudio Naranjo, Andrew Schelling, Gilles Farcet,
and others.
ISBN: 1-890772-87-4 $108.00

To order, call 800-381-2700, or visit our website: www.hohmpress.com

OTHER TITLES OF INTEREST FROM HOHM PRESS

Gasping for Air in a Vacuum:
Poems and Prayers to Yogi Ramsuratkumar
by Lee Lozowick
The second extraordinary volume of Lee's poems to Yogi
Ramsuratkumar written from 1998-2004. With essays and
commentaries from distinguished spiritual teachers including:
Llewellyn Vaughan-Lee, Robert Svoboda, Jakusho Kwong Roshi,
John Welwood, and others.
ISBN: 1-890772-45-3 $145.00

As It Is: A Year on the Road with a Tantric Teacher
by M. Young
A first-hand account of a one-year journey around the world in
the company of tantric teacher, Lee Lozowick.
ISBN: 0-934252-99-8 $29.95

Praying Dangerously: Radical Reliance on God
by Regina Sara Ryan
This book re-enlivens an age-old tradition of prayer as an
expression of radical reliance on God. Contains a chapter on the
prayer of Yogi Ramsuratkumar and Lee Lozowick.
ISBN: 1-890772-06-2 $14.95

The Woman Awake:
Feminine Wisdom for Spiritual Life
by Regina Sara Ryan
Insight on the spiritual path from great women from all the
world's great spiritual traditions. Includes a section on Mataji
Krishnabai, the devotee of Papa Ramdas, and Devaki Ma, the
devotee of Yogi Ramsuratkumar.
ISBN: 0-934252-79-3 $19.95

To order, call 800-381-2700, or visit our website: www.hohmpress.com

SELECT CONTACT INFORMATION

To learn more about Yogi Ramsuratkumar
or to visit centers devoted to his work:

USA:

Triveni (Hohm Sahaj Mandir), c/o Hohm Press: 800-381-2700.
Or write, Hohm Community, PO Box 31, Prescott, Arizona, U.S.A.
Contact, Paul.

INDIA:

The Yogi Ramsuratkumar Ashram Trust, Agrahara Collai, 1833/1,
Chengam Road,Tiruvannamalai, Tamil Nadu. Telephone, 04175-
237567. Email: yrsk@md4.vsnl.net.in

Triveni II, Hohm Sahaj Trust, 95 Chengam Road, Ramana Nagar,
Tiruvannamalai, Tamil Nadu. Contact: Volker or Ute Augustyniak

Bharatamata Gurukula Ashram & Yogi Ramsuratkumar Indological
Research Centre, Bangalore. Email: sadhurangarajan@vsnl.com.
Contact: Sadhu Prof. V. Rangarajan
Sister Nivedita Academy, 118, Big Street, Triplicane, Chennai 600
005. Phone and Fax: (91) 44 8546135. Email :
sadhurangarajan@vsnl.com. Contact: Sadhu Prof. V. Rangarajan

Yogi Ramsuratkumar Manthralayam, Kanimadam 629 401,
Kanyakumari. Contact: Sri Ponkamaraj

Other centers in Kumarakoil, Hosur, Srivillipurtur, Tuticorin, and
other locations, contact the Yogi Ramsuratkumar Ashram Trust,
Tiruvannamalai

FRANCE:

Ramji Association, 86260 St. Pierre de Maille, France.
Contact: Clint or Brindavan Callahan

MAURITIUS:

The Yogi Ramsuratkumar Bhavan, Royal Road, Calebasses,
Pamplemousses, Mauritius. Phone and Fax: (230) 243 56 52;
Email: cKrishna@bigfoot.com. Contact: Krishna Carcelle

SOUTH AFRICA:

Sister Nivedita Academy South Africa, Smt. Sherita Kommal, 12,
Sardine Road, Seatides. P.O. Box 139, Desainagar 4405, KwaZulu
Natal, South Africa. Phone: (27) 322 41163